10 0453520 4

KU-998-722

Formal Theories
of the Commonsense World

ablex
series in
artificial
intelligence

Jerry R. Hobbs, Editor

Formal Theories
of the
Commonsense World

Jerry R. Hobbs
and
Robert C. Moore

Editors
SRI International
Menlo Park, California

NOTTINGHAM UNIVERSITY LIBRARY

ABLEX SERIES IN ARTIFICIAL INTELLIGENCE

ABLEX PUBLISHING CORPORATION
NORWOOD, NEW JERSEY

Second Printing 1988   1004535204

Copyright © 1985 by Ablex Publishing Corporation

All rights reserved. No part of this publication may be reproduced, stored in a retrieval system, or transmitted, in any form or by any means, electronic, mechanical, photocopying, microfilming, recording, or otherwise, without permission of the publisher.

Printed in the United States of America.

Library of Congress Cataloging in Publication Data
Main entry under title:

Formal theories of the commonsense world.

  (Ablex series in artificial intelligence)
  Includes bibliographies and index.
  1. Artificial intelligence.   2. Physics—Philosophy.
3. Reasoning.   4. Knowledge, Theory of.   I. Hobbs,
Jerry R.   II. Moore, Robert C., 1948–   .
III. Series.
Q360.F66   1985   001.53′5   85-1357
ISBN 0-89391-213-1

Ablex Publishing Corporation
355 Chestnut Street
Norwood, New Jersey 07648

Contents

Dedication:
To John McCarthy

We would like to dedicate this collection to John McCarthy, who literally invented the enterprise the book is about—formalization of our commonsense knowledge of the everyday world. McCarthy's work on this problem spans more than twenty-five years, first appearing in print with the classic paper "Programs with Common Sense" in 1959. While the development of philosophical logic in this century has led to some isolated examples of formalization of "philosophically interesting" concepts (e.g., C. I. Lewis's axiomatizations of the concepts of necessity and possibility), McCarthy was the first to realize that the development of computer systems exhibiting general intelligence would require a systematic analysis and formalization of virtually all our ordinary, commonsense knowledge.

McCarthy's influence on current thinking can be gauged by the fact that over half the papers in this volume cite his work and that three of the authors have been his students, either formally or informally. John McCarthy played a particularly important role in encouraging my own work in this area. In 1976 I was a graduate student in the Artificial Intelligence Laboratory at the Massachusetts Institute of Technology, conducting research on the application of formal deductive methods to problems of commonsense reasoning. At the time there was little expertise or interest in this topic among the MIT faculty, so Marvin Minsky got in touch with McCarthy to see whether he might know what to do with me. McCarthy very generously gave me a research assistantship at the Stanford Artificial Intelligence Laboratory, with complete freedom to pursue whatever line of research I wished. McCarthy and several of his co-workers were interested in logics of knowledge, a problematic area to which I had also given some thought. With McCarthy's encouragement, I wrote a dissertation on that topic, which is summarized in Chapter 9 of the present volume.

John McCarthy's many other accomplishments in artificial intelligence and computer science are almost too well known to mention: prominent among them are the invention of the LISP programming language and his pioneering work on time-sharing and on the mathematical theory of computation. In many cases, dedication of a volume such as this to a prominent researcher constitutes a kind of official recognition of the end of that researcher's productive career. That is manifestly not the case with McCarthy, for he continues to work on and write about a wide range of topics. He is currently one of the leading contributors to the rapidly developing study of ''nonmonotonic'' reasoning processes, concentrating especially on a form of nonmonotonic reasoning, devised by him, called ''circumscription.'' It would not be at all surprising if another such volume should appear in ten or fifteen years, also dedicated to John McCarthy, consisting of new papers inspired by his work and ideas in the coming decade.

—Robert C. Moore

Preface to the Series

Jerry R. Hobbs, Series Editor

This is the first volume in the new Ablex Series on Artificial Intelligence. My intention, when with some reluctance I took on the editorship of the series, was to have each volume organized around a central, exciting new idea in artificial intelligence. I felt the idea should be one that had been around for only a few years, but had generated a new and lively area of research. It should be an idea that had not necessarily reached the community as a whole but had inspired enough research to fill a book of papers by a dozen or so good people. Most of all, it should be an idea that promised to be very productive of future research.

I think this volume succeeds in achieving these aims. The motivating idea is, as the title says, the construction of formal theories of the commonsense world— formalizing the ways ordinary people conceptualize various aspects of the world around them. The subsequent volumes in the series that are in preparation are similarly organized around new areas of research with a great deal of forward thrust. My hope is that this series will stimulate the development of this kind of innovative research in artificial intelligence.

Introduction

Jerry R. Hobbs

Artificial Intelligence Center
SRI International
Menlo Park, California

1 Knowledge of the Commonsense World

We are capable of intelligent action, in part, because we know a great deal. If intelligent programs, or robots, are to be constructed, they too must have a great deal of knowledge. In most artificial intelligence (AI) systems, some knowledge of particular problem domains has been encoded, but most of this work has been too specific to be of much use to the field in general. There is a certain minimum of "core knowledge", however, that *any* reasonably sophisticated intelligent agent must have to make its way in the world. This is not knowledge of the world as science perceives it, but the "commonsense theories" of the world that ordinary people have—their everyday beliefs about what the world is like. Large-scale efforts in encoding this core, commonsense knowledge are just beginning, and our aim for this volume has been to gather together some of the most significant examples of this work. The volume focuses not so much on *how* various concepts should be represented or on *how* the knowledge is to be used, but simply on *what* facts should be included.

What must the intelligent agent know? Let's consider an example. Suppose I wanted to build a robot that, without specifically gearing for the task, I could send down to the SRI cafeteria for a salad and a sandwich. What would *it* have to know? First, some basic principles about location, shape, motion and causality, and their realizations in buildings, offices, hallways, elevators, and elevator buttons. It would need a fairly accurate image of its physical self if it is to figure out whether it can fit through a doorway or maneuver a staircase. We might want this knowledge to be fine-grained enough that it could decide whether to take the elevator or the stairs, depending on what floor the elevator is located on. Once outside (SRI's cafeteria is in a separate building), it must thread a narrow path on the sidewalk between the grass, which would be difficult and socially unacceptable to travel on, and the parking lot, where it would risk an encounter with a car. It would need to know about sidewalks, lawns, parking lots, risk, and what cars look like and what they can do.

In the cafeteria, things become more complicated. At the salad bar, it must know how to deal with multiple pieces of a flexible material (lettuce) with a rather

complex tool (the salad tongs). It must know about liquids of varying and problematic viscosities (salad dressings) and granular substances like croutons and
bacon bits. When ordering the sandwich, the robot enters a different kind of world:
the world of social interactions. It needs to know where to go for what purposes—
that it cannot go into the kitchen, for example, and that it must wait in line at the
sandwich counter. It must know about social roles—that one may ask the cafeteria
employee to make a sandwich, but not another customer, although it may ask
another customer for change. It must know about social responsibility—that it
cannot ask for a sandwich to be made and then refuse to pay for it. Finally, when it
reaches the cash register, it needs at least the rudiments of commonsense econom-
ics. It must know the coinage system and typical prices if it is not to tempt people to
take advantage of it.

One could read this example as a demonstration of the impossibility of constructing an intelligent agent. I, along with the contributors to this volume, would read it
rather as an indication of the scope and significance of the project of encoding core
knowledge about the physical, psychological and social worlds. It is a large project
but an important one, and I believe that when we know enough about how to
proceed, there will be people enough to do it.

Patrick J. Hayes issued an early call to this enterprise in his seminal paper, "The
Naive Physics Manifesto" (Hayes, 1979b). This volume begins with a revised
version of that paper, "The Second Naive Physics Manifesto". In it Hayes discusses many of the same issues from the vantage point of five years later. One of the
most critical issues is that of finding what he calls "clusters". To construct even an
initial "theory of the commonsense world" is an immense task. It would be easier
if we could divide it into the construction of a number of isolated subtheories. This
is not possible, since our knowledge is intertwined with such complexity. But he
argues that relatively isolated subtheories, or clusters, can be located. He then lists
some of the most important clusters roughly in the order in which they should be
tackled, and offers some tentative suggestions about how one might begin.

Most of the remainder of this volume can be viewed as a development of Hayes's
program. There are of course gaps in this volume, some due to the accidents of
editorship, some because the research just hasn't been done. One of the gaps,
largely but not entirely of the former kind, is the domain of spatial relationships.
Excellent work has been done on this problem (e.g., Kuipers, 1978; McDermott &
Davis, 1981; Davis, 1983). My view is that we should aim for an axiomatization of
spatial relationships, shape, texture, and motion that, as a test of adequacy, satisfies
three very different criteria. It should mesh well with the view of space that seems to
be implicit in language (Talmy, 1983), and hence lend itself to a treatment of spatial
metaphor; metaphors should be seen as appealing to the same predicates as literal
discourse about space, but with many of the ordinarily appropriate inferences suspended. The axiomatization should link up with vision research; the predicates
produced by a perceptual component should be explicated in the theory. And it
should be adequate for detailed discussions of geography. The most likely way to
fulfill these criteria is to define carefully a topology of space built around the

notions of the location of an entity at another entity, containment, change, nearness, and partial orderings. The topology should have a theory of granularity as an essential part. It would then support most of the metaphorical uses of spatial relationships. On top of this, one would build a kind of Cartesian geometry that would support our more precise uses of spatial reasoning, including perceptual processing and reasoning about geography.

Once we have space, we need to fill it with objects and substances. The notion of "substance" is one that has troubled both philosophers and AI researchers. Harry Bunt's chapter presents his theory of substances, built around what he calls "ensembles". This notion is based on the "part–whole" relationship and subsumes both continuous substances and collections of discrete individuals. Bunt demonstrates how the theory can be used in certain language understanding and knowledge representation problems.

When it comes to axiomatizing the actual behavior of substances, liquids prove to be among the most troublesome. Liquids change their shape and position with ease, and it is difficult to decide on individuating criteria. Patrick J. Hayes, in Chapter 3, takes on this challenge as a good test case for the possibility of naive physics. The task he sets for himself is to axiomatize enough of the naive physics of liquids to explain, among other things, the "simple" fact that when a glass with liquid in it is tipped above a table, the liquid will eventually flow out of the glass onto the table and, if there is enough of it, off the edge onto the floor.

These two chapters only scratch the surface of a very rich topic. To see what a more complete theory would have to encompass, think of the following materials: metal, concrete, wood, rubber, cloth, beads, sand, powder, chocolate, water, smoke, and air. A theory of substances would have to specify the diverse transformations they undergo or fail to undergo due to physical processes like cutting, joining, heating, and so on. These materials are located along at least one continuous scale, and it would be a significant achievement to construct a commonsense theory of substances in which the differences in their properties could be explained by the variation of a few parameters.

The task of understanding the behavior of complex physical systems and, in particular, tracing lines of causality, constitutes a very important problem. A robot moving about in the world must make quick decisions about the approximate outcome of events on the basis of incomplete, qualitative information. This capability is crucial if robotics is to succeed, and Johan de Kleer and John Seely Brown's chapter and Kenneth D. Forbus's chapter are concerned with this. Physics provides methods for computing precisely what will happen in our environment provided certain idealizations hold and certain precise measurements are available. But usually the idealizations are far from appropriate in real situations and precise measurements aren't available. How do we—and how can a robot—get by? The authors of these chapters explore methods for determining the possible outcomes of events, given whatever information we can glean. It is especially intriguing to note in these chapters, de Kleer and Brown's in particular, that the authors are beginning to get a grasp on the elusive notion of causality.

Among the physical objects in our lives, perhaps the most important are artifacts, the objects we create to carry out some function. Charles F. Schmidt, in his chapter, is concerned with representing the knowledge about a few specific artifacts and their functions that we would need in order to use them. He is especially interested in the role this knowledge plays in planning. As Schmidt says, "Some of the properties of commonsense knowledge can best be understood by the functions this knowledge must fulfill under its conditions of use."

Physical processes, events, and actions take place in time, and the temporal relations among them must usually be considered in attempting to understand the world and in planning for action. James F. Allen and Henry A. Kautz are concerned in their chapter with a formal account of time. By basing their theory on intervals rather than points in time, they attempt to capture some of the crucial features of how we conceptualize time, especially the varying granularities at which we are able to view it. Their aim is to support the reasoning necessary for certain kinds of story understanding and problem solving.

Drew McDermott, in his chapter, assumes a previously developed axiomatization of time and constructs a theory of action within its framework. He views the planning process as a kind of deduction. The planning process must be capable of handling hierarchical decomposition of actions and of planning for future events. This point of view leads him to construct an axiomatization of several critical aspects of actions, including formalizations of the notions of subtask, success, failure and feasibility.

There is much more in the purely physical world that must be axiomatized. We can take the name of any scientific discipline and attach the word "naive" to it—naive botany, naive zoology, naive ecology. Or naive meteorology: How do ordinary people conceptualize the weather? What are the principal weather conditions and how are they characterized in terms of such determinants as temperature, cloud cover, and precipitation? Naive geology: It would be desirable to axiomatize the commonsense facts about rocks and land forms that underpin the knowledge of an expert system such as Prospector (Duda, Gaschnig, & Hart, 1979). Similarly, research described in this volume on physical processes and artifacts is just a prelude to characterizing the structure and operation of such complex physical systems as automobiles.

All of these chapters are explorations of naive physics, broadly construed. But theories of naive psychology must also be formulated for our intelligent agent. Fundamental to this is an axiomatization of knowledge, belief, and mutual belief. These are essential for reasoning about how other intelligent agents will act. Moreover, mutual belief is the foundation on which a commonsense theory of the social world must be built. The chapters by Robert C. Moore and Kurt Konolige begin to address these issues.

Moore's chapter is concerned with representing the facts about knowledge and its relation to action. He axiomatizes knowledge and action in terms of an underlying possible world semantics, shows how this formulation handles some classical philosophical problems with knowledge contexts, and gives examples of reasoning in which knowledge is required for action and in which action results in knowledge. This work is more than merely another commonsense theory formally axiomatized; it begins to get at the very heart of what it is to be an intelligent, rational agent.

Konolige takes a more intuitive approach in which beliefs and the reasoning process are themselves actually represented. This enables him to deal with the facts that people do not believe all the logical consequences of what they believe, and that people are able to reason about other people's failures to reason properly. These are necessary directions for research to take if we are to have robots that can reason about other agents' thought and action.

Much, much more needs to be done in commonsense psychology and sociology. There are a number of concepts we appeal to in our attempts to understand other people. We attribute to people not only beliefs but values and emotions as well. We describe them in terms of tendencies and character traits. There is a large repertoire of concepts out of which we construct the various theories of the people we encounter.

The cornerstone of theories of the social world must be axiomatizations of mutual belief and the domain of communicative acts. Some work has already been done on these domains (McCarthy, 1979; Perrault & Allen, 1980; Appelt, 1982), but there has been almost no work on the higher domains that depend on them. I believe that the next essential step is to gain a better understanding of what might be called "microresponsibility"—the responsibility we have in everyday transactions for the truth of our assertions and the sincerity of our requests, the responsibility that gives continuity to our social life. This can presumably be explicated to some degree in terms of the reasons for mutual belief and the consistency of communicative acts across time. On this basis commonsense theories of longer-term social interactions would be constructed, including characterizations of friendship, relations among colleagues, power relationships, marriage, elementary economic transactions, and the structure of groups and organizations. What does it mean to work for SRI, for example? These domains are of course immensely complex, but simply stating the uncontroversial core of such conceptualizations would be a significant advance. It is essential to remember that in axiomatizing the social world, just as in axiomatizing the physical world, we are not trying to characterize things as they really are, but rather the way people ordinarily conceive them.

The last two chapters of the book deal not so much with the content of specific theories as with challenges for or evaluations of the whole enterprise. Jaime G. Carbonell and Steven Minton raise two issues that the other authors ignore: metaphor and learning. Is the formal approach employed by the other authors adequate for dealing with the problems of metaphor and learning? The two problems are not unrelated, for one of the most powerful tools for learning a new domain is to use a previously mastered theory as a metaphor for the new domain. One creates a new theory by applying the old theory to the new domain and learning what second-order adjustments to make where the old theory does not fit. Carbonell and Minton further argue that the process of inference itself can be seen in terms of a very concrete physical metaphor, the metaphor of "balance".

The volume closes with a discussion by David Israel of several issues that arise in connection with the enterprise, especially the controversy over the use of first-order logic. He points out that a commitment to the notation and semantics of first-order logic does not necessarily entail a commitment to its proof theory, and argues that an intelligent agent surely must have global "reasoning" processes that rely upon but are not identical with standard deductive techniques.

2 Related Research

There are several research efforts that are closely related to the naive physics project, and it might be worthwhile to consider how they differ from it. The first is work, principally in psychology, on "mental models". Workers in "mental models" research seek to elucidate the models people seem to use when they solve problems in some moderately complex domain, such as physics or arithmetic. This research is closely related enough to the naive physics project that Gentner and Stevens's *Mental Models* (1983) contains papers by several of the contributors to the present volume. But the principal emphasis in that work has been on differences between novices and experts and is often aimed at developing educational techniques for helping novices become more like experts. Our aim, by contrast, is to construct machines that are as good as novices. We emphasize the formalization of solutions to problems that anyone can solve. A second difference is that the mental-model researchers wish to model as accurately as possible the way peple actually do things. A common technique is to collect protocols. We, at least in the short term, are happy to have any theory, regardless of how accurately it models people, provided it is formally adequate. Our goal is often technological: we want to program computers, not model people. But even where we are motivated by the psychological problem, protocols are of limited use, for we are attempting to model a level of cognitive processing which is so basic it is frequently below the level of consciousness. People are likely to have very poor intuitions about what they know at this level. Finally, the computer imposes upon us a degree of formality that the mental-model researchers do not have to satisfy. Whereas they are able to specify their mental models in rather informal terms, we must encode the knowledge in some precisely defined logical notation if it is to be useful to a computational agent.

A second closely related area is AI research on expert systems. There is some overlap here as well. The first version of the "Naive Physics Manifesto" was published in a book on expert systems (Michie, 1979). Expert-system researchers, like us, must codify large amounts of knowledge, and they require the same degree of formality that we do. The principal difference is that they are after expert knowledge, while we are after naive knowledge, or perhaps, knowledge in domains in which everybody is an expert. Normally, they do not encode the basic knowledge that underlies the expertise. An expert system in geology may know the characteristics of a good prospect site without knowing that a rock is a physical object and that a geologist is a person. Moreover, as de Kleer and Brown say, "Expert systems usually cannot solve simpler versions of the problems they are designed to solve''. This may be a good way to build practical systems, but it is not good as a model of flexible intelligence.

A bit farther afield is research in cognitive anthropology, where researchers attempt to discover the belief systems that people in other cultures operate under (Frake 1980; Agar, 1971; Hutchins, 1981). An obvious distinction here is that whereas they are interested in other cultures, we are interested in our own. While they are concerned with elucidating aspects of belief systems that differ from ours, we seek to elucidate levels of knowledge that are so basic that they are possibly common to all cultures. Moreover, we require a greater degree of formality. In fact, one can understand this requirement in terms of the mandate of ethnography. It is the job of anthropologists, or ethnographers, to communicate the nature of another culture to members of their own culture. Hence, they focus on the differences between the two cultures and describe the differences in terms of the similarities. We must communicate commonsense knowledge to the computer, which knows nothing beyond how to compute. Thus we must express *all* the commonsense knowledge and it must be in formal, computable terms.

Finally, work on lexical semantics in linguistics and psychology can be seen as related to this enterprise. Although it has never become a coherent program of research, excellent investigations have been conducted by Charles Fillmore (1971), Ray Jackendoff (1976), George Miller and Philip Johnson-Laird (1976), and Len Talmy (1983), among others. This work has generally not been cast in a logical framework, but it is fairly straightforward to do so. One can view the lexical decomposition of a word as an inference one can draw, rather than as a special sort of linguistic operation. However, lexical semanticists typically insist on a distinction between linguistic knowledge and general knowledge, feeling that if one admits general knowledge, the problem of specification becomes intractable. Their ''axiomatizations'' are therefore typically small. By contrast, most of us do not see the difference between linguistic and general knowledge as significant, whatever that means for tractability.

3 Decisions and Difficulties

A researcher who undertakes the axiomatization of a commonsense domain will face a number of decisions and difficulties. The first decision that must be made is what formalism to use. Should it be predicate calculus or some special-purpose representation language? Most of the contributors have chosen some variant of the former. Predicate calculus is as powerful a representation language as any other that has been devised by AI researchers. The others are either equivalent to it or something less (Hayes, 1979a). Moreover, it is said to provide a universal medium for comparison of various researchers' work. The semantics of the notation is well understood; by looking at the formulae we can tell something of how they will be used. This is often not true of less highly developed representation languages. But predicate calculus is not necessarily as universal as sometimes claimed. Within the constraints of predicate calculus there is a great deal of play in how things will be formulated. The conceptual analyses that underlie different axiomatizations—for example, ontological questions like whether such things as events or possible worlds exist—can make axiomatizations look radically different even when they use the same notation. Furthermore, we cannot tell from the notation everything about how formulas will be used in a complex AI system. Intelligence is not deduction alone, but deduction controlled and augmented by higher "reasoning" processes (Israel, this volume).

The very unconstrained nature of predicate calculus leads some researchers to choose other formalisms. Often the constraints imposed by a language suggest solutions to problems. If only a narrow set of options is exercised in an unconstrained language, a more constrained language may be more natural and allow knowledge to be expressed more succinctly. In addition, special-purpose notations may indicate more explicitly the special-purpose deduction procedures that will use them. As Hayes admits, "idiosyncratic notations may sometimes be useful for idiosyncratic subtheories." Our concern in this volume is for facts, not notation, but sometimes getting the facts right requires notational maneuvers.

My own feeling is that the choice of a representation language is not a serious issue, as long as it is clear what the consequences are of different ways of expressing something—for example, by explicitly stating the notation's relation to predicate calculus. In organizing this volume we have tried to veer away from this issue—to focus on the facts encoded, not on the language they are encoded in.

The next and perhaps most important problem faced by the researcher is one that is mentioned by Hayes and Israel, but not seriously addressed in *any* of the chapters: how do we decide what facts to put into the knowledge base, and how do we know we have it right? How do we determine the content of a knowledge base, and how is it to be validated? Hayes suggests that "naive physicists" will develop an exquisitely acute sense of the appropriateness of proposed axioms, and this is undoubtedly true. But that can't be the final word. Certain formal properties of our axiomatizations may help in determining content. Thus, we can eliminate some gaps in our axiomatizations by making sure that the predicates used in an axiom are richly explicated elsewhere in the theory. Hayes also suggests that it may be possible to interview people about their naive theories of the world. I doubt, however, that we will be able to learn about the theories to the level of detail that AI research requires. A method I have tried is to look for the knowledge that seems to be presupposed by the uses of a word in a domain, as a way of determining what should be included in the knowledge base (Hobbs, 1984). This is useful if the knowledge base is for a natural language processing system; it is not clear whether there is an equivalent method for robotics.

One important guide to selecting the content of one's axiomatization is what might be called "key problems". Enough knowledge of the domain must be encoded for solutions to the key problems to be found. Thus, Hayes in Chapter 3 is concerned with axiomatizing the naive physics of liquids to the extent of being able to predict that water poured from a glass will eventually spill off a table onto the floor. McDermott sets for himself the goal of planning the solution to a moderately difficult problem in chess. Schmidt aims for the solution of an everyday planning problem, and this motivation underlies Allen and Kautz's work as well. Moore is concerned with solving problems that involve knowing the combination of a safe and what one learns from litmus paper. Konolige considers several variants of the Three Wise Men problem, which has for some time been a major challenge to the adequacy of representation schemes for knowledge and mutual knowledge. None of these problems is especially interesting in itself. Rather they serve as benchmarks for research. By setting the solution of a key problem as a research goal, one has something concrete by which to test the adequacy of one's theory. The key problems don't let the researcher get away with overly simple approaches.

Some of the chapters exhibit another aim that influences the content of the axiomatization—to reduce the number of primitive concepts to a minimum. Allen and Kautz attempt to characterize time solely in terms of durations, eliminating instants. Bunt reduces set membership to the "part-of" relation for ensembles. Hayes, on the other hand, says about the naive physics program, "It is not proposed to find a philosophically exciting reduction of all ordinary concepts to some special collection of concepts". I tend to side with Hayes, believing that the first priority is to encode the facts, although not objecting to elegant reductions when they are achieved.

Most of the contributors to this volume have in mind applications to robotics, while others are interested in natural language processing. These orientations can have a significant influence on the content of a theory. My guess is that where one's concern is robotics, then one's naive physics will be more like real physics, the kind of simplified physics that we find in the chapters by de Kleer and Brown and by Forbus. There are likely to be deep axiomatizations of the cores of subtheories in terms of predicates that are either far from English words or very idealized versions of intuitive concepts. The subtheories may have a high ratio of axioms to predicates; the subtheories will consist of a few concepts well explicated. If one's primary concern is natural language processing, however, the resulting axiomatizations will be closer to our intuitive theories of the world, the ones we seem to presuppose when we talk about the world, and less like those of real physics. The axiomatizations will have the precisely worked out cores, but they will be at a rather shallow level. The predicates will be closer to English words in their meaning. There will be a low ratio of axioms to predicates, and many predicates will have only one or two axioms, expressing how their meanings differ by only a shade from the meaning of some other predicate.

Another theme that in many chapters affects the style of axiomatization is a concern for efficient deduction. It is, for example, one of Allen and Kautz's motivations for their special-purpose treatment of time. Moore rejects the syntactic treatment of knowledge in favor of a possible worlds approach, in part because of his concern for the computationally explosive properties of the former. Much of Konolige's effort is devoted to overcoming some of these difficulties. However, since we know little about what classes of inferences will be most useful, another research strategy would be to build a large knowledge base, use it in a variety of complex tasks, and then determine empirically what classes of inferences most need special-purpose deduction techniques. Hayes expresses this view when he says, "I think we should take our axioms unrestricted for a while, until we can see more realistically what sorts of restriction we shall have to impose on their inferential behavior to achieve practical systems."

How are we to judge the success of an axiomatization? The obvious answer is that it is successful insofar as it enables our robot to succeed in the world. If our robot is to be successful, it ought to have true beliefs, and for this reason we should be interested in the semantics of the notation—the connection between the notation and the world.

But truth is relative to a theory of the world. If we assume that the proper description of the world is in terms given by quantum electrodynamics, then we are perhaps closer to the "correct" theory of the world, but the semantics of most notational systems will be, at the least, formidable. On the other hand, one can assume a more "intuitive" ontology, one that is isomorphic to the language we use to talk about the world. Here the specification of the semantics is easy, even trivial, but the theory of the world is known to be wrong, so that "true" beliefs do not in any way guarantee success in the world. Typical approaches to semantics are much closer to the latter end of the spectrum—one assumes the reality of such things as individuals, like John, of rather complex set-theoretic constructions, of numbers, and sometimes of times, locations, possible worlds, states, and events. My guess is that this ontology is generally too far from scientific truth to ensure success and too sparse to help in specifying the semantics of any but the most closely related constructs. For reasons like these, I find myself quite skeptical about whether specifying the semantics of our notation will go very far in ensuring the success of our robot. But I suspect I am in the minority here; Hayes argues the opposite case persuasively. It is certainly true that specifying the semantics gives the reader at least some idea of how the notation is going to be used. Insofar as concern for semantics means that the axiomatization of a domain in a formal language must proceed hand in hand with thinking clearly about the domain, who could argue against it?

But there is a further use of semantics in this enterprise, a heuristic use, that establishes another criterion for the success of an axiomatization. When we display a model for a set of axioms, we have proved its consistency. Now many researchers in AI have argued that consistency of axiomatizations is not something we should particularly strive for. It is quite unlikely that people have a consistent collection of beliefs. I find myself sympathetic with this point of view. It is probably more appropriate to allow inconsistencies and to devise means by which the agent can back away from contradictions when they are encountered. That is, reasoning, in Israel's sense, would be able to deal with the inconsistencies even though deduction would not.

Nevertheless, since deduction is the most basic operation that the agent would do, we are only asking for trouble if we allow inconsistencies in axiomatizations where we could otherwise avoid them. Among other things, an inconsistency guarantees that we have incorrect beliefs. How inconsistencies may be avoided, therefore, becomes a matter of some interest. Bunt, in his chapter, uses an obviously inappropriate semantics in an interesting way to establish the consistency of a theory. A theory of composite objects is shown to have as one of its models the set of ordered pairs of sets and open-interval series of the real line.

Such moves are possible for isolated subtheories, but proving the consistency of a very large collection of axioms, comprised of highly interconnected subtheories, is a severe problem. One might argue that since the physical world will be a model of such a large-scale axiomatization, the consistency of the axiomatization will follow. But there is a reason real physics is not the same as naive physics—naive physics is wrong. It is useful, indeed essential, for an intelligent agent constrained to act in real time, moving about in a world full of uncertainty, where the idealizations of real physics are seldom encountered. But it is nevertheless wrong, when the world is examined with care and in detail, and so the physical world will *not* be a model for our theory.

The most likely outcome for the consistency problem is that we will be able to prove the cores of most subtheories consistent, when they are considered in isolation, with their interconnections with other subtheories removed. We may also be able to show how adding axioms of certain types does not destroy consistency. But it is unlikely that we will be able to prove the consistency of the whole. The situation will be not unlike the one we find ourselves in with respect to the debugging of large computer programs. We cannot in general prove that no bugs remain, but we do eventually become assured that whatever bugs there are do not ordinarily affect the performance of the system. If procedures for backing away from contradictions are available, this "degree of consistency" may be all that is necessary.

4 A Final Qualm

Let me close on an uneasy note. I occasionally have misgivings about this volume. The papers in it are formal, sometimes forbiddingly so. Is this what AI will come to be? Will future students of AI have to face books as dense in mathematical notation and as bloodless in presentation as those I faced, say, in algebraic topology, as a graduate student in mathematics? AI has been fun up to now because it has been easy to find quick solutions to obviously relevant problems. Everywhere we've turned we've found unclaimed territory ready to yield treasures to our way of looking at things. Is the heavy hand of formalism now going to put an end to all this, burying insights in mires of notation?

I think increased formalism is necessary if our field is to become a mature discipline. Formalization is a tool that forces us to examine our ideas closely. It is a way of discovering unintended consequences of theories and a way of standardizing results for dissemination. But we must be wary of the imperialism of formal logic, the tendency of formalizers to look down on informal work, an instantiation of the more general condescension of the hard sciences toward the soft. Garbage can be formalized, and often has been. Formalization is a trick that can be learned. It is no substitute for insight.

References

Agar, Michael (1971). *Ripping and Running: A Formal Ethnography of Urban Heroin Addicts.* New York: Academic Press

Appelt, Douglas E. (1982). "Planning Natural-Language Utterances to Satisfy Multiple Goals," SRI Artificial Intelligence Center Technical Note 259, SRI International, Menlo Park, California.

Davis, Ernest (1983). "Reasoning and Acquiring Geographic Knowledge," Ph. D. Thesis, Yale University.

Duda, Richard, John Gaschnig, & Peter Hart (1979). "Model Design in the Prospector Consultant System for Mineral Exploration," in *Expert Systems in the Micro-electronic Age,* Donald Michie, ed. Edinburgh, Scotland: Edinburgh University Press, pp. 153–167.

Fillmore, Charles (1971). "Verbs of Judging: An Exercise in Semantic Description," in *Studies in Linguistic Semantics,* Charles Fillmore and D. Terence Langendoen, eds. New York: Holt, Rinehart, Winston, pp. 273–289.

Frake, Charles (1980). *Language and Cultural Description: Essays by Charles O. Frake,* A. S. Dil, ed. Stanford: Stanford University Press.

Gentner, Dedre, & Albert L. Stevens, eds. (1983). *Mental Models.* Hillsdale, NJ: Erlbaum.

Hayes, Patrick J. (1979a). "The Logic of Frames," in *Frame Conceptions and Text Understanding,* D. Metzing, ed. (Walter de Gruyter and Company), Berlin, West Germany: Walter de Gruyter, pp. 46–61.

Hayes, Patrick J. (1979b). "The Naive Physics Manifesto," in *Expert Systems in the Micro-electronic Age,* Donald Michie, ed. Edinburgh, Scotland: Edinburgh University Press, pp. 242–270.

Hobbs, Jerry R. (1984). "Sublanguage and Knowledge," to appear in *Sublanguage: Description and Processing,* Ralph Grishman and Richard Kittredge, eds. Hillsdale, NJ: Erlbaum.

Hutchins, Edwin L. (1981). *Culture and Inference: A Trobriand Case Study.* Cambridge, MA: Harvard University Press.

Jackendoff, Ray (1976, winter). "Toward an Explanatory Semantic Representation," *Linguistic Inquiry,* Vol. 7, No. 1, pp. 89–150.

Kuipers, Benjamin (1978). "Modeling Spatial Knowledge," *Cognitive Science,* Vol. 2, No. 2, pp. 129–154.

McCarthy, John (1979). "Formalization of the Two Puzzles Involving Knowledge," unpublished manuscript.

McDermott, Drew, & Ernest Davis (1984, March). "Planning Routes through Uncertain Territory," *Artificial Intelligence,* Vol. 22, No. 2, pp. 107–156.

Michie, Donald, ed. (1979). *Expert Systems in the Micro-electronic Age,* Edinburgh, Scotland: Edinburgh University Press.

Miller, George A., & Philip N. Johnson-Laird (1976). *Language and Perception* Cambridge, MA: Belknap Press of Harvard University Press.

Perrault, C. Raymond, & James F. Allen (1980, July–December). "A Plan-Based Analysis of Indirect Speech Acts," *American Journal of Computational Linguistics,* Vol. 6, No. 3–4, pp. 167–182.

Talmy, Leonard (1983). "How Language Structures Space," in *Spatial Orientation: Theory, Research, and Application,* Herbert Pick and Linda Acredolo, eds. New York: Plenum, pp. 225–282.

1 The Second Naive Physics Manifesto

Patrick J. Hayes

Cognitive Science
University of Rochester
Rochester, New York

1 Preface

Five years ago I wrote a paper, "The Naive Physics Manifesto", complaining about AI's emphasis on toy worlds and urging the field to put away childish things by building large-scale formalizations, suggesting in particular that a suitable initial project would be a formalization of our knowledge of the everyday physical world: of naive physics (NP). At that time, I felt rather alone in making such a suggestion (which is why the paper had such a proselytizing tone) and quite optimistic that success in even this ambitious a project could be achieved in a reasonable time scale. As this volume testifies, both feelings are no longer appropriate. There is a lot of work going on, and there is more to be done than I had foreseen. A whole layer of professionalism has emerged, for example, in the business of finding out just what people's intuitive ideas are about such matters as falling rocks or evaporating liquids, a matter I had relegated to disciplined introspection. In 1978, I predicted that the overall task was an order of magnitude (but not ten orders of magnitude) more difficult than any that had been undertaken so far. I now think that two or three orders of magnitude is a better estimate. It's still not impossible, though.

My old paper now seems dated and, in places, inappropriately naive on some deep issues. The following is a revised version which attempts to correct some of these shortcomings, and repeats the points which need repeating because nobody seems to have taken any notice of them.

This is a revised version of the original, not a sequel to it. Since several years have passed, some of the passion may have gone, being replaced with (I hope) more careful discussion.

2 Introduction

Artificial intelligence is full of 'toy problems': small, artificial axiomatizations or puzzles designed to exercise the talents of various problem-solving programs or

1

representational languages or systems. The subject badly needs some non-toy worlds to experiment with. In other areas of cognitive science, also, there is a need to consider the organization of knowledge on a larger scale than is currently done, if only because quantitatively different mental models may well be qualitatively different.

In this document I propose the construction of a formalization of a sizable portion of common-sense knowledge about the everyday physical world: about objects, shape, space, movement, substances (solids and liquids), time, etc. Such a formalization could, for example, be a collection of assertions in a first-order logical formalism, or a collection of KRL units, or a microplanner program, or one of a number of other things, or even a mixture of several. It should have the following characteristics.

2.1 Breadth

It should cover the whole range of everyday physical phenomena: not just the blocks world, for example. Since in some important sense the world (even the everyday world) is infinitely rich in possible phenomena, this will never be perfect. Nevertheless, we should *try* to fill in all the major holes, or at least identify them.

It should be reasonably detailed. For example, such aspects of a block in a block world as shape, material, weight, rigidity and surface texture should be available as concepts in a blocks-world description, as well as support relationships.

2.2 Density

The ratio of facts to concepts needs to be fairly high. Put another way: the units have to have *lots* of slots. Low-density formalizations are in some sense trivial: they fail to say enough about the concepts they mention to pin down the meaning of their symbols at all precisely. Sometimes, for special purposes, as for example in foundational studies, this can be an advantage: but not for us.

2.3 Uniformity

There should be a common formal framework (language, system, etc.) for the whole formalization, so that the inferential connections between the different parts (axioms, frames, . . .) can be clearly seen, and divisions into subformalisations are not prejudged by deciding to use one formalism for one area and a different one for a different area.

I (still) believe that a formalization of naive physics with these properties can be constructed within a reasonable time-scale. The reasons for such optimism are explained later. It is important however to clearly distinguish this proposal from some others with which it may be confused, because some of these seem to be far less tractable.

3 What the Proposal Isn't

3.1

It is *not* proposed to make a computer program which can 'use' the formalism in some sense. For example, a problem-solving program, or a natural language comprehension system with the representation as target. It is tempting to make such demonstrations from time to time. (They impress people; and it is satisfying to have actually *made* something which works, like building model railways; and one's students can get Ph.D.'s that way.) But they divert attention from the main goal. In fact, I believe they have several more dangerous effects. It is perilously easy to conclude that, because one has a program which *works* (in some sense), its representation of its knowledge must be more or less *correct* (in some sense). Now this is true, in some sense. But a representation may be adequate to support a limited kind of inference, and completely unable to be extended to support a slightly more general kind of behavior. It may be wholly limited by scale factors, and therefore tell us nothing about thinking about realistically complicated worlds. Images as internal pictures and the STRIPS representation of actions by add and delete lists are two good examples. I suspect that the use of state variables to represent time is another. Such representational devices are traps, tempting the unwary into dead ends where they struggle to overcome insurmountable difficulties, difficulties generated by the representation itself. I now believe, although I know this view is very controversial, that the famous frame problem is such a difficulty: an apparently deep problem which is largely artifact.

I emphasize this point because there is still a prevailing attitude in AI that research which does not result fairly quickly in a working program of some kind is somehow useless or, at least, highly suspicious. Of course implementability is the ultimate test of the validity of ideas in AI, and I do not mean to argue against this. But we must not be too hasty.

This is no more than a reiteration of John McCarthy's emphasis, since the inception of AI as a subject, on the importance of representational issues (McCarthy 1957, McCarthy & Hayes 1969). In 1969, McCarthy proposed the "Missouri Program", which would make no inferences of its own but would be willing to check proposed arguments submitted to it: a proof checker for common sense. Those who find it repugnant to be told to ignore programming considerations may find it more congenial to be urged to imagine the project of building a proof *checker* for naive physics.

3.2

It is *not* proposed to develop a new formalism or language to write down all this knowledge in. In fact, I propose (as my friends will have already guessed) that first-order logic is a suitable basic vehicle for representation. However, let me at once qualify this.

I have no particular brief for the usual syntax of first-order logic. Personally I find it agreeable: but if someone likes to write it all out in KRL, or semantic networks of one sort or another, or OMEGA, or KRYPTON, or what have you; well, that's fine. The important point is that one *knows what it means*: that the formalism has a clear *interpretation* (I avoid the word 's*m*nt*cs' deliberately). At the level of interpretation, there is little to choose between any of these, and most are strictly weaker than predicate calculus, which also has the advantage of a clear, explicit model theory, and a well-understood proof theory.

I have pointed out elsewhere (Hayes 1977, 1978) that virtually all known representational schemes are equivalent to first-order logic (with one or two notable exceptions, primarily to do with nonmonotonic reasoning). This is still true in 1983, but I should perhaps emphasize that care is needed in making comparisons. First, in claiming equivalence, one is speaking of representational (expressive) power, not computational efficiency. Given a simple "dumb" interpreter (i.e. a "uniform" theorem-prover), these may be at odds with one another. The moral is that simple, dumb interpreters are a bad idea, and interpreters should be sensitive to 'control' information, meta-information about the inferential process itself. This idea brings its own representational problems. I am not arguing that these should be ignored. On the contrary, they raise some of the most important questions in AI. But until we have some idea of the sorts of inferences we might want to control, speculation on the matter is premature. Second, in making comparisons between systems one must exercise care. Many "computational" systems have invisible, buried, assumptions about their domain, not explicitly documented in publications, which must be rendered explicit in a logical axiomatization.[1] Third, the use of logic imposes almost no restrictions on the kinds of thing about which we wish to speak: sequences of actions or views of a room or plans or goals, etc., are all perfectly fine candidates. One must not let lack of imagination in axiomatizing lead one to conclude that logical formalisms are weaker than some of the more superficially baroque systems which AI has devised. (In particular, first-order logic can be taken to quantify over some properties, functions and relations and still be essentially first-order. What makes it higher-order is when its quantifiers have to range over all^2 properties, functions and relations, a condition which cannot be enforced without something like a rule of λ-abstraction or a comprehension schema.)

Finally, let me emphasize that idiosyncratic notations may sometimes be useful for idiosyncratic subtheories. For example, in sketching an axiomatic theory of fluids (this volume) I found it useful to think of the possible physical states of fluids as being essentially states of a finite-state machine. This summarizes a whole lot of lengthy, and rather clumsy, first-order axioms into one neat diagram. Still, it *means* the same as the axioms: first-order logic is still, as it were, the reference language. It is essential that there be some standard reference language in this way, so that the different parts of the formalism can be related to one another.

---

[1] This touches on a basic terminological ambiguity. Shall we regard an axiom as a statement *in* a logic; or as a new *rule* to be *added to* the logic, so that the logic is somehow made stronger but the axiomatization is not enlarged? One always has the option: the second route tends to lead to less expressive but operationally more efficient systems, since a rule can often be neatly characterized as an axiom with a restriction imposed on its use, so that less can be inferred from it. I think we should take our axioms unrestricted for a while, until we can see more realistically what sorts of restriction we shall have to impose on their inferential behavior to achieve practical systems.

[2] There are two versions, in fact: "all nameable", which you get with the rule or schema, and "all", which can't be enforced by any schema or rule or computational device of *any* kind, since the set of theorems is then not recursively enumerable. If anyone claims to have implemented a reasoning system which can handle full higher order reasoning, he is wrong.

3.3

It is not proposed to find a philosophically exciting reduction of all ordinary concepts to some special collection of concepts (such as sets, or Goodmanesque "individuals", or space–time points, or qualia.) Maybe some such reduction will eventually turn out to be possible. I think it extremely unlikely and not especially desirable, but whether or not it is, is not the present issue. *First* we need to formalize the naive worldview, using whatever concepts seem best suited to that purpose—thousands or tens of thousands of them if necessary. Afterwards we can try to impose some a priori ontological scheme upon it. But until we have the basic theory articulated, we don't know what our subject matter is.

Now, this is not to say that we should not exercise some care in avoiding unnecessary proliferation of axioms, or some aesthetic sensibility in designing axioms to give clean proofs and to interact as elegantly as possible. But these are matters of general scientific style, not ends in themselves.

4 Theories, Tokens and Closure

Let us imagine that a NP formalization exists. It consists of a large number of assertions (*or*: frames, scripts, networks, etc.) involving a large number of relation, function and constant symbols (*or*: frame headers, slot names, node and arc labels, etc. From now on I will not bother to reemphasise these obvious parallels). For neutral words, let us call these formal symbols *tokens,* and the collection of axioms the *theory* (in the sense of 'formal theory' in logic, not 'scientific theory' in history of science).

The success of a NP theory is measured by the extent to which it provides a vocabulary of tokens which allows a wide range of intuitive concepts to be expressed, and to which it then supports conclusions mirroring those which we find correct or reasonable. People know, for example, that if a stone is released, it falls with increasing speed until it hits something, and there is then an impact, which can cause damage if the velocity is high. The theory should provide tokens allowing one to express the concept of releasing a stone in space. And it should then be possible to infer from the theory that it will fall, etc.: so there must be tokens enabling one to express ideas of velocity, direction, impact, and so on. And then these same tokens must be usable in describing other kinds of circumstance, and the theory support the appropriate conclusions there, and so on. We want the overall pattern of consequences produced by the theory to correspond reasonably faithfully to our own intuition in both breadth and detail. Given the hypothesis that our own intuition is itself realized as a theory of this kind inside our heads, the NP theory we construct will then be equipotent with this inner theory.

More subtle tests than mere matching against intuition might be applied to an NP theory. Consequences which are *very* obvious should have shorter derivations then those which require some thought, perhaps. If, in proving *p* from *q*, the theory must make use of some concept token, perhaps psychologists can devise an experiment in which the "activation" of that concept can be tested for, while people are deciding whether or not q, given p. Pylyshyn (1979) discusses ways in which intermediate psychological states might be investigated: I will not discuss them further here, but focus instead on questions connected with getting a theory constructed in the first place.

The practical task of building such a theory begins with some 'target' concepts and desired inferences. Take the familiar example of formalising a world of cubical wooden blocks on a flat table, with the goal of being able to reason about processes of piling these into vertical stacks and rearranging such piles by moving blocks from place to place: the familiar blocks world. Notice that we have put quite a constraint on what inferences we are interested in. An actual tabletop of blocks admits of many more interesting and complicated activities: building walls and pyramids, pushing blocks around horizontally, juggling, etc.; but we deliberately exclude such matters from consideration for now.

I will go through this toy world in detail, in order to illustrate some general points. It is not intended as a serious exercise in naive physics. First, we obviously need the concept of block (a predicate $Block(b)$), and there will be several states of the little universe as things are moved, so we also need that concept ($State(s)$). A block will be on some other block or on the table in every state ($On(b,c,s)$, and the name $table$): four tokens so far, and now we can write some axioms, such as:

$$\forall s,b.\ State(s) \wedge Block(b) \supset$$
$$(\exists\ c.\ Block(c) \wedge On(b,c,s)) \vee On(b,table,s) \tag{1}$$

(We could have done it differently: for example, a function $below(b,s)$ instead of the relation On, so that $On(b,c,s)$ translates into $below(b,s) = c$. Or a function $above(b,s)$, with the obvious meaning, and a constant, air, so that $above(b,s) = air$ corresponds to: $\forall c. {\sim} On(c,b,s)$, and being careful never to apply $above$ to the table. We could have decided not to use states at all, but to have thought of each block as having a temporal history. No doubt other variations are possible. (In the future, I will—to save paper and to improve readability—omit such antecedents as $Block(b)$ and $State(s)$ from formulae. It is straightforward to enrich the logic to a many-sorted logic in which this omission is syntactically normal. The concepts are there, though, and need inferential machinery of one kind or another, so they should be shown in the "reference language".)

Now, to describe change we need the idea of a state-transition. There are several ways to do this. We could have a relation $Next(s,t)$ between states, for example, or a function $next(s)$, corresponding to the intuitive feeling that one moment follows another, and there is always a unique next thing that will in fact happen (*que sera, sera*). Or we might say that, since we are talking about actions, and there are usually several things one *might* do in a given situation, so there are several different next-states. This leads to McCarthy's idea—now standard—of actions as state-to-state functions. We might have actions $pickup(b,s)$ and $putdown(b,s)$, for example. The result of picking up b is a state in which b is no longer on anything but rather is held in the hand:

$$Held(b,pickup(b)) \tag{2}$$

$$Held(b,s) \supset \forall x. \sim On(b,x,s) \tag{3}$$

We must now modify (1) by adding $Held(b,s)$ as a third possibility. The result of putdowning on b is that whatever is held gets to rest on b; provided of course there is nothing there already. To make this neater, let's define $Clear$:

$$Clear(x,s) \equiv \forall c. On(c,x,s) \lor x=table \tag{4}$$

Then we can say:

$$Held(b,s) \land Clear(c,s) \supset On(b,c,putdown(c,s)) \tag{5}$$

(This still doesn't explain what $putdown(c,s)$ is like if nothing is $Held$ in s. We might decide there are two sorts of states, those in which the hand is holding something and those in which it is empty, and insist that $putdown$ applies only to the former. Or we might just say that:

$$\forall x \cdot \sim Held(x,s) \supset putdown(c,s) = s \tag{6}$$

We can now begin to see how the desired kinds of conclusion might follow. If we know that A is on C on the table and B is on the table and A and C are clear, then we can infer from (2) that after a suitable pickup, A is held. Unfortunately, we can't conclude that B is still clear: C may have jumped onto it, as far as our axioms are concerned. (Consider a world of jumping blocks, or stackable frogs, in which every time one is lifted, the one beneath hops onto a different block. This is a possible world, and all five of the axioms are true in it. So, nothing that they say rules this possibility out.) This is a tiny illustration of the notorious frame problem (McCarthy & Hayes 1969). We need to say that during a pickup of a block, no other On relations change.

Now, for the first time, we don't need to introduce any new tokens. We have a rich enough vocabulary at hand to state our axiom:

$$On(b,c,s) \supset \forall d. \sim On(b,c,pickup(d,s)) \lor b = d \tag{7}$$

Here, $\lor$ is exclusive-or, so that if b is not d, then $On(b,c)$ must still be true in $pickup(d,s)$; and we are sure that $\sim On(b,c,pickup(b,s))$ under any circumstances. Notice that the block picked up might itself carry others, and they go right along with it.

Given (7), we can quickly conclude that B is still clear and still on the table, so we can now putdown onto it and have a state in which A is on B—no longer clear, by (4)—and C is clear . . . well, not quite, since putting down might yet disturb things. But we can fix this with an even simpler frame axiom:

$$On(b,c,s) \supset On(b,c,putdown(d,s)) \tag{8}$$

and we can now discuss states reached by picking up and putting down things all over the place, as we desired. Given a sufficiently complete description of a layout of blocks, and a goal of some other configuration, then if there is a sequence of block movements which get us from the former to the latter, then this theory will show that there is.

For some time now we have not needed to introduce any other tokens. We can do the changes by adding or modifying axioms, working entirely in the given vocabulary. This collection of tokens (*block, table, state, on, held, pickup, putdown*) is enough to work with. Alternative worlds can be constructed within it. It is a large enough collection to support axioms describing general properties of the universe we have in mind, and descriptions of particular worlds in enough detail to allow the sorts of conclusion we wanted to be inferred. No subset will do the job, as we have seen:[3] but this is just enough to let us say what needs saying. We have reached what might be called a *conceptual closure*. This phenomenon is familiar to anyone who has tried to axiomatize or formalize some area. Having chosen one's concepts to start on, one quickly needs to introduce tokens for others one had not contemplated, and the axioms which pin down their meanings introduce others, and so on: until one finds suddenly there are enough tokens around that it is easy to say enough "about" them all: enough, that is, to enable the inferences one had had in mind all along to be made.

This sort of closure is by no means trivial. Suppose we had tried to use *next(s)*, following the idea that world-states are, after all, linearly ordered; then it becomes quite hard to achieve. We can say that a block may stay where it is, or become picked up:

$$On(b,c,s) \wedge \forall x. \sim Held(x,s) \supset$$
$$On(b,c,next(s)) \vee Held(b,next(s)) \tag{9}$$

and we can insist that only one is held at once:

$$Held(b,s) \wedge Held(c,s) \supset b=c \tag{10}$$

---

[3] I omitted *clear* deliberately. It has an explicit definition and could be eliminated entirely at no real cost of expressive power. Having that token makes axioms more compact and deductions shorter, but it does not enable us to say anything new, since we could have replaced it everywhere else by its definition and gotten an equivalent set of axioms. Definitions don't add to the expressive power of a theory.

But putting down is more difficult. If we say

$$Held(b,s) \wedge Clear(c,s) \supset On(b,c,next(s)) \tag{11}$$

then the held block has been put down into every clear space. We certainly want to say that the held block is put down in one of the potential putdown sites:

$$Held(b,s) \supset \exists \ c. \ Clear(c,s) \wedge On(b,c,next(s)) \tag{12}$$

But we now have no way of inferring that the held block can actually be placed in any particular clear place. This axiom is consistent with a world in which blocks can be placed only on the table, for example, or in which blocks are always released from on high and falleth gently upon some random stack or other. There is no way within this vocabulary to describe one possible future state's properties as distinct from those of a different possible future state. We have no way of stating the properties we need: closure eludes us. It can be achieved, but only by bringing possible futures in by the back door.

Our theory, though closed, is by no means perfect. As stated, it can support all the inferences we had in mind. Unfortunately, it can also support some others which we didn't have in mind. For example, nothing in the axioms so far prevents two successive pickups, giving a handful of blocks (or, somewhat less plausibly, a handful of towers of blocks). This would be fine, except that (5) has it that anything held is deposited by a putdown, thus leaving several blocks on one; but they were supposed to be all the same size. The neatest way to fix this is to modify (2), say as follows:

$$\forall \ x. \ \sim Held(x,s) \supset Held(b,pickup(b,s)) \tag{13}$$

We can also insist that only single blocks are picked up by adding $Clear(b,s)$ as another antecedent condition. Again: if a block is $Clear$, then we can pick it up—its still $Clear$—and put it down on $itself$: there's nothing in (5) to prevent this. (Consider a zero-gravity world in which blocks can be released in space, and they then just hang there: and say that in this case the block is On itself. Clearly all the axioms are satisfied in this world too.) So to rule this out we need another axiom, and to modify (5) slightly. Finding other such bugs is left as an exercise for the reader.

It is important to bear such negative properties of a formalization in mind even though they make the formalizer's life more complex. It is easy to overlook them.

5 Meanings, Theories and Model Theory

In developing this toy theory I have several times used an example world to show that something we wanted to follow didn't, or that something we didn't want to be true might be. This ability to interpret our axioms in a possible world, see what they say and whether it is true or not, is so useful that I cannot imagine proceeding without it. But it is only possible if there is an idea of a *model* of the formal language in which the theory is written: a systematic notion of what a possible world is and how the tokens of the theory can be mapped into entities (or structures or values or whatever) in such worlds. We have to be able to *imagine* what our tokens *might* mean.

Now this semantic metatheory may be relatively informal, but the more exactly it is defined, the more useful it will be as a tool for the theory-builder. The main attraction of formal logics as representational languages is that they have very precise model theories, and the main attraction of first-order logic is that its model theory is so simple, so widely applicable, and yet so powerful.

A first-order model is a set of entities and suitable mappings from tokens to functions and relations, of appropriate arity, over it.[4] Any collection of things will do: for example, for our blocks world, I could take the collection of papers on my desk, and interpret *On* to be the relation which holds between two pieces of paper when one partially or wholly overlaps the other, and *pickup* to be the action of picking up, and so on. (In fact, this isn't a model, because my desk is too crowded: axiom (5) is false. But it would be if I tidied my desk up.)

This is very satisfying, since we have found a model which is very close to the original intuition. But there are other models. Consider a table and a single block and the two states, one—call it *A*—with the block on the table, and the other—call it *B*—with the block held above the table. Let *pickup* and *putdown* denote the functions $(A \rightarrow B, B \rightarrow B)$ and $(B \rightarrow A, A \rightarrow A)$ respectively, let *Held* be true just of

---

[4] This is usually presented, in textbooks of elementary logic, in a rather formal, mathematical way: and this fact may have given rise to the curious but widespread delusion that a first-order model is merely another formal description of the world, just like the axiomatization of which it is a model; and that the Tarskian truth-recursion is a kind of translation from one formal system to another (e.g. Wilks 1977). This is quite wrong. For a start, the relationship between an axiomatization and its models (or, dually, between a model and the set of axiomatizations which are true of it) is quite different from a translation. It is many-many rather than one-one, for example. Moreover, it has the algebraic character called a Galois connection, which is to say, roughly, that as the axiomatization is increased in size (as axioms are added), the collection of models—possible states of affairs—decreases in size. It is quite possible for a large, complex axiomizations to have small, simple models, and vice versa. In particular, a model can always be gratuitously complex (e.g. contain entities which aren't mentioned at all in the axiomization). But the deeper mistake in this way of thinking is to confuse a formal description of a model—found in the textbooks which are developing a mathematical approach to the metatheory of logic—with the actual model. This is like confusing a mathematical description of Sydney Harbour Bridge in a textbook of structural engineering with the actual bridge. A Tarskian model can *be* a piece of reality. If I have a blocks-world axiomatization which has three block-tokens, '*A*', '*B*', and '*C*' and if I have a (real, physical) table in front of me, with three (real, physical) wooden blocks on it, then the set of those three blocks can be the set of entities of a model of the axiomatization (provided, that is, that I can go on to interpret the relations and functions of the axiomatization as physical operations on the wooden blocks, or whatever, in such a way that the assertions made about the wooden blocks, when so interpreted, are in fact true). There is nothing in the model theory of first-order logic which a priori prevents the real world being a model of an axiom system.

the block in state *B*, and let *On* be true just of the block and the table in state *A*. All the axioms are true, so this is a possible world. This one is much simpler than my desk, and its existence shows that the axioms really say rather less than one might have thought they did: specifically, they say nothing about *how many* blocks or states there are, or about the direction of time's arrow.

One can find other very simple models, for example models made of dots being moved on a screen—so the theory says nothing about the three-dimensionality of the world.

This illustrates how the existence of a model theory for our formal language is not just a methodological convenience. It tells us what our formalizations could mean and hence, what they couldn't mean. We may think that we have captured some concept in a theory, but unless the theory is sufficiently rich to guarantee that *all* its models reveal the kind of structure we had in mind, then we are deluded: *a token of a theory means no more than it means in the simplest model of the theory.*

Returning to methodology for a moment, a crucial property of this way of characterizing meaning is that it transcends syntactic and operational variations. A given theory might be realized operationally in innumerable ways. Even ignoring heuristic 'control' issues, we have such variations as natural deduction rules, or semantic tableaux or Hilbert-style axiomatizations. We can make the theory look like a semantic network or a collection of frames or MOPS or any one of innumerable other variations. None of these variations will give the theory an ounce more expressive power. None of them *could* ever make good a representational inadequacy of the theory. It is easy to lose sight of this basic and uncomfortable truth. Thinking model-theoretically helps us to keep it in mind.

It also gives us a powerful theoretical tool. For example, I mentioned earlier that defined concept tokens, such as *Clear,* added no real expressiveness to a theory. This seems kind of intuitive once it is pointed out, but it has a quite conclusive model-theoretic statement (Beth's definability theorem) which completely settles the matter, and frees up time for more productive discussions.

An objection to the idea of models goes as follows. Any particular formalization or implementation consists entirely of the expressions and the inference rules or procedures which manipulate them. The idea of a model, and the mappings which relate expressions to denotations, etc., are just metatheorists' ideas, imposed from without. But we could have a different model theory for the same formal language, and declare that *this* semantic theory assigned meanings to the formal symbols. (e.g., see D. Israel, this volume.) And who is to say which of the many possible semantic theories is the right one?

But the relationship between a model theory and the (purely formal) inference rules or procedures attached to the formal language is not arbitrary in this way. Each model theory sanctions certain inferences (the ones that preserve truth in those models) and not others. And, sometimes, we also get the converse, viz., if some assertion is true in all those models, then the rules will indeed eventually declare it so. This is the content of the completeness theorem for a formal language. We should treasure completeness theorems: they are rare and beautiful things. Without them, we have no good justification for our claims that we know how our theories say what we claim they say about the worlds we want them to describe. To emphasize this, consider enriching the formal language by introducing a new kind of symbol, say a quantifier M which I claim means 'most' so that $MxP(x)$ means P is true of *most* things. I can easily give a model theory: $MxP(x)$ is true in a model just when P is true of more than half the universe (with a little more subtlety for infinite domains, but let that pass). I can *claim* this, but the claim is premature until I can describe some mechanism of inference which captures that interpretation, generating all the inferences which it justifies and none which it refutes. And this might be difficult. For some model theories we know it is impossible.

A model theory can determine the actual meaning of the logical symbols of the formal language, but it does not determine the actual meaning of the tokens. The only way to do that is by restricting the set of possible models of the theory, for example by adding axioms. All we can say of a token is that in this model it means this, in that one it means that. There is no single 'meaning' of a formal token (unless there is only a single model): we cannot point to something and say, *that* is the meaning.

We might restate the goal of building a formal theory as being that of ensuring that all the models of the theory are recognizable as the kind of possible world we were trying to describe, so that in each one, each token denotes what it should. But this notion of meaning raises a well-known philosophical specter, a second objection to a model-theoretic view of meaning. For no model theory can specify what *kinds* of entity constitute the universes of its models. It refers only to the presence of functions and relations defined over a set, not to what the set is a set *of*. And we could always make our universes out of entirely unsuitable things, in particular the tokens themselves.

Suppose we have a 'suitable' model of a theory. Make a ghost model as follows. Let each name denote itself. Every token which should denote an operation on things, interpret it rather as an operation on the *names* of things, whose result is the expression which would have referred to the thing got by performing the operation on the things named, so that for example a unary function symbol f denotes the function on expressions which takes the expression 'e' to the expression '$f(e)$', '$g(h(a))$' to '$f(g(h(a)))$', and so on. And interpret each relation symbol as that relation on expressions which is true when the relation is true of the thing named by the expressions in the 'suitable' model: so that 'P' denotes the predicate which is true of the symbol 'a' just if '$P(a)$' is true in the first model. In general, whenever you need to decide a question of fact, go and check in the ''suitable'' model to see what its facts are, and use those.

There is one of these ghostly (Herbrand) models for every model, and it makes exactly the same axioms true. So there could be no way of adding axioms (or frames or scripts or demons or MOPS or anything else, just to re-emphasize the point) which could ensure that all a theory is talking about might not be its own symbols.

This is an important point, considered as a criticism of a theory of meaning. Indeed, no formal operations, no matter how complex, can ever ensure that tokens denote any particular kinds of entity. There are, I think, three ways in which tokens can be attached to their denotations more rigidly (so to speak). One: if the token is itself in a metatheory of some internal part of the theory, then the connection can simply be directly made by internal, formal, manipulations. Formally, these are "reflection principles", or rules of translation between a language and its metalanguage.

Two: if the theory is in a creature with a body—a robot, like us—then some of the tokens can be attached to sensory and motor systems so that the truth of some propositions containing them is kept in correspondence to the way the real world actually is. These tokens—they might include the concept *vertical* connected to the inner ear, and those of a whole intricate theory of lighting and surfaces and geometry and texture and movement connected with visual perception, and a whole other collection associated with proprioceptive awareness of the body's position in space—have a special status. We might say that the body's sensorimotor apparatus *was* the model theory of this part of the internal formalization.

Three: tokens could be attached to the world through language. Again, let the theory be built into a physical computer, one without senses, but with a natural-language comprehension and production system. The tokens of the internal theory are now related to English words in the way we expect, so that the deep semantic meaning of a sentence is a collection of axiomatic statements in the formalism. Such a system could talk about things to other language users and could come to learn facts about an external world by communicating with them. Assuming that *their* beliefs and conversations really were about things—that they managed to actually refer to external entities—then I think we would have no reason to refuse the same honor to the conversing system.

These matters require and deserve fuller discussion elsewhere. But I suggest that for the purposes of developing a naive physics, this whole issue can be safely ignored. We can take out a promissory loan on *real* meanings. One way or another, parts of our growing formalization will have eventually to be attached to external worlds through senses or language or maybe some other way, and ghost models will be excluded. We must go ahead trying to formalize our intuitive world; paying attention indeed to the complexity and structural suitability of our models, but not worrying about what sort of stuff they are made from.

We have then to be ready to repay the loan, by looking out for areas of axiomatization where the tokens might be attachable to perceptual or motor or linguistic systems. For example, ideas connected with time must make some contact with our internal "clocks" of various sorts. Much of our intuitive knowledge of force and movement comes from *what it feels like* when we push, pull, lift and move. Much of our knowledge of three-dimensional space is connected with how things *look*; and so on.

6 Discovering Intuitions and Building Theories

We have been assuming all along that we are able to interpret tokens of the theory in intuitive terms. But this assumes that we can identify our own intuitive concepts sufficiently clearly to assign them to tokens. In practice, building axiomatic theories is in large part an exploration and clarification of our own intuitions. Just as professional grammarians tend to acquire an astonishingly acute sense of exactly which syntactic constructions are acceptable to a native speaker, so naive physicists will need to develop an acute sense of intuitive reasonableness of descriptions of the everyday physical world. It is not at all an easy thing to do.

Consider the earlier toy blocks-world example. It might be argued that here is a small theory with complete conceptual closure. But it is closed only with respect to the very limited range of inferences we required initially; this is exactly what makes it a toy theory. Try to expand it to deal with our own ideas of putting things on things. We have the token *On*: what exactly did that mean? It had a component of pure geometry, referring to the spatial arrangement of the blocks. It also seemed to have some idea of support contained within it: if A is on B, then B is holding A up; B is the reason why A isn't falling, it is bearing A's weight. Now these are very different ideas. For example, the geometric *On* is asymmetrical (nothing is on anything which is on it—although it doesn't seem that this should be an axiom so much as a consequence of some more basic spatial theory), but the support *On* can be, e.g., two long blocks leaning on one another. They come together here in that the geometric *On* implies the support *On,* because blocks are rigid and strong, so they will bear weight without deforming or breaking. And this is because the stuff they are made of has these properties. To emphasize the separateness of these two ideas, imagine the alternative possible world with no gravity. The geometry is unchanged, but the 'support' idea is absent. So they must have distinct subtheories.

Both concepts are linked to clusters of others which we have not yet begun to formalize. The experience of doing so may well sharpen our sense of what the concept is, perhaps separating it out further into several slightly (or very) different ideas, each requiring its own axiomatic connections to the rest of the theory.

We have taken a proposed concept and seen it as a blend of two distinct components. As well as this analytic "division" of concepts there is what we might call a process of "broadening"; extending the range of a concept, trying it out in other areas where it seems natural. For example, imagine four blocks arranged in a compact square on the table, with adjacent faces in contact (the very fact that you can do that says a lot about the richness of the spatial-geometry part of our internal theories) and place a fifth block neatly on top, in the center. What is this block on? We might say it is on *each* of the other blocks, but this is a very different notion (e.g. pick up one of the lower blocks). Perhaps it is on the set of the four blocks . . . but a set hardly seems the kind of thing that can bear weight, and anyway only some sets will work. Perhaps we should abandon the notion of *on* altogether in this case in favor of some other, more subtle, relationship between the blocks. But it seems intuitively clear that the top block *is* on *something,* in much the same way that it could be on one block. The only reasonable conclusion, I believe, is that the fifth block is indeed on a (single) thing, which is made up of the four other blocks. By arranging them thus in a compact square, one has created a new object; we might call it a platform. (If someone points to it and asks; what is *that*?, the question is quite intelligible: there is some *thing* there. One might of course answer: nothing, its just four blocks.) So blocks can be on other things than blocks and tables. Its the same concept, but using it in a different situation forces a reevaluation of what can be said about it. We need to be able to state some criterion of put-on-ability, which seems to be having a firm horizontal surface. But now we have a new concept, that of a surface. This requires more axioms to relate it to existing concepts, and these in turn introduce other concepts (edge, side of a surface, direction, adjacency, contact, the object-surface relation, etc.: see Chapter 3, this volume, "Naive physics I:Ontology for Liquids", for a first attempt at such a list) and these require more axioms, each typically introducing other concepts, and so on. Conceptual closure becomes much harder to achieve: perhaps impossible to achieve completely.

This is what typically happens when one extends the scope of a concept. Closure is fragile, sensitive to the demands placed on the theory. Toy theories achieve it only by having very restricted demands placed on them. In developing naive physics we expect far more of the theory, forcing it to be larger and making closure more remote. There is a constant tension between wanting a closed theory and wanting to pin down the meanings of tokens as precisely as we can: between closure and breadth.

This example illustrates an important and basic fact about the enterprise of knowledge representation. We want breadth and density: but you can't have the density without the breadth. If we want the theory to say a *lot* about a concept, the only way to do so is to relate that concept to many others. If there are many axioms in the theory which contain a certain token, there must ipso facto be many other tokens to which it is axiomatically related. It is exactly this, being tightly caught in a dense web of inferential connections to other parts of the theory, which gives a token meaning, by cutting out unwanted implausible models. And this is what we want, since the goal of the axiomatizing enterprise is to produce a theory from which we can rapidly draw the many conclusions corresponding to our intuitions, and this inferential richness goes along with model-theoretic constraint.

It is easy to find other things wrong with the toy blocks world: it was always just a toy, in any case, and we will now abandon it. But its limitations illustrate a serious general problem of how to get naive physics done.

A completed theory would be huge (a guess: between 10^4 and 10^5 tokens). It would be conceptually closed,[5] but it seems overwhelmingly likely that no reasonably sized subtheory of it will be. Such a subtheory would be completely isolated

---

[5] In fact, it wouldn't really. To *really* capture the notion of "above" it is probably not enough to stay even within naive physics. One would have to go into the various analogies to do with interpersonal status, for example. (Judge's seats are raised: Heaven is high, Hell is low: to express submission, lower yourself, etc.) Only a very broad theory can muster the power (*via* the Galois connection of model theory) to so constrain the meaning of the token '*above*' that it fits to our concept *this* exactly. (Imagine a world in which the 'status' analogy was reversed, so that to be below someone was to be dominant and/or superior to them. That would be a possible model of naive physics, but not of the larger theory of common sense: and it would be a very different world from ours.)

from the rest of the theory: the meanings of its tokens would not be affected by the way in which the other axioms imposed interpretations on the rest of the tokens. It seems much more likely (it is in any case the most conservative assumption) that the whole theory is bound together, so that the meaning of any token depends on all of the rest of the theory.[6] But then how can we judge the correctness or suitability of part of such a theory? Since at any intermediate stage of theory construction there will be tokens not yet axiomatized, the process of formalizing those concepts may force changes in their correspondence to intuition and these changes might require our earlier partial theories to be rewritten. The toy blocks world's concepts came apart and its axioms became inappropriate to the new meanings, when we divided it into separate geometric and physical components, for example. Anyone who has tried to expand the scope of an existing representation will recognize the problem, but the methodology being urged here seems to preclude all the usual solutions.

One response is to proceed by enlarging the toy problems. On this approach we will work on progressively more ambitious subtheories, but always with a clear boundary on the kinds of inferences which the theory is expected to support. This approach is however very dangerous, since it can get caught in conceptual traps, as noted earlier. A technique might work well in a limited domain, and be applicable—with increasing difficulty—to a wider and wider range of phenomena, but be ultimately wrong. It is perilously easy to go on putting off consideration of the examples which clearly demonstrate its futility: one always plans to get to those later. Our toy blocks world embodies several such errors, notably the use of state–state functions to denote actions (completely unusable when several things are happening at once: see section 7).

Another response is to search for a small kernel theory of basic concepts, to which all others can be reduced by suitable definitions. Put another way: suppose we had a finished naive physics and eliminated all tokens which were explicitly defined in terms of others (as *clear* was in the blocks world), kept on doing this to the limit, and looked at what was left. This reduced theory must be conceptually closed, since the original one was: call it the kernel. Now, perhaps this is a smallish theory (less than a thousand tokens, say) so that to get it all done would be a feasible project. Filling in the rest can then be done piecemeal as needed, since adding definitions of new tokens does not affect the meanings of the old tokens; there can be no forced revision of the kernel axiomatization. This is the ''semantic primitives'' idea exemplified in the work of R. Schank and Y. Wilks.

It is worth pointing out that such a small kernel theory supporting a much larger

---

[6] Some authors argue that cognitive structure consists of a large number of isolated units, with very weak connections between them. DiSessa (1983) for example refers to P-prims, which are ''simple . . . monolithic . . . knowledge structures whose meanings . . . are relatively independent of context''. But this is a very strong and optimistic assumption, and a dangerous one. If cognitive structure is really all fragmented and we don't assume that it is, then we will discover that it is. If however it is all bound together and we assume fragmentation, we will probably be unable to see (or express within our formalism) important aspects of its structure.

This issue is quite distinct, by the way, from the issue of ''modularity'' discussed by Fodor (1983). This entire discussion is concerned with the contents of Fodor's impenetrable non-modular central system.

theory by means of mere definitions does exist. It is axiomatic set theory, and it supports virtually the whole of pure mathematics. We have had 60 years to get used to the idea, but it is incredible that such an audacious program should have so nearly succeeded: a tiny theory (2 tokens and perhaps 8 axioms: details vary) enables one to define a large number of mathematical concepts, and then provides enough inferential power that the properties of these things follow from their definitions. The induction principle for the integers, for example, is not an axiom, but a *theorem* whose truth can be established within set theory.

Maybe such a small kernel can be found for our conceptual theory, but I very much doubt it. It seems a priori implausible that our knowledge of the rich variety of the everyday world could be merely a collection of lemmas to some small set of concepts. And there is a more technical objection, borne out by experience with schemes of scientific primitives. To pin down a concept exactly requires a rich theory and hence a large theory: exactness entails density which entails breadth, as noted earlier. It follows that a small theory which is conceptually closed and yet has a wide scope cannot be detailed. The concepts it discusses must be at a high level of generality not very tightly constrained by the theory. But then, if all else we have are definitions, we will never be able to get at the details. As Wilks (1977) says, no representation in terms of primitives can be expected to be able to distinguish between hammers, mallets and axes. But we must, somehow.

A third response, less idealistic but I think inevitable, is to accept the problem as real and find ways to live with it. We must build theories which are only partially closed. Some tokens will not yet have their meanings axiomatically specified: they will represent directions for future investigation. We will, indeed, always be in danger of having later theory construction come back and force an alteration in our present work, perhaps scrapping it entirely. The best we can hope for is to develop a good sense of style and scope in choosing groups of concepts and in formulating their subtheories.

Breadth seems to be crucial. If a concept makes intuitive sense in a wide variety of circumstances, but its candidate theory somehow presupposes a more limited framework, then something is wrong. Either the concept has several parts or cases, one of which is provisionally captured by the theory: or, more likely, the theory is limited by some inappropriate restriction (e.g. that blocks can be put only on other blocks) and needs to be recast in different terms. Applying this breadth criterion as a heuristic guide when building theories is what most clearly distinguishes this from the toy-worlds approach. Sometimes one has to accept a limitation for no better reason than that one can see no way to make progress without it, but this is to be resisted, rather than taken as a guiding principle.[7]

So far, I have assumed that concepts have been initially identified by no more

---

[7] Although perhaps one could not fight *too* hard. It is quite plausible that we might have several minitheories in our heads for some concepts. Perhaps we use one, oversimplified but useful, theory—a general utility version—and also special-purpose theories to handle idiosyncratic cases (such as porous solids in a theory of liquids). Or, more interestingly, a more sophisticated theory which can handle a very wide range of phenomena but is invoked only when needed (such as an atomic theory to explain porosity, c.f. Lucretius).

than careful introspection. Other more objective and disciplined ways are also available. Detailed examination of the meanings of English spatial prepositions (Herskowitz 1982) provides many clues. Driving introspection deeper by sensitive interviews (Gentner & Stevens 1983) can uncover the outlines of whole inner theories. Showing subjects simplified physical situations (or tricking them with excruciatingly realistic ones: Howard 1978) and finding their intuitive predictions can clearly reveal centrally important concepts (such as "impetus", McCloskey 1983).

Many parts of the psychological and linguistic literature are ripe with clues. But one has to exercise great care. It is very difficult to make a *direct* connection between any aspect of overt behavior and any small part of the conceptual theory, if the present account is anything like correct. Single concepts may not emerge as English words, for example. Natural language is for communication, the internal language of thought is for thinking—in our model, inference-making in a highly parallel computer. These are vastly different requirements and so the languages can be expected to be very different. A communication language must be compact (since it has to be encoded as a time sequence, and time is short) but it can afford to be highly context sensitive in the way it encodes meaning (since the recipient is a powerful processor and shares a great deal of the context): neither applies to the internal language.

A word like "in" seems to expand into a whole complex of ideas when examined in detail: we must attempt to build a coherent formal theory of these before making judgements about the appropriateness or otherwise of the expansion, since tokens in isolation are meaningless (and they *seem* to be meaningful: see McDermott 1977).

7 Clusters

Concepts will not be evenly spread throughout a theory. Some groups of concept-tokens will have many tight axiomatic connections within the group, relatively few outside. Think of a graph with tokens as nodes, linked by an arc if there is an axiom containing both of them: call it the axiom-concept (a-c) graph. Then this graph, while connected, will have some areas more densely connected than others. Call such a collection a cluster. Our job as theory-builders is made easier if we can identify clusters: these are as close as one can get to isolated subtheories.

Identifying clusters is both one of the most important and one of the most difficult methodological tasks in developing a naive physics. I think that several serious mistakes have been made in the past here. For example, causality is, I now tend to think, not a cluster: there is no useful, more-or-less self-contained theory of causality. "Causality" is a word for what happens when other things happen, and what happens, depends on circumstances. If there is liquid around, for example, things will often happen very differently from when everything is nice and dry. What happens with liquids, however, is part of the liquids cluster, not part of some theory of "what-happens-when". This is not to say that the concept of causality is useless, but that it is an umbrella term for a large variety of particular relationships, each of which has its own detailed cluster of supporting theory, and its meaning is parasitic on theirs. If *all* you know is that A caused B, about all you can conclude is that A was before B.

Mistakes like this are hard to overcome, since a large conceptual structure can be entered anywhere. The symptom of having got it wrong is that it seems hard to say anything very useful about the concepts one has proposed (because one has entered the graph at a locally sparse place, rather than somewhere in a cluster). But this can also be because of having chosen one's concepts badly, lack of imagination, or any of several other reasons. It is easier, fortunately, to recognise when one is in a cluster: assertions suggest themselves faster than one can write them down.

A good strategy seems to be to work on clusters more or less independently at first: the meaning of the tokens in a cluster is more tightly constrained by the structure of a cluster than by the links to other clusters. It seems reasonable therefore to introduce concepts, which occur definitely in some other cluster, fairly freely, assuming that their meaning is, or will be, reasonably tightly specified by that other cluster. For example, in considering liquids, I needed to be able to talk about volumetric shape: assuming—and, I now claim, reasonably—that a shape cluster would specify these for me. Of course, their occurrence in the liquids cluster does alter their meaning: our concept of a horizontal surface would hardly be complete if we had never seen a large, still body of water—but the assumption of a *fairly* autonomous theory of shape still seems reasonable, at least as a working hypothesis.

The rest of this section discusses some likely clusters and some of the difficulties and issues which arise in formalizing them.

7.1 Places and Positions
Consider the following collection of words: inside, outside, door, portal, window, gate, way in, way out, wall, boundary, container, obstacle, barrier, way past, way through, at, in.

I think these words hint at a cluster of related concepts which are of fundamental importance to naive physics. This cluster concerns the dividing up of three-dimensional space in pieces which have physical boundaries, and the ways in which these pieces of space can be connected to one another, and how objects, people, events, and liquids can get from one such place to another.

There are several reasons why I think this cluster is important. One is merely that it seems so, introspectively. Another is that these ideas, especially the idea of a way through and the things that can go wrong with it, seem widespread themes in folklore and legend and support many common analogies. Another is that these ideas have cropped up fairly frequently in looking at other clusters, especially liquids and histories (see below). Another is that they are at the root of some important mathematics, viz. homotopy theory and homology theory. But the main reason is that *containment limits causality*. One of the main reasons for being in a room is to isolate oneself from causal influences which are operating outside, or to prevent those inside the room from leaking out (respectively: to get out of the rain, to discuss a conspiracy). A good grasp of what kind of barriers are effective against what kinds of influence seem to be a centrally useful talent needed to be able to solve the frame problem.

There is another, closely related, idea which could be called a *position* (although the meanings of the English words "place" and "position" do not exactly coincide with the two concepts I am trying to distinguish). A position is a point within a space defined by some coordinate frame for that space. This need not necessarily be a Cartesian frame (in fact, it is rarely so), just some way of referring to parts of the space (such as the back, center and front of a stage, or a hotel room numbering system). A position is a place you can be *at*; a place is a place you can be *in*. Places always have boundaries, positions usually do not. (Although the boundary may not be marked by a physical barrier, it *is* there, and there is a clear notion of crossing it and getting into the place. Territorial animals have the same idea.) A position in a space is essentially pointlike in that space's coordinate system (i.e. it has no internal structure), but it may itself be a place, in which case its interior is a new space with its own coordinate system defining positions within it. The internal coordinate system need have no relation to the external one, even when there is no physical boundary. For example, one can be *in* a corner of a room, a place whose orientation is radially outwards, but the room's natural coordinate system might be in terms of a back and a front, left and right.

A room in an apartment in an apartment building is a place which is a position in the interior of a place which is a position in the interior of a place . To be *in* the kitchen is to be *at* a position in the apartment (so answers the question: where are you?), and to be *in* the city is to be *at* a position in the state or country (so also answers the question, *if* the space being discussed is this larger one). This mutual nesting of places and positions can get very deep.[8] Notice that if one place is inside another then it must be a position within the latter. (After all, it must be *somewhere, right?*)

To get in or out of a place is to follow a path which must intersect the boundary. (This is the basic property of boundaries.) A path must consist of empty space, so if anything can get in or out, then there must be a part of the boundary of a place which is not solid: the door or portal, the *way* in or out. It follows that a way to prevent entry or exit is to ensure that there are no holes in the boundary of a place.

7.2 Spaces and Objects

Places and positions are concerned with space in the large, space to be in. But there is also a collection of concepts to do with local small-scale space, the space between and around solid objects. The two interact, if only in that suitable solid arrangements can define places, by being a boundary. But there seem to be some concepts and difficulties special to the small scale.

---

[8] Perhaps arbitrarily many or perhaps only seven plus or minus two.

For naive physics, vertical gravity is a constant fact of life, so vertical dimensions should be treated differently from horizontal dimensions: "tall" and "long" are different concepts. An object's shape is also often described differently (width and length; or depth—from the wall—and width or length along the wall: width if one thinks of the object as being put against the wall, length if one thinks of it as running along the wall). I suspect—the details have not been worked out—that these differing collections of concepts arise from the reconciliation of various coordinate systems. A wall, for example, defines a natural coordinate system with a semi-axis along its normal.

An important aspect is the relationship of surfaces to solids and edges to surfaces. The different names available for special cases indicates the richness of this cluster: top, bottom, side, rim, edge, lip, front, back, outline, end. Roget's Thesaurus (class two, section two) supplies hundreds more. Again, these are not invariant under change of orientation, especially with respect to the gravity vertical. Such boundary concepts are also crucial in describing the shape of space, and are the basis of homology theory and differential geometry. There is an obvious connection to the notion of place, in that places have boundaries. Let Δ be the function which defines the boundary of any piece of space: then $\Delta^2 p$ is the boundary of the boundary of p. If there is a gap in the boundary, then $\Delta^2 p$ is then outline of that gap (the door frame, for example). Homology theory takes it as axiomatic that $\Delta^2 = 0$, and studies the algebraic properties of triangulations which divide space into discrete pieces.

One concept which I currently find especially vexing is that of touching. Intuitively, it seems quite clear. Two bodies can touch, and when they do, there is *no space* between them: this could even be a definition of touching. It is also clear that they do not (usually) merge together or become attached or unified into one object: each retains the integrity of its bounding surface. And it also seems intuitively clear that the surface of a solid object is part of the object: the surface of a ballbearing is a *steel surface,* for example. And, finally, the local space we inhabit does seem to be a pseudo metric space (in the technical sense), i.e. there is a (fairly) clear notion of distance between two points. Unfortunately, taken together, these intuitions are incompatible with the basic assumptions of topology, and it is hard to imagine a more general theory of spatial relationships. Briefly, the argument goes: a pseudo-metric space is normal, which is to say that if two closed sets of points are disjoint, then there are disjoint open sets each containing one of them. (Intuitively, two closed sets cannot touch without having some points shared between them.) But if objects contain their surfaces, then they are closed sets: so they can never touch.[9]

---

[9] It may be felt that this concern with mathematical technicalities is out of place in judging the appropriateness of an axiomatization, since people don't think about mathematics in everyday affairs. This reaction is mistaken, however. We are judging the goodness of fit between a formal theory and intuitive reasoning. Intuition seems quite clear on all these matters of touching, which, when formalized, easily yield consequences which are the formal translates of very unintuitive ideas. That the formal derivation uses mathematical ideas is irrelevant to the failure of the match between theory and intuition.

My treatment of surfaces and contact in chapter 3 (this volume) escapes this problem by saying that when objects touch there is an infinitesimally thin layer of space (the "directed surface") between them. This works up to a point, but seems unintuitive and in any case does not address the basic issue, which is that our intuitive local space is, indeed, probably not a topological space.

It is certainly not three-dimensional Cartesian space, which contains such wildly implausible objects as space-filling curves and the Alexander Horned Sphere. Many mathematical intuitions at the basis of geometry and real analysis (from which topology is an abstraction) seem to be at odds with the way we think about everyday space. The idea of a point is itself one which people with no mathematical training seem to find difficult, or even incoherent.[10] As with many of the pathological constructions, the difficulty seems to arise from taking reasonable intuitions to unreasonable lengths by introducing infinite limits of one kind or another: infinitely small spots, or infinitely thin lines; surfaces which have no thickness *at all,* yet are actually there, etc. (see section 7.8). Intuitive space has a definite "grain" to it: when distances get *too* small, they cease to exist. It is a tolerance space (Zeeman 1962; Poston 1972) rather than a topological space.

All of this intricacy came from taking the idea of "touching" seriously, and illustrates again the way in which trying to capture one concept with some breadth of application can force major changes to large parts of the growing theory.

7.3 Qualities, Quantities and Measurements

Many everyday things have some properties which are more intrinsic than others, and might be called the possession of certain *qualities*. Objects have sizes, weights, colors; spaces have volumes; some objects have heights, others lengths. All of these qualities seem to exist independently of the entities which possess them. We can discuss heights, colors or smells as things in their own right: they form *quality spaces*. The set of possible heights is a quality space, as is the set of possible flavors.

There does seem to be a general theory of quality spaces. It always makes sense to consider the extent to which two qualities are alike: the degree of similarity between them. (Even when the answer is trivial, the question is never incoherent.) Thus there seems to always be a notion of "distance" defined on a quality space. Similarly, all quality spaces seem to have a tolerance. If two qualities are *very* similar, they become indistinguishable. (This may be the basic structure, as every tolerance defines a natural notion of distance between qualities to be the smallest number of steps by which one quality can be transformed into the other, each step being invisible under the tolerance. Poston (1972) develops this idea very thoroughly.) Many quality spaces are dense, in the sense that given any two distinct

---

[10] I think this consists in large part of becoming able to simply ignore the clash with raw intuition, rather than reconcile it. A point has position but no extent. How many are there in a 1-inch square, then? Such questions have no answer, and the training enables one to face this situation with equanimity. If points really were common-sense dots, there would have to be an answer.

qualities there is a third somewhere between them. (Colors are dense, but smells and flavors aren't, I think.) Some spaces (colors, notably) seem to be structured in terms of a subset of prototype qualities, the others being defined by their distances from the prototypes. Some seem to be naturally n-dimensional, for some small n: others not.

Some quality spaces can be measured; i.e. there are functions (usually more than one) from them to a *measuring scale,* a linearly ordered set of some kind (e.g. the positive integers, the rational unit interval, the set {small, smallish, medium, tallish, tall}). Such measure functions (feet, meters) induce an order structure on the quality space (but it may not be a strict linear order). We can use this apparatus to talk about quantities: heights and distances are quantities, colors and smells aren't. We can write for example:

meters(height(Bill)) = 3.8

feet(height(Bill)) = 5.9

roughly(height(Bill)) = tallish

Notice that we can discuss heights directly, for example by writing

height(Bill) > height(Fred)

where the ordering relation $>$ is that which is induced by the measuring functions *feet* and *meters.* (If we used the similar relation induced by the measuring function *roughly,* then this would say something like: Bill is *clearly* taller than Fred.) One remark which may be apposite here is this. It is often argued that "common sense" requires a different, fuzzy logic. The examples which are cited to support this view invariably involve fuzzy measuring scales or measure spaces. This, I believe, is where fuzziness may have a place: but that is *no* argument for fuzzy truth-values.

7.4 Change, Time and Histories
The now classical approach to describing time and change, invented first by J. McCarthy (1957), uses the idea of a state or situation (or: world-state, time instant, temporally possible world, . . .). This is a snapshot of the whole universe at a given moment. Actions and events are then functions from state to state. This framework of ideas is used even by many who deny that their formalism contains state variables, and has been deliberately incorporated into several AI programming languages and representational systems. We used it in the toy blocks world earlier. But a slightly broader view condemns it.

Consider the following example (which Rod Burstall showed me many years ago, but I decided to put off until later). Two people agree to meet again in a week. Then they part, and one goes to London, while the other flies to San Francisco. They both lead eventful weeks, each independently of the other, and duly meet as arranged. In order to describe this using world-states, we have to say what each of them is at just before and just after each noteworthy event involving the other, for each world-state encompasses them both, being a state of the whole world. But this is clearly silly.

All we need to know about the other persons history is that at the time of their appointment it is contained in the same place as the first persons, and this can be established by its own train of reasoning. When their histories intersect, indeed, then the interactions between them need to be taken into account in an adequate description; but not until then.

There are other problems with the "situations" ontology (it is very hard to give a reasonable account of continuous processes, for example: see Allen, 1983 for some more), but this alone is enough to indicate that it is not a suitable foundation for a theory with any breadth.

Events happen in time, but also in space—they have a where as well as a when. They are four-dimensional spatiotemporal entities. So are objects, which have a position and shape and composition at a given time or period, which may differ at other times, and have temporal as well as spatial boundaries. All of which suggests that a basic ontological primitive should be a piece of spacetime with natural boundaries, both temporal and spatial. I will call these things *histories*. All the spatial concepts previously introduced can now be seen as instantaneous spatial cross-sections of histories. Thus, a place is a place-history at a time, and an object in a situation is that situations intersection with that objects history. Histories begin and end: the event of putting four blocks together in a square is the beginning of the history of a platform, and the end of that platform is when and where they are separated from one another. Situations themselves, perhaps now better referred to as time-instants, are themselves histories, although of a very special kind, being spatially unbounded and having temporal boundaries defined by the events between which they are fitted.[11] At the other extreme, spatial features which are permanent—notably, permanent places—are histories which are temporally unbounded but spatially restricted. Most objects in the common sense world fit between these extremes. Examples include the inside of a room during a meeting, Lyndon Johnson while he was president (this is an episode in the longer history of the man), Lac Leman (a permanent history) and the trajectory of USAir flight 130 from Washington to Rochester last Wednesday. This last is an example of a history which is more complicated in shape than just the direct algebraic product of a spatial object and a time-period. The projection of a trajectory onto the spatial reference frame is a path (e.g. an air traffic corridor), but the plane was only in a bit of it at each moment: its history slopes in spacetime.

The situations-actions language can be translated uniformly into a language which talks of histories, by replacing

---

[11] If time's passing is represented by a measuring scale, then we might say that time-instants form a quantity space with the measure function defined by a clock. On this account, the division of the conceptual time into discrete situations can be seen as the structuring of the past induced by the clock from the scale. This is how we make appointments to meet: they depend on there being a public clock and associated measuring scale.

$$R(o_1,\ldots,o_n,s)$$

by

$$R(o_1@s,\ldots,o_n@s)$$

where @ is the function which intersects a history and a time-instant, yielding a purely spatial object. But it is often more natural to describe histories and their relationships in other ways. The chapters "Liquids", in this volume, employs the histories ontology to describe an aspect of the world which I do not think could possibly be adequately approached using the situations ontology.

There are several kinds of history, and one does not expect that there will be a very rich theory of histories in general. Such as it is, it seems to be concerned with the relationships between histories and their boundaries, a sort of naive geometry of spacetime. Consider for example a stationary object being hit by a moving one and moving itself as a result. There are at least three histories involved in describing this: two successive episodes of the first object and one—that before the collision— of the second object. Call them *A1, A2* and *B*. The temporal boundary between *A1* and *A2* is a purely spatial entity which itself has a spatial boundary (the surface of the object-at-that-moment: notice that this is the same as the surface-of-the-object at that moment, because space and time are orthogonal) which is in contact with the (isotemporal) surface of the last moment of *B*. Something evidently crossed that boundary ("impetus" (McCloskey 1983), probably) and put the first object into a different state: for if nothing had, then there would be no difference between *A1* and *A2*. The event—itself a tiny history—which took place at the point of contact consisted of some kind of transfer between *A* and *B*, and so must have involved their boundaries, and this is the only place in spacetime where their boundaries intersect.

This vignette of analysis and the "liquids" axiomatization both illustrate a style of axiomatic description in which histories are classified into types and the kinds of relationship they can have with one another are defined by the nature of their boundary surfaces. Reasoning about the dynamics resembles a process of fitting together a jigsaw of historical pieces in an attempt to fill out spacetime, invoking interface properties of spatial and temporal boundaries at every stage. This appears to be a powerful and general technique, perhaps in part because it adapts so readily to constraint-propagation methods. Forbus (1981) uses a similar idea by partitioning space, as does Allen (1983) by classifying kinds of temporal interval. It depends on the use of *taxomonies,* i.e. listings of all the possible kinds of history of a certain type (all the kinds of falling history, or all the kinds of time interval, or all the ways in which a thing can be supported).[12]

---

[12] I think there are six. It can be resting on something which is bearing its weight; hanging from something; attached to something; floating on liquid; floating in the air—if it weighs nothing, and then only for a while—or flying, which takes continual effort.

7.5 Energy, Effort and Motion

There seems to be a significant distinction between events which can "just" happen, and those which require some effort or expenditure of energy to keep them going. The difference between falling and being thrown lies almost exactly in this, as far as I can tell. One importance of the distinction lies in the fact that if no effort is expended, then the second kind of history is ruled out, which eliminates a whole class of possibilities from consideration.

This notion of energy is not the physicists one: it is notoriously not conserved, for example (as in hitting ones head against a brick wall, or becoming exhausted by holding a heavy weight). Since real physics has taken the original term away from ordinary language, there are a number of informal terms in use: "oomph", and the German "schwung".

Typically, sources of schwung are of finite capacity and become exhausted in time, although may be self-replenishing. Also typically, schwung can exert force and thereby produce motion (or perhaps one should say rather that it can *become* motion, and pushing is *giving* the schwung = force = impetus to the object, c.f. the brief example given earlier).

McClosky (1983) and Clement (1982) have demonstrated convincingly what anyone who has talked to children knows informally, that naive physics is pre-Galilean. I can still remember the intellectual shock of being taught Newtonian laws of motion at the age of 11. How could something be moving if there were no forces acting on it: but yet, the argument was compelling: for if a surface was completely frictionless then nothing would stop a sliding object. My internal theory had a contradiction at its very center, the realization of which was acutely distressing. Another very convincing intuition is that heavy objects fall faster than light ones.[13]

I believe there are actually two ways of conceptualizing motion, which may be analogous to the distinction between large scale space and local metric space: as a displacement or as a trajectory. A displacement is a change of position, and requires constant effort to maintain: when the effort stops, the motion stops. They are changes of position, having no dynamic or geometric properties. In real-physics terms, they are dominated by friction. Trajectories are the motions of things with impetus. They are smooth motions along paths with a definite shape, and they keep going until they are stopped (when there may well be an impact, in which some or all of the schwung is transferred to other things). Displacement motion is Greek, trajectory motion is Galilean. Concepts such as going, coming, arriving, leaving, to, from, are connected with the former, concepts such as aiming, impact, speed (a

---

[13] Galileo's own argument why not is beautiful. Consider, he says, a stone cracked in half, falling alongside an identical one not split. Let the two halves separate just slightly. Will the split stone then suddenly decelerate? Surely not. If so, let the two halves just drift together and momentarily reunite: will it then accelerate? I tried this argument out on an intelligent ten year old, but he was unconvinced, arguing that the two halves would drift apart *vertically*, one falling faster than the other, even though they were identical. Why?—because two things *never* fell at *exactly* the same rate. Exasperated by this extraordinary obtuseness, my colleagues and I improvised a demonstration using two pennies. Within the limits of experimental error we could achieve at the dinner table, the child was right.

quantity space), towards, away from, are connected with the latter. Displacements are really mere transitions from their beginnings to their endings, whereas trajectories have a definite *shape,* and can be extrapolated in space and time. Speed is crucial. Walkings are displacements, but runnings have some of the quality of trajectories, and skiings are definitely trajectories. That position changes during the history is true of both kinds of movement, of course: if all we know is that Harry went to the store, it may have been either kind of motion.

7.6 Composites and Pieces of Stuff

Physical objects have many properties and relationships, many of them concerned with external attributes of the object such as shape or position. One category, however, concerns how objects are composed, what they are made of. As far as I can judge, all naive-physical objects are either a single piece of homogenous stuff, or are made up as a composite out of parts which are themselves objects. The essence of a composite is that its component parts *are* themselves objects, and that it can (conceptually if not in practice) be taken apart and reassembled, being then the same object. Examples of composites include a car, a cup of coffee, a house, four bricks making a platform. Examples of homogenous objects are a bronze statue, a plank of wood, the Mississippi, a brick. Homogenous objects have no parts, and can only be taken apart by being broken or divided in some way, resulting in *pieces*. Unlike parts, pieces have no independent status as objects in their own right, and the object has no natural internal boundaries which separate them: it comprises a *single* piece of stuff.

The physical characteristics of a composite depend on those of its parts, but also on the way in which they are arranged. There is a whole collection of concepts which have to do with putting parts together into assemblies: ways of attaching, strength and stability of connections, kinds of relative movement which are possible, how shapes can fit together, adhesive or frictional or lubricated relations between surfaces, etc.: one could put the whole of mechanical engineering in here. Central to the theory of composites is that this is *all* it depends on, so that if a composite is taken apart and reassembled so as to restore all the internal relations exactly, then it will behave in exactly the same way. And it will be the same object. Indeed, parts can be replaced with others—a new engine in a car—and the composite still be considered the same object.[14] A composite is more than the set of its parts. If we have a kit of parts for a model airplane, then after assembly all the parts are still there, but the aircraft exists *as well* as the parts, with its own unique properties. (Notice that the kit then no longer exists. It was also a composite, but of a different kind: not an assembly.)

A homogenous object comprises a single piece of stuff, but is not the same thing as the piece of stuff, since the criteria by which we individuate objects are different

---

[14] Borderline cases suggest themselves. If one simultaneously replaces everything but the body shell of a car, is it the same car? I think one can say yes, or could alternatively claim that this was a new car: but in that case, the body has been taken *from* the original car.

from those for pieces. If a statue is melted, the resulting pool is the same piece of (the same) stuff, but a very different object. In fact, the statue is gone forever. Even if the same metal is used in the same mold, the result is a new object. This contrasts sharply with the norm for composites, in which the set of parts is otherwise analogous to the piece of stuff. Pieces of some homogenous objects can be replaced by more of the same stuff and the object retain its identity. This is most obvious for liquid objects such as rivers, but applies also to solid objects, to a more limited extent. If a statue is broken and repaired, its the same statue (compare reassembling a car), although it has invisibly changed, and may now be a composite of the pieces of its former self (contrast reassembling a car).[15] But a piece of stuff is the piece it is, and cannot be added to or subtracted from without becoming a different piece.

Some of the properties of a homogenous object are properties of the object *qua* object (size, shape), others are properties of the piece of stuff it comprises (*amount of stuff*:[16] compare number of parts in a composite; color, surface hardness, rigidity). So long as the object remains the same piece, these both remain unchanged, but when they come apart, some properties can change. Many rivers change color with the seasons: topping up a cup of coffee increases the amount of coffee in the (same) cupful: freezing water produces an ice cube.

This last illustrates the distinction between stuffs and physical states (solid, liquid, paste, powder, jelly—a preliminary attempt at a complete list produced over a hundred distinctions). Many stuffs can be put into a different physical state (by heating, cooking, grinding, squeezing, drying, etc.), and much of manufacturing depends on using such transitions to manipulate the object/piece distinction. An example is provided by casting. Take many small pieces of copper and heat them in a crucible. When the copper melts, each piece becomes liquid. Liquids can have no shape, so the copper objects which were the pieces cease to exist. Liquid objects in the same space merge together, so a new, larger, liquid copper object is produced. Now put this stuff into a mold—liquids take the shape of their containers, so the piece of copper now has this shape—and let it cool. Now it is a solid piece of copper and still an exact fit to the mold, so its shape is that of the mold. A new object has been created: an axehead, say. It may have seemed almost like a miracle four thousand years ago.

The parallel distinctions between an object and the piece of stuff which it is, and between a composite and the collection of parts which make it up, make it easy to see why a theory might fail to understand conservation of amount or number during manipulations which change the shape or physical layout of an object or group: for amount is a property of the *piece* (or collection), not the object. If that concept is not

---

[15] Primitive atomic theory could be summarized as the idea that homogenous objects are really composites of atoms, and only atoms are truly homogenous (Lucretius). This explains why the recast statue is a new object: the interatomic relationships have changed. If one could get each atom back in the right place, it *would* be the same statue.

[16] Amount is a more basic idea than mass or volume. It takes considerable education to learn to distinguish these.

available, there is no special reason why amount should be preserved, and many examples where it clearly isn't: rivers can get bigger and cause floods, for example. But when the concept is available and is used properly, conservation of amounts is *very* obvious, since amount of stuff in a piece is a property of the piece: and it is the very *same* piece after the transformation as before: *nothing* about it has changed. An ontological shift such as this may provide a convincing amount of the well known phenomenon, first noted by Piaget, of children's sudden acquisition of the "concept" of conservation. Notice however that conservation is not a concept, but a theorem.

7.7 Individuation

Establishing criteria for individuation must be done not only for objects but also for spaces, times, histories, quantities and any other kind of individual in our conceptual universe. When do we ascribe the status of being an individual thing to a piece of the world, since even the purely physical world can be carved up into pieces in arbitrarily many ways? I do not think there is a single neat answer, and there need not be: every kind of thing can have its own kind of reason for being a thing. But there do seem to be some general criteria.

We cut up spacetime into pieces so as to (a) keep important interactions as localized as possible: places are pieces of habitable space which are insulated from one another (by distance or by barriers); objects have a complete bounding surface which separates them from the rest of the world, and (b) to make the interactions as describable as possible. A square of blocks is a platform—a composite object—if we plan to stand something on it; for in that case we need its top surface to describe the *on* relation, so we need the object whose surface this is.

Solid objects have a shape (perhaps one that can change within some constraints, like that of an animal) and, while composites can have pieces replaced and retain their integrity, they tend to stay fairly stable. Liquid objects, on the other hand, are defined by their solid containers, and may be in a state of continual overhaul, like a river. The full story is more complex, however, since if the river dries up and refills it is the same river, while if I drink all my coffee, I go to get *another* cup.

This difference between an object and the piece of stuff which it comprises seems to run through many parts of naive physics, and perhaps all of common sense reasoning. The general phenomenon is that one history is an episode of two different histories, each corresponding to a different way of identifying an individual. "Liquids", this volume, describes a particularly intricate example: pouring one glass of water into another.

An important general point is that we do not want anything like universal individualhood. Common sense is prolix—many kinds of entity—but also very conservative—very few entities of each type. This contrasts with more "universal" schemes such as nominalism, in which *any* piece of spacetime can be an individual, allowing such things as the sphere of radius 20 meters centered on my left thumbnail *now,* during the month of August 1980 (say). Devotees of higher-order logic as a representational vehicle should realize that when one quantifies over all properties, this similarly means *all* (describable) properties, such as being further north than the oldest plumber born in Philadelphia. Axiomatic theories must be very careful of comprehension axioms and schemes which guarantee the existence of entities: they should always state the relationship of the new thing to the other things on whose existence it was predicated. Thus we can speak of the space *between* two walls or *behind* a door, the falling history which is just *after* and *beneath* the moment and place where the object loses its support, and so on. In each case the relations which define the existence of the new entity also attach its boundaries to existing objects.

The use of public global metric coordinate frames restores unrestricted comprehension by the back door, for by using these we can describe the "undescribable" entities: *any* piece of three-dimensional space, such as an air traffic corridor. The resulting ontological freedom and uniformity may be why coordinate systems are so essential in (real) science.

7.8 A Sense of Scale

We seem to be remarkably good at imagining big and small things. One can imagine oneself inside a dolls house, or cupping the galaxy in ones hands. It is as though all our spatial intuitions have a free size parameter, which, while having a normal everyday default setting, can be adjusted so as to bring other things into their range. The incredible shrinking woman had the misfortune to have her actual size controlled by it. We sophisticated adults know this is impossible, but the idea certainly makes conceptual sense, which it would not if things and spaces had fixed sizes in our conceptual world.

This sliding size scale seems to be one of the sources of the intuition of continuity in the physical world, and of such geometric abstractions as points and lines. A dot, no matter how small, does have a size (or we wouldn't be able to see it, for example). Imagine it blown up, or equivalently oneself shrunk to match, and it would become an area, a place to be in. Then that space has tiny dots in it, being just like ordinary space. These are invisible in real space, or course, but they are certainly *there,* for how could it be otherwise? Just turn up the magnification and one would see them. And it must be like that all the way down, since one could always keep on turning the magnification up. That second-level dots are invisible in real life is shown from the observation that real dots are invisible from the next level *up*, achieved by looking at something from a long way away, so that it becomes small. Since—a basic assumption about scale change—it doesn't really matter which level one is at, the interlevel relationships must be transparent to shrinking and expansion as well. Mathematical points are now infinitely small dots, which are things that would appear dotlike at *all* levels. They aren't real physical things, because any real thing has a size and so would eventually stop looking like a dot, but points always resist magnification.

8 Getting It Done

One objection to the naive physics proposal is that it is impossibly ambitious: that we don't know enough about formalizations to embark on such a large representational task; that it would take centuries, etc. Ultimately the only answer to such objections is make the attempt and succeed, so all I can do here is to convey my reasons for feeling optimistic. There are five.

The first is based on my experiences in tackling the "liquids" problem, which I had long believed was one of the most difficult problems in representation theory. The idea of quantifying over pieces of space (defined by physical boundaries) rather than pieces of liquid, enabled the major problems to be solved quite quickly, to my surprise. The key was finding the correct way of individuating a liquid object: the criterion by which one could refer to such a thing. I believe a similar concern for individuating criteria may well lead to progress in other clusters as well.

The second reason for optimism is the idea of histories outlined earlier. I believe that formalizations of the physical world have been hampered for years by an inadequate ontology for change and action and that histories begin to provide a way round this major obstacle.

The third reason is based on the no-programming methodology already discussed. To put it bluntly: hardly anybody has tried to build a large, epistemologically adequate formalization. We may find that, when we are freed from the necessity to implement performance programs, it is easier than we think.

The fourth reason is that, as the papers in this volume and (Gentner & Stevens, 1983) attest, physical intuitions seem to be relatively accessible by such techniques as in-depth interviewing. This was surprising (to me) and encouraging. A common view in AI is that, while expertise is "surface" knowledge and can be extracted by the expert system builders fairly easily, common sense knowledge is "deeper", more firmly buried in native machinery, and that to extract it would be much more difficult if not impossible. But it seems not: basic physical intuitions are near the "surface".[17]

The fifth reason is that there is an obvious methodology for getting it done, and this methodology has, in recent years, proved very successful in a number of areas.

Within AI, it has come to be called 'knowledge engineering', but essentially the same technique is used by linguists. It works as follows. In consultation with an 'expert' (i.e. a human being whose head contains knowledge: one knows it does because he is able to do the task one is interested in), one builds a preliminary formalization, based upon his introspective account of what the knowledge in his head is. This formalization then performs in a particular way, and its performance is compared with that of the expert. Typically it performs rather badly. The expert, observing this performance of the formalization in detail, is often able to pinpoint more exactly the inadequacies in his first introspective account and can offer a more detailed and corrected version. This is formalized, criticized and corrected: and so on. Typically, the expert, continually confronted with the formal consequences of his introspections, becomes better at detailed introspection as time goes by.

In "knowledge engineering", the expert is a specialist of some kind, and the formalization is, typically a collection of condition-action rules which can be run on a suitable interpreter: a very modular program, in a sense. In linguistics, the for-

---

[17] Probably this whole depth metaphor is a mistake, like every other simple metaphor of the mind.

malization is a grammar of some sort which assigns syntactic structures to sentences, and the expert is a native speaker. In both areas, the technique has proven extremely successful.

I believe this process of formalization, confrontation against intuition, and correction, can also be used to develop naive physics. Here is a domain in which we are all experts, in the required sense. The performance of a formalization is, here, the pattern of inferences which it supports. Performance is adequate when the "experts" agree that all and only the immediate, plausible consequences follow from the axioms of the formalization.[18] It seems to be sound to have several "experts" involved, as it is easy to miss some obvious distinctions when working alone.

The sheer size of a plausible formalization should give one pause, however. To even write down ten thousand axioms is not a light task. This can only be a group effort.

The ideal way to make progress is to have a committee. Each member is assigned what seems to be a cluster, and has to try to formalize it. They tell one another what they require from the other clusters: thus the "histories" cluster will need some "shape" concepts, and the "assemblies" cluster will need some "histories" concepts, and so on. Fairly frequently, the fragmentary formalizations are put together at a group meeting, criticized by other members (in their common-sense "expert" role), and tested for adequacy. I anticipate that some clusters will dissolve, and new ones will emerge, during these assembly meetings.

Initially, the formalizations need to be little more than carefully worded English sentences. One can make considerable progress on ontological issues, for example, without actually formalizing anything, just by being *very* careful what you say. The "mental modelling" field is at this stage now. But soon it will be necessary to formalize these insights and unify them into the common framework of a broad theory, and this is a new kind of task. It is here that the importance of a common reference language becomes clear, for it is only through this that the minitheories can be related to one another. It seems that this could be a real problem, because everybody has their own favorite notation. Many people find frame-like notations agreeable: others like semantic networks, etc. There is no reason why these, or even more exotic formalisms, should not be used: the only important requirement is that the inferential relationships between the various formalisms should be made explicit. In practice, this means that they should all be translatable into predicate calculus: but this is no problem, since they all are.

All of the suggestions and assumptions I have made are as conservative and minimal as possible. First-order logic is a very simple, basic, no-frills language. Other more structured ideas (procedural representations, frames, p-prims, concep-

---

[18] In fact, this is a weak notion of adequacy: the stronger notion would be that the derivations of the plausible consequences were also plausible. Attempting to use this stronger notion gives rise to severe methodological problems, since it requires one to have "second-order" introspections. Linguistics has an exactly analogous notion of strong adequacy for a grammatical theory, and suffers exactly similar methodological difficulties.

tual entities, scripts, . . .) make stronger assumptions about the representational language. It is *pessimistic* to assume that the a-c graph is connected, and that there is no small collection of primitive concepts. Maybe such special properties of the internal cognitive structure will emerge: but we should discover them, not assume them.

9 Why It Needs To Be Done

In the earlier version of this paper I argued at length that tackling a large-scale project such as this is essential for long-term progress in artificial intelligence. I will briefly review those arguments here, before turning to other reasons why large-scale formalization of "mental models" (Gentner & Stevens 1983) is of basic importance to other parts of cognitive science.

For AI there are three arguments: the importance of scale effects, the need to develop techniques of inference control, and the motivation of adequate representational languages.

AI has the aim of constructing working systems. This might be taken as the defining methodology of the field, in fact, in contrast to cognitive psychology. But there is a real danger in applying this criterion too early and too rigorously, so that a doctoral thesis must demonstrate a working program in order to be acceptable. Several areas of AI have outgrown this state, but work on knowledge representation is only just beginning to. As I have argued earlier, scale limitations mean that no matter how many short forays into small areas we make, we will never get an adequate formalization of commonsense knowledge. We have to take density seriously, and density requires breadth.

That weak, general techniques of controlling inference are inadequate to cope with the combinatorially explosive search spaces defined by large-scale assertional databases is now a matter for the textbooks. The moral is that the inference-makers need to be informed about what they are doing; they need a theory of control. I will not emphasize this point here, but note that the really large spaces which broad, dense formalizations yield may need qualitatively different metatheories of control, or other search processes entirely. I believe that the study of inferential control (which subsumes many questions of system architecture generally) is one of the most important facing AI at present. *But until we have some dense theories to experiment on, we won't know what the real problems are.* Many of the current ideas on controlling deductive search may be useful only on relatively sparse spaces; contrariwise, richly connected spaces may present new opportunities for effective strategies (the widespread use of relaxation, for example, may become newly effective). It would be interesting to find out, but something like naive physics has to be done first, otherwise our control theories will be little more than formalizations of the weak, general heuristics we already have.[19]

---

[19] The felt need for a nontrivially complex axiomatization to try out search heuristics on was my original motivation for embarking on this whole enterprise.

I will bet that there are more representational languages, systems and formalisms developed by AI workers in the last ten years than there are theories to express in them. This is partly because of the pressure to implement already mentioned, but is also due to a widespread feeling that the *real* scientific problems are concerned with how to represent knowledge rather than with what the knowledge is. When inadequacies arise in formalizations, the usual response is to attribute the cause less to the formalization than to a limitation of the language which was used to express it. [20] Many major recent efforts in the development of special knowledge representation languages are concerned with issues which have to do with the structure of the theories which are to be expressed in them. KLONE, for example appears to be a complex notation for describing interrelationships between concepts in a theory, including those between a concept and its constituent parts. The scientific questions of interest are to do with these relationships, not the idiosyncrasies of any particular notation for recording them. But all of this could be carried out in first order logic. The KLONE authors attribute considerable importance to the distinction between the structure of individual concepts on the one hand and the relationships between concepts on the other. In our terms this amounts to an extra layer of structural distinctions added on top of the simple axiomatic theory. Whether or not the distinction is worthwhile, it should not obscure the need to construct the underlying theory itself first. [21]

Progress in building nontrivially large axiomatizations of commonsense knowledge is also of importance to other fields than AI. Any theorizing about cognition has to take into account the structure of the internal theories which—if the whole computational view of mind is anything like correct—support it. If this is taken seriously, then large parts of cognitive and developmental psychology and psycholinguistics must refer to internal conceptual structures. This is a truism of cognitive science by now, but what is less widely appreciated is the need to be sensitive to the

---

[20] This may be connected with the fact that in computer science generally, development of programming languages is a respectable academic concern, while the development of particular programs isn't. After all, who knows what a language might be used for, especially a *general-purpose* language? And knowledge representation systems are almost invariably proud of their generality. This attitude is especially easy to comprehend when the Krep language is considered a species of programming language itself, which was a widespread confusion for several years.

[21] The deliberate eschewal of control (= computational) issues in the naive physics proposal represents a very *conservative* approach to questions of such structuring. First order logic makes very weak assumptions about the structure of theories couched in it, almost the weakest possible. They can be summarized as: the universe consists of individual entities, with relations between them. Nothing is said about the nature of the entities. (An attempt to find an area where this "discreteness" assumption breaks down was what led me to the liquids formalization, and an individualization assumption was, unexpectedly, crucial to its success.) It makes no assumptions whatever about control. Any insight into theory structure which is obtainable within naive physics must be readily transferable to more elaborate notations or systems of representation, therefore. It seems wisest, at this early stage in the development of large "knowledge bases", to be as conservative as possible. One might think that attempting to use first-order logic as a representational vehicle would be doomed to failure by its expressive inadequacy. In fact, however, the limitations seem to be on our ability to think of things to say in it.

details of these inner theories. Much work concerns itself with broad hypotheses about the functional architecture of cognitive structure, without paying attention to the detailed inferences which constitute the internal activities of the system. Some work assumes very simple internal theories, expressed in terms of "schemata", for example, or as an associative network of concept-nodes. But we know that internal theories, if they exist at all, must be extremely large and complex; and we know that we do not yet have any very reliable ideas about their structure, still less about their dynamics. Under these circumstances it seems risky at best to attempt to relate observable behavior to general hypotheses about cognitive structure. Word meanings in psycholinguistic theorizing, for example, often seem to be regarded as atomic entities related by some kind of association. But, as much AI work on language understanding even in restricted domains has shown, words must map into internal concepts in very complex and idiosyncratic ways, and the concepts themselves must be embedded in a network of internal theory, even to make possible such elementary operations as pronoun disambiguation or the interpretation of indirect speech acts.

The medieval alchemists had much empirical knowledge, and very grandiose but simple theories, and some success in relating the two together. Their view of the world attempted to make direct connections between philosophical and religious ideas and the colors and textures of the substances in their retorts. Modern chemistry began when the search for the Philosophers Stone was abandoned for the more modest goal of understanding the *details* of what was happening in the retorts. Cognitive Science is sometimes reminiscent of alchemy. We should, perhaps, give up the attempt to make grand, simple theories of the mind, and concentrate instead on the details of what must be in the heads of thinkers. Discovering them will be a long haul, no doubt, but when we know what it is that people know, we can begin to make realistic theories about how they work. Because they work largely by using this knowledge.

10 Is This Science?

The earlier manifesto ended on a note of exquisite methodological nicety: whether this activity could really be considered *scientific*. This second manifesto will end on a different note. Doing this job is necessary, important, difficult and fun. Is it really scientific? Who cares?

Acknowledgments

It is impossible to name all the people who have contributed to these ideas. I would, however, like to especially thank Maghi King, who let me get started; and Jerry Hobbs, who made me finish.

References

Allen, J. (1983). Towards a general theory of action and time, *AI Journal* (to appear).

Clement, J. (1982). Students preconceptions in introductory mechanics. *American Journal of Physics,* January.

DiSessa, A. (1983). Phenomenology and the evolution of intuition, in Gentner & Stevens, *Mental Models.* Hillsdale, NJ: Erlbaum.

Fodor, J. (1983). *The modularity of mind.* Bradford Books.

Forbus, K. (1981). *Qualitative reasoning about space and motion* (TR-615). Cambridge, MA: MIT AI Laboratory.

Gentner, D., & Stevens, A. (Eds.). (1983). *Mental models.* Hillsdale, NJ: Erlbaum.

Haak, S. (1973). Do we need fuzzy logic? Unpublished manuscript, University of Warwick, England.

Hayes, P. (1977). In defense of logic. *Proc. 5th IJCAI Conference,* MIT.

Hayes, P. (1978). The naive physics manifesto. In (Ed.), *D. Michie Expert systems in the micro-electronic age* Edinburgh, Scotland: Edinburgh University Press.

Herskowitz, A. (1982). *Space and the prepositions in English: regularities and irregularities in a complex domain.* unpublished doctoral dissertation, Stanford University, Stanford, CA.

Howard, I. P. (1978). Recognition and knowledge of the water-level principle. *Perception, 7,* 151–160.

McCarthy, J. (1957). Situations, actions and causal laws. *(AI-Memo* 1). Artificial Intelligence Project, Stanford University, Stanford, CA.

McCarthy, J., & Hayes, P. (1969). Some philosophical problems from the standpoint of artificial intelligence. In D. Michie & B. Meltzer, (Ed.), *Machine Intelligence 4.* Edinburgh, Scotland: Edinburgh University Press.

McCloskey, M. (1983). Naive theories of motion, in Gentner & Stevens, *Mental Models.* Hillsdale, NJ: Erlbaum.

McDermott, D. (1977). Artificial intelligence and natural stupidity. In J. Haugeland (Ed.), *Mind Design* Bradford Books.

Poston, T. (1972). *Fuzzy geometry.* unpublished doctoral dissertation, University of Warwick, England.

Pylyshyn, Z. (1979). Computational models and empirical constraints. *The Behavioral and Brain Sciences, 3,* 111–132.

Wilks, Y. (1977). *Good and bad arguments about semantic primitives.* (Memo 42). Edinburgh, Scotland: Department of Artificial Intelligence, University of Edinburgh.

Zeeman, C. (1962). The topology of the Brain and Visual Perception. In K. Fort (Ed.), *Topology of 3-manifolds* Englewood Cliffs, NJ: Prentice-Hall.

2 The Formal Representation of (Quasi-) Continuous Concepts

Harry Bunt

Computational Linguistics Unit
Department of Language and Literature
Tilburg University, The Netherlands

1 Introduction

Continuous and quasi-continuous concepts form an integral part of our knowledge of the commonsense world and play an important role in everyday life.

For instance: Your tea is cold, and there's no more hot water, and your computer program still doesn't work as it should; you had better take some time to figure out what the problem is. Perhaps you can get some help from Jeff. And all that traffic noise. Maybe you should switch on the radio and find some pleasant music. Or go out and get some fresh air—sometimes the best way to solve a problem.

Each of these considerations and experiences involve objects of phenomena that we perceive not as consisting of discrete elements, but as having a more or less homogeneous, continuous structure: tea, water, time, help, traffic noise, music, air. These experiences are of an everyday, commonsense nature, and the ability to build up and maintain internal representations of them is of obvious importance both for humans and for AI programs meant to operate in realistic task domains. However, the representation of knowledge of this kind presents fundamental problems, both of a conceptual nature and of a formal one.

To begin with, consider the knowledge that there's no hot water, and compare this with the knowledge that there are no clean cups. The latter could be represented in a logical language by an expression like:

$$\sim \exists x \in \text{CUPS: CLEAN}(x) \tag{1}$$

The terms in capitals are meant to represent the notions "cups" and "clean," where CUPS is the name of a set, the set of all cups, and CLEAN that of a predicate. One would think that "there's no hot water" has a similar logical structure as "there are no clean cups," so we should look for a logical representation similar to Formula(1), something like:

$$\sim \exists x \in \ldots : \text{HOT}(x) \tag{2}$$

37

But now the question as to what we should fill in for the dots arises. The logical language requires that this be a description of a set, but what set could we say to correspond to "water?" The set of H_2O molecules? The set of water drops? Intuitively, it seems wrong altogether to look for a set since water does not seem to have a discrete nature like cups; suggestions for a discrete structure in terms of molecules or drops seem highly artificial. For some of the "continuous" notions mentioned above, such as time, help, or music, and in general for nonmaterial continuous notions, the artificiality of a discrete description would perhaps even be stronger. Besides, why should we allow ourselves to be forced by a logical language to do something artificial?

It would seem natural, then, to look for a way of representing knowledge involving continuous objects that is not based on an ontology of discrete objects and collections of them. However, virtually all the representation schemes devised by logicians, cognitive psychologists, or those working in AI have such a discrete basis, as they all have their roots in set theory. Hayes correctly complains: "Every representational formalism I know which has even the glimmerings of a clear semantics, is based on the idea of individual entities and relationships between them" (Hayes, chapter 3, this volume).

We thus have a problem here, and one of fundamental importance for the realization of any AI program that is to understand natural language sentences about a realistic domain of discourse, to interpret visual scenes in the real world, to plan actions for moving around in that world, or to reason about it. Hayes (1974) was one of the first to signal this problem, but it has so far received little attention in AI, cognitive psychology, logic, or formal semantics.

Up to now, we have only considered the representational problems that continuous concepts present from an intuitive point of view. But putting these intuitions aside, one might ask whether it would be technically possible to fill in a set description for the dots in Formula (2) and arrive at a representation that is at least *formally* adequate, having the right logical properties. Or whether we could find some other formally correct representation, different from Formula (2) but still in purely set-theoretical terms. I will argue that the suggestions to this effect that have been made in the literature are inadequate and that, if an adequate set-theoretical representation can be given at all, it certainly is not going to be in a simple and transparent way, comparable to the use of set concepts in the representation of discrete objects.

This means that we have to face two problems. One is the design of a representational formalism for continuous notions, the second is the "interfacing" of this formalism with a set-based formalism for representing "discrete" notions. The *interface problem* arises for several independent reasons.

One is that, in language understanding or in reasoning about interacting agents, it is necessary to be able to represent knowledge fragments, possibly involving continuous concepts, together with an indication of who possesses the knowledge, who thinks that someone else has that knowledge, etc., as in "I think he doesn't know that his tea is cold." Formalisms for representing propositional attitudes like "knowing that", such as those suggested by Moore (1980) or by Bunt (1984b) have a set-theoretical semantic basis. This calls for an *embedding* of a "continuous" representational formalism within a set-based one.

Another is that it should be possible to represent knowledge involving both continuous and discrete notions. This calls for a *combination* of the "continuous" and the "discrete" representational formalism.

Third it is too simple to divide concepts into discrete and continuous categories. There are many objects that we conceive in either way. Water is a case in point: on the one hand, we usually think about water in a "naive" way, as a continuous substance; on the other hand, we can also think about water as a collection of H_2O molecules. There are many examples of this kind. We usually think of sugar as a continuous substance, but we switch to a discrete view when watching a fly eating a sugar grain. Another large class of examples is provided by mass nouns: furniture, footwear, jewelry, luggage. These terms are used when the individual constitutive pieces are of no relevance, for instance, in expressing the knowledge "the lorry carries two tons of furniture." But when it comes to expressing some knowledge about your personal articles of furniture or pieces of luggage, a count noun is used instead: "there are six chairs and two tables in the lorry." This calls for the possibility of having two *alternative representations* of the same or closely related knowledge, and the possibility of relating and transforming the one into the other.

To satisfy all these interface requirements, there really seems to be only one possibility: we must have one general representational formalism that can accommodate alternative views, allowing both "continuous" and "discrete" representations and meaningful mixtures of the two. In the following section, I will describe such a formalism, called Ensemble Theory.

The observation that we often have alternative conceptions of the same things (water/H_2O molecules, sugar/sugar grains, jewelry/jewels), not only applies to a limited class of concepts. One might be inclined to think, for instance, that onions are objects we typically have a discrete conception of, but then consider the sentence

(3) Don't put too much onion in the salad.

Here we are clearly thinking in terms of onion as the "continuous substance" that individual onions are, so to speak, spatio-temporally coherent parts of. The generality of the phenomenon that we may have alternative views is illustrated by a hypothetical machine invented by Pelletier in 1974, called the Universal Grinder. This machine can chop any object into a homogeneous mass, turning a steak into steak, a book into book, an apple into apple, etc. Conversely, one can imagine an inverse sort of machine, that we might call the Universal Packer, which takes a continuous stream of any substance as input and produces discrete portions of it in appropriate packings. This machine illustrates a phenomenon we all know from making a shopping list: 2 butter, 4 beer, 1 marmelade. Here we think of entities, usually considered as homogeneous masses, in a discrete way. The Universal

Grinder and the Universal Packer show that for a wide variety of things, of which one might think at first that our knowledge is definitely either in terms of discrete objects or in terms of continuous substances, alternative conceptions are used in certain contexts.

The dual conception we may have of things has a reflection in language. Compare the two views on "onion" reflected in the following expressions:

(4a) Don't put too much onion in the salad.

(4b) Don't put too many onions in the salad.

Words that are used as "onion" in sentence (4a) are called *mass nouns,* those used as in sentence (4b) *count nouns.* In English, and in many other languages, most common nouns can be used in either way, though some nouns are primarily used as count nouns (house, book, dream, event), while others are primarily used as mass nouns (water, sand, knowledge, traffic), and still others are used about equally much either way (cake, rope, stone, fish). When using a noun in the count way, the speaker refers to something as if it has a discrete structure in terms of individual elements; when using the same noun as a mass noun he refers to the same thing as if it is a continuous substance (see Bunt, 1979; 1981a for more details). Therefore, the task of representing the semantic content of natural language expressions involving mass nouns is very much the same as that of representing knowledge fragments involving entities, viewed as continuous. Indeed, going back to our example (2), the task of representing the knowledge that there is no hot water entails the same problems as that of giving a semantic representation to the sentence "There's no hot water." The representational formalism of Ensemble Theory, previously mentioned, was developed in the context of building language-understanding programs (the PHLIQA question answering system, see Bronnenberg, et al., 1980; and the TENDUM dialogue system, see Bunt, 1982, 1984a) that generates semantic representations in formal logical languages.

In subsequent sections, I will first review the work on the formal semantic representation of mass noun expressions, as far as relevant to the issues of knowledge representation. This will bring out clearly what problems arise if the representation of such knowledge is to be in a rigorously defined formalism. I will then describe ensemble theory and compare it with standard set theory and with the calculus of individuals, a formalism originally defined by Lesniewski (1927–31; 1929) under the name mereology, and redefined later by Leonard and Goodman (1940). Finally, I will discuss the possibility of using ensemble theory as the basis of a representational formalism in which the problems we have noted may be overcome.

2 Representational Formalisms in Mass Noun Semantics

The proposals that have been reported in the literature for representing the semantic content of expressions with mass nouns can be divided into two categories: those attempting to devise representations in terms of a classical set-based formalism, and those invoking a special formalism. The most prominent proposals in the latter category are the one by Parsons (1970), in which a formalism of "substances" is sketched, and various proposals to invoke mereology. I will consider the most relevant representational issues in (a) the set-based proposals, (b) Parsons' proposal, and (c) the mereology-based proposals.

2.1 Set-based Representations

Of the ways that have been suggested to use sets for representing mass noun denotations, there is in the first place the suggestion that expressions like "There is water on the floor," "This is butter," "Unload the furniture," be viewed as elliptic for "There is a puddle of water on the floor," "This is a dollop of butter," and "Unload this batch of furniture," and interpreted correspondingly. Suggestions to this effect can be found in Strawson (1959) and Clarke (1970). Clearly, the choice of an appropriate "individuating standard" (puddle, dollop, batch) must depend on the circumstances; for example, "sugar" will have to be construed as "lumps of sugar" in some contexts, as "grains of sugar" in others, and as "shipments of sugar" in still other contexts. This context-dependence makes the proposal rather unattractive; moreover, it runs into fundamental difficulties. The following example illustrates this.

If we take some ice cubes from the refrigerator, crush them, and put them into a glass of coke, we may say:

(5) The ice in the coke is the same ice that was in the refrigerator before.

This would be a true sentence about some ice, yet there is no individuating standard that can be used to represent this, since the identity stated by the sentence is not an identity of the pieces of ice involved, but an identity of the totalities of ice made up of whatever pieces involved.

Further criticism of the attempts in this direction can be found in Cartwright (1965) and Pelletier (1974).

If context-dependent individuating standards do not work satisfactorily, the next move is naturally to look for context-independent individuating standards. Such standards would then have to be artificial, since we just saw that natural standards, supplied by the language ("dollop," "lump," "batch") do not work in general. Moreover, these standards would have to be small enough to ensure that nothing of the denotation gets lost. "Water" could denote the set of H_2O molecules, "furniture" the set of chairs, tables, etc, and "sugar" the set of sugar grains. I have not seen any serious proposal for such an approach, though it would seem to encounter fewer formal difficulties than the use of context-dependent individuating standards. Presumably, this is due to the fact that it would so obviously run counter to our intuitions. To consider H_2O molecules as the referents of "water" seems quite counterintuitive; something like "drops" would seem better, but has the problem that a drop can be split into smaller drops, and the same is true of any other part we can name without making use of technical terms from physics or chemistry. Moreover, for abstract nouns like "leisure," "damage," or "time," for which no minimal parts are assumed to exist, this proposal must fail.

An approach that does not run into these problems is to treat a mass term *m* as denoting the set of all objects that can be said "to be *m*." This approach has been suggested by Cartwright (1965) and Grandy (1973), and it is also the basis of the proposals of Pelletier (1974) and ter Meulen (1980), in which an intensional representation language is used. These proposals assume an ontological category of "quantities" used for the denotation of a mass noun (see also Parsons's proposal below for the concept of quantities). The most detailed of these is ter Meulen (1980), who has worked out a suggestion by Montague (1973). Two ways of using a mass noun are distinguished, called "nominal" and "predicative." The nominal use is that of a proper name of an abstract entity, a "substance," the predicative use that of a predicate which is true of those entities that are "quantities" of that "substance." Examples of the nominal use of a mass noun are:

(6a) Gold has atomic number 79.

(6b) Water is a liquid.

and examples of predicative use:

(7a) My tooth is filled with gold.

(7b) There's no water on the moon.

Montague has suggested that different denotations be assigned to nominal and predicative mass nouns: a nominal mass noun denotes a *property* (in the technical sense of the term in possible-worlds semantics), and the same noun used predicatively denotes the *set of quantities* which, in the world under consideration, have that property. Nominal and predicative use are thus semantically related in that the nominal term denotes the intension of the predicative term. Assuming that the nominal use of a mass noun can indeed be treated as denoting the intension of the predicative term, only the proposed treatment of predicative mass terms is relevant here, according to which these terms denote sets of quantities. The difference between count terms and mass terms is then that mass terms denote sets of quantities whereas count terms denote sets of individuals. The question arises as to what the difference is between quantities and individuals. Montague (1973) suggests that there is no difference at all.

> (8) "The question naturally arises whether portions of substances are full-fledged physical objects like tables and rings (together with physical compositions of these). Perhaps. At least I see no clear-cut arguments to the contrary." (p. 291)

Ter Meulen (1980) deviates from Montague at this point and takes the view that there is a fundamental distinction in that quantities have a homogeneous internal structure, which individuals do not necessarily have:

> (9) In some respects quantities of stuff are quite like individuals. Individuals are objects in space-time, and so are all quantities of stuff. They are in this sense part of

the same physical reality. . . . But quantities of substances are in many other respects to be distinguished from individuals. The first most striking difference between quantities and individuals is the fact that the quantities of any substance can be divided into smaller parts that are also quantities of the same substance. Similarly the quantities of some substance can become part of a larger quantity of the same substance. . . . The fact that quantities can be divided into quantities of the same substance together with the fact that any number of quantities of some substance can become part of a new quantity of the same substance is a logical property characteristic of quantities only. (pp. 67–68)

To account for the internal structure of quantities, the proposal includes a great number of axioms (three for each mass noun). This proposal, and any proposal to the effect that a (predicative) mass term denotes a set of quantities, runs into problems when it comes to giving adequate representations to quantified mass nouns and definite descriptions.

For the problems in representing definite descriptions with mass nouns, consider the noun phrase

(10) The gold on the table.

Let Q_{gold} designate the set of all quantities of gold (the set of all objects that can be said 'to be gold'), and let ONTABLE be a predicate constant. Now we can choose between two ways of representing (10): either we treat "gold" like a singular count noun, i.e., we consider (10) as a paraphrase of "The golden object (gold quantity) on the table," and represent it as:

$$(\iota x) (x \in Q_{gold} \text{ \& ONTABLE}(x)) \tag{11}$$

or we treat "gold" like a plural count noun, i.e., we regard (10) as a paraphrase of "The golden objects (gold quantities) on the table" and represent it as:

$$\{x | x \in Q_{gold} \text{ \& ONTABLE}(x)\} \tag{12}$$

If we choose the first alternative we run into the difficulty that, when there is some gold on the table, it is in general incorrect to say that there is *one* quantity of gold on the table since a quantity of gold in general contains many other quantities of gold. Thus the representation (11) is incorrect, as is further corroborated by the fact that we can quantify over a noun phrase like (10), saying, for instance,

(13) All the gold on the table was shiny.

Montague and Ter Meulen suggest that this problem can be solved by introducing the notion of "the largest" of the quantities under consideration. Says Montague (1973):

(14) I would take "the" in "the gold in Smith's ring" as the ordinary singular definite article, so that "the *X*" has a denotation if and only if *X* denotes a unit set, and in that

> case "the X" denotes the only element of that set. But is there not a conflict here? It would seem that there are many portions of gold in Smith's ring. . . . The solution is I think to regard "in" as in one sense . . . amounting to "occupying" or "constituting." Then "gold in Smith's ring" comes to "gold constituting Smith's ring," denotes the set of maximal portions of gold that are "in" (in the more inclusive sense) Smith's ring, and hence denotes a unit set. (p. 290–291)

He suggests further that the linguistic and extralinguistic context be consulted to determine whether volume, weight, or some other dimension should be used for comparing quantities in size. This is of course not a satisfactory solution. First, it is unclear what mechanisms could provide the necessary linguistic and extralinguistic contextual information and, most importantly, it seems quite wrong that the analysis of sentences like

(15) The snow in the garden is beautiful

should force us to introduce such notions as volume or weight to determine what snow is being considered. But how else should we construe the notion "maximal portion of?" I think the analysis should be such that this portion is identified by logical means, for instance, in the Example (15), as that quantity of snow which is in the garden and has all other quantities of snow in the garden as parts. However, this analysis requires a formal part–whole relation among quantities, which does not belong to the set-theoretical framework.

The second aforementioned alternative is to interpret the noun phrase (10) as the set of gold quantities on the table. Sentence (13), "All the gold on the table was shiny," can then be represented in a straightforward way by a universal quantification over this set. But now we get into trouble if the noun phrase is the argument of an amount predicate, as in

(16) The gold on the table weighs 7 ounces.

Suppose we have in our representation language a function "WEIGHT" which has such values as "7 ounces". (For the present I will not bother about the formal status of "7 ounces;" this is discussed in section 4). Treating "the gold on the table" as "the gold quantities on the table" would lead to the analysis that the sum of the weights of the gold quantities on the table is 7 ounces:

$$\text{SUM} \left(\{y|(\exists z)\, (z \in \{x|x \in Q_{\text{gold}} \ \& \ \text{ONTABLE}(x)\} \ \& \right.$$
$$\left. y = \text{WEIGHT}(z)\}\right) = 7 \text{ ounces} \tag{17}$$

Of course, this analysis is wrong, since the set $\{x|x \in Q_{\text{gold}} \ \& \ \text{ONTABLE}\,(x)\}$ contains many overlapping quantities whose weights would be counted many times. To prevent this from happening, we should not apply the WEIGHT function to the elements of the set and then perform a summation of the weights, but we should first perform a "summation" of the quantities involved and then apply the WEIGHT function. However, this "summation" of quantities is an operation that cannot be carried out within a purely set-theoretical framework.

2.2 Parsons' "Substances"

Parsons (1970) has proposed an approach to mass term semantics that differs from all other proposals both in its representational formalism and in the underlying ontological view. This ontological view has been criticized heavily for its complexity (see e.g. Burge, 1972; Moravcsik, 1973; Pelletier, 1974); in a later paper (1975), Parsons has withdrawn some of the details of the original proposal, simplifying his ontology.

Parsons (1970) calls the entities, denoted by mass terms, "substances," and introduces this notion as follows: ". . . I will use the word 'substance' in the chemist's sense—to stand for any material" (p. 365).

To understand what is meant by this, we must briefly consider Parsons's ontology (1970), in which entities at three levels are distinguished: (a) physical objects, (b) bits of matter, and (c) substances. The notions "bit of matter" and "substance," and the relation between them are explained as follows:

> (18) The notion of a bit of matter being *a quantity of* a substance is a primitive notion in my analysis. I can explain it roughly as follows: A substance, like gold, is found scattered around the universe in various places. Wherever it "occurs", we will have a bit of matter which *is a quantity of* gold. This somewhat vaguely delimits the extension of the relation "is a quantity of". Another such delimitation is the following: if it is true to say of an object (a physical object) that it 'is gold', then the matter making it up will be *a quantity of* gold. (p. 367)

Bits of matter are conceived as mereological individuals (see below); of the substance notion only a quasi-formal characterization is given, by means of the following analogy. Noting the formal similarity between the sentences, "Men are widespread" and "Water is widespread," and observing that the count noun case is usually viewed as involving a predicate applied to a class, Parsons (1970) suggests that

> (19) . . . in general, to talk about substances, we need some sort of higher-order terminology like class terminology in the case of count nouns. . . . I suggest then, that we introduce a "substance abstraction operator," on a par with the class abstraction operator. Let us use σx [. . .] for the substance abstraction operator. Inside the brackets go formulas which are true of quantities of a substance (pursuing the analogy suggested above). The resulting term is to refer to that substance which has as quantities all and only things which the formula inside is true of; i.e., we are to have: $x Q \sigma y$ [. . . y . . .] if and only if . . . x . . . (pp. 374–375)

For instance, the nominal complex "muddy water" is analyzed as:

$$\sigma x \ [\text{MUDDY}(x) \text{ and } x \ Q \ w] \tag{20}$$

i.e., as the substance formed by those objects that are muddy and that are a quantity of water.

Unfortunately, the substance notion as defined by (19) is a logically inconsistent concept. For when we have two bits of matter m_1 and m_2, which are both quantities of a substance M, then the bit of matter formed by m_1 and m_2 is also a quantity of M, "formed by m_1 and m_2" understood as the mereological sum of the individuals m_1 and m_2. Now problems arise since there is no guarantee that the property inside the brackets . . . y . . . is always conserved upon taking the mereological sum. Take, for instance, the property of being small: if m_1 and m_2 are small, the bit of matter that they form together does not need to be small. Therefore, substances as defined by (19) in general also contain quantities that do *not* have the property inside the brackets, and consequently the concept of a substance containing those and only those quantities having a certain property is not a well-defined concept.

2.3 The Use of Mereology, or the Calculus of Individuals

Mereology was developed by Lesniewski between 1911 and 1922 as an alternative to set theory, which at the time still struggled with antinomies. Unfortunately, Lesniewski's writings were extremely inaccessible and several of his most important papers appeared only in Polish. Therefore, Leonard and Goodman (1940) reformulated mereology, as they say, "in a more usable form, with additional definitions, a practical notation, and a transparent English terminology." The authors call their reformulation of mereology the "Calculus of Individuals."

Leonard and Goodman (1940) introduce the notion of an *individual* by contrasting individuals with sets ("classes") in the following way:

> (21) An individual . . . we understand to be whatever is represented in any given discourse by signs belonging to the lowest logical type of which that discourse makes use. . . . The concept of an individual and that of a class may be regarded as different devices for distinguishing one segment of the total universe. . . . In both cases, the differentiated segment is potentially divisible, and may even be physically discontinuous. The difference in the concepts lies in this: that to conceive a segment as an individual offers no suggestion as to what these subdivisions, if any, must be, whereas to conceive a segment as a class imposes a definite schema of subdivision into subclasses and members. (p. 45)

The authors argue that domains of discourse can often not be modeled adequately in set-theoretical terms, because set theory has no formal relations for describing the internal structure of individuals: "The ordinary logistic defines no relations between individuals except identity and diversity. A calculus of individuals that introduces other relations, such as the part–whole relation, would obviously be very convenient" (Leonard & Goodman 1940, p. 46).

There is one primitive notion in mereology, the dyadic relation "is disjoint with." In terms of this primitive, the relation "part-of" is defined as follows: An individual x *is part of* an individual y iff any individual disjoint with y is disjoint with x.

The choice of the relation "is disjoint with" as primitive is motivated by the possibility of formulating a very concise axiom system, but from a practical point of view mereology is best seen as a formalism defining the properties of a part-of relation.

Various proposals have been put forward in the linguistic and philosophical literature to use mereology in the representation of mass noun expressions. Quine (1960) and Moravcsik (1973) are classics in this area, and mereology also plays a role in various other proposals. The essence of these proposals is that mereological wholes are used to formalize the intuitive idea of a substance, and the part–whole relation of mereology as the interpretation of the relation between a quantity and a substance. Thus, in Quine's proposal the sentence, "This puddle is water" is represented as

$$p \subseteq \text{WATER} \tag{22}$$

where p represents "this puddle", $\subseteq$ the mereological part–whole relation, and WATER the mereological whole of all water. In the Leonard-Goodman terminology, p and WATER both represent individuals.

The various mereology-based proposals differ in that in some of them a mass noun is always represented by a mereological individual, while in others this depends on the syntactic position of the noun; moreover, in some proposals certain restrictions are imposed on the part–whole relation or on the mereological individuals used as mass noun denotations. Each of these proposals runs into certain problems (see Bunt 1981a); let me point out here two general problems with the use of mereology as a representational formalism.

One problem is that mereology does not have such a thing as an *empty* object. This means that mereology cannot be used for describing the extension of a mass noun with "empty reference," such as "phlogiston," "ambrosia," or "unicorn" (in "I had some unicorn for lunch today"). Montague (1973) has argued that it is the existence of mass nouns with empty extension that requires a complete treatment of mass nouns to be intensional; however, if intensions of mass nouns are functions from possible worlds to mereological extensions, the absence of an empty mereological object is an equally serious problem for an intensional treatment.

An awkward consequence of the absence of an empty object is that, while there is a concept in mereology analogous to the union in set theory (the "sum" or "fusion" of two or more individuals), there is no counterpart of the intersection. This is because the intersection of two disjoint individuals, that is two individuals having no common parts, would be undefined.

A second, fundamental problem in connection with any proposal to use mereology as a representational formalism has to do with the interface problem previously mentioned.

Mereology was developed by Lesniewski as part of a comprehensive logical framework for the foundations of mathematics. This framework consisted of a hierarchy of three axiomatic systems, called "Prototethics," "Ontology," and

"Mereology." Protothetics and Ontology together formed a system of logic, comparable in scope and power to the system of Principia Mathematica; Mereology was meant to be an alternative to set theory. Now a fundamental issue to decide when mereology is invoked is whether the other parts of Lesniewski's logical framework are called into play as well; if not, mereology has to be "interfaced" with the usual logical framework based on modern set theory. None of the authors on mass term semantics who propose the use of mereology has given attention to this problem.

Leonard and Goodman's alternative axiomatization of mereology is formulated in set-theoretical terms; therefore, their system is formally defined only in combination with set theory. They do not discuss the integration of set theory and mereology explicitly, but the suggestion is that the axioms of the calculus of individuals could simply be added to an axiomatization of set theory.

Even if it can be done in a formally correct way, this would not be satisfactory. The part–whole structure of the individuals has the same logical properties as the part–whole structure of sets as defined by the subset-relation. Adding the axioms of calculus of individuals to those of set theory therefore leads to an axiom system in which a part–whole structure is defined twice: once indirectly, via the axioms for the membership-relation, and once directly by the mereological axioms. Moreover, there remain such problems as whether and how the set-theoretical union or the mereological sum could be applied to a mixture of sets and individuals, as would be needed for the representation of certain complex expressions involving both count terms and mass terms, and similarly for intersections. Also, the question arises whether the empty set can play the role of the missing empty individual in mereology.

The following example illustrates the interface problem for mass noun semantics. In Quine's proposal (1960), some adjectives should be considered as mass terms and be treated semantically in the same way as mass nouns:

> (23) . . . in attributive position next to a mass term the adjective must be taken as a mass term: thus "red" in "red wine." The two mass terms unite to form a compound mass term. When we think of the two component mass terms as singular terms naming two scattered portions of the world, the compound becomes a singular term naming that smaller scattered portion of the world which is just the common part of the two. (p. 104).

In other words, an adjective–mass noun combination such as "red wine" is interpreted as the overlap of the mereological wholes denoted by "red" and "wine." Now what if we have a mass noun modified by an adjective like "small," that is treated not as a mass noun but as a count noun, denoting a set? Since the overlap of a set and a mereological whole is undefined, this does not provide a way of interpreting such adjective–noun combinations. Quine's escape—that such adjectives "simply tend not to occur next to mass terms" (Quine, 1960, p. 104)—is not good enough, as is shown by examples such as "There's some small furniture in the doll's house" (see Bunt, 1980 for further details).

3 Ensemble Theory

Continuous concepts, or concepts viewed as if they were continuous ("quasi-continuous concepts"), do have some internal structure. When we consider the water in the pond, or the time needed to do something, we conceptually select a certain part of the water continuum or the time continuum, so we must assume a continuum to have a part–whole structure. We find this reflected in language in that restrictive modifiers (adjectives, relative clauses) when applied to a mass noun have the semantic function of selecting a certain part of the mass noun denotation, and the semantic function of quantifiers like "some" or "all," when applied to a mass noun, is to pick out some or all the parts of the denotation.

Accordingly, ensemble theory is designed around a concept of part–whole. It turns out to be possible to define many useful concepts such as "union," "intersection," and "emptiness" on the basis of the part–whole relation. For instance, the "intersection" of two ensembles can be defined as the "largest" common part C of A and B, "largest" in the sense that any ensemble D, which is also a common part of A and B, is a part of C.

In designing ensemble theory, I have attempted to achieve two goals simultaneously. One is to meet the requirement that ensembles have a part–whole structure which is not necessarily "atomistic," the other is to solve the "interface problem" with classical set theory.

To achieve both goals, the concept of "atomic ensembles" is defined and a second primitive concept is introduced, the "unicle–whole" relation, for describing the internal structure of atomic ensembles. An ensemble is atomic if it has no other nonempty parts than itself, and is not empty. These notions are defined in such a way that ensembles that are built up of atomic parts are formally indistinguishable from sets. But there are also ensembles that are not built up of atomic ones and do not have an atomistic structure. Those ensembles that do not have any atomic parts at all will be used to model continuous substances. By allowing both kinds of ensembles, we obtain a formalism that includes set theory but has more than that: it also contains ensembles without an atomistic structure.

The formalism constructed in this way has a considerable elegance, I think, in that it has *one* part–whole relation, of which the subset relation is a special case, that it has *one* empty object, serving both as empty ensemble and as empty set, that it has *one* concept of "union," applicable to any collection of ensembles, and of which the union of a collection of sets is a special case, etc.

In order to be sure that this formalism is mathematically coherent and does not suffer from internal consistency problems, a full axiomatization of ensemble theory has been carried out. This is described in detail in Bunt (in press).

In the rest of this section, the most important points of ensemble theory will be discussed in a rather informal way, ensembles will be compared with sets and with mereological individuals, and a formal model for ensemble theory will briefly be considered.

3.1 The Part–whole Relation

At the basis of ensemble theory is a part–whole relation that will be designated by the symbol $\subseteq$. This relation is a primitive of the theory, therefore the elementary logical properties we want it to have must be *postulated*. One of these properties is *transitivity:* if A is part of B, and B is part of C, then A is also part of C. The "axiom of transitivity" postulates this property:

$$(\forall\ x,\ y,\ z)\ ((x \subseteq y \text{ and } y \subseteq z) \rightarrow x \subseteq z) \tag{24}$$

Another basic property is that every ensemble should be a part of itself. We shall see below that this does not have to be postulated separately, but that it follows as a special case from more general axioms.

An obviously important notion that we should have in the theory is the notion of *equality*. Equality of ensembles is defined as mutual inclusion:

$$x = y =_D x \subseteq y \text{ and } y \subseteq x \tag{25}$$

It will frequently be relevant to consider only those parts of an ensemble that are not equal to that ensemble. It is therefore convenient to define a notion "proper part": y is a proper part of x if y is a part of x not equal to x. This relation is symbolized as '$\subset$'. Its formal definition is:

$$y \subset x =_D y \subseteq x \text{ and } \sim (y = x) \tag{26}$$

One of the requirements on ensemble theory previously mentioned is the necessity for a concept of *emptiness*. This is defined as the property of having no other parts than itself:

$$\text{EMPTY}\ (x) =_D (\forall y)\ (y \subseteq x \rightarrow y = x) \tag{27}$$

From the transitivity of the part–whole relation, it follows that all parts of an empty ensemble are empty. On the basis of axioms, which will be considered later, it can be proved that there *exists* an empty ensemble, and that an empty ensemble is part of every ensemble. From this, it follows that there exists only *one* empty ensemble. It will be designated by the symbol ϕ.

Among the ideas we should be able to express formally in ensemble theory is that of the whole, formed by a number of parts. Suppose, for instance, we have a collection C of three samples of water: w_1, w_2, and w_3. The whole formed by w_1, w_2, and w_3 is that water sample W that has w_1, w_2, and w_3 as parts, and of which every part is made up of water from these three samples. The latter restriction can be formalized as the condition that every nonempty part of W "overlaps" with (has a nonempty part in common with) at least one of the samples in the collection C. An ensemble with these properties will be called a *merge* of C. It can be proved that for every collection C of ensembles there is exactly one ensemble which is a merge of

C, hence we may speak of *the merge of C*. It is denoted by $\cup(C)$, and if C is a finite collection $x_1, x_2, \ldots, x_n$, the notation $x_1 \cup x_2 \cup \ldots \cup x_n$ is also used. The merge of a collection of ensembles is an analogue of the set-theoretical notion of the union of a collection of sets.

The merge $\cup(C)$ is the "minimal" ensemble having all members of C as parts, minimal in the sense that $\cup(C)$ is a part of any ensemble having all members of C as parts. In the following, the term "minimal" will be used always in this sense: by saying that x is "the minimal ensemble having property P" is meant that x is a part of every other ensemble also having the property P. For any property P there is always at most one minimal ensemble having that property.

An ensemble-analogue of the notion of intersection can be defined in a similar way. If C is a collection of ensembles, the *overlap* $\cap(C)$ of C is the minimal ensemble that includes the common parts of all the members of C. Due to the minimality requirement in the definition, there is only one overlap of a collection of ensembles, hence we may speak of *the overlap of C*.

An ensemble-analogue of the set-theoretical notion of complement can be defined as well; it is called *completion*. Given two ensembles x and U such that $x \subseteq U$, the completion of x relative to U is defined as the minimal ensemble $\bar{x}^U$ such that

$$x \cup \bar{x}^U = U \tag{28}$$

Again, due to the minimality of the completion it is always uniquely determined.

The operations $\cup$, $\cap$, and $^{-U}$ on ensembles have the same properties of associativity, commutativity, and reciprocity as the corresponding operations on sets. More specifically, if $C(E)$ is the collection of all parts of an ensemble E, the sixtuple

$$(C(E), \cup, \cap, ^{-E}, \phi, E) \tag{29}$$

is a Boolean algebra.

One of the most useful theorems that can be derived from the ensemble axioms is the following:

(30) For every ensemble x and condition P, there exists exactly one ensemble which is the minimal ensemble having all x-parts for which P is true as parts.

The notation

$$[z \subseteq x: P(z)] \tag{30}$$

is used to denote this ensemble. Its characteristic properties are thus, on the one hand, that it includes all x-parts with the property $P(z)$:

$$(\forall y) ((y \subseteq x \text{ and } P(y)) \rightarrow y \subseteq [z \subseteq x: P(z)]) \tag{31}$$

and on the other hand that it is part of any ensemble that includes all x-parts with the property P.

It can be proved that the ensemble $[z \subseteq x: P(z)]$ is equal to the merge of those parts of x having the property P. In other words, $[z \subseteq x: P(z)]$ is *the ensemble formed by all x-parts with the Property P*.

3.2 Atoms, Unicles, and Members

Set theory cannot be developed on the basis of a part–whole relation only. The limitations of what can be done on the basis of the part–whole (subset) relation only become clear when we try to establish the axiom for determining the extension of a set. It is customary in set theory to posit an "axiom of extensionality" like:

$$A = B \leftrightarrow (\forall x) (x \in A \leftrightarrow x \in B) \tag{32}$$

The precise form of the axiom depends on the details of the logical framework in which the axiom system is formulated, see Fraenkel, Bar-Hillel, Levy, & Dalen, 1973, pp. 25–30.) We might try to formulate such an axiom in terms of the subset relation, for example, as:

$$A = B \leftrightarrow (\forall x) (x \subseteq A \leftrightarrow x \subseteq B) \tag{33}$$

i.e., two sets have the same extension if and only if they have the same subsets. However, such an axiom is not adequate, as we can see by considering sets with only one element. Suppose $A = \{a\}$ and $B = \{b\}$. Now Axiom (33) would say that A and B are coextensional if they have the same subsets; well, which subsets do they have? A has the subsets ϕ and A, B has the subsets ϕ and B. Trivially, ϕ is a common subset of A and B, so the question whether $A = B$ turns on whether $A \subseteq B$ and $B \subseteq A$. But that is just what we are trying to establish! So we see that (33) is of no help in determining whether two atomic sets are coextensional. Of course, what we have to do in this case is to assess whether their *members* are the same. It turns out that the extensionality relations between sets can be described correctly in terms of the subset relation for all sets except for those that are atomic (singletons); for the latter, one must consider their members.

In view of this, I now introduce a second primitive which will have the effect that the whole of set theory can be built into ensemble theory. This primitive is called the *unicle–whole relation* and is symbolized as $\in$.

To explain the significance of this relation, I first define the notion of an *atomic ensemble* as follows:

(34a) An ensemble is atomic iff it has no other parts than ϕ and itself, and is not empty.

The notation $AT(x)$ will be used to express that x is atomic; formally:

$$AT(x) =_D (\forall y) (y \subseteq x \rightarrow (y = \phi \lor y = x)) \text{ and } x \neq \phi \tag{34b}$$

The significance of the unicle–whole relation is expressed by an axiom postulating that, on the one hand, for every atomic ensemble x there is exactly one ensemble y standing in the unicle–whole relation to x:

$$(\forall x)\ (AT(x) \rightarrow (\exists!y)\ (y \subseteq x)) \tag{35a}$$

and that, on the other hand, there is no such object for an ensemble which is not atomic:

$$(\forall x)\ (\sim AT(x) \rightarrow\ \sim (\exists y)\ (y \subseteq x)) \tag{35b}$$

The unique object, standing in unicle–whole relation to an atomic ensemble x, will be called *the unicle of x*. The word "unicle" is a contraction of "unique element."

With the help of the unicle–whole relation, we can formulate an *axiom of extensionality* for ensembles, that tells us when an ensemble x is part of an ensemble y. The axiom stipulates that this is the case whenever all parts of x are parts of y and, in case x is atomic, whenever x's unicle is the unicle of some part of y. In formula:

$$(\forall x,y)\ (((\forall z)\ (z \subseteq x \rightarrow z \subseteq y)\ \lor\ (\forall z)\ (z \subseteq x \text{ and } z \subseteq y)) \rightarrow x \subseteq y) \tag{36}$$

From this axiom it follows immediately that the empty ensemble is part of every ensemble, and that every ensenble is part of itself and hence equal to itself.

Given the primitive relations part–whole and unicle–whole we can define an ensemble concept, corresponding to that of the singleton set containing a certain element. From the axiom of extensionality it follows that two atomic ensembles are equal if they have the same unicle. In other words, if x is an (atomic) ensemble with unicle z, then any other ensemble with unicle z is equal to x. An (atomic) ensemble is thus uniquely determined by its unicle, and so we may speak of "the ensemble with unicle z." This ensemble will be called *the singleton (ensemble) of z* and will be designated by $\{z\}$.

As mentioned, by adding the unicle–whole relation we obtain the full power of set theory. This can be seen by using the two primitive relations to define an ensemble counterpart of the element relation of set theory. This is done as follows. A relation called *member–whole*, symbolized as $\in$, is defined by:

$$x \in y =_D (\exists z)\ (z \subseteq y \text{ and } x \subseteq z) \tag{37}$$

In other words, x is a member of y if and only if x is the unicle of some part of y.

Since every ensemble is part of itself, it follows that the unicle of an ensemble is a member of that ensemble. It also follows that the empty ensemble has no members, since in order to have a member z it would need to have an atomic part with z as unicle; however, ϕ has no atomic parts since all its parts are empty.

An important theorem that can be derived from the ensemble axioms is the following:

(38) For every ensemble x and condition P, there exists exactly one ensemble which is the minimal ensemble having all x-parts for which P is true as members.

(Cf. Theorem (30)!) The notation

$$\{z \in x: P(z)\}$$

is used to denote this ensemble. Its significance will become clear below.

Does the member–whole relation, defined here, represent the same concept as the element relation in set theory? The typical test for this would seem to be whether, for any x and y:

$$x \subseteq y \leftrightarrow (\forall z) (z \in x \rightarrow z \in y)$$

In ensemble theory, this equivalence does not hold for all x and y, however, but only for those that have the internal structure of a set. This will be discussed in more detail below.

A concept that will be indispensable in the application of ensemble theory is that of the collection of all parts of a given ensemble. This is brought into ensemble theory via the *axiom of powers*, which asserts that for any given ensemble x there is a minimal ensemble having the parts of x as members:

$$(\forall x)\ (\exists P)\ (\forall y)\ (y \subseteq x \rightarrow y \in P) \tag{39}$$

(The notation $(\exists P)\ (..P..)$ means: there is a minimal ensemble P such that $(..P..)$.) This ensemble, uniquely determined by its minimality, is called *the power (ensemble) of* x, and designated by $\mathcal{P}(x)$.

By merging the members of $\mathcal{P}(x)$, i.e., the parts of x, we obtain x itself again, as it should be:

$$\cup\ (\mathcal{P}(x)) = x \tag{40}$$

It was already mentioned that the ensemble denoted by $[z \subseteq x: P(z)]$, i.e. the ensemble made up by the x-parts with property P, is the merge of those parts. We can now express this precisely:

$$[z \subseteq x: P(z)] = \cup\ (\{z \in \mathcal{P}\ (x): P(z)\}) \tag{41}$$

3.3 Continuous and Discrete Ensembles

We now consider two types of ensembles that are of particular importance for the application of ensemble theory to formal semantics, so-called "continuous" and "discrete" ensembles.

It is convenient to first introduce a few special cases of the part–whole relation, which will turn up frequently in the discussion. We already introduced the relation "proper part of" as "part of and not equal to," and symbolized as $\subset$. Another useful restriction besides "not equal to" is that of not being empty. I therefore define the relation *nonempty part of,* symbolized as $\subseteq°$, by:

$$y \subseteq° x =_D y \subseteq x \text{ and } {\sim}(y = \phi) \tag{42}$$

Also useful is the combination of the two restrictions in a relation "nonempty proper part of." I call this relation *genuine part of* and symbolize it as $\subset°$. Its formal definition is:

$$y \subset° x =_D y \subset x \text{ and } {\sim}(y = \phi) \tag{43}$$

With the help of these specialized part–whole relations, the concept of "continuity" is defined as follows. An ensemble is *continuous* if it is not empty and each of its nonempty parts has a genuine part. Formally, x is continuous iff:

$$x \neq \phi \text{ and } (\exists z) (z \subseteq° x \to (\forall w) (w \subset° z)) \tag{44}$$

In a continuous ensemble one can, so to speak, continue ad infinitum to take ever smaller nonempty parts. In that sense, *a continuous ensemble has no minimal parts.* A continuous ensemble differs in this respect from a set: in a set one can take smaller and smaller parts, in the sense of nonempty proper subsets, until one gets down to the atomic subsets, but there it comes to an end.

Since a continuous ensemble does not have atomic parts, it follows that *a continuous ensemble has no members.*

If x is a continuous ensemble and y a nonempty part of x, then by the continuity of x, y has a genuine part z. Due to the transitivity of the part–whole relation, this z is a nonempty part of x. Therefore, z too has a genuine part. This means that y satisfies the definition of continuity, and so we may conclude that every nonempty part of a continuous ensemble is continuous.

If we have two continuous ensembles x and y, then their merge $x \cup y$ is also continuous. This is so because, according to the definition of merge, every nonempty part of $x \cup y$ overlaps with x or with y. If, for instance, $z \subseteq° x \cup y$ and $z \cap x \neq \phi$, then by the continuity of x, $z \cap x$ has a genuine part w. By the definition of overlap, $w \subseteq° z$ and $w \subseteq° x$, etc.

Similarly, it can be proved that the overlap of two (or more) continuous ensembles is continuous, and that the completion of a continuous ensemble relative to a continuous ensemble is again continuous.

I believe the continuous ensemble is an appropriate concept for modeling entities that do not have atomic parts, such as time and space, and the denotations of many abstract mass nouns.

Continuous ensembles have a kind of antipodes in those ensembles that are called *discrete.* The definition is: an ensemble is discrete if it is equal to the merge of its atomic parts. Formally, x is discrete if

$$x = \cup (\{z \in \mathcal{P}(x) : AT(z)\}) \tag{45}$$

Continuous and discrete ensembles are antipodes in that a discrete ensemble is completely built up from atomic parts, whereas a continuous ensemble has no atomic parts at all.

The empty ensemble is trivially equal to the merge of its atomic parts (which is ϕ because there are no such parts), so ϕ is discrete.

By Equation (40), the merge of the atomic parts of an atomic ensemble x is x itself. Hence atomic ensembles are discrete.

It can be proved that any part of a discrete ensemble is discrete, that the merge of two (or more) discrete ensembles is again a discrete ensemble, that the overlap of two discrete ensembles is again a discrete ensemble, and that the completion of a discrete ensemble relative to a discrete ensemble is again discrete.

Is every ensemble either continuous or discrete? No, there is a third case. The merge of a continuous and a discrete ensemble is neither discrete nor continuous. An ensemble that is neither discrete nor continuous has a continuous part and a nonempty discrete part. Such ensembles are called *mixed*. In fact, continuous and discrete ensembles are special cases; in general, an ensemble has both a continuous part and a nonempty discrete part.

If x is a mixed ensemble, its discrete part (or, more accurately, its largest discrete part) is $\mathcal{D}(x) = \{z \in x: z = z\}$ and its (largest) continuous part is $\mathcal{C}(x) = [z \subseteq x: z \neq \phi \ \& \ (\forall y: y \subseteq^\circ x \rightarrow (\exists w) (w \subset^\circ z))]$. The merge of these two gives us the whole ensemble:

$$x = \mathcal{C}(x) \cup \mathcal{D}(x) \tag{46}$$

In general, every ensemble is equal to the merge of its (largest) discrete part and its (largest) continuous part.

3.4 Ensembles, Sets, and Individuals

A discrete ensemble can be proved to be completely determined by its members, that is, for any two discrete ensembles x and y:

$$x \subseteq y \text{ iff } (\forall z) (z \in x \rightarrow z \in y) \tag{47}$$

This means that the classical axiom of extensionality for sets holds for discrete ensembles.

Does this also mean that discrete ensembles are in fact sets? Elsewhere (Bunt, in press), I have proved the following: Let EXT be the list of axioms defining ensemble theory. Let ETX* be ETX extended with the "axiom" saying that all ensembles are discrete. By adding this axiom we restrict ensemble theory to a theory of discrete ensembles only. Let ZFX be the list of axioms defining classical Zermelo-Fraenkel set theory. Then all the axioms of the list ZFX can be derived from ETX* and vice versa. Hence the axiom systems ETX* and ZFX define the same objects. In other words, *discrete ensembles are formally indistinguishable from sets*. Set theory is thus incorporated in ensemble theory.

The part–whole relation as defined by the axioms of ensemble theory has the same logical properties as that defined in mereology, so one might well ask what differences there are.

One point of difference we have seen: There is an empty ensemble, which is a part of every ensemble. In addition, there is the following difference: A nonempty ensemble that has no proper parts is, by definition, atomic and therefore, by the axiom of unicles, it has a unicle. We can introduce the concept of atomicity in mereology in a similar way as in ensemble theory, defining an individual as atomic if it has no other parts than itself, but then, since there is no unicle concept, an "atomic individual" does not have any internal structure. In Bunt (1981a) I have shown that this difference can be removed, if desired, by relaxing the ensemble axiom of unicles slightly. As it stands, it postulates that every atomic ensemble has a unicle and that other ensembles do not have unicles. This may be relaxed to saying just that only atomic ensembles may have unicles—dropping the requirement that *every* atomic ensemble must have a unicle. We then get two kinds of atomic ensembles, with and without a unicle. The latter can be proved to have precisely the same properties as mereological individuals (if we disregard the role of the empty ensemble). Therefore, if so desired not only set theory but also mereology can be incorporated in ensemble theory.

3.5 An Interpretation for Ensemble Theory

In going through the above exposition of ensemble theory, the reader has perhaps got the feeling that everything seems to go quite smoothly. Even so, there are two fundamental questions concerning this whole enterprise that have to be faced. The first is whether we can be certain that ensemble theory is a logically coherent system, free of hidden inconsistencies, and if it is, the second question is whether ensemble theory really offers something not already available in other formalisms, notably in set theory.

The way to show the soundness of an axiomatic system is to specify a so-called *interpretation* (or *model*), i.e., a domain of objects with familiar properties and relations that are shown to satisfy all the axioms. The variables and individual constants (like ϕ) occurring in the axioms are interpreted as denoting objects in the domain, and the relation symbols as denoting relations in that domain. Once it has been established that the objects in the interpretation domain have all the properties expressed by the axioms, it follows automatically that they also satisfy any theorem that can be derived from the axioms. In Bunt (in press) an interpretation of ensemble theory is discussed in detail; here I will only briefly describe an interpretation, omitting most of the formal details and proofs, in which we have interpretations of continuous ensembles. This suffices to show that ensemble theory indeed offers us something beyond set theory.

This interpretation is in terms of intervals on the real line (which, in turn, can be taken as a model of time or any other linearly ordered continuum).

An open interval (a,b), i.e., that portion of the real line between *a* and *b,* the end points not included, always encloses a smaller open interval. Interpreting the $\subseteq$ relation as the enclosure of intervals, open intervals would thus seem appropriate interpretations of continuous ensembles. The merge of two ensembles is then interpreted as the result of "welding together" the corresponding intervals. For instance, if x denotes the interval (a,c) and y the interval (b,d), then the merge of x and y denotes the interval (a,d), as in the following diagram:

$$
\begin{array}{lll}
x: & \text{------}\!\!-\!O\!\!-\!\!-\!\!-\!\!-\!\!-\!\!-\!O\text{----------} & \\
 & \quad a \qquad\qquad c & \\
y: & \text{--------------}O\!\!-\!\!-\!\!-\!\!-\!\!-\!\!-\!\!-\!O\text{--------} & (48) \\
 & \qquad\qquad b \qquad\qquad d & \\
x \cup y: & \text{------}\!\!-\!O\!\!-\!\!-\!\!-\!\!-\!\!-\!\!-\!\!-\!\!-\!O\text{--------} & \\
 & \quad a \qquad\qquad\qquad d &
\end{array}
$$

However, if x denotes the interval (a,b) and y the interval (c,d), disjoint with (a,b), then the merge $x \cup y$ comes out as the *interval series* consisting of (a,b) and (c,d):

$$
\begin{array}{lll}
x: & \text{------}\!\!-\!O\!\!-\!\!-\!\!-\!O\text{--------------} & \\
 & \quad a \quad\; b & \\
y: & \text{----------------}O\!\!-\!\!-\!O\text{--------} & (49) \\
 & \qquad\qquad\quad c \quad\; d & \\
x \cup y: & \text{------}\!\!-\!O\!\!-\!\!-\!\!-\!O\text{----}O\!\!-\!\!-\!O\text{--------} & \\
 & \quad a \quad\; b \quad\; c \quad\; d &
\end{array}
$$

Therefore, continuous ensembles should be interpreted more generally as interval *series* (open subsets of R), rather than as single intervals.

To ensure that the interpretation reflects the Boolean properties of the merge, overlap and completion when restricted to continuous ensembles, the interpretation domain is restricted to those interval series containing no intervals with a common left–right boundary point. The interpretation domain, thus restricted, will be referred to as RE (for "regular-open subsets of R", as the technical term is). Moreover, the "welding together" of intervals is construed in such a way that any common left–right boundary points are *included* in the result. This is illustrated in the following diagram:

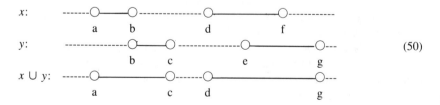

$$(50)$$

So much for the interpretation of continuous ensembles. For discrete ensembles, we can construct interpretations in the way usual in set theory, where one starts out with some object a and subsequently builds up $\{a\}$, $\{\{a\}, a\}$, etc. The crucial step in the construction of an interpretation for ensemble theory consists in the recognition that *mixed* ensembles are the "normal" case of an ensemble in the sense that, in general, an ensemble has both a continuous and a discrete part; this can be taken into account in the interpretation by assigning to an ensemble a *pair* consisting of two objects, one interpreting the continuous part and one interpreting the discrete part. Therefore the domain U of the interpretation is construed as a collection of pairs, where one of the elements in a pair is an interval series from RE. The domain is recursively defined by the following two clauses:

(51)   1. If z belongs to RE and ϕ is the empty set, then the pair (ϕ,z) belongs to U.
      2. If z belongs to RE and y is a subset of U, then the pair (y,z) belongs to U.

The pairs that form the domain U are assigned to ensembles in such a way that the pair (d_x,c_x) is the denotation of the ensemble x if d_x is the denotation of the discrete part of x and c_x the denotation of the continuous part. Continuous ensembles, having empty discrete parts, are interpreted as pairs, (ϕ,z); discrete ensembles as pairs $(y,\varnothing)$, where $\varnothing$ denotes the "empty interval series" on the real line (empty subset of R). The empty ensemble has the interpretation $(\phi,\varnothing)$.

To interpret the ensemble primitives $\subseteq$ and $\in$, two relations in the domain U are defined.

First, using the symbol $\leq$ for the inclusion relation among interval series, a part–whole relation $\subseteq_U$ is defined as follows:

$$(d_x,c_x) \subseteq_U (d_y,c_y) \text{ iff } d_x \text{ is a subset of } d_y \text{ and } c_x \leq c_y \tag{52}$$

Secondly, the relation $\in_U$ is defined as:

$$(d_x,c_x) \in_U (d_y,c_y) \text{ iff } d_y \text{ is the singleton set } \{(d_x,c_x)\} \text{ and } c_y = \varnothing \tag{53}$$

The triple $M = (U, \subseteq_U, \in_U)$ is then an interpretation of ensemble theory. The formal proof of this requires us to verify that all the axioms of ensemble theory are true statements about the domain U if ensemble variables are assigned domain elements as indicated and where, if x and y are ensembles with denotations x' and y', respectively, the elementary statements $x \subseteq y$ and $x \in y$ are interpreted as $x' \subseteq_U y'$ and $x' \in_U y'$, respectively. This has been done in detail in Bunt (in press); here I will only consider the proofs of two of the axioms that have been mentioned above: the axiom of transitivity Axiom (24) and the axiom of unicles Axiom (34).

Let x, y, and z be three ensembles such that $x \subseteq y$ and $y \subseteq z$. The axiom of transitivity then asserts that it is implied that $x \subseteq z$. To verify that this axiom is satisfied in the interpretation $M = (U, \subseteq_U, \in_U)$, we have to do the following. Let $x' = (d_x,c_x)$ be the denotation of x, $y' = (d_y,c_y)$ that of y, and $z' = (d_z,c_z)$ that of z. We have to show that from the premises $x' \subseteq_U y'$ and $y' \subseteq_U z'$ it follows that $x' \subseteq_U z'$. Well, $x' \subseteq_U y'$ means that d_x is a subset of d_y and $c_x \leq c_y$; likewise $y' \subseteq_U z'$

means that d_y is a subset of d_z and $c_y \leq c_z$. From the transitivity of the subset relation, it follows that d_x is a subset of d_z, and from the transitivity of the interval inclusion relation, that $c_x \leq c_z$. Therefore, $x' \subseteq_U z'$.

The axiom of unicles speaks of atomic ensembles; we should therefore first consider what objects in the interpretation domain correspond to atomic ensembles.

Atomic ensembles are discrete, so they denote pairs $(a,\varnothing)$, with $a \neq \phi$. The definition of an atomic ensemble stipulates that every nonempty part of it equals it; in the interpretation domain this means that for every pair $(b,\varnothing)$ with $b \neq \varnothing$, if $(b,\varnothing \subseteq_U (a,\varnothing)$ then $(b,\varnothing) = (a,\varnothing)$. By the definition of $\subseteq_U$, this means that every nonempty subset b that is a subset of a is equal to a. In other words, any element of a is also an element of any nonempty subset of a. Together with $a \neq \phi$, this implies that a can only have one element: $a = \{e\}$. Therefore, atomic ensembles correspond to pairs of the form $(\{e\},\varnothing)$.

From the definition of the $\in$ relation, it follows immediately that e is the one and only object in U such that $e \in_U (\{e\},\varnothing)$; and that for pairs that are not of the form $(\{e\},\varnothing)$, there is no object p such that $p \in_U (\{e\},\varnothing)$. This is precisely what the axiom of unicles says.

4 The Use of Ensemble Theory

Like set theory, ensemble theory is a framework in which fundamental concepts are defined and which can be the basis for a large variety of representational formalisms. Quite in the spirit of Hayes's discussion of representational formalisms in "The Naive Physics Manifesto," I consider logical languages here as representational formalisms, leaving questions of semantic memory organization and other "implementation" issues aside. The complete defintion of the syntax and semantics of a representation language, would go beyond the scope of the present paper (see Bunt, in press); instead, I will just consider the core part of such a language obtained by extending a classical set-based representation language to include ensemble concepts. The use of ensemble theory is then illustrated by considering the representation of certain knowledge fragments in this language, involving definite descriptions, universal and existential quantification, and amount predicates applied to continuous substances. Finally, the possibilities of transforming from a "continuous" to a "discrete" representation or vice versa are discussed.

4.1 An Ensemble-based Representation Language
As a starting point, I take a set-based language containing the following constructions:

1. The standard constructions of propositional logic (conjunction, negation, etc.).
2. Function application, including predication (application of a function with the values TRUE and FALSE).

3. Restricted universal and existential quantification, i.e., quantifications where the variable is restricted in its range to a given set. Such quantifications are represented by expressions like: $\forall x \in S: P(x)$.
4. Lambda abstraction. An expression of the form: $(\lambda x: E(x))$ represents the function assigning to a value v of the variable x the value of the expression E, with any occurrence of x in E evaluating to v.
5. Selection. Given a set S, those elements are selected for which a given proposition is true. For instance, $\{x \in \text{MEN}: \text{DUTCH}(x)\}$ represents the Dutchmen.
6. Tuple formation. Expressions of the form $< a_1, a_2, \ldots, a_n >$ represent n-tuples. This construction is used for functions with more than one argument; for instance, BROTHER ($<$ John,Peter $>$) represents the proposition that John and Peter are brothers.
7. Tuple-element selection. Given an n-tuple T, the expression T_i, with $i < n$, represents the ith element of T. For instance, $<$ John,Peter $>_2$ represents Peter.

The language is a *typed* one, which means that every expression has a logical type, simple or complex. For instance, the constant "John" has a simple type, whereas expressions denoting sets, functions, or tuples have complex types. Since type considerations will play a minor role in this paper, the type system is not considered here.

To this set-theoretical nucleus the following ensemble-theoretical constructions are added:

8. Restricted universal and existential part quantification. For any ensemble E and proposition P, the expressions $\forall x \subseteq^\circ E: P(x)$ and $\exists x \subseteq^\circ E: P(x)$ represent quantified statements where the variable x ranges over the parts of E.
9. Part selection, selecting those nonempty parts of a given ensemble for which a certain proposition is true. For these constructions the notation $[x \subseteq^\circ E: P(x)]$ is used.
10. Power set construction. Given an ensemble E, $\mathscr{P}(E)$ represents the set of all parts of E (see Axiom (39)).

I will refer to this language as "EL" (Ensemble Language).

4.2 Definite Descriptions
The tea in your cup is, intuitively speaking, an object that we view on the one hand as structurally similar to the object(s) denoted by "the books on your desk," due to the way in both cases a predicate acts on an argument, but on the other hand also as different in that it seems most natural to view the books on your desk as discrete, separate things, whereas the tea in your cup is most naturally viewed as one thing. This one thing is what Montague had in mind when he suggested that definite

descriptions with mass nouns be represented by "the maximal portion (quantity) of . . ." (see quotation (14)).

Ensemble theory now gives us the instruments to formalize the idea of "maximal portion," while at the same time retaining the structural similarity between the tea in your cup and the books on your desk. This surprising possibility is realized by using the EL construction called "part selection," representing the tea in your cup as:

$$[x \subseteq^\circ \text{TEA: IN}(< \text{cup}, x >)] \tag{54}$$

In the previous section we have seen that the ensemble denoted by this expression is the unique object made up of the tea samples which are in the cup. Or, to put it differently, it is the merge of all the tea samples in the cup. Now if s_1 and s_2 are two such samples, their merge $s_1 \cup s_2$ is another one. Therefore, the entire ensemble denoted by (54) is also in the cup:

$$\text{IN}(< \text{cup}, [x \subseteq^\circ \text{TEA: IN}(< \text{cup}, x >)]>) \tag{55}$$

Moreover, it is the *maximal* tea sample which is in the cup, for if T is any such sample then $T \subseteq \text{TEA}$ and $\text{IN}(< \text{cup}, T >)$, therefore T belongs to the set $\{(t \in \mathcal{P}(\text{TEA}): \text{IN}(< \text{cup}, t >)\}$. We have seen that (54) is the merge of this set, and by the definition of the merge of a set of ensembles all the ensembles involved are part of the merge. Therefore, $T \subseteq [x \subseteq^\circ \text{TEA: IN}(< \text{cup}, x >)]$.

Note that this argument depends on the assumption that the merge of two samples of tea in the cup is again in the cup. Designating the predicate of being in the cup by P, this assumption can be formulated as the property:

$$P(x) \& P(y) \rightarrow P(x \cup y) \tag{56}$$

This property is sometimes called the *cumulativity* of the predicate (Bunt, 1980, after Quine 1960). It may seem rather a coincidence that we have a predicate with that property, but this is not quite so. As I have argued elsewhere (Bunt, 1980), a predicate that does not have the property of cumulativity cannot be used to restrict a continuous ensemble in a sensible way. For instance, "light" (not heavy) is such a predicate; indeed, it cannot be used in a definite description such as "The light sand from this bag," in the same way as "The dry sand from this bag" to identify certain sand. In the case of predicates like "light," I think the intuition that the definite description refers to the "maximal portion" satisfying the predicate in question no longer prevails.

As to the formal similarity between the tea in your cup and the books on your desk, there is an obvious similarity between the concept of the ensemble $[z \subseteq^\circ E: P(z)]$, made up by the parts of E with the property P, and the set-theoretical notion for which the notation $\{z \in S | P(z)\}$ is often used: the set made up by the members of S with the property P. The similarity comes out in the following implications:

$$y \in S \text{ and } P(y) \rightarrow y \in \{z \in S | P(z)\} \tag{57a}$$

$$y \subseteq^{\circ} E \text{ and } P(y) \rightarrow y \subseteq^{\circ} [z \subseteq^{\circ} E: P(z)] \tag{57b}$$

It is worth emphasizing that there is also a crucial *difference* between the two notions, namely that the implication (57a) may be reversed, but implication (57b) may not. That is, in set theory we have

$$y \in \{z \in S | P(z)\} \rightarrow y \in S \text{ and } P(y) \tag{58a}$$

but in ensemble theory it is in general *not* the case that

$$y \subseteq^{\circ} [z \subseteq^{\circ} E: P(z)] \rightarrow y \subseteq^{\circ} E \text{ and } P(y) \tag{58b}$$

In particular, from $y \subseteq^{\circ} [z \subseteq^{\circ} E: P(y)]$ it follows that $y \subseteq^{\circ} E$, but not that $P(y)$. Ensemble theory is fundamentally different at this point from Parsons's theory of "substances."

4.3 Quantified Knowledge

The representation of quantified knowledge concerning a continuous substance presents special problems, especially in the case of "quantitative quantification" by means of an amount predicate. Universally and existentially quantified predications of a continuum are simply represented in EL by means of the restricted part-quantification constructions. For instance, that all the tea in your cup is cold can be represented by:

$$\forall x \subseteq^{\circ} [y \subseteq^{\circ} \text{TEA}: \text{IN}(< \text{cup}, y >)]: \text{COLD}(x) \tag{59}$$

Similarly, restricted existential part quantification is used to represent that there is some cold tea in the cup:

$$\exists x \subseteq^{\circ} [y \subseteq^{\circ} \text{TEA}: \text{IN}(< \text{cup}, y >)]: \text{COLD}(x) \tag{60}$$

Note that in the existential part quantification it is essential that the relation $\subseteq^{\circ}$, nonempty part-of, is used rather than the general part-of relation $\subseteq$. In universal part quantification and part selection, it makes no difference which of the two relations is used; I have chosen the $\subseteq^{\circ}$ relation throughout just for the sake of obtaining a uniform notation.

Note that, by representing universal and existential quantifications for continua this way, the structural similarity between the representations of definite descriptions for discrete collections and continua, is carried a step further. Again the role of the $\in$ relation in the discrete case is played by the $\subseteq^{\circ}$ relation in the continuous case.

Special problems come in view when we realize that universal and existential quantification are, in fact, two special cases of quantification, the general phenomenon being that something is predicated, in the case of a discrete collection, of a certain number or fraction of the elements in the collection and, in the case of a continuum, of a certain amount or fraction of the continuum. Whereas in the discrete case we can express quantitative knowledge in terms of the (absolute or relative) number of elements for which a certain predicate holds, in the continuous case we need a way of *measuring amounts* (absolute and relative) of a continuum. We find this reflected in natural language in the use of amount expressions for making quantitative statements involving mass nouns, such as:

(61a) This bottle contains 2 liters of wine.

(61b) There's more than 20 kilos of sand in this bag.

Can we represent such knowledge in a similar way as numerically quantified knowledge concerning a discrete collection? In the discrete case we can devise a set-theoretical representation using the concept of cardinality, representing, for instance, that a certain bag contains 20 apples by:

$$|\{x \in \text{APPLES}: \text{IN}(< \text{bag}, x >)\}| = 20 \tag{62}$$

In the continuous case we first have to formalize what is meant by amounts, like 2 liters or 20 kilos, and secondly we have to find a way of using that in a way similar to the way numbers are used to measure the cardinality of a set. A way of doing this has been worked out in Bunt (1978), the basic idea being the following. The units, used in measuring amounts, are categorized as weight units, length units, volume units, duration units, etc. A set of units of the same category together with a specification of their numerical relations (1 inch = 2.54 cm, 1 min = 60 sec, etc.), called "conversion factors", can be used to define a system of measurement called a *dimension*, Given a dimension D and two of its units u_1 and u_2, a relation $=^D$ is defined between pairs consisting of a positive rational number and a unit as follows:

$$< n_1, u_1 > =^D < n_2, u_2 > \text{ iff } n_2/n_1 \text{ is the conversion}$$
$$\text{factor relating } u_1 \text{ to } u_2 \tag{63}$$

It is easy to see that the relation $=^D$ is an *equivalence relation;* therefore, it defines such equivalence classes as $\{< 2, \text{liters} >, < 2000, \text{cm}^3 >, < 3.51, \text{pint} >\}$. My proposal is to treat "2 liters" as denoting this equivalence class, and in general to treat amounts as denoting equivalence classes of this kind.

It is readily seen that, if an equivalence class contains a pair $< 0, u_i >$ with numerical component zero, then all the pairs in this equivalence class have the numerical component zero. I call this equivalence class the *null amount* of the dimension D, and represent it by $\varnothing_D$. For every dimension a *measure function* μ_D is introduced, which has amounts of that dimension as its values. A measure function is defined here as a function with the following properties (where x and y range over ensembles):

1. $\mu_D(x) = \varnothing_D$ if and only if $x = \phi$
2. $\mu_D(x \cup y) = \mu_D(x) + \mu_D(y)$ if $x \cap y = \phi$
3. $\mu_D(\{x\}) = \mu_D(x)$ (64)

To represent amounts, I extend the representation language EL with the relevant measure functions and with a construction combining numerical expressions and unit names into "amount expressions," having equivalence classes of a certain dimension as denotations. The following notation will be used to represent that the measure function of dimension D, applied to an ensemble E, has as value the equivalence class to which $< n,u >$ belongs:

$$|E| = < n - u >_D \tag{65}$$

For example, we can represent that the bottle contains two liters of wine by:

$$\|[x \subseteq^\circ \text{WINE: IN}(< \text{bottle}, x >)]\| = < 2\text{-liters} >_V \tag{66}$$

('V' indicating the volume dimension), and that there's more than 20 kilos of sand in the bag by:

$$\|[x \subseteq^\circ \text{SAND: IN}(< \text{bag}, x >)]\| > < 20\text{-kgs}>_W \tag{67}$$

(W for weight). Note that the latter representation makes sense because amounts of the same dimension can be compared, added, subtracted, etc. (see Bunt, 1978).

The concepts of amount, dimension, and measure function have been defined in a quite general way here, so that they can be used not only in relation to continuous substances, but also in relation to individual objects and collections of them. I will return to this point below, when discussing the transformation between continuous and discrete representations.

Comparing the formulas (62) and (66), it may be noted that the structural similarity in the representation of structurally similar knowledge involving discrete and continuous concepts, already achieved for definite descriptions and universal and existential quantification, has now also been achieved for quantitative knowledge.

4.4 Continuous and Discrete Representations and Their Relations

We have seen that an adequate representational formalism is required to allow for alternative representations of what is essentially the same knowledge, but which differ in whether some of the concepts involved are viewed as continuous or as discrete. Moreover, the representational formalism should support operations on the representation structures that bring out in what respects alternative representations do represent the same knowledge. For these operations, we can think either of two alternative representations both being stored, in which case the relevant operations include that of finding the discrete counterpart of a continuously represented fragment and vice versa, or of only one representation being stored and the other being created as the need arises. I have opted for the latter possibility here, conceiving the creation of one representation, given the alternative one, as a transformation process. So we shall consider operations *transforming* one representation to the other.

Representation transformations should, of course, be logically correct in the first place, but there is more. Hayes (1978) has pointed out that the representation of realistic knowledge domains always requires a great deal of related knowledge about the same concepts to be represented. This means that, if the system that uses the knowledge base switches from a continuous to a discrete view on certain concepts or vice versa, this generally involves the transformation of not just one little fragment, like the representation of a single proposition or description, but of a considerable *amount of knowledge*. In terms of the representational formalism as a logical language (i.e., neglecting such aspects as memory organization), this means that we have to consider the transformation of possibly large *collections of expressions*, involving a possibly large number of related terms: set or ensemble constants, individual constants, function and predicate constants, etc. Now switching from a discrete to a continuous view, or vice versa, seems to be something that humans are capable of doing easily and instantaneously, rather than as a process where all the pieces of knowledge are transformed one by one. It would clearly be attractive if an artificially intelligent system could also make the transition at one blow, so to speak. This poses additional constraints on the transformation operations and their inputs and outputs. For if the continuous view on certain knowledge includes fragments $c_1, c_2, \ldots c_n$ which have to be transformed into $d_1, d_2, \ldots d_n$ in such a way that the transformation $c_1 - d_1$ is performed by a completely different operation than the transformation $c_2 - d_2$, and the transformation $c_3 - d_3$ again by a different operation, and so on, then it is inconceivable that the switch of perspective can be accomplished instantaneously. Rather, there should be just one transformation rule, or a very small set of simple rules, that can be applied to all fragments. I will now show that this can be achieved by using ensemble-based representations as indicated above.

Consider the following example. There is a bowl of more than 2 kilos of rice on the table. It comes from Thailand. The rice at the bottom of the bowl has been baked a little too much, and has a brown colour. I take the following knowledge fragments to be transformed from continuous to discrete representation and vice versa.

(68)   1.   There's more than 2 kilos of rice in the bowl.
       2.   All the rice in the bowl comes from Thailand.
       3.   Some of the rice in the bowl is brown.

According to what has been suggested above, these fragments have the following continuous and discrete representations, where the (*c*) expressions pertain to the continuous view and the (*d*) expressions to the discrete one.

1(c) $\|[x \subseteq^\circ$ RICE: IN($<$ bowl, $x >$)]$ > < $ 2-kilos $>_w$

1(d) $\|\{x \in$ RICEGRAINS: IN($<$ bowl, $x >$)$\}| > < $ 2-kilos $>_w$

2(c) $\forall y \subseteq^\circ [x \subseteq^\circ$ RICE: IN($<$ bowl, $x >$)]: FROM ($<$ Thail, $y >$)

2(d) $\forall y \in \{x \in$ RICEGRAINS: IN($<$bowl, $x >$)\}: FROM ($<$ Thail, $y >$)

3(c) $\exists y \subseteq^\circ [x \subseteq^\circ$ RICE: IN($<$ bowl, $x >$)] : BROWN(y)

3(d) $\exists y \in \{x \in$ RICEGRAINS: IN($<$ bowl, $x >$)\} : BROWN(y)

Comparing the representations (c) and (d), we observe the following systematic differences.

1a. Wherever the relation $\subseteq^\circ$ occurs in the (c) representation, the relation $\in$ occurs in the corresponding (d) representation, and vice versa.

1b. Wherever [. . .] occurs in the (c) representation, { . . . } occurs in the corresponding (d) representation, and vice versa.

2. Wherever the term RICE occurs in the (c) representation, the term RICE-GRAINS occurs in the corresponding (d) representation, and vice versa.

We thus have two kinds of differences: structural ones and differences in constants. (Strictly speaking, we also have variables of different types, with correspondingly different predicates; I will neglect this complication here.) The structural differences do not really have two separate aspects (1a) and (1b), since the notations [. . .] and { . . . } have been defined in combination with the $\subseteq^\circ$ and $\in$ relations, respectively. Therefore, it is better to say that the structural differences are that wherever the EL constructions of selection, universal and existential quantification occur in the (d) representations, the constructions of part selection, universal and existential part quantification occur in the (c) representations, and vice versa.

The transformation of all the representation fragments from one perspective to the other can therefore be accomplished by simple syntactic and lexical operations, consisting of uniformly replacing EL constants, spotted with the help of the type system, and general ensemble constructions by their discrete counterparts. In this way, large sets of representation fragments can indeed be transformed in one blow. (It is especially tempting to think of this process as two alternative modes of "reading" the EL expressions, but this idea would have to be explored further if it is to be more than just a metaphor.)

For switching from the continuous to the discrete view there is yet another way of achieving the transformations in one blow, which I find particularly elegant. It consists in *purely lexical* substitutions, in which continuous ensemble constants are replaced by their discrete counterparts as above, and every predicate $P(a1, . . . ,x, . . . ak)$, where x is a variable ranging over the parts of a continuous ensemble, occurring as ith argument of P, is transformed into: ($\lambda z: \forall y \in z_i:$

$P(z1, \ldots, y, \ldots z_k))$, where z is a variable ranging over k-tuples and z_j represents the jth element of z. Applied to the description

$$[x \subseteq^\circ \text{RICE: IN}(< \text{bowl}, x >)] \tag{70}$$

representing the rice in the bowl on the continuous view, this transformation gives the result

$$[x \subseteq^\circ \text{RICEGRAINS: } (\lambda z: \forall\, y \in z_2: \text{IN}(< z,y >))(< \text{bowl}, x >)] \tag{71a}$$

which, by λ-conversion, is simplified to

$$[x \subseteq^\circ \text{RICEGRAINS: } (\forall\, y \in x: \text{IN}(< \text{bowl}, y >))] \tag{71b}$$

We have seen in section 3.2 that the ensemble, represented here, is the same as the merge of the set of parts in question, so (71b) is equivalent to:

$$\cup \, (\{x \in \mathscr{P} \text{ (RICEGRAINS): } (\forall\, y \in x: \text{IN}(< \text{bowl}, y >))\}) \tag{71c}$$

It is easily seen that the merge of these subsets of rice grains is equal to the merge of the singleton subsets $\{y\}$ of which the unique element y satisfies $\text{IN}(< \text{bowl}, y >)$; so (71c) is equivalent to:

$$\cup \, (\{x \in \mathscr{P} \text{ (RICEGRAINS): } \exists y \in \text{RICEGRAINS: } x = \{y\} \text{ and}$$
$$\text{IN}(< \text{bowl}, y >)\}) \tag{71d}$$

This merge is of course just the set of rice grains in the singletons, so (71d) is equivalent to

$$\{x \in \text{RICEGRAINS: IN}(< \text{bowl}, x >)\} \tag{71e}$$

This is the simplest EL representation of the rice in the bowl on the discrete view.

It is easily verified that this procedure also works for the transformations 2c–2d and 3c–3d and that, owing to the properties of measure functions, the representation 1d is equivalent to saying that the sum of the weights of the individual rice grains is 2 kilos.

The representation (71b), obtained by purely lexical transformations that keep the overall structure of the representation the same, is equivalent to the final representation (71e). Therefore, from a strictly logical point of view the transformation to (71b) is all that needs to be done; the remaining transformation steps merely serve to bring the representation in a simpler and more familiar form. I have included the transformation to a simpler form because I think the strictly logical point of view is not necessarily the only relevant one, and considerations of simplicity may also play a role. It may be considered a disadvantage of this transformation method that certain equivalence transformations have to be carried out if we want to obtain the simplest representation. It should be kept in mind, though, that the reasoning system using the knowledge base must have the capability to perform such operations anyway; therefore, the only additional mechanism required for this way of changing perspective is that of lexical lookup.

I think these examples show that ensemble theory can be a useful basis for a representational formalism that gives us the possibility not only to build up correct representations of knowledge involving (quasi-) continuous concepts, but also to make instantaneous shifts between a discrete and a continuous representation of sizeable bodies of knowledge.

References

Bronnenberg, W. J., Bunt, H. C., Landsbergen, S. P. J., Scha, R. J. H., Schoenmakers, W. J., & Utteren, E. P. C. van (1980). The question answering system PHLIQA1. In L. Bolc (Ed.), *Natural communication with computers* London: McMillan; München: Hanser Verlag.

Bunt, H. C. (1978). A formal semantic analysis of mass terms and amount terms. In J. Groenendijk & M. Stokhof (Eds.), *Amsterdam papers in formal grammar* (Vol. II). Amsterdam: the University.

Bunt, H. C. (1979). Ensembles and the formal semantic properties of mass terms. In F. J. Pelletier (Ed.), *Mass terms.* Dordrecht: Reidel.

Bunt, H. C. (1980). On the why, the how, and the whether of a count-mass distinction among adjectives. In J. Groenendijk, T. Janssen, & M. Stokhof (Eds.), *Formal methods in the study of language.* Amsterdam: Mathematical Centre.

Bunt, H. C. (1981a). *The formal semantics of mass terms.* Unpublished doctoral dissertation, University of Amsterdam, Amsterdam, The Netherlands.

Bunt, H. C. (1981b). *Rules for the interpretation, evaluation, and generation of dialogue acts.* IPO Annual Progress Report *16,* gg-107.

Bunt, H. C. (1982). *The IPO dialogue project.* SIGART Newsletter *80,* 60–61.

Bunt, H. C. (1984a). The resolution of quantificational ambiguity in the TENDUM system. Paper presented at COLING84, Stanford, California.

Bunt, H. C. (1984b). Data module nets as a formalism for knowledge representation. Paper presented at 5th Amsterdam Colloquium.

Bunt, H. C. (in press). *Mass terms and model-theoretic semantics.* Cambridge, England: Cambridge University Press.

Burge, R. T. (1972). Truth and mass terms. *Journal of Philosophy, 69* (10).

Cartwright, H. M. (1965). Heraclitus and the bath water. *Philosophical Review, 74,* 466–485.

Clarke, D. S. (1970). Mass terms as subjects. *Philosophical studies, 21,* 25–29.

Fraenkel, A. A., Bar-Hillel, Y., Levy, A., & Dalen, D. van (1973). *Foundations of set theory.* Amsterdam: North-Holland.

Grandy, R. (1973). Response to Moravcsik. In Hintikka et al. al. (Eds.), *Approaches to natural language,* Dordrecht: Reidel.

Hayes, P. J. (1974). *Some problems and nonproblems in representation theory.* Paper presented at AISB Summer Conference, University of Sussex, England.

Hayes, P. J. (1978). The naive physics manifesto. In D. Michie (Ed.), *Expert systems in the microelectronic age.* Edinburgh, Scotland: Edinburgh University Press.

Leonard, H. F., and Goodman, N. (1940). The calculus of individuals and its uses. *Journal of Symbolic Logic, 5,* 45–55.

Lesniewski, S. (1927–31). O podstawach matematyki. *Przeglad Filozoficzny, 30,* 164–206; *31,* 261–291; *32,* 60–101, *33,* 75–105, *34,* 142–170.

Lesniewski, S. (1929). Grundzüge eines neuen Systems der Grundlagen der Mathematik. *Fundamenta Mathematicae, 14,* 1–81.

Montague, R. (1973). The proper treatment of quantification in ordinary English. In K. J. J. Hintikka, J. M. E. Moravesik, & P. Suppes (Eds.), *Approaches to natural language.* Dordrecht: Reidel.

Moore, R. C. (1980). *Reasoning about knowledge and action* (SRI Technical Note No. 191).

Moravcsik, J. M. E. (1973). Mass terms in English. In Hintikka et al. (Eds.), *Approaches to natural language.* Dordrecht: Reidel.

Parsons, T. (1970). Mass terms and amount terms. *Found. of Language, 6,* 363–388.

Parsons, T. (1975). Afterthoughts on mass terms. *Synthese, 31,* 517–521.

Pelletier, F. J. (1974). On some proposals for the semantics of mass terms. *Journal of Philosophical Logic, 3,* 87–108.

Pelletier, F. J. (Ed.). (1979). *Mass terms.* Dordrecht: Reidel.

Quine, W. V. O. (1960). *Word and object.* Cambridge, MA: M.I.T. Press.

Strawson, P. F. (1959). *Individuals.* London: Methuen, also unpublished doctoral dissertation, Harvard University, Cambridge, MA.

ter Meulen, A. G. B. (1980). *Substances, quantities, and individuals.* Unpublished doctoral dissertation, Stanford University, Stanford, CA.

3 Naive Physics I: Ontology For Liquids

Patrick J. Hayes

Cognitive Science
University of Rochester
Rochester, New York

Here I discovered water—a very different element from the green crawling scum that stank in the garden but. You could pump it in pure blue gulps out of the ground, you could swing on the pump handle and it came out sparkling like liquid sky. And it broke and ran and shone on the tiled floor, or quivered in a jug, or weighted your clothes with cold. You could drink it, draw with it, froth it with soap, swim beetles across it, or fly it in bubbles in the air. You could put your head in it, and open your eyes, and see the sides of the bucket buckle, and hear your caught breath roar, and work your mouth like a fish, and smell the lime from the ground. Substance of magic—which you could tear or wear, confine or scatter, or send down holes, but never burn or break or destroy.

—From "Cider with Rosie", by Laurie Lee

1 Introduction

This paper is a first essay in "Naive Physics", the attempt to create a formalisation of common-sense knowledge of the physical world. The general background and overall aims are explained in chapter 1, this volume, "The Second Naive Physics Manifesto".

The choice of liquids as a first subject may seem arbitrary and obscure. It was made because liquids have seemed for some time to present some very difficult unsolved problems for formalizers. Liquids have, for example, no definite shape, and they merge and split and move in mysterious ways. As expected, I have been forced to develop many other concepts in order to talk of liquids: geometry, time, change, shape among them. None of these is fully investigated here, but we have made a start. In a sense, since the space of concepts is so richly connected, it probably doesn't matter where one starts: every cluster leads into other clusters.

I use first-order logic as the formal language. However, readers to whom logic is either unfamiliar or unattractive should be able to follow most of the ideas by reading the text and looking at the pictures. The same ideas and concepts could be expressed in any one of many formal languages.

A brief note on the logical language used. We use the full predicate calculus with equality, not just clausal form. We use all the usual connectives, and exclusive *or* (written $\dot\vee$), which is often very useful. The usual precedence rules are used: $\sim$ binds more tightly than $\wedge$, $\vee$, or $\dot\vee$; these more than $\supset$ or $\equiv$; and quantifiers have the widest scope of all. Brackets or layout will override these conventions. I will assume $\wedge$, $\vee$, and $\dot\vee$ to be variadic. Note that $A \dot\vee B \dot\vee C$ means

$$(A \wedge \sim B \wedge \sim C) \vee (\sim A \wedge B \wedge \sim C) \vee (\sim A \wedge \sim B \wedge C)$$

so that $\dot\vee$ is not associative.

Some "higher-order" quantifications will be used: these are to be regarded only as syntactic sugarings of related first-order expressions. Predicate and relation names will be capitalised; constant, variable and function names not. Free variables are understood to be universally quantified with the whole axiom as scope.

The only other syntactic curiosity is restricted quantification, for which we use an epsilon, for example:

$$\forall t \in I.\ P(t)$$

We assume that the underlying logic has a fairly sophisticated sort structure, so that relations and functions are defined only on particular combinations of sorts of their arguments. I will indicate types informally by the consistent use of special variable names, such as *ar* for arrivals, *le* for leavings and *h* for histories: see Cohn (1983) for a more formal description of the necessary logic.

2 Individuals and Individuation

Every representational formalism I know which has even the glimmerings of a clear semantics, is based on the idea of individual entities and relationships between them. The individuals need not be *physical* individuals; they may be abstract "things" like *the color green* or *the German nation* or *the concept of man* or *the number zero*. They may only exist in some imaginary world, like *the King of France who would be on the throne now if there hadn't been any revolution*: indeed, they may actually *be* an imaginary world, or a state of it. They may be arbitrarily big or arbitrarily small, real or platonic, compact or spread out; still they are *individuals*: separate entities, each not to be confused with any other entity. They partake in relations with other such crisp *individuals*: physical relations such as being inside of, having as color, and abstract relations such as being in 1:1 correspondence with, or bearing an analogy to, or being a physical property.

Many problems in the philosophy of logic turn on the question of how we *identify* individuals: how they are individuated. Intuitively, certain properties of a thing serve to distinguish it from other things and to identify it as being the thing that it is, while other properties of the thing are merely properties that it happens to have. Thus, my car is a Malibu, like many other Malibu's, but it has several properties—

its chassis number, its registration plate, the dent in the rear door, etc., which, taken together, I use to identify it as being mine.

To distinguish properties of a thing which are essential to it from properties which are merely properties, in this way, is to espouse what Quine calls *essentialism*. He evidently regards it as incompatible with Science, a view with which we can happily agree, while using essentialism wholeheartedly ourselves.

However, the fundamental criteria for individuating a complex object cannot be such superficial properties as those I have mentioned, for they can change. For example, take my car. If it were stolen, its bodywork and driver's seat repaired, its engine and chassis numbers filed off, and resprayed, then all the properties by which I identify it would be false of it; and yet it would still be my car, the very same Malibu. I think what we have to say here is that it is my car because it has continuously *been* my car through all the intervening history. It was my car when it was stolen, and repairing, respraying, etc., are not operations which destroy the identity of a car: ergo, it is still my car. It still would be my car, indeed, if every single piece of it had been replaced, so that it had no part in common with the car that had been stolen from me. (If I could demonstrate this spatiotemporal continuity to a court, it would I think agree that the car was mine, however altered in appearance it seemed.)

The point of this is to illustrate the fact that spatiotemporal continuity is the criterion for determining the identity of complex assemblies: for these can have parts replaced but still retain their identity.

Consider now *pieces* of solid stuff, like metal bars or wooden blocks. Every solid physical object is either a piece of solid stuff, or else an assembly which is made up of a finite number of other solid physical objects. We can state this formally:

$$\forall x.Solidobject(x) \supset Assembly(x) \qquad (1a)$$
$$\bigvee \exists m.Stuff(m) \wedge Rigid(m) \wedge madeof(x)=m$$

$$Assembly(x) \supset \exists x_1,...,x_n.Part(x,x_1) \wedge ... \wedge Part(x,x_n) \qquad (1b)$$
$$\wedge Solid(x_1) \wedge ... \wedge Solid(x_n)$$

Here, *madeof* is a function between a solid undecomposable physical *thing* and a *substance*. (Substances, like *wood*, can be thought of either as abstract individuals—the essence of woodiness—or as worldly, solid but rather spread-out individuals; all the wood in the world. This latter is the nominalist idea developed by Goodman (1966), according to which our relation *madeof* is thought of as meaning *being-a-part-of* (in a rather different sense from our *part*). The platonist–nominalist division between ways of thinking of substances need not concern us here: it is sufficient for our purpose that substances exist as individuals, and can be quantified over.) It is amusing to try to find counterexamples to (1). Two steel bars welded with brass? A muscle-tendon-bone junction? A bar which is steel at one end but aluminium at the other, with a smooth transition between them? I think we always make a *conceptual* division into well-defined parts, even when exact boundaries (as in muscle-tendon-bone) are hard or impossible to place exactly.

I think that *being the same piece* of stuff is the basic individuating property for solid pieces. Thus, a wooden brick is an object, an individual; and it comprises a certain unique *piece* of wood, distinguishable from other pieces of (the same) wood. The block *is* the piece of wood; and every piece of wood is an object. Notice how this differs from the criterion for individuating an assembly.

These objects, moreover, are fairly *enduring*. They can be destroyed (cutting, crushing, burning . . .) and created (cutting, forging, molding . . .) but only by recognizable actions and events. They do not appear and vanish by accident, casually, without anyone noticing, as it were: the events which mark their creation and destruction are nameable, describable entities. They have a beginning and an end. It is possible to keep track of them.

3 The Problem With Liquids

But for liquids, this is far less plausible. Axiom (1) fails immediately: think of a half-melted triple-decker ice cream cone, for example. We can distinguish water, the generic stuff, from a particular piece of water, just as with solid substances. But the criteria for identifying pieces of water do not seem to be the same as for pieces of solids. Lake Leman, for example, has the Rhone flowing in one end and out the other, so it certainly isn't the same piece of water from day to day, yet we feel it is the same *lake*.

Consider a glass containing 100 cc of water. We could say this *piece of water* was an object. Now we pour 10 cc into another glass: now there are *two* objects, and neither is identical to the first one. Now pour it back: there is one object again. Is it the same object as that with which we began? It would seem so, since it is the same water and the same glass, and it has all the same properties as the former. But then, we have individuals which cease to exist and reappear later, which is rather worrying.

Perhaps we should say that a glass of water is like an assembly, so that we can replace bits by others without changing its identity. After all, we could take a car completely to pieces and then reassemble it, and it would be the same car. And this would let Lake Leman be an object, albeit in a state of continuous overhaul.

But what are the components of these assemblies? Presumably, smaller pieces of water. Presumably then one could say, after pouring the 10 cc back, that the 100 cc contained two *parts*, one of 10 cc and one of 90 cc. Now pour out 20 cc and pour it back. It now contains another two parts: one of 80 cc and one of 20 cc. None of these four parts is the same as another, so they must *overlap*. Clearly, by repeating this sort of argument one sees that any piece of water must be an assembly of a very large (maybe infinite) number of very small (maybe infinitesimal) pieces, with no structure: a wholly disorganized assembly, like a powder.

Now, this *is* a good way to look at liquids, but it seems overly sophisticated for everyday use, and gives rise to many problems of its own (one can't *see* the separate grains, for example, and this requires an explanation). Moreover, these liquid assemblies, unlike such well-made things as cars, come apart and reassemble at the slightest provocation. It seems hardly possible to keep track of their existence: they can come apart or recombine by accident, as it were.

And in any case, there is another problem, for sometimes we seem to use the other ontology. We can say, this water (in this glass) came out of the tap. But this requires us to treat the water in the glass as a particular *piece* of water, not a mere assembly: for if I pour some water from the sewer into it, then it's the same assembly, having merely grown somewhat (think of adding seat covers to my car): but it's a very different piece of stuff.

Pieces of liquid, then, are objects which give rise to considerable difficulty. It's not clear what they *are*. We will revisit this question in section 10, but before then will try to do without pieces of liquid altogether. It turns out that one can get a long way by talking only about the pieces of space or space–time which contain liquid, and how they can be connected to one another. And this geometric approach gives one good way to individuate liquid objects, as discussed in section 10.

4 Doing Without Liquid Individuals: Containment

The first idea is to avoid talking about *pieces of liquid* altogether, and to refer, rather, to *containers,* which may be full of liquid, to distinguish one piece of liquid from another. More exactly, we will introduce a notion of *contained space* which may contain some liquid. A notion of *quantity* or *amount* is naturally introduced at the same time. In this way we can talk about *the 20 cc of water in this cup* or *the 10 cc of water in that cup* in a natural way without being committed to the view that such a 20 cc or 10 cc of water *is* an individual thing.

By a *contained space* we will mean some connected volume of three-dimensional-space which has a contiguous rigid boundary (at least) below it and around it. As a first, temporary approximation, we will also assume that the substance comprising the boundary is impermeable and has no leaks. Examples include the inside of a cup or a dish or a jug or a bath; the bed and banks of a lake or a pond; the interior of a paint tin or a petrol can. Notice we distinguish between the *container,* which is a solid object, or part of a solid object, and the *contained space,* which is *not* a physical object but is characterized by a certain capacity and by being in a certain relation to a container.

Let us say that if *c* is a container then *inside(c)* is the space it contains: *inside* is a function from containers to their contained spaces. We will also need to be able to refer to some liquids being in a certain place. If *s* is a contained space and *l* a liquid (in the generic sense—a *liquid stuff* such as water or oil), then we will refer to the *amount* of *l* in *s*. We assume that there is a function *amount(l,s)* from liquids and contained spaces, to entities called *amounts* which are abstract "quantities". We will assume that the set of amounts is (partially) ordered and has a zero element, *none*. Thus, "there's whisky in the jar" can be represented:

amount(whisky,inside(jar)) > none.

Notice that we have nowhere spoken of the piece of whisky in the jar as an individual entity: *whisky* here is a generic liquid stuff. We can measure quantities by *measure functions,* which are functions to some *measure space* from quantities. (We will take measure space to be the positive reals for the moment, but there is considerable interest in extending the notion to other structures, such as finite discrete sets, tolerance spaces and catastrophes. This will be discussed more fully elsewhere.) For example, litres is a measure function, and we can write

$$liters(amount(whisky,inside(jar)))=0.83$$

to say there is 0.83 litres of whisky in the jar.

We have to distinguish amounts from numbers in order to allow different measure functions: 0.83 liters is 1.46 pints, for example, and a heaped tablespoonful is about an ounce. We can express general conversions:

$$liters(x)=1.76 \times pints(x)$$

In any case, it seems a good idea on general grounds to have a prenumerate notion of *quantity,* independent of any quantitative measurement. We also have the axiom :

$$Measurefun(q) \supset q(none) = 0 \tag{2}$$

(I have deliberately not distinguished between mass and volume. I believe the distinction to be fairly sophisticated. Thus, we could introduce notions of the mass of a given amount of liquid *l,* and the volume of a given amount of liquid *l,* and refuse to have any scales of *amounts,* only masses and volumes. I think something like this is what happens in the heads of kids who learn about density for the first time. It is a difficult concept, requiring a fairly thorough overhauling of one's ontological apparatus. The density of liquid *l* is the ratio of the mass of a given amount of liquid *l* to the volume of the same amount. It is by no means *a priori* obvious that it is independent of the amount. I have observed exactly this difficulty in teaching this concept to a child: he couldn't believe, at first, that the density of a big rock would be the same as that of a little piece of the same material. (His problem had been exacerbated by his having been taught in school that the mass of a body was "the amount of it there is", a description he—quite reasonably—could not distinguish from that of the volume.))

We will need the notion of the *capacity* of a container, i.e. the maximum amount it can contain. It is in fact more convenient to introduce a notion of *amount of space,* and define *capacity(s),* where *s* is a contained space, to be the amount of space it comprises. We then have the axiom

$$none \leq amount(l,s) \leq capacity(s) \tag{3}$$

and we can define

$$Full(s,l) \equiv amount(l,s) = capacity(s) \qquad (4)$$

Consider now a lake. This is a contained-space defined by geographical constraints. Lake Leman, for example, is the space contained between the Jura Mountains, Lausanne, the Dent d'Oche, Thonon, and the Rochers de Naye, below the 400-meter contour (more or less). Its container is the surface of the earth under it, i.e. the *lake bed*. I think the only way to describe lakes, rivers and ponds in the present framework is to say that they are contained-spaces which are full of water: that is, the space ends at the surface of the water. To be *in* the lake is then, reasonably, to be immersed in water, while to be *on* the lake is to be immediately above the water and supported by the lake (cf. *on the table*), which seems reasonable. Thus a lake is full by definition.

It might seem that we have essentially resuscitated our original ontology of pieces-of-water under a different name. But not so. For with *this* ontology, Lake Leman is a fixed object in geographical space whereas in the pieces-of-water ontology, it would be constantly changing, since the Rhone flows in one end and out the other; it would be a phenomenon, not an object.

One can make several objections. I will consider two.

1. If the Rhone were to dry up and Lake Leman drain away, we would say the Lake had gone, but the *space* would still be there: so 'Lake Leman' must refer to the water, not the space. No. Because a lake, on our account, is a space full of water, and its top is the surface of the water. Thus, as the lake drained away, we would have its space shrinking and when all the water had gone, so would have the lake. Notice in this connection the distinction between a lake (or a river) and the lake valley (river bed). The latter is a container, the former a contained space. But, in general:

$$capacity(lake) < capacity(inside(lake\text{-}valley)).$$

For rivers, the analogous inequation is the no-flooding condition.

2. Since Lake Leman (for example) is, on our account, merely a *space*, how can it support a boat? Perhaps the water supports the boat. But we want to avoid saying that any particular *piece* of water supports the boat. But, on the other hand, the water in my bath (say) does not support the boat in any way, and we want this to be quite clear. The only way to handle this for now, is to say that, in fact, the *lake* supports the boat: that is, the space supports it. But it only does so *because* it is full of water, so that an empty space would not support a boat. Thus, boats float on lakes and ponds *because* lakes and ponds are full of water.

A naive axiom might be something like this:

$$On(t,su) \,\&\; Top(su,s) \;\&\; \exists l.Full(s,l) \supset Floatable(t)$$
$$\equiv Supports(s,t) \qquad (5)$$

where *Floatable* is supposed to relate to some (as yet unspecified) theory of buoyancy.

Notice that axiom (5) makes no reference to density. Again I believe a concern for variable density arises only at a very sophisticated level of understanding. It also ignores the way in which floating objects are partly submerged.

All in all, agreeing to swallow some artificiality, the idea of avoiding liquid objects by talking about pieces of space seems to work reasonably well for nicely contained liquid. Before considering other situations liquid can be in, we will develop some apparatus for describing geometrical relationships.

5 Space: Places, Enclosures and Portals

(The concepts outlined in this section really belong in a 'geometry' cluster, and will be described more fully elsewhere. The present account should be taken merely as a sketch.)

Three-dimensional space can be described in a very large number of ways. We can use one of many coordinate systems, for example. Any heuristically adequate description must, however, distinguish the description of the shape of an object, or internal arrangement of a space such as the interior of a room, from the description of where this object or space is located in a larger arrangement or coordinate system. A box has a certain shape—occupies a certain piece of space—independently of where it is in a building (more or less). This point deserves more elaboration, but I mention it here only to emphasize that any kind of global coordinate system is heuristically inadequate: We need a notion of a *piece* of space, and how such pieces can be related and connected to one another. In this section I will develop a theory of such pieces, and how they connect to one another, which is entirely topological, and does not depend upon or use any metric ideas or coordinate system.

A contained space is such a piece which is inside a container. Thus, the inside of a cup is the *same* piece of space, in the same relation to the cup, wherever the cup happens to be. So if the cup is moved across a room, its inside moves with it. If the cup is rotated about a horizontal axis, however, the circumstances inside it are liable to change. Indeed this is generally true, for the global gravity vertical runs through all places. (This vertical direction is obviously of great evolutionary importance, since our bodies have an apparatus of great delicacy whose sole purpose is to detect it: the semicircular canals in the inner ear.) I will therefore distinguish three independent aspects of the spatial disposition of an object: its *shape,* its *position* in some larger spatial framework, and its *orientation* with respect to the gravity vertical. Only the first and last will be of great concern to us. I will assume that such concepts as vertical, top, bottom, horizontal, etc., can be used without further comment: they all refer to the global gravity vertical.

We need to characterize the shape of containers. Intuitively, a container is a solid object which *surrounds* a space, so that there is no way out; or, perhaps, so that the only way out is at the top. So we need the notion of "a way out", which I will call a *portal*: that is, a piece of surface which links two pieces of space and through which objects and material can pass.

There seem to be two different ways to describe this. We can say that a portal is a *common face* of the spaces on either side of it, and is itself free space, i.e. is occupied by no solid lamina. Or we can say that it is a surface through which one can pass from (a point in) one space to (a point in) the other, i.e. such that there is a free-space path from one space to the other which intersects it. (Suitably tightened up, these two definitions are, in fact, equivalent: an intuitively obvious fact which is quite hard to prove.)

These two properties of a portal reflect two fundamentally different approaches to the qualitative description of spatial arrangement and connection, which might be called the space/surface approach and the point/path approach. There are distinct topological theories which arise from each: respectively, homology theory and homotopy theory (see for example Hocking & Young 1961).

From homology theory we borrow the idea of a *face*. A face of a spatial or spatiotemporal entity is a piece of space of one lower dimension which forms part of its boundary. Thus, for example, the surface of a wall of a room is a face of a room: the edge of a tabletop is the face of the tabletop, which is itself a face of the table, considered as a solid object. We will write $Face(s_1, s_2)$ in formulae.

There is a basic fact which we will make implicit use of: in a space of dimension n, a piece of space of dimension n-1 is a face of exactly two pieces of dimension n: it has two sides. (For any $k < n$-1, this fails: a piece of dimension k can be a face of an indefinite number of pieces of dimension $k + 1$. Take $n = 3$, $k = 1$, and consider the spine of a book, for example; or $n = 4$, $k = 2$, and consider a tabletop on which a number of bricks are successively placed and removed in turn.) We can make use of this fact by defining a function *toso* ("the other side of"), such that:

$$Face(f, v) \equiv Face(f, toso(f, v)) \tag{6}$$

$$toso(f, toso(f, v)) = v \tag{7}$$

The function *toso* is, by our discussion above, defined only in suitable dimensions. Thus, if f is a point and v part of a line, then $toso(f, v)$ is the other half of the line. If v is a piece of 3-space or an object, then $toso(f, v)$ is another piece of space.

Let us say that a face f of v is a *Top* (of v) if its surface normal has a positive vertical component, similarly for *Bottom*. Then *toso* reverses direction:

$$Top(f, v) \supset Bottom(f, toso(f, v)) \tag{8}$$

(From which the contraposition also easily follows, so we could replace implication by equivalence.) We will also need:

$$\sim Face(s) \tag{9}$$

A solid object defines a piece of space which it (just) fills. Such a piece of space can however be surfacelike, a lamina, as in a sheet of metal. We will want to say that such an object is the face of the spaces of both sides of it. But we will also want to be able to distinguish such an object from its surfaces, since we will want to be able to say whether or not they are wet. I will distinguish therefore a surface (which may or may not be occupied by an object) from the two *directed surfaces* which are its sides. It is convenient to assume that solid objects (considered as pieces of space) contain their boundaries (faces), but that pieces of free space do not: the former can be seen as closed, the latter open, sets in metric, Euclidean, three-dimensional space, in the sense of topology. We can think of a solid object as having an open interior and a "skin" composed of its faces: laminar objects are "all skin". (The topological foundations of such an intuitive geometry deserve closer attention.)

Let us say that $In(s_1,s_2)$ if the piece of space s_1 is wholly contained in s_2, and let $space(o)$, where o is an object, be the space occupied by o. Then we can say:

$$s = space(o) \equiv (\forall f.Face(f,o) \supset In(f,s)) \tag{10}$$

It is convenient to treat *space* as a coercion function in formulae, so that if an expression 'e' naming an object occurs in an argument-place requiring a space or surface, it is taken to mean '$space(e)$'. With this convention, we can often mention objects as though they were pieces of space, writing for example $In(o_1,o_2)$. We will do this without further comment from time to time. We can define:

$$Free(s) \equiv \sim\exists o.In(s,o) \tag{11}$$

and we have

$$In(s,s) \tag{12a}$$

$$In(s_1,s_2) \wedge In(s_2,s_3) \supset In(s_1,s_3) \tag{12b}$$

Now consider two (open) pieces of space separated by a connecting face. There are four possibilities. If the face is free then so must both spaces be (for if one were solid then it would contain the face), so the face is a portal. Or just the face might be a laminar object. Or one piece of space might be the space of an object, containing the face, and the other be free. Or both spaces might be full, in which case we have two objects joined along a face (see Figure 1).

$$
\begin{aligned}
Face(f,v) \equiv \quad & \\
& Free(f) \wedge Free(v) \wedge Free(toso(f,v)) \\
\vee\ & \exists o.f = space(o) \wedge Free(v) \wedge Free(toso(f,v)) \\
\vee\ & \exists o.In(f,o) \wedge (Free(v) \wedge toso(f,v) = space(o) \\
& \qquad \vee Free(toso(f,v)) \wedge v = space(o)) \\
\vee\ & \exists o_1,o_2.v = space(o_1) \wedge toso(f,v) = space(o_2) \wedge Joined(o_1,o_2,f)
\end{aligned}
\tag{13}
$$

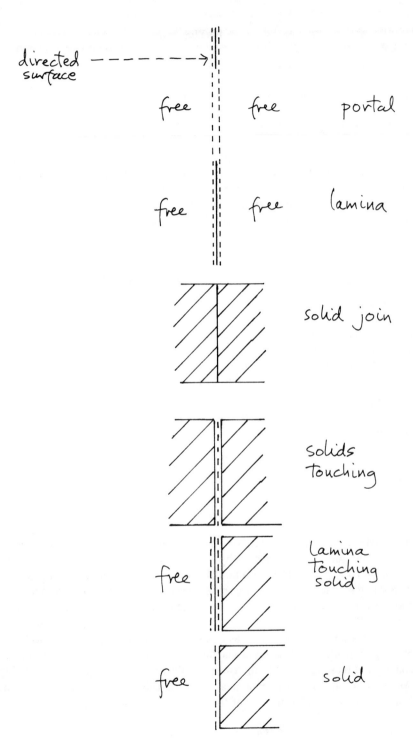

Figure 1. Surfaces and directed surfaces

$$Joined(o_1,o_2,f) \equiv Face(f,o_1) \wedge Face(f,o_2) \wedge o_1 \neq o_2 \tag{14}$$

This last case is the only interpenetration we allow:

$$In(s,o_1) \wedge In(s,o_2) \supset Joined(o_1,o_2,s) \stackrel{.}{\vee} o_1=o_2 \tag{15}$$

We can now, at last, characterize some containers. A closed container, the simplest case, is a solid object o which encloses a space we will call $inside(o)$. (Note that $inside(o)$ is not In the object o, but rather is enclosed by it: an empty glass bottle encloses air but all the space In it is full of glass.) I will not attempt a complete axiomatization of $inside$, but we do have:

$$Closedcontainer(o) \wedge Face(f,inside(o)) \supset In(f,o) \tag{16}$$

which gives some flesh to the idea of enclosure; and of course

$$Free(inside(o)) \tag{17}$$

These alone have some interesting consequences. Assume for example $Closedcontainer(ob)$ and $Face(f,inside(ob))$. Then from (16) we can conclude $In(f,ob)$ and hence $\sim Free(f)$, by (11). Now, checking the various cases in (13), applied to f and $inside(ob)$, the first is ruled out; and the last is ruled out by (17)—since if $inside(ob)$ is $space(o_1)$ then it is not $Free$, by (12a) and (11)—and in the third case, the first subcase, which has $inside(ob) = space(o)$, is similarly eliminated. Hence only two cases remain, either:

$$\exists o. \; f=space(o) \wedge Free(inside(ob)) \wedge Free(toso(f,inside(ob)))$$

or

$$\exists o. \; In(f,space(o)) \wedge toso(f,inside(ob))=space(o) \wedge Free(inside(ob))$$

In the first case, since (16) implies that $In(f,ob)$, we have $In(space(o),ob)$, ie $In(o,ob)$. But then, since $In(o,o)$ by (12a), we can conclude from (15) that $Joined(o,ob,o) \stackrel{.}{\vee} = ob$. The definition (14) of $Joined$ rules out the first possibility since nothing is a face of itself, so we are obliged to conclude that $o = ob$. A similarly tortuous piece of reasoning, using (15), (6) and (17), establishes that $o = ob$ in the second case also. The first case then has f, the face of the inside, being the object ob, so that ob is a laminar object such as a gas can, while the second case has f being merely a part of ob, which has nontrivial thickness: a solid object with a cavity, like a coconut. And these are exactly the two possible ways to make a closed container.

More interesting are *open* containers, i.e. those with (at least) one portal. If there is just one, we will call it the *top* of the container, so that we can say:

$$Opencontainer(o) \supset Free(top(o)) \wedge$$
$$\forall f. \; Face(f,inside(o)) \supset In(f,o) \stackrel{.}{\vee} f=top(o) \tag{18}$$

We could now define some more familiar ideas, for example:

$$Brim(e,o) \equiv Face(e,top(o)) \tag{19}$$

(This is the first nontrivial use of lower-dimensional Faces). Notice that *top*, unlike *Top* introduced earlier, is independent of orientation. We can define a very useful notion of "right way up" (Rwu) by saying:

$$Rwu(o) \equiv Top(top(o),o) \tag{20}$$

(It is important to realize that *Top*, and hence *Rwu*, are not relations which are intrinsic to an object. Unlike most of what we have considered they are liable to be altered when the object is moved around in space.)

We will also need other kinds of containment, such as leaky containers (those with a portal lower than the top) and channels (like a container, but with portals at both its ends). Unfortunately to describe these adequately requires metric ideas. (For example, a tin with a small hole in the base is a leaky tin, but a tin with the bottom missing isn't a container at all, although it could be a channel.) I will not go into this in detail here. Our use of the function *inside* will be taken to imply that the object defines a space in some way, and we will introduce categories of such objects as we need them. For a start,

$$Container(o) \equiv Closedcontainer(o) \vee (Opencontainer(o) \wedge Rwu(o)) \tag{21}$$

Before leaving geometry, we need the notion of a side of a surface. We will define a *directed surface, $d(f,v)$* where f is part of a face of v. The idea is that such an object is an arbitrarily thin, open, lamina on the v side of the face f. (Since Euclidean space is normal, i.e. Hausdorff and compact, such a lamina *can* be arbitrarily thin.) We extend *toso* by defining

$$toso(d(f,v)) = d(f,toso(f,v)) \tag{22}$$

then we have

$$toso(toso(d(f,v))) = d(f,v)$$

And if we assert

$$In(d(f,v),v) \tag{23}$$

then we can easily derive

$$In(toso(d(f,v)), \ toso(f,v))$$

We will extend *In* to directed faces in the obvious way, so that

$$In(f_1,f_2) \equiv In(d(f_1,v),d(f_2,v)).$$

If *o* is a solid object and *f* a face of *o*, then the directed face *d(f, toso(f,o))* is an *outer* face of *o*. If *o* is a laminar container then we can define an outer directed face of *o* to be *d(f,toso(inside(o)))* where *f* is part of *o:*

$$Outer(d,o) \equiv \exists f.Face(f,o) \land d=d(f,toso(f,o))$$
$$\lor$$
$$In(f,o) \land d = d(f,toso(f,inside(o)))\qquad(24)$$

The first case is a solid object *o*, the second a laminar container. We can then say that two objects are *touching* if they share an outer directed face:

$$Touching(o_1,o_2) \equiv \exists d.\ Outer(d,o_1) \land Outer(d,o_2)\qquad(25)$$

i.e. *d* is an arbitrarily thin free space separating the objects. Notice how this differs from a join along a shared face.

Since a solid object not attached to anything else is, by our definitions, completely surrounded by free space, we can define *surround(o)* to be this space. Thus we have

$$Free(surround(o))\qquad(26)$$

$$Outer(d,o) \supset In(d,surround(o))\qquad(27)$$

$$Free(s) \land In(o,s) \supset In(s,surround(o))\qquad(28)$$

Similarly, if *v* is a free volume bounded by a solid face *f*, then the directed face *d(f,v)* will be called an *inward* face of *v:*

$$Inward(d,v) \equiv \exists f.\ Face(f,v) \land d=d(f,v)\qquad(29)$$

Figure 1 illustrates the ways in which spaces, surfaces, objects and directed surfaces can be related to one another.

Later we will need to consider edges and surfaces in some detail, and in order to talk of directions on a surface we will need the concept of a *directed edge*. This is, of course, merely the 1-dimensional version of a directed surface, and we will write *d(e,f)*, where *e* is an edge which is part of the boundary of the piece of surface *f*. All the above axioms apply unchanged, so that *d(e,f)* is *In* the surface *f*. We will use *inward* and *outer* for edges and surfaces also.

However, the full story is more complicated, since directed surfaces themselves, being essentially two-dimensional entities, have edges and hence directed edges.

We must distinguish an edge of a surface from the corresponding edge of the directed surface immediately above it. For example, the latter may be free when the former, being inside a solid surface, is not. One can think of an edge of a directed surface as being an arbitrarily low "fence" on the appropriate side of the underlying surface, and a directed edge of a directed surface is then one side of this fence. It is possible that the edge be solid but both directed surfaces on either side of it be free: this is a "wire" raised on a surface, as in a cloisonné enamel, or a pattern of hedges seen from the air.

Suppose v is a volume of space, f a face of it and e an edge of f. Then $d(e,f)$ is a directed edge which, by (23), is *In* the surface f. The side of f towards v is $d(f,v)$; $d(e,v)$ is the edge of this side (notice, *not* a directed edge), i.e. the "fence" above the edge e on the v side of the surface f. The *directed* edge of the directed surface $d(e,v)$ corresponding to $d(e,f)$ is $d(d(e,v),d(f,v))$, which we will abbreviate by $d(e,f;v)$.

The situation is illustrated in Figure 2, an inspection of which may help convince the reader of the reasonableness of the following axioms.

$$Face(e,f) \wedge Face(f,v) \supset Face(d(e,v),d(f,v)) \tag{30}$$

$$toso(d(e,v),d(f,v)) = d(toso(e,f),v) \tag{31}$$

It follows from these and earlier axioms that the other side of a directed edge of a directed face is what one would expect:

$$
\begin{aligned}
toso(d(e,f;v)) &=_{df} toso(d(d(e,v),d(f,v))) \\
&= d(d(e,v),toso(d(e,v),d(f,v))) & \text{by (22)} \\
&= d(d(e,v),d(toso(e,f),v)) & \text{by (31)} \\
&=_{df} d(e,toso(e,f);v)
\end{aligned}
$$

The identity just proven should be compared to (22).

Notice that, by (23), $d(e,f;v)$ is in $d(f,v)$ and hence in v. Thus if one is on one side of a fence, one is *In* the airspace above the ground.

Finally, let us briefly consider corners of objects and edges of laminas. If e is a corner of o, then it is a face of two faces of o. In this case we will say that these two faces are each on the other side of e from the other: thus, *toso* does not distinguish between a line on a surface and a corner, or between convex and concave corners. It would be consistent to say that if e is an edge of a lamina f then $toso(e,f)$ was f itself. (This would be the limiting case as the corner was made sharper.) We will not adopt this convention, however, but will merely say in this case that $toso(e,f)$ is *Free*. Indeed, we can usefully define *Edge* by:

$$Lamina(o) \supset (Edge(e,o) \equiv Face(e,o) \wedge Free(toso(e,o))) \tag{32}$$

6 The Fifteen States of Liquids

The contained-space ontology seems to work reasonably well for liquids contained safely in bounded volumes. However, as any child knows, this is not the normal condition of liquids, and typically, is a state which requires some care to maintain. Left to themselves, liquids flow and stick to things, and are liable to finish up in a different place from that in which they began. It is not clear whether the ontology which serves for contained fluids can be usefully extended to fluids which are running around loose, or are divided up into fine particles, etc. . . .

Let us try to make a taxonomy of the possible states liquid can be in. I will begin by drawing as many distinctions as possible, thus dividing the space of possibilities up into lots of little boxes (Figure 3).

Liquid can be in *bulk,* or it can be *finely divided* as in a spray, mist, droplets or rainfall. It can be *lazy* or *energetic*. (An object or state or process is *energetic* if it requires effort to maintain; *lazy* otherwise, i.e. if it can ''just happen''. I believe this distinction is of considerable importance throughout naive physics. For example, water falling is lazy, but flying upwards through the air, as in a fountain, is energetic.) It can be supported or unsupported. If it is supported, it can be in a space (*inside* some object), or on a surface (i.e. *In* the directed surface on one side of the surface). It can be moving or still: obviously, still liquid is lazy. Of the 32 logical possibilities, only 15 are physically possible, even allowing such outré possibilities as mist being blown along a tube.

There are a few other possibilities, such as liquid soaked up in a sponge or cloth, or suspended by surface tension across the holes in a metal mesh, or free-floating bubbles, but I shall ignore these. In fact, I shall ignore all except the *lazy bulk* states (the top left hand group in Figure 3) in what follows, in order to keep the presentation to a reasonable length. I do not expect the extension to the remaining states to give rise to any deep problems.

We handled containment, without using liquid objects, by referring to pieces of space which *contain* liquid. A similar device works for wet surfaces. We can use the apparatus of directed surfaces. Let f be a solid face of a free volume v: then to say that f is wet is to say that $d(f,v)$ contains some amount of liquid. It is convenient to use the same function *amount* as before. We can also have a notion of capacity, and can use the same function name;

$$Wetby(d,l) \equiv capacity(d) \geq amount(l,d) > none \qquad (33)$$

Here, we must give the phenomenon a name since it is possible for a surface, unlike a container, to support *more* than its capacity: this is when the liquid flows across the surface.

Our geometry now enables us to make several useful inferences. For example, if one surface touches another wet surface, then the first one will be wet also, since to

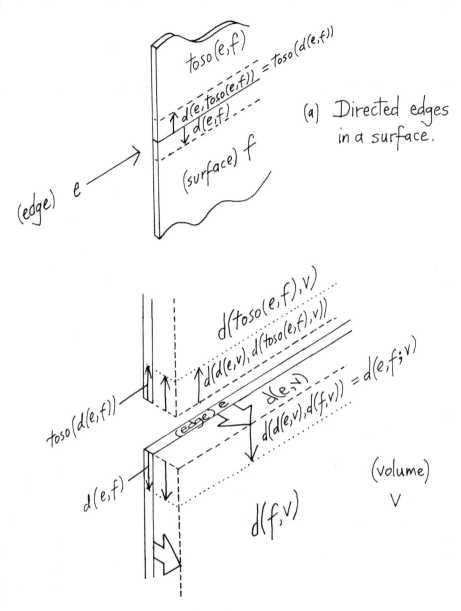

Figure 2. Directed edges and surfaces
(a) Directed edges in a surface.
(b) Directed surfaces, and edges and directed edges of directed surfaces.

LAZY STILL	LAZY MOVING	ENERGETIC MOVING		
Wet surface	Flowing down a surface, e.g. a sloping roof.	Waves lapping shore (?) jet hitting a surface (?)	ON SURFACE	BULK
Contained, in container	Flowing along a channel, e.g. river.	Pumped along pipeline.	IN SPACE	BULK
	Falling column of liquid, e.g. pouring from a jug, or waterfall.	Waterspout, fountain, jet from hosepipe.	UNSUPPORTED	BULK
Dew, drops on a surface.			ON SURFACE	DIVIDED
Mist filling a valley (?)	Mist rolling down a valley (?)	steam or mist blown along a tube (?)	IN SPACE	DIVIDED
Mist, cloud.	Rain, shower.	spray, splash, driving rain.	UNSUPPORTED	DIVIDED

Figure 3.   The possible physical states of liquid

touch a surface is to share the intervening directed surface. More exactly, we can easily show that:

$$Touching(o_1,o_2) \wedge (\exists d.\ Outer(d,o_1) \wedge Wetby(d,l))$$

$$\supset$$

$$\exists d'.\ Outer(d',o_2) \wedge Wetby(d',l)$$

Similarly, we can, with a little more work, show that an object immersed in liquid is *really* wet, all over. For this we need:

$$In(s_1,s_2) \wedge Free(s_1) \wedge Full(s_2,l) \supset Full(s_1,l) \tag{34}$$

Now suppose $In(o,s)$, $Full(s,l)$ and $Outer(d,o)$. Then $In(surround(o),s)$ and $In(d,surround(o))$, by (28) and (27). Hence by (34) (twice), $Full(d,l)$. Thus if someone falls in the lake, he will be as wet as he can get, all over. Finally, it is left as an exercise for the reader to show that if a container is full, then its inside is wet.

Both a wetting and a containment have more structure than we have so far described. If a contained-space contains liquids then there is a surface, which is a horizontal plane (below the *top* of an open container), such that the space below the surface is full (and above it is empty) even though the contained space as a whole is not full. Similarly, if a (directed) face contains liquid, then the chances are that there is a patch of the face which is full and is properly contained in the face. The edge of such a patch is analogous to the surface of the liquid in a container (but has, regrettably, no such tidy property as horizontality.) (It is also possible for a surface to be merely damp, all over. I will ignore this possibility for now but it would figure more prominently if we considered mists, spray and rain.)

An open container will spill if the surface of the liquid reaches the edge of its supports, i.e. a free face of it. In both cases, this can happen while the whole space is not yet full, (by tipping an open container, for example). We need a way, therefore, of talking about the full parts of containments and wettings, which we will call a *wet*.

$$amount(l,s) > none \supset \tag{35}$$
$$In(wet(s),s)$$
$$\wedge\ amount(l,wet(s)) = capacity(wet(s)) = amount(l,s)$$
$$\wedge\ (contained(s) \supset$$
$$\exists p.Horizontal(p) \wedge (Top(su,wet(s)) \supset In(su,p)))$$

(This allows, for example, a U-shaped container, in which the liquid has two tops). Now the spilling criterion can be simply stated: $wet(s)$ shares a face with a portal of s.

The three remaining cases, involving movement and change, cannot be handled by talking only of pieces of space. We need the concept of things that *happen*, rather than merely *are*. In the next section I develop some new apparatus for talking about time and change, which is to a large extent an extension, into the fourth dimension, of the geometric ideas of section 5.

7 Change and Movement: Histories

The now traditional approach to the description of change, due to McCarthy (1959, McCarthy & Hayes 1969), introduces the notion of a time-instant or "situation". Relations whose truth-value is time-dependent are made to depend upon the situation as well as their "static" arguments. A detailed account of the logic of this technique is in (Hayes 1971). Exactly the same idea underlies the familiar context-as-possible-world style of using such systems as Conniver and the tense logics developed by philosophical logicians (see for example Prior 1968: for the connections between tense-logics and the situation calculus, see McCarthy & Hayes 1969, part 4).

I will here use a rather different approach based on the idea of a *history*. A history differs from a situation in being restricted spatially and extended temporally: it is a connected piece of space-time in which "something happens", more or less separate from other such pieces. Histories, unlike situations, have a *shape:* much of this section will be devoted to ways of describing their shape.

Examples of histories include the inside of a room during the afternoon, a horserace and the pouring of water from one cup into another. The idea is that a history shall contain an event, isolating it temporally and spatially from other events. We include the special case in which nothing happens at all.

A *state* (an idea we have already used) is an instantaneous "slice" of a history at a certain time-instant. For most histories, there are two distinguished states called the *start* and the *finish,* between which the history exists. An action *a* defines a class of histories: if *s* is a state which is the start of one, then $do(a,s)$ is the state which is the end of it. A state is not a situation, as it has a limited spatial extent and a spatial shape. It is a very thin history.

Almost all the histories we consider in this paper are in a particularly simple class, consisting of a certain piece of space in which something happens for a certain length of time: they are *rectangular*. (Contrast for example a movement through space, which "slopes" in space–time). It makes sense therefore to speak of the place *where* a history takes place: if *h* is a (rectangular) history then *where(h)* is that place. Similarly, *when(h)* is the time-interval during which *h* takes place. (It is convenient to define *when* to be the open interval, so that it does not include its endpoints. It often happens that some condition is true throughout a history except at its endpoints, at which transient phenomena take place.)

If *h* is a history and *t* a time-instant (we assume a global timescale of some sort with an inequality defined on it), the $h @ t$ (read: *h* at *t*) is the "slice" of *h* at *t*. This is a state, that is, a spatial entity at a particular time. Notice that a state is not merely a place, but has an associated time-value: sometimes we will write a state as a pair $\langle p,t \rangle$ where *p* is a place or other spatial entity and *t* a time-instant.

To avoid confusion, one must keep clearly in mind the distinctions between a four-dimensional history or state, a three-dimensional spatial entity (a place, a piece of space or an object), and a time-instant. We can illustrate these diagrammatically as in Figure 4(a), in which the three spatial dimensions have been reduced to two, so that time can be represented as the third dimension. (This is a graphical convention we shall use subsequently.) Spatial entities belong on the space axes, time-instants on the time-axis, and histories and slices in the center of the diagram.

There is a fundamental extensionality axiom:

$$(when(h_1) = when(h_2) \wedge \forall t \in when(h_1). \; h_1@t = h_2@t) \supset h_1 = h_2 \tag{36}$$

Notice however that we do not rule out the possibility that one history could be an episode of two distinct histories, or could be *In* two distinct histories.

Now we are in the real four-dimensional world, purely spatial entities can be seen for the abstractions that they are. There are no objects, only instantaneous states of objects. We will henceforth assume that *all spatial relations apply to slices*, including *Face* and *In*.

Figure 4(b) illustrates some useful relationships between histories. An episode is a proper temporal part of a history. We can define:

$$Episode(h_2,h_1) \equiv begin(h_2) > begin(h_1)$$
$$\wedge \; end(h_2) < end(h_1)$$
$$\wedge \; \forall t \in when(h_2). \; h_2@t = h_1@t \tag{37}$$

and clearly we have:

$$start(h) = sl(h,begin(h)) \tag{38}$$

$$finish(h) = sl(h,end(h)) \tag{39}$$

The other two relationships are extensions of three-dimensional spatial relationships along the time axis, like the writing in a stick of rock candy. It is convenient to use the same relation names. We have:

$$In(h_2,h_1) \equiv when(h_1)=when(h_2)$$
$$\wedge \; \forall t \in when(h_1). \; In(h_2@t,h_1@t) \tag{40}$$

$$Face(h_2,h_1) \equiv when(h_1)=when(h_2)$$
$$\wedge \; \forall t \in when(h_1).Face(h_2@t,h_1@t) \tag{41}$$

This extension of *Face* and *In* from spatial entities to histories is a generally useful device, and we will use it more generally. If R and f are any relation or function on spatial entities (objects, pieces of space, pieces of surface) then the use of R or f applied to histories will be taken to mean that the histories in question are contemporary (have the same *when*) and that R holds between corresponding slices, or the value of f is that when applied to the contemporary slice throughout:

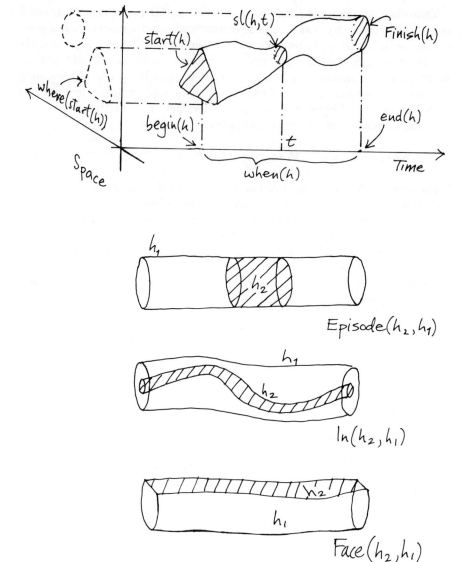

Figure 4. Some relationships between histories

$$R(h_1,\ldots,h_n) \equiv \quad when(h_1)=when(h_2)=\ldots=when(h_n)$$
$$\wedge \; \forall t \in when(h_1). \; R(h_1@t,\ldots,h_n@t) \tag{42a}$$

$$f(h_1,\ldots,h_n)=h_0 \equiv \quad when(h_0)=when(h_1)=\ldots=when(h_n)$$
$$\wedge \; \forall t \in when(h_0). \; f(h_1@t,\ldots,h_n@t)=h_0@t \tag{42b}$$

This useful convention enables us to succinctly state that certain properties of a spatial entity do not change during a certain time period.

Notice that, although we have introduced *Face* and *In* applied to histories as an abbreviation convention, in fact they are literally true in four-dimensional space, i.e. if $Face(h_2,h_1)$ then h_2 is in fact a (three-dimensional: two spatial dimensions + time) face of h_1 in four-dimensional space. The history of a cube, for example, has six such faces—the histories of its faces in three-dimensional space—and two other faces, the *start* and *finish:* eight in all. (Nonrectangular histories can have somewhat more complicated shapes, however.)

Relations on slices play here the same role that fluents play in the situation calculus. Where one would write $R(o_1, \ldots o_n,t)$ in the situation calculus, we will write $R(o_1@t, \ldots, o_n@t)$.

A physical object is a three-dimensional entity which has an associated history representing the life-span of the object: a slice of this history (which we will call the *life* of the object), *is* the object at a given time. If the object is rigid, then its shape is constant, so we can (using the convention just introduced) apply shape descriptors to its history. We might for example assert *spherical(h)*, where h is the history of a ballbearing. In line with the open–closed distinction for spaces and objects, the history of a solid object (unlike other histories) includes its start and finish: thus, a solid object contains *all* its faces.

A special case which will be useful later is a history during which no change takes place at all. We will call this an *enduring*. Given a three-dimensional entity o, and a time-interval I, *endure(o,I)* is defined by the following:

$$when(endure(o,I)) = I \tag{43}$$
$$\forall t \in I.\ endure(o,I)@t = \langle o,t \rangle \tag{44}$$

Clearly an enduring is rectangular.

If f is some function of spatial entities, then we will say that f is *Increasing* in h if:

$$Increasing(f,h) \equiv \forall t,t' \in when(h).\ t < t' \supset f(h@t) < f(h@t') \tag{45}$$

and similarly for *Decreasing*.

8 Histories of Lazy Bulk Liquid

There are five possible lazy bulk histories, shown in Figure 5. The two static ones may be mere endurings, in part: a cup full of liquid, or water spilt on a table, sitting doing nothing for a period. But they may also have less trivial episodes. A cup may be filled or emptied. The wetness on a table may spread, or it may dry up. These changes do not take place randomly, however. A cup will fill only if liquid enters it from somewhere else. Similarly, the three kinds of movement all have ends which are faces through which liquid is passing, and the liquid must go to, or come from, somewhere else. We need to be able to keep track of these comings and goings.

Let f be a face of v: a *leaving* (from v through f) is a history whose where is the directed face $d(f,v)$, and during which liquid passes from v into f. (v may be a volume or a directed surface, the latter corresponding to liquid leaving a surface along its edge.) Similarly an *arriving* (into v through f) is a history of liquid emerging from f into v.

It is tempting to say that *toso* of an arriving is a leaving, and vice versa, but this is true only if the face is a portal. A leaving at a solid surface is more complicated, since the liquid stays on the surface. In this case, we can say that the edge of the leaving is itself a leaving into the directed surface surrounding the leaving. That is, liquid is injected into the surrounding directed face. For this to be possible, we must also allow arrivings and leavings whose *where*s are directed faces of directed edges.

The connections between all these can be stated as:

$$where(h)=d(f,y) \wedge Free(f) \supset (Leaving(h) \equiv Arriving(toso(h))) \tag{46}$$

$$where(h)=d(f,y) \wedge Leaving(h) \wedge \sim Free(f) \supset \tag{47}$$
$$\exists e,h'. \ Face(e,f) \wedge Free(d(e,v))$$
$$\wedge \ where(h')=d(e,f;v)$$
$$\wedge \ when(h')=when(h)$$
$$\wedge \ Leaving(h')$$

In (46) we are using the convention described earlier: in applying the spatial function *toso* to the history h we mean to denote a history contemporary with h whose every slice is *toso* of the instantaneous slice of h. The analogous relationship has had to be spelled out in (47) for lack of a suitable spatial relationship name. It will be convenient to introduce one in what follows. Let us say that if f is a solid face of free v, and e is a face of f such that $d(e,v)$ is free, then $d(e,f;v)$ is a *Splat* of d (f,v):

$$Splat(d(e,f;v),d(f,v)) \equiv Free(v) \wedge \sim Free(f) \wedge Free(d(e,v)) \tag{48}$$

Then (47) above can be replaced by :

$$where(h) = d(f,v) \wedge \sim Free(f) \supset$$
$$Leaving(h) \equiv \exists h'. \ Splat(h',h) \wedge Leaving(h') \tag{49}$$

where we rely on the convention to establish contemporaenity of h and h', cf. (46).

Arrivings and leavings will be the 'glue' with which we attach other liquid-containing histories to one another.

All the possible lazy bulk histories, their episodes and geometric relationships, are illustrated in Figure 5. Before giving the axioms, I will briefly discuss each case.

A wetting can merely endure: or it can spread (i.e. its *wet* can increase in size) if there is an arriving into it; a spreading will spill iff it reaches a free edge of its support. It can also dry up: this is the only change which does not require an arriving or leaving.

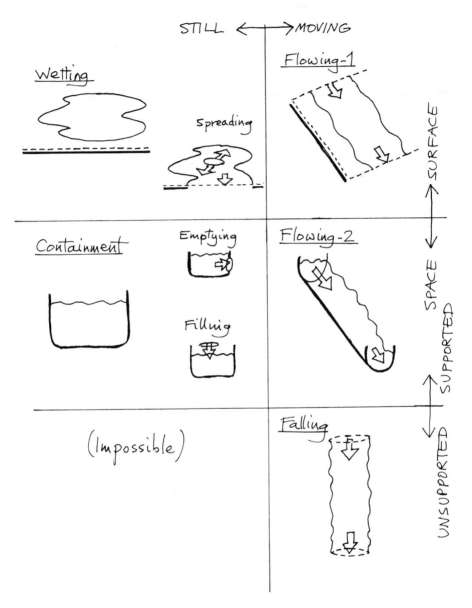

Figure 5. Lazy bulk liquid histories

A containment may merely endure, or it may fill—this needs an arriving—or it may empty, if (and only if) there is a portal below its surface. It is of course possible for a containment to have an arriving and a leaving simultaneously, as Lake Leman has the Rhone flowing in one end and out the other. In this situation, it is both a filling and an emptying, at once.

Neither containments nor wettings can appear or disappear suddenly. The three movements can, however: if one pours water from a jug, the column of water appears instantly, and vanishes as suddenly when the pouring stops. Flowings also, we will assume, establish themselves with no time lag and vanish promptly when their supporting conditions fail. This is of course not accurate, but it will serve as a first approximation.

All three movement histories are similar in that they require an arriving at one end and a leaving at the other, the former higher than the latter (because we are assuming laziness), and their direction is from the former to the latter. They are all endurings: there is no change in them during their lifetimes. As wettings and containments contain *amounts* of liquid, so the three movements have associated *rates;* as, we will assume, do arrivings and leavings. We will use a function *rate(l,h)* which is supposed to take values in some suitable quantity space. The three movements differ only in their shape and support relationships.

To axiomatize all this we start by listing the possible histories.

$$Wetness(h) \wedge \sim Moving(h) \wedge \exists v.where(h){=}d(support(h),v)$$
$$\bigvee (Containment(h) \wedge \sim Moving(h) \wedge where(h){=}inside(support(h)))$$
$$\bigvee (Flowing1(h) \wedge Moving(h) \wedge \exists v.where(h){=}d(support(h),v))$$
$$\bigvee (Flowing2(h) \wedge Moving(h) \wedge where(h){=}inside(support(h)))$$
$$\bigvee (Falling(h) \wedge Moving(h) \wedge \sim Supported(h))$$

This axiom should really have an antecedent setting out the "bulk, lazy" conditions, but this will be omitted here.

Considering now wetnesses, we can say

$$Wetness(h) \supset amount(begin(h)){=}amount(end(h)){=}none$$
$$\wedge \ \forall t \ \epsilon \ when(h). \ Wetby(h@t) \tag{51}$$

(Here we have omitted the 'liquid-stuff' parameter from *amount* and *Wetby*. We will continue to omit this from now on, to make the formulae neater.)

Instantaneous wetnesses are impossible:

$$Wetby(h@t) \supset \exists h'.Wetness(h') \wedge Episode(h,h') \tag{52}$$

Next, the possible episodes of a wetness; another taxonomy:

$$Wetness(h') \wedge Episode(h,h') \equiv \tag{53}$$
$$Merewet(h)$$
$$\bigvee Drying(h)$$
$$\bigvee Spreading(h)$$

Taking these in turn, we have:

$$Merewet(h) \equiv \exists w \ . \ Wetby(w) \wedge h = endure(w,when(h)) \tag{54}$$

$$Drying(h) \supset Decreasing(amount,h) \tag{55}$$

Notice that *amount* here is a functional parameter.

$$Spreading(h) \supset \exists ar.Arriving(ar) \wedge Inward(ar,h) \tag{56}$$
$$\wedge \; (Increasing(amount,h)$$
$$\vee \; \exists le.Leaving(le) \wedge Inward(le,h))$$

It can't spread unless there is a supply, and either it gets bigger, or pours off the edge somewhere. Notice, *this* is not exclusive choice.
Containments are in many ways similar.

$$Containment(h) \supset \quad amount(start(h))=amount(finish(h))=none \tag{57}$$
$$\wedge \; Contained(h)$$

(making use of the convention in (42a) for the base case $n=1$)

$$Contained(h@t) \supset \exists h'.Containment(h') \wedge Episode(h,h') \tag{58}$$

The taxonomy of containment episodes:

$$Containment(h') \wedge Episode(h,h') \equiv \tag{59}$$
$$Merecontain(h)$$
$$\vee \; (Filling(h) \vee Emptying(h))$$

Notice that fillings and emptyings are not exclusive. Taking each case in turn, again:

$$Merecontain(h) \equiv \exists c.Contained(c) \wedge h=endure(c,when(h)) \tag{60}$$

$$Filling(h) \supset \exists ar.Arriving(ar) \wedge Inward(ar,h) \tag{61}$$
$$\wedge \; (Increasing(amount,h)$$
$$\vee \; \exists le.Leaving(le) \wedge Inward(le,h))$$

$$Emptying(h) \supset \exists le.Leaving(le) \wedge Inward(le,h) \tag{62}$$
$$\wedge \; (Decreasing(amount,h)$$
$$\vee \; \exists ar.Arriving(ar) \wedge Inward(ar,h))$$

There is apparently complete symmetry between fillings and emptyings (in fact, leavings and arrivings are not exactly dual to one another, as we will see), unlike spreadings and dryings. In fact, a spreading is exactly analogous to a filling, but a drying has no counterpart for bulk containment (it would be evaporation), and it is impossible to *empty* a wet surface.

Notice the exclusive-or's in axioms (61) and (62). These entail that in a filling with a leaving, the amount does not increase, and similarly does not decrease in an emptying with a leaving. This is an idealisation which allows baths to overflow and leak, but does not allow one to fill a leaky bath. It means that in an episode which is both a filling and an emptying (and therefore has both a leaving and an arriving), the amount neither increases nor decreases: Lake Leman is a good example.

We know from axiom (47) that liquid cannot leave through a solid face. We need however to state the contrapositive, that it *will* leave through a portal, given the chance. There are three ways: a free edge of a wetness' wet, a free face of a containment's wet, or the free edge of a face of a containment's wet (the edge of an overflowing bath, for example). The first two can be covered together:

$$\sim Moving(h') \wedge Episode(l,h') \supset \tag{63}$$
$$(Face(f,wet(h)) \wedge \sim Top(f,wet(h)) \wedge Free(f)$$
$$\equiv Leaving(d(f,h))$$

(This uses the convention in (42) heavily. For example, the face f is a history, as are the entities $wet(h)$ and $d(f,h)$: and these are all exactly contemporary with the episode h during which liquid is leaving.)

$$(Containment(h') \vee Flowing2(h')) \wedge Episode(h,h') \supset \tag{64}$$
$$(Face(f,wet(h)) \wedge Face(e,f) \wedge Free(e) \wedge (\sim Free(f) \vee Top(f,h))$$
$$\equiv Leaving(d(e,f;toso(f,h)))\ )$$

We cannot use *Splat* to shorten axiom (64), since the face f may well be free, as in an overflowing bath.

Now the movements:

$$Movement(h) \supset Arriving(in(h)) \wedge Leaving(out(h))$$
$$\wedge\ Inward(in(h),h) \wedge Inward(out(h),h)$$
$$\wedge\ height(in(h)) > height(out(h))$$
$$\wedge\ direction(h) = \langle in(h),out(h)\rangle \tag{65}$$

in and *out* are the (directed) ends of the movement. We can regard these as Skolem functions: it is handy to have names for these arrivings and leavings. So handy, in fact, that I will use them for spreadings, fillings and emptyings also.

There is not much more to be said about these moving histories, as their only episodes are themselves. It is useful to characterise the shape of fallings.

$$Falling(h) \supset Vertical(direction(h))$$
$$\wedge\ where(in(h)) = d(top(h),where(h))$$
$$\wedge\ where(out(h)) = d(bottom(h),where(h)) \tag{66}$$

We can emphasize their simplicity by:

$$Movement(h) \supset h = endure(where(h),when(h)) \tag{67}$$

Notice this entails that the *rate* of a movement history is constant throughout.

Finally, we need to say that these arrivings and leavings are all there are.

$$Arriving(ar) \supset \exists h. \ (Spreading(h) \wedge Inward(ar,h)) \tag{68}$$
$$\vee \ (Filling(h) \wedge Inward(ar,h))$$
$$\vee \ (Moving(h) \wedge ar=in(h))$$

$$Leaving(le) \supset \exists le'. \ Leaving(le') \wedge Splat(le,le') \tag{69}$$
$$\vee$$
$$\exists h.(Emptying(h) \wedge Inward(le,h))$$
$$\vee \ (Moving(h) \wedge le=out(h))$$
$$\vee \ (Spreading(h) \wedge Inward(le,h))$$

One could go on, introducing a notion of rate of change of quantity, to relate rate of flow (our *rate*) and rate of change, but I will ignore this. However, we do need to relate amounts to the sizes of the wet parts of a containment or wetting.

$$Increasing(amount,h) \equiv \tag{70}$$
$$\forall t,t' \in when(h). \ t<t' \supset In(wet(h@t),wet(h@t'))$$

$$Decreasing(amount,h) \equiv \tag{71}$$
$$\forall t,t' \in when(h). \ t<t' \supset In(wet(h@t'),wet(h@t))$$

We could, in fact, regard *wet* as a quantity scale, the measure space being the set of pieces of three-dimensional space. The appropriate inequality is of course just *In,* so that axioms (70) and (71) could be written simply as

$$Increasing(amount,h) \equiv Increasing(wet,h) \tag{72}$$

$$Decreasing(amount,h) \equiv Decreasing(wet,h)$$

We have also

$$amount(s)=capacity(s) \equiv et(s)=s \tag{74}$$

which is, in fact, the crux of the matter, as we will see.

9 Some Examples

The theory so far, together with a little extra geometry and analysis (which we will not attempt to formalize) enables one, given a description of a physical setup involving liquids, to infer quite detailed knowledge about the future, past or surroundings of the set-up. In this section we will consider a few examples.

Suppose an open container with no leaks is empty, but at time *t* a falling history begins whose *bottom* is the free top of the container: for example, you turn on the bath tap with the plug in. By axiom (46), this leaving has an arriving on its other side, which is an inward-directed face of the inside of the bath. By axiom (59), there must be a filling inside the bath, so the *amount* of water increases: axiom (61). So long as the tap keeps running, it will go on increasing. Let us suppose that eventually the bath is full, i.e. it contains its capacity. Then, by (74), its *wet* is its inside. But the top of it is a face of its inside, with a free edge: and so by axiom (57) the amount of water in it cannot exceed its capacity, but by axiom (61) it must either increase or there must be a leaving somewhere. (Notice that if the container were closed—a tank being filled along a pipe, say—then the same line of reasoning would insist on there being a leaving which could not possibly occur, by axioms (47) and (16). One can conclude from this contradiction, by *modus tollens,* that the arriving must cease to exist at that time, and hence that the flowing-2 along the supply pipe, etc. (working backwards) must cease also. And this is, of course, exactly what happens, assuming the tank doesn't burst.)

So, the bath will overflow. We can describe this in more detail. *Toso* of the leaving is an arriving. Now there are two cases, depending on whether the bath is a lamina or a more solid affair. If a lamina, this *toso* is in free space, so we have an arriving in free space, which can only (by axioms (68) and (50) and assuming that free space doesn't support anything), be the top of a falling. If the rim of the bath is a corner, however, then *toso* of the leaving is a directed edge along the outside surface of the bath (see axiom (19)): again, by axioms (68) and (50), this can only be the arriving of a flowing-1, or a spreading. Either is possible: the latter if the bath is sunk into a flat floor onto which the water spreads; the former if the outside slopes downwards.

We could follow the water even further, but let us consider another example. There is a horizontal floor which is dry (amount = none) at time *t,* but at some later time is wet. What happened in between? Well, there must be a wetness history *h* surrounding the later moment, by axiom (52). Now, by (51), this wetness's start must be later than *t,* and *h* must have started dry. Its first episode could only have been a spreading, therefore (this requires the "analysis" mentioned earlier: specifically, if $t_1 < t_2$, $f(t_1) = 0$ and $f(t_2) > 0$, then f is increasing in $\langle t_1, t_2 \rangle$), and therefore must, by (56), have had an arriving at an edge of it, and by (46) there must have been a leaving on the other side of this. Now this leaving is directed along the surface, and can either be part of a *Splat,* or the *out* of a flowing-1, if there is a suitable sloped surface nearby, or of another spreading, or an "edge-type" leaving from an emptying, as described in axiom (64). All of these are possible: a Splat could result from something pouring or flowing-2 onto the floor: a flowing-1 could have been, for example, water running down a vertical side of a box: the spreading could have run off the edge of a laminar sheet on the floor: the emptying could have been a leaky paint tin.

As a final example, consider a cup of milk held above a table, which is a horizontal lamina suspended above the floor. There are no other liquids and no other surfaces. The cup is rotated slowly about a horizontal axis: what will happen? At first, nothing. But after a while (this requires more geometry than we have developed), the *top* of the *wet* in the cup will reach the edge of the rim. At that moment, by axiom (64), a leaving history will start and the containment in the cup will enter a leaving episode. Assuming the cup to be a lamina, *toso* of this leaving will, by axiom (46), be an arriving in free space, which can therefore by axioms (68) and (50) only be the top of a falling. Since a falling is vertical and the cup is above the table, the bottom of this falling is part of the surface of the table, directed upwards. Therefore, by (49), the free edge of this part will be a leaving also (Splat), and by (46) will have an arriving on its other side, into the top of the table. This could only be, by axiom (68) a directed face of a spreading or a flowing-1: but the latter is impossible since the table is horizontal, so there must be a spreading on the table. Although this has taken a while to infer, it takes place instantaneously:the emptying in the cup and the spreading on the table begin at the same instant. As the milk is spreading over the table, the amount of it there is increasing, and the amount in the cup is decreasing. The spreading is therefore expanding across the table, by axiom (72). This configuration may continue until the cup is empty (amount = none), at which time the emptying, and hence the leaving, arriving, falling, leaving, leaving and arriving (working down) must also cease, and the spreading reverts to a mere wetness. Or, the spreading may reach the edge of the table, before the cup runs dry. In this case a leaving comes into existence along the edge, by axiom (63). The spreading may or may not cease to expand (axiom (56)), but in any case there is again an arriving into free space on the other side, and hence, by similar reasoning, a falling onto the floor, a splat, and a spreading there. When the cup runs out now, both spreadings instantly revert to mere wettings, in which state they will remain, unless they become dryings. The whole sequence is illustrated in Figure 6.

Notice incidentally that since, when the cup was full of milk, its inside surface was wet, this state of wetness must have been a slice of a wetness history, by (52): and this wetness history may continue, even though the containment which gave rise to it has vanished. So the inside of the cup will also be wet, in the final state, unless it has dried. (If we had quantitative concepts we could say that dryings were always slow, which would ensure that the inside were wet.) Notice also that if the table had been a solid cube instead of a lamina, we could have inferred that the milk, on reaching its top edge, would have flowed-1 down its side before spreading across the floor, not fallen.

The finite taxonomies play a crucial role in this sort of reasoning. Given that an arriving exists in some geometric configuration, for example, axiom (50) will usually enable one to infer what sort of history it has to be a face of, because the configuration will typically be consistent with only one of the possibilities listed here. One reasons by a combination of two inferential processes: establishing the existence of a history (typically an arriving or leaving) because some other one exists; and deciding that a certain history must be of some sort because its properties are incompatible with all the other possibilities, and it must be *one* of them. (The reader may be reminded of the Waltz filtering algorithm here, or of Sherlock Holmes, or of relaxation, or a winner-take-all network.) I believe this taxonomic approach to common-sense reasoning is of fundamental importance.

I do not want to leave the impression that there are no problems. Rain flowing off

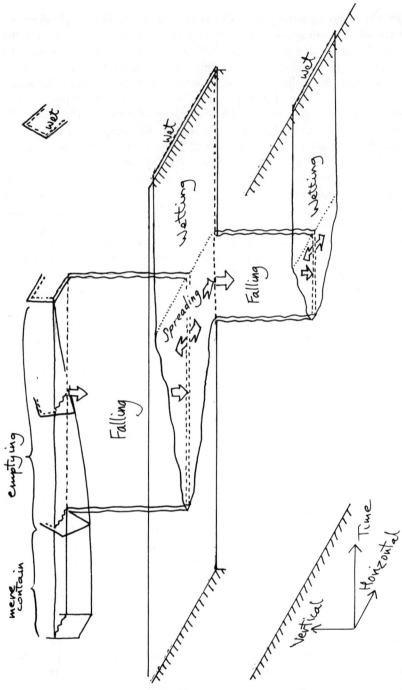

Figure 6. Pouring a cup of milk onto a table

a roof into a gutter, and a tin with many small leaks, are just two examples which I can see no way to handle reasonably.

10 Liquid Individuals Revisited

We have managed to avoid pieces of liquid, throughout this quite extensive development, by always talking of pieces of space or space-time which *contain* some liquid. One could go further and avoid talking of solid objects, indeed, by using a similar idea of pieces of space filled with solid stuff, but that would be artificial. (However, the idea of *the space occupied by* an object seems to be of general utility.) Unfortunately, we have had to swallow some similar artificialities with liquids, at least in the case of liquids in bulk. It seems somewhat peculiar, for example, to have a *space* supporting, or being supported by, a solid object (as in flotation and containment). And it seems odd to be unable to say, when one glass of water is poured into another, that it is the *same* water in the second glass that was in the first glass. Some of this artificiality can be avoided by carefully allowing fluid objects back into our ontology. The preceding development will not have been wasted, however, since liquid histories can plausibly be the criteria by which we individuate liquid objects, thus neatly avoiding the ontological nightmare discussed in section 3.

The idea, then, is that any history (of a certain kind) actually contains a (single) liquid object, which fills the history and lasts as long as it does. Contrariwise, every liquid object fills some history. For example, Lake Leman is now an object, made of water, with a flat top: and it is this object which supports the boat and is supported by the lake bed. It is a single individual object even though of different molecules from one week to the next: it is individuated by its history, its spatiotemporal 'position'. Similarly, a glassful of water is the same object while the glass is being filled, although its size is increasing: and it ceases to exist when the water is emptied out into another glass. A bath being filled and emptied contains a single, unique liquid object—*the* bathwater. A river is an object, similarly, as is Niagara Falls, or the puddle of milk on the floor.

Looked at in this way, then, all the preceding discussion has really been about liquid objects, how they relate to one another and to solid objects in space, and how they can be created and destroyed. We have overcome the ontological nightmare by analyzing in some detail how to keep track of liquid objects.

This idea of liquid objects coexisting with histories still does not allow us to say that the water in this glass used to be in that glass, or that this water came out of the tap. For liquid objects are not identified by being the same piece of liquid (like pieces of solid stuff), but by spatiotemporal continuity (like assemblies: in fact we can explain liquids as limiting cases of powders, which can actually be regarded as unorganized assemblies). In order to express these assertions we need a different sort of liquid individual: *a piece of liquid*. This is meant to be a particular collection of molecules, a piece of stuff.

A given liquid object may or may not be a piece of liquid, and a piece of liquid may or may not be a liquid object. For example, a river is not a piece of liquid, but some water in a glass is. While we are pouring water from one glass into another, there is one piece of liquid present, the same one that there was when it was contained in the first glass, but there are three liquid objects: one, shrinking, in the top glass, and another, growing, in the bottom glass; and a falling. None of these four individuals is the same as another.

We can summarize the criteria for individuating pieces of liquid by considering spatial boundaries. Any history consisting of a piece of space and a time interval such that no liquid crosses the boundary of the space during the interval, defines a piece of liquid, viz. all the liquid in the space during that interval. Notice that we do not require that the "piece" be spatially connected. It is convenient also to have a notion of one piece of liquid (or of stuff in general) being *part* of another.

Consider a glass of water and a glass of ink being mixed in a third glass to get colored water. There are three containment histories here, defining three liquid objects. But we can also say that *the* water and ink from the first two glasses were pieces of liquid which are now part of the piece of liquid which coincides with the final liquid object: for, consider a volume enclosing all three glasses but no other liquid, and consider the piece of liquid it contained: the water and the ink were parts of this piece, and it is the same piece at the end of the history (in which all three containments, and the intervening pourings, traversals, etc., are enclosed) as it was at the beginning, so they are still part of it.

We can use the notions of arrivings and leavings, introduced earlier, to specify this no-boundary-crossing criterion. Let us say that a history is *closed* if no face of it is an arriving or leaving. Then a closed history containing liquid defines a piece of liquid.

Pieces of liquid, unlike liquid objects, are eternal. Consider pouring a glass of water into a lake. The liquid object which was in the glass ceases to exist: but the piece of water is now part of the lake. (To see this, imagine a surface enclosing a glass and the lake, and consider *the* piece of water inside this surface during the pouring.) *It* still exists, although one would be very hard put to separate it out again. Such "separability" is irrelevant to the identity of a piece of liquid.

This ontology of pieces of liquid is very much more sophisticated than the earlier one of liquid objects. To handle it well requires one to reason in terms of *imaginary* surfaces in space, for a start. Conservation of amount is a trivial consequence of this ontology. (For example, if I pour water from one glass into another, it is the *same* piece of water, so of course it must be the same amount, if—as we should—we make *amount* a function of pieces of liquid rather than liquid objects.) We know from the work of Piaget that conservation arises quite late in childrens' development. This may, I suggest, be due to the preconservation child not having access to this more sophisticated ontology for mass terms. Conservation is far less obvious for liquid objects: indeed, I cannot see any very plausible way of expressing it without some very involved assumptions about rates of flow.

We must now be careful in using equality. Consider (again) a cup full of water.

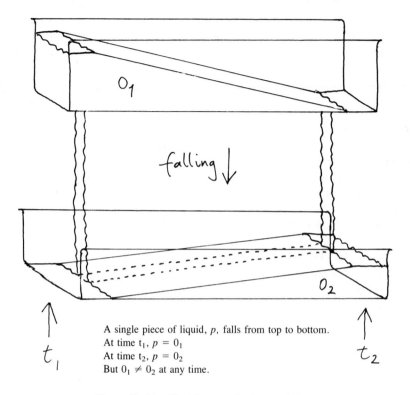

A single piece of liquid, p, falls from top to bottom.
At time t_1, $p = 0_1$
At time t_2, $p = 0_2$
But $0_1 \neq 0_2$ at any time.

Figure 7. Liquid objects and pieces of liquid

This is a liquid object (filling a containment), and it is also a piece of liquid. We might say that $o = p$, where o denotes the liquid object and p the piece of liquid: for these are both the same object. However, this equality may change in the course of time. If part of the water is poured out of the cup into another, then we have the *same* liquid object in the first cup, but a different piece of water (part of the original piece), say p'. If now the rest of the water is poured into the second cup, this contains a *new* liquid object, o' say, which is the same thing as the *original* piece of water p (see Figure 7).

Liquid objects endure through time, as do pieces of liquid. It always makes sense to equate two liquid-object expressions, or two piece-of-liquid expressions, independently of time. But since the criteria for individuating such objects are different, it makes sense to equate a liquid-object expression and a piece-of-liquid expression only during a time-period when these criteria agree. Such an equality *must* be understood as temporary, as liable to change in truth-value.

This phenomenon is more complicated than the case of an object ceasing to have a certain time-dependent property, as when a person ceases to be mayor. Unlike this familiar case (which can be adequately handled by the state- or situation-variable idea), we have here a strange symmetry. The equation $o = p$ can be equally validly taken as asserting *both* that $\lambda x \cdot x = p$ is true of the enduring object o, but in a time-dependent way (i.e. is a fluent), *and* that $\lambda x \cdot o = x$ is true of the enduring object p, but similarly. After the equation becomes false, both o and p still exist, but they have separated.

This phenomenon is not, in fact, special to liquids. It occurs wherever different, rival criteria of individuation are simultaneously in use. My car, for example, is at any instant the same as a particular collection of components: but this identity is time-dependent. A description such as ''the regulator that used to be in my car before I had it replaced'' uses both ways of individuating ''car'', as an enduring assembly and a contingent collection of parts.

It may strike the reader, as it did me at first, that this all seems extremely unnatural. After all, the water in a glass is what it is: how can it be two different things at the same time? Surely, one feels, this baroque way of speaking must be an artifact: in the actual real world, things just *are*. But I now believe that such naive ontological realism is unfounded. In the *actual* real world, there are no *a priori* individuals at all. The universe can be conceptualized as a continuum, perhaps a huge quantum-mechanical wave function. Divisions of it into conceptual individuals are made by us, by our language, not by nature. And then of course, there is no reason at all why we may not carve up the universe's space–time fabric into overlapping pieces, if it is convenient to do so.

11 Further Works

The theory of liquids developed in sections 4 to 9, although I think quite useful, is by no means fully satisfactory and represents only an initial foray. I believe the geometric ideas, especially the concept of *Face* and of d (direction), and the basic approach of using histories to describe change, are likely to survive subsequent developments. The rest is less secure, however, and there are many problems. These will be made clearer only by attempting to extend the theory to a wider range of concepts. Some obvious directions are:

1. The introduction of metric ideas into the geometry, and the development of a suitable topology
2. An account of shape and a theory of the deformability of liquid objects
3. The introduction of non-lazy histories such as fountains and splashes (including an account of pressure, force and impact: for example, a *Splat* is usually an impact on the non-free face, hence the name)
4. A theory of liquid flow based on the idea of a path or trajectory *along which* liquid can flow: this would be based on homotopic ideas, as the account here is based on homological ideas
5. An account of rates and rates of change (which should be linked with metric ideas, so that liquid will flow only *slowly* through a small hole or across a surface)
6. A more detailed account of the interrelations between solid and liquid surfaces: for example, how flotation and lubrication work

I hope to investigate some of these in subsequent work, as well as other areas of naive physics altogether. Finally, I am grateful to Ray Turner for pointing out that to establish the consistency of a large axiom system may not be an altogether trivial task.

Acknowledgments

This paper, with minor changes, originally appeared as Memo 35 of the Institut pour les Etudes Semantiques et Cognitives, Universite de Geneve. It was written while the author was visiting the Institut in 1978.

The early development of some of these ideas was supported by the U.K. Science Research Council on grant number B/RG/61198. I would also like to thank the Dalle Molle foundation and the University of Geneva for financial support, and the Directrice of the Institut, Mme M. King, for inviting me to visit. Maggie King, Mimi Sinclair, Henri Wermus and Giuseppe Trautteur gave me many useful ideas and criticisms. Bob Welham and Jerry Hobbs made many useful criticisms and suggestions. Finally, I would like to thank my wife, Jackie Hayes, for her support, for being a never failing source of reliable intuitions, for much constructive criticism, and for not complaining at retyping the manuscript four times because of my mistakes.

References

Cohn, T. (1983) Improving the Expressiveness of Many-Sorted Logic. *Proc. AAAI*, Washington, D.C.

Goodman, N. (1966). *The structure of appearance*. New York: Bobbs Merrill.

Hayes, P. (1971). A logic of actions. *Machine intelligence 6*. Edinburgh: Edinburgh University Press.

Hocking, J., & Young, G. (1961). *Topology*. Boston: Addison-Wesley.

McCarthy, J. (1959). Situations, actions & causal laws. (Memo 2). Stanford University, Stanford A.I. Project.

McCarthy, J. & Hayes, P. (1969). Some philosophical problems from the standpoint of artificial intelligence. *Machine Intelligence 4*, Edinburgh: Edinburgh University Press.

Prior, A. N. (1968). *Past, present & future*. Oxford: Clarendon Press.

4 A Qualitative Physics Based on Confluences*

Johan de Kleer
John Seely Brown

Intelligent Systems Laboratory
Xerox Palo Alto Research Center
Palo Alto, California

1 Introduction

Change is a ubiquitous characteristic of the physical world. But what is it? What causes it? How can it be described? Thousands of years of investigation have produced a rich and diverse physics that provides many answers. Important concepts and distinctions underlying change in physical systems are state, cause, law, equilibrium, oscillation, momentum, quasistatic approximation, contact force, feedback, etc. Notice that these terms are qualitative and can be intuitively understood. Admittedly they are commonly quantitatively defined. The behavior of a physical system can be described by the exact values of its variables (forces, velocities, positions, pressures, etc.) at each time instant. Such a description, although complete, fails to provide much insight into how the system functions. The insightful concepts and distinctions are usually qualitative, but they are embedded within the much more complex framework established by continuous real-valued variables and differential equations. Our long-term goal is to develop an alternate physics in which these same concepts are derived from a far simpler, but nevertheless formal, qualitative basis.

The motivations for developing a qualitative physics stem from outstanding problems in psychology, education, artificial intelligence, and physics. We want to identify the core knowledge that underlies physical intuition. Humans appear to use a qualitative causal calculus in reasoning about the behavior of their physical environment. Judging from the kinds of explanations humans give, this calculus is quite different from the classical physics taught in classrooms. This raises questions as to what this (naive) physics is like, and how it helps one to reason about the physical world.

In classical physics, the crucial distinctions for characterizing physical change

---

*A version of this paper has previously appeared in the *Artificial Intelligence Journal,* and appears here by permission of the publisher, North Holland Publishing Company, Amsterdam, The Netherlands.

are defined within a nonmechanistic framework and thus they are difficult to ground in the common sense knowledge derived from interaction with the world. Qualitative physics provides an alternate and simpler way of arriving at the same conceptions and distinctions and thus provides a simpler pedagogical basis for educating students about physical mechanisms.

Artificial intelligence and (especially) its subfield of expert systems are producing very sophisticated computer programs capable of solving tasks that require extensive human expertise. A commonly recognized failing of such systems is their extremely narrow range of expertise and their inability to recognize when a problem posed to them is outside this range of expertise. In other words, they have no common sense. In fact, expert systems usually cannot solve simpler versions of the problems they are designed to solve. The missing common sense can be supplied, in part, by qualitative reasoning.

A qualitative causal physics provides an alternate way of describing physical phenomena. As compared to modern physics, this qualitative physics is only at its formative stages and does not have new explanatory value. However, the qualitative physics does suggest some promises of novelty, particularly in its explicit treatment of causality—something modern physics provides no formalism for treating.

Our proposal is to reduce the quantitative precision of the behavioral descriptions but retain the crucial distinctions. Instead of continuous real-valued variables, each variable is described qualitatively—taking on only a small number of values, usually $+$, $-$, or 0. Our central modeling tool is the qualitative differential equation, called a confluence. For example, the qualitative behavior of a valve is expressed by the confluence[1] $\partial P + \partial A - \partial Q = 0$ where Q is the flow through the valve, P is the pressure across the valve, A is the area available for flow, and ∂Q, ∂A, and ∂P represent changes in Q, A, and P. The confluence represents multiple competing tendencies: the change in area positively influences flow rate and negatively influences pressure, the change in pressure positively influences flow rate, etc. The same variable can appear in many confluences and thus can be influenced in many different ways. In an overall system each confluence must be satisfied individually. Thus if the area is increasing but the flow remains constant, the pressure must decrease no matter what the other influences on the pressure are. A single confluence often cannot characterize the behavior of a component over its entire operating range. In such cases, the range *must* be divided into subregions, each characterized by a different component state in which different confluences apply. For example, the behavior of the valve when it is completely open is quite different from that when it is completely closed. These two concepts, of confluence and of state, form the basis for a qualitative physics, a physics that maintains most of the important distinctions of the usual physics but is far simpler.

In presenting our qualitative physics, we rederive a large number of the concepts of classical physics. As the derivation is often novel, we simplify matters by drawing most of our examples from the same device: the pressure-regulator (see

---

[1]We make no attempt to keep the units consistent.

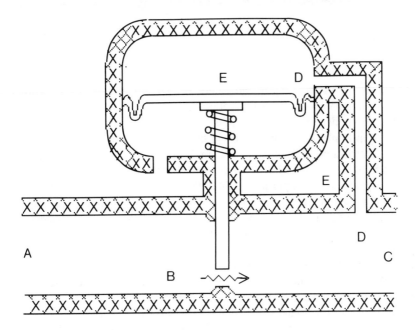

Figure 1. Pressure-regulator

Forbus & Stevens, 1981). The pressure-regulator[2] illustrated in Figure 1 is a device whose purpose is to maintain a constant output pressure (at C) even though the supply (connected to A) and loads (connected to C) vary. An explanation of how it achieves this function might be: *"An increase in source (A) pressure increases the pressure drop across the valve (B). Since the flow through the valve is proportional to the pressure across it, the flow through the valve also increases. This increased flow will increase the pressure at the load (C). However, this increased pressure is sensed (D) causing the diaphragm (E) to move downward against the spring pressure. The diaphragm is mechanically connected to the valve, so the downward movement of the diaphragm will tend to close the valve thereby pinching off the flow. Because the flow is now restricted the output pressure will rise much less than it otherwise would have."*

This explanation characterizes the essential idea underlying the operation of the pressure-regulator that is designed to achieve a kind of homeostasis by sensing its own output and adjusting its operation. Systems that operate on this principle are subject to oscillation due to phase delay in the sensing and destructive feedback when used inappropriately. The foregoing explanation and analyses of feedback action are all derivable from our qualitative physics. No quantitative or analytical

---

[2]More sophisticated considerations than discussed in this paper dictate that most actual pressure-regulators be designed quite differently, but this figure accurately illustrates the central feedback action of regulators.

analysis is required, yet it is possible to identify the essential characteristics of the pressure-regulator's operation.

1.1 Envision

One of the central tenets of our methodology for exploring the ideas and techniques presented in this paper is to construct computer systems based on these ideas and compare their results with our expectations. Except when noted otherwise, everything has been implemented and tested in this way. The program ENVISION has been run successfully on hundreds of examples of various types of devices (electronic, translational, hydraulic, acoustic, etc.). Although we view constructing working programs as an important methodological strategy for doing research, the existence of a working implementation contributes little to the conceptual coherence of the theory. In this paper we focus on presenting the ideas of our conception of naive physics. We therefore leave out extensive examples, computer printouts or the algorithms that produce them.

Although the algorithms ENVISION uses are not the primary focus of this paper, a brief description of its inputs, outputs, and success criteria clarifies the stage for the following conceptual presentations. ENVISION's basic task is to derive function from structure for an arbitrary device. It relies on a single library of generic components and uses the same model library to analyze each device. The input to ENVISION is a description of a particular situation in terms of (a) a set of components and their allowable paths of interaction (i.e., the device's topology), (b) the input signals applied to the device (if any), and (c) a set of boundary conditions which constrain the device's behavior. ENVISION produces a description of the behavior of the system in terms of its allowable states, the values of the system's variables, and the direction these variables are changing. Most importantly, it produces complete causal accounts and logical proofs for that behavior. Both of these analyses provide explanations of how the system behaves with the causal analysis also identifying all possible feedback paths.

The success criteria for ENVISION are also important. Our physics is qualitative and hence sometimes underdetermines the behavior of a system. In these cases, ENVISION produces a set of behaviors (we call these interpretations). At a minimum, for a prediction to be correct, one of the interpretations must correspond to the actual behavior of the real device. A stronger criterion follows from observing that a structural description, abstracted qualitatively (i.e., the device topology), of a particular device implicitly characterizes a wide class of different physically realizable devices with the same device topology. The stronger criterion requires that (a) the behavior of each device in the class is described by one of the interpretations, and (b) every interpretation describes the behavior of some device of the class.

1.2 Organization

The remainder of this paper is divided into five major sections, each addressing a particular aspect of our qualitative physics. Each can be read as a separate unit.

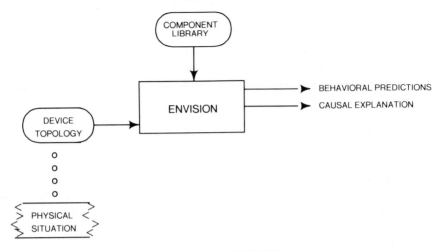

Figure 2. ENVISION

Section 2, "Naive Physics," introduces the subject of naive physics and discusses some of its methodological considerations. We present the major paradigmatic assumptions that underlie the architectures and organizations of the remaining sections. Section 3, "Modeling Structure," presents the techniques by which we can model the generic behavior of individual components of a device. We discuss the basic modeling primitives: the qualitative differential equation (confluence) and the notion of qualitative state. Section 4, "Prediction of Behavior," discusses algorithms to determine the behavior of a composite device from the generic models of its individual components. In this section, we introduce the distinction of behavior within a state from behavior between states. The algorithms determine *what* the behavior is, not an explanation of it. In Section 5, "Explanation of Behavior," we present a form of logical explanation of behavioral predictions—a kind of proof using a natural deduction scheme. The logical explanation turns out to be unsatisfactory as it makes no ontological commitments, just epistemological ones. In Section 6, "Causality and Digital Physics," we present a completely different kind of explanation, one which explains device behavior in terms of *how* the device itself achieves its behavior. This information-processing view of causality may also serve as the basis for an alternate kind of physics.

We present a new unifying framework: the qualitative differential equation. This new research builds on the ideas of qualitative value, component models, and envisioning developed in earlier investigations (de Kleer & Brown, 1981; de Kleer & Brown, 1983). These concepts and our methodology are discussed in more detail in our earlier papers. Some of the important concepts developed in this paper are:

- *Quasistatic approximation.* Most modeling, whether quantitative or qualitative, makes the approximation that behavior at some small time scale is unimportant. In modern thermodynamics, this concept is central to the definition of equilibrium. Until now, qualitative physics has treated this modeling issue in both an ad hoc and tacit manner. In our formulation, quasistatic assumptions play a theoretically motivated and explicit role.

- *Causality.* The behavior of a device is viewed as arising from the interactions of a set of processors, one for each component of the "device." The information-passing interactions of the individual components are the cause-effect interactions between the device's components. Within this framework, causal accounts are defined (as interactions that obey certain metaconstraints) and their limitations explored.

- *Mythical causality and mythical time.* Any set of component models makes some assumptions about device behavior (i.e., quasistatic assumptions) and hence cannot, in principle, yield *causal* accounts for the changes that must occur between equilibrium states of a system. In order to handle this problem we have defined new notions of causality and time (i.e., mythical causality and mythical time) cast in terms of information-passing "negotiations" between processors of neighboring components.

- *Generalized machines.* Many physical situations can be viewed as some kind of generalized machine, whose behavior can be described in terms of variable values. These variables include force, velocity, pressure, flow, current, and voltage.

- *Proof as explanation.* Physical laws, viewed as constraints, are acausal. We discuss how a logical proof of the solution of a set of constraints is a kind of acausal explanation of behavior.

- *Qualitative calculus.* Qualitative physics is based on a qualitative calculus, the qualitative analog to the calculus of Newton and Leibniz. We define qualitative versions of value, continuity, differential, and integral.

- *Episodes.* Episodes are used to quantize time into periods within which the device's behavior is significantly different.

- *Digital physics.* Each component of a physical system can be viewed as a simple information processor. The overall behavior of the device is produced by causal interactions between physically adjacent components. Physical laws can then be viewed as emergent properties of the universal "programs" executed by the processors. A new kind of physical law might thus be expressible as constraints on these programs, processors, or the information-flow among them.

2 Naive Physics

There is a growing amount of research in the area of naive physics, although often under different titles (e.g., qualitative process theory, qualitative physics, common sense knowledge, or mechanistic mental models: Hayes, 1979; Forbus, 1981, 1982; Kuipers, 1982a, 1982b; de Kleer, 1975, 1979a,b; de Kleer & Brown, 1981, 1983). All propose formalizing the common sense knowledge about the everyday physical world, but each views this task rather differently. It is thus important to make clear what the current enterprise is all about. Naive physics is in itself an ambiguous term. Is it just bad physics? Is it psychology? Artificial intelligence? Physics? All these questions deserve to be asked and we take pains to answer them.

Naive physics concerns knowledge about the physical world. It would not be such an important area of investigation if it were not for two crucial facts: (a) people are very good at functioning in the physical world, and (b) no theory of this human capability exists that could serve as a basis for imparting it to computers. Modern science, which one might think should be of help here, does not provide much help. Although the modern mathematics in which most physical laws are expressed is relatively formal, the laws are all based on the presupposition of a shared unstated commonsense prephysics knowledge. Hence, it is not surprising that artificial intelligence has been rather unsuccessful at building systems that require physics problem-solving. The knowledge presented in textbooks is but the tip of the iceberg about what actually needs to be known to reason about the physical world (de Kleer, 1975). Even the physicist will agree that he is not using his formal physics when avoiding an automobile collision or jumping back from his seat after someone has spilled hot coffee on the table. This is hardly an indictment of modern physics— why should it address itself to a subject area that every scientist takes as given? The formalisms of modern physics[3] do not provide much direct help; we need to look elsewhere.

Naive physics, as a theory, bears a resemblance to modern physics in two ways. First, it makes explicit claims about the knowledge necessary for deriving, from relatively meager evidence about the world, the kinds of common sense conclusions that modern physics takes as given. Second, naive physics makes claims about what constitutes information-rich idealizations about the world. For example, in Newtonian physics a crucial idealization is the notion of point mass; in our physics, direction of change is a crucial idealization.

Our naive physics is also an idealization in other senses. It is not intended to be a psychological theory per se—although we use observations of human behavior as hints. We are not concerned with human foibles. Nor do we focus on one domain in particular, nor on one particular set of laws for a domain. Rather, we are concerned with the general *form* of those laws and the calculi for deriving inferences from the laws.

As in the naive physics of Hayes, the actual mechanisms used to derive inferences is of secondary importance, although we do want to characterize properties of the derivational apparatus. Unlike Hayes, we consider accounting for *how* the physical system achieves its behavior a proper task of naive physics; note that he does not view the world as a collection of devices, and thus distinguishing "how" from "what" carries little weight in his framework. Our physics is based on viewing the world as a machine (albeit a very complex one).

---

[3]Although some informal attempts are being made for pedagogical purposes such as "physics for poets" or texts such as *Conceptual Physics* (Hewitt, 1974).

The main goal of our qualitative physics is to provide a theoretical framework for understanding the behavior of physical systems. We are particularly interested in prediction and explanation. It should be possible to predict (an important kind of inference) the future behavior of the physical system. It should also be possible to explain how the device achieves the predicted behavior. This kind of explanation is not based on *how* some algorithm constructs predictions, but rather *how* the device produces the behavior. To answer this latter kind of "how" question requires an ontological commitment to nature as mechanism.

Our qualitative physics is based on a number of fundamental principles or paradigmatic assumptions. We briefly discuss each of these assumptions in turn, but first we need to make explicit the reasons why we chose dynamical systems (i.e., hydraulic, electrical, rotational, etc. systems) as a set of domains to focus our initial inquiry into qualitative physics.

2.1 Our Basic Strategic Move

The essence of doing physics is modeling a physical situation, solving the resulting equations and then interpreting the results in physical terms. Modeling a physical situation requires a description of its physical structure. Although there does not exist a general methodology for describing the structure of all physical situations, system dynamics[4] (Cochin 1980; Shearer, Murphy, & Richardson, 1971; Karnopp & Rosenberg, 1975) fortunately, provides a methodology for describing a large and interesting collection of physical systems. Thus we initially focus our attention on this class of situations and on how behavior arises from structure and do not worry much about the extremely difficult issue of modeling more general physical situations. This move combined with our use of causality as an ontological principle results in a very mechanistic world view. Every physical situation is regarded as some type of physical device or machine made up of individual components, each component contributing to the behavior of the overall device.

2.2 Qualitativeness

The variables used to describe the behavior of the device can only take on a small predetermined number of values, and each value corresponds to some interval on the number line. Using a small number of values instead of a dense set of numbers means some information must be lost. However, our goal is to make a judicious choice for the qualitative intervals such that as little information as possible about the important features of device functioning is lost. Thus the divisions between intervals are best chosen to be at singularities such as at zeros and discontinuities. As such, the formalisms underlying our qualitative calculus relates to the branch of mathematics that characterizes the qualitative behavior of systems of differential equations, i.e., catastrophe theory (Poston & Stewart, 1978).

---

[4]We mean the formalisms used in linear systems theory, not that of Forrester. System dynamics is used to model the behavior of dynamical systems of all types (e.g., mechanical, electrical, fluid and thermal) starting with a description of the system in terms of lumped ideal elements which interact through ideal interconnections.

By taking the qualitative approach, some loss of information cannot be avoided. Sometimes so much information is lost that it is not possible to determine unambiguously the qualitative behavior. Although the consequences of ambiguity are important, the definitions and concepts we define are not significantly affected by the presence of ambiguity. Therefore, in the main flow of this paper we usually assume no ambiguity. In the appendices we discuss the subtle consequences of ambiguity that are important, but tangential, to the main arguments in this paper.[5]

2.3 Structure to Function
We want to be able to infer the behavior of a physical device from a description of its physical structure. The device consists of physically disjoint parts connected together. The structure of a device is described in terms of its components and interconnections. Each component has a type, whose generic model (i.e., laws governing its behavior) is available in the model library. The task is to determine the behavior of a device given its structure and access to the generic model in the model library.

2.4 No-Function-in-Structure
The goal is to draw inferences about the behavior of the composite device solely from laws governing the behaviors of its parts. This view raises a difficult question: where do the laws and the descriptions of the device being studied come from? Unless we place some conditions on the laws and the descriptions, the inferences that can be made may be (implicitly) preencoded in the structural description or the model library.

The *no-function-in-structure* principle is central: the laws of the parts of the device may not presume the functioning of the whole. Take as a simple example a light switch. The model of a switch that states, "if the switch is off, no current flows; and if the switch is on, current flows," violates the no-function-in-structure principle. Although this model correctly describes the behavior of the switches in our offices, it is false as there are many closed switches through which current does not necessarily flow (such as, two switches in series). Current flows in the switch only if it is closed and there is a potential for current flow. One of the reasons why it is surprisingly difficult to create a "context-free" description of a component is that whenever one thinks of how a component behaves, one must, almost by definition, think of it in some type of supporting context. Thus the properties of how the component functions in that particular supporting context are apt to influence subtly how one models it.

2.5 Classwide Assumptions
Those assumptions that are idiosyncratic to a particular device must be distinguished from those that are generic to the entire class of devices. For example, the

[5]Our earlier work (de Kleer & Brown, 1983) focused almost exclusively on the problem of ambiguities and how representing ambiguities (i.e., multiple interpretations) can be useful in producing robust troubleshooting systems that handle faults that fundamentally alter the underlying mechanism of the device.

explanation of the pressure-regulator's behavior ignored turbulence at the valve seat. Brownian motion of the fluid molecules, and the compressibility of the fluid; these are however all reasonable assumptions to make for a wide class of hydraulic devices. We call such assumptions *classwide* assumptions, and they form a kind of universal resolution for the "microscope" being used to study the physical device.

Given this definition for classwide assumptions, the no-function-in-structure principle can be stated more clearly: the laws for the components of a device of a particular class may not make any other assumptions about the behavior of the particular device that are not made about the class in general. An example of an undesirable nonclasswide assumption would be if the law for the valve stated that the area available for flow decreases as pressure goes up. This law is valid for the valve in the pressure-regulator, not for valves in general.

Although as originally phrased, no-function-in-structure is unachievable, its essential idea is preserved through the use of classwide assumptions. A presupposition behind no-function-in-structure is that it is possible to describe the laws and the parts of a particular device without making any assumptions about the behavior of interest. There is no neutral, objective, assumption-free way of determining the structure of the device and the laws of its components. The no-function-in-structure demands an infinite regress: a complete set of engineering drawings, a geometrical description, and the positions of each of its molecules all make some unwarranted assumptions for some behavior that is potentially of interest. Thus we admit that assumptions in general cannot be avoided in the identification of the parts and their laws, which is why classwide assumptions are crucial.

Classwide assumptions play two important roles in our qualitative physics. First, they play a definitional role. Formalizing the idealization (i.e., qualitative physics) demands that we be explicit about which assumptions we are making. Second, and as important but not discussed in this paper, they are important for building expert systems. In constructing an expert system to design, operate, or troubleshoot complex devices, it is critical to clearly state what assumptions are being used in modeling the given device. Thus, when the unexpected situation or casualty occurs, these assumptions can be examined to determine whether the "knowledge base" can be relied on.

The most common kind of classwide assumption is that behavior of short enough duration can be ignored. Under this assumption the "settling" behavior by which the device reaches equilibrium after a disturbance need not be modeled. As "short enough" is a relative term, this assumption can be made at many levels. This assumption plays a major role in studying the heating and cooling of gases. In classical physics, it is called the quasistatic approximation. For example, the lumped circuit formulation of electronics makes the quasistatic assumption that the dimensions of the physical circuit are small compared to the wavelength associated with the highest frequency of interest. Other examples of classwide assumptions are that the mean free path of the fluid particles is small compared to the distances over which the pressure changes appreciably and that the rate of change of the fields is not too large.

A particular set of classwide assumptions will suggest a procedure for determining the structural decomposition of a given situation into its constituent parts. The most common and well-known procedure is the derivation of a schematic for an electrical circuit. The procedure is well-known, and usually tacit; all electrical engineers will agree whether a particular schematic is an accurate description of the circuit. In fact, the schematic is now considered a description of the structure of the electrical device. The situation is analogous in other domains such as acoustics, fluids, etc., but not as clean as it is for electronics.

Providing a coherent theory of classwide assumptions would involve another paper in itself. For the purpose of this paper, it is sufficient to recognize they exist and to provide some examples. By and large we employ the same classwide assumptions that are used in introductory system-dynamics and classical mechanics texts. Some typical classwide assumptions have already been mentioned. Some others are: all masses are rigid and do not deform or break; all flows are laminar; there are always enough particles in a pipe so that macroscopic laws hold; currents are low enough not to destroy components; and magnetic fields are small enough not to induce significant currents in physically adjacent wires. Under these kinds of classwide assumptions, wires, pipes, cables, linkages can be modeled as ideal connections. Note that our formalisms do not presume those classwide assumptions. It is possible to model a string as a part that breaks at a certain tension or a wire as melting away at a certain current. It is just that commonly one chooses not to model strings and wires this way.

Classwide assumptions determine the kinds of interactions that can occur between parts. Under the usual classwide assumptions of electronics, the only way two capacitors can interact is through wires. However, if the electric fields are strong enough each capacitor will affect the distribution of charges in the other. Thus neighboring, physically distinct parts can become coupled thereby changing the connectivity of the parts and the types of interactions that can occur between them.[6]

A sophisticated reasoning strategy, not discussed in this paper, concerns when and how to change the classwide assumptions when reasoning about a particular device. Such concerns are critical for troubleshooting where faults can force devices into fundamentally new modes of operation (Brown, Burton, & de Kleer, 1982; Davis, Shrobe, Hamscher, Wickert, Shirley, & Polit, 1982). However, even a simple analysis can sometimes require departures from the usual set of classwide assumptions. For example, it is sometimes important to remove a classwide assumption for some localized part of the device, such as two wires running close together, which should be modeled as a transmission line. A fluids example of this phenomena is discussed in the next section.

---

[6]A single device can be modeled using various sets of classwide assumptions. Each such set leads to a different collection of device parts and different models for these parts (including their interconnections). Therefore, violation of no-function-in-structure can occur in the models for a part type or in the identification of the parts of a device. These two kinds of violations are arguably indistinguishable.

2.6 Locality

The principle of *locality* demands that the laws for a part cannot specifically refer to any other part. A part can only act on or be acted on by its immediate neighbors and its immediate neighbors must be identifiable a priori in the structure. To an extent, locality follows from no-function-in-structure. If a law for part of type A referred to a specific neighboring part of type B, it would be making a presupposition that every device which contained a part of type A also contained a part of type B. The locality principle also plays a crucial role in our definition of causality. Our theory does not apply to distributed parameter systems, where the locus of causal interactions cannot be determined a priori.

2.7 The Importance of the Principles

Violating the no-function-in-structure principle has no direct consequences on the representation and inference schemes presented later in the paper. Although the form of the structure and the laws are chosen to minimize blatant violations of the no-function-in-structure principle, it is possible to represent and draw inferences from arbitrary laws—in fact, it is too easy.

Without this principle, our proposed naive physics would be nothing but a proposal for an architecture for building handcrafted (and thus ad-hoc) theories for specific devices and situations. It would provide no systematic way of ensuring that a particular class of laws did or did not already have built into them the answers to the questions that the laws were intended to answer. That is not to say that the handcrafted theories are uninteresting—quite the reverse, and the architecture pro-

Table 1.   ICONS

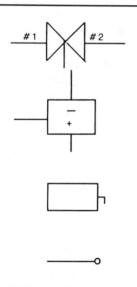

A valve, viewed in isolation, has no distinguished inputs or outputs so the two fluid terminals are labeled #1 and #2. The bottom terminal controls how much area is available for flow within the valve.
A pressure sensor takes as input the pressure from the conduit attached to terminal + to the conduit attached to terminal −, and produces an output signal proportional to it. In the pressure-regulator, increased pressure results in less area available for flow, so the − terminal is attached to the regulator's output and + terminal to the fluid reference.
By convention, most pressurelike variables have a common reference. For electrical systems it is ground, for mechanical system it is the fixed reference frame, and for fluid systems it is the main-sump. This is the icon for the main-sump. Note that, the strictly speaking a reference is a conduit, not a component.
Terminals indicate those terminals which are connected to the external world about which no information is provided in the device topology.

posed in this paper may well be appropriate for this task. This is especially true for constructing an account of the knowledge of any one individual about the given physical situation. We are doing something quite different; we want to develop a physics—not a psychological account—which is capable of supporting inferences about the world.

Another purpose for the principles is to draw a distinction between the "work" our proposed naive physics does and the "work" that must be done (outside of our naive physics) to identify the parts and laws. Only after making such a distinction is evaluation possible. Without making the distinction, a reader could always ask, in response to some complexity in an example, "Why didn't they model it differently?"; or in response to some clever inference in an example, "They built this into their models." As the principles define what can and what cannot be assumed within the models, the criticisms implied by these two questions are invalid. Of course, the principles themselves are open to challenge.

3 Modeling Structure

3.1 Device Structure

Our approach is reductionist: the behavior of a physical structure can be completely accounted for by the behaviors of its physical constituents. We distinguish three kinds of constituents: materials, components and conduits. Physical behavior is accomplished by operating on and transporting materials such as water, air, electrons, etc. The components are constituents that can change the form and characteristics of material. Conduits are simple constituents which transport material from one component to another and cannot change any aspect of the material within them. Some examples of conduits are pipes, wires and cables.

The physical structure of a device can be represented by a topology in which modes represent components and edges represent conduits. Figure 3 illustrates the device topology of the pressure-regulator diagrammed in Figure 1. In this device topology, the conduits IN and OUT transport material of type fluid and conduit FP transports material of type force. In order to avoid ambiguity, the following is a description of the topology of Figure 3 in a textual rather than graphical form. It is important to note that there is no information in the names of any of the components and conduits, these have been chosen (as well as the geometry of Figure 3) solely for the reader's benefit. Each component is described by *name:type[conduits]*, where *name* is solely used to refer to the component, *type* is the generic type of the component, and *conduits* are the names of the conduits to which the terminals of the component are connected. Whenever there might be an ambiguity the conduits are prefixed by *terminal:* indicating the particular component terminal the conduit is attached to.

T1:terminal[IN]

T2:terminal[OUT]

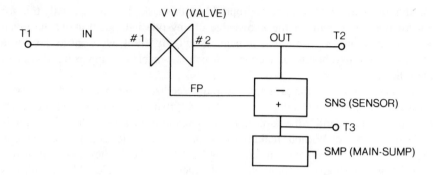

Figure 3: Device topology of the pressure-regulator

T3:terminal[SMP]

SNS:sensor[+ : SMP, − : OUT, FP]

VV:quantity-valve(#1 : IN, #2 : OUT, FP]

Behavior is described in terms of the attributes of the material. Most behavior can be described by dual attributes, one pressurelike and the other flowlike. For a fluid, the attributes are pressure and volumetric flow; for electricity, voltage and current; for translational conduits, velocity and force; for rotational conduits, angular velocity and torque.

By definition, conduits only transport, but do not process, material. Furthermore, we make the simplification that a conduit only transports one type of material. A conduit has a very simple structure: a collection of attachments to components with each attachment taking place at a terminal. For example, a flowlike attribute is associated with every such terminal, and a pressurelike attribute is associated with the entire conduit.

Conduits are poor for modeling distributed parameter systems (e.g., heat flow in a slab) or fields (e.g., gravitational field of the sun). In limited cases, where the paths of causal interaction can be determined *a priori,* a conduit can be used to model the effects of a field.

Unlike conduits, components process and transform material. The behavior of a component can either be modeled by a set of formal laws or by an interconnected set of lower-level components. In this latter case, the lawful behavior of the component emerges from the behavior of the lower-level device. Conduits can also be viewed as more detailed devices, but it is rarely profitable to do so.

3.2 Qualitative Variables
An attribute represents a set of variable entities (e.g., a variable and its integrals and derivatives with respect to time), each of which can be referenced in a law. Unlike quantitative variables, qualitative variables can only take on one of a small number

of values. This set of possible values is determined by the quantity space (Forbus, 1982) it participates in. "$[. . .]_Q$" is used to indicate the qualitative value of the expression within the brackets with respect to quantity space Q. Each qualitative value corresponds to some interval on the real number line. These regions are completely determined by the laws and typically are disjoint.

The most important property of a quantity is whether it is increasing, decreasing or unchanging (or, equivalently, its derivative is positive, negative or zero). This simple, but most important, quantity space consists of only three values: $+$, $-$ and 0. $+$ represents the case when the quantity is positive, 0 represents the case when the quantity is zero, an $-$ represents the case when the quantity is negative. This quantity space is notated: "$[. . .]_o$." More generally, the simple quantity space of x $< a$, $x = a$, and $x > a$ is notated by "$[. . .]_a$." Thus, $[x]_0 = +$ iff $x > 0$, $[x]_0 = 0$ iff $x = 0$, and $[x]_0 = -$ iff $x < 0$.

Addition and multiplication are defined straight-forwardly (as $[. . .]_0$ is so common it is abbreviated $[. . .]$):

Table 2. $[X] + [Y]$

	$[X]$: $-$	0	$+$
$[Y]$:			
$-$	$-$	$-$	
0	$-$	0	$+$
$+$		$+$	$+$

Note that although $[xy] = [x][y]$, $[x + y] \neq [x] + [y]$.

This $+$, 0, $-$ value set is surprisingly versatile. For example, if we need to distinguish x with respect to landmark value a we define a new variable $y = x - a$. Then, $[y] = +$ corresponds to $x > z$, $[y] = 0$ corresponds to $x = a$, and $[y] = -$ corresponds to $x < a$.

"x is increasing" in the formalism is $[dx/dt] = +$. This notation tends to be cumbersome both for typography and computer input-output. Thus, ∂x is used as an abbreviation for $[dx/dt]$, and more generally $\partial^n x$ for $[d^n x/dt^n]$. Note that unlike in quantitative calculus, $\partial^{n + 1}x$ cannot be obtained by differentiating $\partial^n x$. One always has to go back to the quantitative definition: $\partial^{n + 1}x = [d^{n + 1}x/dt^{n + 1}]$. This fact has dramatic impact on the form of the component models.

It is important to note that ∂x and $[x]$ are only instantaneously independent. As time passes, $[x]$'s changes are governed by ∂x (i.e., integration). The laws must be time-invariant. Thus every law applies to a time-instant, and no law may depend on the value of the time variable. (Laws describing behavior over time require explicit integrals in their formulation.) The topic of time is described in more detail in its own section as it plays a central role in our qualitative physics.

The simplicity of this algebra is deceptive and the algebra of Tables 2 and 3 is often misunderstood. The change of a quantity is often confused with the change in the magnitude value of a quantity (i.e., whether it is moving towards or away from

Table 3. $[X] \times [Y]$

	[X]:	−	0	+
[Y]:				
		−	+	0	−
		0	0	0	0
		+	−	0	+

zero). For example, if x changes in value from -6 to -7 its value is decreasing, even though its magnitude is increasing from 6 to 7. Thus, the statements "x is increasing" and "$-x$ is decreasing" are equivalent: $[x] = -[-x]$. $[d^2x/dt^2] = [x]\partial x = +$ if x is moving away from zero, and $[x]\partial x = -$ if x is moving towards zero.

3.3 Qualitative Calculus

Some component laws must be described in terms of derivatives. In our physics, a simple theory of qualitative integration is constructed from the qualitative versions of continuity, Rolle's theorem, and the mean value theorem of the standard differential calculus.

Time, always the independent variable, is also quantized, but in a very different way than the qualitative values. In particular, the distinctions for values of time are not determined a priori but become determined as a consequence of analyzing the confluences. The actual value of the time variable is irrelevant, the only important property is the (partial) ordering of time values. Thus many of the theorems in the standard calculus, when applied to functions of time, are the axioms of time for ours.

- *Qualitative values.* Generally, the qualitative values a variable can have are $A_0 \ldots A_z$, representing disjoint abutting intervals that cover the entire number line (the $A_0 = -$, $A_1 = 0$, $A_2 = +$ value set is an instance of this definition). The ends of the intervals can either be open or closed and the difference between being open and being closed is crucial. The left end of A_0 must be $-\infty$. If the right end of A_k is open, the left end of A_{k+1} must be closed. If the right end of A_k is closed, the left end of A_{k+1} must be open. The right end of A_z must be ∞.
- *Continuity.* As a function of time, every variable changes continuously: If $[X(T_1)]_Q = A_k$ and $[X(T_2)]_Q = A_m$, then for every A_n between A_k and A_m there exists some time $T_1 < T < T_2$ such that $[X(T)]_Q = A_n$. Put intuitively, no variable may jump over a qualitative value.
- *Mean value theorem.* Qualitative versions of Rolle's theorem and the mean value theorem also hold. If $[X(T_1)] = [X(T_2)]$ where $T_1 < T_2$ then $\partial X(T_i) = 0$ for some $T_1 \leq T_i \leq T_2$. If $T_1 < T_2$ then there exists a T_i such that $\partial X(T_i) = [X(T_2)] - [X(T_1)]$. However, as time is quantized, these well-known theorems can be stated far more strongly. In particular, as time is not dense, it makes sense to speak of two successive times. Call T' the time immediately after T.

If $[X(T)] = [X(T')] = C$ where C is the qualitative value representing a point on the number line, then $\partial X(T) = 0$.

These theorems form the basis for reasoning about time in our qualitative physics. Consider some examples using the $+$, $-$, 0 value set. $[X(T)] = +$ followed by $[X(T')] = -$ violates continuity. In most contexts[7] the mean value theorem can be restated as $[X(T')] = [X(T)] + \partial X(T)$. Thus if $[X(T)] = 0$ and $\partial X(T) = +$, then $[X(T')] = +$. If $[X(T)] = +$ and $\partial X(T) = +$ or $\partial X(T) = 0$, then $[X(T')] = +$. On the other hand, if $[X(T)] = +$ and $\partial X(T) = -$, $[X(T')]$ either remains $+$ or becomes 0. We discuss these issues in far greater detail in a later section.

3.4 Models

The component model characterizes all the potential behaviors that the component can manifest. The lawful behavior of a component is expressed as a set of confluence equations. Each model confluence consists of a set of terms which must sum to a constant: $\Sigma T_i = C$. A term can be a variable (i.e., an attribute), the negation of a variable, or the product of a "constant" and a variable. Consider the form of the confluence $\partial P + \partial A - \partial Q = 0$. This confluence consists of three terms, ∂P, ∂A, and $-\partial Q$, which sum (we presume a $+$, 0, $-$ value set) to zero. For naturalness sake, we sometimes write the confluence $[x] - [y] = 0$ as $[x] = [y]$.

A set of values satisfies a confluence if either (a) the qualitative equality strictly holds using the arithmetic of Tables 2 and 3, or (b) if the left-hand side of the confluence cannot be evaluated as in the following case. When $\partial P = +$ and $\partial A = -$, the confluence $\partial P + \partial A - \partial Q = 0$ is satisfied because $\partial P + \partial A$ has no value. A set of values contradicts a confluence if (a) every variable has a value, (b) the left hand side evaluates, and (c) the confluence is not satisfied. Thus $\partial P = +$, $\partial A = +$, and $\partial Q = -$ is contradictory. Note that by this definition a confluence need neither be satisfied nor contradicted if some of the variables do not have assigned values.

3.4.1 The Notion of Qualitative State.

Confluence alone is an inadequate modeling primitive. The value model $\partial P + \partial A - \partial Q = 0$ violates fidelity: if the valve is closed, no flow (Q) is possible, the area (A) available for flow is unchanging, and the pressure (P) across the valve is unconstrained; but the confluence states that if $\partial A = 0$ and $\partial Q = 0$ then $\partial P = 0$. Thus $\partial P + \partial A - \partial Q = 0$ is too specific a model. It violates the no-function-in-structure principle by assuming the valve is never closed. Using confluences alone, no model for the valve exists which does not violate the no-function-in-structure principle.

The second qualitative modeling primitive is qualitative state. Qualitative states

---

[7] If T is an instant and $\partial X(T) = 0$ this formulation of the mean value theorem is technically incorrect. More generally, $[X(T')] = [X(T)] + \partial^n X$ where n is the first nonzero derivative order. However, for many systems, and, in particular, the examples discussed in this paper, if $[X(T)] = 0$ and $\partial X(T) = 0$ then $\partial^n X(T) = 0$ for all n. So we will always use $[X(T')] = [X(T)] + \partial X(T)$. This issue is discussed in (de Kleer & Bobrow, 1984).

divide the behavior of a component into different regions, each of which is described by a different set of confluences. The notion of state is often not necessary in quantitative analysis since a single mathematical equation can adequately model the behavior of the component. Nevertheless it is often convenient to introduce state into quantitative analysis in order to delineate regions where certain effects are negligible or to form piecewise approximations. On the other hand, in the qualitative regime the notion of state is absolutely necessary, since it is often not possible to formulate a *single* qualitative equation set which adequately characterizes the behavior of the component over its entire operating range.

In order to satisfy the no-function-in-structure principle the region of operation is solely specified in terms of inequalities among variables (but not derivatives and integrals). These inequalities must always be of the form x op y, where op is one of $>$, $=$, $<$, $\leq$ or $\geq$ and x and y are nonderivative variables or symbolic constants. For example, the closed state of a valve is defined by the condition $[a = 0]$, stating that if the component is in state CLOSED there is no area available for flow and if there is no area available for flow the component is in state CLOSED. For each qualitative state, the component model provides the confluences which govern the behavior in that state. These specifications correspond to the quantity conditions of qualitative process theory (Forbus, 1982). However, we do not use his more general notion of a global quantity space for the entire device, instead we use a simpler, local quantity space for each component which suffices for our qualitative physics.

The full model for the valve is (the general form of the model is *state:[specifications], confluences*):

OPEN: $[A = A_{MAX}],[P] = 0,\ \partial P = 0$

WORKING: $[0 < A < A_{MAX}],[P] = [Q],\partial P + \partial A - \partial Q = 0$

CLOSED: $[A = 0]$, $[Q] = 0,\partial Q = 0$.

In state OPEN, the valve functions as a simple conduit, there is no pressure drop across it, and the flow through it is unconstrained. Neither can the pressure across it change—that can only be caused by a change in position of the valve. The state CLOSED is the dual to state OPEN. In it the valve completely disconnects the input from the output. There is no flow through the valve and the pressure across it is unconstrained. The flow through it cannot change without changing the area available for flow.

3.4.2 Pure and Mixed Models. The model confluences are not always simple sums. The correct confluence for the WORKING state of the valve is actually $\partial P + [P]\partial A - \partial Q = 0$ not $\partial P + \partial A - \partial Q = 0$ as stated earlier. This can be illustrated by examining the case where P is negative. The basic behavioral characteristic of the valve is that an increase in area available for flow always reduces the *absolute value of the pressure drop across the valve*. If the pressure drop is a positive value, an increase in area decreases the drop to zero (as in the previous analysis). If the pressure drop is a negative value, an increase in area increases the drop to zero. Thus the second term of the valve confluence is $[P]\partial A$ not ∂A.

We call a confluence, which is a simple sum of variables, *pure* (e.g., $\partial P + \partial A - \partial Q = 0$) as opposed to a sum of products, which we call *mixed* (e.g., $\partial P + [P]\partial A - \partial Q = 0$). It is always possible to construct pure models from mixed ones by adding qualitative states. For example, the state for which $\partial P + [P]\partial A - \partial Q = 0$ holds can be split into three states thereby producing a pure model: One in which $P > 0$ so that $\partial P + \partial A - \partial Q = 0$, one in which $P = 0$ so that $\partial P - \partial Q = 0$, and one in which $P < 0$ so that $\partial P - \partial A - \partial Q = 0$. The resulting pure model is formally equivalent to the mixed one and the solution methods function as well for mixed models as well as for pure ones, but we generally presume the models to be pure. The pure five-state valve model is:

OPEN: $[A = A_{MAX}],[P] = 0,\partial P = 0$

WORKING-+: $[0 < A < A_{MAX}, P > 0],[P] = [Q],\partial P + \partial A - \partial Q = 0$

WORKING-0$[0 < A < A_{MAX}, P = 0],[P] = [Q],\partial P - \partial Q = 0$

WORKING--$[0 < A < A_{MAX}, P < 0],[P] = [Q],\partial P - \partial A - \partial Q = 0$

CLOSED: $[A = 0],[Q] = 0,\partial Q = 0.$

This model illustrates, that for pure models, the set of all confluences can be divided into those involving solely derivatives and those involving solely the variables themselves.

3.4.3 Constructing the Component Models.

Although the confluences can be derived from common sense knowledge of component behavior, most are or can be viewed as adaptations of the conventional physical model. Often that adaptation is direct. For example, conservation of fluid for a pipe is exactly $q_{in} - q_{out} = 0$ and the corresponding confluence is $[q_{in}] - [q_{out}] = 0$. If the physical model is a linear function, $\Sigma c_i x_i = c_0$ where the c_i are constants, the confluence is $\Sigma[c_i][x_i] = [c_0]$. In general, a quantitative equation can be transformed to a qualitative one by rules of the following form: $[e_1 + e_2] \Rightarrow [e_1] + [e_2]$, $[e_1 e_2] \Rightarrow [e_1][e_2]$, $[0] + [e] \Rightarrow [e]$, $[0][e] \Rightarrow [0]$, $[+]]e] \Rightarrow [e]$, and $[-][e] \Rightarrow - [e]$. Additionally, if e is a constant, or always of the same sign, substitute its qualitative value.

The original physical model need not be linear. The flow rate through an orifice is given by (Cochin, 1980, p. 797):

$$Q = CA\sqrt{\frac{2P}{\rho}}, P > 0$$

where Q is the flow rate through the orifice, C is the discharge coefficient of the orifice, P is the pressure across the valve, and ρ is the mass density of the fluid. Transforming:

$$[Q] = [C][A]\left[\sqrt{\frac{2P}{\rho}}\right] = [+][+]\left[\sqrt{\frac{2P}{\rho}}\right] = [P].$$

To obtain the confluence for the changes we must first differentiate the quantitative equation and then transform it. Differentiating:

$$\frac{dQ}{dt} = C\sqrt{\frac{2P}{\rho}}\frac{dA}{dt} + \frac{CA}{\rho}\sqrt{\frac{\rho}{2P}}\frac{dP}{dt}.$$

Transforming,

$$\partial Q = [C]\left[\sqrt{\frac{2P}{\rho}}\right]\partial A + [C][A]\left[\sqrt{\frac{\rho}{2P}}\right][P]\partial P.$$

Simplifying,

$$\partial Q = [P]\partial A + [A][P][P]\partial P.$$

As $P > 0$ and $A > 0$ we get

$$\partial Q = \partial A + \partial P.$$

The transformation process introduces component states in two ways. First, the original quantitative equation may be based on states. For example, the preceding valve model holds only for $P > 0$. Second, state specifications can be introduced to remove ambiguities. For example, the transformation $[e_1 + e_2] \Rightarrow [e_1] + [e_2]$ loses information. This information may be regained. For example, $[e_1 + e_2]$ may be $+$ if $x > A$ in which case it is worth introducing a component state. In general, If the physical model is of the form $\Sigma[f_i]\partial x_i = [f_0]$, then it may be worth analyzing the regions of $[f_i]$ and introducing component states for each.

Another method is to linearize via the Taylor expansion producing an equation of the form $\Sigma g_i(dx_i/dt) = g_0$ where g_0 represents the contributions of higher-order derivatives. This equation is then transformed into a collection of states corresponding to the regions of g_i each with its individual confluences. Thus, provided that the original physical model is well-behaved, there is a simple procedure for determining the qualitative states and confluences for a component type.

3.4.4 The Laws for Connections. The laws for flowlike variables are based on the fact that conduits are always completely full of material and incompressible (by definition), and therefore any material added through one terminal must result in material leaving by some other terminal. In other words, material is instantaneously conserved. This rule is called the *continuity condition*.[8] For electrical circuits, it is

---

[8]From system dynamics.

called Kirchoff's current law; for fluid systems, the law of conservation of matter; for thermal systems, the law of conservation of energy.[9] The continuity condition requires that the sum of the current, forces, heatflows, etc., into a conduit (and most components) be zero. As these rules are simple sums they apply to the derivatives of attributes too. These can all be expressed as confluences.

As the value of the pressurelike variable in a conduit is the same everywhere in the conduit, there are no pressure laws for individual conduits or components. Furthermore, if there are no structural loops in the device (i.e., there is only one path of conduits and components between every two components), no pressure laws are needed. For these devices the continuity condition alone completely specifies the qualitatively significant behavior of the material in the conduits. Few devices have this property however. Most interesting devices contain many structural loops. For these loops, the behavior of the material has an additional relevant property. No matter which path the material takes from component A to B, the sum of the individual pressure drops along each path must be equal. This is called the *compatibility* condition.[10] For example, if the pressure between conduits A and B is x and the pressure between conduits B and C is y, then the pressure between conduits A and C is $x + y$ (and thus qualitatively $[x] + [y]$). Compatibility requires equal voltages, velocities, etc., at points where the components are connected.

It is a simple matter to construct all the continuity and compatibility equations from a device topology. However, this set of equations is usually highly redundant. In quantitative analysis every extra equation introduces added complexity, and therefore a great deal of effort is taken to ensure that a minimal number of equations are included. In the qualitative domain, the computational effort manipulating $+$, 0 and $-$ is insignificant. However, the addition of redundant equations have a numerous of unfortunate side-effects for generating explanations and detecting feedback.[11] Therefore, as in the quantitative case, there is a motivation for having all the equations be independent.

Only a few of the possible compatibility and continuity confluences are necessary to establish the compatibility and continuity conditions for the entire device. There are a number of theorems in system dynamics that indicate exactly how many equations are necessary and how to choose them. Most of those theorems are false in the qualitative domain, and we have not yet completed the theoretical analysis to determine how many confluences are actually necessary (n "independent" confluences in n variables do not necessarily have a unique solution). We include a continuity confluence for every component and a compatibility confluence for every

---

[9]Assuming the common, and somewhat misleading, convention in which the two variables are taken to be temperature and heatflow. Better would be temperature and entropyflow.

[10]Again, from system dynamics.

[11]For example, in generating explanations redundant equations result in multiple explanations (derivations) for the same behavior. These explanations are superficially different, but essentially identical. Also, the behavior a redundant equation with three or more variables produces often looks superficially like feedback.

three conduits (between which paths exist and transport the same object type). This usually produces a few redundant confluences, but we have never found a case where adding more conduit confluences provided more information about behavior.

3.4.5 A Model of the Pressure-Regulator.

We have developed all the necessary modeling primitives. The specific confluences governing the behavior of the device can be constructed from the device topology, the library of component models and the composite device state. Assuming that the valve is in a state in which $P > 0$ and $0 < A < A_{MAX}$ (state WORKING-+), the derivative confluences for the pressure-regulator form seven confluences in eight variables. The pressure-regulator has only two components, each of which is modeled by one confluence. The remaining confluences describe the behavior of the material. We state all the confluences in terms of the variables of the pressure-regulator (Figure 4). The subscripts on the variables indicate which terminals and conduits of the device topology the variable refers to. The confluence for the valve is

$$\partial P_{IN,OUT} - \partial Q_{\#1(VV)} + \partial X_{FP} = 0$$

where $P_{IN,OUT}$ is the pressure drop from input to output, $Q_{\#1(VV)}$ is the flow from terminal #1 into the valve, and ∂X_{FP} is the position of the valve control and is

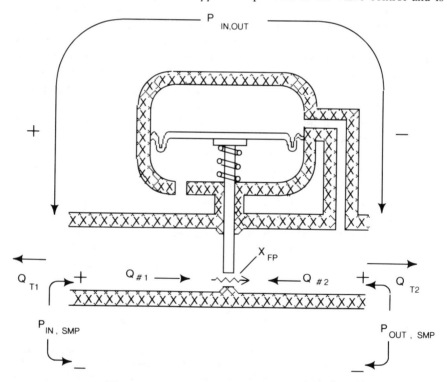

Figure 4. Variables of the pressure-regulator

qualitatively equal to area available for flow. The confluence for the pressure sensor is

$$\partial X_{FP} + \partial P_{OUT,SMP} = 0$$

where $P_{OUT,SMP}$ is the pressure at the output of the pressure-regulator. The position of the valve (equivalently the area available for flow) varies inversely with output pressure. As the pressure-regulator contains very few components, only one confluence is needed to establish the compatibility condition:

$$\partial P_{IN,OUT} + \partial P_{OUT,SMP} - \partial P_{IN,SMP} = 0.$$

The pressure-regulator has three conduits (IN, OUT and SMP) and one component (VV) that processes fluid. We write continuity confluences for all except SMP (whose continuity confluence is redundant):

$$\partial Q_{T2} + \partial Q_{\#2(VV)} = 0$$
$$\partial Q_{T1} + \partial Q_{\#1(VV)} = 0$$
$$\partial Q_{\#1(VV)} + \partial Q_{\#2(VV)} = 0.$$

A load is connected to the pressure-regulator

$$\partial Q_{T2} - \partial P_{OUT,SMP} = 0$$

Our interest in how change comes about results in a focus on the derivative variables. However, it is also possible to model the qualitative values of the device's variables. These values, although they do not direct indicate change, help determine the state of device and hence which derivative confluences apply. This confluence set is very similar to the derivative confluence set. The valve is modeled by three confluences. Unless the valve is completely open or closed, it is simply acting as a fluid resistor obeying the qualitative version of Ohm's Law:

$$[P_{IN,OUT}] - [Q_{\#1(VV)}] = 0$$

Since area is, by definition, always positive:

$$[X_{FP}] = +$$

In state WORKING-+ $P > 0$:

$$[P_{IN,OUT}] = +.$$

Note that given the usual input condition $[P_{IN,SMP}[= +, [P_{IN,OUT}] = +$ necessarily follows given the remaining confluences. The confluence for the pressure sensor is more complex:

$$[X_{FP}] + [P_{OUT,SMP}] = +$$

This confluence, coupled with the corresponding derivative confluence characterizes thresholding effect. The remaining confluences are identical. The compatibility confluence is:

$$[P_{IN,OUT}] + [P_{OUT,SMP}] - [P_{IN,SMP}] = 0$$

The three continuity confluences are:

$$[Q_{T2}] + [Q_{\#2(VV)}] = 0$$
$$[Q_{T1}] + [Q_{\#1(VV)}] = 0$$
$$[Q_{\#1(VV)}] + [Q_{\#2(VV)}] = 0$$

Lastly, the pressure-regulator is connected to a positive load:

$$[Q_{T2}] - [P_{OUT,SMP}] = 0$$

As a comparison, consider all of the confluences grouped by component and conduit:

$$\partial P_{IN,OUT} - \partial Q_{\#1(VV)} + \partial X_{FP} = 0$$
$$[P_{IN,OUT}] - [Q_{\#1(VV)}] = 0$$
$$[X_{FP}] = +$$
$$[P_{IN,OUT}] = +$$
$$\partial X_{FP} + \partial P_{OUT,SMP} = 0$$
$$[X_{FP}] + [P_{OUT,SMP}] = +$$
$$\partial P_{IN,OUT} + \partial P_{OUT,SMP} - \partial P_{IN,SMP} = 0$$
$$]P_{IN,OUT}] + [P_{OUT,SMP}] - [P_{IN,SMP}] = 0$$
$$\partial Q_{T2} + \partial Q_{\#2(VV)} = 0$$
$$[Q_{T2}] + [Q_{\#2(VV)}] = 0$$
$$\partial Q_{T1} + \partial Q_{\#1(VV)} = 0$$
$$[Q_{T1}] + [Q_{\#1(VV)}] = 0$$

$$\partial Q_{\#1(VV)} + \partial Q_{\#2(VV)} = 0$$

$$[Q_{\#1(VV)}] + [Q_{\#2(VV)}] = 0$$

$$\partial Q_{T2} - \partial P_{OUT,SMP} = 0$$

$$[Q_{T2}] - [P_{OUT,SMP}] = 0$$

The fact that these two sets of confluences are similar should not be surprising. If the underlying quantitative model is linear, i.e., all the equations of the form $\Sigma g_i x_i = g_0$ differentiation produces an almost identical expression except for the fact that g_0 is now zero. This is of course not true of the valve, the only nonlinear component of the pressure-regulator.

3.4.6 The Dependence of Device Topology on Connection Laws. The way conduit and component were distinguished in the beginning of this section was purposefully vague; both components and conduits transport and process material. Conduits are simply an abstraction for those pieces of the device whose behavior is modeled extremely simply. Usually, constituents such as wires, pipes, linkages, shafts, etc., only serve the role of communicating information between the more complex components. The compatibility and continuity conditions define what can be modeled as a conduit. The components of a device are necessarily disjoint and thus must share information in order to operate. This sharing cannot be through other components. This is the role of the conduits—they are the informational glue that connects the device together.

The compatibility and continuity conditions follow primarily from the definition of what it means to be connected. Thus modeling the intuitively obvious physical connections will not have the expected result if that physical connection does not obey compatibility or continuity. A simple example illustrates this point. Consider the situation of Figure 5. The pipe cannot be modeled as a conduit if the behavior of interest is the change of fluid level in the tanks. The compatibility condition is violated because the pressure at the left-hand side is different than the pressure at the right-hand side. It is not acting as a simple communicator of information. To analyze the device effectively, the pipe must be modeled as having a finite flow rate (i.e., modeled as a valve). The modified device topology is illustrated by Figure 6. The two conduits now obey the compatibility condition without contradiction: the bottom of tank A is at the same pressure as the left-hand side of the valve and the bottom of tank B is at the same pressure as the right-hand side of the valve.

This example illustrates a violation of a classwide quasistatic assumption: the material in the pipe takes as much time to reach equilibrium as the composite device. Thus this particular pipe cannot be modeled as a conduit. This example is a direct analog of the violation of a classwide assumption of electronics that occurs when two capacitors charged to different potentials are placed in parallel. In these two cases, there is a violation of no-function-in-structure: wires are usually modeled

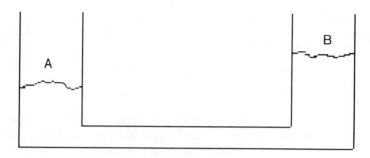

Figure 5. Two tanks

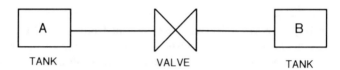

TANK   VALVE   TANK

Figure 6. A device topology for Figure 5

as connections, but that model predicts behavior incorrectly. Knowledge of the behavior of the device is needed to determine what the structure is. No procedure for determining the device topology is foolproof, but every failure can be attributed to a violation of a classwide assumption—as occurred in the previous two examples. However, at present we have not found an effective way to determine whether a topology that describes a particular device violates some classwide assumption; this is a topic of ongoing research.

4 Prediction of Behavior

In order to better understand the technical issues concerning how the behavior of a device is derived from its structure, it may help first to sketch the intuitions underlying our formal theory. Our central concern is with change. That is, what causes a device to move from one equilibrium state to another, how does that change transpire and how can it be explained in terms of the laws defining the given equilibrium state? Our approach involves decomposing a device's behavior into two dimensions, one being its interstate behavior, the other being its intrastate behavior. From this perspective, a device changes state when one or more of its variables (i.e., a pressure, a current, etc.) exceeds some threshold that defines that state. Thus part of determining when a device changes state requires determining which thresholds are being exceeded and from that determining possible target transitions. *But what causes a variable to change in the first place?* Determining this requires figuring out what the first-order time derivatives are within the current state. The qualitative values of these derivatives act as "tendencies" that sum over infinitesimal time intervals that cause a variable to change from its present value. These derivatives constitute intrastate behavior, "forces," or said differently, the agents of change. Thus the time derivatives that are operative within an equilibrium state can eventually lead to a variable changing its value enough to cause that qualitative state to change. In Section 5, we discuss another kind of causality—mythical causality—that explains how a qualitative change in one derivative "causes" another derivative to change all within the (potentially infinitesimal) time interval.

It is also possible to determine indirectly what the first order derivatives must have been within a given state by comparing the values of the variables in the state and its successor state. In that approach, primacy is given to the state transition, itself, from which the values of the derivative can be deduced. However, in our scheme, primacy is given to the tendencies (i.e., values of the derivatives) operating within a state, from which the possible successor states can be determined. Thus our approach must accept the burden of deducing these tendencies directly from structural properties of the device and perturbations to its inputs.

The passage of time is modeled by episodes. Within an episode each component, viewed as a pure model, remains in the same state and all the device's variables keep on changing in the same way (i.e., the derivative variables do not change[12]). In the first set of examples, we tend to use pure models and derivative variables rarely change during a state; thus the states and episodes of a device are in one-to-one correspondence. Their fundamental difference lies in the fact that state is a mode of behavior of a device while an episode is a period of time during which the device is always in the same mode.

The approach outlined in this section does not result in a comprehensive causal account, for there is no causal explanation of the intrastate behavior. Constructing such explanations is discussed in Part 5.

4.1 Intrastate Behavior
To determine the behavior within an episode, an assignment of $+$, 0, and $-$ to the variables must be found that satisfies the confluences of the device. Given the operating context where $[P_{IN,SMP}] = +$, it must be the case that the regulator is in state [WORKING-+] or [OPEN]. The $[x]$ column of Table 4 lists the only assignment of values to variables that satisfies the confluences. Given an input signal of $\partial P_{IN,SMP} = +$, there is only one assignment of values to variables that satisfies the derivative confluences for that state. (By coincidence, these two value sets are identical.)

Before discussing the types of algorithms that produce such a solution, consider the information contained in it. At first blush, it does not appear as if it contains very much information. However, it does capture the essential characteristic that the valve is closing ($\partial X_{FP} = -$). Admittedly, it does not state that the output pressure

---

[12]As a consequence of ambiguity, the derivative values may change while no component changes state. In addition mythical time places an ordering upon the changes of values as a device changes state.

Table 4. Intrastate Behavior
of the Pressure-Regulator

x	$[x]$	∂x
$P_{IN,SMP}$	+	+
Q_{T1}	−	−
Q_{T2}	+	+
$Q_{\#2(VV)}$	−	−
$Q_{\#1(VV)}$	+	+
X_{FP}	−	−
$P_{IN,OUT}$	+	+
$P_{OUT,SMP}$	+	+

does not change ($\partial P_{OUT,SMP} = +$), but the fact that $\partial P_{IN,OUT} = +$ indicates the output pressure is not rising as fast as the input pressure, which indicates some attenuation. Of course, this solution does not explain why the valve is closing. We discuss this issue when we attempt to "push a level" of detail in the analysis.

To determine the behavior (i.e., Table 4), the set of confluences must be solved. Each confluence is a constraint, and thus the problem of determining behavior is a constraint satisfaction problem. Unfortunately, simple propagation methods do not work. For example, consider propagation of constraints as a constraint satisfaction method: (a) start with a given, (b) find some as yet unsatisfied constraint and see if it can be used to determine a value for another variable, (c) repeat. In the foregoing example, the given is $\partial P_{IN,SMP} = +$, but there is no other constraint that provides additional information. The only other constraint that even mentions $\partial P_{IN,SMP}$ is $\partial P_{IN,OUT} + \partial P_{OUT,SMP} - \partial P_{IN,SMP} = 0$, but nothing is known about the values of $\partial P_{OUT,IN}$ or $\partial P_{OUT,SMP}$. Nevertheless, unless $\partial P_{IN,OUT} = +$, the remaining confluences are contradictory. (This is a common problem for all local propagation schemes. We call such systems of simultaneous equations which cannot be solved by substitution alone inherently simultaneous (de Kleer and Sussman, 1980).)

The seemingly obvious way around this problem is to solve the constraints using algebraic symbol manipulation. This is analogous to the situation where x + y = 3 and 2x + y = 4 in which x must be 1 and y must be 3 although there is no sequence of simple propagations that can determine this. One resolves such inherent simultaneity by subtracting x + y = 3 from 2x + y = 4, which yields x = 1. The analogous strategy fails in the qualitative domain because the operations outlined in Table 2 don't satisfy the field axioms which are required to do this kind of equation solving. ENVISION uses a combination of constraint propagation and generate and test to find all the solutions to the confluence equations.

Numerous schemes, for example, relaxation or generate and test can be used to solve sets of inherently simultaneous confluence equations. But because the qualitative calculus does not satisfy the field axioms multiple solutions result (note that just because our calculus is "qualitative" does not, in itself, necessitate it producing ambiguous analyses). Multiple solutions often exist even when there are as many "independent" confluences as qualitative unknowns. These multiple solutions are not just an artifact of our calculus, but are an important part of our theory.

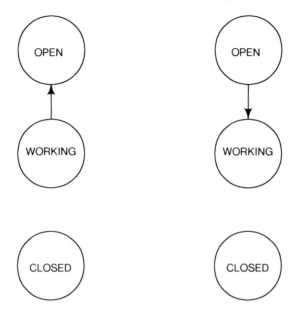

Figure 7. State diagrams for the pressure-regulator with decreasing and increasing input. The spring and mass are not modeled and the load is presumed to be finite. Each circle represents a state and each edge represents a possible transition from one state to another. The contradictory state CLOSED is included purely for expository purposes—in all following examples contradictory states are deleted. This state is contradictory because there is no solution to the model confluences for that state.

Each solution describes a behavior which can potentially occur in the actual operation of the modeled device.

We call each prediction resulting from the same set of confluences an *interpretation*. The issue of interpretations is a complex topic in its own right and is discussed in further detail in Appendix A.

4.2 Interstate Behavior
The allowable states of a device are a subset of the cross-product of all the states of its constituent components. The interstate behavior is the possible transitions between these states. Thus the total solution to a set of qualitative models for the device, namely, a complete description of its behavior, is a set of assignments[13] of values to variables, one set for each composite device state. In addition, the total solution also specifies the state transitions and their causes. This latter information is illustrated graphically by a state transition diagram. (Figure 7 is an example of a state diagram, the details of which are discussed later.)

Legal transitions between states are characterized by a set of conditions derived

---

[13]Sets of assignments of values to variables if there is more than one interpretation for the confluences for a particular state.

from the qualitative calculus. A sketch of the algorithm for constructing the total solution is as follows. Every composite device state is identified and the confluences solved for each in order to determine the qualitative values of each of the derivatives. The values of the derivatives indicate which direction the device's variables are changing and can thus be used to determine whether some state specification may cease to be valid and a transition occur. For example, suppose device state A has specification $[X < A]$ and solution $\partial X = +$ and device state B has specification $[X \geqslant A]$, then the state change from A to B is allowable.

Although the interstate behavior looks much like a result of a simulation, it is not. Instead, it simultaneously describes behaviors under all possible initial conditions of the generic device. The total solution is used to determine the behavior of a particular device using the initial conditions to determine the starting state and tracing through the possible state transitions. The state diagrams are always of finite size, but a particular device, given appropriate operating conditions, can undergo an infinite number of state transitions, never coming to rest in any one state. This is the case with oscillators. The state diagram can also include ambiguities concerning possible state transitions. As a consequence, to determine the precise behavior of a particular device requires additional information. Nevertheless, the total solution describes all possible behaviors of all devices of the generic type *and no others*.

4.2.1 The State Diagram. An example of interstate behavior can be illustrated in the operation of the pressure-regulator whose valve is modeled by the simplified model:

OPEN: $[A = A_{MAX}]$, $[P] = 0$, $\partial P = 0$

WORKING: $[0 < A < A_{MAX}]$, $[P] = [Q]$, $\partial P + \partial A - \partial Q = 0$

CLOSED: $[A = 0]$, $[Q] = 0$, $\partial Q = 0$.

This simple valve model has three states: OPEN, WORKING, and CLOSED. As the valve is the only component of the pressure-regulator that has state, the composite device, likewise, has only three states: [OPEN], [WORKING], and [CLOSED]. Suppose the input pressure is decreasing and the pressure-regulator is in state [WORKING], then $\partial X_{FP} = +$, which causes A, the cross-sectional area available for flow to increase. This raises the possibility that $A < A_{MAX}$ may no longer hold. If that happens, the state ends, and the device transitions into a new one with the valve pinned in state OPEN. In this state, the pressure-regulator provides no regulation at all because the input pressure is less than the regulator's target output pressure. The resulting state diagram is illustrated in Figure 7(a). Figure 7(b) illustrates the diagram in the case where the input pressure is increasing.

This example, although extremely simple, illustrates the task of drawing inferences concerning the termination of states and the determination of the next state. Note that no input disturbance can cause the valve to move to or from state CLOSED. In this device, every increase in input pressure results in a decrease in area available for flow. But even if the input pressure continues to grow unboundedly, the area will never become zero (if it were zero, the output pressure would be zero and hence the action of the sensor could be holding the valve closed). For any finite pressure, the area will be nonzero. Only as pressure tends to infinity does the area approach zero as the mathematical limit. This is a counterexample to the seductive fallacy that infinite sums of nonzero values always diverge. The point to be made here is that even though the qualitative algebra is extremely simple, it nevertheless concerns derivatives, integrals, and time, and one must be careful lest one fall into the well-known pitfalls concerning infinitesimals.

Figure 9 illustrates some of the more complex properties of a state diagram (the details are discussed later). States can have multiple outgoing edges because of qualitative ambiguity. Multiple ingoing edges correspond to cases where there is more than one route for reaching the state. Because derivative variables have one of three values, and the number of states in which any component can be is bounded, there are only a finite number of possible behaviors and possible episodes. Thus unbounded sequences of states can be represented by closed paths in the state diagram.

4.2.2 Improved Spring and Valve Models. The previous models for the pressure-regulator are too simple to illustrate interstate behavior. With the more detailed models presented in this section *it is possible to make.inferences about equilibrium, oscillation, ringing and dissipation in the pressure-regulator solely from the qualitative models and the qualitative differential calculus.* Although in pushing a level the classwide assumptions have been changed, the device topology of Figure 3 remains essentially the same. The same connection laws hold for force and velocity: as connections (points at which two or more physical objects attach) are massless, forces for every connection sum to zero (continuity), and velocities for attached parts must match (compatibility). Thus force and velocity fit into the connection scheme outlined earlier. (However, one usually doesn't think of any "material" carrying this information. This material is momentum and it has all the usual properties of material. For example, momentum can be thought of as having flow; see diSessa, 1979.)

The model for the pressure sensor is extremely simple. It relates pressure directly to force:

$$\partial P = \partial Q.$$

The effects of a force on an object with mass is based on Newton's law $f = ma$. As mass is always positive and unchanging, the confluence equation for this behavior is:

$$[F] = \partial V.$$

∂V is the qualitative derivative of velocity. This is a mixed confluence equation relating a derivative to a nonderivative so an object with mass can be modeled as three states:

$F > 0$: $[F > 0]$, $\partial V = +$

$F = 0$: $[F = 0]$, $\partial V = 0$

$F < 0$: $[F < 0]$, $\partial V = -$.

The model for a spring is the dual (interchange V and F) of that for an object with mass and is derived from Hooke's law $f = kx$ or $dF/dt = kv$:

$\partial F = [V]$.

This is also a mixed confluence equation which can be modeled as three states

$V > 0$: $[V > 0]$, $\partial F = +$

$V = 0$: $[V = 0]$, $\partial F = 0$

$V < 0$: $[V < 0]$, $\partial F = -$.

The model for the valve is the same as the one used earlier, except for the fact that ∂A is the time derivative of distance (assuming area is proportional to the distance the valve is open) and hence it is a velocity (notated V). The confluence is thus still mixed (Q is flow rate):

$\partial P - [V] - \partial Q = 0$.

To construct a pure model such confluences must be modeled by three states, resulting in a valve model with nine states. For simplicity, we only consider three of them.

$V > 0$: $[0 < A < A_{MAX}, P < 0, V > 0]$, $\partial P - \partial Q = +$

$V = 0$: $[0 < A < A_{MAX}, P < 0, V = 0]$, $\partial P - \partial Q = 0$

$V < 0$: $[0 < A < A_{MAX}, P < 0, V < 0]$, $\partial P - \partial Q = -$.

4.2.3 Total Solution for Expanded Pressure-Regulator. Figure 9 is a static diagram for the behavior of the pressure-regulator based on these models. This diagram is produced by ENVISION using the rules discussed earlier. Table 5 describes the results of analyzing each of the nine global device states with an input signal of $\partial P_{IN,SMP} = +$. The new device topology (see Figure 8) is like that of Figure 3 but explicitly includes the spring and the valve's mass (which we model by a separate object-with-mass component). Compared to the earlier analysis (Figure 4), there are four new variables, $\partial F_{\#1(S)}$ and $\partial F_{\#2(S)}$ are the forces pulling at the spring from either side, $\partial F_{A(M)}$ is the force pushing the valve's mass, and ∂V_{FP} is the upward velocity of the point where the valve's mass, spring, and stem attach. The behavior in some of the states is ambiguous and hence all interpretations are stated. For example, state 3 has 5 interpretations.

The device begins in state $V = 0, F = 0$. The confluences describing the behaviors of the valve's mass, valve, and spring are obtained from the models just presented. As $V = 0$ the confluence describing the pressure-regulator is

$$\partial P_{IN,OUT} - \partial Q_{\#1(VV)} = 0.$$

Also, as $V = 0$, the spring obeys the confluence

$$\partial F_{\#1(S)} = 0.$$

Since $F = 0$, the applicable valve mass confluence is

$$\partial V_{FP} = 0.$$

The remaining confluences are the same for every state. The confluence for the pressure sensor is

$$\partial P_{OUT,SMP} + \partial F_{\#1(S)} + \partial F_{A(M)} = 0.$$

The remaining confluences are similar to those presented with Figure 4.

$$\partial F_{\#1(S)} + \partial F_{\#2(S)} = 0$$
$$\partial P_{IN,OUT} + \partial P_{OUT,SMP} - \partial P_{IN,SMP} = 0$$
$$\partial Q_{T1} + \partial Q_{\#1(VV)} = 0$$
$$\partial Q_{T1} + \partial Q_{\#2(VV)} = 0$$
$$\partial Q_{\#1(VV)} + \partial Q_{\#2(VV)} = 0$$
$$\partial Q_{T2} - \partial P_{OUT,SMP} = 0$$
$$\partial P_{IN,SMP} = +$$

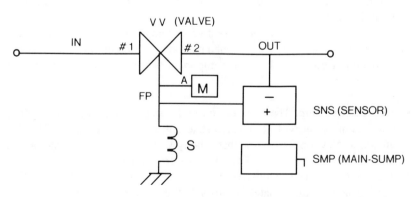

Figure 8. Device topology of the pressure-regulator with mass and spring

State:	1	2	3	4	5	6	7	8	9
State	$V = 0$	$V = 0$	$V < 0$	$V < 0$	$V < 0$	$V = 0$	$V > 0$	$V > 0$	$V > 0$
Specifications:	$F = 0$	$F < 0$	$F < 0$	$F = 0$	$F > 0$	$F > 0$	$F > 0$	$F = 0$	$F < 0$

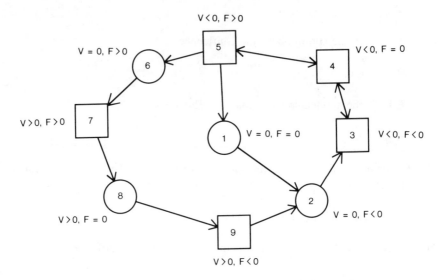

Figure 9. State diagram for the pressure-regulator with continuing input signal, mass, spring, and no friction. Circles indicate momentary states, and squares indicate states that may exist for all interval of time.

4.2.4 Constructing the State Diagram.
Constructing the state diagram is analogous to solving a set of simultaneous differential equations characterizing the behavior of a physical system. The process of constructing a particular state transition is equivalent to performing an integration involving the first-order derivatives operating in the original state. The process for constructing the state diagram outlined in this section, in essence, performs an integration of the set of differential equations describing the composite device.

As in quantitative analysis, there are diverse solution strategies, each applicable to a particular problem type. We present a number of different rules for constructing the state diagram, each based on some important property of the qualitative calculus.

- *The causality rule.* The most basic rule for constructing the state diagram is that a component will not change state unless it is acted upon. (This is our analog to Newton's first law that a body will continue in its state of rest or uniform velocity until acted on by an external force.)
- *The limit rule.* The qualitative mean value theorem is $[X(T')] = [X(T)] + \partial X(T)$ where T' immediately follows T; thus unless some ∂X is nonzero, the

Table 5. All Pressure-Regulator Solutions

State:	1	2	3	4	5	6	7	8	9
State	$V=0$	$V=0$	$V<0$	$V<0$	$V<0$	$V=0$	$V>0$	$V>0$	$V>0$
Specifications:	$F=0$	$F<0$	$F<0$	$F=0$	$F>0$	$F>0$	$F>0$	$F=0$	$F<0$
Interpretation:	1	1	1 2 3 4 5	1 2 3 4 5	1 2 3 4 5	1	1 2 3	1 2 3	1 2 3
$\partial Q_{T1} =$	−	−	− − − 0 +	− − − 0 +	− − − 0 +	−	− − −	− − −	− − −
$\partial Q_{T2} =$	+	+	+ + + 0 −	+ + + 0 −	+ + + 0 −	+	+ + +	+ + +	+ + +
$\partial Q_{\#1(VV)} =$	+	+	+ + + 0 −	+ + + 0 −	+ + + 0 −	+	+ + +	+ + +	+ + +
$\partial Q_{\#2(VV)} =$	−	−	− − − 0 +	− − − 0 +	− − − 0 +	−	− − −	− − −	− − −
$\partial P_{IN,OUT} =$	+	+	+ + + + +	+ + + + +	+ + + + +	+	+ 0 −	+ 0 −	+ 0 −
$\partial P_{OUT,SMP} =$	+	+	+ + + 0 −	+ + + 0 −	+ + + 0 −	+	+ + +	+ + +	+ + +
$\partial F_{\#1(S)} =$	0	0	− − − − −	− − − − −	− − − − −	0	− − −	− − −	− − −
$\partial F_{\#2(S)} =$	0	0	+ + + + +	+ + + + +	+ + + + +	0	− − −	− − −	− − −
$\partial F_{A(M)} =$	−	−	− 0 + + +	− 0 + + +	− 0 + + +	−	+ + +	+ + +	+ + +
$\partial V_{FP} =$	0	−	− − − − −	0 0 0 0 0	+ + + + +	+	+ + +	0 0 0	− − −

state cannot terminate. Only if $\partial X \neq 0$, may X move to its limit.[14] Thus every increasing variable ($\partial X = +$), which is bounded above ($X < A$), can produce a state termination. Similarly, every decreasing variable ($\partial X = -$) which is bounded below ($X > A$) can produce a state termination. There is no other way a state transition can occur.

- *The ordering rule.* Qualitative variables vary continuously, e.g., suppose ∂X $= +$ and the state could terminate by violating $x < m$ for component E or by violating $x < n$ for component B (the interesting case occurs when E and B are different components), and $n < m$. As x varies continuously, the only possible change for x is from $x < n$ to $n \leq x < m$. Thus component B changes state first.

- *The equality change rule.* If $\partial X(T)$ is nonzero and $[X(T)] = A$, where A is a point interval $[k,k]$ then the state terminates immediately. For example, if $[X]$ $= 0$ and $\partial X = +$ then the device must immediately move to a state where $[X]$ $= +$. This rule applies in two situations: (a) where a model specification of the current state is of the form $[X = A]$ and (b) where $[X]$ is determined to be 0 by solving the confluences. (Forbus, 1982, calls this the equality change law.) Such momentary states play an important role and are specially marked.

With minor modification, these same rules apply to state specifications that refer to two variables, e.g., $x < y$ or $x = y$. The case of $x < y$ is transformed in $z = y - x$ and $z > 0$. If the introduced variable is unevaluable all cases must be considered. For example, in the case of $z = y - x$ and $z > 0$ the possibilities $\partial z = +$ and $\partial z = 0$, which cannot cause state change, and $\partial z = -$, which can cause state change must be considered. Similarly, $x = y$ is transformed to $z = x - y$ and $z = 0$.

The remaining rules restrict the results of the first four. Each applies to two states and the transition between them.

The epsilon ordering rule. Any change introduced by the equality change rule occurs first. For example, if $[X]$ is changing from 0 to $+$ and $[Y]$ is changing from $+$ to 0, then $[X]$ changes first. The rationale is that if $[Y]$ is $+$, then $Y > \epsilon > 0$. As $Y(T)$ is a continuous function, it will take some finite time to change by ϵ but the change of X happens instantly.

- *The contradiction avoidance rule.* Contradictions arise if the confluences are unsatisfiable, or two state specifications of different components have an empty intersection. If a state is contradictory in either way, a transition to it is impossible as well. This rule determines the valve cannot close, i.e., even though the area available for flow is decreasing it will never reach 0. Consider what would happen if the valve closed. If the valve closes then $[X_{FP}] = 0$, and by the valve and continuity equations $[Q_{T1}] = [Q_{T2}] = [Q_{\#1(VV)}] = [Q_{\#2(VV)}]$ $= 0$. Using the confluence for the load, this implies $[P_{OUT,SMP}] = 0$. Substituting into the sensor equation $[X_{FP}] + [P_{OUT,SMP}] = +$ we get $0 + 0 = +$ which

---

[14]Note earlier footnote for the case $[x] = \partial x = 0$.

is impossible. Therefore, the valve cannot close and all transitions to this state cannot happen.

- *The continuity rule* Each variable varies continuously. For each variable, $[X(T)]$ must be adjacent to $[XCT')]$ otherwise the transition is impossible (similarly $\partial X(T)$ must be adjacent to $\partial X(T')$ and so on).

- *The mean value rule.* The mean value theorem must hold for every variable if the transition is to be possible. For each variable, $X,[X(T')] = [X(T)] + \partial X(T)$. (This rule holds as a consequence of previously defined rules.)

- *The feedback rule.* Knowledge about the feedback behavior of the device provides a crucial amount of information about the transition (the procedure for recognizing feedback is presented later). A negative feedback path that contains no"momentum" components cannot overshoot. In cases of positive feedback, certain transitions cannot happen because the device will actively prevent the transition from happening. (The constraint satisfaction algorithm discussed earlier cannot detect feedback, but causal analysis, discussed later can.)

Appendix B discusses a procedure (which our program ENVISION uses) to construct the state diagram. It also handles cases where a global device state has multiple interpretations.

4.2.5 ENVISION's Analysis. The following is ENVISION's brief analysis of each of the states and state transitions between them. For each state, the component(s) that may change state due to some threshold being reached are listed followed by the global device state changes which are possible. The state numbers correspond to those used in Figure 8. The following analysis is simplified by avoiding reference to interpretations. The states are labeled by the specifications of the individual component states thereby equating the states of the valve and the valve's mass (both sets of state specifications reference velocity in exactly the same way). Constructing this simplified state diagram requires only three rules. The causality rule limits the transitions to those components undergoing some change, the limit rule specifies in which direction (if any) component changes occur, and the equality change rule indicates which states are momentary (indicated by the words "immediately changes state" in the explanation). The ordering rule does not apply because the state specifications are too simple. If we had not made the simplification that the valve's mass and the spring change state in lock step, the contradiction avoidance rule would have applied. The reason the valve and spring change state in lock step is that both depend directly on the position of the valve, this position controls both the amount of material flowing and the stretch on the spring. If transitions within states had been considered (e.g., see Figure 18), the continuity rule would have been needed. The mean value rule holds automatically and the feedback rule is inapplicable in this example.

At any given time, the state is determined by the values of velocity V_{FP} and force $F_{A(M)}$. State 1 is dependent on $V_{FP} = 0$ and $F_{A(M)} = 0$ thus; the values of ∂V_{FP} and

$\partial F_{A(M)}$ determine the next state transition (if any). Table 5 indicates that $\partial V_{FP} = 0$ so the valve's mass cannot change state. However, the fact that $\partial F_{A(M)} = -$ means that $F_{A(M)}$ immediately becomes negative, thus causing the valve's mass to change state immediately. The new confluence for the valve's mass is $\partial V_{FP} = -$.

The analysis as printed out by ENVISION:

In state 1, $V = 0$, $F = 0$

Because $\partial F_{A(M)} = -$, M immediately changes state to $F < 0$.
The device immediately changes state to 2 $V = 0$, $F < 0$

In state 2, $V = 0$, $F < 0$

Because $\partial V_{FP} = -$, S and VV immediately changes state to $V < 0$.
The device immediately changes state to 3 $V < 0$, $F < 0$

In state 3, $V < 0$, $F < 0$

The value of $\partial F_{A(M)}$ is ambiguous.
If $\partial F_{A(M)} = +$, M may change state to $F = 0$.[15]
The device may change state to 4 $V < 0$, $F = 0$

In state 4, $V < 0$, $F = 0$

The value of $\partial F_{A(M)}$ is ambiguous.
If $\partial F_{A(M)} = -$, M immediately changes state to $F < 0$.
If $\partial F_{A(M)} = +$, M immediately changes state to $F > 0$.
Therefore, the device may change state to one of:
5 $V < 0$, $F > 0$, 3 $V < 0$, $F < 0$

In state 5, $V < 0$, $F > 0$

The value of $\partial F_{A(M)}$ is ambiguous.
If $\partial F_{A(M)} = -$, M may change state to $F = 0$.
Because $\partial V_{FP} = +$, S and VV may change state to $V = 0$.
Therefore, the device may change state to one of:
6 $V = 0$, $F > 0$, 1 $V = 0$, $F = 0$, 4 $V < 0$, $F = 0$

In state 6, $V = 0$, $F > 0$

Because $\partial V_{FP} = +$, S and VV immediately changes state to $V > 0$.
Because $\partial F_{A(M)} = -$, M may change state to $F = 0$.
Therefore, the device must immediately change state to one of:
8 $V > 0$, $F = 0$, 7 $V > 0$, $F > 0$.

In state 7, $V > 0$, $F > 0$

Because $\partial F_{A(M)} = -$, M may change state to $F = 0$.
The device may change state to 8 $V > 0$, $F = 0$.

In state 8, $V > 0$, $F = 0$

Because $\partial F_{A(M)} = -$, M immediately changes state to $F < 0$.
The device immediately changes state to 9 $V > 0$, $F < 0$.

In state 9, $V > 0$, $F < 0$

Because $\partial V_{FP} = -$, S and VV may change state to $V = 0$.
The device may change state to 2 $V = 0$, $F < 0$
Said less baroquely: In the starting state 1, the valve is unmoving and the force

---

[15]If ∂F is 0 or $-$ no state change can happen.

from the sensor and from the spring are in balance. An increase in input pressure produces an increase in output pressure, which is sensed by the sensor and produces an increased downward force on the valve (state 2). The transition is mandatory, as even an infinitesimal change in value at zero must cause it to become nonzero. The increase of downward force on the valve (the coordinate system is chosen so that open valve positions correspond to positive distances and a closed valve is characterized by zero distance) causes the valve to acquire velocity and hence the valve begins to close (state 3). This transition is also mandatory because the velocity is being changed away from zero. In state 3, the value of the force on the valve is ambiguous. The closing of the valve could reduce the output pressure enough to equal the force of the spring, causing a transition to state 4. On the other hand, the rise in input pressure could continue to dominate behavior and thus the output pressure continues to rise. The same sort of situation arises in the two following states. Depending on the functional relationship between the input pressure, the input pressure function itself and the gain of the feedback loop, the system may move back and forth between these three states. If the pressure rise does not dominate, the moving valve will reduce the output pressure enough so that the restoring force of the spring is greater than the force exerted by the pressure. If the input pressure rise becomes negligible the pressure-regulator will continue to oscillate through states 2–9 (as suggested in Figure 8 and verified by the analysis underlying Figure 10).

4.2.6 Physical Rationale for the New Component Models. With the models used in the pressure-regulator examples before section 4.2.2, it is impossible to analyze the behavior of the pressure-regulator at small time durations. The particular quasistatic approximation demands that a change of output pressure "instantly" results in a change of valve setting. The models we had been using are inherently incapable of describing the oscillatory and feedback behavior of the device. We needed to "push a level" of detail and model behavior at smaller time gradations if

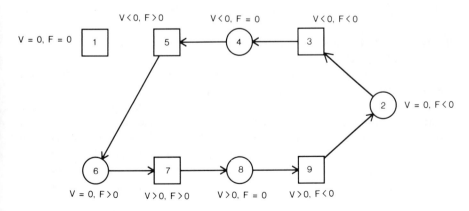

Figure 10. No input signal, no friction

oscillation is to be evidenced. (In Section 6 we present an alternative strategy for determining the presence of feedback and oscillation based on "mythical causality," which does not require pushing a level.)

The time delay introduced by removing the quasistatic approximation is not the result of some explicit time delay in some component, but rather the direct consequence of the particular physical laws and the mathematical properties of integrals and derivatives. When small time durations are involved, the mass of the valve itself, although very small, must be taken into consideration. An increase in pressure increases the force on the mass of the valve. This force produces an acceleration on the valve that results in a velocity that in turn results in a change of position of the valve *after some time has elapsed.* Once the valve is given a nonzero velocity, it starts to close.

To operate successfully, the valve must also contain a spring, which provides a restoring force by tending to open the valve. At equilibrium, the force provided by the pressure of the fluid on the diaphragm equals the restoring force of the compressed spring. As pressure increases, the force of the diaphragm increases, causing the forces on the valve to become unbalanced and forcing it to seek a new equilibrium position. The valve moves in the direction of closing the valve, thereby simultaneously increasing the restoring force of the spring and decreasing the force delivered by the pressure until these two forces balance. There is, however, one more effect that complicates matters: *momentum.* As the valve reaches equilibrium position it will have some nonzero velocity and as it has mass it will continue to move past this equilibrium position. Eventually the valve will reach its maximum overshoot position and will start moving back to equilibrium, but again it will overshoot. This ringing, or oscillation, around the new equilibrium position continues indefinitely unless there are some dissipative effects.

4.2.7 Uses of the State Diagram. The state diagram is a complete description of all possible interstate behaviors of the generic device. It represents every possible interstate behavior the device can manifest, and enumerates how the device changes from one behavioral pattern to another. The state diagram can be used to directly answer "what happens" type questions. The intrastate behavior is characterized by the assignment of values to variables, which satisfies the confluences of the state. The combined structure can be used to answer a variety of types of questions about device behavior in addition to basic prediction. The structure can be used to answer questions about whether something could happen. For example, to determine whether the output pressure could rise, each state is checked to see whether the pressure rises in that state, and then a further check is made to see whether any of those states can be reached given the initial conditions. State A can be reached from state B if there exists a sequence of transitions from A to B. Far more interesting inferences can be drawn about the state diagram concerning oscillation and energy dissipation, but we present those after describing how the state diagram can be constructed.

Figure 9 indicates the system oscillates through states 2–9. A direct examination

Table 6. Solution Given No Imput Signal, No Friction

State:	1	2	3	4	5	6	7	8	9
State	$V = 0$	$V = 0$	$V < 0$	$V < 0$	$V < 0$	$V = 0$	$V > 0$	$V > 0$	$V > 0$
Specifications:	$F = 0$	$F < 0$	$F < 0$	$F = 0$	$F > 0$	$F > 0$	$F > 0$	$F = 0$	$F < 0$
$\partial Q_{T1} =$	0	0	+	+	+	0	−	−	−
$\partial Q_{T2} =$	0	0	−	−	−	0	+	+	+
$\partial Q_{\#1(VV)} =$	0	0	−	−	−	0	+	+	+
$\partial Q_{\#2(VV)} =$	0	0	+	+	+	0	−	−	−
$\partial P_{IN,OUT} =$	0	0	+	+	+	0	−	−	−
$\partial P_{OUT,SMP} =$	0	0	−	−	−	0	+	+	+
$\partial F_{\#1(S)} =$	0	0	−	−	−	0	+	+	+
$\partial F_{\#2(S)} =$	0	0	+	+	+	0	−	−	−
$\partial F_{A(M)} =$	0	0	+	+	+	0	−	−	−
$\partial V_{FP} =$	0	−	−	0	+	+	+	0	−

of Table 5 shows the second-order derivatives (i.e., the column differences between the first-order derivatives). The extrema of the variables occur within those states where the first-order derivatives can be zero (e.g., $\partial V_{FP} = 0$ in state 4) where $\partial X = 0$ and whether these are a maxima or minima can be determined by the second order derivatives. For example, the velocity of the valve achieves a downward maximum in state 4 which is a momentary state at which the forces of the spring and pressure-sensor perfectly balance ($[F_{A(M)}] = 0$). The position of the valve (whose value is the same as the force on the spring ($F = kx$)), has extrema in states 6 and 2 which are momentary states where the velocity of the valve is 0.

The state diagram for a device is a representation of the overall functioning of the generic device. Although it is constructed solely from the component models, many features of the global operation of a device only become evident in the structure of the state diagram. The state diagram is thus a representation of device behavior that itself can be examined to gain further insight into device functioning. In particular, issues such as oscillation, ringing, energy dissipation, and stability are identifiable as particular patterns in the state diagrams. Thus our qualitative physics is able to detect the presence of these important functional characteristics.

State diagrams reveal a great deal more about the potential behaviors of the device. Figure 10 is the state diagram for the pressure-regulator when there is no applied input signal. It shows that if the pressure-regulator starts at quiescence ($V = 0, F = 0$) it will remain there (because in this state all the derivatives are also zero). If the device is in this quiescent state the only solution to the confluence equations is that every derivative variable is zero. If the pressure-regulator starts in a nonquiescent state, it can never reach quiescence. Again this is directly deducible from the confluences. For each state, there is no solution to the confluence equations which results in a change of operating region to the quiescent state. Note that this deduction is possible solely from the component models themselves, models which do not reference or contain any idea of quiescence.

Any movement in the valve is resisted by imperfections in its components. A

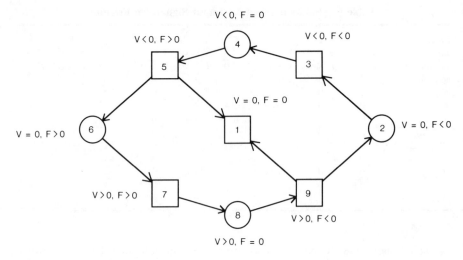

Figure 11. State diagram with no input signal, friction

simple law that describes this effect is $df/dt = k(dV/dt)$, i.e., any change in velocity produces a corresponding increase in force acting against the change in velocity. (This is the mechanical analog to Ohm's law.) The resulting state diagram is illustrated in Figue 11. It shows that it is now possible for the pressure-regulator to reach an equilibrium state and once it reaches it no further movement is possible.

The law of the form $F = kv$ is an instance of a general class of dissipative laws — laws which dictate that the device must lose energy. Hence oscillations involving[16] dissipative components must eventually damp out and ones that do not contain dissipative laws must not. However, it is possible to draw these kinds of inferences from constructing state diagrams and then analyzing their topological structure. The changed state diagram is solely the result of adding a component with the law $\partial F = \partial V$. This component model does not contain any explicit hint about damping or energy dissipation (i.e., no violation of no-function-in-structure). The major difference between Figures 11 and 10 is that the device may reach the quiescent state thus terminating the oscillation. From physics we know that the oscillation *must* eventually damp out, but our qualitative physics cannot capture this fine-grained detail.

4.2.8 Qualitative vs. Quantitative Techniques. Two interesting comparisons emerge between techniques used for qualitative analysis and those used for solving differential equations in physics. First, the usual quantitative analysis techniques produce solutions whose *form* we can interpret as being oscillatory, damped, etc. But this requires an interpretation of the solution. The qualitative techniques pre-

---

[16]And, of course, no sources of energy.

Table 7.   Solution Given No Imput Signal, Friction

State:	1	2	3	4	5	6	7	8	9
State	$V=0$	$V=0$	$V<0$	$V<0$	$V<0$	$V=0$	$V>0$	$V>0$	$V>0$
Specifications:	$F=0$	$F<0$	$F<0$	$F=0$	$F>0$	$F>0$	$F>0$	$F=0$	$F<0$
Interpretation:	1	1	1	1	1 2 3	1	1	1	1 2 3
$\partial Q_{T1} =$	0	0	+	+	+++	0	−	−	−−−
$\partial Q_{T2} =$	0	0	−	−	−−−	0	+	+	+++
$\partial Q_{\#1(VV)} =$	0	0	−	−	−−−	0	+	+	+++
$\partial Q_{\#2(VV)} =$	0	0	+	+	+++	0	−	−	−−−
$\partial P_{IN,OUT} =$	0	0	+	+	+++	0	−	−	−−−
$\partial P_{OUT,SMP} =$	0	0	−	−	−−−	0	+	+	+++
$\partial F_{\#1(S)} =$	0	0	−	−	−−−	0	+	+	+++
$\partial F_{\#2(S)} =$	0	0	+	+	+++	0	−	−	−−−
$\partial F_{A(M)} =$	0	+	+	+	− 0 +	−	−	−	− 0 +
$\partial V_{FP} =$	0	−	−	0	+++	+	+	0	−−−
$\partial F_{\#2(D)} =$	0	+	+	0	−−−	−	−	0	+++
$\partial F_{\#1(D)} =$	0	−	−	0	+++	+	+	0	−−−

sented in this section provide a procedure for constructing such interpretations. However, instead of operating on a given quantitative solution, our techniques operate directly on the qualitative laws that describe the behavior of components.

Second, the construction of the state diagram provides an example of how the combinatorial symbol manipulation capabilities of a computer can be used to provide an analytic tool. The power of this tool comes to light when one can introduce an arbitrary number of "nonlinear" distinctions for an individual component and have these distinctions (i.e., states) then be collapsed through interactions between neighboring components as governed by the rules for constructing the state diagram. Thus this tool provides a new mechanism for analyzing nonlinear systems.

5 Explanation of Behavior

Qualitative physics is concerned with both prediction and explanation. Explanations should be testable, compelling and succinct. By testable, we mean that it is possible to syntactically identify valid explanations. Thus, in particular, an explanation may not contain hidden assumptions about the behavior of the device. An explanation must be compelling and leave no doubt as to the validity of its conclusions. We could define an explanation as the execution trace of whatever algorithm is used to make the prediction. Although this form of explanation certainly meets the foregoing two desiderata, explanations are intended to communicate information and thus they also should be succinct. One structure that meets the two criteria of compellingness and succinctness is logical proof.

An explanation consists of a sequence of statements, $E_1, E_2, \ldots$, where each statement is justified by statements previous in the sequence. The confluences provided by the component models and the input signal(s) provide the givens. The justifications are in terms of simple logical inference steps on the statements. The explanation is expressed as a proof in a natural deduction system (Suppes, 1957). In this system the theorem is the prediction and the proof is the explanation; thus a theory of "explanation" (or at least a taxonomy of different kinds of structures for explanation) can be discovered from examining the different kinds of proof structures.

Each line of the proof consists of a line number (so it can be referenced), a statement, a justification of the statement, and a set of premises upon which the statement depends. The following is part of an explanation of why the valve starts to close (i.e., $\partial X_{FP} = -$) when an input pressure rise is applied (i.e., $\partial P_{IN,SMP} = +$) when the pressure-regulator is in its "normal" mode of operation (i.e., the valve is in state WORKING-+).

(1)	$\partial X_{FP} + \partial P_{OUT,SMP} = 0$	Given	{}
(2)	$\partial Q_{T2} - \partial P_{OUT,SMP} = 0$	Given	{}
(3)	$\partial Q_{\#2(VV)} + \partial Q_{T2} = 0$	Given	{}
(4)	$\partial Q_{\#1(VV)} + \partial Q_{\#2(VV)} = 0$	Given	{}
(5)	$\partial Q_{\#1(VV)} = +$	Premise	{5}
(6)	$\partial Q_{\#2(VV)} = -$	Substitution 5,4	{5}
(7)	$\partial Q_{T2} = +$	Substitution 6,3	{5}
(8)	$\partial P_{OUT,SMP} = +$	Substitution 7,2	{5}
(9)	$\partial X_{FP} = -$	Substitution 8,1	{5}

This explanationproof can be rendered into English as follows (the givens have been put in a more natural order). Suppose the flow into the inputside of the valve is increasing (5). As the valve conserves material (4), the flow into the outputside of the valve must be decreasing (6). As no material is gained or lost in the connection from the output of the valve to the output of the pressure-regulator (3), the flow out of the outputside of the pressure-regulator is increasing (7). As the flow through the load is proportional to the pressure across it (2), this results in an increased output pressure (8). This output pressure is sensed (1), and the area available for flow is reduced (9).

(All the explanationproofs presented in this paper are constructed automatically by our program, i.e., lines 1–9 are a verbatim output. The English text is added by us for expository purposes. Our program, ENVISION, takes a description of the physical structure of the device and a library of component models, constructs a model for the overall device, solves the model thereby making predictions, and produces explanations as illustrated.)

This particular explanation used three kinds of justifications corresponding to the application of three inference rules. "Given" indicates that the statement is a confluence obtained from the models or from the applied input signal. "Substitution $n_1, \ldots, n_i, m$'' indicates that value assignments $n_1, \ldots, n_i$ are substituted into confluence m. "Premise" indicates an arbitrary unsubstantiated assignment introduced to make the explanation go through. Note that lines 1–9 do not explain the necesity of $\partial X_{FP} = -$ because the underlying premise (5) $\partial Q_{\#1(VV)} = +$ has not been substantiated. In a conventional natural deduction system one would derive the statement

$$(9') \quad \partial Q_{\#1(VV)} = + \supset \partial X_{FP} = - \qquad \text{CP 9,5} \qquad \{\}$$

by conditional proof. Namely, if it can be shown that $\partial Q_{\#1(VV)} = +$ then $\partial X_{FP} = -$. In English: suppose the flow into the inputside of the valve is increasing, then the area available for flow is reduced. However, from the three inference rules, there is no way to show that $\partial Q_{\#1(VV)} = +$ necessarily follows.

5.1 The Crucial Role of Indirect Proof

It can, however, be shown that $\partial Q_{\#1(VV)} = +$ by arguing that $\partial Q_{\#1(VV)} \neq +$ is contradictory and thus by *reductio ad absurdum* (abbreviated RAA), $\partial Q_{\#1(VV)} = +$, namely by an indirect proof. As a qualitative variable can have only three values it is sufficient to show that $\partial Q_{\#1(VV)} = 0$ is contradictory and $\partial Q_{\#1(VV)} = -$ is contradictory. We need to introduce three new types of inference rules. "Unique Value n,m" indicates that the assignments of lines n and m directly contradict each other. "RAA n,m" indicates the contradictions of line n and m force an assignment by reductio ad absurdum. "Discharge $n,m_1, \ldots, m_i$" indicates that the assignments of lines $m_1, \ldots, m_i$ can be used to remove unsubstantiated premises from line n. "RAA" and "Discharge" derive directly from natural deduction systems. "Unique Value" is a short-hand for a lemma derived from a simple axiomatization of equality: every variable must have one and only one value. More formally:

$$x = + \lor x = 0 \lor x = -$$

$$x = + \supset x \neq - \land x \neq 0$$

$$x = 0 \supset x \neq + \land x \neq -$$

$$x = - \supset x \neq 0 \land x \neq +$$

With this additional inferential machinery, i.e., the machinery of indirect proof, we can proceed to prove or explain why the valve will start to close when the input pressure is increased. The remaining 21 steps of the proof for the pressure-reg-ulator's behavior discharge the assumption that $\partial Q_{\#1(VV)} = +$. Note that some of the confluences only play a role in the discharging, hence they do not appear in the proof until these steps.

(10)	$\partial P_{IN,OUT} - \partial Q_{\#1(VV)} + \partial X_{FP} = 0$	Given	$\{\}$
(11)	$\partial P_{IN,OUT} + \partial P_{OUT,SMP} - \partial P_{IN,SMP} = 0$	Given	$\{\}$
(12)	$\partial Q_{\#1(VV)} = 0$	Premise	$\{12\}$

(13)	$\partial Q_{\#2(VV)} = 0$	Substitution 12,4	$\{12\}$
(14)	$\partial Q_{T2} = 0$	Substitution 13,3	$\{12\}$
(15)	$\partial P_{OUT,SMP} = 0$	Substitution 14,2	$\{12\}$
(16)	$\partial P_{IN,SMP} = +$	Given	$\{\}$
(17)	$\partial P_{IN,OUT} = +$	Substitution 16,15,11	$\{12\}$
(18)	$\partial X_{FP} = -$	Substitution 12,17,10	$\{12\}$
(19)	$\partial X_{FP} = 0$	Substitution 15,1	$\{12\}$
(20)	False	Unique Value 18,19	$\{12\}$
(21)	$\partial Q_{\#1(VV)} = -$	Premise	$\{21\}$
(22)	$\partial Q_{\#2(VV)} = +$	Substitution 21,4	$\{21\}$
(23)	$\partial Q_{T2} = -$	Substitution 22,3	$\{21\}$
(24)	$\partial P_{OUT,SMP} = -$	Substitution 23,2	$\{21\}$
(25)	$\partial P_{IN,OUT} = +$	Substitution 16,24,11	$\{21\}$
(26)	$\partial X_{FP} = -$	Substitution 21,25,10	$\{21\}$
(27)	$\partial X_{FP} = +$	Substitution 24,1	$\{21\}$
(28)	False	Unique Value 26,27	$\{21\}$
(29)	$\partial Q_{\#1(VV)} = +$	RAA 28,20	$\{\}$
(30)	$\partial X_{FP} = -$	Discharge 9,29	$\{\}$

In English: Suppose the flow into the inputside of the valve were not increasing, but unchanging (12). Then by conservation (4), the flow into the outputside of the valve is also unchanging (13), and again by conservation (3), the output flow of the pressure-regulator is unchanging (15). As flow through the load is proportional to the pressure across it (2), there is no output pressure change (15). Now, we are given that the pressure-regulator input pressure is rising (16), and since the difference of pressure-regulator input and output pressures appears across the valve (11), the increased input pressure appears across the valve (17). In the situation where there is no change in flow and there is an increase in pressure, there must (10) be a decrease in area available for flow through the valve (18). On the other hand, if there is no change in output pressure there cannot be a (1) a change in area (19). Thus assuming that the flow is unchanging leads to a contradiction (20), the flow cannot be unchanging. The only possibility that remains is that the flow into the valve is decreasing (21). By an identical line of argument, (21–28), that assumption also leads to a contradiction. Hence by indirect argument the flow into the inputside of the valve is increasing (29). Thus the area available for flow is decreasing (30).

The intuitive notion of a compelling explanation can now be stated precisely, namely, one which does not depend on any undischarged premises. In the previous example, (30) $\partial X_{FP} = -$ must necessarily follow. Qualitative analysis can sometimes be ambiguous, thus it is not always possible to discharge all the premises. Consider the case where the input pressure is lower than the output pressure (i.e., in state WORKING--). In this situation all the confluences remain the same except the valve confluence:

$$\partial P_{IN,OUT} - \partial Q_{\#1(Vv)} - \partial X_{FP} = 0$$

This is the same confluence as line (10) in the above explanationproof, except that the sign of the area change is inverted. This is because of the behavioral characteristic of the valve that an increase in area available for flow always reduces the *absolute value of the pressure drop*. If the pressure drop is a positive value, an increase in area decreases it towards zero (as in the previous analysis). If the pressure drop is a negative value, an increase in area increases it towards zero. The resulting analysis is ambiguous, in principle, and no unique value can be found for ∂X_{FP}. The following are explanationproofs for the two possible values for ∂X_{FP}.

(1)	$\partial X_{FP} + \partial P_{OUT.SMP} = 0$	Given	{}
(2)	$\partial Q_{T2} - \partial P_{OUT.SMP} = 0$	Given	{}
(3)	$\partial Q_{\#2(VV)} + \partial Q_{T2} = 0$	Given	{}
(4)	$\partial Q_{\#1(VV)} + \partial Q_{\#2(VV)} = 0$	Given	{}
(5)	$\partial Q_{\#1(VV)} = -$	Premise	{5}
(6)	$\partial Q_{\#2(VV)} = +$	Substitution 5,4	{5}
(7)	$\partial Q_{T2} = -$	Substitution 6,3	{5}
(8)	$\partial P_{OUT.SMP} = -$	Substitution 7,2	{5}
(9)	$\partial X_{FP} = +$	Substitution 8,1	{5}

(1)	$\partial X_{FP} + \partial P_{OUT.SMP} = 0$	Given	{}
(2)	$\partial Q_{T2} - \partial P_{OUT.SMP} = 0$	Given	{}
(3)	$\partial Q_{\#2(VV)} + \partial Q_{T2} = 0$	Given	{}
(4)	$\partial Q_{\#1(VV)} + \partial Q_{\#2(VV)} = 0$	Given	{}
(5)	$\partial Q_{\#1(VV)} = +$	Premise	{5}
(6)	$\partial Q_{\#2(VV)} = -$	Substitution 5,4	{5}
(7)	$\partial Q_{T2} = +$	Substitution 6,3	{5}
(8)	$\partial P_{OUT.SMP} = +$	Substitution 7,2	{5}
(9)	$\partial X_{FP} = -$	Substitution 8,1	{5}

(We could also show that $\partial X_{FP} \neq 0$.) The point is that no proof exists for discharging or contradicting the assumptions of either line 5. *When the analysis is ambiguous, compelling explanations cannot, in principle, exist.*

Allowing assumptions in explanation opens the floodgates to an extremely serious problem: arbitrarily many explanations are now syntactically valid and appear plausible. By allowing unsubstantiated premises we, in effect, allow a proof for $A \supset B$ to be an explanation of B. If A is false, the implication is still valid but the proof may provide no information about the validity or the plausibility of B. It is impossible to tell from an explanation alone whether or not its outstanding assumptions can be ruled out. It is hard to show that a particular premise will not be discharged or contradicted. For example, in the foregoing two proofs no further sequence of statements can contradict or discharge the remaining assumptions (without, of course, introducing other assumptions which themselves cannot be discharged, etc.). In general, to show that the theorem $A \supset B$ and its explanationproof is the best result achievable requires showing that A is neither necessarily true nor false. (From a model theory point of view, the theory has at least two *logical interpretations*.) If A were true, we would have a compelling explanation of B alone. If A were false, $A \supset B$ is trivially true. However, one cannot tell from a proof for $A \supset B$ whether it is also possible to determine the validity of A. An even more difficult result to explain is that the given set of interpretations is complete, i.e., there exist no other theorems of the form $A \supset B$ for a behaviorally different B and for which A cannot be proved to be true or false.

For most devices, no explanation exists within the calculus which does not include premises. However, the local ambiguity can often be resolved because the device's behavior exhibits no global ambiguity (i.e., the premise can often be discharged). Thus there are two fundamentally different roles for assumptions which are locally indistinguishable. An assumption either can represent a global ambiguity or can be a temporary construction to enable an explanationproof to go through. The latter type of local ambiguity arises because the system is inherently simultaneous.

5.2 Proof as Explanation

There are four undesirable characteristics of explanationproof that are symptomatic of its inadequacy as a theory of explanation: (a) the introduction of premises into an explanation is unmotivated and arbitrary; (b) indirect proofs are intuitively unsatisfying; (c) explanationproofs are nonunique; and (d) explanationproofs may be causally inverted. We explore each of these in detail.

Premises are introduced because of local ambiguity but can often be resolved because the device's behavior exhibits no global ambiguity. Even so, the premise must be introduced arbitrarily in the explanationproof (and later discharged). Although this might seem plausible if the device's behavior were globally ambiguous, it seems questionable that explanations of unambiguous behavior should be so arbitrary. As the choice of assumption is not determined, usually many different assumptions will independently lead to valid explanations of the same behavior.

Indirect arguments are counterintuitive. One would like explanations to consist of steps, each describing correct behavior which follows by applying a component model rule to functionings described in earlier steps (something like the proof but without RAA). Neither is the case for indirect explanationproofs. The steps may refer to hypothetical functionings which do not actually occur and a justification might be RAA. Indirect proofs explain a consequence by showing that all alternative consequences do not happen, and thus cannot establish a simple relationship between a cause and its effect.

The same conclusion can have many proofs, none of which can be identified as the "correct" one. Hence, there may be multiple explanationproofs of a device's functioning. Although it might make sense in a few cases to have two or three explanations of how a device behaves, it makes little sense to have multiple explanations of a device's behavior *at the same grain size of analysis*. Remember that we are considering explanations of the same behavior in terms of the same component models. Multiple explanations can sometimes arise because the confluences are redundant, but more commonly arise due to the arbitrary choice of premise. In our framework there usually exist an extremely large number of syntactically acceptable valid proofs, but it is straightforward to eliminate most of them by employing a minimality condition. However, there still remain roughly fifteen different explanations of the pressure-regulator's unambiguous behavior, corresponding to the different minimal combinations of premises that can be introduced to analyze the device. A particularly undesirable one is obtained by introducing premises about ∂X_{FP}. The explanation is now totally indirect.

(1)	$\partial X_{FP} = -$	Premise	$\{1\}$
(2)	$\partial Q_{\#2(VV)} + \partial Q_{T2} = 0$	Given	$\{\}$
(3)	$\partial P_{IN,OUT} - \partial Q_{\#1(VV)} + \partial X_{FP} = 0$	Given	$\{\}$
(4)	$\partial P_{IN,OUT} + \partial P_{OUT,SMP} - \partial P_{IN,SMP} = 0$	Given	$\{\}$
(5)	$\partial X_{FP} + \partial P_{OUT,SMP} = 0$	Given	$\{\}$
(6)	$\partial X_{FP} = 0$	Premise	$\{6\}$
(7)	$\partial P_{OUT,SMP} = 0$	Substitution 6,5	$\{6\}$
(8)	$\partial P_{IN,SMP} = +$	Given	$\{\}$
(9)	$\partial P_{IN,OUT} = +$	Substitution 8,7,4	$\{6\}$
(10)	$\partial Q_{\#1(VV)} = +$	Substitution 6,9,3	$\{6\}$
(11)	$\partial Q_{\#1(VV)} + \partial Q_{\#2(V2)} = 0$	Given	$\{\}$
(12)	$\partial Q_{\#2(VV)} = -$	Substitution 10,11	$\{6\}$
(13)	$\partial Q_{T2} = +$	Substitution 12,2	$\{6\}$
(14)	$\partial Q_{T2} - \partial P_{OUT,SMP} = 0$	Given	$\{\}$
(15)	$\partial Q_{T2} = 0$	Substitution 7,14	$\{6\}$

(16)	False	Unique Value 15,13	{6}
(17)	$\partial X_{FP} = +$	Premise	{17}
(18)	$\partial P_{OUT,SMP} = -$	Substitution 17,5	{17}
(19)	$\partial P_{IN,OUT} = +$	Substitution 8,18,4	{17}
(20)	$\partial Q_{\#1(VV)} = +$	Substitution 17,19,3	{17}
(21)	$\partial Q_{\#2(VV)} = -$	Substitution 20,11	{17}
(22)	$\partial Q_{T2} = +$	Substitution 21,2	{17}
(23)	$\partial Q_{T2} = -$	Substitution 18,14	{17}
(24)	False	Unique Value 23,22	{16}
(25)	$\partial X_{FP} = -$	RAA 24,16	{}

In English: Suppose the area available for flow were not changing (6). Then the sensor does not (5) sense any output pressure change (7). As the input pressure is rising, this rise must (4) appear across the valve (9). If the area available for flow is unchanging and the pressure across the valve is increasing, the flow into the input-side of the valve must (3) be increasing (10). As the valve conserves material (11) the flow into the outputside of the valve is decreasing (12) and as the output connection also conserves material (2), the flow out of the output of the pressure-regulator must be increasing (13). However, it was shown earlier that the output pressure was unchanging (7), and hence there can be (14) no change in flow through the load (15). This contradiction shows that the area available for flow must be changing (16). On the other hand, suppose the area available for flow is increasing (17), then the sensor must sense (5) a decrease in output pressure (18). An increase in input pressure and a decrease in output pressure dictate (4) the valve pressure decrease (19). By the same argument used in (10–13), the flow out of the pressure-regulator increases. However, it was shown earlier that the output pressure was decreasing (18), and hence there can be (14) no increase in flow through the load (23). This contradiction shows that the area available for flow cannot be increasing (24). As the area must be changing, and cannot be decreasing, it must be increasing (25).

In this explanation we see another undesirable feature of indirect explanations: the steps in the explanation do not follow any notion of causal order. The explanation proceeds from output to input. The key problem is that the explanationproof explains *why* the device must behave not *how* it behaves—the latter is the task of causal explanations.

6 Causality and Digital Physics

6.1 Causality

An explanation of device behavior may take many forms. For example, explanationproofs explain behavior in terms of inference steps within a formal system. By causal account, we mean a particular kind of explanation that is consistent with our intuitions for how devices function, i.e., causality. Device behavior arises out of time-ordered, cause-effect interactions between neighboring components of the device. In these last two sections of the paper we attempt to derive a notion of causality within our qualitative framework. Our goal is to define a notion of causality that will make it possible to account for the behavior described in explanationproofs in a causal manner like that of a state diagram.

The state diagram embodies the classical notion of causality. Every change of state is attributable to a change in a specific variable: effects have unique causes. Action is local as the variable causes state change in adjacent components: the cause is structurally near the effect. The states are time-ordered: a cause comes before the effect. The state diagram is unique not depending on external arbitrary choices of variables as explanationproofs do.

While the state diagram provides causal explanations of state termination, it does not provide causal explanations of behavior within a state, i.e., why the behavior is what it is within a state. Few of the causal criteria hold for an explanationproof which describes behavior within a state. In an explanationproof, the reasons for a variable's value are nonunique. RAA, which is necessary, is nonlocal. There is no time-order among the settings for the variables. And there are multiple explanationproofs of any particular variable value.

Why introduce the notion of causality when the predictive theory seems sufficient for accounting for behavior within a state? We want a theory that describes *how* devices function when there are no state changes and not just what their behavior is. The confluences and the solution algorithms say nothing about *how* the device functions. Instead the confluences are merely constraints on behavior and the algorithm a method of constraint satisfaction. The explanationproof says little about how the device functions, and instead only proves that the particular instance of constraint satisfaction is correct. In short, it embodies the epistemological principle, "There is a reason for everything" at the expense of the ontological principle, "Everything has a cause."

Before delving into a detailed discussion of how causal explanations are produced, let us review the reasons why we care about creating them, both from an ontological and an epistemological perspective. Causality as a theory of how devices function provides many advantages. Because it is a theory of how the device achieves its behavior rather than just what its behavior is, it provides an ontologically justified connection between the structure of the device and its functioning. It is now possible to ask what functional changes result from hypothetical structural changes (a task important in troubleshooting). Without causality this question could only hope to be answered by a total reanalysis. (Thus, causality also provides an approach to solving the frame problem (Hayes 1979).) Because it describes how behavior is achieved by the device, more information about the behavior can be uncovered. For example, feedback, which alters the behavior of the device, can only be recognized definitively by understanding how the device achieves its behavior. This is because feedback is a property of functioning, not of behavior. Since causality is a universal mode of understanding functioning it provides a medium by which the functioning of a device can be explained, by a designer to a user, by a teacher to a student, etc. Finally, since causal accounts are so universally adopted as the model of understanding, most common patterns of causal interactions around individual components have been identified and abstracted and often form the basic elements of the technical vocabularies of a given field. These abstractions are a kind of *canonical form* which can be used as indices into other knowledge about device behavior. For example, a transistor operating in the mode in which the base is the causal input and the collector the causal output has a technical name called the common-emitter configuration. Once a transistor's configuration has been identified as being an instance of the common-emitter (amplifier) then one knows important things about that circuit's gain and frequency response—things that would be impossible to derive from the prediction of the qualitative behavior alone.

6.2 Two Impediments to Causality

We want to devise a theory of causality which can explain behavior within a state, i.e., when there is no component state change involved. Two related problems concerning time and RAA make it difficult to define a coherent notion of intrastate causality that meets our intuitive criteria. Consider the analytical model for the valve discussed earlier

$$Q = CA \sqrt{\frac{2P}{\rho}}.$$

This equation is based on the assumption that any change in flow occurs simultaneously with any change in pressure. Of course, this is an approximation. Although it may be true that a change in pressure somehow causes a change in flow a moment later (through perhaps a pressure wave), this inference draws on knowledge about fluids not expressed in that equation. Mathematical laws of this type do not admit any such temporal or causal inferences.

Time-order remains a problem in the qualitative domain. Consider the confluence $\partial P - \partial Q = 0$. From this, one can infer that if $\partial P = +$ then $\partial Q = +$. But it is incorrect to say that $\partial Q = +$ was caused by $\partial P = +$, because ∂Q has to become $+$ simultaneously with ∂P becoming $+$. If ∂Q cannot be $+$, ∂P cannot be $+$.

The basic intuition behind our notion of a causal account is that the behavior of the device is produced by interacting individual processors — one processor per component. Each processor (a) has limited ability to process and store information, (b) can only communicate with processors of neighboring components, (c) acts on its neighbors which in turn act on their neighbors, and (d) contributes only once to any particular behavior for each disturbing influence.

Each processor is programmed to satisfy the model confluences. Whenever all but one of the values around a component is known, it will (if possible) determine the last one. For example, if the model confluence were $\partial Q = \partial P_{in} - \partial P_{out}$ it would produce $\partial Q = +$ if it discovered from its immediate neighbors that $\partial P_{in} = +$ and $\partial P_{out} = 0$. Note that the logical power of these combined processors operating in this

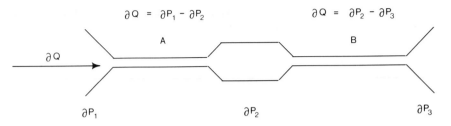

Figure 12. Two narrow pipes (constrictions) in series

fashion is no greater than the natural deduction schemes described earlier without RAA. As the inclusion of RAA is critical to attaining completeness, programming the processors in this manner is inadequate for realizing the behavior of certain devices. Consider an example of two narrow pipes (i.e., constrictions not conduits) connected in series as illustrated in Figure 12. The models are simplified to reference only flow variable ∂Q. Suppose $\partial P_3 = 0$ and $\partial P_1 = +$. The processor for constriction A cannot determine ∂Q or ∂P_2 because the value of only one of its confluence variables is known. The case for constriction B is similar. However, given $\partial P_3 = 0$ and $\partial P_1 = +$, then $+$ is the only possible value for ∂P_2. Suppose it were not. Then, either $\partial P_2 = 0$ or $\partial P_2 = -$. If $\partial P_2 = 0$, then the program for constriction B produces $\partial Q = 0$, and the processor for constriction A produces $\partial Q = +$. These two values are contradictory, hence ∂P_2 cannot be zero. If $\partial P_2 = -$, the processor for constriction A produces $\partial Q = +$, and the processor for constriction B produces $\partial Q = -$. Again a contradiction. Thus $\partial P_2 = +$ by a reductio ad absurdum argument. (This is exactly the type of problem that made it impossible to construct an explanationproof of the behavior of the pressure-regulator; the first proof of Section 5 could not go through without introducing some assumption ($\partial Q_{\#1(VV)} = +$).) There seems to be no way to change the confluences (nor their form) to satisfy locality and fidelity while avoiding the use of RAA.

The impediment to causality raised by RAA is not easily avoided. It is not solely a property of our qualitative physics. Consider the quantitative analysis of Figure 12. The equations describing the behavior are (for brevity we use dx to refer to the time derivative of x).

$$dP_3 = 0 \tag{1}$$

$$dP_1 = a > 0 \tag{2}$$

$$dQ = k(dP_1 - dP_2) \tag{3}$$

$$dQ = k(dP_2 - dP_3) \tag{4}$$

These are four equations in four unknowns. There is no way to solve these equations one at a time. Both equations 3 and 4 reference unknowns dQ and dP_2. To solve this system, equations 3 and 4 have to be considered simultaneously. Equations 1 and 2 are easily eliminated through substitution:

$$dQ = k(a - dP_2) \tag{5}$$

$$dQ = kdP_2 \tag{6}$$

Equating 5 and 6 gives

$$kdP_2 = k(a - dP_2)$$

which can be solved

$$dP_2 = a/2.$$

Thus the quantitative analysis also cannot be done in single steps and requires something like RAA to determine a solution.

Even if we "push a level" the RAA problem is not avoided. Suppose the constrictions are modeled as a sequence of smaller constrictions. If the same constriction model is used, the RAA problem only becomes more complex as one is required for each constriction fragment. Of course, if the fragment is modeled as a simple pressure transporter (i.e., $\partial P_{in} = \partial P_{out}$), each smaller constriction can directly communicate a pressure rise without using RAA. Although, this model successfully shows that the P_2 rises and seems intuitively compelling, it is only a post-hoc rationalization. This simple constriction fragment model does not, in general, predict correctly. For instance, in this same example, as P_2 rises, so must P_3, but this cannot be since P_3 is fixed as a given. The simple model (i.e., $\partial P_{in} = \partial P_{out}$) only applies in limited situations, e.g., all cases where $\partial Q = 0$, but the confluence gives no aid in identifying these situations. The correct model for the constriction fragment at this level is $\partial Q = \partial P_{in} - \partial P_{out}$, but nothing is gained by pushing a level and keeping the component models the same.

A more appropriate way to "push a level" is to model the material in the constrictions as having momentum and the constrictions themselves as having storage capacity. A quantitative analysis of this behavior results in a fourth-order differential equation. The essential characteristic of the solution is that it is oscillatory (but damped). The pressures and amounts in the two constrictions rise and fall repeatedly, but each time the rise is a little less than the previous time and the fall is not as far. Each constriction can contain more or less material and once the material starts to move left or right it gathers momentum and overshoots its quiescent position. Thus not much has been gained. In order for this lower-level system to "find" the higher-level equilibrium solution requires repetitive oscillation back and forth of material between the two constrictions. This kind of "negotiation" does not satisfy the one interaction per disturbance criterion for a causal account.

This lower-level or finer-grain analysis can also be done qualitatively. Each constriction is described by two mixed confluences one characterizing momentum and the other storage capacity. As a result there are four mixed confluences resulting in a state diagram with 81 states. Thus two immediate problems come to the fore. First, the resulting state diagram has additional states and state transitions which can only be resolved with unavailable lower-level information. Second, even if the ambiguities could be resolved, it would show behavior of no interest at the original level. For example, if the "correct" state trajectory could be determined through the ambiguous state diagram, it would be a lengthy sequence representing a damped oscillation to the final values, not a simple direct state transition to the final values. In summary, pushing a level brings up distinctions about which we have no information at the original grain-size and results in an extremely complex state diagram most of whose details are of no conern. Pushing a level may introduce more harm than good.

All these complications and impediments concerning causality come as a result of asking the question "How does change come about?" Modern physics tends to side step this question by adopting a modeling perspective which cannot, in principle, account for change. The central thermodynamical principle that underlies the construction of almost every model is that of quasistatic approximation: the device is presumed always to be infinitesimally near equilibrium. Of course, if the actual device behavior is examined in sufficient detail, one must observe some nonequilibrium intermediate states, otherwise the device could not change state! It is extremely important to note that his problem does not come from the particular laws we have been working with but rather the form of these laws. As was practically illustrated in the previous paragraphs pushing a level without changing the form of the laws does not help. It does not help, because it cannot help. Therefore, in our physics we do not futilely change the level of analysis to obtain causality, but rather change the interpretation of the laws.

6.3 The Correspondence Principle of Mythical Causality

"Time and space are not things but orders of things."—Gottfried Leibniz.

Our solution is to leave the original models unchanged, but define a new kind of causality (which we call *mythical* causality) that describes the trajectory of nonequilibrium "states" the device goes through before it reachieves a situation where the quasistatic models are valid. We introduce the idea of mythical time, which has most of the properties of conventional time, except that it imposes a partial not total order. No conventional time passes between mythical time instants. During mythical time instants, the component laws may be violated, but eventually (in mythical time) all the component laws must hold again.

The component laws and the definition of mythical time are insufficient to unambiguously specify what occurs during the mythical time instants, and a set of criteria must be laid down to restrict some of the options. These additional criteria help to *reconstruct* what the behavior below the quasistatic level *must have been* if the world were causal. The first criterion is to *presume* that the causal action below the grain-size of analysis (of the classwide assumptions) is of a similar form as the causal action that is explicitly represented in the state diagrams. Thus, interactions are local, a cause is always before an effect, every effect has a cause, etc.

The second criterion is deceptively simple: whatever behavior occurs below the quasistatic level, the values of the variables must start with one set of equilibrium values and eventually reach another. We assume that this intervening behavior is as simple as possible.

A difference between the causal action above the grain-size level and below it is that the first takes time and the second does not. If A causes B, we will always say B occurs after A, but no time need pass between A and B. We call causal action below the grain-size level mythical causality and time flow below the grain-size level mythical time.

Mythical causality is, of course, summarizing physical action taking place at a lower level. As discussed in the previous section, no model of the form we have been discussing is adequate. Here is one approach adapted from Feynman, Leighton, and Sands (1963). Assume that the constriction is made of a sequence of *identical* constriction fragments, each having "momentum" and "storage capacity." The idea is that every constriction fragment gets a small piece of the total "momentum" and "storage capacity." So far we have made one simplifying assumption (all fragments are identical) and one complicating assumption (many fragments), and the analysis is still subject to the just stated problems. Now take the limit, that is, break the constriction into an "infinite" number of fragments where each piece has an infinitesimal amounts of "momentum" and "storage capacity." If the mathematics is done correctly, the resulting equation describing the behavior of the constriction is

$$u_{tt} = c^2 u_{xx}.$$

Where $u(x,t)$ is either the pressure or flow at position x at time t. u_{tt} is the second partial derivative of $u(x,t)$ with respect to t and u_{xx} is the second partial derivative of $u(x,t)$ with respect to position. This expression is known as the wave equation because its only solutions are of the form

$$u(x,t) = f(x - ct).$$

This is a wave because as time passes the overall pattern of values of u just shifts with velocity c, e.g., as t changes from 0 to 1 the values of $u(0,0)$, $u(1,0)$, and $u(2,0)$ become the values for $u(0,c)$, $u(1,c)$, and $u(2,c)$. Applying this equation to the constriction (under appropriate boundary conditions) results in a solution of a wave traveling back and forth between the component producing the effect and the component which is recipient of the effect. The wave itself traverses the constriction undiminished, but every time the receiving component reflects it back the amplitude is slightly reduced and the wave eventually damps out. We can interpret this solution as a kind of negotiation underlying RAA that sends information back and forth between the causing and caused component in order to decide what the equilibrium effect will be. Of course this view is an interpretation of the observed wave transmissions and reflections and is not explicit in the mathematics.

6.4 The Causal Process

Having dealt with some conceptual objections we now return to the main theme: how can the processors be programmed such that the informational interactions between neighboring processors satisfy our desiderata for causality? Before proceeding, let us summarize the stage of development we have reached. The device is initially presumed to be at equilibrium, i.e., the confluences of all the component processors are satisfied. Then a disturbance arrives which causes a disequilibrium. The device then equilibrates in mythical time until an equilibrium is again established. At mythical time instants, the confluences are not necessarily satisfied. Quite the opposite; *it is the violation of the confluences that result in causal action.* In the previous subsections, we presented various schemes for programming the processors, none of which met our desiderata for causality. In these subsections, we introduce additional processor architecture and a set of heuristics that enable the processors to meet our desiderata for causality.

We extend the architecture to allow the processors to distinguish between a new equilibrium value and an old equilibrium value. Furthermore, for a single disturbance each variable can change value exactly once, from its old equilibrium value to its new equilibrium value. (Note that the new equilibrium values are not necessarily different than the old equilibrium values.) Each processor is programmed to produce new equilibrium values that satisfy its component's confluences. Whenever all but one of the new equilibrium values of a component confluence are known, the final variable is set to its new equilibirum value (as dictated by our qualitative arithmetic).

One result of this processor architecture is that the set of variables with new equilibrium values grows monotonically in mythical time, while the set of old equilibrium values decreases monotonically. In addition the set of new equilibrium values is topologically connected (with respect to the device's structure), and slowly grows outwards from the initial disturbance. Therefore, there is always a well-defined *fringe* of processors between the new and old equilibrium values.

This approach does not prevent the processors from becoming ''stuck'' in the sense of needing RAA (as demonstrated by Figure 12). Indeed, the need for RAA is inescapable—a fundamental challenge to the classical notions of causality. Suppose we introduce RAA, but in a limited form. A processor can introduce an assumption[17] by assigning $+$, $-$, or 0 value to a variable, but only if: (a) it is just beyond the fringe, i.e., it still has an old equilibrium value and a component confluence exists linking this variable to a variable having a new equilibrium value; and (b) every other processor on the fringe is also stuck. This severely restricts RAA, avoiding spuriously introducing assumptions for already known variables,

---

[17]This is an oversimplification. More accurately, it is the variables which are ''stuck,'' not the processors.

variables remote from the fringe and variables directly determinable without introducing additional assumptions. Although this solution severely limits the introduction of RAA, it is still needed: Every time all the fringe processors are stuck, one of the stuck processors must be arbitrarily selected and be allowed to arbitrarily assign +, −, or 0 to one of its variables such that it becomes unstuck. Because of this arbitrariness, the same device behavior may have many causal accounts. Thus RAA is still there with a vengeance.

At this stage in our research we do not have any principled way of distinguishing between these multiple accounts or identifying which ones are causal. Our desiderata of causality underconstrains the possibilities. To get around this obstacle, in the next section we introduce three heuristic rules for good guessing. Crucially, these rules are just part of the programming of the processors; they do not require access to global information and hence do not violate our desiderata for causality. We employ these three rules to push the fringe causally forward whenever it's stuck. In the next sections we present and make plausibility arguments for these rules, but we have no independent justification for them, except that they work for most of the cases we have tried (the cases on which they fail can be characterized). The causal account produced using them is a representative element of the equivalence class of possible causal accounts using the RAA scheme of the previous paragraph. We thus call these three rules the canonicality heuristics.

The canonicality heuristics, or "rules for good guessing," turn out to be better than one might think to be reasonable given that they were chosen empirically. They largely eliminate ambiguity and the necessity for backtracking yet produce causal accounts for all the possible behaviors. The rules eliminate ambiguity in that for most fringes of stuck processors, the rules introduce a single assumption, no less, and no more. This is somewhat remarkable because these processors are topologically disjoint and thus cannot make their "guesses" by consulting each other. Using these heuristics, we have never seen a case where an entire fringe got stuck (although we can easily invent pathological cases). In the few cases where assumptions are introduced (by multiple processors), the order rarely turns out to matter because the ensuing propagations do not interact (i.e., "race"). If the propagations do "race," then unwanted ambiguity in causal attributions results. In addition, the rules eliminate backtracking because the guesses are rarely wrong (i.e., in the sense that there does not exist an assignment of values to the remaining old equilibrium values which satisfies the confluences).

This state of affairs is not perfect. Although we propose no solutions to the outstanding problems, it is important to summarize how the theory of mythical causality we have arrived at is unsatisfactory. First, we have proposed no mechanism by which the processors on the fringe decide they are all stuck, except by postulating some kind of global polling that violates locality. Second, the canonicality heuristics seem to work, but not for any reason we yet understand. Do these rules reflect a property of the physical world, or perhaps just a cultural property of how humans understand? Third, the canonicality heuristics sometimes produce ambiguity (which is not too bad), but sometimes produces a wrong value (if backtracking which is antithetical to our desiderata for causality is not introduced).[18]

These objections make it impossible to "causally simulate" the behavior of a device. In our study of this theory, we have therefore taken a different approach. Our program ENVISION constructs *all* possible behaviors and *all* causal accounts for those behaviors which satisfy our theory of mythical causality. In this way, we sidestep the final objections. Ambiguity is not a problem: ENVISION produces all accounts. The problem of wrong values is sidestepped by eliminating all accounts that eventually contain contradictions. The price we wind up paying for this is that the resulting causal accounts do not have the compelling force of an explanationproof: A particular causal account does not indicate why alternate behaviors and causal accounts are not possible. The causal accounts produced by ENVISION are often just extremely good rationalizations.

The inability to "causally produce" a causal account of a device's behavior is not a fatal flaw from either an AI or psychological viewpoint. From a psychological perspective there is no reason to expect that the kind of problem solving that underlies constructing a causal account of how a device behaves would in its own right be causal—that is, never need to have access to global information, to backtrack from a decision, etc. Said differently, the problem solving underlying the construction of a causal account need have no relationship to the nearly trivial problem solving involved in executing a causal simulation. Envisioning is not just simulation. However, from a physics perspective the inability to causally produce a behavior is fatal. After all, nature seems to be able to determine what to do next in ways that satisfy our causal criteria. The need for RAA, as discussed previously, dashed that hope. Here, we have been exploring how to minimize the RAA damage in order to bring the machinery to produce a causal account into maximal alignment with the causal account itself. We can argue for this on the basis of simplicity alone, or from the point of view of probing the limits of causality in a digital physics.

6.5 Canonicality Heuristics

There may be many sets of canonicality heuristics that work. Ours, however, have one very important additional property: they have been abstracted from the kinds of argument people tend to use, i.e., from verbal and written explanations of device behavior. Therefore, a causal account generated by these three heuristics, in addition to having the desirable characteristics of causality, is the one human experts use. Thus the explanations generated are ones human's prefer. Of course, this set of particular heuristics is not only good for explanation, but as it is the conventional

---

[18]The fourth objection is the most serious, but also the least obvious: we propose no mechanism for dealing with intrinsic ambiguity resulting from multiple interpretations. Presumably a particular physical device has a single behavior and, in addition, the behavior of this particular device has a single causal account. (Note that a different physical device may have the same behavior, yet have a different causal account for this behavior.) However, both the behavior and its causal account are ambiguous in our formulation. How can a particular physical device select amongst the possibilities proposed by our theory?

terms our culture uses to explain behavior, it is at the base of the hierarchical abstract language our engineering culture uses to describe device behavior. Thus, for example, an expert AI system using our terminology can have access to the functional vocabularies and libraries engineers use. It is an intriguing question whether the particular set of rules and heuristics presented here are necessary as well as sufficient for accounting for device behavior.

On the one hand we want enough heuristics to be able to predict the behavior of all devices, while on the other hand we want them to be as few and as simple as possible. Furthermore, the heuristics should not predict behaviors which are not physically realizable.

Metaphorically speaking, the device can be viewed as the surface of a lake. The water surface is completely flat—the device is at equilibrium. The input disturbance corresponds to dropping a pebble in a lake which causes a wavefront to propagate from the spot where the pebble is dropped disturbing the surface of the entire lake. Complicating matters are the obstacles in the lake which cause the waves to reflect and interact with each other. The values of the device's variables correspond to the heights of the water at different places.

The wave on the lake surface metaphor best conveys the difficulty and the intuition behind the three heuristics that solve the problem. Take the simple case where a single disturbance propagates outwards without reflecting from intervening objects. The wave propagating outwards divides the surface into three regions: the region through which the wavefront has already passed, the region that no wave has yet reached and the region at the boundary between these two. The region that the wave has already passed has reestablished a new equilibrium, and the region it yet has to reach remains at its original equilibrium. As the wave propagates, the old equilibrium region decreases and the new equilibrium region increases. Eventually the new equilibrium completely dominates. The only disequilibrium exists exactly at the wavefront itself. A component "balanced" on the wavefront is partly within the region of the "old equilibrium" and partly in the region of the "new equilibrium." How does the component behave in this third region?

The confluence models apply directly to the equilibrium regions, and as a consequence of our correspondence principle, the equilibrium confluence models also apply to the third region. The confluences underdetermine what happens in the disequilibrium region. As a disturbance first reaches a component, some of its variables may be known, but not enough to apply a confluence. In exactly those situations where RAA is required in the logical analysis, the processors get "stuck," but the metaphorical wave continues on. The three heuristics are based on the intuition of an expanding wavefront, and prevent the processors from ever becoming stuck.

The confluence cannot capture the characteristic that a wavefront causes the new equilibrium to dominate the old. For components on the wavefront, behavior at connections within the new equilibrium region cause behavior at connections within the old equilibrium and dominate it. This is how the wave moves. At the moment the wave passes a component the new equilibrium values are assumed to be dominant (i.e., causal) and the old equilibrium values are assumed to be causally insignificant (i.e., as if they were zero). If some of the old equilibrium inputs are assumed to be zero, the confluences immediately apply and the processors are no longer "stuck." Now as the wave passes, the region of new equilibrium values grows slightly covering the old equilibrium values still attached to the component. Although the old equilibrium values are taken as zero, they need not be zero or become zero; more than likely they are not. The point is that just before the wave passed their values were insignificant with respect to the new equilibrium values and after the wave passed their values are consistent with the confluences. The heuristics capture the behavior of components in the short "blip" in which variables switch from their old equilibrium values to their new equilibrium values.

In summary, each heuristic applies only as a wavefront passes a component and introduces a particular assumption that allows the processors to continue propagating the disturbance *as if it were a wave*. The processor architecture and its associated criteria, define the form of mythical causal accounts, the heuristics dictate their content. Different sets of heuristics would result in different causal accounts although their form would be identical. These differing causal accounts are all of the same behavior but each may assign a different sequence of cause-effect interactions that produces it. Said differently, a theory of causality must assign causal directions to every possible interaction between components, but different sets of heuristics will assign different directions. Without any canonicality heuristics, the notion of causality would be very weak for it would admit many causal accounts for exactly the same behavior.

Significantly, the three canonicality heuristics apply for all disciplines (fluid, electrical, acoustic, rotational, etc.). They are presented here in terms of the pressure-regulator and thus are stated in terms of pressure and flow. In electrical systems, the same heuristics apply, but for voltage and current, etc.

The heuristics presented here will not always work for devices which contain negative resistances (e.g., in the mechanical domain an object with negative mass—easily stated in confluences but rare in the world). As negative resistances do occur, the heuristics can be modified to work for these as well although that is beyond the scope of the paper. We believe (but cannot prove) that the heuristics presented in the next section will work for all devices which do not contain negative impedance, have one disturbance, and have a single common reference.[19]

The component heuristic. If one "pushes" or "pulls" on one side of a component and nothing else is known yet to be acting on the component, the component responds as if the unknown actions are negligible.

Suppose the input disturbance has propagated to a change in a pressurelike variable at some component, say conduit 1 of component D (see Figure 13). (The pressure is changing significantly with respect to some common reference such as the main-sump, ground, etc.) Further, suppose that the disturbance has not yet

---

[19]An example of a device for which the heuristics, even embellished to handle negative resistance, fail are mechanical widgets which do analog multiplication (without logarithmic inputs, of course).

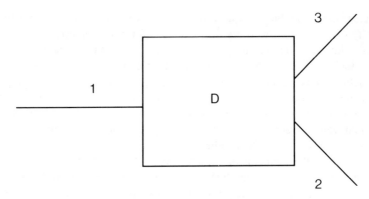

Figure 13. Component D

reached conduits 2 and 3. In this case, it seems reasonable to assume that whatever behavior results in conduits 2 and 3 is caused by the disturbance in conduit 1 propagated through component D. Although the behavior of D may depend on the pressure between conduits 1 and 2 (e.g., a pressure drop) and thus be inapplicable, it is plausible to assume that conduit 2 changes in response to conduit 1. The pressure change between conduits 1 and 2 is thus assumed to be the same as that between conduit 1 and the common reference. Thus component D will exhibit some behavior.

This heuristic is illustrated in the causal argument for the pressure-regulator. ENVISION states an application of the component heuristic as (see Figure 14): *The PRESSURE between conduits IN and OUT is increasing.*

Assume that the change in P#1(PRESSURE from terminal #1 to reference SMP) of QUANTITY-VALVE VV causes a corresponding change in P(PRESSURE between terminals #1 and #2).

The confluence for the valve is $\partial P + \partial A - \partial Q = 0$, where ∂P refers to the pressure across the valve—the pressure from conduit IN to conduit OUT. The input pressure rise is with respect to the reference conduit SMP, not conduit OUT. Therefore this confluence cannot be directly used. However, the disturbance has not yet reached conduit OUT, so its pressure cannot be changing with respect to the main-sump as the system is still at equilibrium there. Therefore the total input pressure rise must appear across the valve.

As the rest of the causal argument for the behavior of the pressure-regulator shows, the pressure at conduit OUT rises as a consequence (which is consistent with the overall causal argument). It is interesting to note that if the pressure rise in conduit OUT had been reached first, the pressure in conduit IN would also be predicted to rise but *the change of flow through the valve would be of opposite sign.* The causal order has a direct effect on the predictions of the heuristics. The latter behavior can arise only if the input disturbance had been applied to the conduit OUT, not to the conduit IN.

An application of an heuristic can be incorrect. There might be an alternate path

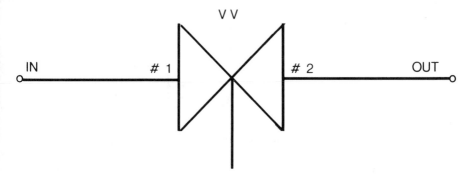

Figure 14. Component heuristic

from the initial input disturbance to terminal #2 of the valve. This might cause the change in pressure drop across the valve or result in the terminal #2 dominating terminal #1.

The conduit heuristic. If some component "sucks" stuff out of a conduit or "forces" stuff into a conduit the conduit's pressure drops or rises respectively.

The conduit heuristic is the only one that relates pressurelike and flowlike variables in a conduit. Like the other heuristic, this relationship describes the behavior of the components attached to the conduit, and not the behavior of the conduit in

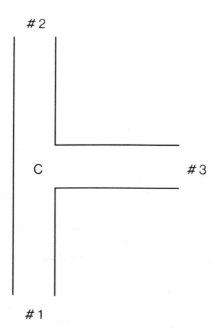

Figure 15. Conduit heuristic

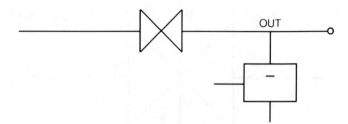

Figure 16. Conduit assumption for pressure-regulator

particular. It does not refer to "compressibility" of the material in the conduit. Suppose the input disturbance has propagated to a change in a flowlike variable of some conduit, say terminal #1 of conduit C (see Figure 15). Further, suppose that the disturbance has not yet reached terminals #2 and #3, nor the pressure of conduit C. In this case it seems reasonable to assume that whatever behavior results in conduit C is caused by the disturbance in terminal #1. The change of pressure in conduit C (with respect to the reference) is assumed to be the same as the change of flow out of terminal #1.

This heuristic is illustrated in the causal argument for the pressure-regulator. ENVISION states the application of a conduit heuristic as:

The PRESSURE between conduits OUT and SMP is increasing.

> *Assume that VOLUMETRIC-FLOW(s) produced by QUANTITY-VALVE VV cause a change in PRESSURE of conduit OUT.*

The conduit OUT has three terminals, one connected to the valve, another to the pressure sensor and yet another to the load. The input disturbance propagates through the valve preducing an increase of flow into the conduit OUT. By the conduit heuristic, the flow pushes up the pressure.

This heuristic is similar to the component heuristic in many ways. We may eventually discover that the flow into the load also increases. If that had been reached first, it would be regarded as pulling the pressure at the conduit OUT down. Thus the causal order has a direct effect on the prediction of the conduit heuristic. The latter behavior can only arise if the input disturbance originates in the load instead of the source of the pressure-regulator.

An application of the conduit heuristic an be incorrect. For instance, the disturbance might reach the conduit first through the valve. There might conceivably be an alternate path from the initial input disturbance to one of the other two terminals of the conduit OUT. This might determine the change in pressure at the conduit directly from the components attached to this conduit or result in the assumption that the changes in flows in these other terminals dominate the effects of the valve terminal.

The confluence heuristic. If some, but not enough, of the variables of a component confluence are known, propagate as if all but one of the unknown variables is zero. (This heuristic does not apply to compatibility and continuity constraints and only makes sense for model confluences having three or more variables—which are relatively rare.)

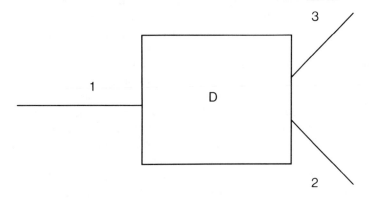

Figure 17. Confluence heuristic

The confluence heuristic is a generalization of the previous two. It applies when some of the quantities mentioned by a component confluence are known, but not enough to make a prediction. Suppose the input disturbance has propagated to a change in a variable at terminal #1 of component D (see Figure 17). Further, suppose that the disturbance has not yet reached terminals #2 or #3. In this case, it seems reasonable to assume that whatever behavior results around component D is caused by the disturbance at terminal #1. Thus the effects of the disturbance at terminal #1 can be predicted by assuming there is no disturbance at terminals #2 or #3.

Suppose the confluence for component D is $\partial x + \partial y + \partial z = 0$, where ∂x is associated with terminal #1, ∂y is associated with terminal #2, and ∂z is associated with terminal #3. From $\partial x = +$, we might assume that ∂y is negligible and that $\partial z = -$. Conversely we might assume that ∂z is negligible and that $\partial y = -$.

This heuristic is illustrated in the causal argument for the pressure-regulator.
The VOLUMETRIC-FLOW into terminal #1 of QUANTITY-VALVE VV is increasing.

Assume, given the confluence rule $\partial P + \partial A - \partial Q = 0$ for QUANTITY-VALVE VV, that the change(s) in P(PRESSURE between terminals #1 and #2) cause a corresponding change in Q(VOLUMETRIC-FLOW into terminal #2).

The valve confluence $\partial P + \partial A - \partial Q = 0$ mentions three variables: ∂Q, the flow through the valve; ∂P, the pressure across the valve; and ∂A, the change in area available for flow. The input pressure increase has propagated to an increase in pressure across the valve. By the confluence heuristic, the area available for flow can be assumed to be negligible and thus the increase in pressure causes an increase in flow through the valve. In the specific case of the valve, the converse (where the area is changed) is impossible as the area is an input-only variable of the valve.

A particular application of the confluence heuristic can be incorrect. However, the prediction of at least one of the possible applications for a particular confluence must hold. For example, from $\partial x = +$ and $\partial x + \partial y + \partial z = 0$, it must be the case that either $\partial y = -$, or $\partial z = -$, or both.

The three heuristics are all very similar. Each embodies the same intuition:

places where the disturbance has not yet reached are not changing. This assumption is only plausible because the device is at equilibrium before the disturbance is applied. Eventually more or different heuristics may be needed, but all heuristics should be of this general form. These three types work for a wide class of devices, but they do not work for all possible devices. In order for the heuristics to apply successfully: the device must be at equilibrium, the disturbance must originate at a single point, the disturbance must either be in a flowlike variable or a pressurelike variable with respect to a common reference conduit, the device must not contain any incremental negative resistances, and the device must have a distinguished conduit which can serve as a reference. By reference, we mean a common return, or sink, for all the material flowing in the conduits. For fluid systems the reference is a main-sump, for electrical systems it is ground, for translational systems it is the fixed reference frame.

6.6 Feedback

One of the additional advantages of mythical causal analysis over simple relaxation or explanationproof is that it is possible to determine the presence and effect of feedback. Relaxation predicts what the behavior would be (i.e., assignments of values to variables) but does not describe how the device achieves that behavior—a causal account does. Thus feedback, which is a characteristic of *how* the device functions, is only detectable using causal analysis.

In the words of Norbert Wiener (1954), "feedback is a method of controlling a system by reinserting into it the results of its past performance." More technically, feedback is defined as the transmission of a signal from a later to an earlier stage. We define feedback as occurring when a sequence of cause-effect interactions produces an effect on antecedents in the sequence. There is no new information to be gained by propagating this feedback signal around the loop again (ad infinitum), it is only important that this event occurs. Thus, once a processor has made a propagation, it becomes quiescent until the next state change no matter what variable values are discovered around it. Feedback is detected by noting when an attempt is made to reactivate it.

Most attempts to reactivate a processor are unimportant. Consider some of the possibilities if reactivation were permitted. When a processor produces a new value, the presence of this new value technically should reactivate the processor, but reactivating the processor could never produce anything different. Sometimes the same value can be produced two different ways, this would again reactivate neighboring processors but to no avail. An intuition behind the causal account is that neighbors act on neighbors until the input disturbance reaches the output. However, a neighbor will usually produce a backwards response as well as passing along the disturbance. For example, if the regulator output pressure across the load is increased, the load responds by drawing more flow from the regulator. This kind of degenerate feedback (which we call reflection) is, in fact, so common that its absence rather than its presence is a sign of something unusual. We define feedback as occurring when the processors of the cause-effect loop also form a loop in the structure (thus ruling out reflections which form a cause-effect loop, but not a structural loop).

Feedback is potentially present when a signal reaches a variable which was assumed to be insignificant according to an heuristic used in one of the signal's antecedents. The analysis of the pressure-regulator required the application of three heuristics, each of which could lead to feedback. The component heuristic (Figure 17) produces increased pressure drop across the valve, which results in increased flow through the valve which produces an increased flow out of the pressure-regulator and hence an increased output pressure. As there is no structural loop, there is no feedback (reflection, perhaps from an attached output load). The conduit heuristic (Figure 15) produces an increased output pressure for which there is no reflection. ENVISION would remark about this, except for the fact that this is a port to the external world about which it knows nothing. The component heuristic (Figure 14) is the only one that results in bona-fide feedback. The confluence for the valve is $\partial P + \partial A - \partial Q = 0$ but only ∂P is known thus far. This heuristic makes the assumption that ∂A is approximately zero, and thus ∂Q must be $+$. This results in increased output pressure which is detected by the sensor producing a decrease in A (i.e., $\partial A = -$). This cause-effect loop corresponds to a loop in the structure and hence represents feedback.

In addition to being able to detect the presence of feedback it is also possible to determine whether it is acting with or against the initial disturbance. In the example, a component heuristic for the valve applied an input disturbance ($\partial P = +$), to the confluence $\partial P + \partial A - \partial Q = 0$, assuming ∂A was insignificant to produce $\partial Q = +$. The subsequent chain of cause-effect interactions produces $\partial A = -$. Consider the effect of $\partial A = -$ would have if ∂P were insignificant. If ∂P were approximately 0, then the confluence would be $\partial A - \partial Q = 0$ and hence $\partial A = -$ would imply $\partial Q = -$. Thus the effect on Q is of opposite sign, and the feedback is negative. Note that $\partial A = -$ cannot completely dominate, because $\partial A = -$ only holds if $\partial Q = +$!

During the causal analysis no additional processing is done for the sake of feedback except that the above facts are noted. Having detected this property of the pressure-regulator's functioning, we can finally say something significant about its regulating action. The presence of negative feedback always reduces the gain of a stage, which is exactly what the pressure-regulator tries to do: lower the amplitude of any disturbance. The lower the gain of the pressure-regulator, the better it regulates pressure.

A causal account can also be represented graphically (see de Kleer & Brown, 1983, and de Kleer, 1979b, for examples). In the causal diagram, a node represents the assignment of a value to a variable and a directed edge represents the causal action of some component processor. Loops in the causal diagram correspond to feedback in the functioning of the device.

7 Summary

Intrastate behavior describes action within a state (i.e., the confluences governing behavior do not change), while interstate behavior describes action between states

Table 8. Summary of Modeling Results

	Acausal	Causal
Level 1:	Table 4	In this Section
Level 2:	Table 5 and Figure 9	

(i.e., as the confluences governing behavior change). We have discussed three techniques for analyzing behavior within a state. The first two, relaxation and natural deduction, produce acausal accounts. The third, which embodies the canonicality heuristics, produces causal accounts. We presented one technique for constructing the state (or episode) diagram. In addition, we have presented two sets of models for the pressure-regulator's components. The first set of models, call them the level 1 models, (first presented in Section 3) did not take account of the spring or the mass of the valve. The second set of models, call these the level 2 models, included models for the mass of the valve and the spring. Table 8 reviews the results of applying the analysis techniques to the different sets of models (we combine relaxation and natural deduction under the heading "acausal"). The result of applying acausal analysis to level 1 models was a simple assignment of values to derivatives (Table 4, Section 3). This analysis was inadequate in that it neither explained how that behavior was produced, nor revealed important characteristics about its operation such as oscillation. We then discussed two approaches to overcoming these shortcomings. The first of these (discussed in Section 4) took the approach of "pushing a level" in order to capture important properties about its operation in a greatly expanded state diagram. The second (discussed in Section 6) introduced mythical causality as an alternative analysis technique and did not "push a level."

It is crucial to observe that the account (causal diagram) produced using causal analysis with level 1 models is very similar to the account (state diagram) produced using acausal analysis with level 2 models. Both reveal important characteristics concerning the operation of the pressure-regulator. In particular, each reveals a loop indicating that the cause-effect interactions eventually fold back on themselves. However, in the causal analysis this is evidenced as feedback, while in the acausal analysis this is evidenced as oscillation. This is because oscillation and feedback are strongly related. Physically speaking, it always takes some time for the output to affect the functioning. Thus, if the output is changing, the device is always correcting its internal functioning based on an output value monitored earlier. As a consequence, all feedback devices tend to over- or undercorrect, thereby producing oscillation. The point is that any device that exhibits feedback necessarily exhibits oscillation when viewed at a lower-level. However, this oscillation often damps out so quickly (i.e., a quasistatic assumption) that it can be ignored.

As both analyses say similar things about the pressure-regulator's behavior, the question rearises whether introducing mythical causality was worth the bother. There are two independent answers to this question. First, note that Figure 9 combined with Table 4 does not explain how the state transitions themselves happen, so there cannot be an unbroken path of cause-effect interactions (covering many states) from the initial input behavior to eventual output. In causal analysis this path is unbroken. Second, the tremendous advantage of mythical causal analysis is that it did not have to "push a level" to detect feedback. Furthermore, in order to "push a level" more complex component models are needed and these might not be available.

7.1 Digital Physics

In a previous section, we discussed how to construct causal accounts for device behavior. These accounts were however constructed by viewing the device from outside. Can we construct a theory for how the device *itself* achieves its behavior? Can the device "decide" what to do next given the constraints that each component processor (a) has access to only local information, (b) has finite memory, and (c) is allowed one cause-effect interaction per disturbance. RAA demands these three cannot be achieved simultaneously. One of these criteria must be relaxed.

If we relax the criteria that the processors only have access to local information, i.e., that they can access as much information about all the components and all the variables as needed, a digital physics is possible although rather uninteresting. Each component processor could contain part of the algorithm discussed in the previous section and thus always make the "correct" assumption about what happens next.

If each processor or inter-processor message is allowed potentially unbounded memory a variety of strategies are available that trade off time against memory requirements. It is possible to include with each value a description of the processing steps that produced it. Then when a contradiction is discovered, this audit trail is consulted to determine which assumption to change. This is equivalent to chronological backtracking and tends to be inefficient in time but relatively efficient in memory usage. In this procedure values will be discovered in their mythical time-order. Another method is to propagate multiple values (only one of which is correct) whenever a choice is encountered. No backtracking is ever required: whenever a contradiction is discovered, values which depend on it are ignored. This strategy trades off memory for a gain in speed.

If more than one cause-effect interaction is allowed per disturbance, the processors can negotiate amongst neighbors in mythical time to determine what happens next. This negotiation process, if it is to succeed at all, needs to be carefully designed as the processors have limited memory. This approach makes an extreme tradeoff, utilizing only local information and little memory at a potentially enormous time cost. A simple negotiation scheme suggested by Hopfield (1982) is based on an idea of local stress or energy. Local energy is defined as how far a variable is away from satisfying all neighboring constraints. If each variable is changed (repetitively) to minimize local energy, the device will eventually find an assignment of values to variables which minimize the local energy for each component. Such a state corresponds to a global energy minimum and thus the device has reachieved equilibrium.

These three approaches are somewhat speculative, but point out some of the ways that a computational approach might be used to account for physical phenomena. Each approach has different predictions. If one of these approaches could be partially validated we would have the basis for a new branch of physics, one in which the flow of information plays as fundamental a role as the flow of energy and momentum.

Acknowledgments

This paper has existed in draft forms for so long (about two and one-half years) that innumerable people have read it and provided useful comments and arguments. We collectively thank them. In particular, the content of this paper benefited from extensive discussions with Ken Forbus, Dan Bobrow and Brian Williams. (This does not imply they agree with the contents however). They read this paper many times and we have incorporated many of their suggestions and good ideas. We also thank Jim Greeno, Russ Greiner, Tom Kehler, Kurt van Lehn, Robert Lindsay, Steve Locke, and Charles Smith for their useful comments. We thank Jackie Guibert for drawing many of the figures. We also thank Dana Bloomberg, Lisa Crupi, Jackie Guibert and Janice Hayashi for drawing figures, proofreading, and copying countless drafts.

Appendix A: Interpretations

Although the pressure-regulator is intended always to be operated under the conditions where the input pressure is higher than the output pressure (i.e., its valve always in state WORKING-+), the component models should correctly predict the behavior of the pressure-regulator under other boundary conditions as well. Otherwise the models for the components are presumed to be part of a working pressure-regulator—a violation of no-function-in-structure. The situation where the output pressure is higher than the input pressure is an unusual operating context for the pressure-regulator, and its behavior illustrates some interesting features. In this situation, all of the same confluences remain in force except that the valve is in state WORKING-- and thus the valve confluence is

$$\partial P_{IN.OUT} - \partial Q_{\#1(VV)} - \partial X_{FP} = 0.$$

Including the input disturbance, there are eight confluences in eight unknowns. Unlike the case when the pressure drop is positive, the pressure-regulator confluences have four solutions. That is there are four different assignments of values to variables that satisfies all the confluences:

Interpretation:	1	2	3	4
$\partial Q_{\#1(VV)} =$	−	+	+	+
$\partial Q_{\#2(VV)} =$	+	−	−	−

$\partial Q_{T2} =$	−	+	+	+
$\partial Q_{T1} =$	+	−	−	−
$\partial P_{IN,SMP} =$	+	+	+	+
$\partial P_{IN,OUT} =$	+	−	0	+
$\partial P_{OUT,SMP} =$	−	+	+	+
$\partial X_{FP} =$	+	−	−	−

The device can only manifest one of these behaviors at a time, but the confluences provide no information about which one is correct. We call these different behaviors for the same episode interpretations. Although these interpretations describe potentially unstable behavior (and hence only occur momentarily if they occur at all), it is possible to design pressure-regulators and to select operating conditions such that each interpretation arises. These potential problems with operating the valve in the reverse of its usual orientation is the reason systems are often designed to prevent such situations from arising.

The set of interpretations is the solution space of the confluences. This solution space describes physical reality in the sense that it specifies the behavior of the generic device. The behavior of every device of the generic type is accounted for within the solution space and every interpretation of the solution space is manifested by some device of the generic type within some operating context. This result is not a desiderata on our modeling but rather a direct consequence of obeying fidelity (and the no-function-in-structure principle) in modeling the individual components of the device correctly. It also provides an interesting example of qualitative prediction. Namely, as we originally modeled the pressure-regulator we had not considered the possibility of operating the pressure-regulator in the "reverse" mode (although a possibility we might have considered as part of some more global context) nor had we ever imagined that there would be multiple possible behaviors.

Interpretations 2, 3, and 4 are nearly identical except for $\partial P_{IN,OUT}$, which is left unconstrained. These three interpretations have the same explanation. As the input pressure rises towards the output pressure ($\partial P_{IN,SMP} = +$) the flow from the high-pressure side decreases ($\partial Q_{\#2(VV)} = -$), and thus the pressure at the output rises ($\partial P_{OUT,SMP} = +$). This increased pressure is sensed and fed back to the valve ($\partial X_{FP} = -$) which closes. This causality is the same as in the normal situation where the input is at higher pressure. In this situation, however, closing the valve reduces the flow from the high-pressure side even further, causing the output pressure to rise even more and thus resulting in positive feedback.

The reason why $\partial P_{IN,OUT}$ cannot be determined for these three interpretations is that there are two tendencies acting on it whose combination cannot be resolved. The valve confluence can be restated as

$$\partial P_{IN,OUT} = \partial X_{FP} + \partial Q_{\#1(VV)}.$$

On the one hand, the increase in flow from the high pressure side ($\partial Q_{\#1(VV)} = +$) tends to cause the pressure at the input to rise with respect to the pressure at the output ($\partial P_{IN,OUT} = +$). On the other hand, the increase in pressure at the output ($\partial P_{OUT,SMP} = +$) causes the valve to close ($\partial X_{FP} = -$), which tends to cause the pressure at the input to drop with respect to the pressure at the output ($\partial P_{IN,OUT} = -$). The result is that the change in pressure difference between input and output is not determinable:

$$\partial P_{IN,OUT} = \partial X_{FP} + \partial Q_{\#1(VV)}$$

$$\partial P_{IN,OUT} = (-) + (+)$$

$$\partial P_{IN,OUT} = ?$$

In this situation no other value depends on $\partial P_{IN,OUT}$ and the ambiguity is completely localized to one variable.

The first interpretation is radically different from the remaining three. As just illustrated, the pressure-regulator contains (potentially unstable) positive feedback. The positive feedback can make a device behave as if it contains a *negative resistance*. (We use the term negative resistance to describe the general situation where a pressurelike variable between two conduits varies inversely with the flow between these two conduits.) It is extremely unusual for an individual component to exhibit negative resistance. A device can exhibit a negative resistance without containing a negative resistor. In interpretation 1 an increased input pressure results in an increased flow *out of* the input, and thus from the point of view of the source, the pressure-regulator is acting like a negative resistance.

A.1 Origin of Ambiguity and its Importance
Depending on one's perspective, ambiguity is either a problem or advantage. Ambiguity is purely a result of inadequate information about the device. However, if we devised a modeling system which was less subject to ambiguity (e.g., the usual quantitative one), more detailed information might always be needed—detailed information that might not be available. Therefore a middle ground must be chosen that can utilize additional information, but does not require it. In this sense, ambiguity is an advantage. Given only the qualitative models, *the solution space of interpretations* is the best, in principle, that can be achieved. The results of the process outlined in Section 4 is thus so much not a prediction of future behavior, but rather a set of options which delimit the possible behaviors. This set of options describes the behavior of the generic device, any particular device will manifest one of the options (at a time).

To see what kind of additional information would be useful, we must examine why qualitative analysis is ambiguous and why quantitative analysis is not. Ambiguity is a consequence of the particular kind of qualitative value set we have chosen to use. In conventional quantitative analysis it is easy to construct n independent equations for n variables of the physical system, and n independent equations are always solvable for n unknowns. There are eight confluences in eight unknowns describing the pressure-regulator's behavior, yet there are four solutions to those confluences. The conventional theorems rely on the field axioms; however, the addition operation of Table 2 does not even form an algebraic group. Hence there is no reason to expect unique solutions.

While it is important to consider what sources of information are available for disambiguation, it is important to define the results of an ambiguous analysis first. An ambiguous analysis produces a set of interpretations, but that set characterizes *every* possibility. Any piece of additional information will serve to reduce the size of this set. To make effective use of new information the starting interpretation set must be complete; otherwise in the cases where the desired interpretation is missing, no additional information can result in a valid analysis.

The contents of Table 2 suggest an additional source of information to deal with ambiguity. The cases where addition is underdetermined could be resolved using information about the ordering of the variables. For example, $[X] + [Y] = +$, if $[X] = +$, $[Y] = -$, and $X > - Y$. Forbus suggests maintaining a partial order data structure among all the variables, and using this ordering information to resolve such ambiguous cases. He calls this partial order the Quantity Space representation. To be effective, the models must also include additional information about inequalities. Nevertheless, only a few of the inequalities will probably be known and therefore the behavior may still be ambiguous or may require drawing very sophisticated inferences about inequalities. For example, suppose we wanted to determine the qualitative value of the sum $X + Y + Z + Q$ where $X = +$, $Y = +$, $Z = -$ and $Q = -$. In the qualitative algebra, this value ($[X[+ [Y] + [Z] + [Q]$) is underdetermined, but if the Quantity Space contained $X > - Z$ and $Y > - Q$ the qualitative value of the sum must be $+$.

Appendix B: A Procedure for Constructing the Expanded Episode Diagram

The existence of multiple interpretations introduces another measure of complexity. Within a given composite device state the device can change its behavior by exhibiting first one interpretation and then another. Thus the same composite state may give rise to multiple episodes.

If the requirement is added that all nonderivative variables be constant during an episode then the procedures outlined in this section work as well for pure as mixed component models. By allowing mixed confluences, more interpretations but less composite states result. For example, suppose we used the mixed value model $\partial P + [P]\partial A - \partial Q = 0$. If $[P]$ is unknown, constraint satisfaction results in six interpretations corresponding to $[P] = +$, $[P] = 0$ and four in which $[P] = -$, but there is only one composite state. Using pure confluences results in three states ([WORKING-+], [WORKING-0] and [WORKING--]) where the third has four interpretations. Both definitions of episode ultimately result in the same number of episodes and the same variable values within them. In both cases time is defined in terms of qualitative state and interpretation. The methods we present work with either representation, although we will generally presume the models are pure.

Here is a procedure, based on the rules of Section 4 that constructs the expanded episode diagram. (This algorithm does not take advantage of the initial device boundary conditions.) First the set of possible composite device states is determined by considering every possible component state. Constraint satisfaction is applied to the confluence set for each such composite state. If there are no solutions, the state is ruled out as contradictory. If there are multiple solutions, each interpretation corresponds to a new episode. Each episode is examined individually to determine under what circumstances it terminates and what the subsequent episode is. Each case $\partial X = +$ where X is bounded above or $\partial X = -$ where X is bounded below indicates a possible transition (always consider only the smallest such bound). In addition, if $X = [c,c]$, the transition is immediate and mandatory. There are sometimes many possible and mandatory transitions for an episode. Except for mandatory transitions, all, some, or none of the transitions may occur. Thus each subset is examined, and the next state is computed on the basis of which thresholds are exceeded. The destination state may have many episodes (corresponding to its interpretations) and a transition is possible to each one as long as no variable need vary discontinuously. In addition, if there are no mandatory transitions out of the state, each episode may transition to an episode of the same state, again as long as no variable changes discontinuously. Figure 18 is the expansion of Figure 9.

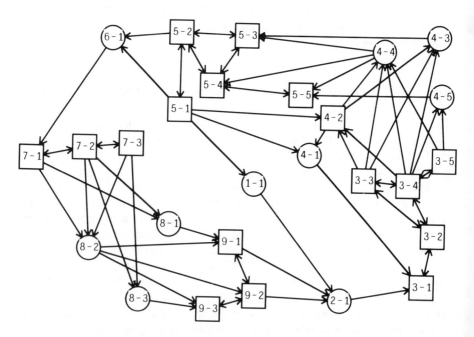

Figure 18. Expanded (of Figure 9) episode diagram for the pressure-regulator with continuing input signal, no friction

References

Brown, J. S., Burton, R. R., de Kleer J. (1982). "Pedagogical, Natural Language and Knowledge Engineering Techniques in SOPHIE I, II and III," in *Intelligent Tutoring Systems*, D. Sleeman and J. S. Brown (Eds.), New York: Academic Press, pp. 227–282.

Cochin, I. (1980). *Analysis and Design of Dynamic Systems*, New York: Harper and Row.

Davis, R., Shrobe, H., Hamscher, W., Wieckert, K., Shirley, M. & Polit, S. (1982). "Diagnosis Based on Description of Structure and Function," *Proceedings of the National Conference on Artificial Intelligence*. Pittsburgh, pp. 137–142.

de Kleer, J. (1975). "Qualitative and Quantitative Knowledge in Classical Mechanics," Artificial Intelligence Laboratory, TR-352, Cambridge, MA: M.I.T.

de Kleer, J. (1979a). "Causal and Teleological Reasoning in Circuit Recognition," Artificial Intelligence Laboratory, TR-529, Cambridge, MA: M.I.T.

de Kleer, J. (1979b). "The Origin and Resolution of Ambiguities in Causal Arguments," *Proceedings of the Sixth International Joint Conference on Artificial Intelligence*, Tokyo, pp. 197–203.

de Kleer, J., & Bobrow, D. G. (1984). "Qualitative Reasoning with Higher-Order Derivatives," *Proceedings of the National Conference on Artificial Intelligence*, Austin, pp. 79–85.

de Kleer, J., & Brown, J. S. (1981a). "Mental Models of Physical Mechanisms and their Acquisition," in *Cognitive Skills and their Acquisition*, J. R. Anderson (Ed.). Hillsdale, NJ: Erlbaum, pp. 285–309.

de Kleer, J., & Brown, J. S. (1981b). "Mental Models of Physical Mechanisms," CIS-3 Cognitive and Instructional Sciences, Xerox, PARC.

de Kleer, J., & Brown, J. S. (1983). "Assumptions and Ambiguities in Mechanistic Mental Models," in *Mental Models*, D. Gentner & A. S. Stevens (Eds.). Hillsdale, NJ: Erlbaum, pp. 155–190.

de Kleer, J., & Sussman, G. J. (1980). "Propagation of Constraints Applied to Circuit Synthesis," *Circuit Theory and Applications*, Vol. 8, pp. 127–144.

DiSessa, A. A. (1979). "Momentum Flow as a World View in Elementary Mechanics," Division for Study and Research in Education, Cambridge, MA: M.I.T.

Feynman, R. P., Leighton, R. B., & Sands, M. (1963). *The Feynman Lectures on Physics*, Vol. 1. Reading, MA: Addison-Wesley.

Forbus, K. D. (1981). "Qualitative Reasoning about Physical Processes," *Proceedings of the Seventh International Joint Conference on Artificial Intelligence*, Vancouver, pp. 326–330.

Forbus, K. D. (1982). "Qualitative Process Theory," Artificial Intelligence Laboratory, AIM-664, Cambridge, MA: M.I.T.

Forbus, K. D., & Stevens, A. (1981). "Using Qualitative Simulation to Generate Explanations," Report No. 4490, Cambridge, MA: Bolt Beranek and Newman.

Hayes, P. J. (1979). "The Naive Physics Manifesto," in *Expert Systems in the Microelectronic Age*, D. Michie (Ed.). Edinburgh, Scotland: Edinburgh University Press.

Hewitt, P. G. (1974). *Conceptual Physics*. Boston: Little, Brown.

Hopfield, J. J. (1982). "Neural Networks and Physical Systems with Emergent Collective Computational Abilities," *Proceedings of the National Academy of Sciences, U.S.A.*, pp. 2554–2558.

Karnopp, D., & Rosenberg, R. (1975). *System Dynamics: A Unified Approach*. New York: Wiley.

Kuipers, B. (1982a). "Commonsense Reasoning About Causality: Deriving Behavior from Structure," Tufts University Working Papers in Cognitive Science No. 18.

Kuipers, B. (1982b). "Getting the Envisionment Right," *Proceedings of the National Conference on Artificial Intelligence*, Pittsburgh, pp. 209–212.

Poston, T., & Stewart, I. (1978). *Catastrophe Theory and its Applications*. London: Pitman.

Shearer, J. L., Murphy, A. T., & Richardson, H. H. (1971). *Introduction to System Dynamics*. Reading, MA: Addison-Wesley.

Suppes, P. S. (1957). *Introduction to Logic*. New York: Van Nostrand.

Wiener, N. (1950). *The Human Use of Human Beings: Cybernetics and Society*. Boston, MA: Houghton Mifflin.

5 The Role of Qualitative Dynamics in Naive Physics

Kenneth D. Forbus

Department of Computer Science
University of Illinois
Urbana, Illinois

1 Introduction

Representing how things change is a central problem in common sense physical reasoning. In classical mechanics *dynamics* describes how forces bring about changes in physical systems. For any particular domain, such as particles or fluids, a dynamics consists of identifying the kinds of forces that act between the classes of objects in the domain and the events that result from these forces.

Similar kinds of theories play an important role in Naive Physics. A theory about the kinds of things that can happen in a domain will be called a *qualitative dynamics*. I claim such theories have a common character, in that they are organized around the notion of *physical processes*. Speaking roughly, a process is something that causes changes through time. Using processes to describe what is happening in a situation enables us to predict how the situation will change and evolve over time.

Qualitative descriptions are important because they provide the ability to reason with incomplete information. Some conclusions can be drawn even with very little information. For example, if we see a container that is partially filled with water sitting on a flame we can conclude that the water might begin to boil soon. Also, we can conclude that if the container is sealed it might blow up as a result of the boiling, an important possibility to forsee. We do not know that it *will* blow up— the information in qualitative descriptions generally only allows proposing alternatives rather than a single prediction. We can then use these alternatives to drive the search for more detailed information (deKleer, 1975), or set up expectations for what we will see (or try to avoid seeing!).

This essay discusses the role of qualitative dynamical theories in Naive Physics. First we will describe the interaction between qualitative dynamics and the rest of Naive Physics. Then we will present some principles by which dynamical theories should be judged, and a catalog of reasoning tasks that rely heavily on qualitative dynamics. Presented next is an overview of Qualitative Process Theory, followed by several examples of how the descriptions it sanctions can be used to represent and reason about physical phenomena. Finally some general conclusions are drawn and open problems discussed.

1.1 Change, Histories, and Processes

Reasoning about the physical world requires reasoning about the kinds of changes that occur and the effects that result. The classic problem which arises is the Frame Problem (McCarthy & Hayes, 1969). Stated simply, the Frame Problem is the problem of knowing what facts remain true and what facts change when something happens. Using the Situational Calculus to represent the changing states of the world requires writing explicit axioms that state what things change and what things remain the same. The number of axioms needed rises as the product of the number of predicates and the number of actions, which means adding a new action can require adding a large number of new axioms. There have been several attempts to fix this problem (Fikes & Nilsson, 1971; Minsky, 1974), but none of them have seemed particularly fruitful. Hayes (1979a) argues cogently that the problem lies in the impoverishment of the Situational Calculus, and has developed the notion of *Histories* as an alternative.

In Situational Calculus, the state of the world at different times is modelled by situations. A situation lasts until some action occurs, and the result of an action is a new situation. The state of the world *during* the action is not modelled. In addition, each situation encompasses the entire world at that time. By contrast, Histories are descriptions of objects that are extended through time but always are bounded spatially. Histories are divided into pieces called *episodes,* corresponding to a particular kind of thing happening to the object.

Histories help solve the Frame Problem because objects can interact only when their histories intersect. Suppose for example we are building a clock in our basement. In testing parts of this gadget we look to see what parts touch each other, what parts will touch each other if they move in certain ways, and so on. By doing so we build descriptions of what can happen to the pieces of the clock. We do not usually consider interactions with the furnace sitting in the corner of the basement, because whatever is happening in there is spatially isolated from us (if it is summer it can also be "temporally isolated").

The assumption that things interact only when they touch in some way also permeates "non-Naive" physics—action at a distance is banished, with fields and particle exchanges introduced to prevent its return. It means that spatial and temporal representations bear most of the burden for detecting interactions. While not simple, developing such representations seems far more productive than trying to develop more clever frame axioms.[1] In particular, qualitative representations of space and time have precisely the desired properties for reasoning with histories—they often allow ruling out interactions, even with very little information.

An explicit theory of processes is needed to exploit the full power of Histories. Histories, by themselves, are inadequate in at least two ways. First, a means of generating histories is needed. To be effective there also must be a way of breaking

---

[1] For an example of Histories in use, see Forbus (1981a) which describes a program called FROB that reasons about motion through space. FROB used a diagram to compute qualitative spatial representations which were used to rule out potential collisions between objects as well as describing possible motions.

up a situation into pieces, each of which can be considered semi-independently. This will be called the *Local Evolution* problem. In the basement example above, we could safely ignore the furnace in the corner and concentrate on figuring out the pieces of the clock we were building would move. The divisions are only semi-independent, because certain kinds of changes can violate the conditions for isolation. For example, if the internal thermostat of the furnace gets stuck and it explodes, we can no longer safely ignore it.[2] The second problem arises because not every intersection of histories leads to an interaction. Dropping a large steel ball through a flame, for example, won't affect its motion even if the flame is hot enough to melt it unless the gasses are going fast enough to impart significant momentum. In other words, there can be several things happening to an object, and these things don't always interact. This will be called the *Intersection/Interaction* problem. Solving these problems in general requires knowing what kinds of things can happen and how they can affect each other—in other words, a theory of processes.

1.2 Reasoning Tasks Involving Dynamics

Aside from the basic role of dynamics in representing change, there are a number of reasoning tasks involving Naive Physics in which dynamics is central. Each of them can be viewed as a different "style" of reasoning with the representations of Naive Physics. The catalog below, while surely incomplete, seems to cover a large proportion of the cases. Examples of inferences from several of these categories will be presented later.

Determining Activity: Inferring "what is happening" in a situation at a particular time. Besides being interesting in its own right, such deductions are also required in the other reasoning tasks below.

Prediction: Inferring what will happen in the future in some situation. We usually must work with incomplete information, so we can only generate the possibilities for what might occur. de Kleer's notion of *envisioning* is a powerful theory about this type of inference.[3]

Postdiction: Inferring how a particular state of affairs might have come about. Hayes (1979b) contains a good example of this kind of deduction. Postdiction is harder than prediction because there are fewer physical constraints on postulating individuals. If we have complete knowledge of a situation and have a complete dynamics, we know what individuals will vanish and appear. But usually there are many ways for any particular situation to have come about. Consider walking back to our basement and finding a small pile of broken glass on the floor. Looking at it we may deduce that a coke bottle was dropped, but we do not know much about its

---

[2] Unless the physical situation is simulated by some incremental time scheme (where everything is pushed forward a small amount at once and then "collisions" are looked for), the reasoning involved in extending histories will be inherently non-monotonic (McDermott & Doyle, 1980).

[3] Useful as it is, envisioning has certain limitations, especially as a sufficient model of human behavior on this task. See Forbus (1983a) for details.

history before that, or about anything else that might have been in the room before we looked. There could have been a troupe of jugglers filling the basement, each manipulating six bottles, and only a minor mishap occurred. The simplest explanation, of course, is that a single bottle was dropped. However, this example illustrates our criteria for simplicity is not due solely to our theories of physics.

Skeptical Analysis: Determining if the description of a physical situation is consistent. An example of this task is evaluating a proposed perpetual motion machine. This kind of reasoning is essential in recovering from inconsistent data and discovering inadequacies in our theories about the world to drive learning.

Measurement Interpretation: Given a partial description of the individuals in the situation and some observations of their behavior, infering what other individuals exist and what else is happening.[4]

Experiment Planning: Planning actions that will yield more information about a situation, given knowledge of what can be observed and manipulated.

Causal reasoning: Computing a description of behavior which attributes changes to particular parts of the situation and particular other changes. Not all physical reasoning is causal, especially as more expert kinds of deductions are considered.[5] Causality is mainly a tool for assigning credit to theories for observed or postulated behaviour. Thus it is quite useful for generating explanations (e.g., Forbus, 1981b), measurement interpretation, planning experiments, and learning (e.g., Forbus & Gentner, 1983).

1.3 Desiderata for Dynamical Theories

There are three properties a qualitative dynamics must have if it is to be useful for commonsense physical reasoning. First, a dynamical theory must explicitly *specify direct effects* and *specify the means by which effects are propagated.* Without specifying what can happen and how the things which happen can interact, there is no hope of solving either the Local Evolution or Intersection/Interaction problems. Second, the descriptions the theory provides must be *composable.* It should be possible to describe a very complicated situation by describing its parts and how they relate.[6] This property is especially important as we move towards a more complete Naive Physics that encompasses several "domains". In dealing with a single kind of reasoning in a particular class of situations an ad hoc domain representation may suffice, but sadly the world does not consist of completely separate domains. Transferring results between several ad hoc representations may be far more complex than developing a useful common form for dynamics theories.[7]

---

[4] Simmons (1982) explores a combination of Measurement Interpretation and Postdiction in reasoning about geology. See also Forbus (1983b).

[5] The experienced elegance of constraint arguments in fact argues against their being central in Naive Physics. Usually some kind of animistic explanation is proposed to justify constraint arguments to non-experts (i.e., "the particle senses which path has the least action").

[6] Producing models with this property is the primary motivation of de Kleer and Brown's "No Function in Structure" principle (de Kleer & Brown, 1983).

[7] Stanfill (1983) describes an initial exploration of linking results from reasoning within multiple domains.

Finally, the theory should allow *graceful extension*. Graceful extension means two things. First, it should be possible to draw at least the same conclusions with more precise data as can be drawn with weak data. Second, the more precise information should allow the resolution of ambiguities which have arisen in reasoning with weak data.

These properties are not independent—for example, specifying direct and indirect effects cleanly is necessary to insure composability. These properties are also not easy to achieve. Graceful Extension is bound up with the notion of good qualitative representations. Qualitative representations allow the construction of descriptions which encompass the possibilities inherent in incomplete information. If designed properly, more precise information can be used to decide between these alternatives as well as perform more sophisticated analyses. Representing quantities by symbols like TALL and VERY-TALL or free space by a uniform grid, for instance, does not allow more precise information to be easily integrated. Note also that while qualitative descriptions are approximations, not all approximations are good qualitative descriptions. Changing a value in a qualitative representation should lead to qualitatively distinct behavior. Consider, for example, heating a pan of water on a stove. Suppose that we represent the value of the temperature of the water at any time by an interval, and the initial temperature is represented by the interval (70.0 80.0), indicating that its actual temperature is somewhere between 70 and 80 degrees fahrenheit. Changing the "value" of its temperature to (75.0 85.0) doesn't change our description of what's happening to it (namely, a heat flow), whereas changing it to (200.0 220.0) changes what we think can be happening to it—it could be boiling as well. While an interval representation makes certain distinctions, they usually are *not* distinctions relevant to physical reasoning.

By defining a basic theory using qualitative representations, we can later add theories involving more precise information—perhaps such as intervals—to allow more precise conclusions. In other words, we would like extensions to our basic theory to have the logical character of extension theories—more information should result in a wider class of deductions, not merely changing details of conclusions previously drawn. In this way we can add theories that capture more sophisticated reasoning (such as an engineer performs when estimating circuit parameters or stresses on a bridge) onto a common base. For example, the Quantity Space description of quantities that will be described below can be seen as an extension theory for the Incremental Qualitative Analysis description of quantities (de Kleer, 1979).

We will return to these properties after discussing Qualitative Process theory, and later discuss them again in regards to more general theories of action.

2 Qualitative Process Theory

Qualitative Process theory (QP) extends the ontology of common sense physical models by introducing the notion of a *physical process*. Processes include things such as flowing, boiling, and stretching that cause changes in physical situations. The collection of active processes constitute the description of "what is happening" in any situation. QP theory provides a language for specifying processes and their effects in a way that induces a natural qualitative representation for quantities and allows both the deduction of what processes occur in a situation and how they might change. Space permits only a brief sketch of the theory; its present status is described in Forbus (1982).

2.1 Basic Concepts

A physical situation is composed of objects and relationships among them. Processes represent the activities that are occuring in physical situations. This means to describe processes we must first introduce some notation for describing objects and quantities. Then we will introduce a notation for processes and elaborate the Qualitative Process theory view of them. Finally we describe some classes of deductions sanctioned by the theory.

2.1.1 Quantities.

The continuous parameters of an object, such as mass, temperature, and pressure, are represented by *quantities*. A quantity consists of two parts, an *amount* and a *derivative*, each of which are *numbers*. Intuitively, the derivative of a quantity is the time derivative, and higher-order derivatives can be expressed by constructing quantities whose amount is equal to the derivative of the original quantity.

The functions A and D map from quantities to amounts and derivatives respectively. Every number has parts *sign* and *magnitude*. The functions s and m map from numbers to signs and magnitudes respectively. The parts of quantities are denoted by the selectors A_s, A_m, D_s, and D_m which map from a quantity to the sign of its amount, the magnitude of its amount, and so forth.

Numbers, magnitudes, and signs take on *values* at particular times. We will use the function M to refer to the value of a quantity or some part of it at a particular time (either instant or interval). For example, we would write:

(M Level(W) t)

to refer to the value of the level of W at time t.[8] Signs can take on the values -1, 0, 1. For purposes of comparison and combination we will assume that the values of numbers and magnitudes behave like elements of the reals ($\mathbb{R}$). The D_s value of a quantity is particularly important because it corresponds to our intuitive notion of how a quantity is changing. To indicate that at time t the level of W is increasing, for instance, we would say

---

[8] We assume Allen's (1982) model of time. To state that a fact is true at or during a particular time t we will use the model operator T (Moore, 1979), such as

(T Cleartop(A) t)

which says "Cleartop(A) is true during time t". For simplicity, we will use T in this exposition only when absolutely necessary.

$$(M\ D_s[level(W)]\ t)\ =\ 1$$

In QP theory, the value of a number is defined in terms of its *Quantity Space*—a collection of inequalities which hold between it and other quantities. (Sometimes we will find it easier to speak loosely of the value of a quantity, rather than the value of a number. In this case we mean the value of the quantity's amount.) The major source of elements in a particular Quantity Space are the various descriptions that involve that parameter. In general the value will be incomplete, which is reflected by the Quantity Space being a partial instead of a total ordering. The Quantity Space is a useful qualitative representation because processes typically start and stop when inequalities between parameters change.[9] For example, if we are describing the states of some piece of stuff the Quantity Space for that stuff's temperature will include elements corresponding to the temperatures at which it melts or boils.

Relationships between quantities (other than simple arithmetic operations) are represented in terms of functional dependencies. We define

$$X \propto_{Q+} Y$$

(read "X is *qualitatively proportional* to Y"), to mean "there exists a function which determines X and is increasing monotonic (i.e., strictly increasing) in its dependence on Y". $\propto_{Q-}$ signifies the same, but with the implicit function being decreasing monotonic (i.e., strictly decreasing) in its dependence on Y. Newton's Second Law, for example, can be written as:[10]

$$acceleration(B) \propto_{Q+} force(B)$$

$$acceleration(B) \propto_{Q-} mass(B)$$

The importance of $\propto_Q$ lies in the minimal assumptions it makes about the form of the function. We do not know exactly what the function is, nor whether or not it depends on other quantities. Monotonicity is required to preserve the sense of a change. If Y goes up then, in the absence of other information, we can conclude that X will go up as well. The cases where we cannot distinguish what change occurs involve multiple functional dependencies, and will be discussed later.

Another other kind of information that can be specified about the function implied by $\propto_Q$'s[11] is a finite set of *correspondences* it induces between points in the

---

[9] This is an application of the *Relevance Principle* of qualitative reasoning. Qualitative reasoning about a continuous thing requires quantization of some sort to induce a finite vocabulary of symbols. The choice of quantization must be chosen to draw the distinctions required by the kind of reasoning being performed. Ignoring this principle leads to ad hoc, inadequate, and unextendable representations.

[10] We will see the reason for choosing this particular form of the constraint law later when discussing causal reasoning.

[11] Qualitative Process Theory also provides a means of naming functions and stating functional dependencies on properties that aren't quantities, but for brevity they are omitted here.

two Quantity Spaces it connects. In Newton's Second Law, for example, we know that when the force is zero then the acceleration will be zero. This fact would be expressed as:

$$\text{Correspondence}((\text{acceleration}(B), \text{ZERO}),$$
$$(\text{force}(B), \text{ZERO}))$$

Correspondences are important because they provide a means of mapping value information (inequalities) from one Quantity Space to another via $\propto_Q$. For example, if the force on the object is greater than zero, then the acceleration must also be greater than zero, by monotonicity of $\propto_Q$.

2.1.2 Objects and States. Objects can come and go, and their properties can change dramatically. Water can be poured into a cup and then drunk, for example, and a spring can be stretched so far that it breaks. Some of these changes depend on values of quantities—when the amount of fluid in a container becomes zero we can consider it gone, and when a spring breaks it does so at a particular length (which may depend on other continuous parameters such as temperature). To model these kinds of changes we will introduce *Individual Views*.

An Individual View consists of four parts. It must contain a list of *Individuals,* the objects which must exist before it is applicable. It has *Quantity Conditions,* which are statements about inequalities between quantities involving the individuals and statements about whether or not certain other Individual Views hold (or certain processes acting, as we will see later), and *Preconditions* which are still further conditions that must be true for the view to hold, and a collection of *Relations* that

---

Individual View Contained-Stuff

Individuals:
      c a container
      s a substance

Preconditions:
      Can-Contain-Substance(s c)

QuantityConditions:
      $A[\text{amount-of-in}(s, c)] > \text{ZERO}$

Relations:
      There is unique $p \in$ *piece-of-stuff*
      amount-of-in(s, c) = amount-of(p)
      s = made-of(p)
      inside(c) = location(p)
      Contained-Stuff(p)

;we will take "amount-of-in" to map from substances and
;containers to quantities

Figure 1. Individual Views describe objects and states of objects. Contained-stuff describes the material of a particular kind inside a container. We will define "pieces of stuff" later on.

```
;Conventions:
;functions are in lower case, relationships and predicates are
;capitalized. Sorts are underlined.

(∀ c ∈ container ∀ s ∈ substance
  (∃ v ∈ view-instance
    c(v) = c ∧ s(v) = s ∧
    (∃ p ∈ piece-of-stuff
    location(p) = inside(c) ∧ made-of(p) = s ∧ Contained-Stuff(p)
    ∧
    (∀ t ∈ time
    [(T Can-Contain-Substance(c, s) t) ∧ (M A[amount-of-in(s, c)] t) > ZERO
        ↔ (T Status(v, Active) t)]
    ∧ [(T Status(v, Active) t) ↔ Exists-In(p, t)
    ;note that physical existence is distinct from logical existence
    ∧ (M amount-of(p) t) = (M amount-of-in(s, c)t)])))))

; note that
(∀ t ∈ time ∀ v ∈ view-instance
        Taxonomy (T Status(v, Active) t), (T Status(v, Inactive) t)))
; where Taxonomy means "exactly one of them is true"

;also,
(∀ p ∈ things ∀ q ∈ quantity-type
    Has-Quantity(p, q) ↔ Quantity(q(p)))
```

Figure 2. Translation of Individual View notation into Logic. Here is the Contained Stuff description of the previous figure translated into logical notation.

are imposed by that view. Figure 1 illustrates a simple description of the fluid in a cup.

For every collection of objects which satisfies the description of the individuals for a particular type of Individual View, there is a *View Instance*, or VI, that relates them. Whenever the Preconditions and Quantity Conditions for an VI hold we will say that it is ACTIVE, and INACTIVE otherwise. Whenever a VI is active the specified Relations hold between its individuals. The Contained Stuff description of the previous figure has been translated into logical notation in Figure 2.

The distinction between Preconditions and Quantity Conditions is important. The intuition is to separate changes that can be predicted solely within dynamics from those which cannot. As we will see below, if we know how a quantity is changing (its D_s value) and its value (specified as a Quantity Space), then we can predict how that value will change. We cannot predict within a purely physical theory that someone will walk by a collection of pipes through which fluid is flowing and turn off a valve. Despite its unpredictability, we still want to be able to reason about the effects of such changes when they do occur; hence Preconditions must be explicitly represented.

2.1.3 Processes. Now that we have a way to describe objects, continuous parameters, and relationships between parameters, we can describe the things that bring about change. A *physical process* is a thing that acts through time to cause changes. Processes are specified by five parts:

- *Individuals:* descriptions of the objects which the process acts on.
- *Quantity Conditions:* Inequality statements and status assignments which must be true for the process to be active.
- *Preconditions:* Statements other than Quantity Conditions that must be true for the process to be active.
- *Relations:* The relationships between the individuals which hold when the process is active.
- *Influences:* Descriptions of the direct effects of the process.

Figure 3 and Figure 4 illustrate two process descriptions. As you can see, a process is a time dependent description very much like an Individual View. In particular, a process acts between any collection of individuals it matches (giving rise to a *Process Instance,* or PI), whenever both the Preconditions and Quantity Conditions are true. The statements in the Relations and Influences fields hold whenever the process is active. What distinguishes a process is that it has *influences*—a set of quantities that it directly affects.

Let us examine the notion of influence in more detail. A changing quantity is said

---

process heat-flow(src, dst, path)

Individuals:
        src an object,Has-Quantity(src, heat)
        dst an object,Has-Quantity(dst, heat)
        path a HeatPath, Heat-Path(path,src,dst)

Preconditions:
        Heat-Aligned(path)

QuantityConditions:
        A[temperature(src)] > A[temperature(dst)]

Relations:
        Let flow-rate be a quantity
        A[flow-rate] > ZERO
        flow-rate $\propto_{Q+}$ (temperature(src) − temperature(dst))

Influences:
        I−(Heat(src), A[flow-rate])
        I+(Heat(dst), A[flow-rate])

;A heat path is defined in terms of objects in contact, and aligned
;indicates that the contact is unbroken. We will ignore heating
;by radiation and by convection.

Figure 3. A Physical Process Definition. Below is a specification of the process of heat flow. Heat flow happens between two objects that have heats and are connected via some path through which heat can flow. The predicate Heat-Aligned is true exactly when heat could flow through the path, named for the analogous predicate in fluid flow.

process boiling(w, hf)

Individuals:
  w a contained-liquid
  hf a process-instance, process(hf) = heat-flow
      $\wedge$ dst(hf) = w

QuantityConditions:
  Active(hf)
  A[temperature(w)] = A[t-boil(w)]

Relations:
  There is g $\in$ *piece-of-stuff*
  gas(g)
  substance(g) = substance(w)
  temperature[w] = temperature[g]
  Let generation-rate be a quantity
  A[generation-rate] > ZERO
  generation-rate $^{\propto}{}_{Q+}$ flow-rate(hf)

Influences:
  I−(heat(w), A[flow-rate(hf)])
  I−(amount-of(w), A[generation-rate])
  I+(amount-of(g), A[generation-rate])
  I−(heat(w), A[generation-rate])
  I+(heat(g), A[generation-rate])

Figure 4. A definition of Boiling. In this simple version, boiling happens to a contained liquid at its boiling temperature (t-boil) that is being heated, and creates a gas made of the same stuff as the liquid. The influence on heat flow models the use of energy from the heat flow for changing state rather than raising its temperature.

to be *influenced.* There are two kinds of influence which can occur. A quantity can be *directly influenced* by a process or processes, in which case we will write either

I+(Q, n)

I−(Q, n)

I±(Q, n)

according to whether the number n is an increasing, decreasing, or unknown influence on the quantity Q. If a quantity is directly influenced, then its derivative is just the sum of the direct influences on it. A quantity can also be *indirectly influenced* by its value being a function of some other quantities which are themselves influenced. If a process P influences some quantity Q and some other quantity R is qualitatively proportional to Q, then we say that P *indirectly influences* R. Figuring out the sign of a derivative from its influences will be called *resolving* its influences. A principle tenet of Qualitative Process theory is that *only* processes directly influence quantities and that functional dependencies are the causes of indirect changes. Thus processes provide the mechanisms of change.

2.1.4 Reprise. The central assumption of Qualitative Process theory is the *Sole Mechanism* assumption, namely:

> *All changes in physical systems are caused directly or indirectly by processes.*

As a consequence, the physics for a domain must include a vocabulary of processes that occur in that domain. This *Process Vocabulary* can be viewed as specifying the dynamics theory for the domain. A situation, then, is described by a collection of objects, their properties, the relations between them, *and* the processes that are occuring. A consequence of the Sole Mechanism assumption is that it allows us to reason by exclusion. If we make the additional assumption that our Process Vocabulary for a domain is complete, then we know what quantities can be directly influenced. If we understand the objects and relationships between them well enough, we know all the ways quantities can be indirectly influenced. Thus we know how the physical world will change. Without this kind of closed world assumption, it is hard to see how a reasoning entity could use, much less debug or extend, its physical knowledge.

2.1.5 Encapsulated Histories. Before moving on to describe the basic inferences sanctioned by QP theory, we need to mention briefly one other kind of behavioral description that will be used below. Some phenomena, such as collisions between moving objects, seem to be most easily described in terms of a piece of history. We will call such descriptions *Encapsulated Histories.* Unlike processes, Encapsulated Histories explicitly refer to a particular sequence of times during which changes take place. While modularity suffers, such descriptions are sometimes all we have of a physical phenomena, especially when faced with a new domain.[12] Encapsulated histories are described by a variant of the notation for processes and Individual Views. An Encapsulated History has Individuals, Preconditions, and Quantity Conditions to declare when and between what they occur. The Relations describe the pieces of histories for the individuals involved. When the Preconditions and Quantity Conditions are true, the histories described in the Relations field are assumed to describe a part of the histories for the individuals.

2.2 Basic Deductions

To be useful, a representation must be computable from other information and in turn sanction other deductions. Several basic deductions involving the constructs of Qualitative Process theory are cataloged below. It may be helpful to skip momentarily to the example in section 3.1, which illustrates these deductions step by step.

---

[12] diSessa's "Phenomenological Primitives" (diSessa, 1983) can probably be written in this form. Encapsulated Histories are also good candidates for the first models people make of a new domain (Forbus & Gentner, 1983).

2.2.1 Finding Possible Processes. A process Vocabulary specifies the types of processes that can occur. Given a collection of individuals and a Process Vocabulary, the individual specifications from the elements in the Process Vocabulary can be used to find collections of individuals which can participate in each kind of process. These *Process Instances* (PI's) represent the potential processes that can occur between a set of individuals. Similarly, the *View Structure* is the collection of all active View Instances at a particular time. Generally whenever we mention ascertaining the status of some description we will implicitly include instances of Individual Views as well as instances of processes.

2.2.2 Determining Activity. A Process Instance has a status of Active or Inactive according to whether or not the particular process it represents is acting between its individuals. By determining whether or not the Preconditions and Quantity Conditions are true, a status can be assigned to each Process (or View) Instance for a situation. The collection of active process instances is called the *Process Structure* of the situation, and the collection of active view instances is called the *View Structure*. The Process Structure represents "what's happening" to the individuals in a particular situation.

2.2.3 Determining Changes. Most of the changes in an individual are represented by the D_s values—intuitively, the direction of change—for its quantities. As stated previously, there are two ways for a quantity to change. A quantity can be directly influenced by a process, or it can be indirectly influenced via $\propto_Q$. (By the Sole Mechanism assumption, if a quantity is uninfluenced its D_s value is 0.) As mentioned above, determining the D_s value for an influenced quantity is called *resolving* its influences, by analogy to resolving forces in classical mechanics.

Resolving a directly influenced quantity involves sorting its influences by sign and determining which collection has the greatest magnitude. Resolving an indirectly influenced quantity involves gathering the $\propto_Q$ statements which implicitly specify it as a function of other quantities. Because the function is only weakly specified, in many cases indirect influences cannot be resolved within the basic theory. An example will make this point clearer. Suppose we have a quantity Q_0 such that in a particular Process Structure it is qualitatively proportional to some quantity Q_1 and inversely proportional to some quantity Q_2. Then if both Q_1 and Q_2 are increasing, then we cannot tell (without additional information) which way Q_0 will be changing. More precisely:

$$Q_0 \propto_{Q+} Q_1 \wedge Q_0 \propto_{Q-} Q_2$$

If we also know that

$$D_s[Q_1] = 1 \wedge D_s[Q_2] = 1$$

then we cannot determine $D_s[Q_0]$, because we do not have enough information to determine which indirect influence "dominates".[13] However, if we had

$$D_s[Q_1] = 1 \wedge D_s[Q_2] = 0$$

then we can conclude that

$$D_s[Q_0] = 1$$

because Q_1 is now the only active indirect influence.

Domain specific and problem specific knowledge will often play a role in resolving influences. We may know that a certain influence can be ignored, such as when we ignore the heat lost by a kettle on a stove to the air surrounding it while being heated to boiling. Our knowledge about particular functions may tell us which way things combine. Suppose for instance that our model of fluid flow included influences to model the changes in heat and temperature that result from mass transfer. In the source and destination temperature would be indirectly influenced due to direct influences on amount-of and heat, and if we knew nothing but the D_s values we could say nothing about how they will change. From physics, however, we know that the temperature of the source is unchanged and the temperature of the destination will rise or fall according to whether the temperature of the source is greater or less than the temperature of the destination.

2.2.4 Limit Analysis. Changes in quantities can result in the Process Structure itself changing. Determining the possible changes in a situation's Process Structure is called *Limit Analysis*. Limit Analysis is carried out by using the D_s values and Quantity Spaces to determine which Quantity Conditions can change.

The first step is to find *neighboring points* within the Quantity Spaces of each changing quantity. One point is a neighbor of another if they are ordered and there is no point known to be between them. (It will help in visualizing what is happening to think of the elements in a Quantity Space as points on a line, with their relative positions determined by the order relationships of the Quantity Space. D_s values correspond to directions of movement along that line.) If there is no neighbor in a direction, then a change in that direction cannot affect any process. The ordering between each neighbor and the current amount of the quantity can be combined with the D_s values of each to determine if the relationship will change. For example, if A is greater than B and A remains constant while B increases, then the relationship can eventually change to equality. If instead A was increasing as well, the next relationship would depend on the ordering between $D_m[A]$ and $D_m[B]$, since A may be

---

[13] The "dominates" is in quotes because the word implicitly assumes Q_1 and Q_2 are separate terms whose sum is part of the function that determines Q_0, and this need not be the case.

increasing faster than B. A neighbor is a *Limit Point* if some process may end there and others begin. Thus the set of possible changes in orderings involving Limit Points determines the ways the current set of active processes might change. The set of single changes plus consistent conjunctions of changes (corresponding to simultaneous changes in Quantity Conditions) forms the set of *Limit Hypotheses*. Each Limit Hypothesis determines a situation called an *Alternate Ending* for the Process Structure, and the one which actually occurs is called the *Next Structure* for that Process Structure.[14]

More than one change is typically possible, as the examples below will illustrate. There are three reasons for this. First, if the ordering within a Quantity Space is not a total order more than one neighbor can exist. Second, a process can influence more than one quantity. Finally, more than one process can be occurring at once. The basic theory does not in general allow the determination of which alternative actually occurs. Using Calculus as the model for quantities, the alternative which actually occurs is the one which takes the minimum time to integrate the quantities involved to their Limit Points. Since the basic theory does not include explicit integrals, this question typically cannot be decided.

There are some special cases, due to the nature of quantities. Consider two quantities A and B which are equal, and C and D which are unequal. If all of the quantities are changing (D_s value of -1 or 1), then the finite difference between C and D implies that the change in the equality between A and B occurs first. In fact, we will assume that the change *from* equality occurs in an instant, while the change *to* equality usually will take some interval. We will further assume that the only time a change *to* equality will take an instant is when the difference was due to a process which acted only for an instant. We will summarize this as the *Equality Change Law:*

> With two exceptions, a Process Structure lasts over an interval of time. It lasts for an instant only when either
> (1). A change from equality occurs in a Quantity Condition or
> (2). A change to equality occurs between quantities in a Quantity Condition that were influenced from equality for only an instant.

The first case assumes that the values of numbers aren't "fuzzy", and the second case assumes that the changes wrought by processes are well-behaved (i.e., no impulses).

Now consider the maximal element (in the sense of set inclusion) of the set of changes which occur in an instant. The Limit Hypotheses which contain this max-

---

[14] This assumes that rates are not infinitesimals, so that if a quantity is moving towards some point in its Quantity Space (i.e., a decreasing difference) it will actually reach that value in some finite time. Note that relaxing this assumption would result in only one additional state in the possibilities returned by Limit Analysis—that the current Process Structure never changes.

imal element are the ones which can occur next, because the duration of an instant is always shorter than the duration of an interval. This means we can sometimes get a unique result from Limit Analysis by using the Equality Change Law. The ability to distinguish between changes in Process Structures that occur in an instant from those which require some time is also essential in distinguishing between true oscillation and dynamic equilibriums (see Forbus, 1982, for details).

Just knowing the possible changes is enough for some tasks, such as envisioning. If required, knowledge outside the scope of Qualitative Process Theory can be used to disambiguate the possibilities. There are several choices, depending on the domain and reasoning task: simulation (Forbus, 1981a), algebraic manipulation (de Kleer, 1975), teleology (de Kleer, 1979), or possibly default assumptions or observations (discussed in Forbus, 1983a).

2.3 Addressing the Problems of Dynamics

Let us see how these notions of quantity, qualitative proportionality, Individual Views, and Process address the problems of qualitative dynamics raised earlier. In particular, we will see how Qualitative Process theory descriptions specify direct and indirect effects, allow composability, and provide graceful extension. Then a technique is proposed for solving the Local Evolution and Intersection/Interaction problems by carving up situations into semi-independent pieces.

Direct and indirect effects are specified by influence statements and statements of qualitative proportionality ($\propto_Q$'s). Each statement provides partial information about how a quantity is changing, and by resolving them we can determine their net effect. Of course, the qualitative nature of the description means that the exact effect cannot always be determined, but this ambiguity can be used to drive the search for more detailed information when relevant.

Process descriptions are composable because the ways of specifying effects do not presuppose their results. Note that a single direct influence does not necessarily determine the sign of the derivative for the quantity it affects, nor does a single qualitative proportionality by itself necessarily determine what a quantity is doing. A closed world assumption that we know all the processes that are occuring (and indeed that we know the kinds of processes that *can* occur) is needed whenever we try to determine what actually affects a quantity. Thus the effects of a new process (or processes engendered by a new individual) are combined by means of shared parameters and additional qualitative proportionalities.

Graceful Extension is satisfied because both the Quantity Space representation for values and the qualitative proportionality representation for functions represent very weak commitments to what the "real world" is like. More detailed representations of quantity will still yield information about ordering, so the additional information can be used to decide between the possible resolutions of direct influences. More detailed information about functions can be interpreted in terms of $\propto_Q$, allowing simple deductions where possible, but the richer information can allow indirect influences to be resolved as well.

I propose that the Local Evolution and Intersection/Interaction problems can be solved with the notion of a *P-component*. Two process or view instances are in the same P-component if (a) they both influence the same quantity or (b) one instance influences a quantity which is mentioned in the Quantity Conditions of another or (c) one instance is mentioned in the Quantity Conditions of another or (d) the other description contains a $\propto_Q$ that propagates an influence of the process. A P-component is an equivalence class, and in fact each P-component constitutes a piece of the situation which can be evolved through Limit Analysis independently of the others. Once Limit Analysis for each P-component has been performed, the histories which result from the alternative endings must be tested to see if, when considered together, they form different P-components. If they do, there has been an interaction and the new P-components must be used to further evolve a description of the system's behavior. In general, we can test for interaction when two histories intersect by first constructing a situation out of slices from episodes which intersect and then seeing whether or not the processes involved lie in distinct P-components. Assuming Qualitative Process theory adequately characterizes qualitative dynamics, these notions should provide a method for carving up a situation into pieces that can be considered in isolation.

3 Examples

Some examples will make the ideas clearer. We will examine several reasoning tasks from the catalog of tasks in section 2.1.5, illustrating along the way the utility of Qualitative Process Theory in modelling commonsense physical phenomena. None of the models presented here should be taken as the last word on their domains—they all represent work in progress rather than a final product. Still, they will suffice to illustrate the dynamical issues involved.

3.1 Modelling Fluids and Flow

The first example illustrates some of the basic deductions sanctioned by QP theory and shows how the dynamical aspects of fluids can be represented. The goal is to use QP theory to determine both what is happening and what will happen to the fluids in the two containers in Figure 5.

First we need to describe "pieces of stuff". Following Hayes (1979b), we will individuate pieces of stuff by what contains them. Figure 6 shows an encoding of various properties of pieces of stuff. Any piece of stuff must be in some state, either solid, liquid, or gas. In Figure 7 these states are described by three Individual Views. We will use the Individual View introduced previously (Figure 1) to describe "contained stuff". The interaction of state and containment is described in Figure 8. Since the containers initially contain some water, we will create individuals corresponding to the water in each container. Call the pieces of stuff in

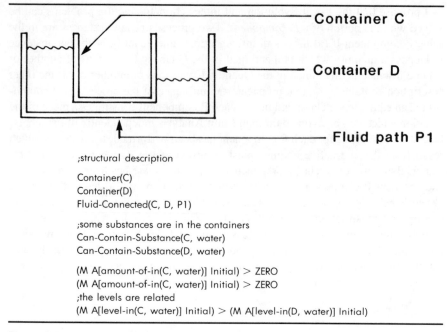

;structural description

Container(C)
Container(D)
Fluid-Connected(C, D, P1)

;some substances are in the containers
Can-Contain-Substance(C, water)
Can-Contain-Substance(D, water)

(M A[amount-of-in(C, water)] Initial) > ZERO
(M A[amount-of-in(C, water)] Initial) > ZERO
;the levels are related
(M A[level-in(C, water)] Initial) > (M A[level-in(D, water)] Initial)

Figure 5. Two partially filled containers. Containers C and D are connected by a pipe. C contains more water than D. In general an ''-in'' suffix indicates a function which maps from a container and a substance to a quantity.

containers C and D WC and WD respectively. We will assume their temperatures are such that they are both liquids. For simplicity we will ignore the liquid in the pipe P1. We will also ignore the precise definition of fluid paths, except to note that P1 is one, connecting the two contained fluids.

Suppose our Process Vocabulary consists of fluid flow, whose description is illustrated in Figure 9. This model is very simple, because it ignores the possibility of different kinds of fluids and the details of how fluids move through the fluid paths (Hayes, 1979b illustrates some of the distinctions that must be drawn).

($\forall$ p $\in$ piece-of-stuff
    Has-Quantity(p, amount-of)
    $\wedge$ Has-Quantity(p, volume) $\wedge$ Has-Quantity(p, pressure)
    $\wedge$ Has-Quantity(p, temperature) $\wedge$ Has-Quantity(p, heat)
    $\wedge$ Substance(madeof(p)) $\wedge$ Place(location(p))
    $\wedge$ temperature(p) $\propto_{Q+}$ heat(p)
    $\wedge$ Has-Quantity(p, t-boil) $\wedge$ Has-Quantity(p, t-melt))

Figure 6. Pieces of Stuff. A piece of stuff is described by several quantities, the substance it is made of, and its location.

Individual-View Solid(P)

Individuals:
      p a piece-of-stuff

QuantityConditions:
      $\sim$ A[temperature(p)] $>$ t-melt(p)

Individual-View Liquid(p)

Individuals:
      p a piece-of-stuff

QuantityConditions:
      A[temperature(p)] $>$ t-melt(p)
      $\sim$ A[temperature(p)] $>$ t-boil(p)

Relations:
      volume(p) $^{\infty}$Q+ amount-of(p)
      t-boil(p) $^{\infty}$Q+ pressure(p)

Individual-View Gas(p)

Individuals:
      p a piece-of-stuff

QuantityConditions:
      $\sim$ A[temperature(p)] $<$ A[t-boil(p)]

Relations:
      temperature(p) $^{\infty}$Q+ pressure(p)
      pressure(p) $^{\infty}$Q+ amount-of(p)
      pressure(p) $^{\infty}$Q- volume(p)
      pressure(p) $^{\infty}$Q+ heat(p)

      ;these $^{\infty}$Q's enforce the implications
      ;of PV=nRT while respecting the directions
      ;of physical effect.

Figure 7. States of Matter. The temperatures at which state changes occur are given by two functions t-melt and t-boil. Making them depend on the piece of stuff represents a weaker commitment than depending on the substance and pressure.

There are two Process Instances in the situation as we have drawn it, one corresponding to flow from C to D and the other corresponding to flow from D to C. To find the Process Structure we must determine which, if any, of them are active. If we assume that the fluid path P1 is aligned—something we generally cannot

;Contained stuff has states as well -

($\forall$ p $\in$ *piece-of-stuff*
  (ContainedGas(p) $\leftrightarrow$ (ContainedStuff(p) $\wedge$ Gas(p)))
  $\wedge$ (ContainedLiquid(p) $\leftrightarrow$ (ContainedStuff(p) $\wedge$ Liquid(p)))
  $\wedge$ (ContainedSolid(p) $\leftrightarrow$ (ContainedStuff(p) $\wedge$ Solid(p)))

;Contained liquids have levels, which are tied to amounts
;and in turn (assuming an open container) determine pressure

($\forall$ c $\in$ *contained-liquid*
  Has-Quantity(c, level) $\wedge$ level(c) $^{\infty}$Q+ amount-of(c)
  $\wedge$ (OpenContainer(space-of(location(c)))) $\Rightarrow$ pressure(c) $^{\infty}$Q+ level(c)))

Figure 8. Effects of state on containment

process fluid-flow(src, dst, path)

Individuals:
    src a contained-fluid
    dst a contained-fluid
    path a fluid path, Fluid-Connected(src, dst, path)

Preconditions:
    aligned(path)

QuantityConditions:
    A[pressure(src)] > A[pressure(dst)]

Relations:
    Let flow-rate be a quantity
    flow-rate $\propto_{Q+}$ (pressure(src) − (pressure(dst))

Influences:
    I+(amount-of(dst), A[flow-rate])
    I−(amount-of(src), A[flow-rate])

;A fluid path is aligned only if either it has no valves or every valve is open
($\forall$ p $\in$ fluid-path
    ((number-of-valves(p) = 0) $\Rightarrow$ Aligned(p))
    $\vee$ ((number-of-valves(p) > 0)
        $\Rightarrow$ ($\forall$ v $\in$ valves(p) Open(v)) $\leftrightarrow$ Aligned(p)))

Figure 9. A Process Description of Fluid Flow. This simple model does not describe the existence and behavior of the fluid within the fluid path.

deduce from dynamical knowledge alone—we only have to know the relative pressures of WC and WD. Assume we deduce from their levels that the pressure in C is greater than the pressure in D.[15] Then the process instance representing fluid flow from WC to WD will be active, and the process instance representing fluid flow from WD to WC will be inactive. Thus the Process Structure is the set consisting of Fluid-Flow (WC, WD, P1).

We must resolve the influences to find out how the quantities are actually changing. In this situation resolving the influences is simple. The fluid flow from C to D is the only cause of direct influences, changing amount-of for WC and WD. Each of them has only one influence, hence

$$D_s[amount\text{-}of(WC)] = -1$$

and

$$D_s[amount\text{-}of(WD)] = \quad 1$$

---

[15] In particular, if the function that determines pressure according to level is the same for all containers, then if the level in one container is greater than another, by $\propto_Q$ the pressure must be greater as well.

Ds[amount-of(WC)] = −1
Ds[volume(WC)] = −1
Ds[level(WC)] = −1
Ds[pressure(WC)] = −1
Ds[heat(WC)] = 0
Ds[temperature(WC)] = 0

Ds[amount-of(WD)] = 1
Ds[volume(WD)] = 1
Ds[level(WD)] = 1
Ds[pressure(WD)] = 1
Ds[heat(WD)] = 0
Ds[temperature(WD)] = 0

Limit Analysis:
                IS: {WC, WD}
            PS: {Fluid-Flow(WC, WD, P1)}

LH: pressure(WC) = pressure(WD)
IS: {WC, WD}
PS: {}

LH: A[amount-of(WC)] = ZERO
IS: {WD}
PS: {}

Figure 10. Resolved Influences and Limit Analysis. The results of resolving influences and Limit Analysis for the situation involving two containers are summarized below. The individuals in the situation are labeled IS, the Process Structure PS, and the Limit Hypothesis LH.

These in turn indirectly influence volume, level and pressure. In fact, each of these quantities has only one indirect influence, so we can conclude that the volume, level and pressure of WC are decreasing, and the volume, level and pressure of WD are increasing. All other quantities are uninfluenced, hence unchanging. Limit Analysis is also easy. The pressures will eventually be equal, which means the fluid flow will stop. It is also possible that the container C will run out of water, thus ending WC's existence (although it is not possible in the particular drawing shown). These results are summarized in Figure 10. This graph of Process Structures can be used to generate a history by first creating the appropriate episodes for objects and processes involved and then selecting one or the other Limit Hypothesis as the end event for that episode. Usually we will just represent the interconnections between possible Process Structures as we have done here. With only a single process and simple relationships between quantities, influence resolution and Limit Analysis are simple and yield unique results. As we will see below, more complex situations give rise to more possibilities, and domain specific information will be required to decide among them.

3.2 Predicting the Future

Let us consider the possible consequences of the situation shown in Figure 11. The situation consists of a container partially filled with water. Initially the lid of the container is open; we stipulate that if boiling ever occurs, the lid will be closed and sealed. A flame, modeled as a temperature source, is placed so that heat can be conducted to the container and water (i.e., there is an aligned heat path between them). What sorts of things can happen?

To begin with, we need the contained substances defined in the previous example and a model of containers. We assume that if the pressure inside the container

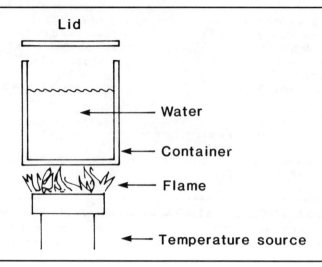

Figure 11. A Simple Boiler

exceeds a particular pressure p-burst(can), the container will explode. Figure 12 describes the container model. We will assume that, in addition to fluid flow, the Process Vocabulary includes heat flow and boiling, as presented previously. We will ignore the rest of the details, such as the nature of heat and fluid paths and the detailed geometry of containers.

We start by assuming that before the heat source is turned on that no processes are active; in other words that all temperatures, pressures, etc. are equal so there are no flows, and that the temperatures are in the appropriate regions of their Quantity Spaces so that no state changes are occurring. (Note that, as usual, we are making a closed world assumption both in assuming our Process Vocabulary is complete and that we know all of the relevant individuals.) Since there is a heat path between the source and the container, if we turn the heat source on and if

$$A[temperature(source)] > A[temperature(water)]$$

there is a heat flow from the source to the water. We ignore the influence of the heat flow on the source by assuming

$$D_s[temperature(source)] = 0$$

The only influence on temperature(can) is that of the heat flow, so

$$D_s[temperature(can)] = 1$$

This in turn causes a heat flow to the air surrounding the container and to the air and the water inside the container. Since we are only thinking about the container and its contents most of these changes will be ignored, and from now on when we refer to

∀ c ∈ *container*
[Has-Quantity(c, volume) ∧ Has-Quantity(c, pressure)
∧ Has-Quantity(c, temperature) ∧ Has-Quantity(c, heat)
∧ (Rigid(c) ⇒ D$_s$[volume(c)] = 0)
∧ (∀ p ∈ contents(c)
        pressure(c) = pressure(p)
        ∧ temperature(c) = temperature(p))]

;note we are assuming instantaneous equilibration
;   within the container

Encapsulated History Explode

Individuals:
        c a container, rigid(c)
        e an episode

Preconditions:
        (T ~ Open-Container(c) e)

QuantityConditions:
        (M A[pressure(c) end(e)) = (M A[p-burst(c)] end(e))
        (M A[pressure(c) during(e)) < (M A[p-burst(c)] during (e))

Relations:
        Let EV1 be an event
        end(e) = EV1
        Terminates(c, EV1)

;Terminates indicates that the object does not exist past
;that particular event

Figure 12. A Simple Container Model. For simplicity we will model a container only as a collection of quantities, a set of pieces of stuff which are its contents, and an Encapsulated History to describe the possibility of it exploding. The geometric information necessary to determine flow paths and the spatial arrangement of the contents will be ignored.

heat flow it will be the flow from the flame to the contained stuff, using the container as the heat path. The temperature Quantity Space that results is illustrated in Figure 13. If A[temperature(source)] > A[t-boil(water)] and the process is unimpeded (i.e., the Preconditions for the heat flow remain true), the next Process Structure to occur will include a boiling.

Suppose the Preconditions for the heat flow continue to be met and boiling occurs. Then by our initial assumptions the lid will be sealed, closing all fluid flow

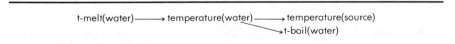

Figure 13. Quantity Space for Water Temperature. The heat flow is increasing the heat, and thus (via $\propto_{Q+}$) the temperature of the water. The lack of ordering information between the temperature of the source and the boiling temperature leads to uncertainty about what will occur next.

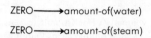

Figure 14. Amount-of Quantity Spaces

paths and thus preventing any flows. The amount-of Quantity Space that results is illustrated in Figure 14. The influence of the boiling on amount-of(water) moves it towards ZERO. So one of the ways the Process Structure might change is that all of the water is converted to steam.

If all the water is converted to steam, the only active process is a heat flow from the heat source to the steam. Thus the sole influence on the heat of the steam is positive, and (because of $\propto_Q$) the temperature also rises. Heat indirectly influences pressure, so the pressure of the steam will also rise. By examining the Quantity Spaces for temperature and pressure we find there are two limit points which may be reached, namely that the temperature of the steam can reach the temperature of the heat source and that the pressure of the container (which is equal to the pressure of the steam) can reach the explosion point. In the first case there are no active processes, and in the second an explosion occurs. We have found one possible disaster, are there more? To find out, we must go back to the boiling episode and check the indirect consequences of the changes in amount-of(steam).

Consider some arbitrary instant I within the boiling episode. Because the steam is still in contact with the water their temperatures will be the same. Since we assumed the container would be sealed when boiling began, there are no fluid paths hence no fluid flows. Therefore during I the only influence on amount-of(steam) and on amount-of(water) is from boiling. So $D_s[\text{amount-of(steam)}] = 1$ and $D_s[\text{amount-of(water)}] = -1$.

Because steam is a gas, there are several indirect influences on temperature(steam) and pressure(steam) (see Figure 7). In particular,

temperature(steam) $\propto_{Q+}$ pressure(steam)

temperature(steam) $\propto_{Q+}$ heat(stream)

pressure(steam) $\propto_{Q+}$ amount-of(steam)

pressure(steam) $\propto_{Q-}$ volume(steam)

pressure(steam) $\propto_{Q+}$ heat(steam)

Assuming the container is rigid, $D_s[\text{volume(can)}] = 0$, and since the spaces of the steam and water are separate and fill the container,

volume(can) = volume(water) + volume(steam)

Since

$D_s[volume(water)] = -1$, $D_s[volume(steam)]=1$ and $D_m[volume(steam)] = D_m[volume(water)]$.

Assume the function that determines pressure(steam) is continuous in amount-of(steam), heat(steam), and volume(steam). Then any particular $D[amount-of(steam)]$ and $D[heat(steam)]$, we can find a corresponding $D[volume(steam)]$ such that

$$(M\ D_s[pressure(steam)]\ I) = 0$$

i.e., the pressure at the end of I will be the same as it was at the start of I. Let β stand for that value of $D[volume(steam)]$. Then

$$(M\ A[volume(steam)]\ end(I)) = (M\ A[volume(steam)]\ start\ (I)) + \beta$$

is necessary for $D_s[pressure(steam)]$ to be zero. A fact about steam is that, at any particular pressure and temperature, the volume of steam is very much greater than the volume of water it was produced from.[16] In other words,

$$D_s[pressure(steam)] = 0 \Rightarrow D_m[volume(water)] << D_m[volume(steam)].$$

But in fact,

$$D_m[volume(steam)] = D_m[volume(water)], \text{ so } D[volume(steam)] < \beta.$$

This means that $(M\ A[volume(steam)]\ end(I))$ will be less than

$$(M\ A[volume(steam)]\ start(I)) + \beta,$$

and because

$$pressure(steam) \propto_{Q-} volume(steam),$$

the pressure of the steam will be greater than it was, i.e.,

$$D_s[pressure(steam)] = 1.$$

Since $D_s[heat(steam)] = 1$, both of the influences on temperature(steam) are positive, so $D_s[temperature(steam)] = 1$.

---

[16] At standard temperature and pressure, about 220 times greater in fact.

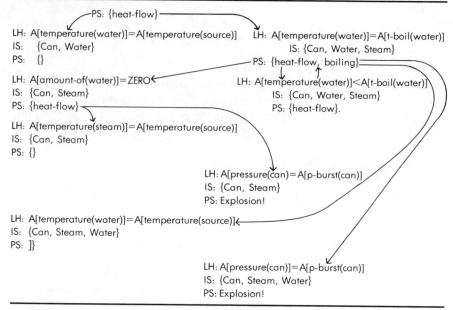

Figure 15. Alternatives for Sealed Container. Here are the Process Structures envisioned for water being heated in a sealed container, generated by repeated Limit Analysis.

So far we have discovered that

$$D_s[pressure(steam)] = D_s[temperature(steam)] = 1.$$

Since the water and steam are in contact their pressures will be equal, and since pressure indirectly affects the boiling temperature, the boiling temperature will also rise. The possible relative rates introduce three cases. If the boiling temperature is rising faster ($D_m[t\text{-boil(water)}] > D_m[temperature(steam)]$) then the boiling will stop, the heat flow will increase heat(water) again, the temperature will rise, and the boiling will begin again.[17] In the other two cases ($D_m[t\text{-boil(water)}] = D_m[temperature(steam)]$ and $D_m[t\text{-boil(water)}] < D_m[temperature(steam)]$) the boiling will continue, albeit at a higher temperature and pressure. In all three cases, the increasing pressure makes $A[pressure(can)] = A[p\text{-burst(can)}]$ possible, in which case the container explodes. The alternatives are summarized in Figure 15. To actually determine which of these occurs requires more information, but at least we have a warning of potential disaster.

---

[17] The astute reader will notice that this situation gives rise to a cycle of states that corresponds to a rising equilibrium rather than an oscillation. The Equality Change Law can be used to distinguish between these types of behavior; see Forbus (1982) for details.

3.3 Analyzing Motion and Stability

Dynamical reasoning involves more than just simulation. By analyzing the possible behaviors of a situation in greater detail we can produce a summary of its behavior and eventual disposition (e.g., Forbus, 1981a). In classical physics these analyses are often concerned with *stability*. Here we will examine a simple situation involving motion, ascertain that it is an oscillator, and perturb it to figure out under what conditions it will remain stable.

3.3.1 A Simple Motion Vocabulary.

First we shall examine how motion can be described within Qualitative Process theory. A simple vocabulary for abstract one dimensional motion will serve as an illustration.

We will need some simple descriptions of spatial relationships. We will use the symbols $+1$ and -1 to denote distinct directions along some axis, and for some quantity Q

Direction-Of(<direction>, Q)

will be true exactly when the sign of Q's amount is the same as the indicated direction. The location of an object will be modeled by a quantity position, and if there is no immobile object directly against an object B in direction dir we will say

Free-Direction(B, dir)

If there is an object in that direction, say C, then we will say

Contact(B, C, dir)

Finally, when some object C lies along direction dir from object B, we will say

Direction-Towards(B, C, dir)

Motion and acceleration are specified as processes in Figure 16. The motion description says that motion will occur when a movable object is free in the direction of its velocity and that velocity is non-zero. Motion is a positive influence on the position of an object, in that if the velocity is positive the position will increase and if negative the position will decrease. Acceleration occurs when a movable object has a non-zero net force in a free direction, and the influence it provides on velocity is qualitatively proportional to the net force and inversely proportional to the mass of the object. Friction (see Figure 17) occurs when there is surface contact, and produces a force on the object which is qualitatively proportional to the normal force and acts in a direction opposite that of the motion.

While this description of motion is Newtonian, Aristotelian and Impetus

---

Process Motion(B,dir)

individuals:
        B an object, Mobile(B)

Preconditions:
        Free-Direction(B, dir)
        Direction-Of(dir, velocity(B))

QuantityConditions:
        A_m[velocity(B)] > ZERO

Influences:
        I+(position(B), A[velocity(B)])

Process Acceleration(B,dir)

Individuals:
        B an object, Mobile(B)
        dir a direction

Preconditions:
        Free-Direction(B,dir)
        Direction-Of(dir, velocity(B))

QuantityConditions:
        A_m[net-force(B)] > ZERO

Relations:
        Let acc be a quantity
        acc $\propto_{Q+}$ net-force(B)
        acc $\propto_{Q-}$ mass(B)
        ; The basic QP version of F = m * a
        Correspondence((acc ZERO)
                        (net-force(B) ZERO))
Influences: I+ (velocity(B) A[acc])

;Recall that a correspondence maps Quantity Space information
;across $\propto_{Q-}$ here, if net-force(B) is greater than ZERO
;we can conclude that Acc is also greater than ZERO

Figure 16. Process Descriptions of Motion and Acceleration. In this abstract motion
vocabulary we ignore the kind of motion occurring (swinging, flying, sliding, etc.) and the
complexities of motion in several dimensions. We assume sign values are assigned to directions along some axis, with magnitudes indicating distance from an arbitrarily chosen origin.

theories[18] can also be described—QP theory constrains the form of dynamics theories not their content.

Collisions are complicated. The reason collisions are complicated is that they are
usually described in terms of a piece of history. We will use an Encapsulated

---

[18] McCloskey (1983) and Clement (1983) argue that naive theories of motion in our culture correspond
to Impetus theories, not Aristotelian theories. Forbus (1982) illustrates process vocabularies for Impetus
and Aristotelian motion.

```
Individual View Moving-Friction
Individuals:
          B an object, Mobile(B)
          S a surface
          dir a direction
Preconditions:
          Sliding-Contact(B,S)
QuantityConditions:
          Motion(B, dir)
Relations:
          Let fr be a quantity
          fr ∝ₐ₊ normal-force(B)
          Aₛ[fr] = −Aₛ[velocity(B)]
          fr ∈ forces-on(B)
```

Figure 17. Friction in Newtonian Motion. Objects have a set forces-on, whose sum is the net force on the object. Friction is modelled by an Individual View rather than a process because it contributes to the force on an object rather than the derivative of force.

History, as described in Section 2. The simplest description of a collision just involves a reversal of velocity, as illustrated in Figure 18. As a simplification we have assumed C is immobile so that we won't have to worry about momentum transfer between moving objects and changes of direction in more than one dimen-

```
Encapsulated-History Collide(B,C,dir)
Individuals:
          B an object, Mobile(B)
          C an object, Immobile(C)
          dir a direction
          E an event
Preconditions:
          (T contact(B, C, dir) start(E))
          (T direction-towards(B, C, dir) start(E))
QuantityCondition:
          (T motion(B, dir) start(E))
Relations:
          (M A[velocity(B)] start(E)) = − (M A[velocity(B)] end(E))
          (M velocity(B) during(E)) = ZERO
          duration(E) = ZERO
          (T direction-towards(C,B,dir) end(E))
          (T contact(B,C,dir) end(E))
;Recall  (T <statement> <time>) means "<statement> is true during <time>"
```

Figure 18. Collision Specification. Sometimes all we know about a situation is the particular kind of behavior that will occur. While violating composability, Encapsulated Histories are the only way to evolve a history in such cases.

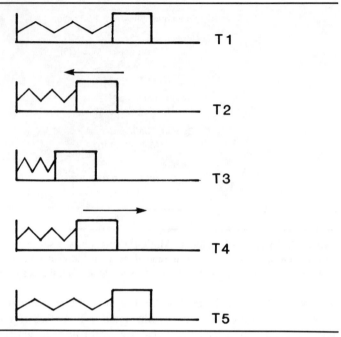

Figure 19. A Sliding Block. Here is a system we will analyze to determine what it does and how different factors, such as whether or not there is friction, affect its behavior.

sion. Even our more complicated models of collisions appear to use such Encapsulated Histories, such as a compound history consisting of contacting the surface, compression, expansion, and finally breaking contact. The type of collision which occurs can be specified by refering to the theory of materials for the objects involved.[19]

The Process Vocabulary for motion presented above is quite abstract. The particular kind of motion—flying, sliding, rolling, or swinging—is not mentioned. These motions would be specializations of the motion process considered above, defined by additional preconditions and relations (sliding and rolling require surface contact and could involve friction, for instance). The advantage of having the abstract description as well as the more detailed ones is that some conclusions can be drawn even with little information. If we kick something and it isn't blocked, for instance, then it will move.

3.3.2 An Oscillator. Consider the block B connected to the spring S in Figure 19. Suppose the block is pulled back so that the spring is extended. Initially we will

---

[19] Forbus (1982) describes how to model simple distinctions between different kinds of materials, such as rigid, elastic, and brittle, with QP theory.

Individual-View Elastic-Object(B)

Individuals:
    B a physical object

Preconditions:
    Elastic-Substance(made-of(B))

Relations:
    Has-Quantity(B, length)
    Has-Quantity(B, internal-force)
    Has-Quantity(B, rest-length)
    D_s[rest-length(B)] = 0
    internal-force(B) $\propto_{Q+}$ length(B)
    Correspondence((internal-force(B) ZERO)
                (length(B) rest-length(B)))

Individual-View Relaxed(B)

Individuals:
    B an elastic object

QuantityConditions:
    A[length(B)] = A[rest-length(B)]

Individual-View Stretched(B)

Individuals:
    B an elastic object

QuantityConditions:
    A[length(B)] > A[rest-length(B)]

Individual-View Compressed(B)

Individuals:
    B an elastic object

QuantityConditions:
    A[length(B)] < A[rest-length(B)]

Figure 20. Descriptions of elastic objects. Intuitively an elastic object stores energy in terms of reversible deformations of shape. The basic view of an elastic object relates the internal force and length, and the other three views describe the states it can be in.

also assume that the contact between the block and the floor is frictionless. What will happen?

We will model the spring S as device satisfying Hooke's Law (see Figure 20). Let displacement(S) be the difference between the block's position and the position at which S is relaxed. Since initially the spring is extended, displacement(S) is greater than ZERO and so the spring will exert a force. Because the block is rigidly connected to the spring, the net force on the block will be negative and since the block is free to move in the direction of the force, an acceleration will occur. The acceleration will in turn cause the velocity to move from ZERO, which will in turn cause $D_s[\text{positive}(B)] = -1$ (in other words, a change of position in the -1 direction). By rigid contact, $D_s[\text{length}(S)] = -1$ and by the $\propto_Q$ relation with displacement, $D_s[\text{net-force}(S)] = -1$. The processes occurring are Motion(B, -1) and Acceleration(B, -1). The next Limit Point reached is A[net-force(S)] = ZERO, which ends the acceleration. The correspondence tells us this occurs when the length of the spring is equal to its rest length, so the spring will become relaxed. The motion, however, will continue. Setting aside the details, the next set of processes are Motion(B, -1) and Acceleration(B, $+1$), with Compressed(S) now true. The only Limit Point in the Quantity Spaces that are changing is the zero velocity point (assuming the spring is unbreakable), so the motion will continue until the velocity is zero. The conclusion that the next set of processes are Motion(B, $+1$) and Acceleration(B, $+1$), followed by Motion(B, $+1$) for an instant and then Motion(B, $+1$) and Acceleration(B, -1) follows in the same way. At the end event of the last Process Structure, the orderings on the Quantity Spaces and the processes evoked are the same as the initial instant. Thus we can conclude that an oscillation is occuring. Note that the active processes must be the same, because the Preconditions might have changed. Figure 21 depicts the envisionment for the oscillator.

Some of the assumptions made in producing the envisionment can now be perturbed to examine the effects of different physical models. For instance, if the spring is crushable or breakable, then there will be Limit Points around rest-length(S) that correspond to the occurance of crushing or breaking. It seems crushing must be ruled out by assumption, since the machinery we have developed so far does not allow us to rule it out via contradiction. However, we can deduce that the spring won't break under the conditions above.

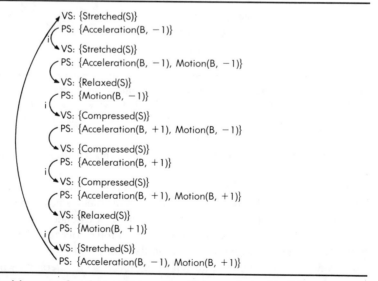

VS: {Stretched(S)}
PS: {Acceleration(B, -1)}

VS: {Stretched(S)}
PS: {Acceleration(B, -1), Motion(B, -1)}

VS: {Relaxed(S)}
PS: {Motion(B, -1)}

VS: {Compressed(S)}
PS: {Acceleration(B, $+1$), Motion(B, -1)}

VS: {Compressed(S)}
PS: {Acceleration(B, $+1$)}

VS: {Compressed(S)}
PS: {Acceleration(B, $+1$), Motion(B, $+1$)}

VS: {Relaxed(S)}
PS: {Motion(B, $+1$)}

VS: {Stretched(S)}
PS: {Acceleration(B, -1), Motion(B, $+1$)}

Figure 21. Envisionment for the oscillator. Transitions marked with "i" occur in an instant, all others require an interval of time.

If we can prove that the block will go out no further than when it started then we can claim that it won't break because it didn't break in the first place. This requires an energy argument. The energy theory we will use is very simple (see Forbus, 1982, for details). To summarize, there are certain types of quantities which are energy-quantities, which are qualitatively proportional to certain other quantities and exist whenever they do. Two such energy quantities are kinetic energy and "spring" energy. For every object there is a total energy, which is the sum of its energy quantities. Process Instances can be defined as energy sources or sinks with respect to a system according to how they influence energy quantities of objects which comprise the system. Energy conservation can be defined in several ways, and for our purposes it is sufficient to say that if there are no sources then the energy of a system doesn't increase over time.

Here the system is the mass and spring combination. At time $t1$ the block is still but the spring is stretched, i.e.,

(M A[velocity(B)] t1) = ZERO

(M displacement(S) t1) > ZERO

which means that

(M total-energy(system) t1) > ZERO

If energy is conserved and there is no influx of energy (i.e., a pattern of influences involving energy quantities where one such quantity inside the system is positively influenced and another such quantity outside the system is negatively influenced), then we know

$\forall t \in ttime$
    After(t, t1)
    $\Rightarrow \sim$ (M total-energy(system) t) > (M total-energy(system) t1)

This means that the block can only go out as far as it was at $t1$, since if it ever went out farther we would contradict the previous statement.

3.3.3 Stability Analysis.

To further analyze this system, we must abstract the processes that occur to form a compound process. We can start by writing an Encapsulated History, but we will also need to define properties of the objects over the piece of history. These properties will include the total energy of the system (total-energy(system)), the energy lost during a cycle (e-loss(system)), and the maximum displacement during a cycle (max-disp(S)). These parameters are chosen because they give rise to energy quantities, as described above. We will assume the Relations for the compound process include:

max-disp(S)(S) $\propto_{Q+}$ total-energy(system)

correspondence((max-disp(S)(S), ZERO), (total-energy(system) ZERO))

To perform an energy analysis we will also want to re-write any inequalities in the Quantity Conditions in terms of energy, to wit:

> QuantityConditions:
> A[total-energy(system)] > ZERO

Thus if the total energy of the system ever reaches ZERO during an occurance of the compound process it will no longer be active. Note that since our Quantity Condition is no longer tied to a particular piece of the history that we cannot use this new model for simulation. Instead, we will use it to analyze global properties of the system behavior.

We can now use the basic QP deductions on this compound process to determine the consequences of perturbing the situation in various ways. Each perturbation is represented by a process which influences one of the parameters which determines the energy of the system. For example, if friction were introduced (i.e., D_s[total-energy(system)] $= -1$), by the Quantity Condition above we can conclude that the oscillation process will eventually stop, and that if the system is pumped so that its energy increases (i.e., D_s[total-energy(system)] $= 1$), that the materials involved in the oscillator may break in some way.[20] Suppose for example the oscillator is subject to friction, but we pump it with some fixed amount of energy per cycle (call it e-pump(system)), as would happen in a mechanism such as a clock. Is such a system stable? The only things we will assume about the friction process in the system is that

> Relations:
> e-loss(system) $\propto_{Q+}$ total-energy(system)
> correspondence((e-loss(system), ZERO), (total-energy(system), ZERO))
>
> Influences:
> I-(total-energy(system), e-loss(system))

recalling that e-loss(system) is the net energy lost due to friction over a cycle of the oscillator process. The loss being qualitatively proportional to the energy is based on the fact that the energy lost by friction is proportional to the distance travelled, which in turn is proportional to the maximum displacement, which itself is qualitatively proportional to the energy of the system, as stated above.

The lower bound for the energy of the system is ZERO, and an upper bound for energy is implicit in the possibility of the parts breaking. The result, via the $\propto_Q$ statement above, is a set of limits on the Quantity Space for e-loss(system). If we assume e-pump(system), the energy which is added to the system over a cycle, is

---

[20] The Tacoma Narrows bridge phenomena, something every engineer should know about.

within this boundary then there will be a value for total-energy(system), call it e-stable(system), such that:

∀ t ∈ *interval*
(M A[total-energy(system)]t) = (M A[e-stable(system)] t)
  ⇒ (M A[e-loss(system)] t) = (M A[e-pump(system)] t)

Note that e-stable(system) is unique because $\propto_Q$ is monotonic. If the energy of the system is at this point, the influences of friction and pumping will cancel and the system will stay at this energy. Suppose

(M A[total-energy(system)] t) > (M A[e-stable(system)] t)

over some cycle. Then because the loss is qualitatively proportional to the energy, the energy loss will be greater than the energy gained by pumping, i.e., D_s[total-energy(system)] = −1, and the energy will drop until it reaches e-stable(system). Similarly, if total-energy(system) is less than e-stable(system) the influence of friction on the energy will be less than that of the pumping, thus D_s[total-energy(system)] = 1. This will continue until the energy of the system is again equal to e-stable(system). Therefore for any particular pumping energy there will be a stable oscillation point. This is qualitative version of the proof of the existence and stability of limit cycles in the solution of a differential equation.

3.3.4 Relationship to Qualitative States. Previous work on representing motion used a *Qualitative State* representation (de Kleer, 1975; Forbus, 1981a), a straightforward abstraction of the notion of state from classical mechanics. Some of the parameters that would appear in a classical description of state are represented abstractly (typically position is represented by a piece of space, and velocity by a symbolic heading). While in classical physics the type of activity is left implicit in the choice of descriptive equations, in the Qualitative State description the type of activity is made explicit. Qualitative States are linked by qualitative simulation rules that map a state into the set of states that can occur next. We can generate a description of all the qualitative states the system can be in as follows: First run the rules on the initial state, producing the set of states that can occur next. Then run the rules on these states in turn, generating still more states. Eventually no new states will be generated, because each component of a Qualitative State can have only a finite number of values, and so there are only a finite (but possibly large) number of distinct states. The graph that results is a rooted directed graph, often containing cycles, called the *envisionment*. Figure 22 illustrates. The envisionment can be used to answer simple questions directly, assimilate certain global assumptions about motion, and plan solutions to more complex questions.

Simulation rules are a very weak form of dynamics theory; they do not explicitly contain the assumptions under which they operate. In the case of motion, they do

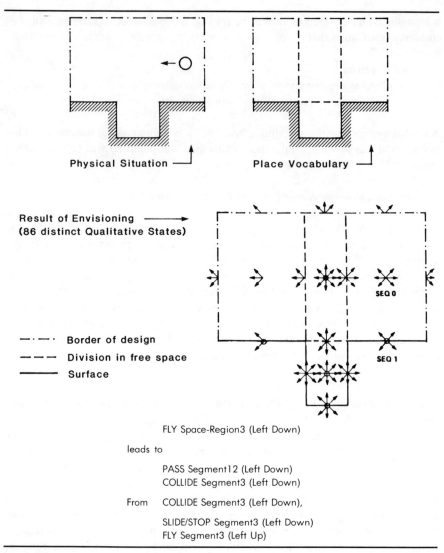

Figure 22. Qualitative State Description of Motion. Consider the ball moving leftwards as depicted below. A qualitative description of space (*Place Vocabulary*) can be computed from the diagram and the possible ways the ball can move given that initial state are depicted schematically over the places they occur. A detailed description of one state and its relationships between other states is also shown.

not allow easy composition to describe more complex systems.[21] However, by comparing Qualitative State representations with QP theory descriptions we can understand them both more clearly.

Consider a Process Vocabulary comprised solely of motion and acceleration. The Limit Analysis for a moving object will include only the possibilities raised by dynamics, such as the acceleration of gravity reversing the velocity of a ball or friction bringing a sliding block to a halt. The possible changes in Process Structure caused by kinematics—such as the ball hitting a wall or the block flying off a table—are not predicted within this vocabulary. To include them would require encoding the relevant geometry in such a way that it can be moved out of the Preconditions and into the Quantity Conditions. To do this, we must first describe space by a *Place Vocabulary*,[22] because we must break space up into distinct pieces that can be reasoned about symbolically. We might then try to use the entities in the Place Vocabulary as elements in the Quantity Space for position. Then the kinematic changes would be discovered by Limit Analysis just as the dynamical ones are.

Unfortunately, things are not so simple. First of all, we need to introduce an ordering between elements of the Place Vocabulary. (This ordering need not be total; we can use ambiguity in the ordering to represent our lack of knowledge about the precise heading of the moving object). For motion in two or three dimensions this requires specifying a direction, since partial orders are only well-defined for one dimension. And because we have specified a direction, we now must also specify the place we are starting from, since that will determine what the neighbors in the position Quantity Space are. (Consider walking out your front door while throwing a ball up in the air. What the ball might hit changes dramatically.) However, this means the place and direction must be included in the specification of the motion process. If we could successfully add such information, an instance of the motion process in this vocabulary would begin to look like a Qualitative State for the same collection of places and type of motion. The qualitative simulation rules would thus roughly correspond to a compilation of the Limit Analysis on this new motion vocabulary.

From this perspective we can see the relative strengths of the two representations. For evolving motion descriptions the Qualitative State representation makes sense, since kinematic constraints are essential to motion. Its "compiled" nature makes the Qualitative State representation inappropriate for very simple deductions (where only part of a Qualitative State is known) and more complex questions involving dynamics or compound systems, such as the example in the previous section.

---

[21] There is potential for confusion, since (de Kleer & Brown, 1983) uses the term "Qualitative State" in a different context. In their physics composability is attained by shared parameters, much as QP theory achieves composability by shared individuals. The Qualitative State representations for motion, however, had no notion of quantity.

[22] Forbus (1981a) describes the principles involved and defines a Place Vocabulary for motion through space in a simple domain.

3.4 Causal Reasoning

We use causality to impose order upon the world. When we think that "A causes B", we believe that if we want B to happen we should bring about A, and that if we see B happening than A might be the reason for it. Causal reasoning is especially important for understanding physical systems, as noted in Rieger and Grinberg (1975) and de Kleer (1979). Exactly what underlies our notion of causation in physical systems is still something of a mystery.

Consider the representations of objects and processes used in physics. Typically equations are used to express constraints that hold between physical parameters. A salient feature of equations is that they can be used in several different ways. For example, if we know "$X = A + B$", then if we have A and B we can compute X, but also if we have X and A we can compute B. It has been noted that in causal reasoning people do *not* use equations in all possible ways (diSessa, 1983; Riley, 1981). Only certain directions of information flow intuitively correspond to causal changes. I propose the following *Causal Directedness Hypothesis:*

> *Changes in physical situations which are perceived as causal are due to our interpretation of them as corresponding to direct changes caused by processes or to propagation of those direct effects through functional dependencies.*

This section will attempt to justify that hypothesis.

First, I propose that causality requires some notion of mechanism. Imagine an abstract rectangle of a particular length and width. If we imagine the same rectangle being longer, it will have greater area. There is no sense of causality in the change from one to the other. However, if we imagine the rectangle to be made of some elastic material and we bring about the increased length by stretching it, then we are comfortable with saying "the increased length causes the area to increase". Qualitative Process theory asserts that processes are the mechanisms which directly cause changes. The quantities that can be directly influenced by processes are in some sense *independent* parameters, because they are what can be directly affected. All other quantities are dependent, in the sense that to affect them some independent parameter or set of independent parameters must be changed. This suggests representing the relationships between parameters in terms of functions rather than constraint relations.

This hypothesis explains a problem that has been observed in programs that reason about physical systems. In generating explanations of physical systems, it is often useful to characterize how the system responds to some kind of change (this variety of qualitative perturbation analysis was invented by de Kleer, who calls it *Incremental Qualitative Analysis*). One way to perform IQ analysis is to model the system by a constraint network, in which the relationships are modeled by "devices" which contain local rules that enforce the desired semantics.[23] The values of

---

[23] These examples are drawn from systems implemented in CONLAN (Forbus, 1981c), a constraint language. The graphical notation for constraint networks is similar to logic diagrams, except that the terminals are given explicit names and the devices are multi-functional. The technique described here is a simplification of de Kleer's algorithms (de Kleer, 1979), which are far more subtle and powerful. de

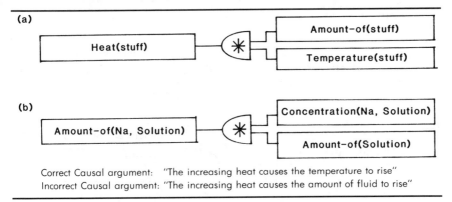

Correct Causal argument: "The increasing heat causes the temperature to rise"
Incorrect Causal argument: "The increasing heat causes the amount of fluid to rise"

Figure 23. Constraint representation of relationships. In the constraint networks below, the boxes (cells) represent quantities. The relationship between the quantities is expressed in terms of a multiplier constraint. (a) is drawn from the model for a piece of "stuff" used in an effort to represent a student's understanding of heat exchangers. (b) is drawn from an IQ model of a kidney to be used in explaining the syndome of inappropriate secretion of anti-diarretic hormone (SIADH).

quantities are modeled by the sign of their change—increasing, decreasing, or constant. To perform an analysis, a value corresponding to a hypothesized change is placed in a cell of the constraint network representing the system. The rules associated with the constraint network are then used to deduce new values for other cells in the network. The propagation of information models the propagation of changes in the system, with dependency relationships between cells corresponding to causal connections. For example, if the value of cell A was used to deduce the value for cell B, the interpretation of the value of cell A being used to deduce the value of cell B is that "The change represented by cell A caused the change represented by cell B". Figure 23 illustrates fragments from two different models.[24] The top fragment states that temperature of some "stuff" is the product of its heat and the amount of it that there is, and the bottom fragment is the definition of sodium concentration in a solution.

It is possible to reach an impasse while building a causal argument—a quantity receives a value, but no further values can be computed unless an assumption is made. The safest assumption to make is that, unless you know otherwise, a quantity doesn't change. The problem lies in determining which quantity to make the assumption about. Suppose we assume that the amount of stuff is constant. Then we would conclude that the increase in heat causes an increase in temperature, which makes sense. However, suppose we assume instead that the temperature remains constant. We are left with the conclusion that a rise in heat *causes* the amount of

---

Kleer's models use directional rules as well as constraint laws, although his theory does not provide any criteria for selecting which direction in a constraint law is appropriate for causal reasoning.

[24] The problem was observed in implementing the model of a student's understanding of a heat exchanger described in (Williams et al., 1983), in my own work on understanding Automatic Boiler Control systems, and in an early version of the kidney model described in Asbell (1982).

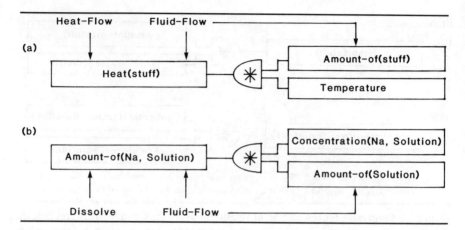

Figure 24. Model Fragments with Possible Process. Here are the models from the previous figure with the quantities annotated with the (likely) processes that might affect them. Note that certain quantities (temperature, concentration) cannot be directly changed. These are *dependent* quantities, and should not be the subject of assumptions in building causal arguments.

stuff to decrease! Barring state transitions, this change does not correspond to our ideas of what can cause what. In the second fragment the problem is more serious—increasing sodium will cause the amount of water to increase, *if* the rest of the kidney is working as it should! To do this requires a complicated feedback mechanism which is triggered by detecting an increased sodium concentration, not by the definition of concentration itself!

The problem lies in the ontological impoverishment of the constraint representation. Temperature and concentration are not directly influenced by processes (at least in most people's Naive Physics)—physically they are *dependent* variables, and thus are not proper subjects of assumptions in constructing causal arguments. Amount of stuff, on the other hand, can be directly affected, so assuming it does not change will avoid generating ill-formed causal arguments. Figure 24 illustrates this.

Of course, the proper assumptions to make concern what processes are active and how indirect influences are resolved. If we do not represent processes, we can only make assumptions about the values of quantities. If we assume a quantity is constant and later discover that assumption is wrong, we are left in the dark about *why* that assumption was wrong. For example, if the amount of stuff turns out not to be constant, we can look for fluid flows or state changes to explain why it isn't. Since processes tend to have more than one effect, there is some chance that the contradiction can lead to discovering more about the system rather than just being a bad guess.

4 Discussion

An intelligent entity must be able to reason about a changing world, often with incomplete information. A common form for the mechanisms of change simplifies this problem considerably. Qualitative Process theory adds the notion of physical process to the ontology of common sense physics to provide such a common form.

The preceeding examples indicate the usefulness of Qualitative Process Theory for reasoning tasks involving dynamics, as well as illustrate how various common-sense phenomena might be modelled. As of this writing Qualitative Process Theory is still under active development, and more thinking and experimenting will be required to fully develop the basic theory, much less a set of extension theories adequate to fully characterize human facility at physical reasoning. Nevertheless, some interesting questions have already arisen. What else do we need to make full use of Processes and Quantity Spaces? Are there any conclusions we can draw concerning reasoning about change in non-physical domains?

First, it should be noted that good ontologies are required. Without appropriate definitions of what can comprise an individual within a domain, such as Hayes' notion of contained fluids, it is impossible to write process descriptions. In addition, the ability of certain processes to create and destroy individuals must also be better formalized. For fluids most of this can be modeled adequately with quantities, but for solid objects descriptions of breaking, gluing, and crushing will require a different mechanism for specifying effects.

Another requirement can be thought of as determining "connectedness". The conditions of "connectedness" are stated in terms of the existence of certain individuals (such as paths) and implicitly (with respect to Qualitative Process theory) in the Preconditions. Each domain will require such notions, akin to (and in some cases, exactly) kinematics. Usually these conditions are spatial, so further developments in qualitative spatial reasoning will be required. It is unclear just how many different useful qualitative descriptions of space there are; all of them will have the form of breaking up objects and pieces of space into pieces (PLACES) according to some criteria that simplifies the kind of reasoning being performed. Building such theories is not simple, but their construction will be richly rewarding in the possibility of connecting our physics with theories of perception and manipulation to truly understand how to reason about the physical world.

There are of course many important kinds of change that are not strictly physical—changes in economic and social properties, for instance. Dynamics is merely a subset of a full theory of action, but it is the most approachable subset. One well known reason is that we agree on what the right answers are. Another reason is that the intentions of actors are not modelled. But now that we have learned more about representing change in the physical world, there is another difficulty of more general domains which has become clearer. The problems of Local Evolution and Intersection/Interaction still apply, and to solve them will require finding ways to specify direct and indirect effects in ways that allow their comparison and combination. There may not in general be such techniques; only time will tell.

References

Allen, J. (1981). "Maintaining Knowledge about Temporal Intervals," TR-86, Computer Science Department, University of Rochester.

Asbell, I. (1982). "A Constraint Representation and Explanation Facility for Renal Physiology," MIT SM Thesis. Cambridge, MA.

Clement, J. (1983). "A Conceptual Model Discussed by Galileo and Used Intuitively by Physics Students," in *Mental Models*, D. Gentner & A. Stevens (Eds.). Hillsdale, NJ: Erlbaum.

de Kleer, J. (1975). "Qualitative and Quantitative Knowledge in Classical Mechanics," TR-352, MIT AI Lab, Cambridge, MA.

de Kleer, J. (1979). "Causal and Teleological Reasoning in Circuit Recognition," TR-529, MIT AI Lab, Cambridge, MA.

de Kleer, J., & Brown, J. (1983). "Assumptions and Ambiguities in Mechanistic Mental Models," in *Mental Models*, D. Gentner & A. Stevens (Eds.). Hillsdale, NJ: Erlbaum.

diSessa, A. (1983). "Phenomenology and the Evolution of Intuition," *Mental Models*, D. Gentner & A. Stevens (Eds.). Hillsdale, NJ: Erlbaum.

Forbus, K. (1981a). "A Study of Qualitative and Geometric Knowledge in Reasoning about Motion," TR-615, MIT AI Lab, Cambridge, MA.

Forbus, K. (1981b). "Using Qualitative Simulation to Generate Explanations," BBN Technical Report No. 4490. (Also in *Proceedings of the Third Annual Conference of the Cognitive Science Society*, August 1981.

Forbus, K. (1981c). "A CONLAN Primer," BBN Technical Report No. 4491.

Forbus, K. (1981d). "Qualitative Reasoning about Physical Processes," in *Proceedings of IJCAI-7*.

Forbus, K. (1982). "Qualitative Process Theory," MIT AI Lab Memo No. 664. (To appear in *Artificial Intelligence*.)

Forbus, K. (1983a). "Qualitative Reasoning about Space and Motion," in *Mental Models*, D. Gentner & A. Stevens (Eds.). Hillsdale, NJ: Erlbaum.

Forbus, K. (1983b). "Measurement Interpretation in Qualitative Process Theory," in *Proceedings of IJCAI-8*.

Forbus, K., & Gentner, D. (1983). "Learning Physical Domains: Towards a Theoretical Framework," in *Proceedings of the Second International Machine Learning Workshop*.

Fikes, R., & Nillson, N. (1971). "STRIPS: A New Approach to the Application of Theorem Proving to Problem Solving," *Artificial Intelligence*, Vol. 2, No. 3.

Hayes, P. J. (1979a). "The Naive Physics Manifesto," in *Expert Systems in the Microelectronic age*, edited by D. Michie (Ed.). Edinburgh, Scotland: Edinburg University Press.

Hayes, P. J. (1979b). "Naive Physics 1—Ontology for Liquids," Memo, Centre pour les etudes Semantiques et Cognitives, Geneva, Switzerland.

McCarthy, J., & Hayes, P. J. (1969). "Some Philosophical Problems from the Standpoint of Artificial Intelligence," *Machine Intelligence 4*, B. Meltzer & D. Michie (Eds.). Edinburgh, Scotland: Edinburgh University Press.

McCloskey, M. (1983). "Naive Theories of Motion," in *Mental Models*, D. Gentner & A. Stevens (Eds.). Hillsdale, NJ: Erlbaum.

McDermott, D., & Doyle, J. (1980). "Non-Monotonic Logic I," *Artificial Intelligence*, Vol. 13, N. 1.

Minsky, M. (1979). "A Framework for Representing Knowledge," MIT AI Lab Memo No. 306.

Moore, R. (1979). "Reasoning about Knowledge and Action, MIT PhD thesis.

Riley, M., Bee, N., & Mokwa, J. (1981). "Representations in Early Learning: The Acquisition of Problem Solving Strategies in Basic Electricity/Electronics," Technical Report, Navy Personnel Research and Development Center, San Diego, CA.

Simmons, R. (1982). "Spatial and Temporal Reasoning in Geologic Map Interpretation," in *Proceedings of the National Conference on Artificial Intelligence*.

Stanfill, C. (1983). "The Decomposition of a Large Domain: Reasoning about Machine," in *Proceedings of the National Conference on Artifical Intelligence*.

Williams, M., Hollan, J., & Stevens, A. (1983). "Human Reasoning about a Simple Physical System," in *Mental Models*, D. Gentner & A. Stevens (Eds). Hillsdale, NJ: Erlbaum.

6 *Partial Provisional Planning: Some Aspects of Commonsense Planning*

Charles F. Schmidt

Department of Psychology
and Laboratory for Computer Science Research
Rutgers University
New Brunswick, New Jersey

1 Introduction

Consider the following somewhat idealized example of the kind of planning that you and I do in pursuing the mundane goals of our everyday lives.

> *Goal:* A recently acquired print, already framed in an aluminum frame, is to be hung on the north wall of my living room between the left corner of the wall and the window.
>
> *Planned Action:* Hang the framed picture in the aforementioned general location.
>
> *Subgoal:* Picture wire is needed across the back of the picture to support it when hung.
>
> *Planned Action:* String the wire through supports on frame and wrap wire.
>
> *Default assumption:* This type of metallic frame already has supports provided for the wire.
>
> *Subgoal:* A support embedded in the wall is needed.
>
> *Analysis:* Type of support depends on type of wall material. Wall material is unknown, and covered with wallpaper.
>
> *Default assumption:* This house was built within the past 10 years; therefore the wall material is probably wallboard.
>
> *Analysis:* Support can be safely embedded in wallboard using plastic anchors. Plastic anchors accept a screw of matching diameter.
>
> *Planned action:* Embed screw in plastic anchor in wall.
>
> *Subgoal:* Obtain a plastic anchor.
>
> *Analysis:* Do I have an unused plastic anchor.
>
> *Fact:* Someone, self or other, recently purchased plastic anchors for use in hanging some other pictures.

227

Default assumption: Plastic anchors are usually sold with several in a packet and unless all are used, some will remain.

Subgoal: Get the plastic anchor.

Default assumption: Tools and hardware are typically kept in the basement in the vicinity of the work bench.

Subgoal: Obtain a screw of appropriate diameter and length.

Default assumption: Box filled with miscellaneous screws and nails typically will contain a screw that will be appropriate for use in a plastic anchor.

Subgoal: Get the screw.

Default assumption: Tools and hardware are typically kept in the basement in the vicinity of the work bench.

Subgoal: Make a hole in the wall for the anchor.

Subgoal: Get one of the hammers.

Default assumption: Tools and hardware are typically kept in the basement in the vicinity of the work bench.

Subgoal: Get the awl.

The example could be continued a bit more to include: determining whether I have picture wire; actions of going to the basement and bringing tools, supports and picture wire to the living room; making the hole; and so on. However, the plan would probably not be worked out in much more detail before I decided that I had planned enough to support the guidance of the actual execution of the plan.

Seemingly simple and certainly mundane scenarios such as these have kept my colleagues and I thinking and wondering about how to represent and use commonsense knowledge in planning and plan recognition for longer than I like to admit (Schmidt, Sridharan, & Goodson, 1978). I suspect that there are enough issues of logic and reasoning lurking in examples such as these to keep many of us busy for some time to come.

But although I have no definitive answers to share with you in this paper, we have implemented a planning system that can mimic some aspects of the reasoning that underlies this example. By relating here some of the details about how knowledge is structured and used in this system, I hope to contribute to the collective task of deepening our understanding of commonsense reasoning.

2 A Digression into Methodology

Before proceeding with this discussion, a few remarks about the way in which we have approached the task of understanding commonsense reasoning should be made. The foregoing example to which we will soon return illustrates one aspect of the approach. The starting point involves a consideration of how commonsense knowledge is used by the holder and creator of that knowledge, namely, the human information processing system. In this case, the use is for planning and supporting the execution of actions. The same knowledge may be put to use in other ways as well, but we choose to focus our investigation on one important use. This focus results in consideration of only part of the story about the contents and function of commonsense knowledge. This is a drawback to our approach, but it also affords an advantage. By looking at one type of use of commonsense knowledge, we can characterize the constraints on its use and the function it must serve. For example, one characteristic of human knowledge about object types is that this knowledge is typically organized within a hierarchical structure. As we proceed in our discussion of commonsense planning we will appreciate the functional utility of this organization in the planning process.

What is meant by constraints here? There are really two types. The first are the relatively invariant constraints imposed by the processing advantages and limitations of the human mind that created this knowledge for its use. Some of the advantages that the mind seems to enjoy are the ability to retain and efficiently retrieve a great deal of general and specific knowledge about the everyday world, and the use of an extremely flexible control structure. The mind's disadvantages seem to be related primarily to a rather limited working memory, and some unreliability in the ability to retrieve specific facts that were known at some point in time.

The second type of constraints that affect the use of commonsense knowledge arise from the world in which humans use this knowledge. On the one hand, our everyday world is an open one. Here nature and others like ourselves create changes quite without notice of or regard to our own current plans and goals. Consequently, we rarely have the luxury of complete knowledge. These changes that we could not foresee may simplify or complicate the plan we had in mind. In either case, a revision of the plan is required. A system that must plan in such an open world must, therefore, attempt to create plans that are easily revised in light of changing circumstances. On the other hand, the everyday world is also a world of convention and standard practice. Artifacts are manufactured with specific purposes in mind and generally the manufacturers of these artifacts are motivated to work out for us some of the interactions that exist between the various artifacts required for many of the tasks we must perform. For example, screwdrivers are made for the different types of screws, which in turn are created to function effectively in different types of material and under differing conditions of required torque. The existence of convention does not guarantee adherence to these conventions. But, again, a planning system that must function in such a world is expected to take advantage of whatever aid the existence of such conventions can give to the planning process.

Consideration of both the internal and external constraints on commonsense planning coupled with an examination of examples of this reasoning alert us to the role, or function, that commonsense knowledge serves. As someone trained in psychology, the biological heuristic that structure and function are often related, seems also to be a valid heuristic for studying commonsense knowledge—itself the product of a natural intelligence. This relation between structure and function in human cognition is probably best documented in the case of linguistic abilities (Lenneberg, 1967). There is no reason to suspect that such relations are confined to only this one aspect of human cognition (cf. Simon, 1981 gives a general discussion of a possible relation between evolution and the structure of complex systems.)

3 Functions and Characteristics

We have characterized a human actor as one who typically lacks the knowledge, time, computational resources, and often also the motivation to create complete and logically correct plans. What is created are what might be called partial and provisional plans. The important functional features of this type of plan is that it provides a basis for:

1. Recognizing when a new fact is relevant to the plan so that the plan may be updated, revised, or discarded
2. The execution and monitoring of the plan

These functional features suggest that the set of expressions that constitute a plan need not refer in a strict and straightforward sense to the "real world." Rather a plan may be more like a working hypothesis derived from a general theory. The hypothesis may be only partially formed in certain of its aspects, but if it is detailed enough to inform us about how to view new incoming information about the "real world," then its function is fulfilled. It is an hypothesis that is constantly being interpreted in light of new facts. We know that in general this is a logically risky strategy. A good hypothesis must be one whose terms and expressions are detailed enough so that determinate interpretations of their validity can be made, but at the same time, a hypothesis should not be so detailed that any mistaken assumption about the facts of the situation necessitates drastic revisions.

This is a delicate balance. It is probably not one which any computational device that must plan in an open world can guarantee. However, some ways of forming such hypotheses or plans will do better than others. Let us now turn to the explicit consideration of what strategies and characteristics of planning might do better than others in this regard.

4 Planning with Incomplete Knowledge

In fact, AI research on planning has indirectly extensively researched the problem of planning with incomplete knowledge. Every planning algorithm has incomplete knowledge at some point during the process of creating a plan. A decision made after another may invalidate the prior decision or an earlier choice may preclude a later choice. The difference is that the planning process that possesses complete knowledge relies on the fact that a truth value can be assigned to an expression when it wishes to evaluate that expression. This allows the planning process to tightly control the order in which subgoals are evaluated and pursued. In contrast, when the knowledge is incomplete, the process itself does not have control of when it will receive an answer to a question about an expression's value.

There are four strategies that can be followed by a planning process when an answer is needed but not forthcoming. One is the rather unimaginative but sometimes necessary solution of simply abandoning an attempt at creating a plan. A second is to plan conditionally. If the set of possible answers to a question needed to choose what to do is known (and not too large), then planning may be continued for each of the possible cases. This strategy has been studied particularly in the context of programming (Luckham & Buchanan, 1974; Warren, 1976; Manna & Waldinger, 1977). A third possibility is to postpone the decision until a later time when an answer might be forthcoming and shift the efforts of planning to another aspect of the plan. This is the strategy which has been most extensively investigated in research on planning. Hierarchical planning and nonlinear planning are both ways of postponing certain aspects of the planning process (Sussman, 1973; Stepankova & Havel, 1976; Sacerdoti, 1977; Stefik, 1980; Wilkins & Robinson, 1981). This research shows that postponing certain classes of decisions often reduces the search that a planner must engage in. A final strategy is not to postpone, but to make an assumption about the value of the unknown expression. The main example of research that involves this strategy is in the area of game playing. Here the assumptions are made using a rational theory of the opponent to determine possible values of an expression.

Except for the case of abandonment, each of these strategies has consequences for the way a plan might be represented. Commonsense planning probably at one time or another utilizes each of these strategies both singly and in combination. How to choose which strategy is an interesting research question which will not be pursued here. What we have pursued is the way in which the combination of the strategies of postponement and assumption might be incorporated in a planning process.

The fragment of planning provided in the example with which we began illustrates the use of both assumption and postponement. In order to develop our understanding of these general ideas, let us look at some of the specific features of this planning fragment.

Consider first how assumptions entered into the planning protocol. The assumptions were not triggered by a global evaluation of what is unknown in the planning context. Rather, they were triggered by specific steps in the planning process. Making assumptions is very much a goal-driven inference process in this example. Second, consider the contents of the assumption. In some cases the assumption involved assigning a truth value to a partially grounded expression. For example, this living-room wall is a type of wallboard was considered to be true by assumption. In other cases, the assumptions seemed to involve something analogous to assigning a truth value to an existentially quantified expression. For example, it was assumed that on this particular metallic frame there are two supports on opposite sides. Third, consider the nature of the assumptive inferences. None were made in what we might term an arbitrary way. They all involved an appeal to rules that seem to be similar in form to what Reiter (1980) refers to as defaults. The rules provided a basis for the conclusion. This basis typically rested on knowledge about how things usually are and also on supporting characteristics of the currently known facts. For example, the assumption that a plastic anchor could be found in the basement rested on the general knowledge that they are typically sold with several to a package. Also it rested on the specific fact that someone recently purchased a package of plastic anchors.

Next consider the various usages of postponement. Both hierarchical and non-linear strategies are exemplified in the same fragment. But there is also another type of postponement that is more striking. This is a strategy which I term a postponement of object or place selection. The simplest case of this involves deferring the choice of how to bind a variable in an expression and implicitly maintaining the disjunctive set of possibilities. The goal statement referred to hanging the picture somewhere between the window and the left corner of the north wall of the living room. The possible locations specified by this expression are known. But the choice among these may depend on the later choice of support as well as aesthetic considerations.

The more complicated type of postponement of object or place selection is created as a kind of side effect of making assumptions about the existence of certain objects in the planning environment. In this case, our knowledge of the facts provides no referent for the variables in the expression that has been introduced by assumption. Consequently, the binding to a known object must be deferred. This seems like a rather strange move if we are conditioned to thinking about planning within the context of complete knowledge. When knowledge is complete, binding a variable allows access to further expressions that characterize the chosen object in the world. In this way, additional information is gained about what must be done to this particular object in order to use it in the plan. For example, by choosing a particular screwdriver for use in the plan we would, in the case of complete knowledge, also be able to retrieve information about its type, location, color, length, and so on.

However, the introduction of such referentially empty statements makes good sense in commonsense planning, because there are two sources of information available for use in planning. One source is, of course, what we do know about the specific world in which we are planning to act. But a second source is in the form of general knowledge about types of objects, the functional interactions between object types (e.g. a philips screwdriver), part–whole relations between objects, interactions between object types and action specifications, and knowledge about how things typically are.

We now have a fairly specific picture of the kind of strategies that we would like to build into our computational experiment on commonsense planning. The remainder of the paper is devoted to describing how a first order approximation was implemented in our planning system.

5 Description Formalism

We have a great many types of things that must be described in a formalism convenient for the computations we wish to carry out in our study of this type of planning. Our work was carried out using the AIMDS system. This is a system designed to facilitate the investigation of knowledge-based reasoning developed by my colleague and collaborator N. S. Sridharan. The work on the planning system was carried out in collaboration first with Sridharan and John Goodson, and then with Sridharan and John Bresina. John Bresina deserves much of the credit for the fact that the planning system actually runs.

An overall discussion of the work on planning is available in (Sridharan, Bresina, & Schmidt, 1983), and a specific discussion of PLANX10 in (Bresina, 1981). The AIMDS system is extensively documented in (Sridharan, 1980). The reader who wishes more details is referred to these sources. Within this paper, I will present only those aspects of the formalism and implementation that bear on the strategies of postponement and assumption. The attempt will be made to keep the discussion as informal as possible without being unnecessarily vague about the syntax and semantics of our representation.

6 Representing Simple Facts

Although we have emphasized what a planner does not know, there are, of course, always specific facts about individual objects that are known. These facts are modeled in PLANX10 as a set of assertions held in a context referred to as the world model, WM. Assertions are names of individuals or constants connected by binary relations. Each such grounded term has a truth value of True, False, or Unknown associated with it. Some examples are:

((SCREW-1 INSIDE CAN-1) T)
A particular screw is inside a particular can.

((SCREW-1 TYPE PHILIPS) T)
This particular screw is a philips screw.

7 Representing Structured Descriptions

In addition to instances and relations, one can define a set of class names and class inclusion relations between the class names. For example, the class names FASTENER and SCREW might be introduced. By declaring that (SCREW AKO FASTENER) the fact that the class of things named screws are included in the class of things named fasteners is made known to the system. Class names are called templates within AIMDS. Instances, constants, class names, typed variables, and relations provide the basic stuff out of which more complex forms are constructed.

```
descform ::= (desc . alist)
    desc ::=  ([quant] tname iname [rspec ...])
       quant ::= THE | A | ALL
       tname ::= template | template-conjunct
              template-conjunct ::= (template ...)
       iname ::= variable | constant
       rspec ::= (relation target ...)
          relation ::= rel | rel-path
             rel-path ::= (rel ...)
          target ::= constant | desc
    alist ::= (binding ...) | NIL
       binding ::= (variable value ...)
```

Figure 1. BNF definition of descform

A more complex form is a description form or Descform. The syntax for a Descform is given in Figure 1. As can be seen in this figure, a Descform consists of
something called a Desc and an Alist. A Desc is a syntactically well-formed expression in the vocabulary provided to the system. The Alist consists of specific
individuals or constants that are associated with the variables that occur within the
Desc. In order to minimize the use of the terms Desc and Descform within the text
of this discussion, we will often refer to a Desc as a general description and to a
Descform as a specific description or description. A Descform allows one to construct a somewhat limited set of the expressions that can be formed in a standard
first-order language. Some examples will clarify this. The Description:

> Desc : (SCREWDRIVER S (TYPE PHILIPS) (ON TABLE T))
> Alist : ((S SCREWDRIVER-1 SCREWDRIVER-2) (T TABLE-1))

expresses that screwdriver-1 or screwdriver-2 is on a particular table-1 and is of the
philips type. Here the Desc consists of the classname, screwdriver, together with
the variable S followed by a list of relations. These relations specify further aspects
of S. The target of type, the first relation in the Desc, is the constant, philips. The
second relation, ON, has as its target the classname, table, and the variable T. This
specifies that the individuals bound to T must be members of the class, table. A
classname need not be mentioned in the target of the relation when the individual is
a constant, since the typing of a constant is unique. If multiple bindings are given
for a typed variable, S in this case, then the form is given a disjunctive interpretation. The list of relations (rspecs), in this case (TYPE PHILIPS) and (ON TABLE
T) receive a conjunctive interpretation.

Negation is introduced through negation of a relation. For example, the screwdrivers on the table that are not philips screwdrivers, would be expressed as:

Desc : (SCREWDRIVER S (NOT-TYPE PHILIPS) (ON TABLE T))
Alist : (T TABLE-1)

In this case, the variable S is unbound and the specific description roughly corresponds to the English statement, "Any screwdriver that is not a philips and is on table-1."

The requirement that an instance be included in more than one class is expressed as a template conjunct which is simply a list of templates. A particular object that is both a picture frame and an antique could be described as:

Desc : ((PICTURE-FRAME ANTIQUE) P)
Alist : (P PICTURE-FRAME-1)

Finally, the language allows a shorthand construction called a rel-path. One might wish to describe the screwdrivers that are on anything that is in turn on the table. This would be expressed as:

Desc : (SCREWDRIVER S ((ON ON) TABLE T))
Alist : (T TABLE-1)

The Descform differs from a logical expression in the sense that the order of the expression has computational significance. Intuitively the idea is that the typed variable or instance that is mentioned at the beginning of the description is the focus of that description. This entity is referred to as the root or source of the relation. The list of rspecs describe relationships between this root and other instances or Descs. Since the target itself can be a Desc, an unlimited amount of embedding is allowed. An example of embedding is given by the description:

Desc: (SCREWDRIVER S (ON (TABLE T) (COLOR RED))))

which describes any screwdriver on a red table.

The fact that these are ordered does not affect the standard semantic interpretation of a specific description. A semantic interpretation of a specific description is obtained by matching the forms in the description against the assertions in WM. If bindings are provided for each variable in the description and if the assertion and appropriate truth value for each of the subexpressions is found in WM, then the match succeeds and the specific description is true of that context. If some variables in the expression are unbound, and if the match succeeds, then the bindings that made the description true are also returned. In this way a query can also return additional information that further specifies the description.

This type of matching as well as other types of matches are carried out by the AIMDS procedure called SEEK. A detailed description of SEEK is provided in Bresina (1981). This function is also involved in the use of general knowledge, which is stored as rules. It is in this context that we will observe a computational effect due to the fact that a description is an ordered expression.

8 Rules

It is to rules that we now turn. Rules are used to represent some of the general knowledge about actions and objects that will be needed to implement our planning system. Rules are organized into named rule sets. This organization is based on the type of function or use that will be made of the rules.

However, rules all have a uniform structure and are retrieved using a single mechanism. A rule consists of three parts. The first part, the Applicability Test (AT), is used to declare the domain of objects over which the rule can be applied. This domain of objects is expressed using a single general description. The second part of a rule, the World Model Test (WMT), consists of a list of general descriptions or the truth value, T. The third part of a rule, the Retrieved Knowledge (RK), is again represented as a single description.

The applicability test is used to select a rule, the world model test provides a way of forcing a conclusion to be conditional on the truth value of certain known facts, and the retrieved knowledge represents the conclusion that may be drawn if the previous two test portions are satisfied.

A simple example of a rule will help to fix these ideas before we discuss them in more detail. The following rule is a way of representing general facts about how to hang picture frames.

```
AT   : (HANG H (OBJ PICTURE-FRAME F))
WMT: T
RK   : (HANG H (USING (WIRE W (TYPE STRANDED))))
```

The rule reads, if some hanging involves a picture frame as an object (the AT component) then that hanging also involves using stranded wire. In this case, there is no world model test. We could modify this and insert

```
WMT : (PICTURE-FRAME F (NOT-PART (OBJECT O (TYPE SUPPORT)
                                          (RELLOC CENTER-
                                          BACK)))
```

This expresses the condition that the picture frame does not have a part which is a support that is centered on its back.

Rules are used to answer questions. In this case, the questions might be thought of rather anthropomorphically as: "I need to hang a picture frame; what else is involved in doing this?" The question is stated as a Descform, for example:

Query-DescForm

Desc : (HANG H (OBJ PICTURE-FRAME F)
        (AT PLACE P))
Alist : ((H HANG-1) (F PICTURE-FRAME-1) (P LRLOC1 LRLOC2))

To determine what rules are relevant to this query, SEEK is used to match the AT-Desc of a rule against the Query-Descform. For this example the match succeeds because the description in the AT portion of the rule is more general than the query description, which includes mention of the location of the action of hanging the picture frame. The match is basically a structural match of these two general descriptions. It succeeds if the general description of the query contains at least all of the features of the general description of the Applicability Test. Although the match is structural, it is not a simple syntactic match. First, the order of the relations does not matter; second, the match succeeds if the class names of the target of a relation match or if those in the description of the query name a class that is included as a subclass in those class names mentioned in the AT-Desc. Note, however, that retrieval, that is, success of the AT match, is dependent on the focus or root of the description of the query and is dependent on the specificity of the list of relations of the query description.

If the AT match succeeds, then the WMT, if any, is carried out with SEEK matching the list of descriptions in the WMT against WM. This is the semantic type of match that was described earlier. Generally, the description of the WMT will include some of the same variables included in the description of the AT part of the rule. The bindings for these variables in the Alist of the Query-Descform are used in matching the descriptions of the WMT part of the rule against WM. Generally, some of the variables in these descriptions in the WMT portion of the rule will be unbound. If this WMT portion succeeds, then bindings for these variables will be added to a Rule-alist which is constructed as a result of successful rule application.

If WMT also succeeds, then the description forming the retrieved knowledge is retrieved along with the rule-alist, and the AT and WMT portions of the rule. We include the entire rule and the Rule-alist in the return, because the AT and WMT parts are used to annotate the support for a particular conclusion. This annotation is needed because new knowledge about this particular action of hanging this picture frame may become known which violates the condition portion of the rule.

9 Types of Knowledge and its Organization

Now that we have defined a framework within which to represent facts, expressions, and general knowledge about objects and actions, we can return to the question of what knowledge to represent and how to organize that knowledge. In thinking about this, we must keep in mind the constraint that at any point in time the facts and knowledge may be incomplete. So we can begin our consideration by asking ourselves the general question, ''What can be done if some needed information is unknown?''

The answer to this general question is simple. There are really only three possible courses of action that can be followed. The first is to simply try to entirely ignore what we are ignorant of. A second possibility is to make a guess or assumption about the unknown information. The third possibility falls between these two extremes. This involves creating some surrogate to stand in the place of the unknown information. This surrogate might be as general as "something belongs here" or it might be an outline which describes what we currently know about what belongs here.

The question is how to gracefully, robustly, and cleverly either ignore, make assumptions about, or create placeholders for the unknown knowledge needed in planning. This knowledge might be ignorance about a fact, about the existence of a particular object, or ignorance of a precondition or outcome associated with an action description.

Before plunging into our answers to this question, let us step back for a moment and take a very general look at human knowledge of the actions and objects involved in everyday activities. Luckily, we do a great deal of talking to one another about our own plans and the plans of others. Our language is replete with words to describe different actions and objects. The objects themselves are often named not on the basis of perceptual characteristics, but rather on the basis of functional ones. We all know the difficulty in giving a definition for "chair" in terms of its visible characteristics. Further, not only do we name many actions and functionally distinct objects, but these names themselves appear to be organized in quite regular ways.

This isn't proof that our mental representation of this knowledge about actions and objects is isomorphic to the structure of corresponding terms in natural language. But a very reasonable conjecture is that commonsense knowledge is at least as structured as that which we can discover through study of our linguistic usage of these terms. Accepting this conjecture, we are encouraged to conjecture further that if the structure exists, then the human mind probably tries to exploit it for use in commonsense planning.

One of the most striking features of these linguistic terms for actions and objects is that they appear to be organized hierarchically. A screw is a kind of fastener and a philips screw is a kind of screw. This "a kind of" notion can be extended further in generality or specificity. Any verb of action can be used to create statements that vary along a dimension of specificity. The statement that the picture was hung on the wall is more specific than the statement that the picture was hung. In addition to optionally specifying various aspects of the action, the statements can also be made more specific by giving a more specific description of one of the objects mentioned. For example, the picture was hung on the wall to the left of the mirror.

From a strictly logical perspective, these features seem somewhat baroque. Hierarchies don't really contribute anything special. And the dependence of an action's meaning on the referents used in filling its arguments is vague at best and perhaps even a bit perverse. Hanging a picture is really quite different from hanging drapes or the laundry. This dependence is often eliminated in planning systems by representing each action type by object-type combination as a separate action, giving what I term an action–object representation of actions.

This strategy closes the set of possible action and object combinations that can be considered in planning. When the number of actions and objects is limited, this strategy works well. However, when the number of actions or objects is large, this strategy becomes inefficient, because knowledge about the commonalities between similar object-action combinations is not represented. In this case, a more appropriate strategy is to leave open this cross-product set of action and object combinations and to encode the knowledge and processes needed to constructively use this open texture. Perhaps this feature of action by object interactions can be turned to advantage in planning with incomplete knowledge.

A further advantage afforded by a hierarchical representation such as this is that it provides a basis for a computational strategy to deal with what is termed the partial match problem (Joshi, 1978; Rosenschein, 1978). When knowledge is incomplete, often only some of the conditions required to select a rule are known. This is the partial match problem. A knowledge structure that holds information in a hierarchy based on specificity of its matching conditions, provides a partial solution to the partial match problem. The position matched in the hierarchy provides both a way of retrieving information appropriate to the current knowledge of the system and a basis for creating an appropriate surrogate or placeholder for further specialization if relevant new knowledge becomes available.

10 Representing Actions and Object Descriptions

Knowledge about action and object dependencies is represented in PLANX10 by distributing the knowledge about an action into rule sets. The rule sets are grouped according to the functional significance of a particular type of action knowledge. The standard knowledge associated with an action is distributed into three sets of rules which we term, Act-Select Rules, Precondition Rules, and Outcome Rules. These rules are all uniformly represented in the rule form discussed earlier.

Act-Select rules are accessed when the Query-Descform represents a goal to be achieved. If the match succeeds, the rule matched returns the name and some or all of the arguments of an act which may achieve the goal of the query. An example for HANG is given as:

ACT-SELECT:
    AT   : (OBJECT O (HUNGON OBJECT P))
    WMT : T
    RK   : (HANG H (OBJ O) (PAT P))

In the retrieved knowledge, OBJ and PAT are relation names used to represent the case slots or arguments representing the different roles objects play in an action.

Precondition Rules are accessed with a Query-Descform, which describes an action and some of its associated case structure. If the match succeeds, then the knowledge about an action's preconditions are retrieved. For example:

PRECONDITION:
    AT   : (HANG H (OBJ O) (PAT P))
    WMT : T
    RK   : (OBJECT O ((AT LOCOF) (OBJECT P)))

This merely states that both O and P must be at the same place.

Outcome Rules are retrieved with the same type of Query-Descform as the Precondition Rules. But in this case, the retrieved knowledge describes outcomes associated with the action. An example is:

```
OUTCOME:
  AT   : (HANG H (OBJ O) (PAT P))
  WMT : T
  RK   : (OBJECT O (SUPPORTED BY (OBJECT P)))
```

One consequence of distributing this knowledge according to its function in planning is that in reasoning about an action, the planning process can focus on some aspects of the action and postpone consideration of other aspects. Thus it provides the framework for a flexible control structure.

Now, the version of HANG used in this example was purposely written in a most general way. As it stands, it is rather uninformative. But if all that is known is that something is to be hung somewhere, then this is quite an appropriate representation of that state of knowledge. Even stated in this general way, an outline is given and a computationally useful placeholder has been created.

11 Action Customization

Placeholders are only useful if there is a way of returning to them when new information becomes available that is relevant to their further specification. Many of the class names for objects are based on functional characteristics. When an object in a plan is further specified, then we can often retrieve information about the class of objects that will participate in the action. The set of rules which we refer to as Act-Customize rules provide for us the means to represent this general knowledge about action by object dependencies.

Two examples of such a rule for HANG are:

```
ACT-CUSTOMIZE:
  AT   : (HANG H (OBJ (PICTURE-FRAME F)) (PAT (WALL W)))
  WMT: (SUPHOOK H)
  RK   : (HANG H (OBJ PICTURE-FRAME F)) (PAT (WALL W)) (ON
(SUPHOOK H)))

  AT   : (HANG H (OBJ (CLOTHING G)) (PAT (CLOSET C)))
  WMT : (HANGER H)
  RK   : (HANG H (OBJ (CLOTHING G)) (PAT (CLOSET C)) (ON (HANGER
H))
```

In the first rule, I use the term SUPHOOK to refer to a class that includes hook, screw, and nail as subclasses. This rule simply involves the general knowledge that this class of object can be involved in hanging the class of objects called picture frames on a wall. The second introduces in an analogous way the object class, hanger, when it is known that clothes and a closet are involved in an action of hanging.

Thus whenever more becomes known about the objects involved in an action, it is possible that the action may be further specified by the knowledge encoded in these Act-Customize rules. If a match is successful then the Precondition and Outcome rules may be interrogated again. Since the Query-Descform is more specific, a more specific rule may be matched and new preconditions or outcomes determined.

12 Creating Place-Holders for Unknown Instances

In the previous examples of Act-Customization rules, a world model test was present. This would have the effect of only allowing the rule to succeed if the world model satisfied the descriptions of WMT. If it succeeded, then a bindings list of possible instances would be available to the planning process.

But we have already noted that knowledge about the existence of certain classes of objects is often unknown. Or the opposite may be the case. The description may be so general at a point in the planning process that almost any instance that is known could be used to satisfy the description.

Again the solution of creating placeholders is suggested. The tactic of simply using a description with the unknown object as the root is useful but not entirely adequate. A particular object mentioned in one action may also be required to participate in other actions in the plan. For example, the wire that is used to hang the picture must be the same wire that is strung and tied across the back of the frame. Or the opposite case must hold. The eyelet attached to the left side of a wooden frame to string the wire through must not be the same eyelet used on the right side of the frame.

For reasons such as these, an unknown or indefinite object cannot be adequately represented simply as a variable in a description. Placeholders for objects mentioned in a description must refer to something, but that something must have an indefinite reference. PLANX10 deals with this by uniformly creating instances which are called plan objects for each object mentioned in a plan.

However, even this solution is not quite general enough. Planning for different actions might each create a description for a particular plan object. At some point in the planning process it may be determined that the two plan objects created in planning the two different actions must be the identical plan object. Since these objects do not exist, they can not be directly compared. They exist only in the sense that associated with each is a description reflecting the local constraints that were required at a point in the planning process. Clearly, what must be done is to compare the descriptions associated with each plan object.

Such a comparison process can be carried out again using SEEK. The result of this comparison can be used to define an ordering based on the specificity of a description over the space of objects. (See Sridharan & Bresina, 1983a for definition of this relation). In order to represent this ordering information a description space is created. It consists of entities referred to as DSNodes. Among the information associated with a DS node are:

1. The Desc of a plan object
2. The Plan-Alist (a list of plan objects bound to the variables in the Desc)
3. The WM-Alist (possibly empty)
4. Links to DSNodes which are more general with respect to the Descs
5. Links to DSNodes which are more specific with respect to the Descs
6. Links to DSNodes which are equal with respect to the Desc but may have different Alists.

All of this structure may appear quite imposing and improbable to some. But the information associated with a DSNode serves several functions in the planning process.

First, the DSNode provides the information about correspondences that have been established at any point in the planning process between plan objects and objects known in WM. This information is held in the Plan-Alist and WM-Alist. If the WM-Alist is empty, then the plan object and its associated description do not yet refer to aspects of WM in any way. At the other extreme, if each plan object on the Plan-Alist corresponds to a unique object on the WM-Alist, then the plan object is uniquely specified in WM and it is referentially complete. By creating plan objects that only indirectly refer to objects in WM; that is, reference depends upon whether a partial or full correspondence currently holds between the two Alists, it is possible to represent the degree of indefiniteness that holds for a plan object at any point in the planning process.

Second, the Desc of a plan object and its associated Plan-Alist allow for the representation of a strictly *functional* characterization of the object. Functional in the sense that what appears in this description is a result of collecting the constraints that arose out of the planning process itself. This functional focus is important, because it provides the information needed to guide a process of *object selection*. In a typical planning process, object selection cannot be separated from the planning process itself. Objects must be bound in order to evaluate a precondition of an action in order to decide whether to subgoal on the precondition. Indefinite descriptions provide the flexibility of deferring object selection until many of the functional constraints have been collected. Or object selection can even be deferred until the time of plan execution.

Finally, the links to more general, more specific, or functionally equivalent Descs provides a basis for substituting one plan object choice for another. If the Desc of a particular DSNode is evaluated against WM, and no object bindings are returned, then an alternative object must be chosen. The links which result from the comparison of Descs yield a space based on *functional similarity*. Further, if the space is relatively dense, a move upward or downward corresponds to a relatively small change in the functional characterization of the object. Choosing a DSNode close to the DSNode that failed will yield a functionally similar candidate plan object for substitution into the existing plan. This allows the use of a heuristic strategy for object substitution that will often minimally affect the validity of the existing plan and, thereby, minimize the number of required revisions to the plan. Since this heuristic can be carried out using only the local structure of the description space, the heuristic can be used without examining the entire dependency structure of the existing plan.

13 Assumptions

The final option for planning with incomplete knowledge involves making assumptions as needed. Discussion of this was postponed until now because assumptions about the truth value of an assertion also typically requires an assumption about the existence of an indefinite object.

The general knowledge used to make assumptions is again encoded in rule form. We have implemented two sets of such rules which are termed Normally True and Normally False rule sets. These rules are typically invoked when a truth value for a precondition of some action is unknown. Consequently, the making of an assumption is not arbitrary, but a byproduct of the planning process.

An example of a Normally True rule is:

    AT   : (WIRE-SUPPORT W (ON (PICTURE-FRAME F)))
    WMT : (PICTURE-FRAME F (TYPE METALLIC))
    RK   : T

This rule may be paraphrased as: Normally it is true that a wire support is found on a picture frame if it is metallic. In this case the retrieved knowledge is simply a truth value. The rule encodes the knowledge that metallic picture frames normally come with supports for the picture wire. The WMT portion of these rules is used to encode the conditions under which the description of the AT part of the rule can normally be expected to have the particular truth value indicated in the rule. Thus, assumptions must have a support. In PLANX10 this support is annotated so that the basis for a particular assumption is retained.

As long as the WMT portion of the rule is tested against WM and allowed to succeed only if it evaluates to true, the chaining of default assumptions is blocked. A deeper strategy of default reasoning can be achieved if the unknown or false components of the WMT list of descriptions are extracted and subject to further analyses.

Consider first the actions that might be called for in the case when a description in this WMT portion of the rule is false in WM. Further default reasoning on this description is blocked because we have a known truth value. Consequently, only two options remain open. One is to attempt to create a plan that changes this description so that it will evaluate to true. This would then allow the default rule to be used to assign a truth value to the original expression that led to the selection of this default rule. This truth value is conditional on the execution of the plan. This option has not been used in PLANX10 because it conflicts with the semantics which are associated with these default rules. These rules are used to encode information about normal states of affairs. The information in the WMT portion of the rule encodes *associations* between the AT and WMT descriptions and a truth value. It does not encode necessary or prerequisite relations. Consequently, an action that established the WMT portion as true will not affect the truth value of the Query-Descform. For example, I may know that philips screws are normally found in the second drawer of my workbench. I also may know that there is a particular screw in the desk drawer in my study, but I do not recall its type. Putting this screw in the second drawer of my workbench would allow the default rule to succeed. But, of course, this is not an effective way of causing a screw to become a philips screw.

The second option for dealing with a false WMT description is to use this information to trigger the selection of a different object for use in the plan. Returning to the above example, this would involve abandoning the screw in my desk altogether and choosing one that is in the second drawer of my workbench. Of course, this necessitates a reexamination of the plan for any aspect of the current plan that depended on this object binding.

Consider next the case where aspects of the WMT test return unknown when tested against WM. Since we are often dealing with indefinite objects in this type of commonsense planning, this is the typical case that we encounter in our use of default rules. There are again two options available. First, consider the case where the unknown description refers to the same, though indefinite, object referred to in the Query-Description. In this case the unknown description may simply be added to the description of the plan object. Thus, the default rule can be used as a means of collecting constraints about the indefinite object. For example, assume now that the query above had referred to an indefinite screw of type philips rather than to the particular screw in my desk drawer. Since this object has no WM reference, the WMT description of the default rule stating that it is in the second drawer of my workbench will return unknown. By adding this description to the description of the indefinite screw, a constraint on future object selection has been added. If this constraint is satisfied when a WM referent is selected, then we may plausibly expect to obtain the desired philips screw.

The second option is to allow the chaining of default rules. In this case the unknown description is used as the Query-Description and the default rules are again consulted. This option is preferred when the object referred to in the initial Query-Description has a reference in WM. This means that a specific object has already been selected. Consequently, one can meaningfully pursue the question of whether this particular object normally satisfies the unknown description returned by the previous evaluation of the WMT portion. For example, in the planning example with which we began this paper, the choice of support for the picture frame depended upon the type of wall material out of which the wall area was constructed. Here we have an example of an interaction between object types, the support and the wall, where the wall already has a definite reference. In this planning protocol a chaining of default rule application was pursued to determine the type of wall material involved. We will return to this example shortly since it illustrates a computational role for dispositional expressions. What should be noted here is that the basis for each default assumption is annotated. Consequently, when chaining is allowed, these anotations provide a basis for controlling and evaluating the inference chain. For example, it provides the information needed to detect a cycle in the inference chain.

14 An Abbreviated and Stylized Trace

A number of pieces of commonsense knowledge have been discussed and cast in a particular computational form. What remains to be done is to provide a recapitulation of this discussion which shows how these pieces fit together to form the puzzle of commonsense planning posed in this paper. What follows then is an abbreviated sketch of the computational moves that could yield the planning protocol with which the paper began.

Figure 2 provides a hopefully readable approximation to the major steps that might underlie the planning protocol. To make this trace easier to follow, I have avoided a strict encoding of the trace into the language of Descforms. Most notably, the Alist notation has been dropped in favor of a notation that uses the name of the binding within the Desc itself. In order to indicate in a rough way the degree of definiteness of an expression, the following conventions are followed in this figure. A constant which is bound to a unique WM object appears in large capitals, one that is not uniquely bound is shown in small capitals, and a constant that is currently unbound to a WM constant is rendered in italics. Relations are shown in small letters. The Preconditions of an action are preceded by the name of the action concatenated with a "P" and a number so that they may be simply referred to at other points in the trace.

The trace begins by using the goal as the Query-Descform against the Goal-Select rules. Since the goal states that a frame and wall are involved, the appropriate sense of HANG is retrieved. This sense of HANG adds the new information that a support must be involved in the action. This support for the frame is unbound to any WM object.

This action Desc now serves as the Query-Descform for accessing the appropriate Precondition rules. Three preconditions are retrieved. The first is rather uninteresting. The second tells us that the support for the frame should be embedded in the center of the wall area where the picture is to be hung. The third introduces three new types of objects; picturewire and supports on the frame for the wire.

Goal: (FRAME hangingon WALLAREA)

Goal-Select Rules Return:
 Action: (HANG H1 (object FRAME) (at WALLAREA) (on *Support*))

Precondition-Rules Return:
 (HANG-P1): (FRAME near WALLAREA)
 (HANG-P2): (*Support* embeddedin (CENTER (partof WALLAREA)))
 (HANG-P3): (*PictureWire* strungon (*PSupport1* (partof FRAME))
                                   (*PSupport2* (partof FRAME)))

   Evaluation of HANG-P3 Returns:
   Unknown from World Model

      Evaluation using Default Inference Returns:
      False with Basis: (FRAME unused YES)

   Goal-Select Rules applied to HANG-P3 Returns:
   Action: (STRING S1 (object *PictureWire*) (on *PSupport1*)
              (on *PSupport2*) (patient FRAME))

Preconditions-Rules Return:
 (STRING-P1): (*Psupport1* attachedto (PSIDE1 (partof FRAME) (backof YES)))
 (STRING-P2): (*PSupport2* attachedto (PSIDE2 (partof FRAME) (backof YES)))
 (STRING-P3): (*PictureWire* near FRAME)

   Evaluation of STRING-P1 and STRING-P2 Returns:
   Unknown from World Model

      Evaluation using Default Inference Returns:
      True with Basis: (FRAME (type METAL))

Evaluation of HANG-P2 Returns:
False from World Model

Goal-Select Rules applied to HANG-P2 Returns:
 Action: (EMBED E1 (object *Support*) (in (CENTER (partof WALLAREA))
                                (using *Instrument*))

Preconditions-Rules Return:
 (EMBED-P1): (*Instrument* near WALLAREA)
 (EMBED-P2): (*Support* near WALLAREA)
 (EMBED-P3): (*Support* embeddable WALLAREA)

   Evaluation of EMBED-P3 Returns:
   Unknown from World

      Evaluation using Default Inference Returns:
      True if ((*Support* type SCREW)
            (WALLAREA (type WALLBOARD)
            (hasembedded (*SSupport* (type ANCHOR))))

         Map into Independent Conjuncts:
         (C1) (*Support* type SCREW)
         (C2) (WALLAREA (type WALLBOARD))
         (C3) (WALLAREA (hasembedded (*SSuport* (type ANCHOR))))

      Evaluation of (C2) Returns:
      Unknown from WM

         Evaluation using Default Inference Returns:
         True with Basis: (WallArea (partof HOUSE (age POSTWWII)))

Act-Customize of EMBED with new knowledge of Wall Type Results in:
 Action: (EMBED E2 (object *Screw*) (in (CENTER (partof WALLAREA
                                   (type WALLBOARD)))) (using *Screwdriver*))

Preconditions-Rules Return:
 (EMBED2-P1): (*Screwdriver* near WALLAREA)
 (EMBED2-P2): (*Screw* near WALLAREA)
 (EMBED2-P3) (*Anchor* embeddedin (CENTER (partof WALLAREA)))

Figure 2. Abbreviated example of partial provisional planning

HANG-P3 is evaluated next and since the frame is unused it is concluded that the frame probably does not have a wire already strung on it. This precondition is then treated as a subgoal and the Goal-Select rules yield the action of stringing the wire through the supports on the frame. Again a default assumption based on the fact that a metallic frame is involved is used to draw the conclusion that STRING-P2 and STRING-P3 are probably true.

Next HANG-P2 is evaluated and known to be false. Goal-Select Rules yield the action of embedding the support in the wall using some sort of instrument. The Precondition rules return EMBED-P3 as the only really interesting precondition. This states that the support must be embeddable in the wall area. This dispositional type of relation is simply a way of alerting the planner to the fact that there is a dependence between the support chosen and the wall.

Luckily, the WMT test portion of the appropriate default rules will hold the needed information about which combinations of support types and wall types will happily embed with each other. After some search through the default rules indexed on this expression, the default rule is found that states that a support is embeddable in the wall if the support is a screw and the wall area is of type wallboard and an anchor is itself embedded in the wall. Since we have a particular wall in mind, the type of wall material is determined by chaining on the default rules and it is decided that it is probably wallboard. Since the support is quite indefinite at this point, we simply accept the constraint that it be of type screw. Finally, since more is now known about this particular embedding action, the Act-Customize rules are consulted. This results in the retrieval of a new and more specific representation of the embed action needed.

Things proceed pretty much in this fashion, so let us leave this abbreviated trace and conclude this recapitulation with some general observations. First, the control flow is of a fairly standard backward-chaining variety. Exotic control regimes are not required to integrate the use of general knowledge into the planning process. We did judiciously avoid pursuing certain preconditions that were concerned about things being near each other. These are deferred by allowing the planner to ignore certain classes of relations that are specified to it. The relation ''near'' has been one of our favorite ones to ignore since in this type of plan those preconditions are among the least problematic.

The most interesting feature of this example is in its use of general knowledge. This knowledge about action–object and object–object dependencies allows the planning to proceed in a highly focussed way despite the planner's relative ignorance about the specific facts of the situation in which the plan will eventually be carried out.

Finally, although for purposes of presentation, postponement and reasoning by assumption were discussed as separate strategies for planning with incomplete knowledge, this example trace shows how these strategies complement each other. Certainly, in the way we have implemented these strategies neither taken alone would yield a great deal of additional planning power.

15 Concluding Remarks

An example of a partial and provisional plan for carrying out an everyday activity served as the starting point for our consideration of some issues of knowledge representation that arise in commonsense planning. It was argued that some of the properties of commonsense knowledge can be best understood by the functions this knowledge must fulfill under its conditions of use.

Since persons must plan with limited knowledge about the planning context and limited processing resources, we argued that this requirement of reasoning with incomplete knowledge strongly influences the nature of commonsense knowledge. Two strategies for dealing with incomplete knowledge were explored—postponement and reasoning by assumptions.

A computational experiment that involved implementing a system that used commonsense knowledge was performed. The experiment identified ways of representing knowledge and organizing commonsense knowledge about actions and objects, which enabled the strategies of postponement and assumptions to be effectively used in planning. The system, PLANX10, itself has many features and mechanisms that were not discussed here and the interested reader is referred to (Sridharan & Bresina, 1982, 1983b). What was presented was simply the representational facilities and processes needed which provide the basis for modelling properties of the example protocol with which we began.

Although we feel that our experiment should be judged to be a qualified success in this regard, clearly there are many issues that require further research and many new questions are raised. Some of these issues we are currently pursuing. A great many questions about the control of planning in this type of context are suggested. When should assumptions be made? When should a postponed portion of the plan be reconsidered? When, if ever, should known facts about the world be ignored in favor of a strategy of postponement?

Planning with incomplete knowledge requires that the planning system be capable of refining and revising its plan as new information becomes available. Can these placeholders created by the strategy of postponement aid in the recognition of the relevance of new facts to the partial plan? Under what conditions is a partial plan easily revised? How can incorrect assumptions be recognized and the plan revised?

None of these questions have an easy answer. But we have been able to see ways in which this framework for representing partial plans might generalize and be used to provide partial and provisional answers to questions such as these.

Acknowledgments

This research was supported by Grant RR-643 to the Rutgers Research Resource on Computers in Biomedicine from the BRP, Division of Research Resources, NIH and by Grant NSF IST 81-19889. The work reported here was done in collaboration with N.S. Sridharan, and John Bresina. John Goodson also contributed importantly to the development of this work in its earlier manifestations. They deserve a lion's share of the credit for whatever the reader finds interesting and correct in this paper. The writer reserves exclusive right to all blame for those aspects the reader finds dull or incorrect. Additionally, I would like to express my appreciation to these individuals as well as Saul Amarel, Ray Reiter and Jerry Hobbs for their helpful comments on this paper.

References

Bresina, J. L. (1981). *An interactive planner that creates a structured, annotated trace of its operation* (Technical Report RU-CBM-TR-123). Rutgers University. Laboratory for Computer Science Research.

Joshi, A. (1978). Some extensions of a system for inference on partial information. In D. A. Waterman, & F. Hayes-Roth (Eds.), *Pattern-directed inference systems*. New York: Academic Press, 1978.

Lenneberg, E. H. (1967). *Biological foundations of language*. New York: Wiley.

Luckham, D. C., & Buchanan, J. R. (1974). "Automatic generation of programs containing conditional statements," in *Proceedings of the Conference on Artificial Intelligence and Simulation of Behavior.*

Manna, Z., & Waldinger, R. (1977). The automatic synthesis of systems of recursive programs, in *Proceedings of the Joint Conference on Artificial Intelligence*, 405–411. Cambridge, MA: MIT.

Reiter, R. A. (1980). Logic for default reasoning. *Artificial Intelligence, 15,* 81–132.

Rosenschein, S. J. (1978). The production system: architecture and abstraction. In D. A. Waterman and F. Hayes-Roth (Eds.), *Pattern-directed inference systems,* New York: Academic Press.

Sacerdoti, E. D. (1977). A structure for plans and behavior (Artificial Intelligence Series). New York: Elsevier North-Holland.

Schmidt, C. F., Sridharan, N. S. & Goodson, J. L. (1978). The plan recognition problem: An intersection of Artificial Intelligence and Psychology. *Artificial intelligence. 11*(1,2), 45–83.

Simon, H. A. (1981). The sciences of the artificial. Cambridge, MA: MIT Press.

Sridharan, N. S. (1980). *Representational facilities of AIMDS: A sampling* (Technical Report RU-CBM-TM-86). Rutgers University, Department of Computer Science.

Sridharan, N. S., & Bresina, J. L. (1982). Plan formation in large, realistic domains, (Available as Rutgers Tech. Rept. RU-CBM-TR-127) *Journal of the Canadian society for computational studies of intelligence/Societe canadienne pour etudes d'intelligence par ordinateur.* 12–18.

Sridharan, N. S., & Bresina, J. L. (1983a). *A mechanism for the management of partial and indefinite descriptions* (Technical Report RU-CBM-TR-134). Rutgers University, Laboratory for Computer Science Research.

Sridharan, N. S., & Bresina, J. L. (1983b). *Knowledge structures for a modular planning system* (Technical Report RU-CBM-TR-133). Rutgers University, Laboratory for Computer Science Research.

Sridharan, N. S., Bresina, J. L. & Schmidt, C. F. (1983). *Evolution of a plan generation system* (Technical Report RU-CBM-TR-128). Rutgers University, Laboratory for Computer Science Research.

Stefik, M. (1980). *Planning with constraints*. Unpublished doctoral dissertation, (Report STAN-CS-80-784). Stanford University.

Stepankova, O., & Havel, I. M. (1976). Incidental and state-dependent phenomena in robot problem solving. *Proceedings of the conference on artificial intelligence and simulation of behavior.* 266–278.

Sussman, G. J. (1973). A Computational model of skill acquisition. Unpublished doctoral dissertation, MIT, Cambridge, MA.

Warren, D. H. D. (1976). "Generating conditional plans and programs," in *Proceedings of the Conference on artificial intelligence and simulation of behavior*. 344–354.

Wilkins, D. E. & Robinson, A. E. (1981). An interactive planning system (Technical Report 245). SRI International

7 A Model of Naive Temporal Reasoning

James F. Allen
Henry A. Kautz

Department of Computer Science
University of Rochester
Rochester, New York

Temporal reasoning is an essential part of most tasks considered as intelligent behavior. In fact, it is so prevalent that it is often not recognized explicitly. In this paper, we shall consider naive temporal reasoning as it is required within two areas: natural language comprehension and problem solving.

For example, consider the following story:

> Ernie entered the room and picked up a cup in each hand from the table. He drank from the one in his right hand, put the cups back on the table, and left the room.

This story contains many explicit temporal relationships. For instance, we are told that Ernie picked up the cups after he entered the room, and that the cups were picked up more or less simultaneously. After they were picked up, he drank from one, and later still he put the cups down more or less simultaneously. There are temporal relationships that are obvious from this story that are not explicitly mentioned as well. For example, we know that he held the cups for more or less the same span of time, and that while he drank from one cup, he was holding the other cup in his left hand.

In problem-solving situations, we see more evidence of temporal reasoning. Consider the simple blocks world in which there is one action, namely picking up a block and moving it to a new location. Assume we are given an initial situation with three blocks on a table and want to construct a tower:

We must reason that putting B on C must precede putting A on B. Looking deeper, however, the above temporal constraint is only valid in a domain in which only one put action can occur at a time. In a domain with two arms, for instance, we should know that the action of putting B on C must complete no later than the action of putting A on B completes, but otherwise they may overlap or be performed simultaneously.

In more complicated domains, temporal reasoning becomes crucial. For instance, assume block A is on a rotating table and hence can only be reached periodically as it passes close to the arm. A plan to put A on B involves waiting for block A to appear and then picking it up while it is available.

All of these examples may seem obvious, but it is not obvious how to explain even such simple examples within existing models in artificial intelligence. This paper outlines a theory of time that accounts for many of the foregoing examples and that appears to be computationally effective. We hope to provide motivation and background for our research effort, leaving the actual details for other papers (Allen, 1981a, 1981b). In the first section, we shall discuss basic issues on the nature of temporal representations and argue for an interval-based approach rather than a point-based approach (i.e., in which time is viewed as analogous to the real line). We shall then provide a brief description of a temporal reasoner we have built and demonstrate it by some examples involving story comprehension. Finally, we shall describe how the model may be applied to problem solving.

1 A Theory of Time Based on Intervals

Let us consider some (generally accepted) intuitions about time. The primary intuition is that times and events are intimately connected. Our perception of time is intimately connected (or identical to) our perception of events. Thus, in the discussion below, we will be discussing the nature of events as much as the nature of time.

1. Most of our temporal knowledge is introduced without explicit reference to a date. By date we mean not only calendar dates (e.g., March 25, 1950), but also times of day (e.g., 12 noon). Temporal information in language is conveyed mostly by tense, order of presentation, and temporal connectives (e.g., "before," "during," "while"). Temporal information in plans is relative to the other actions in the plan rather than to a specific date (e.g., action A must occur before action B).

   The same emphasis on relative information over precise quantization occurs in considering durations of time. It is more common to learn that event A took longer than event B, than that A took 35 minutes versus B taking 15.

2. Given that we know an event E occurred over time T, we believe that by considering the event more closely we could in fact break down E (and hence the time T) into subevents (and hence subtimes). For example, the event of walking to school can be decomposed into a series of events consisting of one step, each of which could be decomposed into moving a leg forward, which could be decomposed into lifting your foot off the ground, pushing it forward, etc. Even events that appear to complete other events (e.g., arriving at school)

can be decomposed (entering the building, opening the door, etc.). So it appears we can always "increase the magnification" and find more structure.

3. Notwithstanding the decomposability of times discussed in 2, it appears that we also often consider time as indivisible. In other words, in a given situation, we often view time as being pointlike. This obviously varies. A historian interested in ancient history might not care ever to break down years into finer divisions (thus a year is "pointlike"); however, a computer engineer may want to consider times as small as or smaller than nanoseconds. To the engineer, a second might be like a century to the historian.

4. Time (or events) appears to be hierarchically organized. For instance, we can detect a hierarchy of times by considering the ambiguous nature of the word 'now.' 'Now' may refer to the time of my writing this sentence, the time of my writing this page, or larger periods such as the time of research projects. The question "What are you working on now?" at a conference refers to a much larger time than the instant the question is asked. If it didn't, one would have to answer "nothing" every time one had an idle moment. Thus, 'now' appears to be ambiguous, and can refer to one of a hierarchy of times based on containment.

These intuitions strongly support the claim that times should be viewed as intervals. What this means simply is that all times can be decomposed into subtimes. This is actually a fairly nontrivial claim, in that it disallows models in which times may be points. Thus we cannot start, for instance, with the real line as a model of the time line and build time intervals from time points as in Bruce (1972) and McDermott (1982). We want to claim that there are no time points in such a strong sense. The major arguments for this are, first, that allowing time points presents us with certain technical difficulties, and second, that we can do without time points.

An annoying characteristic of allowing time points in the strong sense is that it presents difficulties in defining the semantics of our temporal logic. For example, consider the time of running a race (call it RR) and the time after the race (AR). These two events are intimately related by definition; the latter interval beings where the former ends. If we allow time points, we must consider whether time intervals are open or closed. We cannot pick one option uniformly. If intervals are open, then there is a time between RR and AR in which the race is neither being run nor is it over. If intervals are closed, then there is a time in which the race is both being run and is over. It has been suggested that this problem can be avoided by a convention that all time intervals are open at a lesser end, and closed at the later end, but this seems completely arbitrary and indicates the model is unintuitive, for each interval would only have one endpoint. In an appropriate model, such a question should never have arisen. Another solution is to claim that it does not make sense for predicates to hold at time points, but this is essentially eliminating time points as useful entities.

Addressing the second point, we don't need to introduce points to explain or elaborate on interval-based descriptions. In the next section we shall introduce seven relations (and their inverses) that completely characterize how two time intervals could be related.

While we want to allow pointlike temporal reasoning, we should not equate this with allowing infinitesimal points in our model. For one thing, we may later reason about the same times that were previously considered to be points as though they are intervals with rich internal structure. This could not be done if the original times were represented as points. We view point-based reasoning as a special case of interval reasoning: by viewing a time as a point we (temporarily) eliminate the possibility that it could overlap another time also viewed as a point. As a consequence the reasoning task would be simplified, for we would be ignoring any internal structure of the time "points." This allows a notion of abstraction somewhat similar to that in hierarchical problem-solving systems such as Sacerdoti's (1977).

Let us move from consideration of the underlying model of time to consideration of models of temporal reasoning. The intuitions discussed above appear to eliminate techniques that depend on constructing dates for each event. In the domains we are considering, such information is not available and cannot be constructed in a reasonable manner. Even allowing "fuzzy dates" (e.g., Vere 1981) will not solve the problem. For instance, assume we know that events A and B did not occur over the same time interval, either A occurred entirely before B or vice versa. There is no way we can assign fuzzy dates to A and B that capture this knowledge. Thus we are left with relative reasoning schemes.

One possibility (even without allowing points) would be to have partial ordering of the start and finish of intervals. Thus, intervals might start at the same time, or one might start before the other. Similarly, we could analyze the endings of intervals. This scheme is theoretically adequate but makes it difficult to define reasoning techniques that reflect our intuitions. For instance, the most common type of reasoning we will perform is considering whether some property P holds at a certain time t. Typically, such information will not be explicitly stored, but will need to be inferred. The key inference rule we desire is:

> If proposition P holds over interval T, and interval t is during T, then P holds over interval t.

Modeling the during relationship using a partial ordering of endpoints makes this inference more complicated. Thus we prefer a representation that explicitly captures such containment information. A further benefit of this organization is that it reflects our intuitions about the hierarchical organization of temporal knowledge. This representation is outlined in the next section.

2 A Representation of Temporal Knowledge

2.1 Reasoning About Intervals
A pair of time intervals can be related in only a small number of ways, such as by the "during" and "meets" relationships discussed above. Thirteen primitive rela-

X equals (=) Y	XXXXXX	
	YYYYYY	

X before (<) Y	XXXXXX	
Y after (>) X		YYYYYY

X meets (m) Y	XXXXXX	
Y met by (mi) X		YYYYYY

X overlaps (o) Y	XXXXXX	
Y overlapped by (oi) X		YYYYYY

X starts (s) Y	XXX
Y started by (si) X	YYYYYYYYY

X during (d) Y	XXX
Y contains (c) X	YYYYYYYYY

X finishes (f) Y	XXX
Y finished by (fi) X	YYYYYYYYY

Figure 1. The Thirteen Primitive Relations

tions, graphically illustrated below in Figure 1, form the basis for all knowledge relating two intervals.

Often the precise relationship between intervals is not known. A complex relation is a disjunction of primitive relations. For example, if we know only that no part of X occurred outside of Y, then X could have been equal to Y, or could have fallen at the start, middle, or end of Y. Thus

X entirely within Y

abbreviates the complex relationship X (= s d f) Y.

Similarly, one can assert that X and Y are disjoint by saying that X is related to Y by any of the primitive relations which have that property: X (< m mi >) Y. Finally, knowing nothing about the relationship between X and Y is equivalent to holding the disjunction of all primitive relations between the two:

X (= < > s si d di f fi m mi o oi) Y

This formulation naturally suggests that our temporal knowledge be organized in a *constraint network*. Such a network is a directed graph, where each node represents an interval. The arc between any two nodes is labeled with the set of primitive relations which are consistent with our knowledge of the relationship of the intervals.

In addition to constraints imposed by world knowledge, the semantics of the temporal representation impose certain binary and ternary constraints. These constraints can be used to complete the graph, as well as reduce the size of label sets on the given arcs.

The binary constraints merely state that the label on an arc from, say X to Y is the inverse of that from Y to X. These constraints are readily derived from the table above, e.g.,

If X (m) Y then Y (mi) X.

The inverse of a set of primitives is the set of inverses of each primitive:

   If X (o s d) Y then Y (oi si c) X.

   More interesting are the ternary constraints, which encode the *transitive* properties of the primitive relations. For example, if X is during Y, and Y is during Z, then
certainly X is during Z. Some other combinations of primitive relations yield only
disjunctive information. Suppose X starts Y, and Z finishes Y. Then X could be
before, meet, or overlap Z:

   If X (s) Y and Y (fi) Z then X (< m o) Z

or, expressed more briefly,

   (s) * (fi) → (< m o)

   The transitive constraints can thus be considered to define a multipication operation over interval relationships. A multipication table for eight of the primitive
relations, shown in Figure 2, is easily constructed. In this table, the three relations
s, f and d are collapsed into the one relation d, and likewise si, fi and di are
collapsed into the one relation di. (For the table for all thirteen relations, see Allen,
1983a.) The product of two complex relations is simply the disjunction of all
products of primitives from the first complex relation with primitives from the
second.

   We now have the basic deductive tools for working with our temporal logic. The
network may be built and updated in various ways (see Vilain, 1982 for an alternative treatment to the one presented here). An algorithm based on *incremental
constraint propagation* is useful for maintaining an updated network as new constraints and queries are dynamically applied.

   Briefly, when a new constraint is asserted, one checks whether it in fact shrinks
the old label set on the specified arc. If so, it (and its inverse) is inserted in the net,
and all transitive relations passing through the arc (and its inverse) are computed.
The process is then applied recursively to the resulting new constraints. Queries
about the relationship of one interval to another are simply answered by inspection.

   The story fragment which began this paper serves to demonstrate interval reasoning. Imagine that temporal assertions are being derived from a text as it is sequentially processed:

   Ernie entered the room and picked up a cup in each hand.

   ENTER (m) HOLDR   (A1)

   ENTER (m) HOLDL   (A2)

In the following, relations marked with A1, A2, etc. are assertions, and those
marked D1, D2, etc. are derived relations. Entering meets both holding events.

Br2C Ar1B	<	>	d	di	o	oi	m	mi
<	<	no info	< o d m	<	<	< o d m	<	< o d m
>	no info	>	> oi d mi	>	> oi d mi	>	> oi d mi	>
d	<	>	d	no info	< o d m	> oi d mi	< m	> mi
di	< o di m	> oi di mi	o oi d di	di	o di	oi di	o di m	oi di mi
o	<	> oi di mi	o d	< o di m	< o m	o oi d di	<	oi di
oi	< o di m	>	oi d	> oi di mi	o oi d di =	> oi mi	o di	>
m	<	> oi di mi	o d m	< m	<	o d	<	d di =
mi	< o di m	>	oi d mi	> mi	oi d	>	d di =	>

Figure 2. The Transitivity Table

Constraint propagation fills in the relationship between the holding events, by multiplying HOLDR (mi) ENTER and ENTER (m) HOLDL:

HOLDR (= s si) HOLDL (D1)

He drank from the one in his right hand—.

DRINK (d) HOLDR (A3)

Drinking is now known to have occurred after entering (by multiplying (A3) and (A1) inverse), but the relationship to holding the second cup is not fully known. We derive:

DRINK (> mi) ENTER (D2)

DRINK (> d f mi oi) HOLDL (D3)

—put the cups back on the table and left the room.

From the first proposition deduced from this statement:

HOLDR (m) LEAVE   (A4)

We infer that leaving occurred after entering and drinking:

DRINK (<) LEAVE   (D4)

ENTER (<) LEAVE   (D5)

HOLDL (< c fi m o) LEAVE   (D6)

Then, adding the final assertion

HOLDL (m) LEAVE   (A5)

lets us derive that the cups were held for the same period of time, and that John drank while holding the second cup as well:

HOLDR (=) HOLDL   (D7)

HOLDL (c) DRINK   (D8)

The constraint propagation algorithm, we see, only derives significant new assertions about the relationships between intervals, and automatically halts when no more can be drawn. Such nice behavior is rather more difficult to obtain when one tries to feed a collection of axioms about time to a general-purpose theorem prover!

The basic propagation algorithm can be elaborated in several ways. It is obviously costly and unnecessary to maintain a complete graph for the constraint network. For example, the system may deal with a number of intervals that occurred yesterday, and a number that occurred today. Rather than explicity link every node in the first group via a "before" arc to every node in second, we introduce *reference intervals*. All of yesterday's intervals can be asserted to be during a certain reference interval, say YESTERDAY, and all of today's intervals to be during TODAY. Finally, YESTERDAY is asserted to be before TODAY. Constraint propagation is not carried through reference intervals. Instead, when a query comes in concerning intervals not directly related, one answers it by climbing up the reference hierarchy. A more thorough discussion of reference intervals (including their use in maintaining a notion of the present) is found in Allen (1981a).

Alternatively, one may desire to ensure that the propagation algorithm is *complete*. Although basic constraint propagation seems to capture most of the inferences that are "obvious" to humans, in certain cases it does not constrain all arcs as tightly as possible. A more complex algorithm that builds a constraint hierarchy (Freuder, 1978) can be shown to fully capture the temporal semantics.

2.2 Reasoning About Durations

An important aspect of time intervals is that they have *durations*. So far, there is no way to assert that interval X lasted for 45 minutes, or that X lasted for twice as long as Y. Such knowledge can have consequences for the interval logic discussed above; for instance, if X has a smaller duration than Y, then X is constrained not to contain Y. This section describes a logic for reasoning about durations, which is separate from, but integrates nicely with, the basic interval logic.

The simplest approach might be to choose a basic unit for durations, say seconds, and assign a real number of those units to every interval. This is clearly inadequate, since knowledge of durations is often approximate:

> The trip lasted *several* hours.
> The reaction takes *two* to *five* minutes to complete.

The next stage might be to use fuzzy numbers for durations. Thus one might encode the second statement above as

REACTION = [120 300] SECONDS

Note that it is somewhat clumsy to use the same units for all durations. The problem is exacerbated when the size of unit is completely inappropriate; for example, encoding knowledge about geological eras in microseconds! Even worse, much knowledge refers to *no* fixed scale:

> Driving across town *takes longer* than walking.
> John ran around the track *three times* while Mary played tennis.

Perhaps suprisingly, all these statements can be represented in a uniform manner. Our solution is to construct a constraint network for duration knowledge (see Davis, 1981, for a very similar treatment of *spatial* knowlege). The nodes are time intervals (as before) and the arcs are labeled with fuzzy numbers, where a fuzzy number is an open or closed interval over the positive real numbers together with infinity. An arc indicates that its source node is a fuzzy multiple of its destination. The example statements could be represented as:

TRIP [2 10] HOURS
REACTION [2 5] MINUTES
DRIVING (1 ∞) WALKING
MARY-PLAY-TENNIS [3 3] JOHN-RUN-AROUND-TRACK

Incremental constraint propagation, using standard fuzzy multipication, can be used to update the constraint network as new information arrives.

The next brief example shows the integration of scaler and relative duration knowledge. Suppose Ernie and Bert travel across town, the first by car, the latter by bus. The bus ride is known to take 30 to 60 minutes.

BUS [30 60] MINUTES (A6)

Other real world knowledge states that the car trip should be faster:

CAR (0 1) BUS (A7)

That is, the car trip is between 0 and 1 times as long. Thus the car trip is between 0 and 60 minutes, exclusive:

CAR (0 60) MINUTES (D9)

Now suppose we learn that the car trip took at least 45 minutes:

CAR [45 ∞) MINUTES (A8)

Propagation then narrows the constraint on the length of the bus ride:

BUS (45 60] MINUTES (D10)

In more complicated situations, certain units (such as the "standard" time units—minutes, hours, weeks, etc.) can be used as *reference durations* to keep the network of managable size.

2.3 A Unified Implementation
A time interval logic system and a duration logic system as described above have been implemented in LISP. Since certain interval logic assertions yield duration information, and vice versa, an interface program links the two systems. The following example demonstrates constraints flowing back and forth between the interval and duration systems as the temporal information gleaned from a story fragment is processed.

Moe and Larry began reading *Principia Mathematica*.

The two reading events could be simultaneous, or one could last longer:

MOE-READ (= s si) LARRY-READ (A9)

Moe read for over an hour.

Now a duration assertion is made:

MOE-READ (1 ∞) HOUR (A10)

Larry stopped reading and fell asleep after 10 minutes.

This statement contains both interval and duration information. The first is the assertion that Larry's sleep follows on the heels of his reading.

LARRY-READ (m) LARRY-SLEEP   (A11)

Next comes the duration assertion:

LARRY-READ [10 15] MINUTE   (A12)

Given an assertion relating hours to minutes,

MINUTE [60 60] HOUR   (A13)

The duration reasoner first deduces Moe's reading time in minutes (or Larry's in hours), and the relationship between the two:

MOE-READ (60 ∞) MINUTE   (D11)

MOE-READ (6 ∞) LARRY-READ   (D12)

When (D12) is added to duration network, the interface program notes that it potentially constrains the interval network as well, since it implies that Moe's reading event could not be during Larry's reading event. So the interval assertion is made:

MOE-READ (< > c si fi m mi o oi) LARRY-READ   (D13)

Combined with (A9) above, this means that Larry's reading must start Moe's.

MOE-READ (si) LARRY-READ   (D14)

Finally, interval constraint propagation adds the fact that Larry's sleeping must have begun while Moe read, but it's not known whether it continued on afterward:

LARRY-SLEEP (d f oi) MOE-READ   (D15)

More elaborate examples can be devised where a duration constraint triggers an interval constraint, which eventually triggers another duration constraint, and so on for several iterations.

3 Problem Solving with the Temporal Reasoner

Given the model of temporal reasoning, we can consider how it affects our approaches to planning and problem-solving systems. Current problem solvers have a quite crude model of time: the world is represented as sets of facts, each set describing an instantaneous slice of time (a state). An action is a function from one state to the next. There is no notion of an action taking any time. A goal description is simply another state. The planner attempts to find a sequence of actions that will transform the initial state into the goal state.

State-based models do not easily allow for the possibility of simultaneous actions, or actions or events not caused by the agent. In addition, the goals described are confined to one time instant. Thus we couldn't express a goal such as "Put block A on B, and then later move A to block C." Goals of this form are not as uncommon as they might seem. For instance, the above goal statement might be the description of how to signal something to another agent.

There are other problems that have been addressed by some systems. For instance, McDermott (1978) allows constraints on the solution to a problem such as, "Don't violate goal x during the solution." Vere (1981) allows events not caused by the agent provided that there is a reasonable estimation of the date at which the event will occur. These are both attempts to introduce more general world models into problem solving. The foregoing temporal reasoner seems to suggest a model of planning that may be able to incorporate all the above and more into one uniform framework.

The model of the world we suggest is that the current state consists of all the planner's knowledge of the present and past, and predictions about the future expressed in an interval-based temporal logic. Planning an action does not update the state of the world but updates the predictions about the world. An action might affect beliefs about the future, the past, or in fact the present. Thus the states in this model are states of the planner's knowledge and independent of the temporal aspects of the world being modeled. We could generalize this further by explicitly introducing a belief predicate and indexing it by time, but this is unnecessary for the present discussion.

In this view, a plan is a collection of assertions viewed as an abstract simulation of some future world, including actions by the agent, other events, actions, and states. Most of these actions, events, and states must be causally related if it is to be a reasonable plan, though it may be simply known that certain events (and states) will occur without any causal explanation.

A goal is a partial description of the world desired. This description is not confined to the world at some specific time. A goal may include sequences of states (get A on B, then later get A on C), restrictions throughout (never let ON(B,C) be true), or any other set of facts expressable in the temporal logic.

Problem solving can be approached along fairly traditional lines. We could use means and analysis, decomposition of actions, etc., (e.g., Ernst & Newell, 1969; Fikes & Nilsson, 1971; Sacerdoti, 1977]). Action descriptions may be quite standard, except that each part of it will be temporally qualified. For the example below, we will use a STRIPs-like action formalism. An interesting side effect of this approach is that the temporal reasoner may do a lot of the problem solving for us. For instance, it will allow for nonlinear plans along the lines of Sacerdoti (1977), and in fact do all the bookkeeping for deriving ordering constraints between actions.

Consider a very simple example. We want to stack three blocks, A, B, and C, starting from a world in which each is clear on the table. While this example is trivial, it allows us to demonstrate our approach in a fairly short space. Thus at the initial time interval I, we have the facts

> holds(CLEAR(A),I)
> holds(CLEAR(B),I)
> holds(CLEAR(C),I).

Our goal description is to build a tower that stands during time interval F. Thus we want

> holds(ON(A,B),F)
> holds(ON(B,C),F).

Note that as this stands, it can be considered to be a (very abstract) plan. It, however, has no causal connections between the initial and final states, so is not considered to be a useful solution. As we go along, we will list the temporal constraints that are added. Our first constraint is that I is before F.

> I $(<)$ F   (A13)

Let us assume Sacerdoti's strategy for conjunctive subgoals: we shall solve each independently and then check for interactions. Each ON(x,y) goal can be achieved by an action PUTON(x,y) that has preconditions that x and y are clear, and an effect that x is on y. With the temporal augmentation, we have

> occurs(PUTON(x,y),t)
>> only if, holds (CLEAR(x),t1) where t finishes t1
>> holds (CLEAR(y),t2) where t finishes t2
>> and the effect is holds (ON(x,y),t3) where t meets t3.

Applying this action description to our first subgoal holds (ON(A,B),F) we introduce the following assertions into the plan for some time TAB:

> occurs(PUTON(A,B),TAB) where I before or meets TAB;
> holds(CLEAR(A),TABp1) where TAB finishes TABp1
> holds(CLEAR(B),TABp2) where TAB finishes TABp2
> holds(ON(A,B),TABe) where TAB meets TABe
>> and F is during TABe

To summarize, the temporal constraints added are:

$$I \; (< m) \; TAB \tag{A14}$$

$$TAB \; (f) \; TABp1 \tag{A15}$$

$$TAB \; (f) \; TABp2 \tag{A16}$$

$$TAB \; (m) \; TABe \tag{A17}$$

$$F \; (s \; f \; d) \; TABe \tag{A18}$$

These relationships can be shown pictorially if we let Time increase from left to right, and use dotted lines to indicate uncertainty as to the position of the ends of intervals. Then the constraints (A14) to (A18) can be shown as in Figure 3. The constraint propagation algorithm infers all the obvious relationships (e.g., TABp1 (m) TABe) implicit in this diagram.

Do the same for an action PUTON(B,C) during time TBC, and we get the constraints:

$$I \; (CV \; m) \; TBC \tag{A19}$$

$$TBC \; (f) \; TBCp1 \tag{A20}$$

$$TBC \; (f) \; TBCp2 \tag{A21}$$

$$TBC \; (m) \; TBCe \tag{A22}$$

$$F \; (s \; f \; d) \; TBCe \tag{A23}$$

Now general world knowledge must come into play. We know that CLEAR(x) and ON(y,x) are mutually exclusive, so if

holds(CLEAR(x),t1) and
holds(ON(y,x),t2)

are true, then it must be the case that t1 and t2 are disjoint, i.e.,

$$t1 \; (< \; > \; m \; mi) \; t2.$$

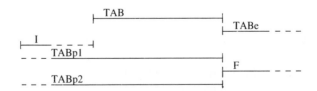

Figure 3. The Intervals Associated with PUTON (*A,B*)

Examining the above plan, we find

    holds(CLEAR(B),TABp2) and
    holds(ON(A,B),TABe),

and so could infer that

    TABp2 (< > m mi) TABe,   (D16)

but these two intervals are already further constrained to be TABp2 (m) TABe, which was derived from constraints in Axioms (A16) and (A17). As a consequence, this has no effect. A constraint that is not already known, however, arises from the facts

    holds(ON(A,B),TABe) and
    holds(CLEAR(B),TBCp1),

giving us

    TABe (< > m mi) TBCp1.   (A24)

However, the constraint (A18) and the constraint TBCp1 (<) F inferred from Axioms (A20), (A22), and (A23) eliminate the possibility that TABe is less than or meets TBCp1. This situation is shown in Figure 4. Thus we are left with the conclusion that TABe is either after or met by TBCp1:

    TABe (> mi) TBCp1.   (D17)

This is shown in Figure 5. The relationship between TAB and TBC, the times of the two PUTON actions, is now constrained to be

    TAB (e di si fi f > mi oi) TBC   (D18)

Thus, PUTON(B,C) must be completed by the time PUTON(A,B) completes. The reason that this constraint is not stronger so far is that there is no implicit assumption that actions cannot be simultaneous in this model. If we add such a constraint

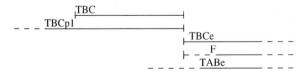

Figure 4. The Results of A18, A20, A22, and A23

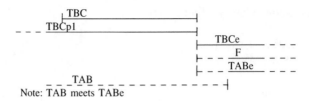

Figure 5. The Result of Adding A24 (Producing D17)

(bringing us in line with most current planning systems), then we have a new constraint that PUTON(A,B) and PUTON(B,C) must be disjoint:

TAB (< > m mi) TBC   (A25)

Of these, only the (> mi) relationships are possible; thus we derive

TAB (> mi) TBC,   (D19)

i.e., PUTON(B,C) must occur before PUTON(A,B). Thus, in effect, we have used the temporal inference machinery together with some general knowledge about the world to capture the action ordering as done by the resolve conflicts critic in Sacerdoti. This final configuration is shown in Figure 6.

As seen in the foregoing examples, actions may take time and may occur simultaneously. In a more complex example using hierarchical planning, as in Sacerdoti, we can model two actions that could occur simultaneously at one level of abstraction, but then when they are decomposed would have ordering constraints on their subparts. It is even possible that the subactions of two abstract actions could be interleaved. For more details on this, see Allen and Koomen (1983).

4 Future Directions

We have presented a model of time based on hierarchically organized time intervals and specified an inference technique based on constraint propagation. This model appears to account for much of the temporal reasoning that is required for story comprehension and problem solving. There are cases where the technique, based on maintaining pairwise consistency between temporal relationships, is inadequate.

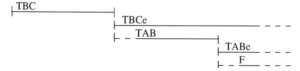

Figure 6. The Final Configuration, with D19

For example, in the problem-solving domain we can allow actions to occur simultaneously, or we can constrain actions of a certain type to occur sequentially. We cannot, however, constrain the domain so that two actions of a certain type may be simultaneous but more than two are not allowed.

For example, consider the state of holding a block. A two-armed robot would be able to hold two objects at one time. In other words, if T1, T2, and T3 are the times of three distinct holding states, then the three can never simultaneously overlap. They may pairwise overlap, however. Such a constraint cannot be expressed in the current system. Generalizing the technique to allow such constraints may be computationally prohibitive. If so, we shall have to introduce special-purpose mechanisms external to the temporal reasoning system to handle such cases.

The other major area of investigation concerns the organization and use of reference intervals in problem solving. Reference intervals are the mechanism for controlling the computation and must be used extensively in an efficient planner. Currently, our reference hierarchy mirrors the action hierarchy: each action has a reference interval which clusters together that action's preconditions, effects, and subactions. Problems arise from interactions between actions. We are considering various ways to adjust the reference hierarchy when such interactions occur.

Acknowledgments

This work was supported in part by the National Science Foundation under Grant IST-8012418, the Defense Advanced Research Projects Agency under Grant N00014-82-K-0193, and the Office of Naval Research under Grant N00014-80-C-0197. We would like to thank Marc Vilain and Hans Koomen for many fruitful discussions concerning this work.

References

Allen, J. F. (1983a). *Maintaining knowledge about temporal intervals* (TR 86). Rochester, NY: U. Rochester, Computer Science Dept. *Communications of the ACM* 26, 11, pp 832–843.

Allen, J. F., (1983b). *A general model of action and time* (TR 97). Rochester, NY: U. Rochester, Computer Science Dept.; to appear, *Artificial Intelligence*.

Allen, J. F. & Koomen, J. A. (1983). Planning using a temporal world model, *Proc., 8th Int'l. Joint Conference on Artificial Intelligence,* Karlsruhe, Germany. pp 741–747.

Bruce, B. C. (1972). A model for temporal references and its application in a question answering program. *Artificial Intelligence, 3,* 1–25.

Davis, E. (1981). Organizing spatial knowledge (TR 193). New Haven, CT: Yale University, Computer Science Dept.

Ernst, G. W. & Newell, A. (1969). *GPS: A case study in generality and problem solving.* New York: Academic Press.

Fikes, R. E. & Nilsson, N. J. (1971). STRIPS: A new approach to the application of theorem proving to problem solving. *Artificial Intelligence, 2,* 189–205.

Freuder, E. C. (1978). Synthesizing constraint expressions. *CACM, 21* (11), 958–965.

McDermott, D. (1978). Planning and acting. *Cognitive Science, 2* (2), 71–109.

McDermott, D. (1982). A temporal logic for reasoning about processes and plans. *Cognitive Science, 6* (2), 101–155.

Sacerdoti, E. D. (1977). *A Structure for plans and behavior.* New York: Elsevier North-Holland.

Vere, S. (1981). *Planning in time: Windows and durations for activities and goals.* Pasadena, CA: California Institute of Technology, NASA Jet Propulsion Laboratory.

Villain, M. (1982). A system for reasoning about time. *Proc., AAAI,* Pittsburgh, PA. pp 197–201.

8 Reasoning about Plans

Drew McDermott

Department of Computer Science
Yale University
New Haven, Connecticut

1 Introduction

This paper is about the relationships between plans, actions, and time. In previous papers (McDermott 1978, 1982), I have proposed some ideas in this area, and here wish to try some new ones.

I begin with some words on methodology. I will be writing a lot of definitions and proofs. This is not because I think that thinking is like proving things. But thinking does appear to rely on "representations," expressions written in a *notation*. Part of the problem of designing a representation is designing the data structures that embody it in a working program. Part of the problem is extracting information from experts (possibly ourselves) in the domain the program works on. These two activities do not exhaust the problem, however. In many domains, once you get beyond simple "production rules," you are often faced with knowledge that is just too hard to be represented using current methods. The representations that result are often *ad hoc* and inert. An "inert" representation is one that rarely reacts with other representations, even when a human observer sees that the resulting inferences would be valuable. A reliable symptom of an inert notation is one whose symbols contain many hyphens; they have internal structure to a human reader, but none to the computer manipulating them.

A way of designing noninert, *robust* notations is that used in McDermott (1982) and Hayes, (Chapter 3, this volume). This is to design a vocabulary of concepts, and focus on the inferences they permit, without worrying at all about the data structures they will ultimately appear as. The prime method is to constrain the meaning of the vocabulary items by writing axioms that contain them. The aim is to restrict the class of models of the axioms (Mendelson, 1964) to those in which the fundamental facts of the domain are true. For instance, it is a key fact about liquids that the amount flowing into a space must be the same as the amount flowing out. The axioms should support this inference.

It is remarkable how often this exercise reveals sticky difficulties, and how easy it is to recognize a breakthrough that allows interesting inferences to flow. (As Hayes, 1979, says, the axioms start to "suggest themselves faster than one can write them down.") Although such methods are still in their infancy, one insight I have gained from them is that data-structuring issues are much easier to attack if the logical issues have been solved in advance.

Proving theorems is obviously an important part of the method, for there is no other way to show that the axioms support the fundamental inferences. This can give rise to misunderstanding, because in real life theorems of this kind are never proven. No one ever has to prove that the amount of liquid flowing into a space is equal to the amount flowing out; the fact is important because it enables you to find oil wells and keep your bathroom from flooding. Presumably a fundamental fact like this is wired into the mechanism for reasoning about liquids. The point of the method is to figure out what to wire in.

I go into these points at such length because the possibility of misinterpretation is especially acute for the domain of action planning. To demonstrate the power of our concepts, we must prove things, and the obvious thing to prove is that a given plan of action will have a desired result. In real life, this is almost never possible. Instead, what we usually do is put together likely-looking plan fragments, attempt to prove that the combination *won't* work, and if we can't, hope for the best.

This is, I think, the right way to view a popular and apparently powerful technique for organizing problem solvers pioneered by Sacerdoti (1975) and Sussman (1975). This technique relies on a catalogue, or *plan library,* of fairly detailed *plans* for accomplishing *tasks.* When a problem solver has more than one task, as it certainly will, since even simple plans consist of several *subtasks,* it must coordinate the execution of the flock of plans it chooses to carry all its tasks out. Planning and execution are interleaved. At any point, the system represents what it plans to do as a *task network,* whose nodes describe tasks, and whose arcs record subtask and "successor" relationships. See Figure 1. (Some of the terminology is from McDermott, 1978.)

In the figure, there is one overall task, "Cook dinner," with subtasks like "Bake cake," "Cook turkey," and "Cook rice." These three can apparently be done in any order, but, of course, there may be interactions between them. Indeed, inspection of the subtasks of "Bake cake" and "Cook turkey" shows that they require

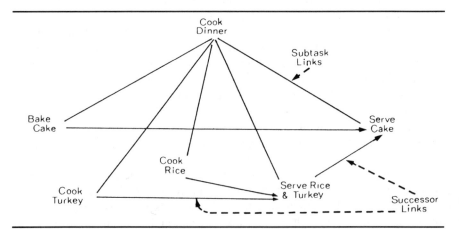

Figure 1. A Task Network

setting the oven on two different temperatures for longish amounts of time. Hence, the two tasks cannot be done completely independently.

The hope for this scheme derives from the expectation that the interactions between plans will be a simple, relatively closed set. If this is so, then the solver can solve problems involving new combinations of subproblems, by adapting their individual plans and cleaning up the interactions.

Unfortunately, progress in this area has been slow. Few interactions besides those originally studied by Sussman and Sacerdoti have been studied systematically. (But see Wilkins, 1984, and Vere, 1983.)

There are several reasons for this slowdown. The one I want to focus on is the "seductive successor link" problem. Pictures like Figure 1-1 are so appealing that one yearns to bring more and more plan types into this format, creating more links if need be.[1] A link shortage is not the fundamental problem here, however; the fundamental problem is that *more interesting plan types resist being decomposed into independently describable subtasks.*

This problem appears as soon as you try to extend Sacerdoti's program NOAH beyond simple blocks-world applications. For instance, consider the following fragment of a plan for calling person P on the phone:

1. Look up P's phone number, $N(P)$.
2. Dial $N(P)$.

Task 2 is not fully specified until 1 is finished (Moore 1980).

A more elaborate example is this plan for loading ballast on a hot-air balloon:

    (repeat until (force up $\leq$ 0)
    (Get a rock R)
    (Put R in the gondola)   )

This is a clear-enough plan. The problem is to see it giving rise to a set of subtasks. Of course, after it is executed, we can divide it into subtasks by counting rock acquisitions, rock transfers, and buoyancy tests, but this is pointless. The whole idea was to break one's amorphous plan of action into easy-to-manage chunks (tasks) in order to plan more effectively and modularly. For example, a NOAH-style "critic" cannot realize that it must move a rock that for some other reason should stay still unless it can see the plan as engendering subtasks for moving particular rocks.

It is important to see what the problem is here. Of course, one can easily make up programming languages in which "Repeat" is a control structure, and one can make robots execute programs in that language. But problem solving involves reasoning about plans, not just executing them. Is there any way to generalize the plans NOAH executes without making them impenetrable?

---

[1] For instance, the "policy scope links" of McDermott (1978).

Another example is the action "Put all the eggs in set E into basket B without breaking any." NOAH can (if it knows how to enumerate E in advance) break this into as many subtasks as there are eggs in E, but, for each subtask, it must treat "Put x in B without breaking it" as a unit. Intuitively, this action consists of two parts: "Put x in B" and "Don't break x."

A radical variant of the "programming-language" idea is the proposal (made by Stan Rosenschein and Robert Moore, personal communication) to replace task networks with logical sentences. They point out that a plan is nothing but a sentence which is true iff the plan is executed successfully. For example, the plan to "Put all the eggs in the basket without breaking any," is just the sentence, "I did put all the eggs in the basket without breaking any," plus the tag: To be made true. The nice thing about this theory is that is does away with all special perplexities about notations for plans, since it reduces them to the general problem of talking about time. For example, "I didn't break x" is just another statement about a time interval. The whole plan would, in the logic developed in McDermott (1982), correspond to the logical formula:

```
(forall (e)
   (and (if (elt e E)
           (and (exists (s2 s3)
                   (and (=< s0 s2 s3 s1)
                        (Occ s2 s3 (put Robot e B))))
                (not (exists (e s2 s3)
                        (and (=< s0 s2 s3 s1)
                             (Occ s2 s3 (break Robot e)))))))))
```

Here I have introduce the term Robot to refer to the planner itself. The formula contains two free variables, s0 and s1 (in addition to the constants E and B, a set of eggs and a basket). As explained in McDermott (1982), s0 and s1 are states of the universe such that s0 temporally precedes or is the same as s1. This is written (=< s0 s1). (=< x y z ...) is true if x, y, z, etc. are states that occur in that order. The *state interval* [s0, s1] can be the site of an event occurrence; it is the set of all instants s such that (=< s0 s s1). The formula (Occ s0 s1 ev) is true if the event type *ev* occurred from s0 to s1. The formula then makes a statement about the interval from s0 to s1, namely, that an occurrence of (put Robot e B) fell in that interval for each egg e, and no occurrence of (break Robot e) did for any egg e. Hence, it states that the robot carried out the plan "Put all the eggs in the basket without breaking any."

The problem with this sweeping generalization from plans to sentences is that it provides no hint as to how to build a problem solver that thinks about plans this way. Intuitively, we can carry out this plan (with no prior experience) by putting together what we know about

- Doing something to a group of objects
- Putting things places
- Avoiding breaking things

But the proposed generalization provides no hint how to break the sentence up in the ways required. (On the other hand, it is just fine for proving that a given sequence of actions would carry out this plan.)

So here is our problem: How to achieve logical robustness without giving up implementability.

2 An Approach

I think the solution must look something like this: the task network picture is correct for tasks that are ready for execution, and is a useful approximation for tasks in the future. The more remote the future, the less accurate the approximation. According to this view, an important job of a problem solver is to revise continually its model, or "time map," of what it is going to do.

For example, before looking up a telephone number, you believe you are going to dial a seven-digit number. After looking it up, you know which number. This is a transition from a partial description of an action to a complete (executable) one. For a loop like that of the balloon-gondola example, you maintain an estimate of how many tasks with action, Put a rock in the gondola, there will be. By the time you are done, this estimate has become accurate.

If this works, then we can salvage the task network idea. The major modification is to realize that the more remote parts of it are to some extent *guesses* about the problem solver's intentions. If they turn out to be drastically wrong, some replanning may be done. I hope that some of the data-base management ideas of Doyle (1979) and me (McDermott, 1983) can help (although they need a lot of extension).

On the other side of the ledger, we will probably have to restrict plan desciptions substantially to meet the requirement that they be factorable into familiar fragments. For instance, we must insist that "Put all the eggs in the basket without breaking any" be factorable into explicit pieces like "Avoid breaking any eggs," such that

1. These pieces are of the sort likely to be found in the "plan library."
2. The relationships between the pieces are familiar.

2.1 The Logical Framework

I will now develop a skeleton of a formal theory that begins to meet these requirements. Before I start, I must review some of the features of the temporal calculus that I will be using (for a fuller treatment, see McDermott 1982). The ontology behind it postulates that the universe consists of a tree of states, or instants. The tree branches in the forward direction. A given state has many futures, but only one past. This reflects the fact that the outcome of many events is indeterminate (Figure 2). Every state has a date that is a real number. The date of state s is denoted by (d s). I will assume obvious properties of real numbers.

A *fact* is something that is true or false at every state. We say that a fact f is true

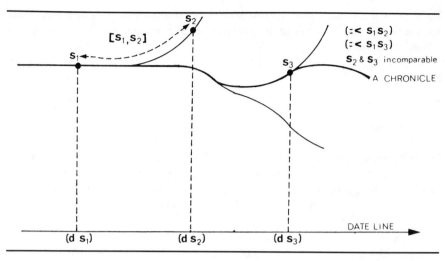

Figure 2. Tree of States

in state *s* by writing (T *s f*). An event is something that can occur over a state interval
[*s1, s2*], the set of all states between *s1* and *s3*, including *s1* and *s2* themselves. We
say that an event *e* occurred over the interval between *s1* and *s2* by writing (Occ *s1
s2 e*).[2] I use "Cambridge Polish," or Lisplike syntax throughout this paper. Constants and variables are represented by symbols. Atomic formulas and terms are
represented by expressions of the form (*f* a_1 a_2 ... a_N), where *f* is a function or
predicate, and the *a*'s are its arguments. Connectives look similar, as in

(not *p*)
(and p_1 p_2 ... p_N)
(or p_1 p_2 ... p_N)
(if *p q*)
(iff p_1 p_2 ... p_N)
(exc p_1 p_2 ... p_N)

Notice that iff ("if and only if") can take any number of formulas as arguments,
and asserts that they all have the same truth value. The last connective, exc (for
"exclusive"), asserts that at most one of its arguments can be true. It is an abbreviation for

(and (if p_1 (not (or p_2 ... p_N)))
    (if p_2 (not (or p_1 ... p_N)))
    (if p_N (not (or p_1 ... p_{N-1}))))

---

[2] In the previous paper, I assumed that facts were literally sets of states, and events sets of state intervals.
This assumption had the advantage of concreteness, but is unnecessary.

I also allow binary predicates to take any number of arguments. So

$$(=< t_1\ t_2\ ...\ t_N)$$

asserts that

```
(and (=< t_1 t_2)
     (=< t_2 t_3)
     ...
     (=< t_{N-1} t_N))
```

Quantified formulas are written as (forall (-vars-) *formula*) or (exists (-vars-) *formula*), with obvious meanings.

Variables are distinguished from constants by appearing in the variable lists of quantifiers, and usually by being lower case. To avoid clutter, if a variable is universally quantified over an entire formula, I will suppress the quantifier and instead prefix every occurrence of it with "?". An example is

```
(if (< ?s1 ?s2)
    (exists (s)
        (< ?s1 s ?s2)))
```

This is equivalent to

```
(forall (s1 s2)
    (if (< s1 s2)
        (exists (s)
            (< s1 s s2))))
```

Variables are *sorted*. A variable beginning with the letter "s" ranges over states. A variable beginning with a doubled letter ranges over a set; ss1 might range over sets of states. Here is a table of all the sorts I will use (many of which I have not explained yet):

s = states
r = real numbers
h = chronicles
p = facts
e = events
k = tasks
a = actions

Capitalized terms beginning with these letters are not variables, but anonymous constants. S1 and S2, for instance, would be used to denote anonymous states.

I will assume casual set theory throughout. The predicate (elt x xx) will be used to state that x is an element of the set xx. Finite *tuples* will also be handy. The tuple of N elements x_1 through x_N is denoted by $<x_1 \ldots x_N>$. The empty tuple is denoted by $<>$.

A key fact of our logic is that states are partially ordered. For details, see McDermott (1982). The ordering branches into the future, but not into the past. A state may have several possible futures, containing states that are not mutually comparable. But it has only one past; any two states before a given state are comparable. A complete branch through this tree is called a *chronicle*. A state s occurring in chronicle h is denoted by (elt s h). See Figure 2.

One consequence of the absence of branching into the past is that any chronicle containing the end of an interval also contains its beginning:

Theorem 1:

```
(if (and (elt ?s2 ?h)
         (=< ?s1 ?s2))
    (elt ?s1 ?h))
```

One consequence of the branching into the future is that to assert that something is inevitable in a state, you must assert that it occurs in all chronicles containing the state. For instance, to assert that after someone is born he will inevitably die, you must say:

```
(forall (s1 s2)
   (if (Occ s1 s2 (born ?person))
       (forall (b)
          (if (elt s2 h)
              (exists (s3 s4)
                 (and (elt s3 h)
                      (elt s4 h)
                      (< s2 s3)
                      (Occ s3 s4 (die ?person)))  )) )))
```

Because this pattern is fairly common, I introduce the following syntactic abbreviation

Definition 1:

```
        (inevitably state (v1 ...vn) formula)
means
        (forall (h)
           (if (elt state h)
               (exists (v1 ...vn)
                  (and (elt v1 h)
```

```
...
(elt vₙ h)
formula) )) )
```

Hence the "inevitability of death" example would be written thus:

```
(forall (s1 s2)
   (if (Occ s1 s2 (born ?person))
      (inevitably s2 (s3 s4)
         (and (< s2 s3)
            (Occ s3 s4 (die ?person)))) )) )
```

Note that (inevitably *s1* (*s2*) ...) does not necessarily imply that *s2* is *after s1*; although this is usually the case, we must state it explicitly.

It will be useful to assume that events occur only over proper intervals:
Axiom 1:

```
(if (Occ ?s1 ?s2 ?e) (=< ?s1 ?s2))
```

In many cases, we are interested only in the state when an event comes to an end, for which we use the predicate EOcc:
Definition 2:

```
(iff (EOcc ?s2 ?e)
   (exists (s1) (Occ s1 ?s2 ?e)) )
```

Another useful predicate is (one-way *e1 e2*):
Definition 3:

```
(iff (one-way ?e1 ?e2)
   (forall (s1 s2)
      (if (Occ s1 s2 ?e1)
         (Occ s1 s2 ?e2)) ))
```

That is, ?e1 is one way ?e2 can happen; whenever ?e1 happens, ?e2 does.

This logic allows events to come in many varieties. Some events occur over extended intervals, while others consume just an instant. Some events (like "Sing for a while") occur over every subinterval during which they occur. I described several different event types in McDermott (1982), focusing on continuous change. In this paper, I will supplement the treatment of the previous paper with some axioms about becoming. This will occupy most of the rest of this section.

An important class of event is the *discrete events*, those whose occurrences are easy to individuate, because they never overlap. Examples of discrete events are "eclipses of the moon," "years," and "chess moves." To define them, we need two subsidiary concepts:

Two intervals *overlap* if one is a subset of the other, or they share more than one point and lie entirely in the same chronicle:

Definition 4:

```
(iff (overlap [?s1, ?s2] [?s3, ?s4])
   (or (=< ?s1 ?s3 ?s4 ?s2)
       (=< ?s3 ?s1 ?s2 ?s4)
       (< ?s3 ?s1 ?s4 ?s2)
       (< ?s1 ?s3 ?s2 ?s4)))
```

Now we can define a *discrete* event as one whose occurrences do not overlap:

Definition 5:

```
(iff (discrete ?e)
   (forall (s1 s2 s3 s4)
      (if (and (Occ s1 s2 ?e)
               (Occ s3 s4 ?e)
               (overlap [s1, s2] [s3, s4]))
          (and (= s1 s3)
               (= s2 s4)))   )))
```

An event is *countable* if any open interval in which it occurs contains an earliest occurrence of it. First we define (occurs-in *s1 s2 s3 s4 e*) to mean that [*s2, s3*] is an occurrence of *e* in the open interval (*s1, s4*):

Definition 6:

```
(iff (occurs-in ?s1 ?s2 ?s3 ?s4 ?e)
   (and (< ?s1 ?s2)
        (=< ?s2 ?s3 ?s4)
        (Occ ?s2 ?s3 ?e)))
```

Now countable is defined thus:

Definition 7:

```
(iff (countable ?e)
   (forall (s1 s4)
      (if (exists (s2 s3)
              (occurs-in s1 s2 s3 s4 ?e)   )
          ; If [s2, s3] is an occurrence of ?e
          ; in the interval [s1, s4]
          (exists (s2 s3)
              ; Then there is an earliest such occurrence
```

```
; in that interval
(and (occurs-in s1 s2 s3 s4 ?e)
     (forall (s5 s6)
          (if (occurs-in s1 s5 s6 s4 ?e)
              (=< s2 s5)) )) )) ))
```

I call this property "countability" because we could enumerate all the occurrences of such an event in an interval by stripping the earliest off repeatedly.

It is hard to think of a natural event that is discrete and yet uncountable. Let us formalize this intuition in this axiom:

Axiom 2:

```
(if (discrete ?e) (countable ?e))
```

Here is a theorem we will use implicitly below:

Theorem 2:

```
(if (and (one-way ?e1 ?e2)
         (discrete ?e2))
    (discrete ?e1))
```

Proof: Assume (one way E1 E2) and (discrete E2). Then clearly E1's occurrences do not overlap, because they are also occurrences of E2. QED

I will use the term *fact predicate* to refer to a function whose range is the set of facts. For instance, in the expression (T S1982 (PRESIDENT REAGAN)), PRESIDENT is a fact predicate that maps an object into the fact true when the object is President. S1982 is a state of the universe at, say, noon on January 1, 1982. In the example, the fact (PRESIDENT REAGAN) was in fact true then.

The term "fact predicate" suggests that the set of terms representing facts can be thought of as a timeless sublanguage. I will encourage this by introducing these notations:

$(- p)$: the fact true when p is false, and vice versa
$(\& \ p_1 \ ... \ p_N)$: the fact true just when facts $p_1, p_2, ...,$ and p_N are true.
$(V \ p_1 \ ... \ p_N)$: the fact true just when one of facts $p_1, p_2, ...,$ or p_N is true.

To indicate that a fact is true over an interval, we use TT:

Definition 8:

```
(iff (TT ?s1 ?s2 ?p)
     (and (=< ?s1 ?s2)
          (forall (s)
               (if (=< ?s1 s ?s2)
                   (T s ?p)) )))
```

The predicate TTopen is used when the endpoints are not included:
Definition 9:

```
(iff (TTopen ?s1 ?s2 ?p)
    (and (< ?s1 ?s2)
        (forall (s)
            (and (< ?s1 s ?s2)
                (T s ?p))  )))
```

Facts change in true value. A fact *p begins* at a state and lasts until another state, or, formally, (begin *s*1 *s*2 *p*), if it is not true before the first state, and is true from the first to the second:
Definition 10:

```
(iff (begin ?s1 ?s2 ?p)
    (and (< ?s1 ?s2)
        (TTopen ?s1 ?s2 ?p)
        ; It is true from ?s1 to ?s2
        (exists (s0)
            ; and false before ?s1
            (and (< s0 ?s1)
                (TTopen s0 ?s1 (- ?p)))  )))
```

It is a theorem that a true fact that has not always been true and stays true for more than a single state has a beginning:
Theorem 3:

```
(if (and (< ?s1 ?s2) (TTopen ?s1 ?s2 ?p))
    (or ; Either it has always been true
        (forall (s')
            (if (=< s' ?s1) (T s' ?p))  )
        ; Or it began to be true
        (exists (s0)
            (and (=< s0 ?s1)
                (begin s0 ?s2 ?p))  )))
```

I will not prove it here, but it follows straightforwardly from the axioms of McDermott (1982).

It will be useful to assume a slightly stronger proposition, that there is a "becoming" event that marks the beginning of a fact's being true. If *p* becomes true, then *p* must be false at the beginning of this event, and true at the end; furthermore, it must remain true for at least a little while in every chronicle containing the event.

Our intuitions about becoming are unclear. On the one hand, we want to preserve the idea that every fact is either true or false at every time. On the other hand, when something is "becoming true," it might be hard to specify its truth value for a while. (For instance, picture someone "becoming an adult.")

This confusion is not entirely central to the problem of designing internal representations. Intuitions about the meanings of English words can often be neglected in trying to build a coherent notation to support reasoning. Nonetheless, there are cases where something take time to become true, and yet it must, if we are to preserve two-valued logic, actually make the transition instantaneously.

The only solution is to accept that every becoming contains a transition point. If *p* becomes true over the interval *s1* to *s2*, then (transition *s1* *s2* *p*) is the term designating the state where the transition occurs. During the intervals on either side of the transition point, we can refer to the uneasy status of *p* by making reference to the ongoing becoming event. That is, before the transition point, we can capture our intuitions that *p* is not "really false," by saying that *p* is "false but becoming true."

Formally:

Axiom 3:

```
(if (Occ ?s1 ?s2 (become ?p))
   (and (T ?s1 (− ?p))
           ; ?p is false at the beginning
           (T ?s2 ?p)
           ; and true at the end;
           (exists (s)
              ; ?p begins to be true at the transition point
              (and (= s (transition ?s1 ?s2 ?p))
                   (TTopen ?s1 s (− ?p))
                   (begin s ?s2 ?p))   )
           ; ?p stays true for a little while after the becoming
           (inevitably ?s2 (s3)
              (TTopen ?s2 ?s3 ?p)   ))   )
```

(The "transition" symbol is functioning here as a Skolem function; it has no further definition than this axiom.)

Intuitively, nothing goes from false to true without becoming true. But we cannot simply assert that there is a becoming between any two states in which a fact has two different truth values. Any fact is either true or false in every state, so that within every becoming there would be an infinite telescoped set of becomings converging on a single point. As I have defined "become," after (become *P*), *P* remains true for some amount of time in every chronicle. See Figure 3.

If there were a becoming between any two points where a fact has different truth values, then the branching of the chronicles would be complex.

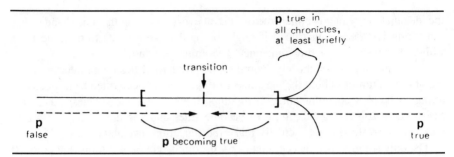

Figure 3. *P* Becomes True

We specifically exclude infinitely telescoped becomings, by asserting that becomings are countable and nonoverlapping:

Axiom 4:

(forall (p) (discrete (become?p)))

Now, to say that every change in truth value is accomplished via a becoming, the first thing we assert is that nothing begins to be true without becoming true:

Axiom 5:

(if (begin ?s1 ?s2 ?p)
   (inevitably ?s2 (s3 s4)
      (and (Occ s3 s4 (become ?p))
           (= ?s1 (transition s3 s4 ?p)))   ))

In English, if ?p begins to be true at ?s1, then in every chronicle in which this happens, there is a become event for which ?s1 is the transition point.

With these axioms, we can prove this theorem:

Theorem 4: If a fact is false, and later true over a non-point interval, then there is a become event between the earlier and later times during which it becomes true:

(if (and (T ?s1 (− ?p))
         (< ?s1 ?s2)
         (TTopen ?s2 ?s3 ?p))
   ; *If ?p goes from false to true and stays true*
   ; *for more than an instant*
   (inevitably ?s2 (s3 s4)
      ; *then inevitably there is a becoming event*
      (and (Occ s3 s4 (become ?p))
           ; *whose transition point falls between*
           ; *?s1 and ?s2*
           (elt (transition s3 s4 ?p) [?s1, ?s2]))   ))

Proof: Let P be the fact in question, and let $S1$, $S2$ and $S3$ satisfy the antecedent of the theorem. By Theorem 3, there must be an SO such that (begin SO $S2$ P). But then by Axiom 5, in every chronicle containing $S2$, there is a become event for P whose transition point is SO. This is the become event called for by the theorem. QED

Note that the theorem does not say that the becoming lies entirely inside the interval [?s1, ?s2]. If it is the case, however, that s3 comes before ?s1, or s4 comes after ?s2, ?p will not change in truth value in the part of the becoming that surrounds [?s1, ?s2].

Hence, by constraining our models a little bit, we can capture the intuition that there are definite events, known as "becomings," that occur when something changes in truth value. With these concepts, we can always make the intuitively simple transition from talking of differences in truth value over time to talking about the events during which the truth values change. I won't make frequent use of this, but there is one place where I talk about "tasks" coming to an end, where it is important.

All of this applies only to facts that stay true for a while. If the temperature changes smoothly from 50 to 60 degrees, we do not need to infer that it "became" 53.14159....

The last topic before going on to the main topic of this paper is that of *action*. An action is an abstract object that, combined with an *agent*, gives an event. For instance, (take *object place*) is an action that an agent can perform, producing the event consisting of that agent taking the object to the place. The term (do *agent action*) denotes the event consisting of the agent performing the action. In McDermott (1982), I dropped the first argument because I never had occasion to talk about more than one agent. Here we will want to talk about domains like chess, so I put the argument back. The constant "Robot" will denote the reasoner itself. That is, the event referred to in McDermott (1982) as (do (take OB1 PL2)) will be referred to here as (do Robot (take OB1 PL2)).

It is significant that actions are treated in this neutral way. I do not require that an action be definable in terms of some change in the facts that it brings about. On the contrary, I want to analyze very abstract actions, like "Avoid moving the block," or "Prevent your opponent from queening his pawn." For further discussion, see McDermott (1982).

2.2 A Logic of Tasks

An action can be performed unintentionally. Intending to perform an action we denote using the fact predicate task: (task *name act*) is a fact that is true when "Robot" is actively engaged in trying to do *act*.[3] We give a name to this attempt so we can say things about it.

The predicate task is like do in that it should involve an agent. However, in this

---

[3] This definition clashes with that of McDermott (1982), as do several of the others given in what follows.

paper we will avoid talking about any tasks but the robot's, so I leave the agent argument out consistently.

The logic of tasks is of interest, because it provides a flexible way of talking about actions. Traditionally, the situation calculus developed by McCarthy modeled an action as altering the truth values of a set of facts. This led to thinking of planning as finding a sequence of actions that would bring about some state of affairs, as early problem solvers like GPS actually did. More recent problem solvers think in terms of representing actions at an abstract level, then refining the description. One of my goals in this section is to provide a clean way of talking about what these problem solvers already do, in hopes that the result will suggest ways of improving them.

There are some obvious constraints on tasks:

Axiom 6:

```
(if (T ?s (task ?k ?a))
  (= ?a (task-act?k)))
```

"Every task has a unique, unchanging action, denoted (task-act *task*)."
Axiom 7:

```
(if (and (T ?s (task ?k1 ?a))
         (T ?s (task ?ks ?a)))
    (= ?k1 ?k2))
```

"There is just one task for a given action at a given time."
Definition 11:

```
(iff (T ?s (is-task ?k))
     (exists (a) (T ?s (task ?k a))))
```

This is the definition of is-task: "*t* is a task just while (task *t* a) is true for some a."
Axiom 8:

```
(if (and (T ?s1 (is-task ?k))
         (T ?s2 (is-task ?k))
         (=< ?s1 ?s2))
    (forall (s)
      (if (< ?s1 s ?s2)
        (T s (is-task ?k)))))
```

"A task remains a task for a single uninterrupted interval in any chronicle."
One aspect of intentions that I neglect completely in this paper is the well known intensionality of intentions. Suppose John intends to write the least prime on the

blackboard (i.e., in the present terminology, has a task to do this). If John has an erroneous idea of what primes are, he may intend to write "3" on the board. In the calculus of this paper, everything is first-order, and, in particular, equals may be substituted freely for equals. Hence the action of writing the least prime on a blackboard is the same as the action of writing "2" on the blackboard, and a task to do one is the same as a task to do the other.

At a given time, the problem solver has a set of tasks that entirely define its intentions. For example, the problem solver might have the following tasks:

```
(T S0 (task K1 (prog <(unscrew lightbulb1)
                      (screwin lightbulb2)
                      (discard lightbulb1)>)))

(T S0 (task K2 (screwin lightbulb2)))
```

That is, it is engaged in two things: a three-step plan, and the task of screwing in a lightbulb. This second task is step 2 of the three-step plan. This coincidence might be an accident: there might be some other reason for screwing in lightbulb2. If it is not an accident, we use the *subtask* fact-predicate to notate this:

```
(T S0 (subtask K2 K1 <2>))
```

This formula says that K2 is the second action of K1.[4] The third argument to *subtask* is a "path expression," a tuple that unambiguously picks out a subpiece of an action. This notion relies on an "abstract syntax" (McCarthy, 1962) for each action-description primitive. For example, prog takes a tuple of steps and denotes the action of doing one after another. Each subaction is indicated by a positive integer. Another example is (while *fact act*). In the action

```
(while (not (nail-driven))
       (repeat (prog <(lift hammer) (drop hammer)>)))
```

we can indicate (lift hammer) using the path expression <act 1>, that is, the first step of the prog, which is the *act* part of the while. The *test* part of the while is the action of testing whether or not the nail is driven. Hence, the path expression <test> is used for subtasks that do this test:

```
(T S0 (task K25 (look-at-nail)))
(T S0 (subtask K25 nail-drive-task <test>))
```

A subtask does not have to be derived from a supertask in this simple way. In fact, to transcend triviality, a working program must contain mechanisms (called

---

[4] More precisely, the action of K2 is the second part of the action of K1. Here and elsewhere in the text I conflate tasks and their actions for the sake of brevity. Of course, I will never do this in formal contexts.

the "plan generators," or the "plan library") that supply actions to carry out other actions when needed. If a subtask is derived this way, we make its path expression <>. So we might have

```
(T S0 (task K26 (replace lightbulb1 lightbulb2)))
(T S0 (subtask K1 K26 <>))
```

I will use the term *syntactic subtask* for a subtask with non-<> path expression; that is, for a subtask whose action is derived from the action of the supertask.
Definition 12:

```
(iff (T ?s (synsubtask ?k1 ?k2))
    (exists (x)
        (and (not (= x <>))
             (T ?s (subtask ?k1 ?k2 x)))   ))
```

"Subtask" is a fact-predicate, because the relationship can change. For one thing,
Axiom 9:

```
(if (T ?s (subtask ?k1 ?k2 ?x))
    (and (T ?s (is-task ?k1))
         (T ?s (is-task ?k2))))
```

"The subtask relationship is true only as long as the two tasks involved are actually tasks."

A task can, of course, be a subtask of more than one supertask. One can kill two birds with one stone. A task can also be a subtask of no other tasks; such a task is called a *top-level task*.
Axiom 10:

```
(if (toplevel-task ?k)
    (forall (s)
        (not (exists (k' x) (T s (subtask ?k k' x))   ))))
```

I introduce the constant Birth to denote the situation at which all top-level tasks began.
Axiom 11:

```
(if (toplevel-task ?k)
    (EOcc Birth (become (is-task ?k))))
```

There were no tasks at all before Birth:

Axiom 12:

```
(forall (s)
    (if (< s Birth)
        (not (exists (k) (T s (is-task k))  )))   )
```

Top-level tasks last forever:
Axiom 13:

```
(if (toplevel-task ?k)
    (forall (s)
        (if (> s Birth)
            (T s (is-task ?k)))  ))
```

What I have in mind for top-level tasks are goals like "Stay alive" and "Avoid hunger." It is something of an idealization to have them all begin at "birth" and go on forever, but it seems a harmless one.

Top-level tasks provide the ultimate rationale for all intentional actions. The reason for an action is the set of all its supertasks. The ultimate reason is the set of top-level tasks of which the action is a sub-sub-...-task. Such ultimate reasons cannot themselves have reasons.

One might suppose that new top-level tasks are created many times. For instance, if you see a truck bearing down on you, you suddenly acquire the task, "Get out of the way." (Schank and Abelson, 1977 call these "P-goals.") However, it will simplify analysis if we assume that the task structure is actually somewhat as shown in Figure 4, where "Avoid getting hit by trucks" is a long-term subtask of "Stay alive." The reason this is an improvement is that it forces us to give reasons for all new tasks; in principle, we can prove that something will never be a task by showing that it could never be a subtask of an existing task. Without this structure, it would be harder to prove anything about the future behavior of the problem solver.

We define the predicate subtask* to be the transitive and reflexive closure of the subtask relation:
Definition 13:

```
(iff (T ?s (subtask* ?k1 ?k2))
    (or (= ?k1 ?k2)
```

```
                    Stay alive
                        ↑
            Avoid getting hit by trucks
                    /           \
            Detect truck  →  Get out of the way
```

Figure 4. Supertasks for Truck Avoidance

```
(exists (k x)
    (and (T ?s (subtask ?k1 k x))
        (T ?s (subtask* k ?k2)))  )))
```

Similarly, we define synsubtask* to be the transitive closure of the syntactic-subtask relation:

Definition 14:

```
(iff (T ?s (synsubtask* ?k1 ?k2))
    (or (T ?s (synsubtask ?k1 ?k2))
        (exists (k)
            (and (T ?s (synsubtask ?k1 k))
                (T ?s (synsubtask* k ?k2)))  )))
```

We would like to have an axiom to the effect that tasks are never unintentional, that is, that every task is a subtask* of some top-level task. However, there are exceptions to this rule, which I will discuss in the next section.

There are just three ways something can cease to be a task: success, failure, or "evaporation." The last category summarizes those cases when a task vanishes from the agenda because it is pointless, due to success or failure of all its supertasks. Consider the task "Poison Daddy Warbucks," which Orphan Annie might have as a subtask of "Get Daddy Warbucks's inheritance." The subtask succeeds if Warbucks is poisoned by Annie; fails if she is thwarted; and evaporates if Warbucks dies from some other cause.

We define (task-end k) to be an event that occurs whenever a task stops being a task:

Definition 15:

```
(iff (Occ ?s ?s' (task-end ?k))
    (Occ ?s ?s' (become (- (is-task ?k)))))
```

Tasks end by success, failure, or evaporation:

Axiom 14:

```
(iff (occ ?s ?s' (task-end ?k))
    (or (Occ ?s ?s' (succeed ?k))
        (Occ ?s ?s' (fail ?k))
        (Occ ?s ?s' (evaporate ?k))))
```

Each of the three ways is further described in what follows.

Success can be defined as follows:

Definition 16:

```
(iff (Occ ?s1 ?s2 (succeed ?k))
    ; ?k succeeds...
```

```
(and (T ?s1 (is-task ?k))
     (Occ ?s1 ?s2 (do Robot (task-act ?k)))
     ; as soon as its action is done by Robot
     (not (exists (s1' s2')
          (and (=< s1' ?s1)
               (< s2' ?s2)
               (T s1' (is-task ?k))
               (Occ s1' s2'
                    (do Robot (task-act ?k))))
     ))))
```

In English, a task succeeds upon the first execution of its action that begins when it is a task.

This definition has the virtue of simplicity, but means that some care is required in defining some tasks. For instance, the action (avoid A), where A is some other action, usually succeeds instantaneously, since it is executed over any interval, no matter how short, in which A is not done. Therefore, when an action like "Pick up a stick, and avoid moving any other stick" is decomposed into pieces, the "Avoid" subtask must be something like "Avoid moving any other stick while executing the 'Pickup' task." If it is analyzed simply as "Avoid moving any other stick," then it will succeed trivially immediately.

Evaporation and failure cannot be defined as tidily as success. We have the following axiom about evaporation:

Axiom 15:

```
(if (Occ ?s1 ?s2 (evaporate ?k))
    (or (T ?s1 (supertaskless ?k))
        (Occ ?s1 ?s2 (become (supertaskless ?k)))))
```

"If a task evaporates, all of its supertasks go away (if it ever had any)."
supertaskless is defined thus:

Definition 17:

```
(iff (T ?s (supertaskless ?k))
     (not (exists (k' x)
          (T ?s (subtask ?k k' x)) )))
```

It would be nice to write an axiom to the effect that, when all the supertasks of a task cease, the task evaporates. However, it is difficult to state such an axiom correctly, because the ending of the supertask could just as well be caused by the success or failure of a subtask. We want to say, "If the supertask ends for reasons having nothing to do with this task, then this task evaporates." This is hard to formalize.

There seems to be no general way to define task failure, except as the only alternative to success and evaporation:

Axiom 16:

```
(exc (Occ ?s1  ?s2 (fail ?k))
     (Occ ?s1  ?s2 (succeed ?k))
     (Occ ?s1  ?s2 (evaporate ?k)))
```

(Recall that exc is a connective stating that at most one of its arguments is true.)
From Axioms 14 and 16 and Definition 16, we can prove
Theorem 5:

```
(if (Occ ?s1  ?s2 (fail ?k))
    (if (= ?a (task-action ?k))
        (forall (s3 s4)
            (if (Occ s3 s4 (do Robot ?a))
                (not (and (=< s4 ?s2)
                          (T s3 (task ?k ?a)))))
    )))
```

"If a task fails, its action has not been done (within the time the task is a task)." If
the action had been done, then by Definition 16, the task would have succeeded,
and would have come to an end, which (Definition 15 and Axioms 4 and 8) can only
happen once.

There ought to be more to say about task failure. For instance, a task fails if its
action becomes impossible (and its supertasks don't cease for some other reason).
But this can't be the definition of failure, since it is easy to think of other cases. We
must rely on detailed accounts of how individual actions can fail.

There are three ways tasks can end. How do tasks begin? This is a more interesting topic, which, alas, I will not address formally in this paper. Intuitively, a task
comes into existence when it is the next step in the best plan for carrying out an
existing task. One problem is that there might be two or more equally good plans;
this is minor, since we can assume that a random choice is made, one action
becoming a task in some chronicles, another in others. A much more serious
problem lies in formalizing what it means for a plan to be best. Suppose we
introduce a "utility measure" on the set of chronicles. The best plan might be the
one that leads to the highest utility. But it might be impossible to know which is best
in this sense at the time decisions have to be made, so we must switch to some
definition in terms of expected utility. This will require a probabilistic analysis.

My neglect of this issue means that I have omitted an important fourth way that a
task might come to an end. A subtask could end because it ceases to be the best way
to carry out a supertask. What this points up is that my analysis of the reasons for
actions is only half the story. The reason for an intentional action is not just the set
of its supertasks, but also the fact that this action is part of the best way to carry out
those supertasks. One can view this paper as a preliminary attempt at analysis that
neglects this dimension. I will return to this topic in the Conclusions.

One other thing to discuss is the consequences of task failure. Past problem solvers have been so single-minded that any failure could cause them to quit. An autonomous robot will in the course of things acquire many tasks, of which it must expect many to fail. Failure is not necessarily a catastrophe. It can happen that a task's failure requires replanning of its supertasks, but it is not necessary. For instance, the action (do-one-of $A1$ $A2$) succeeds if either $A1$ or $A2$ is done. The failure of $A1$ may not affect the success of the overall enterprise at all. In fact, there is no contradiction in having an action (hopetofail A), which has one subtask with action A, such that the supertask succeeds if and only if the subtask fails. An example of such a task structure would be the task of testing a rope, which a mountain climber might carry out with a subtask, "Cause the rope to break by putting all your weight on it." If this task fails, the test succeeds.

A problem solver will often have two tasks, such that both cannot be achieved. Resolving such *task conflicts* is a key issue in the design of planners. Unfortunately, an analysis of this issue will not be possible until we devise a way of talking about one plan being better than another.

2.3 Feasibility

We can make a small step toward solving these problems by attempting to analyze the concept of *action feasibility*, which is somewhat simpler than the mess of problems I described above.

One analysis is that an action is feasible if there is a chronicle in which it is performed. There are two problems with this idea:

1. It omits the concept of the chronicle being due to choice by the problem solver. I can win the lottery by this definition, but winning the lottery is not feasible in any useful sense.
2. It neglects the problem solver's current plan. It is feasible for me to rob a bank, but it would upset my other tasks, like "Stay out of jail."

To address these problems, I introduce the concept of "feasibility relative to a set of tasks." (feasible a kk) is true in a state if trying a would succeed without causing any of the tasks in the set kk to fail. This might seem like a step into obscurity, since "trying" appears to involve notions of subjective "effort." But we already have this problem in trying to formalize what a "task" is. Formalization can never narrow down the meanings of two concepts like this completely, but it helps us to explore all the interrelationships between them. The key interrelationship is that to have a task with a given action is to be trying to do that action.

Now let us define the function (reltry a kk), which denotes the action of trying a without causing any task in the set kk to fail. We call the set kk the *boundary task set* of the action, and each element a *boundary task*. Intuitively, the boundary tasks have "higher priority" than other tasks while the attempt to do a is made. However, I will not formalize this idea, except to require that a failure of a boundary task counts as a failure of the "reltry."

To do this action is to have a task with action *a*:
Axiom 17:

```
(if (Occ ?s1 ?s2
        (do Robot (reltry ?a ?kk)))
    (and (begin ?s1 ?s2
                (task (reltrytask ?s1 ?a ?kk) ?a))
         (EOcc ?s2
               (task-end
                  (reltrytask ?s1 ?a ?kk)))))
```

As I said, the idea is to explicate trying by relating it to the task concept. reltrytask is a Skolem function, which denotes the task with action *A* that exists by virtue of the robot's attempt to do *A*. A particular reltry is defined by an action, a set of boundary tasks, and the occasion on which it occurs. So the Skolem function must have three arguments; the result is to give the name (reltrytask *s a kk*) to the task with action *a* corresponding to the execution of (reltry *a kk*) that begins in *s*. Its lifetime coincides with the execution of that action. It is important to note that the reltry action may or may not itself be the action of some task.

For instance, suppose that I want to reason about the feasibility of robbing a bank, with boundary task *J* = "Stay out of jail". I posit that I execute (reltry (rob-bank) {*J*}). This assumption entails my having a task with action (rob-bank). The name of this task is (reltrytask *current-state* (rob-bank) {*J*}). If this task would succeed, then robbing a bank is feasible.

Although I use "reltrytask" as a common noun in this paper, such tasks are not distinguished from other tasks in any way, except possibly origin. Indeed, the whole concept would not be worth much if reltrytasks did not share the properties of tasks in general. Their only peculiarity is that they come into being when the problem solver tries to do something, and nothing stops the problem solver from *trying* to do anything, anytime. (More on this below.) But I have already admitted that the origin of tasks in general is obscure.

It is easy to confuse this concept with some others. The distinguishing feature of reltrytasks is that they are "artificial"—they are used to test feasibility, and hence must be allowed to come into existence at any time. There are superficially similar actions without this property. For example, consider the action (avoid-while *a b*), which is done whenever one does *a* without doing *b*. (Example: (avoid-while (eat-dinner-out) (spend-more-than-$20)).) This action can arise as part of a plan, like any other. It will have two syntactic subtasks:

> K1, with action *a*
> and K2, with action (avoid-during *b* K1)

Contrast this avoid-while construct with (reltry *a* {*k*}):

- With a reltry, the boundary tasks must already be in existence. "Stay out of jail" is one (of thousands) of one's normal background tasks.

- The reltry does not arise as a part of a plan to do something. To reason about feasibility, we must be able to posit a task attempted for no reason at all.
- The relationship between a reltry and its reltrytask is unusual. Intuitively, the action (reltry a ...) causes the task (reltrytask ... a ...) to exist.

The reltry action is, in a way, neither intentional nor unintentional. It is not done by accident, or unconsciously, but, on the other hand, it is not done for a reason either. Once initiated, it corresponds to a task for carrying out the action it is a reltry of. This formal concept is an attempt to capture the intuition that, although one never does anything without a reason, one *could*.

This is why the axiom we wanted in the last section, that every task is a subtask* of a top-level task, is too strong. Reltrytasks do not count as top-level tasks, but they are not subtasks of anything, either. Furthermore, we must permit such reltrytasks to exist; that is, for any given action and state of the world, the theory must have models in which that action is actually attempted in that state, leading to chronicles in which the attempt succeeds, or fails, or evaporates. See Figure 5.

If such models were ruled out, as they would be by an axiom that said that all tasks were for a reason, then a conditional of the form "If a is attempted, then ..." would be trivially true because its antecedent would be false.

It will be convenient to stipulate that the subtasks of reltrytasks themselves count as reltrytasks:

Axiom 18:

```
(if (and (= ?k0 (reltrytask ?s0 ?a ?kk))
         (T ?s1 (subtask ?k1 ?k0 ?x))
         (begin ?s0 ?s1 (task ?k1 ?a)))
    (= ?k1 (reltrytask ?s0 ?a ?kk))   ))
```

Now we are finally in a position to state the axiom that the ultimate reason for every task is some set of top-level supertasks. The only exceptions, we can now state, are tasks whose ultimate reasons are reltrytasks; by Axiom 18, these will be reltrytasks themselves:

Axiom 19:

```
(if (T ?s (task ?k ?a))
    ; Every task
```

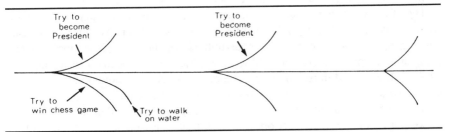

Figure 5. A Reltrytask Any Time You Want It

```
(or (exists (ks)
   ; is a subtask* of a top-level task
     (and (subtask* ?k ks)
          (toplevel-task ks))  )
   ; or is a reltrytask
     (exists (s kk)
       (= ?k (reltrytask s ?a kk))     )))
```

Put another way, every task is for an ultimate reason, or is an expression of irrational whim.

The concept of evaporation must be altered to apply it to a reltrytask. A reltrytask ceases to be appropriate when one of the boundary tasks succeeds or evaporates (whereas an ordinary task ceases to be appropriate when all its supertasks go away). Formally:

Axiom 20:

```
(if (exists (k)
       (and (elt k ?kk)
            (Occ ?s1 ?s2 (task-end k))
            (exists (s3)
              (TTopen s3 ?s2
                (is-task (reltrytask ?s0 ?a ?kk)))
            )))
    (Occ ?s1 ?s2
       (evaporate (reltrytask ?s0 ?a ?kk))))
```

A reltry and its associated tasks play a role like that of a "test particle" in physics: a hypothetical entity introduced into a situation that reacts to it without disturbing it. To determine if an action is feasible, we posit that it is tried, and see if we can deduce that it is successful.

We have to be quite careful about the way this is done, in order to avoid fallacies like this one: Suppose that $A1$ and $A2$ are both feasible, because if either is tried, it succeeds. Then suppose both are tried simultaneously. This event qualifies as a try of each separately, so we can conclude that both will happen, and hence that it is feasible that both can be done simultaneously. Since $A1$ might be "Leave the room," and $A2$ might be "stay in the room," you see the problem.

Therefore, we want to make the criterion be that an "isolated reltry" of an action would succeed. An *isolated* reltry is one that occurs without any other crazy tasks popping up, including especially other reltries. In the example of the previous paragraph, the proofs that $A1$ and $A2$ were feasible would depend on what happened when each was tried in isolation from the other. As desired, nothing could then be concluded about a situation in which both were tried at once.

We can't isolate a reltry too much, however, or the result will be useless; as soon as we put a complex task network around a task, the isolation condition will no longer hold, and feasibility will not allow us to conclude anything.

This is a deep problem, which I do not pretend to solve completely here. It is closely related to the whole problem of counterfactual conditionals (Lewis, 1973). A counterfactual is of the form, "If so-and-so were true, then . . . ," where so-and-so is not true. The problem is that the most plausible situations in which P is true may not be a superset of the most plausible situations in which (and P Q) is true. Analogously, the problem with defining feasibility is that the plausible situations in which A is tried may include too much or too little.

My partial solution is to allow only the following two categories of "extra" reltrytasks to pop up while a reltrytask is being attempted:

1. subtasks and
2. syntactic supertasks

of the "test particle" task.

The rationale for the first category is that a task that occurs as part of the plan for carrying out the test task cannot interfere with it (or, if it does, we want that to block the feasibility proof). In a proof that it is feasible to win the election of 1984, we will posit a reltrytask to win it. We forbid weird new reltrytasks like "Run naked down Pennsylvania Avenue," but we allow subtasks like "File for candidate status by January, 1983."

The rationale for the second category is that supertasks constructed "syntactically" out of this task and other subtasks have no independent meaning except for the correct execution of the subtasks, so their presence should not cause any problems. In a proof that it is feasible to win the election of 1984, we are allowed to introduce supertasks like (prog <(win 1984), (win 1988)>) without adverse effects.

We summarize all this with the following definition of *isolated reltry:*
Definition 18:

```
(iff (Occ ?s1 ?s2 (isolated-reltry ?a ?kk))
   ; An isolated-reltry event occurs
   (and (Occ ?s ?s2
            (do Robot (reltry ?a ?kk)))
        ; whenever a reltry occurs such that
        (forall (s3 s4 a' kk')
          (if (and (=< ?s1 s3 ?s2)
                   (overlap [?s1, ?s2] [s3, s4])
                (Occ s3 s4
                   (do Robot
                      (reltry a' kk'))))
             ; any other overlapping reltry
             (or (TT s3 s4
                    (subtask*
                       (reltrytask s3 a' kk')
                       (reltrytask ?s1 ?a ?kk)))
```

```
; is either a subtask or
; a syntactic supertask
(TT s3 s4
    (synsubtask*
        (reltrytask ?s1 ?a ?kk)
        (reltrytask s3 a' kk')))))        )))
```

We use this in the definition of *feasibility:* ?a is feasible if an isolated reltry of ?a would result in neither the failure of ?a or of any boundary task:

Definition 19:

```
(iff (T ?s (feasible ?a ?kk))
    (forall (s2)
        (if (Occ ?s s2
                (isolated-reltry ?a ?kk))
            (and (not
                    (EOcc ?s2
                        (fail
                            (reltrytask
                                ?s ?a ?kk))))
                (forall (k)
                    (if (elt k ?kk)
                        (not (EOcc ?s2
                                (fail k))))
            )))   ))
```

We do not count against feasibility those cases where a boundary task succeeds or evaporates.

One might suppose that *all* stray tasks should be forbidden during a reltry, not just other reltrytasks. Couldn't the task ''Run nude down Pennsylvania Avenue'' occur naturally? Yes, it could, which is precisely why we can't rule it out of court. Consider proving that ''Don't drink any water for 30 days'' is feasible with respect to {''Stay alive''}. In the course of things, the task ''Drink some water'' will come into being as an essential subtask of ''Stay alive.'' The proof of feasibility will therefore fail, as it should, because the reltrytask will clash with a new subtask of a boundary task. What this example shows is that proofs of feasibility must reckon with the ecology of ordinary tasks. What we can exclude are new, arbitrary reltrytasks being injected into the situation. This will be a real issue in the chess example examined below, where we will have to prove that clashing tasks do not arise.

At first glance, it seems like my definition of feasibility requires one to prove an awfully strong statement. Surely ordinary mortals are never in a position to prove their plans feasible this way. Of course, they aren't. As I have emphasized before, the fact that one proves theorems in papers like this does not imply that people prove theorems of the same kind. In most cases, many actions are feasible without our even guessing it, let alone proving it. Where proof is possible, however, the representation ought to support it.

A related point is that often people carry out actions knowing full well that they are not feasible in this sense, because they might fail. People select plans because of low expected cost/benefit ratios, or because they can't think of anything better to do, not because the plans are provably feasible.

To demonstrate how feasibility works, consider the action (prog $<a_1 \ldots a_N>$), which I have mentioned before. Intuitively, such an action consists of doing the given actions in order, and is feasible if each one leaves the universe in a state where the next is feasible. To prove this, we will need two basic axioms.

First, we give the basic definition of prog. It will simplify matters if we analyze instead the concept (prog2 $a1$ $a2$), an action done when $a1$ is done followed by $a2$, since the more general prog can be analyzed in terms of prog2 straightforwardly. I hope it will not be confusing if I state the theorems in terms of (prog $<a1$ $a2>$):

Definition 20:

```
(iff (Occ ?s0 ?s1 (do ?x (prog <?a1 ?a2>)))
    (exists (s2 s3)
        (and (=< ?s0 s2 s3 ?s1)
            (Occ ?s0 s2 (do ?x ?a1))
            (Occ s3 ?s1 (do ?x ?a2)))  ))
```

The definition states that the prog is done over any interval in which the first action is followed, not necessarily immediately, by the second.

What we want to prove is this theorem:

Theorem 6: If *A1* is feasible in *S0* wrt *KK,* and *A2* is feasible wrt *KK* after every execution of *A1* in *S0,* then (prog $<A1$ $A2>$) is feasible wrt *KK* in *S0.* Formally:

```
(if (and (T ?s0 (feasible ?a1 ?kk))
        (forall (s1)
            (if (Occ ?s0 s1 (do Robot ?a1))
                (T s1 (feasible ?a2 ?kk)))  ))
    (T ?s0 (feasible (prog <?a1 ?a2>) ?kk)))
```

If this theorem seems obvious, it's because you have in mind the simple definition of feasibility that we rejected, that *A* is feasible if doing it might happen. That definition neglected the intentions of the problem solver. The definition we wound up with remedies this defect by talking in terms of tasks as well as actual outcomes. Clearly, we are going to have to describe the "intention structure" of a prog as well as its "action structure." To appreciate this point, consider the action (accidentally *A*), which is executed whenever the robot does *A* without having any task with action *A*. The "action structures" of (prog $<A1$ $A2>$) and (accidentally (prog $<A1$ $A2>$)) are identical, yet it is clear that the latter is never feasible. (That is, it's intuitively clear, although to prove it would require some axioms.)

In order to present the "intention structure" of a prog, we need a couple of definitions. First, I define (subtasks *task set*), which asserts that a given set contains all and only the subtasks of a given task:

Definition 21:

```
(iff (T ?s (subtasks ?k ?kk))
   (forall (ks)
      (iff (exists (s)
              (T ?s (subtask ks ?k x)))
           (elt ks ?kk))  ))
```

Second, I define the concept of being the *sole subtask* of a given supertask at a moment. To be a "sole subtask" is to bear the full weight of the supertask; the only way the supertask can fail is for the sole subtask to fail:

Definition 22:

```
(iff (T ?s (solesubtask ?k0 ?k1 ?a1 ?x))
   (and (T ?s (task ?k1 ?a1))
        (T ?s (subtask ?k1 ?k0 ?x))
        (T ?s (subtasks ?k0 {?k1}))
        ; If the supertask ?k0 fails,
        ; the subtask ?k1 does, too
        (forall (s1 s2)
           (if (and (=< s1 ?s s2)
                    (Occ s1 s2
                         (fail ?k0)))
               (Occ s1 s2 (fail ?k1)))
   )))
```

This is mainly a convenient abbreviation, which will be of use here and in section 3. There is nothing particularly momentous about the group of concepts that are abbreviated. The last clause of the definition is not vacuous, however, A task with the peculiar action (hopetofail A) presumably would have a single subtask with action A, such that failure of the supertask is accompanied by *success* of the subtask.

Now we can describe the subtask structure of a prog task, which is what you would expect: a task to do a prog is accomplished by a subtask to do its first step, then a subtask to do its second step:

Axiom 21:

```
(if (begin ?s1 ?s2
           (task ?k0 (prog <?a1 ?a2>)))
    ; If ?k0 is a prog
    ; task in state ?s2
    (or (exists (k1)
```

```
(begin ?s1 ?s2
        (solesubtask ?k0 ?k1
                          ?a1 <1>))
)
```
; *then either* ?a1 *is*
; *still in progress*
```
(exists (k1 K2 s3)
    ; or ?a1 is done and
    ; ?a2 is in progress
    (and (not (= k1 k2))
         (< ?s1 s3 ?s2)
         (begin ?s1 s3
                (solesubtask ?k0 k1
                                 ?a1 <1>))
         (begin s3 ?s2
                (solesubtask ?k0 k2
                                 ?a2 <2>))))
))))
```

It is a consequence of this axiom and the definition of solesubtask that a prog fails only if one of its subtasks fails. We already know from Definition 20 that a prog is successful (i.e., actually executed; see Definition 16) iff its actions are done in order. It is not hard to see that this is equivalent to each subtask succeeding. Suppose that the first action is done. Then by Definition 16 and Axiom 14, the first subtask will end successfully. Then by Axiom 21, the next subtask will begin immediately. The execution of the second action will terminate the second subtask and the supertask simultaneously. We can conclude:

Theorem 7: A prog task fails only if one of its subtasks fails, and succeeds only if all of its subtasks succeed.

Now we can go back and prove the "obvious" theorem about prog feasibility. Let $[S0, S1]$ be an interval over which (prog $<A1\ A2>$) is reltried, such that any other thing reltried is either a subtask of the prog, or a syntactic supertask. (See Figure 6.) That is, the reltry is isolated.

There will be a reltrytask for the prog, and hence (Axiom 21) there will be a task for $A1$ starting at $S0$, and (Axiom 18) this will be a reltrytask. $A1$ is feasible in $S0$, so the task will succeed. This may seem obvious, but think about it for a second. To use the feasibility of $A1$, there must be no other reltrytasks except subtasks and syntactic supertasks of $A1$. But we assumed (see the figure) that all reltrytasks were subtasks or syntactic supertasks of the prog reltrytask. Any syntactic supertasks of the prog task are automatically syntactic supertasks of the $A1$ task, and any subtasks of the prog task are subtasks of the $A1$ task, since it is (Axiom 21) the *only* immediate subtask of the prog task. Therefore, we can conclude that the $A1$ task will not fail, and neither will any of the boundary tasks. By Axiom 22, the prog task will not fail either.

There are several possible fates of $A1$ and the boundary tasks. If any boundary

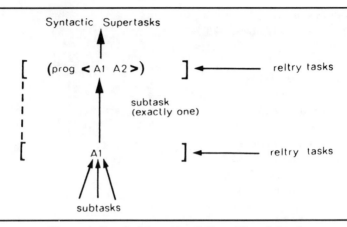

Figure 6. Proof of Prog Feasibility—First Subtask

task ends without failing, then the prog task will evaporate, and we can conclude that the prog is feasible. If the *A1* task evaporates, then (Axiom 15), the prog task must evaporate, and hence the prog is feasible.

The only remaining possibility is that the *A1* task succeeds, leaving the universe in a state *S2* between *S0* and *S1*. Now *A2* becomes a task, which is feasible. A similar analysis to that for *A1* leads to the conclusion that either a boundary task will end, or everything will evaporate, or *A2* (and hence the prog) will succeed. In any case, the prog will not fail and the boundary tasks will not fail, so the prog is feasible. QED

As another example, consider the action of waiting for something to happen. (do *agent* (wait *event*)) occurs over any interval that ends in an occurrence of the event:

Definition 23:

```
(iff (Occ ?s1 ?s2 (do ?x (wait ?e)))
    ; ?e has been awaited successfully
    (exists (s3)
        (and (=< ?s1 s3 ?s2)
            (Occ s3 ?s2 ?e)
            ; as soon as it happens for the first time
            (not (exists (s4 s5)
                    (and (=< ?s1 s4 s5)
                        (< s5 ?s2)
                        (Occ s4 s5 ?e)) )))  ))
```

(The name wait is perhaps inappropriate for this action, which has little in common with what is meant by the English word. But it will do, so long as you keep its peculiar properties in mind, such as the fact that all agents wait for all events that actually occur.)

As with prog, we must state under what circumstances a waiting task will fail. The following axiom states that a task to wait for an event fails when it becomes true that the event will never happen:

Axiom 22:

```
(if (and (= (task-act ?k) (wait ?e))
         (EOcc ?s (fail ?k)))
    (forall (s1 s2)
       (if (=< ?s s1 s2)
           (not (Occ s1 s2 ?e)))   ))
```

This may seem a little strong, since it allows you to wait forever without the waiting having failed.

These axioms allow us to prove the following theorem, which will be useful later:

Theorem 8: In an arbitrary state *S0*, if *E* is a discrete event that is certain to happen, and *KK* is a set of tasks such that the failure of any task in *KK* must be preceded by an occurrence of *E*, then waiting for *E* is feasible in *S0* with respect to *KK*.

The proof is fairly obvious.

The axioms I have outlined encourage the following style of reasoning about feasibility: we posit an attempt (a *reltry*) of an action, and we rule out failure of the *reltrytask*. For this to work, we will have to have exhaustive lists of the ways things can fail.

Of course, one ought to be able to show that something is feasible by showing that (under prevailing circumstances) another action will suffice to perform it, and show that this action is feasible. This is not a theorem of the current system, so we make it an axiom:

Axiom 23:

```
(if (and (T ?s (feasible ?a1 ?kk))
         (forall (s2)
            (if (Occ ?s s2 (do Robot ?a1))
                (Occ ?s s2 (do Robot ?a2)))   ))
    (T ?s (feasible ?a2 ?kk)))
```

Let us use the name *local entailment* to describe the relation between ?a1 and ?a2 described in the antecedent of this conditional. ?a1 locally entails ?a2 in state ?s, in that executing ?a1 implies that you executed ?a2.

Finally, there are many axioms about feasible actions. For instance, the action "Raise your right hand" is just known to be feasible (subject to caveats, such as that the agent not be handicapped, that the boundary tasks not be very strange, and so forth). From this you can conclude that if you tried to raise your hand, you would raise your hand. No plan (decomposition into subtasks) is required. Philosophers

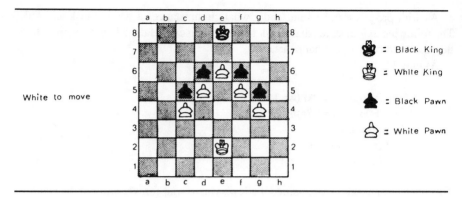

Figure 7. A Chess Problem

use the term ''basic action'' for a feasible action that can be done without any plan (see Goldman, 1970).

3 An Example

To show the utility of these ideas, I will discuss a problem posed by John McCarthy (personal communication, from a well-known type of chess problem). Consider the chess situation of Figure 7. I will call this state of affairs S0, although you must remember that this constant refers to an arbitrary snapshot of a board position that actually lasts until White makes a move; an uncountable set of other states go by during this time, during which the chess position doesn't change (although other things in the world will).

White can win, by the following argument: WK can get to a5, because if BK leaves the rectangle with corners c8 and g7 (an area I will call the ''cage''), then the pawn at e6 will queen. But then WK can get to b6, because if BK is anywhere but c7, white can move to b6 in one step, and if BK is at c7, white can move to a6, then b6. By similar arguments, WK can get to c6, and then to either d6 or d7; and then the pawn at e6 can queen.

This argument is informal, but reasonably convincing. (It omits many details; for instance, can White avoid stalemate?) There must be another argument that considers every possible move sequence, and shows that White can choose a winning one. (That is, this argument would mirror a minimax algorithm applied to this situation.) Such an argument would be tedious, but the most obvious axiomatization of chess, in which the only actions are piece moves that get you from one position to the next, seemingly gives you no choice. McCarthy's problem is to find an axiomatization that permits the simple argument. (To keep it simple, I will feel free to use what McCarthy calls ''chess lemmas,'' obvious theorems of chess, which might have complex formal proofs.)

I will discuss an approach to part of McCarthy's problem within the framework I have outlined. The part I will be concerned with is step one, showing that the white king can get to a5. (The remaining steps are more straightforward.) The interesting thing about this step is that the reasoning is "continuous": it talks about the white king moving toward a5 while the black king moves around in the "cage," completely neglecting the fact that these moves occur as interleaved jumps.

I choose chess as an example domain mainly because its formality allows us to prove things. As I mentioned in section 1, this may mislead you into thinking that proofs of this kind play an important role in thinking; that we routinely prove that our plans will work. Of course, we don't. But a good test of the power of formal concepts is their ability to support proofs when, intuitively, proofs ought to be possible.

Another reason to look at chess is that games require planning, more than most current game-laying programs do. Perhaps this paper will stimulate improvements. One program, Wilkins's (1980) PARADISE already creates plans. Some of the plans I look at below are essentially the same as those generated by Wilkins's seminal program.

White's plan seems to be this, which I will call P1[5]:

```
(interrupt (move WK a5)
          (outside BK cage)
          (move WP/e6 e8))
```

where the action (interrupt *a1 p a2*) is defined as an action that is executed in one of two ways: One is for *a1* to be executed without *p* ever becoming true. The other is a little more complex. This is for *p* to become true before *a1* is complete, and for *a2* to be executed as a result, with the attempt to execute *a1* being dropped. Formally:

Definition 24:

```
(iff (Occ ?s1 ?s2 (do ?x (interrupt ?a1 ?p ?a2)))
    ; There are two ways it can be executed:
    (or ; By having the action ?a1 be executed
       (and (Occ ?s1 ?s2 (do ?x ?a1))
            (not (exists (s) (and (< ?s1 s ?s2)
                                  (T s ?p))  )))
       ; Or by having the interrupt condition become
       ; true, and then have ?a2 get executed
       (exists (s3 s4)
          (and (< ?s1 s3 ?s2)
               (Eocc s3 (become ?p))
```

---

[5] The notation WP/e6 is informal, and has the awkward feature that it tends to give the same object different names at different times. While it would be possible to make it work by using "fluents" (McCarthy, 1958; McDermott, 1982), it would be simpler just to give the pawns standard names. For clarity to humans, however, I will stick with the informal notation.

```
; Note: it must become true before
; ?a1 is completed
(not (exists (s5)
          (and (=< ?s1 s5 s3)
               (Occ ?s1 s5
                    (do ?x ?a1)))   ))
(=< s3 s4 ?s2)
(Occ s4 ?s2 (do ?x ?a2)))   ))))
```

As with other actions, we must give the "intention structure" of an interrupt as well as the "action structure." Any interrupt task has at most two subtasks, "main" and "oops":

Axiom 24:

```
(if (begin ?s1 ?s2 (task ?k (interrupt ?a1 ?p ?a2)))
    (or (and (TTopen ?s1 ?s2 (- ?p))
             (exists (ks)
                 (begin ?s1 ?s2
                     (solesubtask ?k ks (until ?p ?a1)
                                        <main>))  ))
        (exists (s3 ks1 ks2)
            (and (< ?s1 s3 ?s2)
                 (T s3 ?p)
                 (begin ?s1 s3
                     (solesubtask ?k ks1 (until ?p ?a1)
                                        <main>))
                 (begin s3 ?s2
                     (solesubtask ?k ks2 ?a2 <oops>)))
    )))
```

This should be compared with the corresponding axiom for prog, Axiom 21. One important similarity is the inference that an interrupt or prog can fail only if one of its syntactic subtasks fails.

In this axiom, I have had to introduce an intermediate task to perform the action (until ?p ?a1). The reason is that the subtask ks, with action ?a1, must evaporate if ?p becomes true, and therefore its supertask must end. Since the interrupt task itself can't end, we insert the until task, which succeeds if ?p becomes true.

until is defined the way prog and interrupt were, by giving its success conditions and task structure.

The success condition for (until *P A*) is for *A* to be executed without *P* becoming true (before the last instant); or for *P* to become true without *A* being executed. Formally:

Definition 25:

```
(iff (Occ ?s1 ?s2 (do ?x (until ?p ?a)))
    (or ; Either ?a is executed before ?p becomes true
```

```
(and (Occ ?s1 ?s2 (do ?x ?a))
     (not (exists (s) (and (< ?s1 s ?s2)
                           (T s ?p))   ))))
; or vice versa
(and (EOcc ?s2 (become ?p))
     (not (exists (s3)
              (and (=< ?s1 s3 ?s2)
                   (Occ ?s1 s3 (do ?x ?a1)))   ))))))
```

The until task has its own subtask structure (see Figure 8):
Axiom 25:

```
(if (and (begin ?s1 ?s2 (task ?k (until ?p ?a)))
         (TTopen ?s1 ?s2 (− ?p)))
    (exists (ks)
       (begin ?s1 ?s2 (solesubtask ?k ks ?a <tryit>))  ))
```

In English, any task with action (until *P A*) has one subtask with action *A*. The supertask fails only if *A* fails before *P* becomes true.

Now let's attempt to show that the plan P1 will work. To do this, we must show that the plan is feasible, and, if it is executed, then either

1. If BK stays in the cage, then WK will reach a5
2. If BK leaves the cage, the pawn will queen

Step one, therefore, is to prove feasibility, but with respect to what set of boundary tasks? How do we rule out White's picking up the plastic piece representing the king, and just moving it to a5? Clearly, White can't do this while continuing to play chess, so "play chess" is one of the boundary tasks. What kind of action is "playing chess"?

Among other problems, this question raises the problem of multiple agents, which I have avoided (cf., for instance, Konolige, 1980). Seemingly, you can't play chess without an opponent. I will resort to a trick here, and treat the opponent, Black, as a random process that makes a move after each move of White's, without having any tasks or plans. This won't work in general, but it works when you're trying to prove White can force a win.[6]

---

[6] It is rather tricky to formalize the whole truth. Playing chess is at first blush a matter of moving plastic pieces subject to certain constraints. Actually, the pieces are only a mnemonic aid. What is really happening is a complicated sequence of ritual speech acts in which speakers agree on a sequence of board positions by communicating what they should be. Usually, speech is not the literal medium of communication, but this is a detail. Note that a "chess game" is a slippery sort of individual. It refers to a particular ritual activity, begun usually with the standard initial chess position. But chess games, unlike baptisms and marriages, are not individuated by their participants and times of occurrence. Two players can play two games at once. In fact, by agreeing that, say, the first five moves of each game will be the same, they can have the two games begin at precisely the same instant. Furthermore, chess games, like

I will go on using "Robot" to refer to the computer, and use "Opponent" to refer to the opposing process that generates the alternate chess moves. Predicates like "task" and "feasible" will implicitly refer to Robot.

There are only two relevant tasks as a backdrop to P1: a task with action (play-chess) and a task with action (win-chess). That is, we will take the robot's goals to be playing chess and winning. We could probably do without the latter, but let's leave it in, since one might play chess without intending to win.

We will treat both of these tasks as solitary activities, in that the opponent always responds as if it were an inanimate natural phenomenon. Playing chess cannot fail; it succeeds when you do (win-chess) or (lose-chess). (win-chess) fails if you do (lose-chess).

Axiom 26:

```
(if (T ?s (task ?k (play-chess)))
    (forall (h)
       (if (elt ?s h)
          (exists (s2)
             (and (elt s2 h) (=< ?s s2)
                  (EOcc s2 (task-end ?k))
                  (or (EOcc s2
                            (do Robot (win-chess)))
                      (EOcc s2
                            (do Robot (lose-chess)))
          )) )) ))
```

Once you are engaged in (play-chess), you may pursue a variety of plans, but the only primitive sub-sub-tasks are of two sorts: make a legal chess move, and wait for your opponent to make one. The following axiom states that every move either culminates a (win-chess); or is followed within a bounded amount of time by a single opponent move, which gives the Robot the task of moving again:

Axiom 27:

```
(if (Occ ?s1 ?s2 (do Robot (chess-move)))
    ; If the robot makes a move
    (or ; Then either it wins
        (and (EOcc ?s2 (do Robot (win-chess)))
             (EOcc ?s2 (do Opponent (lose-chess))))
        ; or, in all chronicles,
```

---

liquids, can split apart with remarkable ease. Having lost, a player can ask to go back a few moves and see how much better he might have done. In sum, a chess game is an individual that exists purely because two people agree that it exists. This may seem like metaphysical mumbo-jumbo, but a robust formalization of all of a person's activities over a given day would have to contain a solution of all these problems, in order to support reasoning about winning one game while losing another.

```
(exists (r km)
    (inevitably ?s2 (s3 s4)
        (and (< ?s2 s3 s4)
            ; The opponent eventually
            ; makes a move
            (Occ s3 s4
                (do Opponent
                    (chess-move)))
            ; (within some bound r)
            (< (d s3)
                (+ (d ?s2) r))
            (or ; and either he wins
                (and (Eocc s4
                        (do Opponent
                            (win-chess)))
                    (EOcc s4
                        (do Robot
                            (lose-chess))))
                ; or the robot must move again
                (Occ s3 s4
                    (become
                        (task km
                            (chess-move))))))
))))
```

Here and later I use the term (chess-move) to denote the action of making a move. There are three sorts of chess-move: moving a single piece to a square, queening, and castling. I will neglect castling here, and introduce notations only for the first two. I will use the function (piece-move *piece square*) to refer to the action of making a single legal move of a piece to a square. Converting a piece upon a move to the last rank is denoted by (piece-move= *piece square new-type*), as in (piece-move= p3 e8 queen).

The action (move *piece square*) refers to the action of moving a piece to a square, regardless of how many moves it takes. This action may be done at the same time as several other chess actions (such as "develop bishops," or "attack center"), and competes with them for moves.

At this point, a thorough analysis would define the various sorts of chess move in detail. There would be axioms of the sort, "If x is a bishop, then moving to so-and-so square is legal if there's nothing in the way (and no check is discovered or in effect already), and the result is to leave x in the new square (and to capture enemy piece y if it used to be there)." I am not going to bother with this, except to make a couple of observations:

- For most purposes, we can treat "legal" as "feasible," and provide axioms that just assert that chess moves are feasible, without breaking a move down into finer actions. Of course, for a person a chess move requires various arm movements; the same movements are involved in illegal as well as legal moves, but an illegal move doesn't count as a move at all.

- One thing to make clear in such axioms is that I can't move my opponent's pieces! One way to do this is to forbid (make unfeasible?) moves of pieces of two different colors during a single game.
- In McDermott (1982) I introduced the concept of "persistence" for describing the effects of actions. For much common-sense reasoning, it is important to infer that the effects last for a while, in the absence of knowledge about forces that would dislodge them. Persistence would be less appropriate for a domain like chess, where we know exactly what sorts of actions will cause effects to cease, and we know when they can occur.

One axiom we will need is that chess moves are discrete events:
Axiom 28:

(discrete (do ?x (chess-move)))

Recall that this entails that in every finite interval there is an earliest chess move.

After all this, we can return to the question of feasibility of plan P1. First, we need a notion of "fact-dependent feasibility." An action is feasible wrt *KK* dependent on a fact *P* if an isolated reltry of that action would avoid failure, providing *P* stays true.
Definition 26:

```
(iff (T ?s (feasible-dep ?a ?kk ?p))
    (and (T ?s ?p)
          (forall (s2)
            (if (and (Occ ?s s2
                          (isolated-reltry ?a ?kk))
                     (or (EOcc s2
                            (fail (reltrytask
                                     ?s ?a ?kk)))
                         (exists (k)
                            (and (elt k ?kk)
                                 (EOcc s2 (fail k)))
                    )))
              (exists (s3)
                 (and (< ?s s3 s2)
                      (not (T s3 ?p)))
    )) )))
```

Lemma 9: In a state *S0*, if A1 is feasible dependent on (- *P*) with respect to *KK*, and if A2 is feasible in the first state in which *P* becomes true after *S0*, then (interrupt A1 *P* A2) is feasible with respect to *KK* in *S0*.

Proof: The proof follows the basic structure of the proof of prog feasibility given earlier.

We use this lemma in the obvious way: First we show that (move WK a5) will succeed unless the black king leaves the cage. Then we show that if he leaves the cage, (move WP/e6 e8) will be feasible.

Carrying out this proof plan is harder than it seems. The original informal argument had some gaps, that, unfortunately, we must try to fill. For instance, why do we assume that the blockaded pawns stay put? If they do not, the geometry of the whole situation changes. And they could move, if White and Black conspired to move them. How do we prove they won't?

We start with two lemmas:

Lemma 10: If WP/e6 doesn't queen, and BK stays in the cage, and WK doesn't move through a4, then the other pawns stay put.

Proof: I will only sketch the proof, since this is basically a "chess lemma." For a pawn to move, there must be nothing in front of it. Therefore, the first thing that can happen is that a pawn is captured. There are three pieces that could take a pawn. For each of them, we assume that the pawns remain uncaptured, and unmoved, and show that the piece cannot take a pawn without one of the conditions becoming satisfied. A subproof needed is to show that the white king can capture a black pawn only by going around the left file, through a4. QED

One step of this proof requires more comment. For a pawn to move, a pawn must be captured. But suppose that this pawn capture is the result of a pawn move, which is the result of a pawn capture, and so on into the past *ad infinitum*. Then there would be no *first* pawn move, and hence the step would fail. There are several reasons this cannot happen, but one obvious one is that chess moves are discrete (Axiom 28), and hence there is always a first pawn move.

Our next proof goal is to show that if the black king does not leave the cage, then it is feasible for the white king to get to a5. There is a problem with proving this, that we anticipated in section 2.3, and postponed. What if, during the move of the white king, White perversely pushes the pawn, allowing it to be taken? Intuitively, this won't happen, but a nice *proof* that it won't is hard to find.

There are two possible approaches: One is to add "Avoid moving the pawn" as an explicit component of the plan. It probably would not be hard to show that the resulting plan is feasible, and the desired constraint would follow automatically.

This seems like a dangerous precedent. If we have to state explicitly everything the problem solver is *not* going to do, we may end up stating a lot of things. Also, it seems unnecessary. If moving the pawn is a bad idea, then of course the problem solver won't do it.

I will pursue this other approach. An action is a "bad idea" if there is no reason to do it, that is, no supertask for which it would be a subtask. In the case of chess moves, we can assert that the only possible reason for a (chess-move) is a (play-chess) supertask (or, as in Axiom 19, a whim):

Axiom 29: Every action of the form (chess-move) is taken only if there is a task with this action, that is either a reltrytask, or a subtask* (play-chess).[7] Formally:

```
(if (Occ ?s1 ?s2 (do Robot (chess-move)))
    (exists (k a)
        (and (TT ?s1 ?s2 (task k a))
             (one-way (do Robot a)
                      (do Robot (chess-move)))
             (or (exists (s kk)
                     (= k (reltrytask s a kk))   )
                 (exists (k0)
                     (TT ?s1 ?s2
                         (& (task k0 (play-chess))
                            (subtask* k k0)))
            )))   ))
```

This axiom is only the first step in proving lemmas we really need, like this:

Lemma 11: If, starting in state *S1* and lasting at least through state *S2*, the only tasks have actions in this list:

```
(play-chess)
(win-chess)
(interrupt (move X loc) p A)
(until p (move X loc))
(move X loc)
```

or are subtasks* of (move *X loc*); and (TT *S1 S2* (- *p*)), (that is, *p* does not become true in the interval [*S1, S2*], and there is a clear *X*-path for the motion in state *S1*, such that, for all *S2'*, (=< *S1 S2'*), the path cannot become blocked without *p* becoming true, then no other piece belonging to the problem solver will be moved during [*S1, S2*].

This is disconcertingly *ad hoc*. But a more general lemma would probably be false. If you relax the "clear path" requirement, then of course you will have to create a clear path, which could require a plan with arbitrary ramifications. If you relax the requirement that these tasks be the *only* ones the problem solver has, then those other tasks might demand some piece movement.

Ad hoc though it is, proving this lemma would be quite tricky, and I will not

---

[7] I will neglect the possibility of bumping a piece accidentally during a real tournament. This is the kind of unlikely occurrence worth neglecting in the formal study of chess. An analysis of Space Invaders, however, would have to deal with such possibilities explicitly, and probably have to bring probabilities in.

attempt it here; I will consider it one of the "chess lemmas." The proof would have
to carefully consider every reason for moving a piece, and show that none of these
reasons can be (move X loc), or be a subtask of (move X loc). This would take us
more deeply into chess and induction than I care to go.

Think about this lemma a bit. It may actually begin to seem false. Suppose that in
the course of moving X the opponent takes my queen, without making p true.
Wouldn't that throw my plans in a tizzy, and force me to re-evaluate?

In practice, of course, it would, which indicates that most chess players rarely
have plans as simple and pure as P1. Most of us instead have plans more like:

> (interrupt (*attack kingside [or queenside, or whatever]*)
>   (*opponent threatening something terrible*)
>   (*go on the defensive*))

(This is the way *I* play chess, which probably accounts for my not winning
much.) Each of the elements is relatively open-ended. That is, there is no tidy
theory of what it means for the opponent to threaten something terrible, a contrast to
P1, where the condition causing an interrupt is the opponent leaving a certain
region. Therefore, it is easy to make mistakes in executing this plan, and hard to
prove when it will work.

In fact, it is a key feature of a plan like P1 that it is to be persevered in even if the
opponent does take the robot's queen. Since we want to be able to have plans like
this, we must make it explicit when the plan is of this kind, and when it isn't.
Otherwise, queen sacrifices would be hard to represent. Therefore, in saying, in the
statement of the lemma, that those four tasks are all there are, I am committed to a
belief that during normal chess play there are quite a few other tasks, like: "Monitor
queen threats; if one is detected, take steps to neutralize it."

Now we can return to the proof that P1 is feasible. I will not bother to be terribly
formal in stating the remaining lemmas and proofs.

Lemma 12: In state S0, it is feasible for WK to get to a5 with respect to {(win-
chess)}, dependent on BK being inside the cage.

Proof: This follows from a straightforward chess lemma to the effect that if a
clear path exists for a piece in a state S (a path for a bishop, of course, being a quite
different thing from a path for a king), and if nothing can happen either to block the
path or end the game without making P false, then it is feasible for the piece to
move, dependent on P. Getting from this lemma to my application of it would
require a careful analysis to show that the game cannot end without the black king
leaving the cage. It would also require the use of Lemmas 10 and 11 to show that the
path cannot become blocked.

Here is roughly how the proof would go: Lemma 11 says that WP/e6 won't move
as long as the path remains clear, which is true if the black king stays in the cage and
the other pawns stay put. Lemma 10 says that the pawns stay put as long as WP/e6
doesn't move. We can combine these by appealing again to the discreteness of chess
moves. If there are any pawn moves of either variety, there must be an earliest such

move. But it would have to be preceded by another one: a move of WP/e6 would have to be preceded by a move of a blockaded pawn, and vice versa. Hence, there is no earliest pawn move, and therefore no pawn move at all. QED

Lemma 13: If BK leaves the cage before WK moves through a4, then it is feasible for the pawn at e6 to queen.

Proof: When BK leaves the cage, then WP/e6 has not budged, and the other pawns are in their initial positions, by an argument similar to that described in the proof of the previous lemma. It is then a straightforward chess theorem that the pawn can get to the last rank and still be a move away from the black king. We put this in our framework by proving that the following plan is feasible:

```
(prog <(piece-move WP/e6 e7)
       (wait (do Opponent (chess-move)))
       (piece-move= WP/e7 queen)
       (wait (do Opponent (chess-move)))>)
```

and that it results in the pawn reaching the back row safely. It will then follow from Axiom 23 that queening the pawn is feasible.

Given our analysis of the feasibility of prog and wait in section 2.3, it is clear that this plan is feasible. We need Axiom 27 to show that waiting is feasible. QED

We can now put these lemmas together to conclude the theorem:

Theorem 14: Plan P1 is feasible in state S0 with respect to {(win-chess)}.

The next step would be to show that executing the plan would actually result in either White having won or his king being at a5. This theorem is not interesting, and the proof would require all of the chess facts I have neglected, so I will stop here.

4 Conclusions

McCarthy's (1958) situation calculus served as the underpinning of much early work in problem solving. It summarized and cleaned up the structure of GPS, and supported more elegant systems like STRIPS and NOAH. Systems like NOAH have, however, structure that is not captured in the original situation calculus. NOAH reasons about task networks as well as states of the world. This is not just a detail; it means that the problem solver represents intentions before they have been realized as atomic actions. In more recent systems (McDermott, 1978; Wilkins, 1982; Stefik, 1980), these intentions have begun to be more complex than simple changes in the state of the world. They include things like:

- Make sure the place you move Block B is not already in use.
- Avoid moving a pawn.
- Minimize the amount of money used in step S.

These intentions, which I have called *tasks,* come in bundles. The basic operation on them is to bring them about. A task like "Queen this pawn" is brought about by queening the pawn. A task like "Avoid letting him queen his pawn" is brought about by queening yours in such a way as to prevent him queening his. We can use the term *execution* for this process of bringing a task about, transforming it from intention to accomplishment, from future to past.

In this paper, I have made a start on some important questions about tasks, such as

- What sorts of bundles do they come in?
- How can you tell when a task is feasible?
- What does it mean for one task to be part of the way of executing another task?
- How do you figure out a way to execute a bundle of tasks?

The picture that is emerging looks like this: At any instant, a problem solver has a set of tasks. Some are "top-level" tasks, of which all the others are *subtasks*. Some tasks have actions that are deomposable into subactions, as (prog $<A_1$ ... $A_N>$) is decomposable into the actions A_1, ..., A_n. These typically give rise to "syntactic" subtasks corresponding to the subactions. If the subactions are carried out in a certain way, the supertask will be successful. Against such a backdrop, an action will be considered *feasible* if a new "test task" (a *reltrytask*) injected into the situation would succeed.

The place where research is now needed is on the last question in my list, How do you figure out a way to execute a bundle of tasks? In the past, problem solvers have taken each task individually, and looked in a "plan library" of some kind for a way to carry it out. Then the separate plans are coordinated. This process is called *task reduction,* because the old task set has been "reduced" to a presumably simpler set of subtasks. At the beginning of the paper, I pointed out how fragile this paradigm is.

Two improvements are necessary:

1. The system must be able to deal with incomplete information about its own task network.
2. Tasks must be reduced in groups when necessary, not always individually.

I have not by any means achieved either of these improvements. But the logic I have developed provides a framework for research.

One question the logic settles is the "seductive successor link" problem. Although such links may be useful in an implementation, their logical function is subsumed by the notion of syntactic subtask. For instance, consider the task network shown in Figure 8.

The (prog ...) has four subtasks, labeled $<1>$, $<2>$, etc. It in turn is the $<$oops$>$ subtask of the interrupt plan. There is no need for a successor link over and above the path expressions.

Note that there is no longer any assumption that all of the subtasks of a task must be done (in an order constrained by successor links) in order for the supertask to be

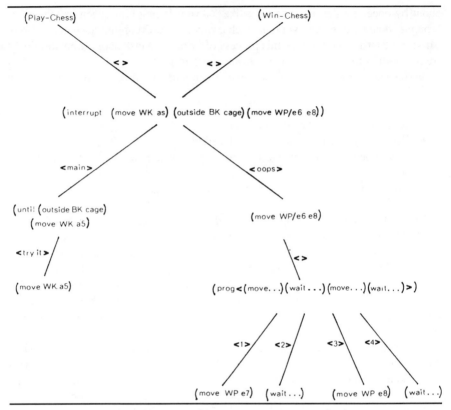

Figure 8. Task Network for Interrupt Task

accomplished. The interrupt is successful if the <oops> subtask is successful. As I
mentioned in section 2.2 we could have an action (do-one-of *A1 A2*), successful if
either subaction were successful, or even (hopetofail *A*), successful when its subaction fails. The only requirement is that the path expressions unambiguously identify
the role of the subtask's success in the success of the supertask.

Another point to make about Figure 8 is that it makes a *prediction* about the
future. There is no reason to plan for the <oops> subtask unless the problem solver
expects (outside k cage) to become true. (One might believe the opponent to be
gullible.) The task network notation should be augmented with an "event network"
of events that are expected to happen, that justify the subtasks' existence.

In general, it is important to distinguish between *current* subtasks and *expected*
subtasks. Previous systems have not made this distinction clearly enough. A subtask, once expected, was sure to become current. We must abandon this assumption. As I mentioned in section 1, a problem solver must continually alter its task
network, filling in and revising pieces as they get closer to execution. This is the
sort of thing problem solvers already do, but their abilities must be broadened. For
an example, let's go back to the gondola we were loading with ballast. One reason

existing systems cannot represent what's happening in this case is that there is no foreseeable set of rock-loadings to be organized into a task network. We should not let this stop us. The problem solver must make the best estimate it can about how many rocks will be needed, and, for instance, reduce the task

(Repeat-until *(force up ≤ 0)*
    <*(get a rock R)*
    (Put R in the gondola)>)

to

{*(Get rock129)*
(Put rock129 in the gondola)
(Get rock504)
(Put rock504 in the gondola)
(Get another rock about that size)
(Put it in the gondola)
(Test whether force up ≤ 0)}

in the case where three rocks seem to be needed. This action then gets factored into six subtasks with obvious actions. Note that the subtasks do not have to be fully stipulated. In this case, the solver has picked out the first two rocks, and judged that finding a third of the same size will be feasible.

The difference between this task reduction and more traditional ones is its shakiness. The subtask relationship is based on an estimate that three rocks will be enough. The problem solver has the duty to make sure that they are.

In many cases, a problem solver will not have a firm estimate of what its own subtasks will be, and will have to do a case analysis, or postpone task reduction until the future becomes clearer.

The second suggestion in my list was to allow tasks to be reduced in groups as well as individually. The logic allows this already. One way to take advantage of it would be to have the "plan library" be indexed by *primary* and *secondary* tasks; the plans for putting something somewhere might be further classified by how gentle they are with breakable things.

Let's look at how this might work with the "eggs and basket" problem. The overall action here is denoted by a term like this:

(while (do-forall (λ (x) (elt x E))
                  (λ (x) (putin x B)))
    (avoid (do-forsome (λ (x) (elt x E))
                       (λ (x) (break x)))))

A problem solver must reduce this to subtasks. Presumably its first step is to break it apart syntactically, into the main action, plus the constraint. It then looks in the plan library for a plan for the main action, favoring those that mention this constraint. If there aren't any, it keeps reducing the main tasks' subtasks, but keeps the constraint around. Finally, when it gets down to subtasks of the form "Grasp x," it presumably will find more than one plan, including one for grasping things that might break. Actually, this sort of thing has already been done by NASL (McDermott 1978), but in an *ad hoc* way. The logic of tasks and subtasks may help generalize and debug the idea.

One thing the task-subtask logic suggests is to think about problem solving "non-psychologically." In a given instant, there is a "best" way of carrying out a set of tasks.[8] Objectively speaking, that becomes a new set of subtasks. Objectively, (task k a) means "I ought to do a," a statement that is either true or false. If it is true, and a' is the best way to do a, then I ought to do a'.

Furthermore, the time at which I discover that I have a task is not usually the time at which I start to have one. In fact, the task reduction inference I just sketched, while it may take time to discover, clearly takes no time to be valid (!), so that task reduction is instantaneous. Given a set of tasks, the inference to a detailed series of subtasks is immediate.

This picture would be more satisfying if we knew how to deal with the fact that the choice of best plan can change. Suppose that the probability of another Great Depression is 0.01, and I have the task, "Maximize wealth." The best way to do this is to put my money in a bank; putting it in a mattress is much worse. But later, if the probability rises to 0.9, the mattress plan may become the best. All of these facts are familiar from decision theory. To import this theory into a logic like the one developed here, we need to find a way to deal with probability and utility.

It may be possible to handle probabilities by providing a measure on "chronicle space." A statement like, "After doing Action A, fact Q will be true with probability p" means that the set of chronicles in which Q is true after A has measure p.[9] It may be possible to analyze utility as a preference among different chronicles (Stan Rosenschein, personal communication). One problem is to reconcile this with the task vocabulary. Intuitively, one would "prefer" chronicles in which more of one's tasks were executed successfully. However, there are several cases where this intuition is violated. Top-level tasks are never finished at all, for instance. And, in general, although the problem solver is supposed to want to expend "effort" on each of its tasks, there is no particular relationship between them and their super-tasks. One may hope one's efforts are in vain.

All of these problems will have to be solved in order to extend the analysis of "task evaporation." In Section 2.2, I said that a task could evaporate only if all its supertasks went away. The other way a task can evaporate is if it ceases to be part of the best plan for all its supertasks, because of a change in the world.

This wasn't so important in my artificial chess world, where probabilities could be ignored. It would clearly be important in more complex domains.

---

[8] Let's ignore the possibility that there are two equally good ways.

[9] I am talking about objective probabilities here. Clearly, there will be cases where it will be hard to classify an uncertainty as due to probabilities or lack of information.

I started the paper by arguing that the original task-reduction paradigm had become too confining, but that abandoning it totally would get us nowhere. It is just too important that actions be decomposed into well-defined subtasks. It now seems that, while there are limits to how far we can take the idea that actions may be decomposed, there is freedom to maneuver within those limits.

Acknowledgments

This research was supported by NSF grant MCS 8013710, and by SRI, where I spent two stimulating weeks in 1982. The ideas in this paper were developed in conversations with Robert Moore, Stan Rosenschein, Ernie Davis, Eugene Charniak, John McCarthy, Stan Letovsky, Yoav Shoham, and others. Thanks to Davis, Letovsky, Shoham, and Jerry Hobbs for many suggestions on improving the presentation.

References

Doyl, J. (1979). "A truth maintenance system," *Artificial Intelligence*, 12, 231–272.

Goldman, Alvin I. (1970). *A Theory of Human Action*. Englewood Cliffs, NJ: Prentice-Hall.

Hayes, Patrick. (1979). The Naive Physics Manifesto. In *Expert Systems in the Microelectronic Age*, D. Michie (Ed.). Edinburgh: Edinburgh University Press.

Konolige, Kurt, & Nils J. Nilsson, Nils J. (1980). "Multiple-Agent Planning Systems," in *Proceedings of the AAAI*. AAAI.

Lewis, David K. (1973). *Counterfactuals*. Oxford: Basil Blackwell.

McCarthy, John. (1958). "Programs with common sense," in *Proceedings of the Symposium on the Mechanization of Thought Processes*. National Physiology Laboratory.

McCarthy, John. (1962). "Towards a Mathematical Theory of Computation," in *Proceedings of the IFIP Congress*. IFIP.

McDermott, Drew V. (1978). "Planning and acting," *Cognitive Science* 2, 71–109.

McDermott, Drew V. (1982). "A temporal logic for reasoning about processes and plans," *Cognitive Science* 6, 101–155.

McDermott, Drew V. (1983). "Contexts and data dependencies: a synthesis," in *IEEE Transactions on Pattern Analysis and Machine Intelligence*, 5, 237–246.

Mendelson, Elliot. (1964). *Introduction to Mathematical Logic*. New York: Van Nostrand.

Minsky, M. (1968). *Semantic Information Processing*. Cambridge, MA: MIT Press.

Moore, Robert. (1980). *Reasoning about knowledge and action*. Technical Report 191, SRI AI Center.

Sacerdoti, E. D. (1975). *A structure for plans and behavior*. Technical Report 109, SRI Artificial Intelligence Center.

Schank, R. C., & Abelson, R. (1977). *Scripts, Plans, Goals and Understanding*. Hillsdale, NJ: Erlbaum.

Stefik, Mark J. (1980). *Planning with Constraints*. Technical Report STAN-CS-80-784, Stanford Computer Science Department.

Sussman, G. J. (1975). *Artificial Intelligence Series*. Volume 1: *A computer model of skill acquisition*. New York: American Elsevier.

Vere, Steven. (1983). "Planning in Time: Windows and Durations for Activities and Goals," *IEEE Transactions on Pattern Analysis and Machine Intelligence*, 5, 246–267.

Wilkins, David. (1980). "Using Patterns and Plans in Chess," *Artificial Intelligence* 14, 165–203.

Wilkins, David. (1984). "Domain Independent Planning: Representation and Plan Generation," *Artificial Intelligence*.

9 A Formal Theory of Knowledge and Action

Robert C. Moore

Artificial Intelligence Center
SRI International
Menlo Park, California

1 The Interplay of Knowledge and Action

Planning sequences of actions and reasoning about their effects is one of the most thoroughly studied areas within artificial intelligence (AI). Relatively little attention has been paid, however, to the important role that an agent's knowledge plays in planning and acting to achieve a goal. Virtually all AI planning systems are designed to operate with complete knowledge of all relevant aspects of the problem domain and problem situation. Often any statement that cannot be inferred to be true is assumed to be false. In the real world, however, planning and acting must frequently be performed without complete knowledge of the situation.

This imposes two additional burdens on an intelligent agent trying to act effectively. First, when the agent entertains a plan for achieving some goal, he must consider not only whether the physical prerequisites of the plan have been satisfied, but also whether he has all the information necessary to carry out the plan. Second, he must be able to reason about what he can do to obtain necessary information that he lacks. AI planning systems are usually based on the assumption that, if there is an action an agent is physically able to perform, and carrying out that action would result in the achievement of a goal P, then the agent can achieve P. With goals such as opening a safe, however, there are actions that any human agent of normal abilities is physically capable of performing that would result in achievement of the goal (in this case, dialing the combination of the safe), but it would be highly misleading to claim that an agent could open a safe simply by dialing the combination unless he actually *knew* that combination. On the other hand, if the agent had a piece of paper on which the combination of the safe was written, he could open the safe by reading what was on the piece of paper and then dialing the combination, even if he did not know it previously.

In this paper, we will describe a formal theory of knowledge and action that is based on a general understanding of the relationship between the two.[1] The question

---

[1] This paper presents the analysis of knowledge and action, and the representation of that analysis in first-order logic, that were developed in the author's doctoral thesis (Moore, 1980). The material in Sections 3.1 and 3.2, however, has been substantially revised.

of generality is somewhat problematical, since different actions obviously have different prerequisites and results that involve knowledge. What we will try to do is to set up a formalism in which very general conclusions can be drawn, once a certain minimum of information has been provided concerning the relation between specific actions and the knowledge of agents.

To see what this amounts to, consider the notion of a test. The essence of a test is that it is an action with a directly observable result that depends conditionally on an unobservable precondition. In the use of litmus paper to test the pH of a solution, the observable result is whether the paper has turned red or blue, and the unobservable precondition is whether the solution is acid or alkaline. What makes such a test useful for acquiring knowledge is that the agent can infer whether the solution is acid or alkaline on the basis of his knowledge of the behavior of litmus paper and the observed color of the paper. When one is performing a test, it is this inferred knowledge, rather than what is directly observed, that is of primary interest.

If we tried to formalize the results of such a test by making simple assertions about what the agent knows subsequent to the action, we would have to include the result that the agent knows whether the solution is acid or alkaline as a separate assertion from the result that he knows the color of the paper. If we did this, however, we would completely miss the point that knowledge of the pH of the solution is inferred from other knowledge, rather than being a direct observation. In effect, we would be *stipulating* what actions can be used as tests, rather than creating a formalism within which we can *infer* what actions can be used as tests.

If we want a formal theory of how an agent's state of knowledge is changed by his performing a test, we have to represent and be able to draw inferences from the agent's having several independent pieces of information. Obviously, we have to represent that, after the test is performed, the agent knows the observable result. Furthermore, we have to represent the fact that he knows that the test has been performed. If he just walks into the room and sees the litmus paper on the table, he will know what color it is, but, unless he knows its recent history, he will not have gained any knowledge about the acidity of the solution. We also need to represent the fact that the agent understands how the test works; that is, he knows how the observable result of the action depends on the unobservable precondition. Even if he sees the litmus paper put into the solution and then sees the paper change color, he still will not know whether the solution is acid or alkaline unless he knows how the color of the paper is related to the acidity of the solution. Finally, we must be able to infer that, if the agent knows (i) that the test took place, (ii) the observable result of the test, and (iii) how the observable result depends on the unobservable precondition, then he will know the unobservable precondition. Thus we must know enough about knowledge to tell us when an agent's knowing a certain collection of facts implies that he knows other facts as well.

From the preceding discussion, we can conclude that any formalism that enables us to draw inferences about tests at this level of detail must be able to represent the following types of assertions:

(1) After A performs ACT, he knows whether Q is true.

(2) After A performs ACT, he knows that he has just performed ACT.

(3) A knows that Q will be true after he performs ACT if and only if P is true now.

Moreover, in order to infer what information an agent will gain as a result of performing a test, the formalism must embody, or be able to represent, general principles sufficient to conclude the following:

(4) If 1, 2, and 3 are true, then, after performing ACT, A will know whether P was true before he performed ACT.

It is important to emphasize that any work on these problems that is to be of real value must seek to elicit general principles. For instance, it would be possible to represent (1), (2), and (3) in an arbitrary, ad hoc manner and to add an axiom that explicitly states (4), thereby "capturing" the notion of a test. Such an approach, however, would simply restate the superficial observations put forth in this discussion. Our goal in this paper is to describe a formalism in which specific facts like (4) follow from the most basic principles of reasoning about knowledge and action.

2 Formal Theories of Knowledge

2.1 A Modal Logic of Knowledge

Since formalisms for reasoning about action have been studied extensively in AI, while formalisms for reasoning about knowledge have not, we will first address the problems of reasoning about knowledge. In Section 3 we will see that the formalism that we are led to as a solution to these problems turns out to be well suited to developing an integrated theory of knowledge and action.

The first step in devising a formalism for reasoning about knowledge is to decide what general properties of knowledge we want that formalism to capture. The properties of knowledge in which we will be most interested are those that are relevant to planning and acting. One such property is that anything that is known by someone must be true. If P is false, we would not want to say that anyone knows P. It might be that someone believes P or that someone believes he knows P, but it simply could not be the case that anyone knows P. This is, of course, a major difference between knowledge and belief. If we say that someone believes P, we are not committed to saying that P is either true or false, but if we say that someone knows P, we are committed to the truth of P. The reason that this distinction is important for planning and acting is simply that, for an agent to achieve his goals, the beliefs on which he bases his actions must generally be true. After all, merely believing that performing a certain action will bring about a desired goal is not sufficient for being able to achieve the goal; the action must actually have the intended effect.

Another principle that turns out to be important for planning is that, if someone knows something, he knows that he knows it. This principle is often required for reasoning about plans consisting of several steps. Suppose an agent plans to use

ACT$_1$ to achieve his goal, but, in order to perform ACT$_1$ he needs to know whether P is true and whether Q is true. Suppose, further, that he already knows that P is true and that he can find out whether Q is true by performing ACT$_2$. The agent needs to be able to reason that, after performing ACT$_2$, he will know whether P is true and whether Q is true. He knows that he will know whether Q is true because he understands the effects of ACT$_2$, but how does he know that he will know whether P is true? Presumably it works something like this: he knows that P is true, so he knows that he knows that P is true. If he knows how ACT$_2$ affects P, he knows that he will know whether P is true after he performs ACT$_2$. The key step in this argument is an instance of the principle that, if someone knows something, he knows that he knows it.

It might seem that we would also want to have the principle that, if someone does not know something, he knows that he does not know it—but this turns out to be false. Suppose that A believes that P, but P is not true. Since P is false, A certainly does not know that P, but it is highly unlikely that he knows that he does not know, since he thinks that P is true.

Probably the most important fact about knowledge that we will want to capture is that agents can reason on the basis of their knowledge. All our examples depend on the assumption that, if an agent trying to solve a problem has all the relevant information, he will apply his knowledge to produce a solution. This creates a difficulty for us, however, since agents (at least human ones) are not, in fact, aware of all the logical consequences of their knowledge. The trouble is that we can never be sure which of the inferences an agent *could* draw, he actually *will*. The principle people normally use in reasoning about what other people know seems to be something like this: if *we* can infer that something is a consequence of what someone knows, then, lacking information to the contrary, we will assume that the other person can draw the same inference.

This suggests the adoption some sort of "default rule" (Reiter, 1980) for reasoning about what inferences agents actually draw, but, for the purposes of this study, we will make the simplifying assumption that agents actually do draw all logically valid inferences from their knowledge. We can regard this as the epistemological version of the "frictionless case" in classical physics. For a more general framework in which weaker assumptions about the deductive abilities of agents can be expressed, see the work of Konolige (Chapter 10, this volume).

Finally, we will need to include the fact that these basic properties of knowledge are themselves *common knowledge*. By this we mean that everyone knows them, and everyone knows that everyone knows them, and everyone knows that everyone knows that everyone knows them, ad infinitum. This type of principle is obviously needed when reasoning about what someone knows about what someone else knows, but it is also important in planning, because an agent must be able to reason about what he will know at various times in the future. In such a case, his "future self" is analogous to another agent.

In his pioneering work on the logic of knowledge and belief, Hintikka (1962) presents a formalism that captures all these properties. We will define a formal logic based on Hintikka's ideas, but modified somewhat to be more compatible with the additional ideas of this paper. So, what follows is similar to the logic developed by Hintikka in spirit, but not in detail.

The language we will use initially is that of propositional logic, augmented by an operator KNOW and terms denoting agents. The formula KNOW(A,P) is interpreted to mean that the agent denoted by the term A knows the proposition expressed by the formula P. So, if JOHN denotes John and LIKES(BILL,MARY) means that Bill likes Mary, KNOW(JOHN,LIKES(BILL,MARY)) means that John knows that Bill likes Mary. The axioms of the logic are inductively defined as all instances of the following schemata:

> M1. P, such that P is an axiom of ordinary propositional logic
> M2. KNOW(A,P) ⊃ P
> M3. KNOW(A,P) ⊃ KNOW(A,KNOW(A,P))
> M4. KNOW(A, (P ⊃ Q)) ⊃ (KNOW(A,P) ⊃ KNOW(A,Q))

closed under the principle that

> M5. If P is an axiom, then KNOW(A,P) is an axiom.

The closure of the axioms under the inference rule modus ponens (from (P ⊃ Q) and P, infer Q) defines the theorems of the system. This system is very similar to those studied in modal logic. In fact, if A is held fixed, the resulting system is isomorphic to the modal logic S4 (Hughes and Cresswell, 1968). We will refer to this system as the modal logic of knowledge.

These axioms formalize in a straightforward way the principles for reasoning about knowledge that we have discussed. M2 says that anything that is known is true. M3 says that, if someone knows something, he knows that he knows it. M4 says that, if someone knows a formula P and a formula of the form (P ⊃ Q), then he knows the corresponding formula Q. That is, everyone can (and does) apply modus ponens. M5 guarantees that the axioms are common knowledge. It first applies to M1–M4, which says that everyone knows the basic facts about knowledge; however, since it also applies to its own output, we get axioms stating that everyone knows that everyone knows, etc. Since M5 applies to the axioms of propositional logic (M1), we can infer that everyone knows the facts they represent. Furthermore, because modus ponens is the only inference rule needed in propositional logic, the presence of M4 will enable us to infer that an agent knows any propositional consequence of his knowledge.

2.2 A Possible-World Analysis of Knowledge

We could try to use the modal logic of knowledge directly in a computational system for reasoning about knowledge and action, but, as we have argued elsewhere (Moore, 1980), all the obvious ways of doing this encounter difficulties. (Konolige's recent work, this volume, suggests some new, more promising possibilities, but the details remain to be worked out.) There may well be solutions to these problems, but it turns out that they can be circumvented entirely by changing the language we use to describe what agents know. Instead of talking about the individual propositions that an agent knows, we will talk about what states of affairs are compatible with what he knows. In philosophy, these states of affairs are usually called "possible worlds," so we will adopt that term here as well.

This shift to describing knowledge in terms of possible worlds is based on a rich and elegant formal semantics for systems like our modal logic of knowledge, which was developed by Hintikka (1962, 1971) in his work on knowledge and belief. The advantages of this approach are that it can be formalized within ordinary first-order classical logic in a way that permits the use of standard automatic-deduction techniques in a reasonably efficient manner[2] and that, moreover, it generalizes nicely to an integrated theory for describing the effects of actions on the agent's knowledge.

Possible-world semantics was first developed for the logic of necessity and possibility. From an intuitive standpoint, a possible world may be thought of as a set of circumstances that might have been true in the actual world. Kripke (1963) introduced the idea that a world should be regarded as possible, not absolutely, but only relative to other worlds. That is, the world W_1 might be a possible alternative to W_2, but not to W_3. The relation of one world's being a possible alternative to another is called the *accessibility relation*. Kripke then proved that the differences among some of the most important axiom systems for modal logic corresponded exactly to certain restrictions on the accessibility relation of the possible-world models of those systems. These results are reviewed in Kripke (1971). Concurrently with these developments, Hintikka (1962) published the first of his writings on the logic of knowledge and belief, which included a model theory that resembled Kripke's possible-world semantics. Hintikka's original semantics was done in terms of sets of sentences, which he called *model sets,* rather than possible worlds. Later (Hintikka, 1971), however, he recast his semantics using Kripke's concepts, and it is that formulation we will use here.

Kripke's semantics for necessity and possibility can be converted into Hintikka's semantics for knowledge by changing the interpretation of the accessibility relation. To analyze statements of the form KNOW(A,P), we will introduce a relation K, such that ($K(A,W_1,W_2)$ means that the possible world W_2 is compatible or consistent with what A knows in the possible world W_1. In other words, for all that A knows in W_1, he might just as well be in W_2. It is the set of worlds $\{w_2 \mid K(A,W_1,w_2)\}$ that we will use to characterize what A knows in W_1. We will discuss A's knowledge in W_1 in terms of this set, the set of states of affairs that are consistent with his knowledge in W_1, rather than in terms of the set of propositions he knows. For the present, let us assume that the first argument position of K admits the same set of terms as the first argument position of KNOW. When we consider

---

[2] Chapters 6 and 7 of More (1980) present a procedural interpretation of the axioms for knowledge and action given in this paper that seems to produce reasonably efficient behavior in an automatic deduction system.

quantifiers and equality, we will have to modify this assumption, but it will do for now.

Introducing K is the key move in our analysis of statements about knowledge, so understanding what K means is particularly important. To illustrate, suppose that in the actual world—call it W_0—A knows that P, but does not know whether Q. If W_1 is a world where P is false, then W_1 is not compatible with what A knows in W_0; hence we would have $\neg K(A, W_0, W_1)$. Suppose that W_2 and W_3 are compatible with everything A knows, but that Q is true in W_2 and false in W_3. Since A does not know whether Q is true, for all he knows, he might be in either W_2 or W_3 instead of W_0. Hence, we would have both $K(A, W_0, W_2)$ and $K(A, W_0, W_3)$. This is depicted graphically in Figure 1.

Some of the properties of knowledge can be captured by putting constraints on the accessibility relation K. For instance, requiring that the actual world W_0 be compatible with what each knower knows in W_0, i.e., $\forall a_1(K(a_1, W_0, W_0))$, is equivalent to saying that anything that is known is true. That is, if the actual world is compatible with what everyone [actually] knows, then no one has any false knowledge. This corresponds to the modal axiom M2.

The definition of K implies that, if A knows that P in W_0, then P must be true in every world W_1 such that $K(A, W_0, W_1)$. To capture the fact that agents can reason with their knowledge, we will assume converse is also true. That is, we assume that, if P is true in every world W_1 such that $K(A, W_0, W_1)$, then A knows that P in

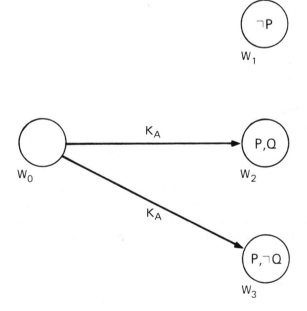

Figure 1. "A Knows That P"
"A Doesn't Know Whether Q"

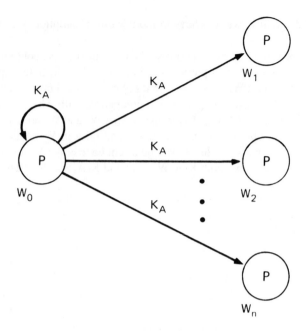

Figure 2. "P is True in Every World That is Compatible with What A Knows"

W_0. (See Figure 2.) This principle is the model-theoretic analogue of axiom M4 in the modal logic of knowledge. To see that this is so, suppose that A knows that P and that (P ⊃ Q). Therefore, P and (P ⊃ Q) are both true in every world that is compatible with what A knows. If this is the case, though, then Q must be true in every world that is compatible with what A knows. By our assumption, therefore, we conclude that A knows that Q.

Since this assumption, like M4, is equivalent to saying that an agent knows all the logical consequences of his knowledge, it should be interpreted only as a default rule. In a particular instance, the fact that P follows from A's knowledge would be a justification for concluding that A knows P. However, we should be prepared to retract the conclusion that A knows P in the face of stronger evidence to the contrary.

With this assumption, we can get the effect of M3—the axiom stating that, if someone knows something, he knows that he knows it—by requiring that, for any W_1 and W_2, if W_1 is compatible with what A knows in W_0 and W_2 is compatible with what A knows in W_1, then W_2 is compatible with what A knows in W_0. Formally expressed, this is

$$\forall a_1, w_1, w_2 (K(a_1, W_0, w_1) \supset (K(a_1, w_1, w_2) \supset K(a_1, W_0, w_2)))$$

By our previous assumption, the facts that A knows are those that are true in every world that is compatible with what A knows in the actual world. Furthermore, the facts that A knows that he knows are those that are true in every world that is

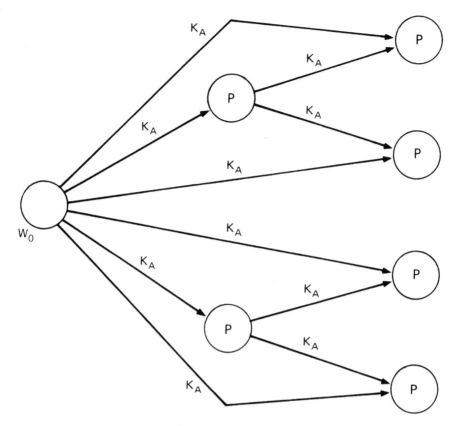

Figure 3. "If A Knows That P, Then He Knows That He Knows That P"

compatible with what he knows in every world that is compatible with what he knows in the actual world. By the constraint we have just proposed, however, all these worlds must also be compatible with what A knows in the actual world (see Figure 3), so, if A knows that P, he knows that he knows that P.

Finally, we can get the effect of M5, the principle that the basic fact about knowledge are themselves common knowledge, by generalizing these constraints so that they hold not only for the actual world, but for all possible worlds. This follows from the fact that, if these constraints hold for all worlds, they hold for all worlds that are compatible with what anyone knows in the actual world; they also hold for all worlds that are compatible with what anyone knows in all worlds that are compatible with what anyone knows in the actual world, etc. Therefore, everyone knows the facts about knowlege that are represented by the constraints, and everyone knows that everyone knows, etc. Note that this generalization has the effect that the constraint corresponding to M2 becomes the requirement that, for a given knower, K is reflexive, while the constraint corresponding to M3 becomes the requirement that, for a given knower, K is transitive.

Analyzing knowledge in terms of possible worlds gives us a very nice treatment

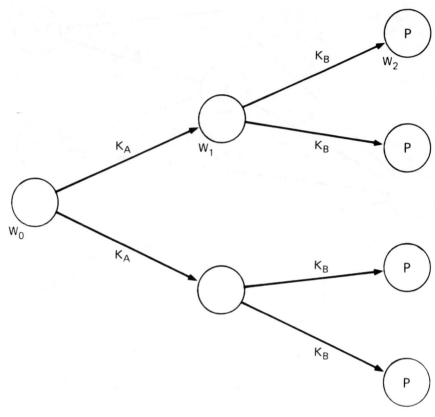

Figure 4. "A Knows That B Knows That P"

of knowledge about knowledge. Suppose A knows that B knows that P. Then, if the actual world is W_0, in any world W_1 such that $K(A,W_0,W_1)$, B knows that P. We now continue the analysis relative to W_1, so that, in any world W_2 such that $K(B,W_1,W_2)$, P is true. Putting both stages together, we obtain the analysis that, for any worlds W_1 and W_2 such that $K(A,W_0,W_1)$ and $K(B,W_1,W_2)$, P is true in W_2. (See Figure 4.)

Given these constraints and assumptions, whenever we want to assert or deduce something that would be expressed in the modal logic of knowledge by KNOW(A,P), we can instead assert or deduce that P is true in every world that is compatible with what A knows. We can express this in ordinary first-order logic, by treating possible worlds as individuals (in the logical sense), so that K is just an ordinary relation. We will therefore introduce an operator T such that T(W,P) means that the formula P is true in the possible world W. If we let W_0 denote the actual world, we can convert the assertion KNOW(A,P) into

$$\forall w_1(K(A,W_0,w_1) \supset T(w_1,P))$$

It may seem that we have not made any real progress, since, although we have gotten rid of one nonstandard operator, KNOW, we have introduced another one, T. However, T has an important property that KNOW does not. Namely, T "distributes" over ordinary logical operators. In other words, $\neg$ P is true in W just in case P is not true in W, (P $\vee$ Q) is true in W just in case P is true in W or Q is true in W, and so on. We might say that T is extensional, relative to a possible world. This means that we can transform any formula so that T is applied only to atomic formulas. We can then turn T into an ordinary first-order relation by treating all the nonintensional atomic formulas as *names* of atomic propositions, or we can get rid of T by replacing the atomic formulas with predicates on possible worlds. This is no loss to the expressive power of the language, since, where we would have previously asserted P, we now simply assert $T(W_0,P)$ or $P(W_0)$ instead.

2.3 Knowledge, Equality, and Quantification

The formalization of knowledge presented so far is purely propositional; a number of additional problems arise when we attempt to extend the theory to handle equality and quantification. For instance, as Frege (1949) pointed out, attibutions of knowledge and belief lead to violations of the principle of equality substitution. We are not entitled to infer KNOW(A,P(C)) from B = C and KNOW(A,P(B)) because A might not know that the identity holds.

The possible-world analysis of knowledge provides a very neat solution to this problem, once we realize that a term can denote different objects in different possible worlds. For instance, if B is the expression "the number of planets" and C is "nine," then, although B = C is true in the actual world, it would be false in a world in which there was a tenth planet. Thus, we will say that an equality statement such as B = C is true in a possible world W just in case the denotation of the term B in W is the same as the denotation of the term C in W. This is a special case of the more general rule that a formula of the form $P(A_1,...,A_n)$ is true in W just in case the tuple consisting of the denotations in W of the terms $A_1,...,A_n$ is in the extension in W of the relation expressed by P, provided that we fix the interpretation of = in all possible worlds to be the identity relation.

Given this interpretation, the inference of KNOW(A,P(C)) from B = C and KNOW(A,P(B)) will be blocked (as it should be). To infer KNOW(A,P(C)) from KNOW(A,P(B)) by identity substitution, we would have to know that B and C denote the same object in *every* world compatible with what A knows, but the truth of B = C guarantees only that they denote the same object in the actual world. On the other hand, if KNOW(A,P(B)) and KNOW(A,(B = C)) are both true, then in all worlds that are compatible with what A knows, the denotation of B is in the extension of P and is the same as the denotation of C; hence, the denotation of C is in the extension of P. From this we can infer that KNOW(A,P(C)) is true.

The introduction of quantifiers also causes problems. To modify a famous example from Quine (1971), consider the sentence "Ralph knows that someone is a spy." This sentence has at least two interpretations. One is that Ralph knows that there is at least one person who is a spy, although he may have no idea who that person is. The other interpretation is that there is a particular person whom Ralph knows to be a spy. As Quine says (1971, p. 102), "The difference is vast; indeed, if Ralph is like most of us, [the first] is true and [the second] is false." This ambiguity was explained by Russell (1949) as a difference of *scope*. The idea is that indefinite noun phrases such as "someone" can be analyzed in context by paraphrasing sentences of the form P("someone") as "There exists a person x such that P(x)," or, more formally, $\exists x(PERSON(x) \wedge P(x))$. Russell goes on to point out that, in sentences of the form "A knows that someone is a P," the rule for eliminating "someone" can be applied to either the whole sentence or only the subordinate clause, "someone is a P." Applying this observation to "Ralph knows that someone is a spy," gives us the following two formal representations:

$$KNOW(RALPH, \exists x(PERSON(x) \wedge SPY(x))) \tag{1}$$

$$\exists x(PERSON(x) \wedge KNOW(RALPH, SPY(x))) \tag{2}$$

The most natural English paraphrases of these formulas are "Ralph knows that there is a person who is a spy," and "There is a person who Ralph knows is a spy." These seem to correspond pretty well to the two interpretations of the original sentence. So, the ambiguity in the original sentence is mapped into an uncertainty as to the scope of the operator KNOW relative to the existential quantifier introduced by the indefinite description "someone."

Following a suggestion of Hintikka (1962), we can use a formula similar to (2) to express the fact that someone knows who or what something is. He points out that a sentence of the form "A knows who (or what) B is" intuitively seems to be equivalent to "there is someone (or something) that A knows to be B. But this can be represented formally as $\exists x(KNOW(A,(x = B)))$. To take a specific example, "John knows who the President is" can be paraphrased as "There is someone whom John knows to be the President," which can be represented by

$$\exists x(KNOW(JOHN,(x = PRESIDENT))) \tag{3}$$

In (1), KNOW may still be regarded as a purely propositional operator, although the proposition to which it is applied now has a quantifier in it. Put another way, KNOW still is used simply to express a relation between a knower and the proposition he knows. But (2) and (3) are not so simple. In these formulas there is a quantified variable that, although bound outside the scope of the operator KNOW, has an occurrence inside; this is sometimes called "quantifying in." Quantifying into knowledge and belief contexts is frequently held to pose serious problems of interpretation. Quine (1971), for instance, holds that it is unintelligible, because we have not specified what proposition is known unless we say what description is used to fix the value of the quantified variable.

The possible-world analysis, however, provides us with a very natural interpretation of quantifying in. We keep the standard interpretation that $\exists x(P(x))$ is true just in case there is some value for x that satisfies P. If P is KNOW(A,Q(x)), then a value for x satisfies P(x) just in case that value satisfies Q(x) in every world that is compatible with what A knows. So (2) is satisfied if there is a particular person who is a spy in every world that is compatible with what A knows. That is, in every such world the same person is a spy. On the other hand, (1) is satisfied if, in every world compatible with what A knows, there is some person who is a spy, but it does not have to be the same one in each case.

Note that the difference between (1) and (2) has been transformed from a difference in the relative scopes of an existential quantifier and the operator KNOW to a difference in the relative scopes of an existential and a universal quantifier (the "every" in "every possible world compatible with . . ."). Recall from ordinary first-order logic that $\exists x(\forall y(P(x,y)))$ entails $\forall y(\exists x(P(x,y)))$, but not vice versa. The possible-world analysis, then, implies that we should be able to infer "Ralph knows that there is a spy," from "There is someone Ralph knows to be a spy," as indeed we can.

When we look at how this analysis applies to our representation from "knowing who," we get a particularly satisfying picture. We said that A knows who B is means that there is someone whom A knows to be B. If we analyze this, we conclude that there is a particular individual who is B in every world that is compatible with what A knows. Suppose this were not the case, and that, in some of the worlds compatible with what A knows, one person is B, whereas in the other worlds, some other person is B. In other words, for all that A knows, either of these two people might be B. But this is exactly what we mean when we say that A does not know who B is! Basically, the possible-world view gives us the very natural picture that A knows who B is if A has narrowed the possibilities for B down to a single individual.

Another consequence of this analysis worth noting is that, if A knows who B is and A knows who C is, we can conclude that A knows whether B = C. If A knows who B is and who C is, then B has the the same denotation in all the worlds that are compatible with what A knows, and this is also true for C. Since, in all these worlds, B and C each have only one denotation, they either denote the same thing everywhere or denote different things everywhere. Thus, either B = C is true in every world compatible with what A knows or B ≠ C is. From this we can infer that either A knows that B and C are the same individual or that they are not.

We now have a coherent account of quantifying in that is not framed in terms of knowing particular propositions. Still, in some cases knowing a certain proposition counts as knowing something that would be expressed by quantifying in. For instance, the proposition that John knows that 321-1234 is Bill's telephone number might be represented as

KNOW(JOHN,(321-1234 = PHONE-NUM(BILL))),   (4)

which does not involve quantifying in. We would want to be able to infer from this, however, that John knows what Bill's telephone number is, which would be represented as

$\exists x$(KNOW(JOHN,(x = PHONE-NUM(BILL)))).   (5)

It might seem that (5) can be derived from (4) simply by the logical principle of existential generalization, but that principle is not always valid in knowledge contexts. Suppose that (4) were not true, but that instead John simply knew that Mary and Bill had the same telephone number. We could represent this as

$$\text{KNOW(JOHN,(PHONE-NUM(MARY) = PHONE-NUM(BILL))).} \qquad (6)$$

It is clear that we would not want to infer from (6) that John knows what Bill's telephone number is—yet, if existential generalization were universally valid in knowledge contexts, this inference would go through.

It therefore seems that, in knowledge contexts, existential generalization can be applied to some referring expressions ("321-1234"), but not to others ("Mary's telephone number"). We will call the expressions to which existential generalization can be applied *standard identifiers,* since they seem to be the ones an agent would use to identify an object for another agent. That is, "321-1234" is the kind of answer that would *always* be appropriate for telling someone what John's telephone number is, whereas "Mary's telephone number," as a general rule, would not.[3]

In terms of possible worlds, standard identifiers have a very straightforward interpretation. Standard identifiers are simply terms that have the same denotation in every possible world. Following Kripke (1972), we will call terms that have the same denotation in every possible world *rigid designators.* The conclusion that standard identifiers are rigid designators seems inescapable. If a particular expression can always be used by an agent to identify its referent for any other agent, then there must not be any possible circumstances under which it could refer to something else. Otherwise, the first agent could not be sure that the second was in a position to rule out those other possibilities.

The validity of existential generalization for standard identifiers follows immediately from their identification with rigid designators. The possible-world analysis of KNOW(A,P(B)) is that, in every world compatible with what A knows, the denotation of B in that world is in the extension of P in that world. Existential generalization fails in general because we are unable to conclude that there is any particular individual that is in the extension of P in all the relevant worlds. If B is a rigid designator, however, the denotation of B is the same in every world. Consequently, it is the same in every world compatible with what A knows, and that denotation is an individual that is in the extension of P in all those worlds.

There are a few more observations to be made about standard identifiers and rigid designators. First, in describing standard identifiers we assumed that everyone

---

[3] "Mary's telephone number" *would* be an approriate way of telling someone what John's telephone number was if he already knew Mary's telephone number, but this knowledge would consist in knowing what expression of the type "321-1234" denoted Mary's telephone number. Therefore, even in this case, using "Mary's telephone number" to identify John's telephone number would just be an indirect way of getting to the standard indentifier.

knew what they referred to. Identifying them with rigid designators makes the stronger claim that what they refer to is common knowledge. That is, not only does everyone know what a particular standard identifier denotes, but everyone knows that everyone knows, etc. Second, although it is natural to think of any individual having a unique standard identifier, this is not required by our theory. What the theory does require is that, if there are two standard identifiers for the same individual, it should be common knowledge that they denote the same individual.

3 Formalizing the Possible-World Analysis of Knowledge

3.1 Object Language and Metalanguage

As we indicated above, the analysis of knowledge in terms of possible worlds can be formalized completely within first-order logic by admitting possible worlds into the domain of quantification and making the extension of every expression depend on the possible world in which it is evaluated. For example, the possible-world analysis of "A knows who B is" would be as follows: There is some individual x such that, in every world w_1 that is compatible with what the agent who is A in the actual world knows in the actual world, x is B in w_1. This means that in our formal theory we translate the formula of the modal logic of knowledge,

$$\exists x(KNOW(A,(x = B))),$$

into the first-order formula,

$$\exists x(\forall w_1(K(A(W_0),W_0,w_1) \supset (x = B(w_1))))).$$

One convenient way of stating the translation rules precisely is to axiomatize them in our first-order theory of knowledge. This can be done by introducing terms to denote formulas of the modal logic of knowledge (which we will henceforth call the *object language*) and axiomatizing a truth definition for those formulas in a first-order language that talks about possible worlds (the *metalanguage*). This has the advantage of letting us use either the modal language or the possible-world language—whichever is more convenient for a particular purpose—while rigorously defining the connection between the two.

The typical method of representing expressions of one formal language in another is to use string operations like concatenation or list operations like CONS in LISP, so that the conjunction of P and Q might be represented by something like CONS(P,CONS('∧,CONS(Q,NIL))), which could be abbreviated LIST(P,'∧,Q). This would be interpreted as a list whose elements are P followed by the conjunction symbol followed by Q. Thus, the metalanguage expression CONS(P,CONS('∧,CONS(Q,NIL))) would denote the object language expression (P ∧ Q). McCarthy (1962) has devised a much more elegant way to do the encoding, however. For purposes of semantic interpretation of the object language, which is what we want to do, the details of the syntax of that language are largely irrelevant. In particular, the only thing we need to know about the syntax of conjunctions is that there is *some* way of taking P and Q and producing the conjunction of P and Q. We can represent this by having a function AND such that AND(P,Q) denotes the conjunction of P and Q. To use McCarthy's term, AND(P,Q) is an *abstract syntax* for representing the conjunction of P and Q.

We will represent object language variables and constants by metalanguage constants; we will use metalanguage functions in an abstract syntax to represent object language predicates, functions, and sentence operators. For example, we will represent the object language formula KNOW(JOHN,$\exists$x(P(x))) by the metalanguage term KNOW(JOHN,EXIST(X,P(X))), where JOHN and X are metalanguage constants, and KNOW, EXIST, and P are metalanguage functions.

Since KNOW(JOHN,EXIST(X,P(X))) is a term, if we want to say that the object language formula it denotes is true, we have to do so explicitly by means of a metalanguage predicate TRUE:

$$\text{TRUE(KNOW(JOHN,EXIST(X,P(X)))).}$$

In the possible-world analysis of statements about knowledge, however, an object language formula is not absolutely true, but only relative to a possible world. Hence, TRUE expresses not absolute truth, but truth in the actual world, which we will denote by W_0. Thus, our first axiom is

L1. $\forall p_1(\text{TRUE}(p_1) \equiv T(W_0, p_1))$,

where $T(W,P)$ means that formula P is true in world W. To simplify the axioms, we will let the metalanguage be a many-sorted logic, with different sorts assigned to differents sets of variables. For instance, the variables w_1, w_2,... will range over possible worlds; x_1, x_2,... will range over individuals in the domain of the object language; and a_1, a_2,... will range over agents. Because we are axiomatizing the object language itself, we will need several sorts for different types of object language expressions. The variables p_1, p_2,... will range over object language formulas, and t_1, t_2,... will range over object language terms.

The recursive definition of T for the propositional part of the object language is as follows:

L2. $\forall w_1, p_1, p_2(T(w_1, \text{AND}(p_1, p_2)) \equiv (T(w_1, p_1) \wedge T(w_1, p_2)))$

L3. $\forall w_1, p_1, p_2(T(w_1, \text{OR}(p_1, p_2)) \equiv (T(w_1, p_1) \vee T(w_1, p_2)))$

L4. $\forall w_1, p_1, p_2(T(w_1, \text{IMP}(p_1, p_2)) \equiv (T(w_1, p_1) \supset T(w_1, p_2)))$

L5. $\forall w_1, p_1, p_2(T(w_1, \text{IFF}(p_1, p_2)) \equiv (T(w_1, p_1) \equiv T(w_1, p_2)))$

L6. $\forall w_1, p_1(T(w_1, \text{NOT}(p_1)) \equiv \sim T(w_1, p_1))$

Axioms L1–L6 merely translate the logical connectives from the object language to the metalanguage, using an ordinary Tarskian truth definition. For instance, according to L2, AND(P,Q) is true in a world if and only if P and Q are both true in the world. The other axioms state that all the truth-functional connectives are "transparent" to T in exactly the same way.

To represent quantified object language formulas in the metalanguage, we will introduce additional functions into the abstract syntax: EXIST and ALL. These functions will take two arguments—a term denoting an object language variable and a term denoting an object language formula. Axiomatizing the interpretation of quantified object language formulas presents some minor technical problems, however. We would like to say something like this: EXIST(X,P) is true in W if and only if there is some individual such that the open formula P is true of that individual in W. We do not have any way of saying that an open formula is true of an individual in a world, however; we just have the predicate T, which simply says that a formula is true in a world. One way of solving the problem would be to introduce a new predicate, or perhaps redefine T, to express the Tarskian notion of satisfaction rather than truth. This approach is semantically clean but syntactically clumsy, so we will instead follow the advice of Scott (1970, p. 151) and define the truth of a quantified statement in terms of substituting into the body of that statement a rigid designator for the value of the quantified variable.

In order to formalize this substitutional approach to the interpretation of object language quantifications, we need a rigid designator in the object language for every individual. Since our representation of the object language is in the form of an abstract syntax, we can simply stipulate that there is a function @ that maps any individual in the object language's domain of discourse into an object language rigid designator of that individual. The definition of T for quantified statements is then given by the following axiom schemata:

L7. $\forall w_1(T(w_1,EXIST(X,P)) \equiv \exists x_1(T(w_1,P[@(x_1)/X])))$

L8. $\forall w_1(T(w_1,ALL(X,P)) \equiv \forall x_1(T(w_1,P[@(x_1)/X])))$

In these schemata, P may be any object language formula, X may be any object language variable, and the notation $P[@(x_1)/X]$ designates the expression that results from substituting $@(x_1)$ for every free occurrence of X in P.

L7 says that an existentially quantified formula is true in a world W if and only if, for *some* individual, the result of substituting a rigid designator of that individual for the bound variable in the body of the formula is true in W. L8 says that a universally quantified formula is true in W if and only if, for *every* individual, the result of substituting a rigid designator of that individual for the bound variable in the body of the formula is true in W.

Except for the knowledge operator itself, the only part of the truth definition of the object language that remains to be given is the definition of T for atomic formulas. We remarked previously that a formula of the form $P(A_1,...,A_n)$ is true in a world W just in case the tuple consisting of the denotations in W of the terms $A_1,...,A_n$ is in the extension in W of the relation P. To axiomatize this principle, we need two additions to the metalanguage. First, we need a function D that maps a possible world and an object language term into the denotation of that term in that world. Second, for each n-place object language predicate P, we need a corresponding n+1-place metalanguage predicate (which, by convention, we will write :P) that takes as its arguments the possible world in which the object language formula is to be evaluated and the denotations in that world of the arguments of the object language predicate. The interpretation of an object language atomic formula is then given by the axiom schema

L9. $\forall w_1, t_1,...,t_n$
$$(T(w_1, P(t_1,...,t_n)) \equiv :P(w,_1, D(w_1, t_1),...,D(w_1, t_n)))$$

To eliminate the function D, we need to introduce a metalanguage expression corresponding to each object language constant or function. In the general case, the new expression will be a function with an extra argument position for the possible world of evaluation. The axiom schemata for D are then

L10. $\forall w_1, x_1 (D(w_1, @(x_1)) = x_1)$

L11. $\forall w_1 (D(w_1, C) = :C(w_1))$

L12. $\forall w_1, t_1,...,t_n$
$$(D(w_1, F(t_1,...,t_n)) = :F(w_1, D(w_1, t_1),...,D(w_1, t_n))),$$

where C is an object language constant and F is an object language function, and we use the ":" convention already introduced for their metalanguage counterparts.

Since $@(x_1)$ is a rigid designator of x_1, its value is x_1 in every possible world. In the general case, an object language constant will have a corresponding metalanguage function that picks out the denotation of the constant in a particular world. Similarly, an object language function will have a corresponding metalanguage function that maps a possible world and the denotations of the arguments of the object language function into the value of the object language function applied to those arguments in that world.

It will be convenient to treat specially those object language constants and functions that are (or can be used to construct) rigid designators. We could introduce additional axioms asserting that such expressions have the same value in every possible world, but we can accomplish the same end simply by making the corresponding metalanguage expressions independent of the possible world of evaluation. So, for object language constants that are rigid designators, we will have a variant of axiom L11:

L11a. $\forall w_1 (D(w_1, C) = :C)$ if C is a rigid designator.

We will similarly treat *rigid functions*—those that always map a particular tuple of arguments into the same value in all possible worlds:

L12a. $\forall w_1, t_1, \ldots, t_n (D(w_1, F(t_1, \ldots, t_n)) = :F(D(w_1, t_1), \ldots, D(w_1, t_n)))$
if F is a rigid function.

Finally, we introduce a special axiom for the equality predicate of the object language, fixing its interpretation in all possible worlds to be the identity relation:

L13. $\forall w_1, t_1, t_2 (T(w_1, EQ(t_1, t_2)) \equiv (D(w_1, t_1) = D(w_1, t_2)))$

3.2 A First-Order Theory of Knowledge

The axioms given in the preceding section allow us to talk about a formula of first-order logic being true relative to a possible world rather than absolutely. This generalization would be pointless, however, if we never had occasion to mention any possible worlds other than the actual one. References to other possible worlds are introduced by our axioms for knowledge:

K1. $\forall w_1, t_1, p_1$
$(T(w_1, KNOW(t_1, p_1)) \equiv \forall w_2 (K(D(w_1, t_1), w_1, w_2) \supset T(w_2, p_1)))$

K2. $\forall a_1, w_1 (K(a_1, w_1, w_1))$

K3. $\forall a_1, w_1, w_2 (K(a_1, w_1, w_2) \supset \forall w_3 (K(a_1, w_2, w_3) \supset K(a_1, w_1, w_3)))$

K1 gives the possible-world analysis for object language formulas of the form KNOW(A,P). The interpretation is that KNOW(A,P) is true in world W_1 just in case P is true in every world that is compatible with what the agent denoted by A in W_1 knows in W_1. Since an object language term may denote different individuals in different possible worlds, we use $D(W_1, A)$ to identify the denotation of A in W_1. K represents the accessibility relation associated with KNOW, so $K(D(W_1, A), W_1, W_2)$ is how we represent the fact W_2 is compatible with what the agent denoted by A in W_1 knows in W_1.

As we pointed out before, the principle embodied in K1 is that an agent knows everything entailed by his knowledge. Since this is too strong a generalization, in a more thorough analysis we would regard the inference from the right side of K1 to the left side as being a default inference. K2 and K3 state constraints on the accessibility relation K that we use to capture other properties of knowledge. They require that, for a fixed agent :A, $K(:A, w_1, w_2)$ be reflexive and transitive. We have already shown this entails that anything that anyone knows must be true, and that if someone knows something he knows that he knows it. Finally, the fact that K1–K3 are asserted to hold for all possible worlds implies that everyone knows the principles they embody, and everyone knows that everyone knows, etc. In other words, these principles are common knowledge.

To illustrate how our theory operates, we will show how to derive a simple result in the logic of knowledge, that from the premises that A knows that P(B) and A knows that B = C, we can conclude that A knows that P(C). Our proofs will be in natural-deduction form. The axioms and preceding lines that justify each step will be given to the right of the step. Subordinate proofs will be indicated by indented sections, and ASS will mark the assumptions on which these subordinate proofs are based. DIS(N,M) will indicate the discharge of the assumption on line N with respect to the conclusion on line M. The general pattern of proofs in this system will be to assert the object language premises of the problem, transform them into their metalanguage equivalents, using axioms L1–L13 and K1, then derive the meta-language version of the conclusion using first-order logic and axioms such as K2 and K3, and finally transform the conclusion back into the object language, again using L1–L13 and K1.

Given: TRUE(KNOW(A,P(B)))
         TRUE(KNOW(A,EQ(B,C)))
Prove: TRUE(KNOW(A,P(C)))

1.	TRUE(KNOW(A,P(B)))	Given
2.	$T(W_0,KNOW(A,P(B)))$	L1,1
3.	$K(D(W_0,A),W_0,w_1) \supset T(w_1,P(B))$	K1,2
4.	$K(:A(W_0),W_0,w_1) \supset T(w_1,P(B))$	L11,3
5.	TRUE(KNOW(A,EQ(B,C)))	Given
6.	$T(W_0,KNOW(A,EQ(B,C)))$	L1,5
7.	$K(D(W_0,A),W_0,w_1) \supset T(w_1,EQ(B,C))$	K1,6
8.	$K(:A(W_0),W_0,w_1) \supset T(w_1,EQ(B,C))$	L11,7
9.	$\quad K(:A(W_0),W_0,w_1)$	ASS
10.	$\quad T(w_1,P(B))$	4,9
11.	$\quad :P(w_1,D(w_1,B))$	L9,10
12.	$\quad :P(w_1,:B(w_1))$	L11,11
13.	$\quad T(w_1,EQ(B,C))$	8,9
14.	$\quad D(w_1,B) = D(w_1,C)$	L13,13
15.	$\quad :B(w_1) = :C(w_1)$	L11,14
16.	$\quad :P(w_1,:C(w_1))$	12,15
17.	$\quad :P(w_1,D(w_1,C))$	L11,16
18.	$\quad T(w_1,P(C))$	L9,17

19. $K(:A(W_0),W_0,w_1) \supset T(w_1,P(C))$ DIS(9,18)

20. $K(D(W_0,A),W_0,w_1) \supset T(w_1,P(C))$ L11,19

21. $T(W_0,KNOW(A,P(C)))$ K1,20

22. $TRUE(KNOW(A,P(C)))$ L1,21

A knows that P(B) (Line 1), so P(B) is true in every world compatible with what A knows (Line 4). Similarly, since A knows that B = C (Line 5), B = C is true in every world compatible with what A knows (Line 8). Let w_1 be one of these worlds (Line 9). P(B) and B = C must be true in w_1 (Lines 12 and 15), hence P(C) must be true in w_1 (Line 16). Therefore, P(C) is true in every world compatible with what A knows (Line 19), so A knows that P(C) (Line 22). If TRUE(EQ(B,C)) had been given instead of TRUE(KNOW(A,EQ(B,C))), we would have had B = C true in W_0 instead of w_1. In that case, the substitution of C for B in P(B) (Line 16) would not have been valid, and we could not have concluded that A knows that P(C). This proof seems long because we have made each routine step a separate line. This is worth doing once to illustrate all the formal details, but in subsequent examples we will combine some of the routine steps to shorten the derivation.

4 A Possible-World Analysis of Action

In the preceding sections, we have presented a framework for describing what someone knows in terms of possible worlds. To characterize the relation of knowledge to action, we need a theory of action in these same terms. Fortunately, the standard way of looking at actions in AI gives us just that sort of theory. Most AI programs that reason about actions are based on a view of the world as a set of possible states of affairs, with each action determining a binary relation between states of affairs—one being the outcome of performing the action in the other. We can integrate our analysis of knowledge with this view of action by identifying the possible worlds used to describe knowledge with the possible states of affairs used to describe actions.

The identification of a possible world, as used in the analysis of knowledge, with the state of affairs at a particular time does not require any changes in the formalization already presented, but it does require a reinterpretation of what the axioms mean. If the variables w_1, w_2,... are reinterpreted as ranging over states of affairs, then "A knows that P" will be analyzed roughly as "P is true in every state of affairs that is compatible with what A knows in the actual state of affairs." It might seem that taking possible worlds to be states of affairs, and therefore not extended in time, might make it difficult to talk about what someone knows regarding the past or future. That is not the case, however. Knowledge about the past and future can be handled by modal tense operators, with corresponding accessibility relations between possible states-of-affairs/worlds. We could have a tense operator FUTURE such that FUTURE(P) means that P will be true at some time to come. If we let F be an accessibility relation such that $F(W_1,W_2)$ means that the state-of-affairs/world W_2 lies in the future of the state-of-affairs/world W_1, then we can define FUTURE(P) to be true in W_1 just in case there is some W_2 such that $F(W_1,W_2)$ holds and P is true in W_2.

This much is standard tense logic (e.g., Rescher & Urquhart, 1971). The interesting point is that statements about someone's knowledge of the future work out correctly, even though such knowledge is analyzed in terms of alternatives to a state of affairs, rather than alternatives to a possible world containing an entire course of events. The proposition that John knows that P will be true is represented simply by KNOW(JOHN,FUTURE(P)). The analysis of this is that FUTURE(P) is true in every state of affairs that is compatible with what John knows, from which it follows that, for each state of affairs that is compatible with what John knows, P is true in some future alternative to that state of affairs. An important point to note here is that two states of affairs can be "internally" similar (that is, they coincide in the truth-value assigned to any nonmodal statement), yet be distinct because they differ in the accessibility relations they bear to other possible states of affairs. Thus, although we treat a possible world as a state of affairs rather than a course of events, it is a state of affairs in the particular course of events defined by its relationships to other states of affairs.

For planning and reasoning about future actions, instead of a tense operator like FUTURE, which simply asserts what will be true, we need an operator that describes what would be true if a certain event occurred. Our approach will be to recast McCarthy's situation calculus (McCarthy, 1968; McCarthy & Hayes, 1969) so that it meshes with our possible-world characterization of knowledge. The situation calculus is a first-order language in which predicates that can vary in truth-value over time are given an extra argument to indicate what situations (i.e., states of affairs) they hold in, with a function RESULT that maps an agent, an action, and a situation into the situation that results from the agent's performance of the action in the first situation. Statements about the effects of actions are then expressed by formulas like P(RESULT(A,ACT,S)), which means that P is true in the situation that results from A's performing ACT in situation S.

To integrate these ideas into our logic of knowledge, we will reconstruct the situation calculus as a modal logic. In parallel to the operator KNOW for talking about knowledge, we introduce an object language operator RES for talking about the results of events. Situations will not be referred to explicitly in the object language, but they will reappear in the possible-world semantics for RES in the metalanguage. RES will be a two-place operator whose first argument is a term denoting an event, and whose second argument is a formula. RES(E,P) will mean that it is possible for the event denoted by E to occur and that, if it did, the formula P would then be true. The possible-world semantics for RES will be specified in terms of an accessibility relation R, parallel to K, such that $R(:E,W_1.W_2)$ means that W_2 is the situation/world that would result from the event :E happening in W_1.

We assume that, if it is impossible for :E to happen in W_1 (i.e., if the prerequisites of :E are not satisfied), then there is no W_2 such that $R(:E,W_1,W_2)$ holds. Otherwise we assume that there is exactly one W_2 such that $(:E,W_1,W_2)$ holds:[4]

R1. $\forall w_1,w_2,w_3,e_1((R(e_1,w_1,w_2) \wedge R(e_1,w_1,w_3)) \supset (w_2 = w_3))$

(Variables e_1, e_2,... range over events.) Given these assumptions, RES(E,P) will be true in a situation/world W_1 just in case there is some W_2 that is the situation/world that results from the event described by E happening in W_1, and in which P is true:

R2. $\forall w_1,t_1,p_1(T(w_1,RES(t_1,p_1)) \equiv \exists w_2(R(D(w_1,t_1),w_1,w_2) \wedge T(w_2,p_1)))$

The type of event we will normally be concerned with is the performance of an action by an agent. We will let DO(A,ACT) be a description of the event consisting of the agent denoted by A performing the action denoted by ACT.[5] (We will assume that the set of possible agents is the same as the set of possible knowers.) We will want DO(A,ACT) to be the standard way of referring to the event of A's carrying out the action ACT, so DO will be a rigid function. Hence, DO(A,ACT) will be a rigid designator of an event if A is a rigid designator of an agent and ACT a rigid designator of an action.

Many actions can be thought of as general procedures applied to particular objects. Such a general procedure will be represented by a function that maps the objects to which the procedure is applied into the action of applying the procedure to those objects. For instance, if DIAL represents the general procedure of dialing combinations of safes, SF a safe, and COMB(SF) the combination of SF, then DIAL(COMB(SF),SF) represents the action of dialing the combination COMB(SF) on the safe SF, and DO(A,DIAL(COMB(SF),SF)) represents the event of A's dialing the combination COMB(SF) on the safe SF.

This formalism gives us the ability to describe an agent's knowledge of the effects of carrying out an action. In the object language, we can express the claim that A_1 knows that P would result from A_2's doing ACT by saying that KNOW(A_1,RES(DO(A_2,ACT),P)) is true. The possible-world analysis of this statement is that, for every world compatible with what A_1 knows in the actual

---

[4] This amounts to an assumption that all events are deterministic, which might seem to be an unnecessary limitation. From a pragmatic standpoint, however, it doesn't matter whether we say that a given event is nondeterministic, or we say that it is deterministic but no one knows precisely what the outcome will be. If we treated events as being nondeterministic, we could say that an agent knows exactly what situation he is in, but, because :E is nondeterministic, he doesn't know what situation would result if :E occurs. It would be completely equivalent, however, to say that :E is deterministic, and that the agent *does not* know exactly what situation he is in because he doesn't know what the result of :E would be in that situation.

[5] It would be more precise to say that DO(A,ACT) names a *type* of event rather than an individual event, since an agent can perform the same action on different occasions. We would then say that RES and R apply to event types. We will let the present usage stand, however, since we have no need to distinguish event types from individual events in this paper.

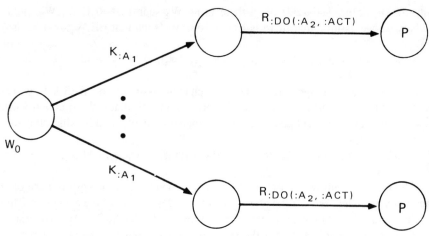

Figure 5. TRUE(KNOW(A₁,RES(DO(A₂,ACT),P))) ≡
$$\forall w_1(K(:A_1,W_0,w_1) \supset$$
$$\exists w_2(R(:DO(:A_2ACT),w_1,w_2) \wedge T(w_2,P)))$$

world, there is a world that is the result of A_2's doing ACT and in which P is true (see Figure 5). Formally, this is expressed by

$$\forall w_1(K(:A_1,W_0,w_1) \supset \exists w_2(R(:DO(:A_2,:ACT),w_1,w_2) \wedge T(w_2,P))),$$

if we assume that A_1,A_2, and ACT are rigid designators.

In addition to simple, one-step actions, we will want to talk about complex combinations of actions. We will therefore introduce expressions into the object language for action sequences, conditionals, and iteration. If P is a formula, and ACT_1 and ACT_2 are action descriptions, then $(ACT_1; ACT_2)$, IF(P,ACT$_1$,ACT$_2$), and WHILE(P,ACT$_1$) will also be action descriptions. Roughly speaking, $(ACT_1; ACT_2)$ describes the sequence of actions consisting of ACT_1 followed by ACT_2. IF(P,ACT$_1$,ACT$_2$) describes the conditional action of doing ACT_1 if P is true, otherwise doing ACT_2. WHILE(P,ACT$_1$) describes the iterative action of repeating ACT_1 as long as P is true.

Defining denotations for these complex action descriptions is somewhat problematical. The difficulty comes from the fact that, whenever we have an action described as a sequence of subactions, any expression used in specifying one of the subactions needs to be interpreted relative to the situation in which that subaction is carried out. For instance, if PUTON(X,Y) denotes the action of putting X on Y, STACK denotes a stack of blocks, TABLE denotes a table, and TOP picks out the top block of a stack, we would want the execution of

(PUTON(TOP(STACK),TABLE); PUTON(TOP(STACK),TABLE))

to result in what were initially the top two blocks of the stack being put on the table, rather than what was initially the top block being put on the table twice. The second occurrence of TOP(STACK) should be interpreted with respect to the situation in which the first block has already been removed. The problem is that, in general, what situation exists after one step of a sequence of actions has been executed depends on who the agent is. If John picks up a certain block, *he* will be holding the block; if, however, Mary performs the same action, *she* will be holding the block. If an action description refers to "the block Mary is holding," exactly which block it is may depend on which agent is carrying out the action, but this is not specified by the action description.

One way of getting around these difficulties conceptually would be to treat actions as functions from agents to events, but notational problems would remain nevertheless. We will therefore choose a different solution: treating complex actions as "virtual individuals" (Scott, 1970), or pseudoentities. That is, complex action descriptions will not be treated as referring expressions in themselves, but only as component parts of more complex referring expressions. In particular, if ACT is a complex action description (and A denotes an agent), we will treat the event description DO(A,ACT), but not ACT itself, as having a denotation. Complex action descriptions will be permitted to occur only as part of such event descriptions, and we will define the denotations of the event descriptions in a way that eliminates reference to complex actions. We will, however, continue to treat actions as real entities that can be quantified over, and simple action descriptions such as DIAL(COMB(SF),SF) will still be considered to denote actions.

The denotations of event descriptions formed from conditional and iterative action descriptions can be defined as follows in terms of the denotations of event descriptions formed from action sequence descriptions:

R3. $\forall w_1,t_1,t_2,t_3,p_1$
$((T(w_1,p_1) \supset (D(w_1,DO(t_1,IF(p_1,t_2,t_3))) = D(w_1,DO(t_1,t_2)))) \wedge$
$(\neg T(w_1,p_1) \supset (D(w_1,DO(t_1,IF(p_1,t_2,t_3))) = D(w_1,DO(t_1,t_3)))))$

R4. $\forall w_1,t_1,t_2,p_1$
$(D(w_1,DO(t_1,WHILE(p_1,t_2))) =$
$D(w_1,DO(t_1,IF(p_1,(t_2; WHILE(p_1,t_2)),NIL)))$

R3 says that performing the conditional action IF(P,ACT$_1$,ACT$_2$) results in the same event as carrying out ACT$_1$ in a situation where P is true or carrying out ACT$_2$ in a situation where P is false. R4 says that performing WHILE(P,ACT) always results in the same event as IF(P,(ACT; WHILE(P,ACT)),NIL), where NIL denotes the null action. In other words, doing WHILE(P,ACT) is equivalent to doing ACT followed by WHILE(P,ACT) if P is true, otherwise doing nothing—i.e., doing ACT as long as P remains true.

To define the denotation of events that consist of carrying out action sequences, we need some notation for talking about sequences of events. First, we will let ";" be a polymorphic operator in the object language, creating descriptions of event sequences in addition to action sequences. Speaking informally, if E$_1$ and E$_2$ are event descriptions, then (E$_1$; E$_2$) names the event sequence consisting of E$_1$ followed by E$_2$, just as (ACT$_1$; ACT$_2$) names the action sequence consisting of ACT$_1$

followed by ACT_2. In the metalanguage, event sequences will be indicated with angle brackets, so that $\langle :E_1, :E_2 \rangle$ will mean $:E_1$ followed by $:E_2$. The denotations of expressions involving action and event sequences are then defined by the following axioms:

R5. $\forall w_1, t_1, t_2, t_3$
$(D(w_1, DO(t_1, (t_2; t_3)))) = D(w_1, (DO(t_1, t_2); DO(@(D(w_1, t_1)), t_3))))$

R6. $\forall w_1, w_2, t_1, t_2$
$(R(D(w_1, t_1)), w_1, w_2) \supset (D(w_1, (t_1; t_2)) = \langle D(w_1, t_1), D(w_2, t_2) \rangle))$

R5 says that the event consisting of an agent A's performance of the action sequence ACT_1 followed by ACT_2 is simply the event sequence that consists of A's carrying out ACT_1 followed by his carrying out ACT_2. Note that, in the description of the second event, the agent is picked out by the expression $@(D(w_1, A))$, which guarantees that we get the same agent as in the first event, in case the original term picking out the agent changes its denotation after the first event has happened. R6 then defines the denotation of an event sequence description $(E_1; E_2)$ as the sequence comprising the denotation of E_1 in the original situation followed by the denotation of E_2 in the situation resulting from the occurrence of E_1. If there is no situation that results from the occurrence of E_1, we leave the denotation of $(E_1; E_2)$ undefined.

Finally, we need to define the accessibility relation R for event sequences and for events in which the null action is carried out.

R7. $\forall w_1, w_2, e_1, e_2$
$(R(\langle e_1, e_2 \rangle, w_1, w_2) \equiv \exists w_3(R(e_1, w_1, w_3) \wedge (Re_2, w_3, w_2)))$

R8. $\forall w_1, a_1(R(:DO(a_1, :NIL), w_1, w_1))$

R7 says that a situation W_2 is the result of the event sequence $\langle E_2, E_2 \rangle$ occurring in W_1 if and only if there is a situation W_3 such that W_3 is the result of E_1 occurring in W_1, and W_2 is the result of E_2 occurring in W_2.[6] We will regard NIL as a rigid designator in the object language for the null action, so :NIL will be its metalanguage counterpart. R8, therefore, says that in any situation the result of doing nothing is the same situation.

5 An Integrated Theory of Knowledge and Action

5.1 The Dependence of Action on Knowledge
As we pointed out in the introduction, knowledge and action interact in two principal ways: (a) knowledge is often required prior to taking action; (b) actions can

---

[6] R7 guarantees that the sequences $<<E_1, E_2>, E_3>$ and $<E_1, <E_2, E_3>>$ always define the same accessibility relation on situations; so, just as one would expect, we can regard sequence operators as being associative. Thus, when we have a sequence of more than two events or actions, we will not feel obliged to indicate a pairwise grouping.

change what is known. In regard to the first, we need to consider knowledge prerequisites as well as physical prerequisites for actions. Our main thesis is that the knowledge prerequisites for an action can be analyzed as a matter of knowing what action to take. Recall the example of trying to open a locked safe. Why is it that, for an agent to achieve this goal by using the plan "Dial the combination of the safe," he must know the combination? The reason is that an agent could know that dialing the combination of the safe would result in the safe's being open, but still not know what to do because he does not know what the combination of the safe is. A similar analysis applies to knowing a telephone number in order to call someone on the telephone or knowing a password in order to gain access to a computer system.

It is important to realize that even mundane actions that are not usually thought of as requiring any special knowledge are no different from the examples just cited. For instance, none of the AI problem-solving systems that have dealt with the blocks world have tried to take into account whether the robot possesses sufficient knowledge to be able to move block A to point B. Yet, if a command were phrased as "Move my favorite block back to its original position," the system could be just as much in the dark as with "Dial the combination of the safe." If the system does not know what actions satisfy the description, it will not be able to carry out the command. The only reason that the question of knowledge seems more pertinent in the case of dialing combinations and telephone numbers is that, in the contexts in which these actions naturally arise, there is usually no presumption that the agent knows what action fits the description. An important consequence of this view is that the specification of an action will normally not need to include anything about knowledge prerequisites. These will be supplied by a general theory of using actions to achieve goals. What we will need to specify are the conditions under which an agent knows what action is referred to by an action description.

In our possible-world semantics for knowledge, the usual way of knowing what entity is referred to by a description B is by having some description C that is a rigid designator, and by knowing that B = C. (Note, that if B itself is a rigid designator, it can be used for C.) In particular, knowing what action is referred to by an action description means having a rigid designator for the action described. But, if this is all the knowledge that is required for carrying out the action, then a rigid designator for an action must be an *executable description* of the action—in the same sense that a computer program is an executable description of a computation to an interpreter for the language in which the program is written.

Often the actions we want to talk about are mundane general procedures that we would be willing to assume everyone knows how to perform. Dialing a telephone number or the combination of a safe is a typical example. In many of these cases, if an agent knows the general procedure and what objects the procedure is to be applied to, then he knows everything that is relevant to the task. In such cases, the function that represents the general procedure will be a rigid function, so that, if the arguments of the function are rigid designators, the term consisting of the function applied to the arguments will be a rigid designator. Hence, knowing what objects the arguments denote will amount to knowing what action the term refers to. We will treat dialing the combination of a safe, or dialing a telephone number as being this type of procedure. That is, we assume that anyone who knows what combination he is to dial and what safe he is to dial it on thereby knows what action he is to perform.

There are other procedures we might also wish to assume that anyone could perform, but that cannot be represented as rigid functions. Suppose that, in the blocks world, we let PUTON(B,C) denote the action of putting B on C. Even though we would not want to question anyone's ability to perform PUTON in general, knowing what objects B and C are will not be sufficient to perform PUTON(B,C); knowing *where* they are is also necessary. We could have a special axiom stating that knowing what action PUTON(B,C) is requires knowing where B and C are, but this will be superfluous if we simply assume that everyone knows the definition of PUTON in terms of more primitive actions. If we define PUTON(X,Y) as something like

    (MOVEHAND(LOCATION(X)));
     GRASP;
     MOVEHAND(LOCATION(TOP(Y)));
     UNGRASP),

then we can treat MOVEHAND, GRASP, and UNGRASP as rigid functions, and we can see that executing PUTON requires knowing where the two objects are because their locations are mentioned in the definition. So, although PUTON itself is not a rigid function, we can avoid having a special axiom stating what the knowledge prerequisites of PUTON are by defining PUTON as a sequence of actions represented by rigid functions.

To formalize this theory, we will introduce a new object language operator CAN. CAN(A,ACT,P) will mean that A can achieve P by performing ACT, in the sense that A knows how to achieve P by performing ACT. We will not give a possible-world semantics for CAN directly; instead we will give a definition of CAN in terms of KNOW and RES, which we can use in reasoning about CAN to transform a problem into terms of possible worlds.

In the simplest case, an agent A can achieve P by performing ACT if he knows what action ACT is, and he knows that P would be true as a result of his performing ACT. In the object language, we can express this fact by

$$\forall a(\exists x(KNOW(a,((x = ACT) \wedge RES(DO(a,ACT),P))))) \supset$$
$$CAN(a,ACT,P)).$$

We cannot strengthen this assertion to a biconditional, however, because that would be too stringent a definition of CAN for complex actions. It would require the agent to know from the very beginning of his action exactly what he is going to do at every step. In carrying out a complex action, though, an agent may take some initial action that results in his acquiring knowledge about what to do later.

For an agent to be able to achieve a goal by performing a complex action, all that is really neccessary is that he know what to do first, and that he know that he will know what to do at each subsequent step. So, for any action descriptions ACT and ACT_1, the following formula also states a condition under which an agent can achieve P by performing ACT:

$$\forall a(\exists x(KNOW(a,((DO(a,(x;\ ACT_1)) = DO(a,ACT))\ \wedge$$
$$RES(DO(a,x),CAN(a,ACT_1,P))))) \supset$$
$$CAN(a,ACT,P)).$$

This says that A can achieve P by doing ACT if there is an action X such that A knows that his execution of the sequence X followed by ACT_1 would be equivalent to his doing ACT, and that his doing X would result in his being able to achieve P by doing ACT_1.

Finally, with the following metalanguage axiom we can state that these are the only two conditions under which an agent can use a particular action to achieve a goal:

C1. $\forall w_1,t_1,t_2,t_3,p_1$
$\quad ((t_2 = @(D(w_1,t_1))) \supset$
$\quad (T(w_1,CAN(t_1,t_3,p_1)) \equiv$
$\quad (T(w_1,EXIST(X,KNOW(t_1,AND(EQ(X,t_3),RES(DO(t_2,\ t_3),p_1))))))V$
$\quad \exists t_4(T(w_1,\ EXIST(X,KNOW(t_1,AND(EQ(DO(t_2,(X;\ t_4)),DO(t_2,t_3)),$
$\quad\quad\quad RES(DO(t_2,X),$
$\quad\quad\quad\quad CAN(t_2,t_4,p_1)))))))))))$

Letting $t_1 = A$, $t_2 = A_1$, and $t_3 = ACT$, C1 says that, for any formula P, if A_1 is the standard identifier of the agent denoted by A, then A can achieve P by doing ACT if and only if one of the following conditions is met: (a) A knows what action ACT is and knows that P would be true as a result of A_1's (i.e., his) doing ACT, or (b) there is an action description $t_4 = ACT_1$ such that, for some action X, A knows that A_1's doing X followed by ACT_1 is the same event as his doing ACT and knows that A_1's doing X would result his being able to achieve P by doing ACT_1.

As a simple illustration of these concepts, we will show how to derive the fact that an agent can open a safe, given the premise that he knows the combination. To do this, the only additional fact we need is that, if an agent does dial the correct combination of a safe, the safe will then be open:

D1. $\forall w_1,a_1,x_1$
$\quad (:SAFE(x_1) \supset$
$\quad \exists w_2(R(:DO(a_1,:DIAL(:COMB(w_1,x_1),x_1)),w_1,w_2)\ \wedge$
$\quad :OPEN(w_2,x_1)))$

D1 says that, for any possible world W_1, any agent :A, and any safe :SF, there is a world W_2 that is the result of :A's dialing the combination of :SF on :SF in W_1, and in which :SF is open. The important point about this axiom, is that the function :COMB (which picks out the combination to a safe) depends on what possible world it is evaluated in, while :DIAL (the function that maps a combination and a safe into the action of dialing the combination on the safe) does not. Thus we are implicitly assuming that, given a particular safe, there may be some doubt as to what its combination is, but, given a combination and a safe, there exists no possible doubt as to what action dialing the combination on the safe is. (We also simplify matters by omitting the possible world-argument to :SAFE, so as to avoid raising the question of knowing whether something is a safe.) Since this axiom is asserted to hold for all possible worlds, we are in effect assuming that it is common knowledge.

Now we show that, for any safe, if the agent A knows its combination, he can open the safe by dialing that combination; or, more precisely, for all X, if X is a safe and there is some Y, such that A knows that Y is the combination of X, then A can open X by dialing the combination of X on X:

Prove: TRUE(ALL(X,IMP(AND(SAFE(X),
                         EXIST(Y,KNOW(A,EQ(Y,COMB(X)))))),
                    CAN(A,DIAL(COMB(X),X),OPEN(X)))))

1. $T(W_0,$
    $AND(SAFE(@(x_1),$
    $EXIST(Y,KNOW(A,EQ(Y,COMB(@(x_1)))))))))$ ASS

2. $:SAFE(x_1)$ 1,L2,L9

3. $\forall w_1(K(:A(W_0),W_0,w_1) \supset$ 1,L2,L7,K1,L11,
    $(:C = :COMB(w_1,x_1)))$ L13,L10,L12

4. $K(:A(W_0),W_0,w_1)$ ASS

5. $:C = COMB(w_1,x_1)$ 3,4

6. $:DIAL(:C,x_1) = :DIAL(:COMB(w_1,x_1),x_1)$ 5

7. $T(w_1,$ L10,L12,L12a,L13
    $EQ(@(:DIAL(:C,x_1)),$
    $DIAL(COMB(@(x_1)),@(x_1))))$

8. $\exists w_2(R(:DO(:A(W_0),$ 2,D1
    $:DIAL(:COMB(w_1,x_1),x_1)),$
    $w_1,w_2) \wedge$
    $:OPEN(w_2,x_1)))$

9. $T(w_1,$ L11,L10,L12a,L9,R2
    $RES(DO(@(D(W_0,A)),$
    $DIAL(COMB(@(x_1)),@(x_1))),$
    $OPEN(@(x_1))))$

10. $T(w_1,$ 7,9,L2
    $AND(EQ(@(:DIAL(:C,x_1)),$
    $DIAL(COMB(@(x_1)),@(x_1))),$
    $RES(DO(@(D(W_0,A)),$
    $DIAL(COMB(@(x_1)),@(x_1))),$
    $OPEN(@(x_1)))))$

11. $K(:A(W_0),W_0,w_1) \supset$ DIS(4,10)
    $T(w_1,$
        $AND(EQ(@(:DIAL(:C,x_1)),$
                $DIAL(COMB(@(x_1)),@(x_1))),$
            $RES(DO(@(D(W_0,A)),$
                $DIAL(COMB(@(x_1)),@(x_1))),$
            $OPEN(@(x_1)))))$

12. $T(W_0,$ 11,L11,K1
    $KNOW(A,$
        $AND(EQ(@(:DIAL(:C,x_1)),$
                $DIAL(COMB(@(x_1)),@(x_1))),$
            $RES(DO(@(D(W_0,A)),$
                $DIAL(COMB(@(x_1)),@(x_1))),$
            $OPEN(@(x_1))))))$

13. $T(W_0,$ 12,L7
    $EXIST(X,$
        $KNOW(A,$
            $AND(EQ(X,$
                $DIAL(COMB(@(x_1)),$
                    $@(x_1))),$
                $RES(DO(@(D(W_0,A)),$
                    $DIAL(COMB(@(x_1)),$
                      $@(x_1))),$
                $OPEN(@(x_1)))))$

14. $T(W_0,$ 13,C1
    $CAN(A,$
        $DIAL(COMB(@(x_1)),@(x_1)),$
        $OPEN(@(x_1))))$

15. $T(W_0,$ DIS(1,14)
    $AND(SAFE(@(x_1)),$
        $EXIST(Y,KNOW(A,EQ(Y,COMB(@(x_1)))))))) \supset$
    $T(W_0,$
        $CAN(A,DIAL(COMB(@(x_1)),@(x_1)),OPEN(@(x_1))))$

16. $TRUE(ALL(X,$ 15,L4,L8,L1
        $IMP(AND(SAFE(X),$
               $EXIST(Y,$
                  $KNOW(A,$
                      $EQ(Y,COMB(X))))))$
        $CAN(A,DIAL(COMB(X),X),OPEN(X))))$

Suppose that x_1 is a safe and there is some C that A knows to be the combination of x_1 (Lines 1–3). Suppose w_1 is a world that is compatible with what A knows in the actual world, W_0 (Line 4). Then C is the combination of x_1 in w_1 (Line 5), so dialing C on x_1 is the same action as dialing the combination of x_1 on x_1 in w_1 (Lines 6 and 7). By axiom D1, A's dialing the combination of x_1 on x_1 in w_1 will result in x_1's being open (Lines 8 and 9). Since w_1 was an arbitrarily chosen world compatible with what A knows in W_0, it follows that in W_0 A knows dialing C on x_1 to be the act of dialing the combination of x_1 on x_1 and that his dialing the combination of x_1 on x_1 will result in x_1's being open (Lines 10–12). Hence, A knows what action dialing the combination of x_1 on x_1 is, and that his dialing the combination of x_1 on x_1 will result in x_1's being open (Line 13). Therefore A can open x_1 by dialing the combination of x_1 on x_1, provided that x_1 is a safe and he knows the combination of x_1 (Lines 14 and 15). Finally, since x_1 was chosen arbitrarily, we conclude that A can open any safe by dialing the combination, provided he knows the combination (Line 16).

5.2 The Effects of Action on Knowledge

In describing the effects of an action on what an agent knows, we will distinguish actions that give the agent new information from those that do not. Actions that provide an agent with new information will be called *informative* actions. An action is informative if an agent would know more about the situation resulting from his performing the action after performing it than before performing it. In the blocks world, looking inside a box could be an informative action, but moving a block would probably not, because an agent would normally know no more after moving the block than he would before moving it. In the real world there are probably no actions that are never informative, because all physical processes are subject to variation and error. Nevertheless, it seems clear that we do and should treat many actions as noninformative from the standpoint of planning.

Even if an action is not informative in the sense we have just defined, performing the action will still alter the agent's state of knowledge. If the agent is aware of his action, he will know that it has been performed. As a result, the tense and modality of many of the things he knows will change. For example, if before performing the action he knows that P is true, then after performing the action he will know that P was true before he performed the action. Similarly, if before performing the action he knows that P would be true after performing the action, then afterwards he will know that P is true.

We can represent this very elegantly in terms of possible worlds. Suppose :A is an agent and :E_1 an event that consists in :A's performing some noninformative action. For any possible worlds W_1 and W_2 such that W_2 is the result of :E_1's happening in W_1, the worlds that are compatible with what :A knows in W_2 are exactly the worlds that are the result of :E_1's happening in some world that is compatible with what :A knows in W_1. In formal terms, this is

$$\forall w_1, w_2(R(:E, w_1, w_2) \supset$$
$$\forall w_3(K(:A, w_2, w_3) \equiv \exists w_4(K(:A, w_1, w_4) \land R(:E, w_4, w_3)))),$$

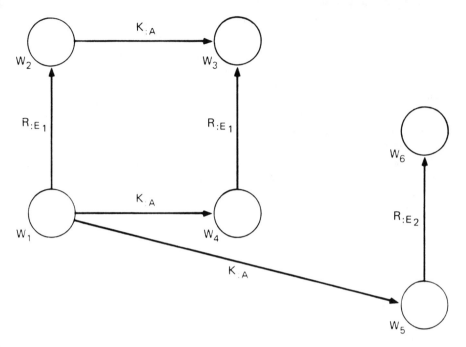

Figure 6. The Effect of a Noninformative Action on the Agent's Knowledge

which tells us exactly how what :A knows after :E_1 happens is related to what :A knows before :E_1 happens.

We can try to get some insight into this analysis by studying Figure 6. Sequences of possible situations connected by events can be thought of as possible courses of events. If W_1 is an actual situation in which :E_1 occurs, thereby producing W_2, then W_1 and W_2 comprise a subsequence of the actual course of events. Now we can ask what other courses of events are compatible with what :A knows in W_1 and in W_2. Suppose that W_4 and W_3 are connected by :E_1 in a course of events that is compatible with what :A knows in W_1. Since :E_1 is not informative for :A, the only sense in which his knowledge is increased by :E_1 is that he knows that :E_1 has occurred. Since :E_1 occurs at the corresponding place in the course of events that includes W_4 and W_3, this course of events will still be compatible with everything :A knows in W_2. However, the appropriate "tense shift" takes place. In W_1, W_4 is a possible alternative present for :A, and W_3 is a possible alternative future. In W_2, W_3 is a possible alternative present for :A, and W_4 is a possible alternative past.

Next consider a different course of events that includes W_5 and W_6 connected by a different event, :E_2. This course of events might be compatible with what :A knows in W_1 if he is not certain what he will do next, but, after :E_1 has happened and he knows that it has happened, this course of events is no longer compatible with what he knows. Thus, W_6 is not compatible with what :A knows in W_2. We can see, then, that even actions that provide the agent with no new information from

the outside world still filter out for him those courses of events in which he would
have performed actions other than those he actually did.

The idea of a filter on possible courses of events also provides a good picture of
informative actions. With these actions, though, the filter is even stronger, since
they not only filter out courses of events that differ from the actual course of events
as to what event has just occurred, but they also filter out courses of events that are
incompatible with the information furnished by the action. Suppose :E is an event
that consists in :A's performing an informative action, such that the information
gained by the agent is whether the formula P is true. For any possible worlds W_1
and W_2 such that W_2 is the result of :E's happening in W_1, the worlds that are
compatible with what :A knows in W_2 are exactly those worlds that are the result of
:E's happening in some world that is compatible with what :A knows in W_1, *and in
which P has the same truth-value as in* W_2:

$$\forall w_1,w_2(R(:E,w_1,w_2) \supset$$
$$\forall w_3(K(:A,w_2,w_3) \equiv (\exists w_4(K(:A,w_1,w_4) \wedge R(:E,w_4,w_3)) \wedge$$
$$(T(w_2,P) \equiv T(w_3,P)))))$$

It is this final condition that distinguishes informative actions from those that are
not.

Figure 7 illustrates this analysis. Suppose W_1 and W_2 are connected by :E and
are part of the actual course of events. Suppose, further, that P is true in W_2. Let W_4
and W_3 also be connected by :E, and let them be part of a course of events that is
compatible with what :A knows in W_1. If P is true in W_3 and the only thing :A
learns about the world from :E (other than that it has occurred) is whether P is true,
this course of events will then still be compatible with what :A knows after :E has
occurred. That is, W_3 will be compatible with what :A knows in W_2. Suppose, on
the other hand, that W_5 and W_6 form part of a similar course of events, except that P
is false in W_6. If :A does not know in W_1 whether P would be true after the
occurrence of :E, this course of events will also be compatible with what he knows
in W_1. After :E has occurred, however, he will know that P is true; consequently,
this course of events will no longer be compatible with what he knows. That is, W_6
will not be compatible with what :A knows in W_2.

It is an advantage of this approach to describing how an action affects what an
agent knows that not only do we specify what he learns from the action, but also
what he does not learn. Our analysis gives us necessary, as well as sufficient,
conditions for :A's knowing that P is true after event :E. In the case of an action that
is not informative, we can infer that, unless :A knows before performing the action
whether P would be true, he will not know afterwards either. In the case of an
informative action such that what is learned is whether Q is true, he will not know
whether P is true unless he does already—or knows of some dependence of P on Q.

Within the context of this possible-world analysis of the effects of action on
knowledge, we can formalize the requirements for a test that we presented in
Section I. Suppose that TEST is the action of testing the acidity of a particular

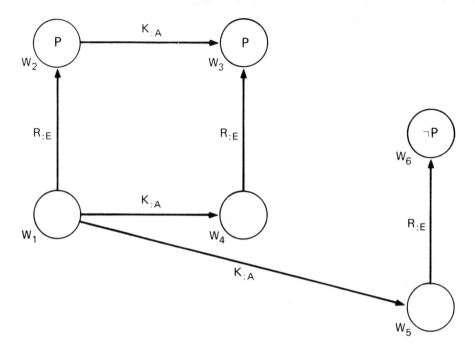

Figure 7. The Effect of an Informative Action on the Agent's Knowledge

solution with blue litmus paper, RED is a propositional constant (a predicate of zero arguments) whose truth depends on the color of the litmus paper, and ACID is a propositional constant whose truth depends on whether the solution is acidic. The relevent fact about TEST is that the paper will be red after an agent A performs the test if and only if the solution is acidic at the time the test is performed:

$$(ACID \supset RES(DO(A,TEST),RED)) \wedge$$
$$(\neg ACID \supset RES(DO(A,TEST),\neg RED))$$

In Section 1 we listed three conditions that ought to be sufficient for an agent to determine, by observing the outcome of a test, whether some unobservable precondition holds; in this case, for A to determine whether ACID is true by observing whether RED is true after TEST is performed:

(1) After A performs TEST, he knows whether RED is true.

(2) After A performs TEST, he knows that he has just performed TEST.

(3) A knows that RED will be true after TEST is performed just in case ACID was true before it was performed.

Conditions (1) and (2) will be satisfied if TEST is an informative action, such that the knowledge provided is whether RED is true in the resulting situation:

T1. $\forall w_1, w_2, a_1$
         $(R(:DO(a_1,:TEST), w_1, w_2) \supset$
         $\forall w_3(K(a_1, w_2, w_3) \equiv$
            $(\exists w_4(K(a_1, w_1, w_4) \wedge R(:DO(a_1,:TEST), w_4, w_3)) \wedge$
            $(:RED(w_2) \equiv :RED(w_3)))))$

If :RED and :TEST are the metalanguage analogues of RED and TEST, T1 says that for any possible worlds W_1 and W_2 such that W_2 is the result of an agent's performing TEST in W_1, the worlds that are compatible with what the agent knows in W_2 are exactly those that are the result of his performing TEST in some world that is compatible with what he knows in W_1, and in which RED has the same truth-value as in W_2. In other words, after performing TEST, the agent knows that he has done so and he knows whether RED is true in the resulting situation. As with our other axioms, the fact that it holds for all possible worlds makes it common knowledge.

Thus, A can use TEST to determine whether the solution is acid, provided that condition 1 is also satisfied. We can state this very succinctly if we make the further assumption that A knows that performing the test does not affect the acidity of the solution.[7] Given the axiom T1 for test, it is possible to show that

ACID $\supset$ RES(DO(A,TEST),KNOW(A,ACID)) and
$\neg$ ACID $\supset$ RES(DO(A,TEST),KNOW(A,$\neg$ ACID))

are true, provided that

KNOW(A,(ACID $\supset$ RES(DO(A,TEST),(ACID $\wedge$ RED)))) and
KNOW(A,($\neg$ ACID $\supset$ RES(DO(A,TEST),($\neg$ ACID $\wedge$ $\neg$ RED))))

are both true and A is a rigid designator. We will carry out the proof in one direction, showing that, if the solution is acidic, after the test has been conducted the agent will know that it is acidic.

Given: TRUE(KNOW(A,IMP(ACID,RES(DO(A,TEST),AND(ACID,RED)))))
          TRUE(KNOW(A,IMP(NOT(ACID),
                          RES(DO(A,TEST),
                                AND(NOT(ACID),NOT(RED))))))
          TRUE(ACID)
Prove: TRUE(RES(DO(A,TEST),KNOW(A,ACID)))

---

[7] We have to add this extra condition to be able to infer that the agent knows whether the solution *is* acidic, instead of merely that he knows whether it *was* acidic. The latter is a more general characteristic of tests, since it covers destructive as well as nondestructive tests. We have not, however, introduced any temporal operators into the object language that would allow us to make such a statement, although there would be no difficulty in stating the relevant conditions in the metalanguage. Indeed, this is precisely what is done by axioms such as T1.

1. $\forall w_1(K(:A,W_0,w_1) \supset$ Given,L1,L4,R2,
    $(:ACID(w_1) \supset$ L2,L9,L12,L11a
       $\exists w_2(R(:DO(:A,:TEST),w_1,w_2) \wedge$
          $:ACID(w_2) \wedge :RED(w_2))))$

2. $\forall w_1(K(:A,W_0,w_1) \supset$ Given,L1,L4,R2,L2,
    $(\neg :ACID(w_1) \supset$ L6,L9,L12,L11a
       $\exists w_2(R(:DO(:A,:TEST),w_1,w_2) \wedge$
          $\neg :ACID(w_2) \wedge \neg :RED(w_2))))$

3. $:ACID(W_0)$ L1,L9

4. $:ACID(W_0) \supset$ 1,K2
    $\exists w_2(R(:DO(:A,:TEST),W_0,w_2) \wedge$
      $:ACID(w_2) \wedge :RED(w_2))$

5. $R(:DO(:A,:TEST),W_0,W_1)$ 3,4

6. $:RED(W_1)$ 3,4

7. $\forall w_2(K(:A,W_1,w_2) \equiv$ 5,T1
    $(\exists w_3(K(:A,W_0,w_3) \wedge$
         $R(:DO(:A,:TEST),w_3,w_2)) \wedge$
    $(:RED(W_1) \equiv :RED(w_2))))$

8. $K(:A,W_1,w_2)$ ASS

9. $K(:A,W_0,W_3)$ 7,8

10. $R(:DO(:A,:TEST),W_3,w_2)$ 7,8

11. $:RED(W_1) \equiv :RED(w_2)$ 7,8

12. $:RED(w_2)$ 6,11

13. $\neg :ACID(W_3) \supset$ 2,9
    $\exists w_4(R(:DO(:A,:TEST),W_3,w_4) \wedge$
       $\neg :ACID(w_4) \wedge \neg :RED(w_4))$

14. $\neg :ACID(W_3)$ ASS

15. $R(:DO(:A,:TEST),W_3,W_4)$ 13,14

16. $\neg :RED(W_4)$ 13,14

17. $w_2 = W_4$ 15,R1

18. $\neg :RED(w_2)$ 16,17

19. FALSE   12,18

20. $:ACID(W_3)$ DIS(14,19)

21. $:ACID(W_3) \supset$ 1,9
    $\exists w_4(R(:DO(:A,:TEST),W_3,w_4) \wedge$
      $:ACID(w_4) \wedge :RED(w_4))$

22. $R(:DO(:A,:TEST),W_3,W_4)$ 20,21

23. $:ACID(W_4)$ 20,21

24. $w_2 = W_4$ 15,22

25. $:ACID(w_2)$ 23,24

26. $K(:A,W_1,w_2) \supset :ACID(w_2)$ DIS(8,25)

27. $R(:DO(:A,:TEST),W_0,W_1) \wedge$ 5,26
      $\forall w_2(K(:A,W_1,w_2) \supset :ACID(w_2))$

28. $TRUE(RES(DO(A,TEST),KNOW(A,ACID)))$ 27,L9,L11a,L12,
                                                           K2,R2,L1

The possible-world structure for this proof is depicted in Figure 8. Lines 1 and 2 translate the premises into the metalanguage. Since A knows that, if the solution is acidic, performing the test will result in the litmus paper's being red, it must be true in the actual world (W_0) that, if the solution is acidic, performing the test will result in the litmus paper's being red (Line 3). Suppose that, in fact, the solution is acidic (Line 4). Then, if W_1 is the result of performing the test in W_0 (Line 5), the paper will be red in W_1 (Line 6). Furthermore, the worlds that are compatible with what A knows in W_1 are those that are the result of his performing the test in some world that is compatible with what he knows in W_1, and in which the paper is red if and only if it is red in W_1 (Line 7). Suppose that w_2 is a world that is compatible with what A knows in W_1 (Line 8). Then there is a W_3 that is compatible with what A knows in W_0 (Line 9), such that w_2 is the result of A's performing the test in W_3 (Line 10). The paper is red in w_2, if and only if it is red in W_1 (Line 11); therefore, it is red in w_2 (Line 12). Since A knows how the test works, if the solution were not acidic in W_3, it would not be acidic, and the paper would not be red, in w_2 (Line 13).

Now, suppose the solution were not acid in W_3 (Line 14). If W_4 is the result of A's performing the test in W_3 (Line 15), the paper would not be red in W_4 (Line 16). But w_2 is the result of A's performing the test in W_3 (Line 17), so the paper would not be red in w_2 (Line 18). We know this is false (Line 19), however, so the solution must be acidic in W_3 (Line 20). If the solution is acidic in W_3, it must also be acidic in the situation resulting from A's performing the test in W_3 (Lines 21–23), but this is w_2 (Line 24). Therefore, the solution is acidic in w_2 (Line 25). Hence, in W_1, A knows that the solution is acidic (Line 26), so in the situation resulting from A's performing the test in W_0, he knows that the solution is acidic (Line 27). In other words (Line 28), A's performing the test would result in his knowing that the solution is acidic.

By an exactly parallel argument, we could show that, if the solution were not acidic, A could also find that out by carrying out the test, so our analysis captures the sort of reasoning about tests that we described in Section 1, based on general principles that govern the interaction of knowledge and action.

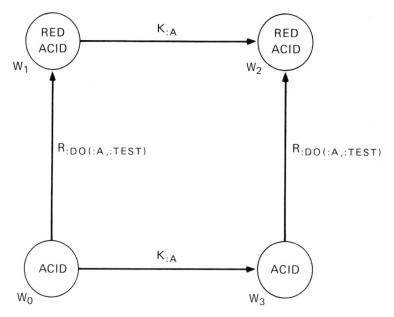

Figure 8. The Effect of a Test on the Agent's Knowledge

Acknowledgments

This research was supported in part by the Air Force Office of Scientific Research under Contract No. F49620-82-K-0031. It has also been made possible in part by a gift from the System Development Foundation as part of a coordinated research effort with the Center for the Study of Language and Information, Stanford University.

References

Frege, G. (1949). "On sense and nominatum," in *Readings in Philosophical Analysis,* H. Feigl & W. Sellars, Eds., pp. 85–102. New York: Appleton-Century-Crofts.

Hintikka, J. (1962). *Knowledge and Belief.* Ithica, NY: Cornell University Press.

Hintikka, J. (1971). "Semantics for propositional attitudes," in *Reference and Modality,* L. Linsky, Ed., pp. 145–167. London: Oxford University Press.

Hughes, G. E., & Cresswell, M. J. (1968). *An Introduction to Modal Logic.* London: Methuen.

Kripke, S. A. (1963). "Semantical analysis of modal logic," *Zeitschrift für Mathematische Logik und Grundlagen der Mathematik,* 9, pp. 67–96.

Kripke, S. A. (1971). "Semantical considerations on modal logic," in *Reference and Modality,* L. Linsky, Ed., pp. 63–72. London: Oxford University Press.

Kripke, S. A. (1972). "Naming and necessity," in *Semantics of Natural Language,* D. Davidson & G. Harmon, Eds., pp. 253–355. Dordrecht, Holland: Reidel.

McCarthy, J. (1962). "Towards a mathematical science of computation," in *Information Processing, Proceedings of IFIP Congress 62,* C. Popplewell, Ed., pp. 21–28. Amsterdam: North-Holland.

McCarthy, J. (1968). "Programs with common sense," in *Semantic Information Processing*, M. Minsky, Ed., pp. 403–418. Cambridge: MIT Press.

McCarthy, J., & Hayes, P. J. (1969). "Some philosophical problems from the standpoint of artificial intelligence," in *Machine Intelligence 4*, B. Meltzer & D. Michie, Eds., pp. 463–502. Edinburgh: Edinburgh University Press.

Moore, R. C. (1980). "Reasoning about knowledge and action," Artificial Intelligence Center Technical Note 191. Menlo Park, CA: SRI International.

Quine, W. V. O. (1971). "Quantifiers and propositional attitudes," in *Reference and Modality*, L. Linsky, Ed., pp. 101–111. London: Oxford University Press.

Reiter, R. (1980). "A logic for default reasoning," *Artificial Intelligence*, 13, 81–113.

Rescher, N., & Urquhart, A. (1971). *Temporal Logic*. Vienna: Springer-Verlag.

Russell, B. (1949). "On denoting," in *Readings in Philosophical Analysis*, H. Feigl & W. Sellars, Eds., pp. 103–115. New York: Appleton-Century-Crofts.

Scott, D. (1970) "Advice on modal logic," in *Philosophical Problems in Logic: Some Recent Developments*, K. Lambert, Ed., pp. 143–173. Dordrecht, Holland: Reidel.

10 *Belief and Incompleteness*

Kurt Konolige

Artificial Intelligence Center
SRI International
Menlo Park, California

1 Introduction

Two artificially intelligent (AI) computer agents begin to play a game of chess, and the following conversation ensues:

> S_1: *Do you know the rules of chess?*
> S_2: *Yes.*
> S_1: *Then you know whether White has a forced initial win or not.*
> S_2: *Upon reflection, I realize that I must.*
> S_1: *Then there is no reason to play.*
> S_2: *No.*

Both agents are state-of-the-art constructions, incorporating the latest AI research in chess playing, natural-language understanding, planning, etc. But because of the overwhelming combinatorics of chess, neither they nor the fastest foreseeable computers would be able to search the entire game tree to find out whether White has a forced win. Why then do they come to such an odd conclusion about their own knowledge of the game?

The chess scenario is an anecdotal example of the way inaccurate cognitive models can lead to behavior that is less than intelligent in artificial agents. In this case, the agents' model of belief is not correct. They make the assumption that an agent actually knows all the consequences of his beliefs. S_1 knows that chess is a finite game, and thus reasons that, in principle, knowing the rules of chess is all that is required to figure out whether White has a forced initial win. After learning that S_2 does indeed know the rules of chess, he comes to the erroneous conclusion that S_2 also knows this particular consequence of the rules. And S_2 himself, reflecting on his own knowledge in the same manner, arrives at the same conclusion, even though in actual fact he could never carry out the computations necessary to demonstrate it.

We call the assumption that an agent knows all logical consequences of his beliefs *consequential closure*. This assumption is clearly not warranted for either mechanical or human agents, because some consequences, although they are logically correct, may not be computationally feasible to derive. This is in fact illustrated by the chess scenario. Unfortunately, the best current formal models of belief on which AI systems are based have a *possible-worlds* semantics, and one of the inherent properties of these models is consequential closure. While such models are good at predicting what consequences an agent could *possibly* derive from his beliefs, they are not capable of predicting what an agent *actually* believes, given that the agent may have resource limitations impeding the derivation of the consequences of his beliefs.

The chess scenario illustrates one source of logical incompleteness in belief derivation, namely, an agent may not have enough computational resources to actually derive some result. We will identify several others in section 2, by presenting a problem in belief representation that we have called the Not-So-Wise-Man Problem, a variation of the familiar Wise Man Puzzle. Not surprisingly, this problem involves reasoning about beliefs an agent does *not* have, even though they are logical consequences of his beliefs. The representational problems posed by the chess scenario and the not-so-wise-man problem cannot be solved within the framework of any model of belief that assumes consequential closure.

In this chapter, we introduce a new formal model of belief, called the *deduction model,* for representing situations in which belief derivation is logically incomplete. Its main feature is that it is a symbol-processing model: beliefs are taken to be expressions in some internal or "mental" language, and an agent reasons about his beliefs by manipulating these syntactic objects. Because the derivation of consequences of beliefs is represented explicitly as a syntactic process in this model, it is possible to take into account the fact that agents can derive some of the logically possible consequences, but in many cases not all of them. When the process of belief derivation is logically incomplete, the deduction model does not have the property of consequential closure.

Symbol-processing models of belief in themselves are not new (see, for example, Fodor, 1975; Lycan, 1981; and Moore & Hendrix, 1979, for some philosophical underpinnings; and McCarthy, 1979; Perlis, 1981; and Konolige, 1982a for AI approaches). The deduction model presented here differs significantly from previous approaches, however, in two respects. First, it is a formal model: beliefs are represented in a mathematical framework called a *deduction structure.* The properties of the deduction model can be examined with some precision, and we do so in section 3. Second, we have found sound and complete logics for the deduction model. One of these, **B**, is presented in section 4, and used in the solution of the problems in section 5. An important property of the deductive belief logic **B** is that it can serve as a basis for building computer agents that reason about belief. We have been able to find a number of interesting proof methods for **B** that have reasonable computational properties. Although the exposition of these methods is beyond the scope of this paper, at the appropriate points we will show how the design of the logic was influenced by computational considerations.

The nature of the deduction model and its logic **B** is further analyzed by comparing **B** to modal logics based on a possible-worlds semantics in section 6. An important result is that the deduction model exhibits a correspondence property: in the limit of logically complete deduction, **B** reduces to a modal logic with possible-worlds semantics. Thus the deduction model dominates the possible-worlds model, while retracting the assumption of consequential closure.

The material for this chapter was abstracted from the author's dissertation work (Konolige, 1984). Because of the limited scope of this paper, we are not able to do more than mention in passing several interesting topics that are part of the deduction model and its logics. Among these are efficient proof methods, the formal semantics and completeness proofs, extensions to **B** that permit quantifying-in, and introspection properties (beliefs about one's own beliefs). Interested readers can consult the dissertation itself for a fuller exposition.

2 Two Problems in the Representation of Belief

In this section, we introduce three ways in which an agent may be incomplete in reasoning from his beliefs: *resource-limited incompleteness, fundamental logical incompleteness,* and *relevance incompleteness.* We argue that it is important for AI systems that reason about belief to be able to represent each of these, and offer two anecdotal problems to support this contention.

> THE CHESS PROBLEM. *Suppose an agent knows the rules of chess. It does not necessarily follow that he knows whether White has a winning strategy or not.*

The chess problem, on the face of it, seems hardly to be a representational problem at all. Certainly its statement is *true:* no agent, human or otherwise, can possibly follow out all the myriad lines of chess play allowed by the rules to determine whether White has a strategy that will always win. What kind of model of belief would lead us to expect an agent to know whether White has a winning strategy? As we stated in the introduction, any model that does not take resource limitations into account in representing an agent's reasoning about the consequences of his beliefs has this behavior. Within such a model, we could establish the following line of argument.

> *Chess is a finite game,[1] and so it is possible, in theory, to construct a complete, finite game tree for chess, given the rules of the game. The question of White's having a winning strategy is a property of this finite game tree. If for every counter Black makes, White has a move that will lead to a win, then White has a winning strategy. Thus White's having a winning strategy is a consequence of the rules of chess that can be derived in a finite number of simple steps. If an agent believes all the logical consequences of his beliefs, then an agent who knows the rules of chess will, by the reasoning just given, also know whether White has a winning strategy or not.*

---

[1]The finiteness of chess is assured by the rule that, if 50 moves occur without a pawn advance or piece capture, the game is a draw.

The chess problem is thus a problem in representing reasoning about beliefs in the face of resource limitations. The inference steps themselves are almost trivial; it is a simple matter to show that a move is legal, and hence to construct any position that follows a legal move from a given position. But while the individual inferences are easy, the number of them required to figure out whether White has a forced win is astronomical and beyond the computational abilities of any agent. We call this behavior *resource-limited incompleteness*. A suitable model of belief must be able to represent situations in which an agent possesses the inferential capability to derive some consequence of his beliefs, but simply does not have the computational resources to do so.

> THE NOT-SO-WISE-MAN PROBLEM. *A king, wishing to know which of his three advisors is the wisest, paints a white dot on each of their foreheads, tells them there is at least one white dot, and asks them to tell him the color of their own spots. After a while the first replies that he doesn't know; the second, on hearing this, also says he doesn't know. The third then responds, "I also don't know the color of my spot; but if the second of us were wiser, I would know it."*

The not-so-wise-man problem is a variation of the classic Wise Man Puzzle, which McCarthy (McCarthy, Sato, Hayashi, & Igarashi, 1978; McCarthy, 1978) has used extensively as a test of models of knowledge. In the classic version, the third wise man figures out from the replies of the other two that his spot must be white. The "puzzle" part is to generate the reasoning employed by the third wise man. The solution is really quite complex and hinges on the ability of the wise men to reason about one another's beliefs. To convince themselves of this, readers who have never tried before may be interested in attempting to solve it before reading the answer below.

> Solution to the Wise Man Puzzle: *the third wise man reasons: "Suppose my spot were black. Then the second of us would know that his own spot was white, since he would know that, if it were black, the first of us would have seen two black spots and would have known his own spot's color. Since both answered that they had no knowledge of their own spot's color, my spot must be white."*

The difficulty behind this puzzle seems to lie in the nature of the third wise man's reasoning about the first two's beliefs. Not only must he pose a hypothetical situation (*Suppose my spot were black*), but he must then reason within that situation about what conclusions the second wise man would come to after hearing the first wise man's response. This in turn means that he must reason about the second wise man's reasoning about the first wise man's beliefs, as revealed by his reply to the king. Reasoning about beliefs about beliefs about beliefs . . . we call reasoning about *iterated* or *nested beliefs*. It can quickly become confusing, especially when there are conditions present concerning what an agent does *not* believe.

In the Wise Man Puzzle, nested belief contributes to the complexity of the reasoning involved. The third wise man must reason about what the second wise man does not know (the color of his own spot); in doing this, he must also reason about the second wise man's reasoning about what the third wise man does not know (the color of *his* own spot). It is particularly annoying and troublesome to keep track of who believes what after several occurrences of not-believing in a statement of nested belief. Because human agents find it so difficult, the Wise Man Puzzle is thought to be a good test of the *competence* of any model of belief. If one can state the solution to the puzzle within the framework of Model X, so the reasoning goes, then Model X is at least good enough to show what might conceivably be concluded by agents in complicated situations involving nested beliefs.

It is possible to solve the Wise Man Puzzle within the confines of belief models that assume consequential closure (see, *e.g.,* McCarthy et al., 1981; McCarthy, 1981; or Sato, 1976). Such models make the assumption that every agent believes other agents' beliefs are closed under logical consequence, and so on to arbitrary depths of belief nesting. While this is an accurate assumption if one is trying to model the competence of ideal agents (which is what the Wise Man Puzzle seeks to verify), it cannot represent interesting ways in which reasoning about complicated nested beliefs might fail for a less-than-ideal agent. This is the import of the not-so-wise-man problem. From the reply of the third wise man, it appears that the second wise man lacks the ability to deduce all the consequences of his beliefs. The representational problem posed is to devise interesting ways in which the second wise man fails to be an ideal agent, and then show how the third wise man can represent this failure and reply as he does.

The not-so-wise-man problem does not seem to fall into the category of resource-limited incompleteness mentioned in the chess problem, since the computational requirements of the inferences are not particularly acute. We can identify at least two other types of incompleteness (there may certainly be more) that are interesting here and would be useful to represent. In one of these, the second wise man may have incomplete inferential procedures for reasoning about the other wise men's beliefs, especially if tricky combinations of *not-believing* are present. Suppose, for instance, the second wise man were to see a black spot on the third wise man, and a white spot on the first wise man (this is the hypothetical situation set up by the third wise man in solving the classic puzzle). If he were an ideal agent, he would conclude from the first wise man's reply that his own spot must be white (by reasoning: *if mine were not white, the first of us would have seen two black spots and so claimed his own as white*). But he may fail to do this because his rules for reasoning about the beliefs of the first wise man simply are not powerful enough. For example, he might never consider the strategy of assuming that his spot was black, and then asking himself what the first wise man would have said. In this case, the second wise man's inferential process, even when given adequate resources, is just not powerful enough in terms of its ability to arrive at simple logical conclusions. To apply an analogy from high-school algebra: a student who is confronted with the equation $x + a = b$ and asked to solve for x won't be able to do so if he doesn't know the rule that subtracting equals from each side leaves the equation valid. It is not that the student lacks sufficient mental resources of time or

memory to solve this problem; rather, his rules of inference for dealing with equa-
tional theories are logically incomplete. To contrast this type of incompleteness
with the resource-limited incompleteness described in the chess problem, we call it
fundamental logical incompleteness.

Another way in which the not-so-wise-man might fail to draw conclusions is if he
were to make an erroneous decision as to what information might be relevant to
solving his problem. Although the Wise Man Puzzle has a fairly abstract setting, it
is reasonable to suppose that actual agents confronted with this problem would have
a fair number of extraneous beliefs that they would exclude from consideration. For
example, the not-so-wise-man might be privy to the castle rumor mill, and therefore
believe that the first wise man was scheming to marry the king's daughter. A very
large number of beliefs of this sort have no bearing on the problem at hand, but
would tend to use up valuable mental resources if they were given any serious
consideration. One can imagine an *unsure agent* who could never come to any
negative conclusions at all, because he would keep on considering more and more
possibilities for solving a problem. This agent's reasoning might proceed as follows: *I can't tell the color of my spot by looking at the other wise men. But maybe
there's a mirror that shows my face. No, there's no mirror. But maybe my brother
wrote the color on a slip of paper and handed it to me. No, there's no slip of paper,
and my brother's in Babylon. But maybe . . .*

McCarthy (1980) first called attention to the problem of representing what is *not*
the case in solving puzzles. In the Missionaries and Cannibals Puzzle, why can't the
missionaries simply use the bridge downstream to get across? A straightforward
logical presentation of the puzzle doesn't explicitly exclude the existence of such a
bridge. And, if it did, we could always come up with other modes of transportation
that had not been considered beforehand and explicitly excluded. McCarthy called
the general problem of specifying what conditions do not hold in a puzzle the
circumscription problem. By analogy, we call the problem of specifying what
beliefs an agent does not have, or does not use in solving a given task, the problem
of *circumscriptive ignorance* (Konolige, 1982b). Without a solution to this representational problem, all agents will be modeled as unsure agents—never able to
reach a conclusion about what they don't believe, even though it is obvious when
the set of relevant beliefs is circumscribed.

Of course, if an agent can circumscribe his beliefs, it is possible that he will
choose the wrong set of beliefs, and exclude some that actually are relevant. The
not-so-wise-man may decide that the beliefs of the first wise man are not germane to
the problem of figuring out his own spot's color. Thus, even though he has all the
relevant information, and even sufficiently powerful inference rules and adequate
resources, he may fail to come to a correct conclusion because he has circumscribed
his beliefs in the wrong way. We call this type of incompleteness *relevance
incompleteness.*

Within a model of belief that assumes consequential closure, it is possible to
represent circumscriptive ignorance, but only in a relatively limited fashion. If
consequential closure is assumed, one can state that an agent is ignorant of some

fact which is not a logical consequence of his beliefs (McCarthy (1978) uses this technique in his solution to the Wise Man Puzzle). But this clearly does not capture the complete conditions of circumscriptive ignorance, since agents are often ignorant of some of the logical consequences of their beliefs, as in the chess scenario.

Modeling relevance incompleteness (or having the third wise man do so) is impossible if it is assumed that the beliefs of agents are consequentially complete. One simply cannot partition the set of beliefs into those that are either relevant or not to a given problem; *all* the consequences of beliefs are believed. If we try to state the conditions of relevance incompleteness within such a model, we can arrive at a contradiction, where a proposition is both believed (because of the assumption of consequential closure) and not believed (because of the condition of relevance incompleteness).

3 The Deduction Model of Belief

The two belief representation problems can be solved within the framework of a formal model of belief that we call the deduction model. In this section we define the model; in the next we introduce a logic family **B** as its axiomatization.

The strategy we pursue is to first examine the way typical AI robot planning systems—STRIPS (Fikes & Nelson, 1971) NOAH (Sacerdoti, 1977), WARPLAN (Warren, 1974), KAMP (Appelt, 1982), *etc.*—represent and reason about the world. This leads to the identification of an abstract *belief subsystem* as the internal structure responsible for the beliefs of these agents. The characteristics of belief subsystems can be summarized briefly as follows.

1. A belief subsystem contains a list of sentences in some internal (''mental'') language, the *base beliefs*.
2. Agents can infer consequences of their beliefs by syntactic manipulation of the sentences of the belief subsystem.
3. The derivation of consequences of beliefs is logically incomplete, because of limitations of the inferential process.

Having identified a belief subsystem as that part of an agent responsible for beliefs, our next task is to define a formal mathematical structure that models it accurately. The decisions to be made here involve particular choices for modeling the various components of a belief subsystem: what does the internal language look like? What kind of inference process derives consequences of the base beliefs? and so on. The formal mathematical object we construct according to these criteria is called a *deduction structure*. Its main components are a set of sentences in some logical language (corresponding to the base beliefs of a belief subsystem) and a set of deduction rules (corresponding to the belief inference rules) that may be logically incomplete. Because we choose to model belief subsystems in terms of logical (but perhaps incomplete) deduction, we call it the *deduction model of belief*.

3.1 Planning and Beliefs: the Belief Subsystem Abstraction

A robot planning system, such as STRIPS, must represent knowledge about the world in order to plan actions that affect the world. Of course it is not possible to represent all the complexity of the real world, so the planning system uses some abstraction of properties of the real world that are important for its task; *e.g.,* it might assume that there are objects that can be stacked in simple ways (the *blocks-world* domain). The state of the abstract world at any particular point in time has been called a *situation* in the AI literature.

In general, the planning system will have only incomplete knowledge of a situation. For instance, if it is equipped with visual sensors, it may be able to see only some of the objects in the world. What this means is that the system has to be able to represent and reason about partial descriptions of situations. The process of deriving beliefs is a *symbol-manipulating* or *syntactic* operation that takes as input sentences of the formal language, and produces new sentences as output. Let us call any new sentences derived by inferences the *inferable sentences,* and the process of deriving them *belief inference.*

It is helpful to view the representation and deduction of facts about the world as a separate subsystem within the planning system; we call it the *belief subsystem.* In its simplest, most abstract form, the belief subsystem comprises a list of sentences about a situation, together with a process for deriving their consequences. It is integrated with other processes in the planning system, especially the *plan deriva-tion process* that searches for sequences of actions to achieve a given goal. In a highly schematic form, Figure 1 sketches the belief subsystem and its interaction with other processes of the planning system. The belief system is composed of the base beliefs, together with the belief inference process. Belief inference itself can be decomposed into a set of inference rules and a control strategy that determines how the rules are to be applied and where their outputs go when requests are made to the belief subsystem.

A belief subsystem defines an agent's beliefs by the action of the inference rules on the base beliefs, under the guidance of the control strategy. Some, but not necessarily all, of the inferable sentences will be beliefs of the agent; which infera-ble sentences are actually beliefs depends on the details of the control strategy and the resources available for belief inference.

There are two types of requests that result in some action in the belief subsystem. A process may request the subsystem to add or delete sentences in its base beliefs; this happens, for example, when the plan derivation process decides which sen-tences hold in a new situation. The problem of updating and revising beliefs in the face of new information is a complicated research issue in its own right, and we do not address it here (see Doyle, 1978 for some related AI research). The second type of request is a query as to whether a sentence is a belief or not. This query causes the control strategy to try to infer, using its rules, that the sentence is follows from the base beliefs. It is this process of *belief querying* that we model in this paper.

The foregoing description of the operation of a belief subsystem is meant to convey the idea that in most formal planning systems there is a tight interaction

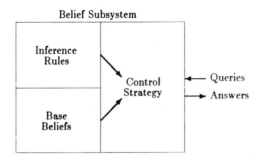

Figure 1. Schematic of a belief subsystem

between belief subsystems and planning. Different systems may deviate from the described pattern to a greater or lesser extent. In some systems, the representation of facts may be so limited, and that of actions so explicit, as to almost obviate the need for belief deduction *per se* (as in some versions of STRIPS). In others, deduction may be used to calculate all the effects of an action by expanding the representation to include situations as objects (as in WARPLAN). Here it is hard to make a clean separation between deductions performed for the purpose of deriving consequences of beliefs and those that establish the initial set of facts about a new situation. However, it is still conceptually useful to regard the belief subsystem as a separate structure and belief derivation as a separate process within the planning system.

3.2 A Formal Model of Belief

The formal mathematical object we use to model belief subsystems is called a *deduction structure*. A deduction structure is a tuple consisting of two sets and will be written as $\langle B, \mathcal{R} \rangle$. The set B is a set of sentences in some language L; It corresponds to the base beliefs of a belief subsystem and its members are referred to as the *base sentences* of the deduction structure. $\mathcal{R}$ is a set of deduction rules for L; these correspond to the inference rules of a belief subsystem. We demand that deduction structures satisfy the following four conditions.

Language Property. The language of a deduction structure is a logical language.

Deduction Property. The rules of a deduction structure are logical deduction rules. These rules are sound, effectively computable, and have bounded input.

Closure Property. The *belief set* of a deduction structure is the least set that includes the base sentences and is closed under derivations by the deduction rules.

Recursion Property. The intended model of deduction structure sentences involving belief is the belief set of another deduction structure.

We discuss each of these properties briefly below. For the interested reader, a more thorough treatment of the mathematical properties of deduction structures is given in the next subsection.

About the only condition we require of L is that it be a *logical* language. Logical languages are distinguished by having a constructable set of syntactic objects, the *sentences* of the language, together with an *interpretation method* (a means of assigning true or false to every sentence with respect to a given state of affairs).

$\mathcal{R}$ is a set of deduction rules that operate on sentences of L. We will leave unspecified the exact form of the deduction rules $\mathcal{R}$, but we do insist that they operate in the normal manner of deduction rules in some proof-theoretic framework. This means that there is the concept of a *derivation* of a sentence, which is a structure built from effective applications of the rules $\mathcal{R}$. If P is derivable from the set of sentences Γ in this manner, we write $\Gamma \vdash_{\mathcal{R}} p$, where $\vdash_{\mathcal{R}}$ is a derivation operator for the rules $\mathcal{R}$. For example, in terms of Hilbert systems (as defined in Kleene, 1967), $\mathcal{R}$ would be a set of logical axioms (zero-premise rules) together with *modus ponens* (a two-premise rule). A sentence p would be derivable from the premise sentences $B = \{b_1, b_2, \ldots\}$ if there were a Hilbert proof of $(b_1 \wedge b_2 \wedge \ldots) \supset p$, using the logical axioms and *modus ponens*.

A deduction structures models beliefs by its *belief set*, which we define as follows.

DEFINITION 3.1: $\mathrm{bel}(\langle B, \mathcal{R}\rangle) =_{df} \{p | B \vdash_{\mathcal{R}} p\}$.

The belief set is composed of all sentences that are derivable from the base set B with the rules $\mathcal{R}$. The derivation operator $\vdash_{\mathcal{R}}$ thus corresponds to the belief inference process of belief subsystems.

For several technical reasons, we restrict the derivation operators allowed in deduction structures to those that satisfy a deductive closure condition. One consequence of this assumption is that the belief set itself obeys a closure property: if the sentence p can be derived from the sentences in a belief set, then it too must be present in the belief set. By making the assumption of deductive closure, the task of formalizing and reasoning about deduction structures is greatly simplified.

It is important to note that deductive closure does not entail *consequential* closure for belief derivation: a set of sentences closed under logically incomplete deduction rules need not contain all logical consequences of the set. This is an important property of deduction structures, and it enables them to capture the behavior of belief subsystems with resource-bounded control strategies.

Finally, we single out certain sentences of the deduction structure for special treatment, namely the ones that themselves refer to the beliefs of agents. In discussing the not-so-wise-man problem in the previous section, we mentioned that one of the key tests of a belief model is its ability to handle nested beliefs by assuming that agents use the model in representing other agents' beliefs; a belief model that has this characteristic is said to have the recursion property. In terms of deduction structures, the recursion property implies that the sentences of the internal language L that are about beliefs should have another deduction structure as their intended interpretation.

3.3 Properties of Deduction Structures

In this subsection, we treat the mathematical properties of deduction structures in some detail, taking care to show how they can model the behavior of belief subsystems of formal AI planning systems.

3.3.1 Language Property.

One restriction we place on the language of deduction structures is that sentences of the language have a well-defined (*i.e.*, truth-theoretic) semantics. Such a requirement seems absolutely necessary if we are going to talk about the beliefs of an agent being *true* of the actual world, or, as we will want to do in discussing the rationality of agents, judge the *soundness* of belief deduction rules. Such concepts make no sense in the absence of an interpretation method—a systematic way of assigning meanings to the constructions of the language. As Moore and Hendrix (1979, parts IV and especially V) note, the interpretation method is not something the agent carries around in his head; a belief subsystem is just a collection of sentences, and computational processes manipulate the sentences themselves, not their meanings. One simply cannot put the referent of "Cicero" into a robot's computation device, even if he (Cicero, of course) were alive. But the attribution of semantics to sentences is necessary if an outside observer is to analyze the nature of an agent's beliefs.

How well do actual robot belief subsystems fit in with the assumption of a logical language of belief? AI systems use a variety of representational technologies; chief among these are frames, scripts, semantic nets, and the many refinements of first-order logic (FOL), including PROLOG and the "procedurally oriented" logics of μ-PLANNER, CONNIVER, QA4, and the like. The representations that fall into the latter category inherit their semantics from FOL, despite many differences in the syntactic form of their expressions. But what can we say about the first three? In surface form they certainly do not look anything like conventional mathematical logics; furthermore, their designers often have not provided anything but an informal idea of what the meanings of expressions in the language are. When, after all, is a pair of nodes connected by a directed arc *true* of the world? As Hayes (1977) has forcefully argued, the lack of a formal semantics is a big drawback for these languages. Fortunately, on further examination it is often possible to provide such a semantics, usually by transliterating the representation into a first-order language (see Woods, 1975; and Schubert, 1976 for a reconstruction of semantic nets in FOL terms; and Brachman, 1980 for a similar analysis of frames).

In discussing human belief, several philosophers of mind have argued that internal representations that count as beliefs must have a truth-value semantics (see Fodor, 1975; Field, 1978; and Moore and Hendrix, 1970, for a discussion of the many intricate arguments on this subject, especially pp. 48ff. of Field and part V of Moore and Hendrix). However, there almost certainly is a lot more to human belief than can be handled adequately within the framework of a logical language. For example, the question of membership in the belief set of a deduction structure is strictly two-valued: a sentence is either a member of the belief set of a deduction structure, or it is not. If it is, then the assumed interpretation is that the agent believes that sentence to be true of the world. Deduction structures thus do not support the notion of *uncertain* beliefs directly, as they might do if fuzzy or uncertain membership in the belief set were an inherent part of their structure.[2]

One further requirement is that L contain expressions referring to the beliefs of agents. Generally we will take this to be a belief operator whose argument is an expression in L.

Finally, it is often the case that we will want to freeze the language of deduction structures in order to study their properties at a finer level of detail, e.g., when looking at the behavior of nested beliefs in general or when giving the particulars of the solution to a representational problem. It is convenient to think of the language as being a *parameter* of the formal model. For every logical language L, there is a class of deduction structures $D(L,\rho)$ whose base sets are sentences of the language L (the parameter ρ will be explained in discussing the recursion property below).

3.3.2 Deduction Property. Rules for deduction structures are rules of inference with the following restrictions:

1. The rule is an effectively computable function of sentences of L.
2. The number of input sentences is boundedly finite.
3. The conclusion is sound with respect to the semantics of L.

These restrictions are those normally associated with deduction rules for classical logic, although, strictly speaking, deduction rules need not be sound, if one is just interested in proof-theoretic properties of a logic without regards to semantics.

The fact that belief deduction rules are effectively computable functions means that they can be very complicated indeed. Mathematical logicians are interested in logics with simple deduction rules (such as Hilbert systems) because it is easy to analyze the proof-theoretic structure of such systems. However, for the purpose of deriving proof methods for commonsense reasoning in AI, it is often better to sacrifice simplicity for computational efficiency. For example, Robinson's *resolution rule* (1979), which employs a matching process called unification, is a complicated rule that has been widely employed in AI theorem-proving. Another important technique is Weyhrauch's *semantic attachment* (1980), a general framework for viewing the results of computation as deduction. And in this paper, we will exploit complicated rules that perform deductions that are relatively "large" with respect to the grain size of the predicates, particularly in solving the chess problem of section 2. Although these "large" deductions could be broken down into smaller steps, it is computationally and conceptually easier to view them as single deductions.

We call an inference rule *provincial* if the number of its input sentences is

---

[2]However, uncertain beliefs could always be introduced into deduction structures in an indirect manner by letting L contain statements about uncertainty, e.g., statements of the form P *is true with probability* 1/2.

boundedly finite; deduction rules are always provincial. We thus do not allow inferences about beliefs that take an infinite number of premises. For example, the following rule of Carnap's is not a valid rule of belief deduction: *if for every individual a: F(a) is a theorem, then ∀x.F(x) is a theorem.*[3] Provincial inference rules have the following interesting property: if α is a consequence of a set of sentences S by the rule, then it is also a consequence of any larger set $S' \supset S$. To see that this must be so, consider that, if a can be derived by the application of provincial rules on the set of sentences S, and S' contains S, then the same derivation can be performed by using S'. Rules that adhere to this property are called *monotonic*. Technically, monotonicity is convenient because it means we can reason about what an agent believes on the basis of partial knowledge about his beliefs. A derivation made using a subset of his beliefs cannot be retracted in the face of further information about his beliefs.

Several types of nonmonotonic (and unsound) reasoning have been of interest to the AI community, specifically

Belief revision: the beliefs of an agent are updated to be consistent with new information (*e.g.*, Doyle, 1978)

Default reasoning: an agent "jumps to a conclusion" about the way the world is (*e.g.*, McCarthy, 1980; Reiter, 1980; McDermott and Doyle, 1980)

Autoepistemic reasoning: an agent comes to a conclusion about the world based on his knowledge of his own beliefs (*e.g.*, Collins, Warnock, Aiello, & Miller, 1975; Moore, 1983)

We are explicitly not trying to arrive at a theory of these forms of reasoning. Indeed, it is helpful here to make the distinction that Israel (1983) advocates between inference or reasoning in general (which may have nonmonotonic properties) and the straightforward deduction of logical consequences from a set of initial beliefs. It is the latter concept only that is treated in this paper.

If we wish to accommodate a nonmonotonic theory formally within the framework of the deduction model, it is possible to do so by viewing its inferences as deduction rules operating on deduction structure theories as a syntactic whole. McCarthy (1980) exploits this approach to formalize a certain type of useful default inference, which he calls *circumscription* (see the description of the not-so-wise-man problem in section 2). In defining the logic **B**, we will show how to formalize *circumscriptive ignorance*, a type of nonmonotonic inference, in this manner.

Deduction rules for belief subsystems must also be sound. A sound deduction rule is one for which, if the premises are true in an interpretation, then the conclusion will be also (see Kleene, 1967). Informally, one would say that sound deduc-

---

[3] I am indebted to David Israel for pointing out this example.

tion rules never deduce false conclusions from true premises. *Modus ponens* is an example of such a rule: if p and $p \supset q$ are true, then q must also be.

Soundness of inference is an important property for robot agents in deriving consequences of their beliefs. We would not want a robot who believed the two sentences

> *All men are mortal.*   (3.1)
> Socrates is a man.

to then deduce unsoundly (and hence believe) the sentence

> *Socrates is not mortal.*   (3.2)

Soundness is not a critical assumption for the deduction model, since none of the major technical results depend on it. In some cases we may wish to relax it, for example, in modeling the behavior of human syllogistic reasoning, which is often unsound (see Johnson-Laird, 1968).

To sum up: deduction structures are restricted to using inference rules which are provincial, sound, and effectively computable. Several interesting types of reasoning, such as reasoning about defaults or one's own beliefs, cannot be modeled directly as deduction rules over sentences. However, they can be incorporated into the deduction model if the input to the rules is taken to be the deduction structure as a whole.

3.3.3 Closure Property. The closure property states that the belief set of a deduction structure is *closed under derivations.* Formally, this amounts to the following conditions on the belief set.

1. $B \subseteq \text{bel}(\langle B, \mathfrak{R} \rangle)$.
2. If $\Gamma \subseteq \text{bel}(\langle B, \mathfrak{R} \rangle)$ and $\Gamma \vdash_{\mathfrak{R}} p$, then $p \in \text{bel}(\langle B, \mathfrak{R} \rangle)$.

Since we have defined the belief set in terms of the belief derivation operator $\vdash_{\mathfrak{R}}$ (Definition 3.1), we can reexpress these as conditions on belief derivation.

> (Reflexivity) $\alpha \vdash_{\rho(i)} \alpha$
> (Closure) If $\Gamma \vdash_{\rho(i)} \beta$ and $\beta, \Sigma \vdash_{\rho(i)} \alpha$, then $\Gamma, \Sigma \vdash_{\rho(i)} \alpha$.

Reflexivity guarantees that the base set will be included in bel, and the closure condition establishes closure of bel under derivation.

The chief motivation for requiring derivational closure is that it simplifies the technical task of formalizing the deduction model. Consider the problem of formalizing a belief subsystem that has a complex control strategy guiding its inferential process. To do this correctly, one must write axioms that not only describe the agendas, proof trees, and other data structures used by the control strategy, but also describe how the control strategy guides inference rules operating on these structures. Reasoning about the inference process involves using these axioms to perform deductions that *simulate* the belief inference process, a highly inefficient procedure. By contrast, the assumption of derivational closure leads to a simple formalization of deduction structures in a logic **B** that incorporates the belief inference process in a direct way. We need not differentiate between a belief as a member of the base set, or as a derived sentence. A sentence that follows from any members of the belief set is itself a belief. The axiomatization of **B** is simplified, since we need only have an operator whose intended interpretation is membership in the belief set. In section 4, we exploit the properties of closed derivational systems to exhibit a complete axiomatization of **B**, using techniques that are manner similar to the *procedural attachment* methods of Weyhrauch (1980).

The closure property is an extremely important one, and we should examine its repercussions closely. A point that we have already made is that derivational closure is not the same as consequential closure. The latter refers to a property of sets of sentences based on their *semantics:* every logical consequence of the set is also a member of the set. The former refers to the *syntactic* process of derivability; if the rules $\mathcal{R}$ are not logically complete, then a set of sentences that is derivationally closed under $\mathcal{R}$ need not be consequentially closed.

One of the key properties of belief subsystems that we wish to model is the incompleteness of deriving the consequences of the base set of beliefs. We have identified three sources of incompleteness in belief subsystems: an agent's belief inference rules may be too weak from a logical standpoint, or he may decide that some beliefs are irrelevant to a query, or his control strategy may perform only a subset of the inferences possible when confronted with resource limitations. The assumption of derivational closure for deduction structures only affects the ability to model incomplete control strategies, since closure demands that all possible deductions be performed in deriving the belief set.

For an important class of incomplete control strategies, however, there is a corresponding complete control strategy operating on a different set of inference rules that produces the same beliefs on every base set. The criteria that defines this class is that the control strategy use only a *local cost bound* in deciding to drop a particular line of inference. By "local" is meant that the control strategy will always pursue a line of inference to a certain point, without regard to other lines of inference it may be pursuing in parallel. Control strategies with a local cost bound are important because their inferential behavior is predictable: all inferences of a certain sort are guaranteed to be made.

Deduction structures can accurately model the class of locally bounded incomplete control strategies by using an appropriate set of logically incomplete deduction rules. A good example is found in the solution of the chess problem in section 5. The agent's control strategy applies general rules about chess to search the game tree to only a limited depth; this is modeled in a deduction structure by using deduction rules that work only above a certain depth of the game tree, and applying them exhaustively.

In belief subsystems whose control strategies have a global cost bound, the concept of belief itself is complicated, since one must differentiate between base beliefs and beliefs inferred with some amount of effort. Deduction structures are only an approximate model of these subsystems, and a language with a single belief operator is no longer sufficient for their axiomatization.

3.3.4 Recursion Property. If belief subsystems adhere to the recursion property, then agents view other agents as having belief subsystems similar to their own. This still leaves a considerable degree of flexibility in representing nested beliefs. For example, an agent John might believe that Sue's internal language is L_1 and that she has a set of deduction rules $\mathcal{R}_1$, whereas Kim's internal language is L_2 and her deduction rules are $\mathcal{R}_2$. In addition, John might believe that Sue believes that Kim's internal language is L_3, and that her rules are $\mathcal{R}_3$. We call the description of a belief subsystem at some level of nesting a *view;* formally, views are sequences of agents' names, so that the view *John,Sue* is Sue's belief subsystem as John sees it. We will often use the Greek letter v to stand for an arbitrary view, and lowercase Latin letters (*i, j, etc.*) for singleton views, which are agents' actual belief subsystems. Since the formal objects of the deduction model are deduction structures, these will be indexed by views when appropriate. For example, the $d_{John,Sue}$ is a deduction structure modeling the view *John,Sue*.

Obviously, some fairly complicated and confusing situations might be described, with agents believing that other agents have belief subsystems of varying capabilities. AI applications often are concerned with scenarios of this sort; *e.g.*, an expert system tutoring a novice in some domain would need a representation of the novice's deductive capabilities that would initially be less powerful and complete than its own, and could be modified as the novice learned about the domain.

We model the recursion property of belief subsystems within the framework of deduction structures by allowing sentences of L to refer to the beliefs of agents. A standard construct is to have a *belief operator* in L: an operator whose arguments are an agent S and a sentence P, and whose intended meaning is that S believes P. According to the recursion property, this means that the belief operator must have a deduction structure as its interpretation. Deduction rules that apply to belief operators will be judged sound if they respect this interpretation. For example, suppose a deduction structure d_v has a rule stating that the sentence "John believes q" can be concluded from the premise sentences "John believes p" and "John believes $p \supset q$." This is a sound rule of d_v if *modus ponens* is believed to be a rule of John's belief subsystem as viewed from the view v, since the presence of p and $p \supset q$ in a deduction structure with *modus ponens* means that q will be derived.

Several simplifying assumptions are implicit in the use of deduction structures to model the nested views of belief subsystems. The language L contains a belief operator that denotes membership in a belief set (its intended interpretation), and so L can describe what sentences are contained in an agent's belief set. However, there is no provision in L for talking about the deduction rules an agent uses. Instead, these nested-belief rules are implicitly specified by the rules that manipulate sentences with belief operators. Consider the example from the previous paragraph. Let us suppose that we are modeling Sue's belief subsystem with the deduction structure d_{Sue}. Because Sue believes that John uses *modus ponens,* a sound rule of inference for d_{Sue} would be the one that was stated above, namely, the sentence "John believes q" could be concluded from the premise sentences "John believes p" and "John believes $p \supset q$." All of the rules that Sue believes John uses are modeled in this way. Similarly, if, in Sue's opinion, John believes that Kim uses a certain rule, this will be reflected in a rule of John's deduction structure as seen by Sue, which in turn will be modeled by a rule in d_{Sue}. The deduction model thus assumes that the rules for each view, though they may be different, are a fixed parameter of the model. We introduce the function $\rho(v)$ to specify deduction rule sets for each view v; thus, for each function ρ and each language L, there is a class of deduction structure $D(L,\rho)$ that formalize the deduction model. If the rules ρ are complete with respect to the semantics of L, then the class is said to be *saturated,* and is written $D_s(L,\rho)$.

A final simplification that is not inherent in the deduction model, but which we introduce here solely for technical convenience, is to assume that all deduction structures in all views use the same language L. There are situations in which we might want to relax this restriction, but it makes the axiomatization less complex in dealing with the problems at hand.

4 The Logic Family B

We now define a family of logics $B(L,\rho)$ for stating facts and reasoning about deduction structures. This family is parameterized in the same way as deduction structures, namely by an agents' language L and an ensemble of deduction structure rules ρ. Each logic of the family is an axiomatization of the deduction structures $D(L,\rho)$.

The language of **B** includes operators for stating that sentences are beliefs of an agent, but not for describing deduction rules of agents. Thus the deduction rules are a parameter of the logic family and are fixed once we decide to use a particular logic of the family. The ensemble function ρ picks out a set of rules for each agent. The reason we chose to make the deduction rules a parameter of **B** is that it is then possible to find efficient proof methods for **B**. One of the interesting features of **B**'s axiomatization is that agents' rules are actually present as a subset of the rules of **B**; proofs about deduction structures in **B** use these rules directly in their derivation.

The logic of **B** is framed in terms of a modified form of Gentzen systems, the block tableau systems of Hintikka. Although they may be unfamiliar to some readers, block tableaux are easy to work with and possess some natural advantages when applied to the formalization of deduction structures. Unlike Hilbert systems, which contain complex logical axioms and simple rules of inference (in the propositional case just *modus ponens*), block tableau systems have simple axioms and a rich and flexible method of specifying deduction rules. We exploit this capability when we incorporate deduction structure rules into **B**.

In this section we first present a brief overview of block tableaux. Then we give the postulates of the family **B**, and a particularly simple subfamily called **BK** that will be used in solving the problems. By the way of example, we prove some theorems of **BK**.

4.1 Block Tableaux

Most of this section will comprise a review for those readers who are already familiar with tableaux systems.

4.1.1 The Base Language L_0. The language of **B** is formed from a base language L_0 that does not contain any operators referring to beliefs. L_0 is taken to be a first-order language with constant terms. An interpretation of L_0 is a truth-value assignment to all sentences (closed formulas) of L_0; this assignment must be a *first-order valuation*, that is, it must respect the standard interpretation of the universal and existential quantifiers as well as the Boolean connectives.

We call L_0 *uninterpreted* if every first-order valuation is an interpretation of L_0; *partially interpreted* if some proper subset of the first-order valuations are interpretations of L_0; and *fully interpreted* (or simply *interpreted*) if there is a singleton interpretation of L_0. A sentence of L_0 is *valid* if and only if it is true in every interpretation of L_0.

We use lowercase Latin or Greek letters (p, q, α, *etc.*) as metavariables that stand for sentences of L_0. A formula of L_0 that possibly contains the free variable x will be indicated by $\alpha(x)$; the formula derived by substituting the constant a everywhere for x is denoted by $\alpha(x/a)$. Uppercase Greek letters ($\Gamma =_{df} \{\gamma_1, \gamma_2, \ldots\}$, $\Delta =_{df} \{\delta_1, \delta_2, \ldots\}$, *etc.*) stand for *finite sets* of sentences of L_0. By p, Γ we mean the set $\{p\} \cup \Gamma$. We also introduce the abbreviation $\sim\Gamma =_{df} \{\sim\gamma_1, \sim\gamma_2, \ldots\}$.

4.1.2 Sequents. Sequents are the main formal object of block tableaux systems.
DEFINITION 4.1: *A sequent is an ordered pair of finite sets of sentences, $\langle\Gamma,\Delta\rangle$. This sequent will also be written as $\Gamma \Rightarrow \Delta$, and read as "$\Delta$ follows from Γ."*

A sequent $\Gamma \Rightarrow \Delta$ *is* true in an interpretation *of its component sentences iff one of γ_i is false, or one of δ_j is true. A sequent is* valid *iff it is true under all interpretations, and* satisfiable *iff it is true in at least one interpretation.*

From the definition of truth for a sequent, it should be clear that a sequent $\Gamma \Rightarrow \Delta$ is true in an interpretation just in case the sentence $(\gamma_1 \wedge \gamma_2 \wedge \ldots) \supset (\delta_1 \vee \delta_2 \vee \ldots)$ is true in that interpretation. Thus, in a given interpretation a true sequent can be taken as asserting that the conjunction of γ's materially implies the disjunction of the δ's.

We allow the empty set ϕ to appear on either side of a sequent, and abbreviate $\phi \Rightarrow \Delta$ by $\Rightarrow \Delta$, $\Gamma \Rightarrow \phi$ by $\Gamma \Rightarrow$, and $\phi \Rightarrow \phi$ by $\Rightarrow$. By the foregoing definition, $\Rightarrow \Delta$ is true (in an interpretation) if and only if one of δ_j is true, $\Gamma \Rightarrow$ is true if and only if one of γ_i is false, and $\Rightarrow$ is never true in any interpretation.

4.1.3 Block Tableaux for L_0. The proof method we adopt is similar to Gentzen's original sequent calculus, but simpler in form. It is called the *method of block tableaux,* and was originated by Hintikka (1955). A useful reference is Smullyan (1968), in which many results in block tableaux and similar systems are presented in a unified form.

A block tableau system consists of axioms and rules (collectively, *postulates*) whose formal objects are sequents. Block tableau rules are like upside-down inference rules: the conclusion comes first, next a horizontal line, then the premises. Block tableaux themselves are derivations whose root is the sequent derived, whose branches are given by the rules, and whose leaves are axioms. Block tableaux look much like upside-down Gentzen system trees. (A more formal definition of block tableaux is given below).

We consider a system τ_0 (see Smullyan (1968), pp. 105–109) that is first-order sound and complete: its consequences are precisely the sentences true in every first-order valuation.

DEFINITION 4.2: *The system τ_0 has the following postulates:*

Axioms: $\qquad\qquad\qquad\quad \Gamma, p \Rightarrow \Delta, p$

Conjunction Rules: $\quad C_1: \dfrac{\Gamma, p \wedge q \Rightarrow \Delta}{\Gamma, p, q \Rightarrow \Delta}$

$\qquad\qquad\qquad\qquad C_2: \dfrac{\Gamma \Rightarrow \Delta, p \wedge q}{\Gamma \Rightarrow \Delta, p \quad \Gamma \Rightarrow \Delta, q}$

Disjunction Rules: $\quad D_1: \dfrac{\Gamma \Rightarrow \Delta, p \vee q}{\Gamma \Rightarrow \Delta, p, q}$

$\qquad\qquad\qquad\qquad D_2: \dfrac{\Gamma, p \vee q \Rightarrow \Delta}{\Gamma, p \Rightarrow \Delta \quad \Gamma, q \Rightarrow \Delta}$

Implication Rules: $\quad I_1: \dfrac{\Gamma \Rightarrow \Delta, p \supset q}{\Gamma, p \Rightarrow \Delta, q}$

$\qquad\qquad\qquad\qquad I_2: \dfrac{\Gamma, p \supset q \Rightarrow \Delta}{\Gamma \Rightarrow \Delta, p \quad \Gamma, q \Rightarrow \Delta}$

Negation Rules: $\quad N_1: \dfrac{\Gamma \Rightarrow \Delta, \sim p}{\Gamma, p \Rightarrow \Delta}$

$\qquad\qquad\qquad\qquad N_2: \dfrac{\Gamma, \sim p \Rightarrow \Delta}{\Gamma \Rightarrow \Delta, p}$

Universal Rules: $\quad U_1: \dfrac{\Gamma, \forall x.\alpha(x) \Rightarrow \Delta}{\Gamma, \alpha(x/a), \forall x.\alpha(x) \Rightarrow \Delta}$

$\qquad\qquad\qquad\qquad U_2: \dfrac{\Gamma \Rightarrow \forall x.\alpha(x), \Delta}{\Gamma \Rightarrow \alpha(x/a), \forall x.\alpha(x), \Delta}$, *where a has not appeared in the tableau*

Existential Rules: $\quad E_1: \dfrac{\Gamma \Rightarrow \exists x.\alpha(x), \Delta}{\Gamma \Rightarrow \alpha(x/a), \exists x.\alpha(x), \Delta}$

$\qquad\qquad\qquad\qquad E_2: \dfrac{\Gamma, \exists x.\alpha(x) \Rightarrow \Delta}{\Gamma, \alpha(x/a), \exists x.\alpha(x), \Rightarrow \Delta}$, *where a has not appeared in the tableau*

Remarks. Note the simple form of the axioms and the symmetric nature of the inference rules (actually, each rule is a rule schema, since Γ, Δ, p, q, and α stand for formulas and sets of formulas of L_0). There is one rule that deletes each logical connective on either side of the sequent. For example, the first conjunction rule deletes a conjunction on the left side of a sequent in favor of the two conjoined sentences; informally, it can be read as "Δ follows from Γ and $p \wedge q$ if it follows from Γ, p, and q." It is easily verified that each rule is *sound* with respect to first-order valuations: if the premises are true in an interpretation, then so is the conclusion.

DEFINITION 4.3: *A block tableau for the sequent $\Gamma \Rightarrow \Delta$ in a system τ is a tree whose nodes are sequents, defined inductively as follows.*

1. *$\Gamma \Rightarrow \Delta$ is the root of the tree.*
2. *If sequent s is the parent node of daughters $s_1 \ldots s_n$, then $s/s_1 \ldots s_n$ is a rule of τ.*

A block tableau is closed if all its leaves are axioms. If there is a closed block tableau for the sequent $\Gamma \Rightarrow \Delta$, then this sequent is a theorem *of the system τ and we write $\vdash_\tau \Gamma \Rightarrow \Delta$.*

A system τ' is called a subsystem *of τ if every rule of τ' is also a rule of τ. If some subsystem τ' of τ has exactly the same theorems as τ, then the rules of τ not appearing in τ' are said to be* eliminable *from τ, or* admissible *to τ'*

Block tableaux are similar to the AND/OR trees commonly encountered in AI theorem-proving systems (see Nilsson, 1980). Rules C_2, D_2, and I_2 cause AND-splitting, while a choice of rules to apply at a tableau node is an OR-split.

Example. Here is a block tableau for the sequent $\exists x.\ Bx \wedge Ax,\ \forall x.\ Cx \supset \sim Bx \Rightarrow \exists x.\ Ax \wedge \sim Cx$.

$$
I_2 \quad
\begin{array}{c}
E_2 \dfrac{\exists x.Bx \wedge Ax, \forall x.Cx \supset \sim Bx \Rightarrow \exists x.Ax \wedge \sim Cx}{
U_1 \dfrac{Be \wedge Ae, \forall x.Cx \supset \sim Bx \Rightarrow \exists x.Ax \wedge \sim Cx}{
E_1 \dfrac{Be \wedge Ae, Ce \supset \sim Be \Rightarrow \exists x.Ax \wedge \sim Cx}{
C_1 \dfrac{Be \wedge Ae, Ce \supset \sim Be \Rightarrow Ae \wedge \sim Ce}{
Ae, Be, Ce \supset \sim Be \Rightarrow Ae \wedge \sim Ce}}}}
\end{array}
$$

$$
N_2 \dfrac{Ae, Be, \sim Be \Rightarrow Ae \wedge \sim Ce}{Ae, Be \Rightarrow Be, Ae \wedge \sim Ce} \qquad\qquad
C_2 \dfrac{Ae, Be \Rightarrow Ce, Ae \wedge \sim Ce}{N_1 \dfrac{Ae, Be \Rightarrow Ce, \sim Ce \quad Ae, Be \Rightarrow Ce, Ae}{Ae, Be, Ce \Rightarrow Ce}}
$$

$$\mathsf{x} \qquad\qquad\qquad\qquad\qquad \mathsf{x} \qquad\qquad \mathsf{x}$$

The sequent to be proved is inserted as the root of the tree. By a series of reductions based on the rules of τ_0, the atoms of the sequent's sentences are extracted from the scope of quantifiers and Boolean operators. Splitting of the tree occurs at the rules I_2 and C_2; otherwise the reduction produces just a single sequent below the line. If a tree is found where the sequents at all the leaves are axioms, then the theorem is proved. Note that the logical inferences are from the leaves to the root of the tree, even though we work backwards in forming the tree. At each junction of the tree, the parent sequent is true in an interpretation if all its daughters are true in that interpretation.

An important connection between theoremhood and logical consequence for sequent systems is the following soundness theorem for tableaux.

THEOREM 4.1: *If* $\Gamma \Rightarrow p$ *is a theorem of* τ *(where p is a single sentence of* L_0*), and all the rules of* τ *are sound, then p is a logical consequence of* Γ.

Proof. If the rules of τ are sound, then every theorem of τ is valid. By Definition 4.1, this means that in every interpretation in which all of Γ are true, p must be also. ∎

4.2 The Language of B

The language of **B** is formed from a first-order base language L_0 by adding modal operators for belief and belief circumscription. We call this language L^B. It is convenient to use L^B also as the agents' language L, since it provides a representation for nested beliefs as required by the recursion property. With this assumption, we can parameterize **B** by the base language L_0, and write $B(L_0, {}_\rho)$ for the logic family.

To form L^B from a base language, L_0, we require a countable set of agents (S_0, S_1, . . .).

DEFINITION 4.4: *A sentence of* L^B *based on* L_0 *is defined inductively by the following rules.*

1. *All formation rules of* L_0 *are also formation rules of* L^B.
2. *If p is a sentence, then* $[S_i]p$ *is a sentence for* $i \geq 0$.
3. *If p is a sentence and* Γ *is a finite set of sentences, then* $\langle S_i : \Gamma \rangle p$ *is a sentence for* $i \geq 1$.

An *ordinary atom* of L^B is a ground atom of L_0; a *belief atom* is a sentence of the form $[S_i]p$, and a *circumscriptive atom* is one of the form $\langle S_i : \Gamma \rangle p$. In the belief atom $[S_i]p$, p is said to be *in the context of* the belief operator. Note that there is no quantification into the contexts of belief atoms, since the argument of a belief operator is always a closed sentence. L^B can be extended to include quantification into belief contexts; such a language has greater representational power and its logic **qB** has a more complex axiomatization. The interested reader is referred to Konolige (1984) for a description of **qB**. Here, the simpler **B** is sufficient for an analysis of the problems.

We will use the abbreviation $[S]\Gamma =_{df} [S]\gamma_1, [S]\gamma_2, \ldots$.

4.2.1 Interpretations.
Interpretations of the language of L^B are formed from interpretations of its base language L_0, together with an interpretation of belief and circumscriptive atoms. The intended meaning of the belief atom $[S_i]p$ is that p is in the belief subsystem of agent S_i; informally, we would say "S_i believes p." Since we are formalizing belief subsystems by means of deduction structures, an in-

terpretation of the belief atoms $[S_i]p$ is given by a deduction structure d_i. $[S_i]p$ is *true* if p is in bel(d_i), the belief set of d_i; otherwise it is *false*.

In addition to representing beliefs of individuals, we use belief atoms to represent common beliefs. A common belief is one that every agent believes, and every agent believes every other agent believes, and so on to arbitrary depths of belief nesting. We reserve the name S_0 for a fictional agent whose beliefs are taken to be common among all agents. The belief atom $[S_0]p$ means that p is a common belief. In terms of deduction structures, its intended interpretation is that p and $[S_0]p$ are in the deduction structure d_i of every agent S_i, $i \geq 0$.

McCarthy (see, for example, McCarthy, 1978) was the first to recognize the common knowledge could be represented by the use of a fictitious agent FOOL whose knowledge "any fool" would know. He used a possible-worlds semantics for knowledge, and so all consequences of common knowledge were also known. The representation of common belief presented here uses an obviously similar approach; it differs only in that common belief rather than common knowledge is axiomatized (common beliefs need not be true), and in having a deduction structure semantics, so that common beliefs need not be closed under logical consequence.

The interpretation of circumscriptive atoms is also given by the deduction structure representing an agent's beliefs. The intended meaning of $\langle S_i : \Gamma \rangle p$ is that p is derivable from Γ in the deduction structure d_i, that is, $\Gamma \vdash_{\rho(i)} p$. The circumscription operator elevates the belief derivation process to a first-class entity of the language (as opposed to belief operators $[S_i]$, which simply state that certain sentences are in or not in the belief set).

While it may not be apparent at first glance, the circumscription operator is a powerful tool for representing situations of delimited knowledge. For example, to formally state the condition, "the only facts that agent S knows about proposition p are Γ," we could use

$$\langle S : \Gamma \rangle p \equiv [S]p \tag{4.1}$$

This assertion states that S believing p is equivalent to S being able to derive p from Γ. The forward implication is uninteresting, since it just says that p is derivable from Γ by agent S, i.e., $[S]\Gamma \supset [S]p$. The reverse implication is more interesting, since it states p cannot be a belief of S *unless* it is derivable from Γ. This reverse implication limits the information S has available to derive p to the sentences Γ, and thus gives the circumscriptive content of (4.1). Note that there is no way to formulate the reverse implication as a sentence of L^B using only belief operators.

The reader should note carefully that the semantics of L^B differs completely from that of most modal languages, in which the argument to the modal operator is usually taken to denote a *proposition* that can take on a truth-value in a possible world. By contrast, arguments to modal operators in the language of **B** denote *sentences* of L, namely themselves. It is important to keep this distinction in mind when interpreting the modal operators of **B**.

4.3 A Sequent System for B

The deductive process that underlies the deduction model is characterized in very general terms by deduction structures and their associated belief sets. Until now we have been content with deliberate vagueness about the exact nature of deduction rules and the derivation process. As stated in section 3, there are five conditions that must be satisfied: the deduction rules must be *effective*, *provincial*, and *sound*, and the derivations *reflexive* and *closed under deduction*. Consider a deduction structure $d_i = \langle B, \rho(i) \rangle$ for agent S_i. If we let the process of belief derivation for d_i be symbolized by $\vdash_{\rho(i)}$, these conditions are as follows.

(Effectiveness) The deduction rules $\rho(i)$ are effectively applicable.
(Provinciality) The number of input sentences to each rule is finite and bounded.
(Soundness) If $\Gamma \vdash_{\rho(i)} \alpha$, then α is a logical consequence of Γ.
(Reflexivity) $\alpha \vdash_{\rho(i)} \alpha$.
(Closure) If $\Gamma \vdash_{\rho(i)} \beta$ and $\beta, \Sigma \vdash_{\rho(i)} \alpha$, then $\Gamma, \Sigma \vdash_{\rho(i)} \alpha$.

Suppose we are given beforehand a derivation operator $\vdash_{\rho(i)}$, satisfying the foregoing conditions, that models an agent S_i's belief subsystem. The central problem in the formulation of **B** is to find tableau rules that correctly implement the meaning of the belief operator $[S_i]$ and the circumscription operator $\langle S_i : \Gamma \rangle$ under $\vdash_{\rho(i)}$.

Consider first the sequent $[S_i]\Gamma \Rightarrow [S_i]\alpha$. Its intended meaning is that, if all of Γ are in S_i's belief set, then so is α. The only possible way that we can guarantee this condition is if α is derivable from Γ, *i.e.*, $\Gamma \vdash_{\rho(i)} \alpha$. If this were not the case, then we could always construct the counterexample $d_i =_{df} \langle \Gamma, \rho(i) \rangle$ in which all of Γ are in d_i but α is not. Thus we can relate the truth of a sequent involving belief operators to derivability in an agent's belief subsystem. This relation is captured by the inference rule

$$A: \frac{\Sigma, [S_i]\Gamma \Rightarrow [S_i]\alpha, \Delta}{\Gamma \vdash_{\rho(i)} \alpha} \ .$$

A is called the *attachment rule*, because it derives results involving the belief operator by attaching sentences about belief to the actual derivation process of an agent. Remembering that the premise is the bottom sequent and the conclusion the top, we can read A informally as follows: "If α is a deductive consequence of Γ in S_i's belief subsystem, then, whenever S_i believes Γ, he also believes α."

To capture the notion of common belief, we need to make a modification to the attachment rule. The intended meaning of the common belief atom $[S_0]q$ is that both q and $[S_0]q$ are in the belief subsystem of every agent. The sequent $[S_0]\Lambda, [S_i]\Gamma \Rightarrow [S_i]\alpha$ will be true if whenever $[S_0]\Lambda$, Λ, and Γ are in the belief set of d_i, α also is. By reasoning similar to that used in deriving the rule A, we can rephrase this in terms of belief derivation. This yields the revised attachment rule A^{CB}.

$$A^{\mathbf{CB}}:\frac{\Sigma,[S_0]\Lambda,[S_i]\Gamma \Rightarrow [S_i]\alpha,\Delta}{[S_0]\Lambda,\Lambda,\Gamma \mathrm{B}_{p(i)}\alpha}$$

In $A^{\mathbf{CB}}$, both Λ and $[S_0]\Lambda$ can be used in the derivation of α. Note that this rule is applicable to the fictional agent S_0. Because S_0's beliefs are intended to be common beliefs, and hence derivable by any agent, it should be the case that the rules $\rho(0)$ are used by every agent. We thus demand that $\rho(0) \subseteq \rho(i)$ for every i.

We can find tableau rules for the circumscription operator in a similar manner. The intended semantics of this operator relates directly to the belief derivation process: $\langle S_i : \Gamma \rangle p$ means that p is derivable from Γ in S_i's belief subsystem, *i.e.*, Γ $\mathrm{B}_{\rho(i)}\, p$. In writing sequent rules, there are two cases to consider, for a circumscriptive atom can appear on the right or left side of the sequent arrow. We thus have the following two rules.

$$Circ_1:\frac{\Sigma \Rightarrow \langle S_i : \Gamma \rangle p, \Delta}{\Gamma \mathrm{B}_{p(i)} p}$$

$$Circ_2:\frac{\Sigma, \langle S_i : \Gamma \rangle p \Rightarrow \Delta}{\Gamma \mathrm{B}_{p(i)} p}$$

The second circumscription rule is the one that is used to show circumscriptive ignorance. It states that if p is not derivable from a set of sentences Γ, then the circumscriptive atom $\langle S_i : \Gamma \rangle p$ is false. Given a statement of the form 4.1, this in turn would imply that S_i was ignorant of p.

We can now give a full axiomatization of the logic family **B**.

DEFINITION 4.5: *The system* $\mathbf{B}(L_{0,\rho})$ *has the following postulates.*

1. *The first-order complete rules* τ_0.
2. *The rules* $A^{\mathbf{CB}}$, $Circ_1$, *and* $Circ_2$.
3. *A closed derivation process* $\mathrm{B}_{\rho(i)}$ *for each agent* S_i, *such that* $\rho(0) \subseteq \rho(i)$ *for every* i.

This axiomatization of **B** is both sound and complete with respect to its deduction structure semantics, as proven in Konolige (1984). It is a compact formalization of the deduction model and useful for theoretical investigations, but we do not use it very much as a representational formalism because of the general nature of the belief deduction process $\mathrm{B}_{\rho(i)}$, which is rather opaque to further analysis. For instance, we might wish to look at the subfamily of **B** in which the rules of $\rho(i)$ that govern nested belief are as strong as $A^{\mathbf{CB}}$. In order to explore the fine structure of S_i's belief deduction process, or to formalize the problems, we need to fix the nature of $\mathrm{B}_{\rho(i)}$ more precisely. The rich set of rules, and the flexibility of tableau derivations, make tableau systems a natural choice here. In the next section we define a particularization of **B**, the logic family **BK**, whose belief derivation process is defined in block tableaux terms.

4.4 The Nonintrospective Logic Family BK

In the logic family **BK**, the belief derivation operator B– is defined as probability in a tableau system.

DEFINITION 4.6: *A sentence* α *is* **BK**-*derivable from premises* Γ $(\Gamma$ B–$_\tau$ $\alpha)$ *if and only if* $\vdash_\tau \Gamma \Rightarrow \alpha$.

We need to show that tableau system derivability as just defined satisfies the five criteria of belief derivation: effectiveness, provinciality, soundness, reflexivity and closure. Consider a sequent system τ made up of sound tableau rules. According to Theorem 4.1, the theorem $\vdash_\tau \Gamma \Rightarrow p$ of τ implies that p is a logical consequence of Γ, so we are assured that $\vdash_\tau$ satisfies the soundness criterion. Provinciality and effectiveness are also satisfied, since the theorems of τ are built by using effectively computable steps that operate on a bounded number of sentences at each step. The observant reader might object at this point that tableau rules may indeed refer to an unbounded number of premise sentences; *e.g.*, any of the rules of τ_0 have this property, since Γ and Δ can stand for any set of sentences. However, each rule of τ_0 is actually a rule *schema:* the capital Greek letters are metavariables that are instantiated with a boundedly finite set of sentences to define a rule.

The closure condition is fulfilled by a special subclass of sequent systems, namely those for which the following rule, Cut^*, is admissible:

$$Cut^*: \frac{\Gamma,\Sigma \Rightarrow \alpha}{\Gamma \Rightarrow \beta \quad \beta,\Sigma \Rightarrow \alpha}$$

To see how this rule guarantees closure, suppose that $\Gamma \Rightarrow \beta$ and $\beta,\Sigma \Rightarrow \alpha$ are both theorems of a sequent system τ for which Cut^* is admissible. Because Cut^* is admissible and both of its premises have closed tableaux, the conclusion $\Gamma,\Sigma \Rightarrow \alpha$ must also be a theorem. This is exactly the closure condition in section 4.3.

Finally, the derivation process will be reflexive $(\alpha \vdash_\tau \alpha)$ if we include the following axiom in the system τ:

$$Id : \Sigma,\alpha \Rightarrow \alpha,\Delta.$$

Thus we only allow a system τ to appear in a deduction structure $d\langle B, \tau \rangle$ if the system is sound, Cut^* is an admissible rule of τ, and Id is an axiom of τ.

An interesting consequence of using tableau derivations in **BK** is that the attachment rule A can now be expressed wholly in terms of sequents, eliminating the derivation operator. To see how this comes about, consider first replacing the belief operator in rule A by tableau provability, as given by Definition 4.6. This yields

$$AK': \frac{\Sigma,[S_i]\Gamma \Rightarrow [S_i]\alpha,\Delta}{\vdash_{\tau(i)}\Gamma \Rightarrow \alpha}$$

where $\tau(i)$ is the set of tableau rules used by agent S_i.

Now $\vdash_{\tau(i)} \Gamma \Rightarrow \alpha$ is true precisely if there is a closed tableau for $\Gamma \Rightarrow \alpha$, using the rules $\tau(i)$. Hence we should be able to eliminate the provability symbol if we add the rules $\tau(i)$ to **B** for the purpose of constructing a tableau for $\Gamma \Rightarrow \alpha$. In order to keep the agents' rules $\tau(i)$ from being confused with the rules of **B**, we add an agent index to sequents to indicate that the tableau rules to be use are for a particular agent. The final version of the attachment rule is

$$AK: \frac{\Sigma,[S_i]\Gamma \Rightarrow [S_i]\alpha,\Delta}{\Gamma \Rightarrow_i \alpha}$$

Agents' rules are expressed using the indexed sequent sign, *e.g.*, if agent S_i were to use C_2, the following rule would be added to **B**.

$$C_2^i: \frac{\Gamma \Rightarrow_i \Delta,p \wedge q}{\Gamma \Rightarrow_i \Delta,p \quad \Gamma \Rightarrow_i \Delta,q}$$

Taking the recursion property of belief subsystems seriously, we can iterate the process just described for the attachment rule. Each agent treats other agents as having a set of tableau rules. In formulating **BK**, there will be a tableau rule set associated with each view (views are discussed in relation to the recursion property in section 3.3). Let us symbolize the set of tableau rules representing the view v by $\tau(v)$.

A sequent $\Gamma \Rightarrow_v \Delta$, with index v, is a statement about the belief subsystem of the view v. For example, if $v = Sue,Kim$, the sequent $\Gamma \Rightarrow_v p$ states that p follows from Γ in Sue's view of Kim's belief subsystem. The deduction rules $\tau(v)$ always have sequents indexed by v in their conclusions (above the line), as in rule C_2^i above. This assures us that they will always be used as rules of the belief subsystem v, and of no other.

The logic **BK** can thus be parameterized by a set of tableau rules for each view, and we write **BK**(L_0,τ) to indicate this. If the sequent $\Gamma \Rightarrow_v \Delta$ is a theorem of the logic **BK**(L_0,τ), it asserts that the sequent $\Gamma \Rightarrow \Delta$ is provable in the view v. We write this as $\vdash_{\mathbf{BK}(L_0,\tau)} \Gamma \Rightarrow_v \Delta$. If this sequent is a theorem for every parameterization of **BK**, we write simply $\vdash \Gamma \Rightarrow_v \Delta$. Note that the presence of the index on the sequent means that we do not have to state explicitly that the set of rules used to derive the theorem were those of the view v. Properties of the actual belief subsystems are always stated using unindexed sequent; for example, to show formally that if an agent believes p, then he believes q, we would have to prove that the sequent $[S_i]p \Rightarrow [S_i]q$ is a theorem of **BK**.

4.4.1 Postulates of BK(L_0,τ). This family is parameterized by a base language L_0 and tableau rules $\tau(v)$ for each view v.

DEFINITION 4.7: *The system* **BK**(L_0,τ) *is given by the following postulates:*

1. *The first-order complete rules τ_0.*
2. *The attachment rule*

$$AK\mathbf{CB}: \frac{\Sigma,[S_0]\Lambda,[S_i]\Gamma \Rightarrow [S_i]\alpha,\Delta}{[S_0]\Lambda,\Lambda,\Gamma \Rightarrow_i \alpha} \ .$$

3. *A set of sound sequent rules τ (v) for each view v that contains the axiom Id, and for which the rule Cut* is admissible. Also, $\tau(v,0) \subseteq \tau(v,i)$ for all views v and agents S_i.*
4. *The circumscription rules*

$$CircK_1: \frac{\Sigma \Rightarrow \langle S_i:\Gamma\rangle p,\Delta}{\Gamma \Rightarrow_i p}$$

and

$$CircK_2: \frac{\Sigma,\langle S_i:\Gamma\rangle p \Rightarrow \Delta}{\nvdash\Gamma \Rightarrow_i p}$$

Remarks. There are three parts to the system $\mathbf{BK}(L_0,\tau)$. The first part is a set of rules that perform first-order deductions about the real world. These rules incorporate the nonsubscripted sequent sign $(\Rightarrow)$.

The second part is the attachment rule $AK^{\mathbf{CB}}$, together with a set of rules formalizing the deductive system of each view. These rules involve the sequent sign $\Rightarrow_v$, since they talk about agents' deductive systems. They can contain rules that have a purely nonmodal import (*e.g.*, rules of τ_0), as well as rules that deal with belief operators. The rule *Cut**, which implements the closure property of belief sets, must be an admissible rule of $\tau(v)$.

The rules $\tau(v)$ of a view v can be incomplete in several ways. They may be first-order incomplete, in which case they cannot be used to draw all the consequences of sentences involving nonmodal operators that they otherwise might (to be first-order complete, it is sufficient for the rules τ_0 to be admissible in a view). They may also be incomplete with respect to the semantics of sentences involving belief operators. To be complete in this respect, a sufficient rule would be $AK^{\mathbf{CB}}$. A view for which this rule is admissible is called *recursively complete*. If every view of a logic $\mathbf{BK}(L_0,\tau)$ is recursively and first-order complete, the logic is called *saturated*. We will symbolize the subfamily of saturated logics by $\mathbf{BK}_s$.

The rule $AK^{\mathbf{CB}}$ is a weak version of the attachment rule $A^{\mathbf{CB}}$ in that it makes no assumptions about the beliefs an agent may have of his own beliefs. For example, we might argue that, if an agent S believes a proposition P, then he believes that he believes it. All he has to do to establish this is query his belief subsystem with the question, "Do I believe P?" If the answer comes back "yes," then he should be able to infer that he does indeed believe P,*i.e.*, $[S][S]P$ is true if $[S[P$ is. However, as far as rule $AK^{\mathbf{CB}}$ is concerned, an agent's own belief subsystem has the same status for him as does that of any other agent. In particular, $AK^{\mathbf{CB}}$ allows an agent to have false and incomplete beliefs about his own beliefs. Other version of $AK^{\mathbf{CB}}$ with stronger assumptions about self-belief are possible (see section 6).

The third part consists of the two circumscription rules. The provability operator can be eliminated from $CircK_1$, but not from $CircK_2$. In order to show that p does not follow from Γ for S_i, we must show that there is no closed tableau for $\Gamma \Rightarrow_i p$. One technique that we use for this in solving the problems is the following. If there is no closed tableau for a *saturated* logic of **BK**, there is no closed tableau for any logic of **BK**. Every theorem of saturated **BK** is a theorem of the normal modal system $K4$ (see section 6), which has a decision procedure based on the methods of Sato (1976). Thus if a sequent is not provable in $K4$, it is not provable in any logic of **BK**.

4.4.2 Some Theorems of BK

THEOREM 4.2: *Let p be derivable from Γ in the view i of* **BK**(L_0,τ). *Then*

$$\vdash_{\mathbf{BK}(L_0,\tau)} [S_i]\Gamma \Rightarrow [S_i]p$$

Proof. In one step, using rule $AK^{\mathbf{CB}}$:

$$AK^{\mathbf{CB}} \; \frac{[S_i]\Gamma \Rightarrow [S_i]p}{\Gamma \Rightarrow_i p}$$
$$\mathsf{X}$$

∎

THEOREM 4.3: *Let v be a recursively complete view of* **BK**(L_0,τ), *and let p be derivable from Γ in the view v,i. Then*

$$\vdash_{\mathbf{BK}(L_0,\tau)} [S_i]\Gamma \Rightarrow_v [S_i]p$$

Proof. In one step, using rule $AK^{\mathbf{CB}}$ of $\tau(v)$:

$$AK^{\mathbf{CB}} \; \frac{[S_i]\Gamma \Rightarrow_v [S_i]p}{\Gamma \Rightarrow_{v,i} p}$$
$$\mathsf{X}$$

∎

Remarks. These two theorems show that **BK** has a weakened analog of the necessitation rule of modal logic (if α is provable, so is $\Box\alpha$). If a nonmodal sentence α is provable in the view i (*i.e.,* $\vdash_{\mathbf{BK}(L_0,\tau)} \Rightarrow_i \alpha$), then, by Theorem 4.2, $[S_i]\alpha$ is provable in the empty view. Since the theorems of $\tau(i)$ are assumed to be sound, α is a tautology, and so must be provable in the empty view.[4] Hence, for those tautologies provable in the view i, necessitation holds. Theorem 4.3 establishes this result for an arbitrary view in which A is an admissible rule. Depending on the exact nature of the rule sets τ, necessitation will hold for some subset of the provable sentences of a particular logic **BK**(L_0,τ).

---

[4]Care must be taken in restricting α to nonmodal sentences, since the semantics of modal operators can change from one view to another (see the discussion of the recursion property in section 3.3).

THEOREM 4.4: $\nvdash [S_i]p \Rightarrow p$

Proof. If p is a primitive sentence, then there is no applicable tableaux rule, and hence no closed tableaux for the sequent.∎

Remarks. The familiar modal logic principle $\Box p \supset p$ (if p is necessary, then p is true) is not a theorem of **BK,** since beliefs need not be true.

THEOREM 4.5: $\nvdash [S_i]p \Rightarrow [S_i][S_i]p$

Proof. The only applicable rule is $AK^{\mathbf{CB}}$:

$$AK^{\mathbf{CB}} \frac{[S_i]p \Rightarrow [S_i][S_i]p}{p \Rightarrow_i [S_i]p}$$

According to the semantics of the deduction model, the sequent $p \Rightarrow_i [S_i]p$ is not valid: just because a sentence p is true does not mean that an agent S_i believes it. Hence, there cannot be any set of sound tableau rules for $\tau(i)$ that causes $p \Rightarrow_i [S_i]p$ to close.∎

THEOREM 4.6: $\nvdash \sim[S_i]p \Rightarrow [S_i] \sim [S_i]p$

Proof. We can apply either N_2 or $AK^{\mathbf{CB}}$. If we apply the latter, we obtain

$$AK^{\mathbf{CB}} \frac{\sim[S_i]p \Rightarrow [S_i]\sim[S_i]p}{\Rightarrow_i \sim[S_i]p}.$$

But $\sim [S_i]p$ is not a valid sentence according to the deduction model, since it would require that no agent believe any sentence. Hence there can be no set of sound tableau rules $\tau(i)$ that derives it.

If we apply N_2 first, we obtain

$$N_2 \frac{\sim[S_i]p \Rightarrow [S_i]\sim[S_i]p}{\Rightarrow [S_i]p,[S_i]\sim[S_i]24S_i]p}$$

There are now two ways to apply $AK^{\mathbf{CB}}$. In one application, we generate the sequent $\Rightarrow_i \sim[S_i]p$, which cannot close. In the other, we generate $\Rightarrow_i p$, which again cannot be derived by any set of sound tableau rules.∎

Remarks. These theorems show that no logic of **BK** sanctions inferences about self-beliefs. If an agent believes p, it does not follow that his model of his own beliefs includes p; this is the import of Theorem 4.5. Similarly, if he does not believe p, he also may not have knowledge of this fact, as shown by Theorem 4.6.

THEOREM 4.7: $\vdash [S_0]p \Rightarrow [S_0][S_0]p$

Proof.

$$AK^{\mathbf{CB}} \frac{[S_0]p \Rightarrow [S_0][S_0]p}{[S_0]p,p \Rightarrow_i [S_0]p}$$
$$\times$$

∎

Remarks. We have proven a simple fact about common beliefs: if p is a common belief, it is a common belief that this is so.

For the circumscriptive ignorance part of **BK**, it is an interesting exercise to show that

$$\langle S_i : \Gamma \rangle p \Rightarrow [S_i]\Gamma \supset [S_i]p \tag{4.2}$$

holds, but the converse doesn't. That is, if p follows from Γ for agent S_i, it must be the case that believing Γ entails believing p; on the other hand, it may be that every time an agent has Γ in his base set he also has p, which would satisfy $[S_i]\Gamma \supset [S_i]p$ without having p derivable from Γ.

THEOREM 4.8: $\vdash \langle S_i : \Gamma \rangle p \Rightarrow [S_i]\Gamma \supset [S_i]p$

Proof. We have the following two tableaux for this sentence.

$$AK^{\mathbf{CB}} \quad I_1 \frac{\dfrac{\langle S_i : \Gamma \rangle p \Rightarrow [S_i]\Gamma \supset [S_i]p}{\langle S_i : \Gamma \rangle p[S_i]\Gamma \Rightarrow [S_i]p}}{\Gamma \Rightarrow_i p}$$

$$Circ_2 \quad I_1 \frac{\dfrac{\langle S_i : \Gamma \rangle p \Rightarrow [S_i]\Gamma \supset [S_i]p}{\langle S_i : \Gamma \rangle p, [S_i]\Gamma \Rightarrow [S_i]p}}{\not{\vdash}\Gamma \Rightarrow_i p}$$

Either p is derivable from Γ using the rules $\tau(i)$, or it isn't. In either case one of these tableaux closes. ∎

Example. We give an example of the use of the circumscription rules to show ignorance. Suppose the agent Sue believes only the sentences P and $P \supset Q$ in a situation; we want to show that she doesn't believe R. Thus we want to prove the sequent $\langle Sue : P, P \supset Q \rangle R \equiv [Sue]R \Rightarrow \sim[Sue]R$.

$$C_1 \frac{\langle Sue{:}P, P \supset Q \rangle R \equiv [Sue]R \Rightarrow \sim[Sue]R}{}$$
$$I_2 \frac{\langle Sue{:}P, P \supset Q \rangle R \supset [Sue]R, [Sue]R \supset \langle Sue{:}P, P \supset Q \rangle R \Rightarrow \sim[Sue]R}{}$$

$$Circ_2 \frac{\langle Sue{:}P, P \supset Q \rangle R \Rightarrow \sim[Sue]R}{\not{\vdash} P, P \supset Q \Rightarrow_{Sue} R} \qquad N_2 \frac{\Rightarrow [Sue]R, \sim[Sue]R}{\dfrac{[Sue]R \Rightarrow [Sue]R}{\times}}$$

If the rules $\tau(Sue)$ are sound, there is no closed tableau for $P, P \supset Q \Rightarrow_{Sue} R$, and so both branches of the tableau close. Note that only the reverse implication half of the equivalence was needed; we have deleted the forward implication from the last part of the proof to simplify it.

5 The Problems Revisited

Using the logic **BK**, we present formal solutions to the two representational problems posed at the beginning of this section. In each case we have tried to avoid solutions that are trivial in the sense that they solve the representational problem, but only at the expense of excluding types of reasoning that might be expected to occur. For example, in the chess problem it would be an adequate but unrealistic solution to credit each player with no deduction rules at all. Instead, we try to find rules that allow a resource-limited amount of reasoning about the game to take place.

5.1 The Chess Problem

To approach this problem, we need to represent the game in a first-order language. Because the ontology of chess involves rather complicated objects (pieces, board positions, moves, histories of moves) we will not give a complete formalization, but rather sketch in outline how this might be done.

We use a multisorted first-order language L_c for the base language L_0. The key sorts will be those for players (S_w or S_b), moves, and boards. The particular structure of the sort terms is not important for the solution of this problem, but they should have the following information. A board contains the position of all pieces, and a history of the moves that were made to get to that position. This is important because we want to be able to find all legal moves from a given position; to do this, we have to have the sequence of moves leading up to the position, since legal moves can be defined only in terms of this sequence. For example, castling can only occur once, even if a player returns to the position before the castle; more importantly, there are no legal moves if 50 moves have been made without a capture or pawn advancement (this is what makes chess a finite game). A move contains enough information so that it is possible to compute all successor boards, that is, those resulting from legal moves.

The *game tree* is a useful concept in exploring game-playing strategies. This is a finite tree (for finite games like chess) whose nodes are board positions, and whose branches are all possible complete games. A terminal node of the tree ends in either a win for White or Black, or a draw. The *game-theoretic value* of a node for a player is either 1 (a win), 0 (a draw), or -1 (a loss), based on whether that player can force a win or a draw, or his opponent can force a win. We use the predicate $M(p,b,k,l,r)$ to mean that board b has value k for player p. The argument l is a depth-of-search indicator, and shows the maximum depth of the game tree that the value is based on. We include the argument r so that M can represent heuristic information about the value of a node; when $r = f$, k is the player's subjective estimate of the value of the node, *i.e.*, he has not searched to all terminal nodes of the game tree. If $r = t$, then k is the game-theoretic value of the board.

We take the formal interpretation of boards, players, and the M predicate to be the game of chess, so that L_c is a partially interpreted language. The rules of the game of chess strictly specify what the game tree and its associated values will be; hence, each predication $M(p,b,k,l,t)$ or its negation is a valid consequence of these interpretations. Any agent who knows the rules of chess, and who has the concept of game trees, will know the game-theoretic value of every node if his beliefs are consequentially closed. In particular, he will believe either $M(S_w,I,l,k,t)$ or $\sim M(S_w,I,l,k,t)$, where I is the initial board; and so he will know whether White has an initial forced win or not.

We represent agents' knowledge of chess by giving tableau rules for L_c. The rules τ_c presented below are one possible choice.

$$Ch_1: \frac{\Gamma \Rightarrow M(p,b,k,l,r),\Delta}{\Gamma \Rightarrow M(p,b_1,k_1,l_1,r_1),\Delta \quad \Gamma \Rightarrow M(p,b_2,k_2,l_2,r_2),\Delta \quad \cdots \quad \Gamma \Rightarrow M(p,b_n,k_n,l_n,r_n),\Delta},$$

where: b_1-b_n are *all* the legal successor boards to b
p's opponent is to move on b
k is the minimum of k_1-k_n
l is $1 +$ (the maximum of $l_1 - l_n$)
r is **t** *iff* all of $r_1 - r_n$ are **t**

$$Ch_2: \frac{\Gamma \Rightarrow M(p,b,k,l,r),\Delta}{\Gamma \Rightarrow M(p,b_1,k_1,l_1,r_1),\Delta \quad \Gamma \Rightarrow M(p,b_2,k_2,l_2,r_2),\Delta \quad \cdots \quad \Gamma \Rightarrow M(p,b_n,k_n,l_n,r_n),\Delta},$$

where $b_1 - b_n$ are *all* the legal successor boards to b
p is to move on b
k is the maximum of $k_1 - k_n$
l is $1 +$ (the maximum of l_1-l_n)
r is **t** *iff* all of r_1-r_n are **t**

$$Ch_3 : \Gamma \Rightarrow M(p,b,k,0,t),\ \Delta,$$

where $k = 1$ if p has a checkmate on his opponent on board b; $k = 0$ if board b is a draw; and $k = -1$ if p's opponent has a checkmate.

$$Ch_4 : \Gamma \Rightarrow M(p,b,k,0,f),\ \Delta,$$

where k is any number between -1 and 1

Ch_1 axiomatizes nodes in the game tree where p's opponent moves. The value of such a node is the minimum of the values of its successor nodes. The argument l is the maximum depth of the subtree searched. r will be **t** only if all the subtrees have been searched for leaf nodes. Ch_2 is similar to Ch_1, except p moves, and the maximum of the successor values is chosen. Ch_3 is the rule for terminal nodes of the tree. Ch_4 is a rule for heuristic evaluation of any node; note that the last argument to M is **f**, which indicates that a terminal node has not been reached. Each agent may have his own particular heuristics for evaluating nonterminal nodes; we can accommodate this by changing the values for k in Ch_4.

As an example of the use of these rules, consider the following tableau proof.

$$Ch_1 \frac{\Rightarrow M(S_w,b,1,2,t)}{\Rightarrow M(S_w,b_1,1,0,t) \quad Ch_2 \frac{\Rightarrow M(S_w,b_2,1,1,t) \qquad\qquad \Rightarrow M(S_w,b_5,1,0,t)}{\Rightarrow M(S_w,b_3,0,0,t) \quad \Rightarrow M(S_w,b_4,1,0,t)}}$$

$$\begin{array}{ccc} \text{x} & \quad \text{x} & \quad \text{x} \\ & \text{x} \qquad\qquad \text{x} & \end{array}$$

(5.1)

This is a proof that the board b has a value 1 for White, searching to all terminal nodes. Boards b_1, b_2, and b_3 all have value 1, so an application of rule Ch_1 yields that value 1 for b (it is Black's turn to move on b). Boards b_1 and b_5 are terminal nodes that are checkmates for White. There are two legal moves from board b_2; one ends in a draw (b_3), the other in a win (b_4) for White. Since it is White's turn to move, rule Ch_2 applies.

The structure of this tableau proof mimics exactly the structure of the game tree from the board b. Indeed, for any subtree of the complete game tree of chess whose root the board b with value k for player p, there is a corresponding proof of $M(p,b,k,l,\mathbf{t})$ using the rules τ_c. In particular, if one of $M(S_w,I,1,l,\mathbf{t})$, $M(S_w,I,0,l,\mathbf{t})$, or $M(S_w,I,-1,l,\mathbf{t})$ is true, there is a proof of this fact. Hence the rules τ_c are sufficient for a player to reason whether White has a forced initial win or not, given an infinite resource bound for derivations. If we model agents as having the rules τ_c, so that $\tau_c \subseteq \tau(v)$ for every view v, the conversation presented at the beginning of this paper would make sense: each agent would believe that everyone knew whether White had a forced initial win.

A simple modification of the rules Ch_1 and Ch_2 can restrict exploration of the entire game tree, while still allowing agents to reason about game tree values using the heuristic axioms Ch_4, or the terminal node axioms Ch_3 if the game subtree is small. All that is necessary is to add the condition that no rule is applicable when the depth l is greater than some constant N. S_w would still be able to reason about the game to depths less than or equal to N, but he could go no further. In this way, a deductively closed system can represent a resource-limited derivation process. The revised rules are

Ch'_1 : Ch_1, with the condition that $l \leq N$.

Ch'_2 : Ch_2, with the condition that $l \leq N$.

With these rules, the proof of (5.1) would still go through for $N \geq 2$, but a proof of $M(S_w,I,k,l,\mathbf{t})$ would not be found if N were low enough to stop search at a reasonable level of the game tree.

The solution to the chess problem illustrates the ability of the deduction model to represent resource bounds by the imposition of constraints on deduction rules. There are other workable constraints for this problem besides depth cutoff: for example, the number of nodes in the tree being searched could be kept below some minimum. Because the structure of proofs mimics the game tree, any cutoff condition that is based on the game tree could be represented by appropriate deduction rules.

5.2 The Not-So-Wise-Man Problem
For this problem we use a base language L_w containing only the three primitive propositions P_1, P_2, and P_3. P_i expresses the proposition that wise man S_i has a white spot on his forehead.

In the initial situation, no one has spoken except the king, who has declared that at least one spot is white. Axioms for this situation are

$$P_1 \wedge P_2 \wedge P_3 \tag{W1}$$

$$[S_0](P_1 \vee P_2 \vee P_3) \tag{W2}$$

$$(P_i \supset [S_j]P_i) \wedge [S_0](P_i \supset [S_j]P_i), \qquad i \neq j, \quad j \neq 0 \tag{W3}$$

$$(\sim P_i \supset [S_j]\sim P_i) \wedge [S_0](\sim P_i \supset [S_j]\sim P_i), \quad i \neq j, j \neq 0 \tag{W4}$$

$$\langle S_i{:}W2\text{-}4,P_j,P_k\rangle P_i \equiv [S_i]P_i, \qquad i \neq j,k \tag{C1}$$

(W1) describes the actual placement of the dots. (W2) is the result of the king's utterance: it is a common belief that at least one spot is white. (W3) and (W4) are schemata expressing the wise men's observational abilities, including the fact that everyone is aware of each other's capabilities. (C1) is the circumscriptive ignorance axiom: the only beliefs a wise man has about the color of his own spot are the three axioms $(W_2\text{-}W_4)$, plus his observation of the other two wise men's spots.

As an exercise of the formalism, especially the circumscription rules, let us show that all agents are ignorant of the color of their own spot in the initial situation.

$$I_2 \dfrac{C_1 \dfrac{CircK_1 \dfrac{\dfrac{C \Rightarrow \sim[S_i]P_i}{[S_i]P_i \supset \langle S_i{:}W2\text{-}4,P_j,P_k\rangle P_i \Rightarrow \sim[S_i]P_i}}{\langle S_i{:}W2\text{-}4,P_j,P_k\rangle P_i \Rightarrow \sim[S_i]P_i}}{\not\vdash W2\text{-}4,P_j,P_k \Rightarrow_i P_i} \quad N_1 \dfrac{\Rightarrow [S_i]P_i, \sim[S_i]P_i}{[S_i]P_i \Rightarrow [S_i]P_i}}{\times} \tag{5.2}$$

We have omitted some irrelevant sentences from the left side of sequents in this tableau. To show that it closes, we must be able to prove that there is no set of sound deduction rules that will enable S_i to deduce P_i from W2, W3, W4, P_j, and P_k. We can prove this for any set of sound tableau rules by showing that $W2\text{-}4, P_j, P_k \Rightarrow_i P_i$ is not provable in the normal modal logic $K4$ (see section 4.4). It is possible to find a $K4$-model in which the sequent $W2\text{-}4, P_j, P_k \Rightarrow_i P_i$ is false, using the methods of Sato (1976); hence this sequent is not provable in any logic of **BK**.

After the first wise man has spoken, it becomes a common belief that he does not know his own spot is white. The appropriate axioms are

$$\sim[S_1]P_1 \wedge [S_0]\sim[S_1]P_1 \tag{W5}$$

$$\langle S_i : W1\text{-}5, P_j, P_k\rangle P_i \equiv [S_i]P_i, \ i \neq j,k \tag{C2}$$

In this new situation, all the wise men are again ignorant of their own spot's color; we could prove this fact, showing that $\vdash C2 \Rightarrow \sim [S_i]P_i$, in a manner similar to the proof in (5.2). S_2 relates his failure to the others, and the new situation has the additional axiom

$$\sim[S_2]P_2 \wedge [S_0]\sim[S_2]P_2 \tag{W6}$$

The third wise man at this point does have sufficient cause to claim his spot is white, but only if the second wise man is indeed wise, and the third wise man believes he is. To see how this comes about, let us prove it in the saturated form of **BK**. We will take the wise men to be powerful reasoners, and set $\tau(v) = \tau_0 + AK^{CB} + CircK_1 + CircK_2$, for all views v. The sequent we wish to prove is $W1\text{--}6 \Rightarrow [S_3]P_3$.

$$
I_2 \cfrac{C_1 \cfrac{C_1 \cfrac{W1\text{--}6 \Rightarrow [S_3]P_3}{W2\text{--}6,P_1,P_2,P_3 \Rightarrow [S_3]P_3}}{W2\text{--}6,P_1,P_2,P_3,P_2 \supset [S_3]P_2 \Rightarrow [S_3]P_3}}{\cfrac{\begin{array}{c}P_2 \Rightarrow P_2 \\ \times\end{array} \quad I_2 \cfrac{C_1 \cfrac{W2\text{--}6,P_1,P_2,P_3,[S_3]P_2 \Rightarrow [S_3]P_3}{W2\text{--}6,P_1,P_2,P_3,[S_3]P_2,P_1 \supset [S_3]P_1 \Rightarrow [S_3]P_3}}{\begin{array}{c}P_1 \Rightarrow P_1 \\ \times\end{array} \quad AKCB \cfrac{W2\text{--}6,P_1,P_2,P_3,[S_3]P_2,[S_3]P_1 \Rightarrow [S_3]P_3}{W2\text{--}6,P_1 \vee P_2 \vee P_3,P_2,P_1 \Rightarrow_3 P_3}}}{}} \tag{5.3}
$$

This part of the proof is mostly bookkeeping. We have used some shortcuts in the proof, omitting some obvious steps and dropping sentences from either side of the sequent if they are not going to be used.

We now must show that S_3's belief subsystem can prove P_3 from the assumptions $W2\text{--}6$ and from the belief that the other two wise men's dots are white (note that we are now using S_3's sequent $\Rightarrow_3$).

$$
I_2 \cfrac{C_1 \cfrac{W2\text{--}6,P_1 \vee P_2 \vee P_3,P_2,P_1 \Rightarrow_3 P_3}{W2\text{--}6,P_1,P_2,P_1 \supset [S_2]P_1 \Rightarrow_3 P_3}}{\cfrac{\begin{array}{c}P_1 \Rightarrow_3 P_1 \\ \times\end{array} \quad I_2 \cfrac{C_1 \cfrac{W2\text{--}6,P_1,P_2,[S_2]P_1 \Rightarrow_3 P_3}{W2\text{--}6,P_1,P_2,[S_2]P_1,\sim P_3 \supset [S_2]\sim P_3 \Rightarrow_3 P_3}}{\cfrac{N_1 \cfrac{\Rightarrow_3 P_3,\sim P_3}{P_3 \Rightarrow_3 P_3}}{\times} \quad N_2 \cfrac{W2\text{--}6,P_1,P_2,[S_2]P_1,[S_2]\sim P_3 \Rightarrow_3 P_3}{W2\text{--}6,P_1,P_2,[S_2]P_1,[S_2]\sim P_3 \Rightarrow_3 P_3,[S_2]P_2}}{AKCB \cfrac{}{W2\text{--}6,P_1 \vee P_2 \vee P_3,P_1,\sim P_3 \Rightarrow_{32} P_2}}}}{}} \tag{5.4}
$$

Note the atom P_3 on the right-hand side of the top sequent; it is equivalent to $\sim P_3$ on the left-hand side, *i.e.*, the assumption that S_3's spot is black. The sequent proof here mimics the third wise man's reasoning, *Suppose my spot were black. . . .* Through the observation axiom $W4$, which is a common belief, this assumption means that S_3 believes that S_2 believes $\sim P_3$. At this point, S_3 begins to reason about S_2's beliefs. Since, by $W6$, the second wise man is unaware of the color of his own spot, a contradiction will be derived if P_2 follows in S_2's belief subsystem.

$$
I_2 \cfrac{C_1 \cfrac{W2\text{--}6,P_1 \vee P_2 \vee P_3,P_1,\sim P_3 \Rightarrow_{32} P_2}{W2\text{--}6,P_1,\sim P_3,\sim P_3 \supset [S_1]\sim P_3 \Rightarrow_{32} P_2}}{\cfrac{\begin{array}{c}\sim P_3 \Rightarrow_{32} \sim P_3 \\ \times\end{array} \quad I_2 \cfrac{C_1 \cfrac{W2\text{--}6,P_1,\sim P_3,[S_1]\sim P_3 \Rightarrow_{32} P_2}{W2\text{--}6,P_1,\sim P_3,[S_1]\sim P_3,\sim P_2 \supset [S_1]\sim P_2 \Rightarrow_{32} P_2}}{\cfrac{N_1 \cfrac{\Rightarrow_{32} P_2,\sim P_2}{P_2 \Rightarrow_{32} P_2}}{\times} \quad N_2 \cfrac{W2\text{--}6,P_1,\sim P_3,[S_1]\sim P_3,[S_1]\sim P_2 \Rightarrow_{32} P_2}{W2\text{--}6,P_1,\sim P_3,[S_1]\sim P_3,[S_1]\sim P_2 \Rightarrow_{32} P_2,[S_1]P_1,[S_1]\sim P_1}}{AKCB \cfrac{}{W2\text{--}6,P_1 \vee P_2 \vee P_3,\sim P_2,\sim P_3 \Rightarrow_{321} P_1}}}}{}} \tag{5.5}
$$

S_2's reasoning (in S_3's view) takes the assumption that the third wise man's spot is black and asks what the effect would be on the first wise man S_1. Since S_1 is also ignorant of the color of his own spot, a contradiction will ensue if the first wise man can prove that his own spot is white, under the assumption $\sim P_3$. The remainder of the proof is conducted in the view 321.

$$D_2 \frac{N_2 \dfrac{W2\text{--}6, P_1 \vee P_2 \vee P_3, \sim P_2, \sim P_3 \Rightarrow_{321} P_1}{W2\text{--}6, P_1 \vee P_2 \vee P_3 \Rightarrow_{321} P_1, P_2, P_3}}{\underset{\times}{P_1 \Rightarrow_{321} P_1, P_2, P_3} \quad \underset{\times}{P_2 \Rightarrow_{321} P_1, P_2, P_3} \quad \underset{\times}{P_3 \Rightarrow_{321} P_1, P_2, P_3}} \qquad (5.6)$$

In pursuing this proof, we have assumed that the second wise man is indeed wise. There are several places in which, with slightly less powerful deduction rules for the view 32, the proof would break down. Each of these corresponds to one of the two types of incompleteness that we identified in the statement of the problem: relevance incompleteness and fundamental logical incompleteness.

Consider first the notion that S_2 is not particularly good at reasoning about what other agents do not believe, a case of fundamental logical incompleteness. One way to capture this would be to weaken the rule N_2 in the following manner:

$$N_2': \frac{\Gamma, \sim p \Rightarrow_{32} \Delta}{\Gamma \Rightarrow_{32} p, \Delta}, \qquad \text{where } p \text{ contains no belief operators.}$$

The modified rule N_2' would not allow deductions about what agents do not know. In particular, it would not allow the transfer of the sentence $\sim [S_1]P_1$ to the left-hand side of the sequent, a crucial step in the tableau (5.5) for the view $\Rightarrow_{32}$.

Note that the modified rule N_2' still allows deductions about what other agents do believe. For instance, if S_2 were asked whether S_1's believing P_1 followed from his believing $\sim P_2$ and $\sim P_3$, S_2 would say "yes," even with the logically incomplete rule N_2' (as in tableau (5.6) above).

A more drastic case of logical incompleteness would result if S_2 simply did not reason about the beliefs of other agents at all. In that case, one would exclude the rule AK^{CB} from S_2's deduction structure. Again, the proof would not go through, because the attachment rule could not be applied in the tableau (5.5).

The notion of relevance incompleteness emerges if the not-so-wise-man S_2 does not consider all the information he has available to answer the king. For example, he may think that the observations of other agents are not relevant to the determination of his own spot, since the results of those observations are not directly available to him. The observational axioms $W3$ and $W4$ enter into the proof tableau (5.5) in two places. Both times the rule I_2 is used to break statements of the form $p \supset [S]p$ into their component atoms. Preventing the decomposition of $W3$ and $W4$ effectively prevents S_2 from reasoning about the observations of other agents. A weakened version of I_2 for doing this is:

$$I_2': \frac{\Gamma, p \supset q \Rightarrow_{32} \Delta}{\Gamma \Rightarrow_{32} p, \Delta \quad \Gamma, q \Rightarrow_{32} \Delta}, \qquad \text{where } p \text{ and } q \text{ are both modal or both nonmodal.}$$

This rule is actually weaker than required for the purpose we have in mind. Consider the observation axiom $\sim P_3 \supset [S_1] \sim P_3$. There are two ways S_2 could use this axiom. If S_2 believes $\sim P_3$, he could conclude that S_1 does also. This is not the type of deduction we wish to prevent, since it means that S_2 attributes beliefs to other agents based on his own beliefs about the world. On the other hand, the axiom $\sim P_2 \supset [S_1]\sim P_2$ is used in a conceptually different fashion. Here it is the contrapositive implication: if S_1 actually does not believe $\sim P_2$, then P_2 must hold. The way this shows up in the proof tableau (5.5) is that $\sim P_3$ appears as an initial assumption on the sequent $W2-5$, P_1, $\sim P_3 \Rightarrow_{32} P_2$, while P_2 is a goal to be proved.

To capture the notion of using an implicational sentence in one direction only, we would have to complicate the deduction rules by introducing asymmetry between the left and right sides of the sequent. This is one of the major strategies used by commonsense theorem provers of the PLANNER tradition (Hewitt, 1972, originated this theorem-proving method). Rather than having implicational rules of the form I_2, typical PLANNER-type systems use something like the following rule.

$$PI: \frac{\Gamma, p, p \supset q \Rightarrow \Delta}{\Gamma, p, q, p \supset q \Rightarrow \Delta}$$

The implicational sentence is used in one direction only in *PI*. If it is desired to make contrapositive inferences, then the contrapositive form of the implication must be included explicitly. The construction of PLANNER-type deduction rules within the tableau framework allows a much finer degree of control over the inference process. A full exposition of such a system is beyond the scope of this paper; the interested reader is referred to Konolige (1984).

In sum, we have shown that it is possible for the deduction model to represent the situation in which not-so-wise-man has less than perfect reasoning ability, preventing the third wise man from figuring out the color of his own spot. Both relevance incompleteness and fundamental logical incompleteness can be captured by using appropriate rules for $\tau(32)$.

6 Other Formal Approaches to Belief

How does the deduction model and its logic **B** compare to other formal models and logics of belief? We examine two alternative approaches in this section: modal logics based on a Hintikka/Kripke possible-worlds semantics, and several different first-order formalizations that treat beliefs as sentences in an internal language.

6.1 The Possible-Worlds Model
The possible-worlds model of belief was initially developed by Hintikka in terms of sets of sentences he called *model sets*. Subsequent to Kripke's introduction of possible worlds as a uniform semantics for various modal systems, Hintikka rephrased his work in these terms (see Hintikka, 1962). The basic idea behind this

approach is that the beliefs of an agent are modeled as a set of possible worlds, namely, those that are *compatible with* his beliefs. For example, an agent who believes the sentences

> *Some of the artists are beekeepers.*
>
> *All of the beekeepers are chemists.*

(6.1)

would have his beliefs represented as the set of possible worlds in which some artists are beekeepers and all beekeepers are chemists.

6.1.1 Representational Issues.

In a possible world for which the sentences (6.1) are true, anything that is a valid consequence of (6.1) must also be true. There can be no possible world in which some artists are beekeepers, all beekeepers are chemists, and no artists are chemists; such a world is a logical impossibility. If beliefs are compatible with a set of possible worlds (i.e., true of each such possible world), then every valid consequence of those beliefs is also compatible with the set. Thus one of the properties of the possible-worlds model is that an agent will believe all consequences of his beliefs—the model is consequentially closed. Hintikka, recognizing this as a serious shortcoming of the model, claimed only that it represented an idealized condition: an agent could justifiably believe any of the consequences of his beliefs, although in any given situation he might have only enough cognitive resources to derive a subset of them.

The assumption of consequential closure limits the ability of the possible-worlds model to represent the cognitive state of agents. Consider, for example, the problem of representing the mental state of agents as described by belief reports in a natural language. Suppose the state of John's beliefs is at least partially given by the sentence

> *John believes that given the rules of chess, White has a forced initial win.*   (6.2)

Since the statement, "*given the rules of chess, White has a forced initial win*" is either a tautology or inconsistent, this would be equivalent in the possible-world model to one of the following belief reports:

> a. *John believes* **t.**
>
> b. *John believes everything.*

(6.3)

Clearly this is wrong; if it turns out that John's belief in White's forced initial win is correct, John has a good deal of information about chess, and we would not want to equate it to the tautology **t.** On the other hand, if John's belief is false and no such strategy for White exists, it is not necessarily the case that all of his beliefs about other aspects of the world are incoherent. Yet there are no possible worlds compatible with a false belief, and so every proposition about the world must be a belief.

The representational problems of the possible-worlds approach stem from its treatment of belief as a relation between an agent and a proposition (*i.e.*, a set of possible worlds). All logically equivalent ways of stating the same proposition, no matter how complicated, count as a report of the same belief. By contrast, the deduction model treats belief as a relation between an agent and the *statement* of a proposition, so that two functionally different beliefs can have the same propositional content.

There is a large philosophical literature on the problems of representing propositional attitudes using possible worlds. Perry (1979) gives an account of some of the more subtle problems inherent in equating belief states with propositions; his analysis does not depend on consequential closure. Barwise (1981) critiques consequential closure in possible-worlds models of perception. By comparison, a good account of the relative advantages of a symbol-processing approach to representing belief can be found in Moore and Hendrix (1979).

6.1.2 The Correspondence Property. It is reasonable to ask how the deduction and possible-worlds models compare in respects other than the assumption of consequential closure. That is, are the saturated deduction models $D_s(L, \rho)$ (whose rules are consequentially complete) significantly different from possible-worlds models for the purpose of representing belief?

The last phrase, "for the purpose of representing belief," is important. The two models are composed of different entities (expressions versus propositions), so we can always use a language that distinguishes these entities, and has statements that are valid in one model and not the other. So the answer to this question depends on the type of language used to talk about the models. Fortunately, the language standardly used to axiomatize possible-worlds models is the same as that of **B**; a modal calculus containing atoms of the form [S[p, in which p refers to a proposition.[5] Thus it is possible to compare the possible-worlds and deduction models by comparing their axiomatizations in modal logic. We have proven the following general property about the two approaches.

Correspondence Property. For every modal logic of belief based on Kripke possible-worlds models, there exists a corresponding deduction model logic family with an equivalent saturated logic.

The correspondence property simply says that possible-worlds models are indistinguishable from saturated deduction models from the point of view of modal logics of belief. To the author's knowledge, this is the first time that the symbol-processing and possible-worlds approaches to belief have been shown to be comparable, in that the possible-worlds model is equivalent to the limiting case of a symbol-processing model with logically complete deduction.

Although space is too short here to give a full proof of this claim, we will give an overview of the most important of the propositional modal logics with a possible-

---

[5]Historically, the axiomatization of modal systems preceded Kripke's introduction of a unifying possible-worlds semantics.

worlds semantics, and their corresponding deductive belief logics (a full exposition and proofs of results mentioned here are in Konolige, 1984).

Modal calculi for the possible-worlds model differ, depending on the particulars of their intended domains. For propositional modal calculi, these particulars center around whether knowledge or belief is being axiomatized, and what assumptions are made about self-beliefs or self-knowledge (a survey of these calculi may be found in Hughes and Cresswell, 1968). The standard propositional modal calculi contain a single modal operator (which we write here as $[S]$) and are expressed as Hilbert systems. Their rules of inference are modus ponens (from p and $p \supset q$, infer q) and necessitation (from p, infer $[S]p$). Axioms are taken from the following schemata.

M1. p, where p is a tautology

M2. $[S](p \supset q) \supset ([S]p \supset [S]q)$

M3. $[S]p \supset p$

M4. $[S]p \supset [S][S]p$

M5. $\sim [S]p \supset [S]\sim[S]p$

$M1$ are the purely propositional axioms. $M2$, also called the *distribution axioms*, allow modus ponens to operate under the scope of the modal operator. $M3$ are axioms for knowledge: all knowledge is true. $M4$ and $M5$ are called the positive and negative introspection axioms, respectively: if an agent believes p, then he believes that he believes it ($M4$); if he doesn't believe p, then he believes that he doesn't believe it ($M5$).

Any modal calculus that uses modus ponens and necessitation, and includes all tautologies and the distribution axioms, is called a *normal modal calculus*. Normal modal calculi have the following interesting property (see Boolos, 1979): if $p \supset q$ is a theorem, then so is $[S]p \supset [S]q$. Interpreting the modal operator $[S]$ as belief, this asserts that whenever q is implied by p, an agent S who believes p will also believe q. As expected, normal modal calculi assume consequential closure when the modal operator is interpreted as belief.

The simplest normal modal calculus is K, which contains just the schemata $M1$ and $M2$. To axiomatize knowledge, $M3$ is included to form the calculus T. Assumptions about self-knowledge lead to the calculi $S4$ ($T + M4$) and $S5$ ($S4 + M5$). McCarthy (McCarthy et al., 1978; McCarthy, 1978) was the first to recognize the utility of modal calculi for reasoning about knowledge in AI systems, and defined three calculi that were extensions to T, $S4$, and $S5$, allowing belief operators for multiple agents. Sato (1976) has a detailed analysis of these calculi as Gentzen systems, and calls them $K3$, $K4$, and $K5$, respectively. He also gives decision procedures for these logics. $K4$ is the calculus used by Moore in his dissertation on the interaction of knowledge and action (Moore, 1980).

The so-called weak analogs to $S4$ and $S5$ are formed by omitting the knowledge axiom $M3$ (this terminology is introduced by Stalnaker, 1980). The weak versions are appropriate for axiomatizing belief rather than knowledge, since beliefs can be false. Levesque (1982) has an interesting dissertation in which he explores the question of what knowledge a data base can have about its own information. Because he makes the assumption that a data base has complete and accurate knowledge of its own contents, the propositional calculus he arrives at is weak $S5$, with the addition of a consistency schema $[S[p \supset \sim[S]\sim p$.

How does the family of logics **B** compare with these propositional model calculi? As with the possible-worlds logics, the deductive belief logics formed from **B** will depend on the assumptions that are made about self-beliefs. In this paper, we have developed the logic family **BK,** which assumes that an agent has no knowledge of his own beliefs. The saturated logic **BK**$_s$, restricted to a single agent, is provably equivalent to K, the weakest of the possible-worlds belief calculi.

We have developed a theory of introspection within the deduction model framework that accounts for varying degrees of self-knowledge about one's own beliefs. This theory is based on the idea that an agent's belief subsystem can query a model of itself (an *introspective belief subsystem*) to answer question of self-belief. Depending on constraints placed on the introspective belief subsystem, it is possible to arrive at two logic families **BS4** and **BS5**. The saturated form of these logics are equivalent in the single-agent case to the modal systems weak $S4$ and weak $S5$.

While we have been interested in the concept of belief throughout this paper, it is possible to define a deductive belief logic based on the related concept of knowledge. One property that distinguishes knowledge from belief is that if something is known it must be true, whereas beliefs can be false. The appropriate tableau axiom for knowledge is

$$K_0 : \frac{\Sigma, [S_i]\Gamma \Rightarrow \Delta}{\Sigma, \Gamma, [S_i]\Gamma \Rightarrow \Delta}$$

Adding K_0 to **B** forms the logic family **K**. Particularizations of **K** with varying degrees of self-knowledge correspond to the propositional modal systems T, $S4$, and $S5$.

We summarize these results in the following table.

	Normal Modal Calculus	Deduction Model Family
Belief	K	**BK**
	weak $S4$	**BS4**
	weak $S5$	**BS5**
Knowledge	T	**KT**
	$S4$	**KS4**
	$S5$	**KS5**

6.2 Syntactic Logics for Belief

There are a number of first-order formalizations of belief or knowledge in the symbol-processing tradition that have been proposed for AI systems. We have labeled these "syntactic" logics because their common characteristic is to have terms whose intended meaning is an expression of some object language. The object language is either a formal language (*e.g.*, another first-order language) or an internal mental language. The logic **B** is also a syntactic logic, although it uses a modal operator, because the argument of the operator denotes a sentence in the internal language. We have chosen to use a modal language for **B** because it has a relatively simple syntax compared to first-order formalizations. It is also less expressive, in that quantification over sentences of the object language is not allowed by the modal syntax.

McCarthy (1979) has presented some incomplete work in which *individual concepts* are reified in a first-order logic. Exactly what these concepts are is left deliberately unclear, but in one interpretation they can be taken for the internal mental language of a symbol-processing cognitive framework. He shows how the use of such concepts can solve the standard representational problems of knowledge and belief, *e.g.*, distinguishing between *de dicto* and *de re* references in belief sentences.

A system that takes seriously the idea that agent's beliefs can be modeled as the theory of some first-order language is proposed by Konolige (1982a). A first-order metalanguage is used to axiomatize the provability relation of the object language. To account for nested beliefs, the agent's object language is itself viewed as a metalanguage for another object language, and so on, thereby creating a hierarchy of metalanguage/object language pairs. Perlis (1981) presents a more physchologically oriented first-order theory that contains axioms about long- and short-term memory. The ontology is that of an internal mental language.

These axiomatic approaches are marred by one or both of two defects—the lack of a coherent formal model of belief, and computational inefficiency. Regarding the first one: the vagueness of the intended model often makes it difficult to claim that the given axioms are the correct ones, since there is no formal mathematical model that is being axiomatized. In arriving at the deduction model of belief, we have tried to be very clear about what assumptions were being made in abstracting the model, how the model could fail to portray belief subsystems accurately, and so on. In contrast, the restrictions that syntactic systems place on belief subsystems are often obscure. What type of reasoning processes operate to produce consequences of beliefs? How are these processes invoked? What is the interaction of the belief subsystem with other parts of the cognitive model? These types of questions are begged when one simply writes first-order axioms and then tries to convey an intuitive idea of their intended content. (To some extent this criticism is not applicable to the formalism of Konolige in (1982a), because here the intended belief model is explicitly stated to be a first-order theory).

A second shortcoming is that efficient means of deduction for the syntactic axiomatizations are not provided. As we have mentioned, a system that is actually going to reason about belief by manipulating some formalization can encounter severe computational problems. Many of the assumptions incorporated into the deduction model, especially the closure property, were made with an eye towards deductive efficiency. The end result is a simple rule of inference, the attachment rule A, that has computationally attractive realizations.[6] On the other hand, formalizations that try to account for complex procedural interactions (as in Perlis's theory of long- and short-term memory), or that use a metalanguage to simulate a proof procedure at the object language level (as in Konolige, 1982a), have no obvious computationally efficient implementation.

7 Conclusion

We have explored a formalization of the symbol-processing paradigm of belief that we call the deduction model. It is interesting that the methodology employed was to examine the cognitive structure of AI planning systems. This methodology, which may be termed *experimental robot psychology,* offers some distinct advantages over its human counterpart. Because the abstract design of such systems is open and available, it is possible to identify major cognitive structures, such as the belief subsystem, that influence behavior. Moreover, these structures are likely to be of the simplest sort necessary to accomplish some task, without the synergistic complexity so frequently encountered in studies of human intelligence. The design of a robot's belief subsystem is based on the minimum of assumptions necessary to ensure its ability to reason about its environment in a productive manner, namely, it incorporates a set of logical sentences about the world, and a theorem-proving process for deriving consequences. The deduction model is derived directly from these assumptions.

The deduction model falls within that finely bounded region between formally tractable but oversimplified models and more realistic but less easily axiomatized views. On the one hand, it is a generalization of the formal possible-worlds model that does not make the assumption of consequential closure, and so embodies the notion that reasoning about one's beliefs is resource-limited. On the other hand, it possesses a concise axiomatization in which an agent's belief deduction process is incorporated in a direct manner, rather than simulated indirectly. Thus the deduction model and its associated logic **B** lend themselves to implementation in mechanical theorem-proving processes as a means of giving AI systems the capability of reasoning about beliefs.

---

[6]Several efficient proof methods are given in Konolige (1984): a decision procedure for propositional **BK** based on the Davis-Putnam procedure (see Chang and Lee, 1973), which is sufficient to solve the Wise Man Puzzle automatically; a resolution method for the quantifying-in form of **B**; and a PLANNER-type deduction system.

Acknowledgments

Many people contributed their time and effort to reading and critiquing this paper. I am especially indebted to Stan Rosenschein, Nils Nilsson, and Jerry Hobbs in this regard.

This research was made possible in part by a gift from the System Development Foundation. It was also supported by Grant N00014-80-C-0296 from the Office of Naval Research.

References

Appelt, D. E. (1982). *Planning natural-language utterances to satisfy multiple goals*, (*SRI Artificial Intelligence Center Technical Note 259*) Menlo Park, Ca: SRI International.

Barwise, J. (1981). Scenes and other situations. *Journal of Philosophy, 78* (7), 369–397.

Boolos, G. (1979). *The Unprovability of consistency*. Cambridge, MA: Cambridge University Press.

Brachman, R. (1980). *Recent advances in representational languages*. Invited lecture at the National Conference on Artificial Intelligence, Stanford University, Stanford, CA.

Chang, C. L., & Lee, R. C. T. (1973). *Symbolic logic and mechanical theorem proving*. New York: Academic Press.

Collins, A. M., Warnock, E., Aiello, N. & Miller, M. (1975). Reasoning from incomplete knowledge, in D. G. Bobrow, & A. Collins (Ed.), *Representation and Understanding*. New York: Academic Press.

Doyle, J. (1978). *Truth maintenance systems for problem solving* (*Artificial Intelligence Laboratory Technical Report 419*). Cambridge, MA: Massachusetts Institute of Technology.

Field, H. H. (1978). Mental representation, *Erkenntnis, 13* 9–61.

Fikes, R. E., & Nilsson, N. J. (1971). STRIPS: A new approach to the application of theorem proving to problem solving. *Artificial Intelligence, 2*(3–4) 189–208.

Fodor, J. A. (1975). *The language of thought*. New York: Thomas Y. Cromwell Company.

Hayes, P. J. (1977). In defence of logic. *Proceedings of the 5th International Joint Conference on Artificial Intelligence,* Cambridge, MA: Massachusetts Institute of Technology.

Hewitt, C. (1972). *Description and theoretical analysis (using schemata) of PLANNER: A language for proving theorems and manipulating models in a robot*. Unpublished doctoral dissertation, Massachusetts Institute of Technology, Cambridge, MA.

Hintikka, J. (19755). Form and content in quantification theory. *Acta Philosophica Fennica 8* 7–55.

Hintikka, J. (1962). *Knowledge and belief*. Ithaca, New York: Cornell University Press.

Hughes, G. E., & Cresswell, J. J. (1968). *Introduction to modal logic*. London, England: Methuen and Company.

Israel, D. J. (1983). The role of logic in knowledge representation. *Computer, 16*(10), 37–42.

Johnson-Laird, P. N. (1980). Mental models in cognitive science. *Cognitive Science, 4,* 71–115.

Kleene, S. C. (1967). *Mathematical logic*. New York: John Wiley and Sons.

Konolige, K. (1982a). A first-order formalization of knowledge and action for a multiagent planning system. In J. E. Hayes, D. Michie, & Y. H. Pao (Eds.) *Machine Intelligence 10* (pp. 120–147). Chichester, England: Ellis Horwood Limited.

Konolige, K. (1982b). Circumscriptive ignorance. *Proceedings of the Second National Conference on Artificial Intelligence*. Pittsburgh, PA: Carnegie-Millon University.

Konolige, K. (1984). *A deduction model of belief and its logics,* Doctoral thesis in preparation, Stanford University Computer Science Department, Stanford, CA.

Levesque, H. J. (1982). *A formal treatment of incomplete knowledge bases (FLAIR Technical Report No. 614)*. Palo Alto, CA: Fairchild.

Lycan, W. G. (1981). Toward a hommuncular theory of believing. *Cognition and Brain Theory, 4*(2) 139–59.

McCarthy, J. (1978). Formalization of two puzzles involving knowledge. Stanford, CA: Stanford University, unpublished note.

McCarthy, J. (1979). First-order theories of individual concepts and propositions. In B. Meltzer & D. Michie (Eds.), *Machine Intelligence 9,* (pp. 120–147). Edinburgh, Scotland: Edinburgh University Press.

McCarthy, J. (1980). Circumscription—*A form of non-monotonic reasoning. Artificial Intelligence, 13*(1,2), 27–40.

McCarthy, J., Sato, M., Hayashi, T., & Igarashi, S. (1978). *On the model theory of knowledge (Stanford Artificial Intelligence Laboratory Memo AIM-312).* Stanford CA:Stanford University.

McDermott, D., & Doyle, J. (1980). Non-monotonic logic I. *Artificial Intelligence, 13*(1,2) 41–72.

Moore, R. C. (1980). *Reasoning about knowledge and action (Artificial Intelligence Center Technical Note 191)* Menlo Park, CA: SRI International.

Moore, R. C. (1983). *Semantical considerations of nonmonotonic logic (SRI Artificial Intelligence Center Technical Note 284)* Menlo Park, CA: SRI International.

Moore, R. C., & Hendrix, G. G. (1979). *Computational models of belief and the semantics of belief sentences (SRI Artificial Intelligence Center Technical Note 187).* Menlo Park, CA: SRI International.

Nilsson, N. (1980). *Principles of artificial intelligence.* Palo Alto, CA: Tioga Publishing Co.

Perlis, D. (1981). Language, computation, and reality *(Department of Computer Science TR95).* Rochester, NY: University of Rochester.

Perry, J. (1979). The problem of the essential indexical. *NOÛS, 13,* 3–21.

Reiter, R. (1980). A logic for default reasoning. *Artificial Intelligence, 13*(1,2) 81–132.

Robinson, J. A. (1979). *Logic: Form and function.* New York: Elsevier North Holland.

Sacerdoti, E. D. (1977). *A structure for plans and behavior.* New York: Elsevier.

Sato, M. (1976). *A study of Kripke-type models for some modal logics by Gentzen's sequential method.* Kyoto, Japan: Kyoto University, Research Institute for Mathematical Sciences.

Schubert, L. K. (1976). Extending the expressive power of semantic nets. *Artificial Intelligence, 7*(2) 163–198.

Smullyan, R. M. (1968). *First-order logic.* New York: Springer-Verlag.

Stalnaker, R. (1980). A note on nonmonotonic modal logic. Cornell University, Department of Philosophy, unpublished manuscript.

Warren, D. H. D. (1974). *WARPLAN: A system for generating plans (Dept. of Computational Logic Memo 76).* University of Edinburgh School of Artificial Intelligence, Edinburgh, Scotland.

Weyhrauch, R. (1980). Prolegomena to a theory of mechanized formal reasoning. *Artificial Intelligence, 13*(1,2), 133–170.

Woods, W. (1975). What's in a link? in D. G. Bobrow & A. Collins (Eds.), *Representation and understanding.* New York: Academic Press.

11 Metaphor and Commonsense Reasoning*

Jaime G. Carbonell
Steven Minton

Computer Science Department
Carnegie-Mellon University
Pittsburgh, Pennsylvania

1 Introduction

The theory that metaphor plays a principal role in human thinking, as well as in linguistic communication, has been argued with considerable force (Lakoff-Johnson, 1980; Johnson, unpublished manuscript; Carbonell, 1982; Burstein, 1980). However, the validity of such a theory is a matter of continuing debate that appears neither to dissuade its proponents nor convince its detractors. Being among the proponents, we propose to develop a computational reasoning system for performing metaphorical inferences. If such a system exhibits cognitively plausible commonsense reasoning capabilities, it will demonstrate, at the very least, the utility of metaphorical inference in modeling significant aspects of naive human reasoning. This paper reviews our initial steps towards the development of a computational model of metaphor-based reasoning.

2 Experiential Reasoning versus Formal Systems

Humans reason and learn from experience to a degree that no formal system, AI model, or philosophical theory has yet been able to explain. The statement that the human mind is (or contains) the sum total of its experiences is in itself rather vacuous. A more precise formulation of experience-based reasoning must be structured in terms of coordinated answers to the following questions: *How* are experiences brought to bear in understanding new situations? *How* is long-term memory modified and indexed? *How* are inference patterns acquired in a particular domain and adapted to apply in novel situations? *How* does a person "see the light" when a previously incomprehensible problem is viewed from a new perspective? *How* are

* This research was sponsored in part by the Office of Navel Research (ONR) under grant numbers N00014-79-C-0661 and N00014-82-C-50767.

the vast majority of irrelevant or inappropriate experiences and inference pattern filtered out in the understanding process? Answering all these "how" questions requires a *process model* capable of organizing large amount of knowledge and mapping relevant aspects of past experience to new situations. Some meaningful starts have been made toward large-scale, episodic-based memory organization (Schank, 1979, 1980, 1982; Lebowitz, 1980; Kolodner, 1980) and toward episodic-based analogical reasoning (Carbonell, 1981b, 1983, 1981a). Bearing these questions in mind, we examine the issue of commonsense reasoning in knowledge-rich mundane domains.

Our central hypothesis is:

> **Experiential reasoning hypothesis:** *Reasoning in mundane, experience-rich recurrent situations is qualitatively different from formal, deductive reasoning evident in more abstract, experimentally contrived, or otherwise nonrecurrent situations (such as some mathematical or puzzle-solving domains).*

In the statement of our hypothesis, we do not mean to exclude experience-rich metaphorical inference from scientific or mathematical thought. Rather, we claim that formal deductive inference is definitely not the dominant process in mundane reasoning. In essence, the experiential reasoning hypothesis states that structuring new information according to relevant past experience is an important aspect of human comprehension—perhaps more important than other aspects studied thus far in much greater depth.

Commonsense, experience-rich reasoning consists of recalling appropriate past experiences and inference patterns, whereas solving abstract problems divorced from real-world experience requires knowledge-poor search processes more typical of past and present AI problem solving systems. Since computer programs perform much better in simple, elegant, abstract domains than in "scruffy" experience-rich human domains, it is evident that a fundamental reasoning mechanism is lacking from the AI repertoire. The issue is not merely that AI systems lack experience in mundane human scenarios—they would be unable to benefit from such experience if it were encoded in their knowledge base. We postulate that the missing reasoning method is based on the transfer of proven inference patterns and experiential knowledge across domains. This is not to say that humans are incapable of more formal reasoning, but rather that such reasoning is seldom necessary, and when applied it requires a more concerted cognitive effort than mundane metaphorical inference.

There is evidence that human expertise, far beyond what we would label commonsense reasoning, draws upon past experience and underlying analogies. For instance, the master chess player is not a better deductive engine than his novice counterpart. Rather, as Chase and Simon (1974) have shown, he commands a vast repertoire of chess-board patterns and associated strategies that comprise his past experience. And, when encountering a new chessboard situation he uses the relevant patterns (which may only partially match the current position) to index the appropriate knowledge. Mechanics problems in physics are often solved by creating a simple mental model—an analog of the real situation—that preserves the significant properties. The model, created on the basis of past experience solving similar problems, is then used to instantiate one or more well-known principles of physics in a familiar manner and thereby obtain a solution (Larkin & Carbonell; Clements, 1982; Carbonell, Larkin, & Reif, 1983).

People's well-developed ability to perform analogical reasoning is at least partly responsible for what we call "commonsense" reasoning. Roughly speaking, *analogical reasoning* is the process by which one recognizes that a new situation is similar to some previously encountered situation, and uses the relevant prior knowledge to structure and enrich one's understanding of the new situation. *Analogical comprehension* is the related process that occurs when the analogy is explicitly stated or otherwise made evident. For instance, understanding "John is an encyclopedia" entails analogical comprehension since the analogy between John and an encyclopedia is explicitly suggested. However, constructing a novel analogy in order to explain some new situation is a different task, which requires searching memory for a previously encountered similar situation. Both of these forms of inference may be labeled commonsense reasoning in so far as they require access to large amounts of past knowledge and reaching conclusions without benefit of formal deduction.

3 Patterns of Metaphorical Inference

A metaphor, simile, or analogy can be said to consist of 3 parts: a *target*, a *source* and an *analogical mapping*. For example:

John was embarrassed. His face looked like a beet.

Here the target is "John's face" and the source is "a beet." The analogical mapping transmits information from the source to the target domain. In this case, the mapping relates the color of John's face to the color of a beet. Our use of the same terminology to describe metaphors, similes, and analogies reflects our opinion that they are all merely different linguistic manifestations of the same underlying cognitive process: analogical reasoning. That is, they differ primarily in their form of presentation rather than in their internal structure. Consequently, although our choice of terminology may indicate that we are centrally concerned with the phenomenon of metaphor, we mean to include simile and analogy as well.

3.1 The Balance Principle

Consider a prevalent metaphor: reasoning about imponderable or abstract entities as though they were objects with a measurable weight. One of several reasoning pattern based on this simple metaphor is the *balance principle*. The physical analog of this reasoning pattern is a prototypical scale with two balanced plates. Large numbers of metaphors appeal to this simple device coupled with the processes of bringing the system into (and out of) equilibrium. First, consider some examples of the basic metaphor, in which the relevant aspects of an abstract concept maps onto the weight[1] of an unspecified physical object.

Arms control is a *weighty* issue.

The worries of a nation *weigh heavily* upon his shoulders.

The Argentine air force launched a *massive* attack on the British fleet. One frigate was *heavily* damaged, but only *light* casualties were suffered by British sailors. The Argentines payed a *heavy* toll in downed aircraft.

Not being in the mood for *heavy* drama, John went to a *light* comedy, which turned out to be a piece of meaningless *fluff*.

Pedergast was a real *heavyweight* in the 1920s Saint Louis political scene.

The crime *weighed heavily* upon his conscience.

The *weight* of the evidence was overwhelming.

3.2 The Physical Metaphor Hypothesis

Weight clearly represents different things in the various metaphors: the severity of a nation's problems, the number of attacking aircraft, the extent of physical damage, the emotional affect on audiences of theatrical productions, the amount of political muscle (to use another metaphor), the reaction to violated moral principles, and the degree to which evidence is found to be convincing. In general, more is heavier; less is lighter. One may argue that since language is heavily endowed with words that describe weight, mass, and other physical attributes, such as height and orientation (Lakoff & Johnson, 1980; Carbonell, 1982b), one borrows such words when discussing more abstract entities for lack of alternate vocabulary. Whereas this argument is widely accepted, it falls far short of the conjecture we wish to make.

> **Physical metaphor hypothesis:** *Physical metaphors directly mirror the inferential reasoning process. Inference patterns valid in physical domains are transformed into inference patterns applicable in different target domains by stripping away physical descriptors but preserving underlying relations such as causality.*

In order to illustrate the validity of this hypothesis, consider a common inference pattern based on the weight of physical objects: The inference pattern is the *balance principle* mentioned earlier as applied to a scale with two plates. The scale can be in balance or tipped towards either side, as a function of the relative weights of objects placed in the respective plates. Inference consists of placing objects in the scale and predicting the resultant situation—no claim is made as to whether this process occurs in a propositional framework or as visual imagery, although we favor the former. How could such a simple inference pattern be useful? How could it apply to

---

[1] Mass is virtually synonymous with weight in naive reasoning.

complex, nonphysical domains? Consider the following examples of metaphorical communication based on this inference pattern:

> The jury found the **weight** of the evidence favoring the defendant. His impeccable record **weighed heavily** in his favor, whereas the prosecution witness, being a confessed conman, carried **little weight** with the jury. **On balance** the state failed to **amass** sufficient evidence for a **solid** case.

> The SS-20 missile **tips the balance** of power in favor of the Soviets.

> Both conservative and liberal arguments appeared to **carry equal weight** with the president, and his decision **hung on the balance.** However, his long-standing opposition to abortion **tipped the scale** in favor of the conservatives.

> The Steelers were the **heavy** pre-game favorites, but the Browns started **piling up** points and accumulated a **massive** half-time lead. In spite of a late rally, the Steelers did not score **heavily** enough to pull the game out.

> The job applicant's shyness **weighed** against her, but her excellent recommendations **tipped the scales** in her favor.

In each example above, the same basic underlying inference pattern recurs, whether representing the outcome of a trial, statements of relative military power, decision-making processes, or the outcome of a sporting event. The inference pattern itself is quite simple: it takes as input signed quantities—whose magnitudes are analogous to their stated "weight" and whose signs depend on which side of a binary issue those weights correspond—and selects the side with the maximal weight, computing some qualitative estimate of how far out of balance the system is. Moreover, the inference pattern also serves to infer the rough weight of one side if the weight of the other side and the resultant balance state are known (e.g., If Georgia won the football game scoring only 14 points, Alabama's scoring must have been *really light*).

Our point is that this very simple inference pattern accounts for large numbers of inferences in mundane human situations. Given the existence of such a simple and widely applicable pattern, why should one suppose that more complicated inference methods explain human reasoning more accurately? We believe that there exist a moderate number of general inference patterns such as the present one which together span a large fraction of mundane human reasoning situations. Moreover, the few other patterns we have found thus far are also rooted on simple physical principles or other directly experienced phenomena.

4 The Role of Metaphor in Common-Sense Reasoning

Recently one of us developed a model of analogical problem-solving (Carbonell, 1983, 1982a) based on the principle that past experience in solving particular classes of problems should play a central role in solving new problems of a similar

nature. At the risk of oversimplification, analogical problem solving can be summarized as a four-stage process:

1. Recalling one or more past problems that bear strong similarity to the new
   problem.
2. Constructing a mapping from the old problem solution process into a solution
   process for the new problem, exploiting known similarities in the two problem situations.
3. Instantiating, refining, and testing the potential solution to the new problem.
4. Generalizing recurring solution patterns into reusable plans for common types
   of problems.

The analogical problem-solving model finessed most of the issues in building a
computationally effective mechanism to recall similar problem solving episodes
from memory but suggested a model built along the lines of Schank's MOPS
(Schank, 1982; Lebowitz, 1980; Kolodner, 1980) that utilized relative invariance
measures (Carbonell, 1982b) as a memory organization principle.

Most of the "action" in the analogical problem-solving model dealt with the
issue of constructing a mapping that would transfer, modify, and augment a solution
from a similar past problem situation to satisfy the requirements of the new problem
situation. Here we propose that the role of metaphors is to capture and communicate
mappings from well-known experiential domains to new, less structured domains.
These mappings often fail to provide deep insight into the target phenomenon they
seek to explain but do provide easily and quickly a shallow level of understanding
sufficient for most common, everyday purposes. For instance, stating that the
prosecutor's evidence was counterbalanced by the defendant's alibi gives us all a
"feel" for the present state of the trial. But consider a situation where you, the
reader, must step in for the temporarily ill prosecuting attorney. Suddenly, your
understanding of the trial is woefully inadequate. Questions arise such as: Just how
did the defense witness counter the prosecutions evidence? Did it undermine the
credibility of our witnesses? Did it beef up the defendant's story? Did new evidence
surface? Does the case now hinge upon a possible breakdown in our chain of
evidence?" (to use other metaphors). Deeper reasoning about a particular topic may
well be metaphorically based, or more deductive in nature. Whether or not a
particular metaphor provides more than a casual level of understanding depends on
the validity of the source as a model, as well as the structure of the mapping
(Gentner, 1980). In the next section, we will examine further the close relationship
between mappings and metaphorical understanding.

5 Metaphorical Inference and The Mapping Problem

Metaphors, similes, and analogies are more than clever ways of restating the obvious. They are extraordinarily concise devices by which a writer can convey new

information, simply by signaling his audience that information in the source domain is applicable to the target domain. Presumably the reader has a coherent body of knowledge about the source and can transfer and adapt this information to the target. This saves both the reader and the writer a good deal of time and cognitive effort. However, before the reader can initiate the transfer, he must identify the correspondences between the two domains and establish exactly what information in the source is applicable to the target, since much of it is clearly inappropriate. This is the central issue in metaphor comprehension; we refer to it as the *analogical mapping problem*.

One might suppose that the reader finds the analogical mapping simply by comparing the source and target domains for similarities. However, several researchers (Carbonell, 1982b; Ortony, 1979) have demonstrated that this *domain comparison* model is in fact too simplistic. Although discovering similarities is an important component of the comprehension process, other strategies must be used as well. Indeed, when learning new material, the reader knows little about the target, hence domain comparison is, by itself, inadequate. Clearly, if the purpose of the metaphor is to transfer information to the target domain from the source domain, then this information does not already exist in the target domain, and hence it can play no part in the comparison process. Furthermore, when one considers requirements for computational tractability, it becomes evidence that there must be strategies to help focus the comparison and constrain the matching process. Focusing limits the complexity of the comparison process and reduces spurious matches between the two domains.[2] Our purpose in this section is to explore some cognitively plausible focusing strategies which might be used to facilitate the construction of analogical mappings.

5.1 Knowledge Acquisition via Analogical Mappings

The following example, found in a children's book, illustrates an explanation in which the reader (presumably a child) is expected to create an analogical mapping and transfer information across domains.

A motorcycle is a vehicle. Like a car it has a motor. But it looks more like a bicycle.

The author attempts to explain the concept of a motorcycle by referring to other, presumably more familiar, objects. But his statement implies much more than is explicitly stated. For instance, it suggests not only that a motorcycle has a motor, but that it has a motor in the same way that a *car* has a motor: that the motor is an internal

---

[2] Implementing domain comparisons in a computer is typically accomplished by attempting to find matches between the representations of the target and source domains. As we shall see in the next section, these representations are typically graphs or equivlalent structures. Although the details of the matching process vary considerably depending on the representation system used, the computation can be quite expensive if performed upon arbitrary domains. Indeed, the related "Subgraph Isomorphism" problem is NP-complete (Garey-Johnson, 1979). Given a precise formulation of the matching problem, it is easy to demonstrate that it too is intractable unless it is bounded in some principled way.

combustion engine, it uses gasoline, it causes the machine to move, etc. The reference to a *car* is essential; consider the effect of substituting "electric shaver" for "car" in the example. (After all, electric shavers have motors too, but their motors are not a means of propulsion). Certainly, drawing an analogy to electric shavers would not be nearly as helpful in communicating what a motorcycle is.

Although analogies, such as the foregoing one, can obviously be used to great advantage in transmitting new information, the reader is often left in the position of not knowing how far to carry the analogy. To a child who has never seen a motorcycle, the previous description of a motorcycle, though informative, is still quite ambiguous. "Does a motorcycle have pedals?" he may ask. In order to gauge the extent of the analogy, to verify which of his inference patterns relevant to cars and bicycles are valid for motorcycles, the child must either read further or find a picture of a motorcycle. A priori, there is no way for him to be sure which inferences to make. But at least the set of sensible questions he may ask will be focused by the analogy. Thus it is reasonable to ask about handlebars or pedals but not about whiskers or wings.

In most mundane situations, knowing which inferences are correct seldom poses a significant problem for people, largely because there are characteristic ways of expressing metaphors so that the mapping problem is easier to solve. The truly novel metaphor is rarely encountered. Through frequent use, many metaphors acquire idiomatic meanings, to a greater or less degree. We refer to these metaphors as *frozen*. "John is a hog" and "Sheila is a dog" both exemplify frozen metaphors. The latter would probably be interpreted as a rude comment concerning Sheila's looks, rather than a compliment on her loyalty, which seems to be an equally reasonable interpretation given only one's knowledge about dogs. Frozen metaphors are easy to understand because the analogical mapping has been (to some degree) precomputed and so does not have to be reconstructed, only remembered and reapplied. Hence neither a complex matching process nor prior knowledge about the target are necessary in order to find the mapping. There is little question of which are the right inferences and which are the wrong ones.

5.2 Salience and Novel Metaphors

If a metaphor is novel, other strategies are available for coping with the complexity of the mapping problem. One way is to focus on *salient* features of the source (Ortony, 1979; Searle, 1979). Consider the example "Billboards are like warts" in which both the target and source are familiar objects. Most people interpret this as meaning that billboards stick out, and are ugly. Their mapping relates attributes that are common to both source and target, but particularly emphasizes those such as "ugliness" that are "high-salient" attributes of warts, the source. It is our contention that by focusing on prominent features and ignoring unimportant ones, the complexity of the mapping problem is reduced.

Restricting the initial mapping to salient features of the source is an effective strategy, even when one's knowledge of the target domain is limited. In fact, it is likely that the salient features are the very ones that should be mapped into the target domain, as is the case the following metaphor:

RTO Inc. is the Freddie Laker of consumer electronics.

Although the target is an unknown company, and the metaphor is novel, it is understandable simply because the source, Freddie Laker of Laker Airlines, has certain outstandingly salient features. Of course, the creator of the metaphor expects that his audience will all have the same opinion as to which of Laker's features are salient. Why certain features are considered universally salient whereas others are not is a difficult problem in its own right, one which we will not pause to consider here.

We have examined two types of metaphors which can be understood in spite of incomplete knowledge of the target: frozen metaphors and metaphors based on the source's salient features. These illustrate just two of the many ways *pragmatic* considerations enable one to bypass much of the complexity of the mapping problem. Occasionally, however, one cannot avoid more complex versions of the mapping problem. For us, this is the most interesting case. It occurs frequently during explanations involving extended analogies, such as when a grade-school mathematics teacher begins his algebra class by proclaiming:

An equation is like a balance. You must keep the same amount of weight on each side of the equals sign. . . .

Certainly there will be students in the class for whom this is a novel idea, and who spend the next 10 minutes desperately trying to find the intended analogical mapping. Or consider a secondary school biology text which begins a chapter on the human nervous system by comparing it to a telephone network. Or a treatise on "Hamlet" whose thesis is that the protagonist's life is a metaphor for adolescence. When confronted with one of these analogies in context, one may need to search for appropriate hypotheses; one's analogical mapping will be elaborated and changed as one's understanding of the target domain grows.

A good example of an extended analogy is provided by Milton Friedman in his *Newsweek* Column (of 12/27/82), in his attempt to explain recent fluctuations in the nation's money supply.

. . . Consider the record: M_1 grew at annual rates of 15.3 percent from October 1981 to January 1982; 1.2 percent from January 1982 to July 1982; 16.3 percent from July 1982 to November 1982. Is it really conceivable that the Fed produced these gyrations on purpose, given its repeated protestations that it was committed to a steady and moderate rate of monetary growth?

Why the gyrations? A better explanation is that the Fed is, as it were driving a car with a highly defective steering gear. It is driving down a road with walls on both sides. It can go down the middle of the road on the average only by first

bouncing off one wall and then off the opposite wall. Not very good for the car or
its passengers or bystanders, but one way to get down the road.

This interpretation raises two key questions: first, why doesn't the Fed replace
the defective steering gear? Second, what course will this defective steering gear
lead to over coming months . . .

This metaphor provides the reader with a clear, albeit simplistic, understanding
of the situation *without requiring much prerequisite knowledge about how the Fed
works.* A possible remedy (replacing the steering wheel) is suggested based on
inferences valid in the source domain. Most important, the passage implies that the
Fed's control over the economy and where it is headed (one can hardly help but use
metaphors here!) is not very accurate. Simply by invoking this metaphor Friedman
communicates his belief that this situation is bad—but not totally disastrous—
without ever having to explain the underlying monetary and fiscal reasons. In fact,
when we informally questioned people about what exactly Friedman is referring to
when he speaks of "walls", most admitted that they weren't really sure. A typical
response was that the "walls" represented some sort of "limits." And yet, these
people felt that they had understood, or gotten the gist of, the metaphor. Apparently
one's analogical mapping does not have to be particularly detailed, as long as *key*
inferences can be made. It seems that once certain connections or *beachheads* have
been established between the target and source domains, people are content to
incrementally elaborate the mapping as they find it necessary during further reading
or problem solving.

5.3 A Classification Based on Processing Requirements
In our discussion thus far, we have identified various analogical mapping strategies
whose applicability depends upon the properties of the metaphor under consideration. We therefore offer the following pragmatic classification, based on what we
believe are meaningful distinctions in the type of processing employed during
comprehension. We caution that these categories should not be viewed as distinct; it
seems more reasonable to view metaphors as occurring along a continuum with
respect the criteria presented below.

- **Frozen Metaphors**—Example: "John is a hog." These have idiosyncratic,
  well-established meanings and therefore require little, if any, analysis or
  domain comparison during comprehension. Spurious inferences, such as John
  having a curly tail, snoutish nose, or a tendency to crawl on all fours, do not
  typically enter the readers's mind.
- **Partially Frozen Metaphors**—Example: "The new evidence weighed heavily in the defendant's favor." The balance metaphor is a partially frozen
  metaphor; the details of the metaphor may vary from instance to instance, but
  the mappings remain fairly standard. Previous experience guides the mapping
  process, and thereby reduces the amount of domain comparison necessary to
  establish a new mapping.

- **Novel One-shot Metaphors**—Example: "RTO electronics is the Freddie Laker of consumer electronics." These metaphors may require a considerable amount of computation in order to construct a satisfactory mapping. Various strategies, such as focusing on salient attributes, are employed both by the writer in creating the metaphor, and the reader in comprehending the metaphor. Typically these metaphors are used once, and then forgotten.
- **Extended Metaphors**—The quote from Friedman (above) is an example of an extended metaphor. These are characterized by a relatively extensive mapping that is incrementally elaborated over time. The metaphor provides a model for reasoning about the target domain. *Scientific* analogies (Carbonell et al., 1983; Gentner, 1980) such as the nervous system/telephone network analogy fall into this category.

6 Representing Metaphors: The LIKE Relation

In the previous paragraphs, we have discussed the problems involved in finding an analogical mapping and making metaphorical inferences. We now turn our attention from the process of comprehension to issues of representation. How do we represent an analogical mapping in a computational model? We know that our representation must satisfy two requirements:

1. The representation must facilitate the transfer of information from the source domain to the target domain.
2. It must be dynamic, enabling the analogy to be elaborated over time.

In this section, we discuss how analogies (and metaphors) can be represented in semantic networks so as to satisfy these requirements. Although our work was motivated by representation languages such as KL-ONE (Brachman, 1979), SRL (Wright & Fox, 1983), NETL (Fahlman, 1979) and KRL (Bobrow & Winograd, 1977), we intend the ideas presented below to be applicable on a broad basis, and therefore make no commitment to any particular representational scheme. The notation presented in our diagrams is meant to be purely illustrative. In a semantic network, knowledge about a domain is encoded as a graph. Typically, the nodes represent *concepts* and the links *relations*.[3] In order to represent an analogy we need a way of indicating that one domain is "like" another domain. For instance, we might want to represent the metaphor "The U.S./Russian arms negotiations is a high stakes poker game." Unfortunately, simply "linking" the target concept to the source concept with a "LIKE" relation (Figure 1) does not provide us with the necessary functionality. We require a means of representing the various correspon-

---

[3] Concepts may be decomposable, in which case a single node can be replaced by a network of lower-level nodes if desired. Exactly how this is managed is of importance to the domain matching process, but it need not concern us greatly for the purposes of this discussion.

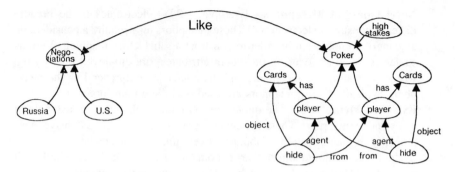

Figure 1. Using a Single LIKE Link to Relate Two Domains

dences between the two graphs so that it is apparent *how* arms negotiations are like a game of poker. Russia and the U.S. are both being compared to poker players, each of which is withholding information from the other, etc. The representation must identify precisely which subconcepts and corresponding relations map into each other. A single link between two domains is just not expressive enough to represent mappings conveying our understanding of the metaphor.

We can attempt to remedy the situation by connecting all the corresponding subconcepts in the two domains with LIKE links. However, this multiple-link solution also fails since the lower-level links have meaning only in the context of the entire analogy. To see why, consider what might occur after representing and storing "The Democrats and the Republicans are like Coke and Pepsi," meaning that they are virtually indistinguishable except by self-chosen labels. One of the assertions contained in the semantic network would be "The Republicans are like Pepsi." In isolation, this fact is meaningless and potentially misleading. We must associate it with its analogical context. But, if only subconcept correspondences are stored, it is impossible to reconstruct the context because there is nothing in the knowledge base that represents the analogy per se. The problem grows worse for more complex analogies because it is increasingly difficult to keep track of the various interrelationships between concepts given the growing forest of LIKE links. Essentially, the multiple-link solution is inadequate because it relies completely on a reductionistic representation for the analogy (see Bobrow and Winograd, 1977 and Schank, 1982 for discussions of more wholistic, reconstructive representations).

In order to represent an arbitrary mapping between two domains, we propose to use a distinct entity, which we term a **mapping structure.** A mapping structure functions as a filter, allowing explicitly specified types of information to be transferred from one domain to another. (In this respect it plays a role similar to that of Winston's transfer frames (Winston, 1978, 1979). A mapping structure identifies the various correspondences in the source and target by providing a skeleton that specifies the analogical mapping in terms of common elements found in both domains. Figure 2 is a schematic which illustrates how the structure serves to

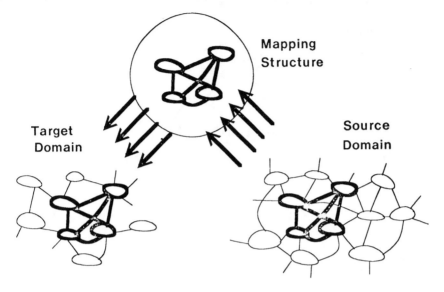

Figure 2. Schematic Illustrating the Role of Mapping Structures

coordinate the mapping by associating the two domains. The small graphs representing the target and source in the figure are meant to reside within much larger semantic networks.

In addition to the role they play in associating the source and target domains, mapping structures serve to organize metainformation about the mapping. Inferences made as a result of the analogy are represented by collections of new nodes in the target domain. These new nodes are associated with *data-dependencies* (Charniak, Riesbeck, & McDermott, 1980; Doyle, 1979) referring back to the mapping structure. (A data-dependency is essentially an indication of how the information was derived.) This enables the mapping structure to be extended incrementally while permitting subsequent verification or retraction of inferences. Because the mapping structure can be modified dynamically, at any particular time it represents the current conception of what the metaphor means. Of course, this implies that the mapping structure must be retained for some unspecified duration. We assume that the mapping structure will be "forgotten" (i.e., discoarded by some autonomous process supporting the representation system) if it does not continue to be accessed as a source of inferences when target domain information is retrieved from or added to memory.

Figure 3 shows a simplified representation for "Bulgaria is a Russian Puppet." The dotted lines around the CONTROL node in the target domain are meant to suggest that this is an inference made as a result of the metaphor. For simplicity, only the directly relevant sections of the target and source domains are actually shown. In addition, several nodes which do not take part in the mapping, such as the FUNNY attribute describing puppets, are included for illustrative purposes. Note

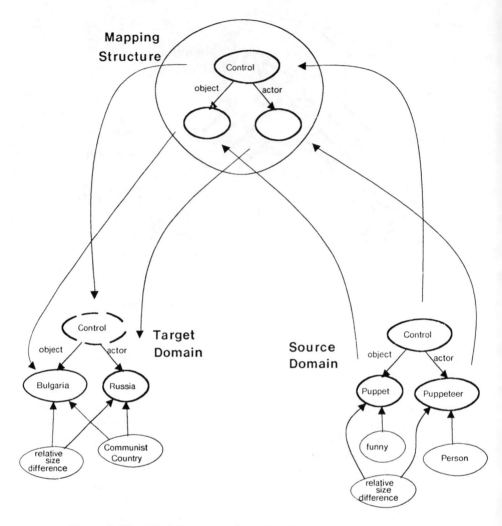

Figure 3. Simplified Representation of "Bulgaria is a Russian Puppet"

that in both the target and the source, there is a node signifying the "relative size differences" of the objects (admittedly a gross representational simplification). Although this node is not part of the mapping, it might very well be included later if the mapping is extended.

As we pointed out in the previous section, a metaphor may become frozen through frequent use. An advantage gained by the use of mapping structures is that we can model computationally this "freezing" process quite naturally. When presented with a novel metaphor, there is no recourse but to construct a brand new mapping structure. However, suppose a metaphor is encountered whose source is similar to the source of a previously understood metaphor. In this case, we can use the mapping structure built earlier as a template to help build the new structure. This constrains the domain comparison process, because the relevant features of the source concept are identified by the preexisting mapping structure. While one must still locate corresponding features in the new target domain, this too may be done efficiently if the two targets are similar.

The statement "John eats like a pig" is a typical example of a frozen metaphor. Notice that it is understandable even though we are using "John" as a generic person. In our model, the mapping structure corresponding to ". . . eats like a pig" is associated with the section of the knowledge network where information about pigs' eating habits is stored. Parsing "John eats like a pig" requires retrieving this mapping structure, noticing the exact correspondence between the source in the structure and the source in the new metaphor, and then instantiating the structure with "John" as the target domain. Instantiation is relatively easy to do, because the mapping structure specifies which nodes map from the source (Carbonell, 1982b). Obviously, we have glossed over many important problems in this description, such as how mapping structures can be retrieved given a source description and whether a new physical copy of the mapping structure must be generated for each instantiation of a frozen metaphor. These questions are being studied at the present time.

7 Generalizing Mapping Structures

In the previous section, mapping structures were proposed as a means for representing arbitrary interdomain correspondences. It is our intention that mapping structures be viewed as data structures which *implement* LIKE relations. That is, a LIKE relation still exists between the source and target domain of an analogy, but it is too complex to be implemented with a simple link. Instead, a more elaborate mechanism is required to represent the internal structure of the analogical relationship. The indirect implementation of an analogical relationship as a data structure declaratively specifying the mapping process provides a necessary extra level of abstraction along its functional dimension. Thus, one can refer to the entire analogy as a unit, or one can access and elaborate the constituent parts of the mapping structure.

At the present time, we are considering other relations that may be better implemented by mapping structures rather than by simple links. Perhaps the most obvious candidate the IS-A relation, which provides a way to structure a knowledge network into a **type hierarchy** so that properties of a class representative can be mapped automatically to members of that class. We refer to this as *vertical* inheritance, because each concept inherits from those above it in the type hierarchy.[4] Historically, vertical inheritance has been used in knowledge representation systems to

---

[4] In AI applications, the type hierarchy is almost never a strict hierarchy, but rather is a *directed acyclic graph* or a *tangled hierarchy,* in which a concept can have more than one superordinate. See Brachman (1977) for an overview of network-based knowledge representation methods.

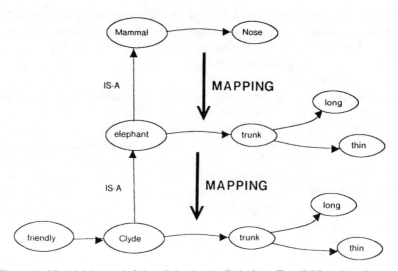

Figure 4. IS-A Links and Other Inheritance Relations Entail Mappings between Concepts

implement certain types of default reasoning. For example, knowing that Clyde is an elephant, and elephants have trunks, a system might use inheritance to infer that Clyde has a trunk.[5]

The IS-A relation requires that a mapping be established between the superordinate and subordinate concepts, so that properties of the superordinate can be inherited by the subordinate (Figure 4). Accordingly, it is natural to use a mapping structure to accomplish this as was done for the LIKE relation. The mapping structure allows us to record what information may be transmitted from a particular superordinate, as well as to indicate explicitly what information *should not* be inherited. Although one assumes by default that all the information in the superordinate is shared by the subordinate, in many cases this can be contradicted. For example, if it is known that "Penguins do not fly," then the PENGUIN node should not inherit the FLIES attribute from BIRD. The mapping structure provides us with a *view* of a penguin as a bird[6] The key point we mean to emphasize is that

---

[5] Other reasons for employing inheritance include space savings, although this is countered by a corresponding time cost during retrieval operations. In addition, updating the knowledge base can be simpler; to add the fact that mammals are warm blooded, only single node must be changed, that of "TYPICAL-MAMMAL," rather than having to find and change each and every node in the network denoting John, Mary, Felix the Cat, saber-tooth tigers, and all other mammals.

[6] Views have played a central role in many knowledge representation schemes, including those of Moore and Newell (1974), Bobrow and Winograd (1977), and Wright and Fox (1983). To indicate the need for more flexible mappings than simple all-or-nothing inheritance, consider the fact that the average mammal may be 3 feet tall, or may range from a ½ in. to 21 ft tall. Whereas we want our concept of "Giraffe" to inherit most of our knowledge of mammals, we clearly do not want to say that the average giraffe is 3 ft tall, nor that giraffes range in height from ½ in. to 21 ft tall. Hence, the IS-A relation

both the LIKE relation and the IS-A relation require mappings between concepts. This similarity has prompted some to describe the analogical mapping process as *lateral inheritance,* since information is mapped laterally between concepts in the type hierarchy. If one accepts this viewpoint, then mapping structures begin to play a broad role in representing complex situations.

8 Towards a Computational Model of Metaphorical Inference

The pervasiveness of metaphor in every aspect of human communication has been convincingly demonstrated by Lakoff and Johnson (1980), Ortony (1979b), Hobbs (1979), and many others. However, with a few exceptions (Hobbs, 1979; Carbonell, 1982b), the creation of a process model of metaphor comprehension and inference has not been of central concern. From a computational standpoint, metaphor has been viewed as an obstacle, to be tolerated at best and ignored at worst. For instance, Wilks (1977) presents a few rules on how to relax semantic constraints in order for a parser to process a sentence in spite of the metaphorical usage of a particular word. From our point of view, this attitude is not surprising, since few AI systems to date have used analogical reasoning as a primary inference method. Analogical reasoning has been viewed as a difficult problem in its own right, which must be solved before it can be incorporated in applications systems (such as parsers and medical diagnosis systems). However, a robust system must be able to operate analogically, especially if intended for naive users, otherwise they would find its lack of "common sense" intolerable. For example, a parser which could not understand metaphors, analogies, or similes would be useful only in the most limited of situations.[7] With these thoughts in mind we have begun initial work towards a parser which can reason metaphorically, and below present the following conceptual steps in the metaphor-recognition parsing process:

1. Identification of the source and target concepts. This is done during the parser's normal, nonmetaphorical operation.
2. Recognition that the input currently being parsed cannot be handled literally and is in fact an instance of a metaphor. This is actually a nontrivial task requiring considerable sophistication. For example, the parser must realize that the input is not simply erroneous. This judgement depends to a large degree on pragmatic considerations.

---

inherits only certain classes of attributes and excludes others; typically intrinsic properties of individual members are inherited whereas aggregate set properties are not. A mapping structure can be used to make explicit statements, such as the one above, regarding the information that may be transmitted from one concept to another via any particular inheritance link (Fox, 1979; Carbonell, 1980).

[7] Skeptics who dispute this claim are invited to examine any source of common everyday text, such as a copy of Time magazine or even the New York Times Financial section, and count the number of metaphors occurring on a single page.

3. Creation of an analogical mapping from the source domain unto the target domain so that corresponding subconcepts in the two domains map to each other. This phase may be broken down further as follows:

   a. Search for a preexisting mapping structure associated with the source domain.

   b. If any such structure is found, check whether it is appropriate with respect to the new target domain. This is done by building incrementally a new mapping structure containing the same nodes as the old structure. As each new node is created a corresponding node in the target domain must be identified.

   c. If no preexisting mapping structure is found for the source, or those that are found prove to be inappropriate for the new target, then a new mapping must be constructed from scratch. A matching algorithm must search the two domains in order to find similarities. In this case, one should use as many heuristics as possible for reducing the amount of domain comparison that must be done. Possible heuristics include focusing on salient concepts in the source, and focusing on certain categories of knowledge which tend to be mapped invariant in meaningful metaphors (Carbonell, 1982b).

4. Once corresponding nodes in the two domains have been identified (by constructing a mapping structure), knowledge from the source can be added to the mapping, thereby generating corresponding inferences within the target domain.[8] In an abstract sense, this mechanism accomplishes an implicit transfer of information from the source to the target. Verification that the metaphorical inferences are compatible with the target domain is an integral part of this process.

Whether or not it is possible to develop a *robust* metaphor comprehension system with today's technology is a matter of debate. Metaphorical understanding requires a potentially vast amount of world knowledge, as well as an efficient way of comparing large domains for similarities. However, we feel that even a fragile, partial model built along these lines is a worthwhile endeavor, since eventually these problems must be solved in order to create a truly intelligent parser and inference system.

In cooperation with work towards a model of metaphor understanding, we are also studying the role that metaphorical inference plays in scientific reasoning. As discussed earlier, metaphorically-based general patterns of inference do not appear

---

[8] We acknowledge that the model as specified does not account for the way people understand metaphors such as "Sally is a block of ice," in which the properties transferred from the source are themselves metaphorical. The metaphor transfers the property "cold" from ice to Mary, but this is a metaphor within a metaphor because we are refering to Mary's personality rather than her temperature. Metaphors occur in all shapes and sizes, and we have not addressed many of the subtler nuances of the phenomenon in this paper. We do believe, however, that the model can be elaborated to handle more sophisticated metaphors without revising the general framework we have presented.

confined to naive reasoning in mundane situations. Gentner (1980) and Johnson (unpublished manuscript) have argued the significant role that metaphor plays in formulating scientific theories. In preliminary investigations, Larkin and Carbonell (1981) and Carbonell, Larkin, and Reif (1983) have isolated general inference patterns in scientific reasoning that transcend the traditional boundaries of a science. For instance, the notion of equilibrium (of forces on a rigid object, or of ion transfer in aqueous solutions, etc.) is, in essence, a more precise and general formulation of the balance metaphor. Reasoning based on recurring general inference patterns seems common to all aspects of human cognition. These patterns encapsulate sets of rules to be used in unison, and thereby bypass some of the combinatorial search problems that plague more traditional rule-based deductive inference systems. The inference patterns are frozen from experience and generalized to apply in many relevant domains.

At the present stage in the investigation, we are searching for general inference patterns and the metaphors that give rise to them, both in mundane and in scientific scenarios. As these patterns are discovered, they are cataloged according to the situational features that indicate their presence. The basic metaphor underlying each inference pattern is recorded along with exemplary linguistic manifestations. The internal structure of the inference patterns themselves are relatively simple to encode in an AI system. The difficulty arises in connecting them to the external world (i.e., establishing appropriate mappings) and in determining their conditions of applicability (which are more accurately represented as partial matches of the situations where apply, rather than as simple binary tests). For instance, it is difficult to formulate a general process capable of drawing the mapping between the "weight" of a hypothetical object and the corresponding aspect of the non-physical entity under consideration, so that the balance inference pattern may apply. It is equally difficult to determine the degree to which this or any other inference pattern can make a useful contribution to novel situations that bear sufficient similarity to past experience (Carbonell, 1983).

9 Conclusions

In this paper we have analyzed the role of metaphors in common sense reasoning. In particular, we showed how the balance metaphor exemplifies metaphorical inference, suggested that inference patterns valid for physical domains might provide the foundation upon which much of human commonsense reasoning rests, and provided the first steps toward a computationally-effective method for representing analogical mappings. However, since the current study is only in its initial stages, the hypothesis that metaphorical inference dominates human cognition retains the status of a conjecture, pending additional investigation. We would say that the weight of the evidence is as yet insufficient to tip the academic scales.

Our investigations to date suggest that intensified efforts to resolve the questions raised in this paper may prove fruitful, in addition to pursuing the following related research objectives:

- Develop an augmented representation language that handles analogical mappings as a natural operation. We intend to start from a fairly flexible, operational language such as SRL (Wright & Fox, 1983). Using this language, we intend to build and test a system that acquires new information from external metaphorical explanations.
- Continue to develop the MULTIPAR multistrategy parsing system (Hayes & Carbonell, 1981a,b) and incorporate within its evolving flexible parsing strategies a means of recognizing and processing metaphors along the lines mentioned in this paper.
- Examine the *extent* to which linguistic metaphors reflect underlying inference patterns. The existence of a number generally useful inference patterns based on underlying metaphors provides evidence against, but does not refute, the possibility that the vast majority of metaphors remain mere linguistic devices, as previously thought. In essence, the existence of a phenomenon does not necessarily imply its universal presence. This is a matter to be resolved by more comprehensive future investigation.
- Investigate the close connection between models of experiential learning and metaphorical inference. In fact, our earlier investigation of analogical reasoning patterns in learning problem solving strategies first suggested that the inference patterns that could be acquired from experience coincide with those underlying many common metaphors (Carbonell, 1982b, 1983).
- Exploit the human ability for experientially-based metaphorical reasoning in order to enhance the education process. In fact, Sleeman and others have independently used the *balance metaphor* to help teach algebra to young or learning disabled children. Briefly, a scale is viewed as an equation, where the quantities on the right- and left-hand sides must balance. Algebraic manipulations correspond to adding or deleting equal amounts of weight from both sides of the scale, hence preserving balance. First, the child is taught to use the scale with color-coded boxes or different (integral) weights. Then, the transfer to numbers in simple algebraic equations is performed. Preliminary results indicate that children learn faster and better when they are able to use explicitly this general inference pattern. We foresee other applications of this and other metaphorical inference patterns in facilitating instruction of more abstract concepts. The teacher must make the mapping explicit to the student in domains alien to his or her past experience. As discussed earlier, establishing and instantiating the appropriate mapping is also the most problematical phase from a computational standpoint, and therefore should correspond to the most difficult step in the learning process.

Clearly, the possible research directions suggested by our initial investigations far outstrip our resources to pursue them in parallel. Our central concerns include the representation and comprehension of metaphorical mappings. But, the use of derived metaphorical inferences embedded within a general reasoning framework is an equally important topic of investigation.

References

Bobrow, D. G., & Winograd, T. (1977). An overview of KRL, a knowledge representation language. *Cognitive Science, 1* (1), 3–46.

Brachman, R. J. (1977). *A structural paradigm for representing knowledge.* Unpublished doctoral dissertation, Harvard University, Cambridge, MA; Also BBN report # 3888.

Brachman, R. J. (1979). On the epistemological status of semantic networks, In N. V. Findler Ed., *Associative networks.* New York: Academic Press.

Burstein, M. H. (1981). Concept formation through the interaction of multiple models, *Proceedings of the Third Annual Conference of the Cognitive Science Society.*

Carbonell, J. G., (1980). Default reasoning and inheritance mechanisms on type hierarchies. *SIGART, SIGPLAN, SIGMOD Joint volume on Data Abstraction.*

Carbonell, J. G. (1981a) A computational model of problem solving by analogy. *Proceedings of the Seventh International Joint Conference on Artificial Intelligence* (pp. 147–152).

Carbonell, J. G. (1981b) Invariance hierarchies in metaphor interpretation. *Proceedings of the Third Meeting of the Cognitive Science Society* (pp. 292–295).

Carbonell, J. G. (1982a) Experiential learning in analogical problem solving. *Proceedings of the Second Meeting of the American Association for Artificial Intelligence,* Pittsburgh, PA. pp. 168–272.

Carbonell, J. G. (1982b) Metaphor: An inescapable phenomenon in natural language comprehension. in W. Lehnert & Ringle (Eds.), *Strategies for natural language processing* (pp. 415–434). Hillsdale NJ: Erlbaum.

Carbonell, J. G. (1983). *Learning by analogy: Formulating and generalizing plans from past experience. in R. S. Michalski, J. G. Carbonell, & T. M. Mitchell (Eds.), Machine learning an artificial intelligence approach.* Palo Alto, CA: Tioga Press.

Carbonell, J. G., Larkin, J. H., & Reif, F. (1983). *Towards a general scientific reasoning engine* (CMU Computer Science Technical Report and C.I.P. #. 445). 1983

Charniak, E., Riesbeck, C., & McDermott, D. (1980). *Artificial intelligence programming.* Hillsdale, NJ: Erlbaum.

Chase, W. G., & Simon, H. A., (1974). Perception in chess. *Cognitive Psychology, 4,* 55–81.

Clements, J. (1982). Analogical reasoning patterns in expert problem solving. *Proceedings of the Fourth Annual Conference of the Cognitive Science Society.*

Doyle, J. (1979). A truth maintenance system. *Artificial Intelligence, 12* (3), 231–272.

Fahlman, S. E. (1979). *NETL: A system for representing and using real world knowledge.* Cambridge, MA: MIT Press.

Fox, M. S. (1979). On Inheritance in Knowledge Representation. *Proceedings of the Sixth International Joint Conference on Artificial Intelligence* (pp. 282–284).

Garey, M., & Johnson, D. (1979). *Computers and intractability, San Francisco, CA: W. H. Freeman.*

Gentner, D. (1980). *The structure of analogical models in science,* (Tech. Report 4451). Bolt Beranek and Newman.

Hayes, P. J., & Carbonell, J. G. (1981a) Multi-strategy construction-specific parsing for flexible data base query and update. *Proceedings of the Seventh International Joint Conference on Artificial Intelligence* (pp. 432–439).

Hayes, P. J., & Carbonell, J. G. (1981b) *Multi-strategy parsing and it's role in robust man-machine communication,* (Tech. Report CMU-CS-81-118). Carnegie-Mellon University, Computer Science Department.

Hobbs, J. R. (1979). *Metaphor, metaphor schemata, and selective inference* (Tech. report 204). SRI International.

Johnson, M. Metaphorical Reasoning. Unpublished manuscript. 1983

Kolodner, J. L. (1980). *Retrieval and organizational strategies in conceptual memory: A computer model*. Unpublished doctoral dissertation, Yale University, New Haven, CT.

Lakoff, G., & Johnson, M. (1980). *Metaphors we live by*. Chicago, IL: Chicago University Press.

Larkin, J. H., & Carbonell, J. G., "*General patterns of scientific inference: A basis for robust and extensible instructional systems* (Proposal to the Office of Naval Research), Office of Naval research Washington D.C. 1981

Lebowitz, M. (1980). *Generalization and memory in an integrated understanding system*. Unpublished doctoral dissertation, Yale University, New Haven, CT.

Moore, J., & Newell, A. (1974). How can MERLIN understand?. in L. Gregg (Ed.), *Knowledge and cognition* (pp. 253–285).

Ortony, A. (1979a) The role of similarity in similes and metaphors. in A. Ortony (Ed.), *Metaphor and thought*. Cambridge, England: Cambridge University Press.

Ortony, A. (Ed.) (1979b) *Metaphor and thought*. Cambridge, England: Cambridge University Press.

Schank, R. C. (1979). *Remdining and memory organization: An introduction to MOPS* (Tech. Report 170). New Haven, CT: Yale University, Comp. Sci. Dept.

Schank, R. C. (1980). *Language and memory. Cognitive Science, 4* (3), 243–284.

Schank, R. C. (1982). *Dynamic memory*, Cambridge, England: Cambridge University Press.

Searle, J. R. (1979) Metaphor, in A. Ortony (Ed.), *Metaphor and thought*. Cambridge, England: Cambridge University Press.

Wilks, Y. (1977) Knowledge structures and language boundaries. *Proceedings of the Fifth International Joint Conference on Artificial Intelligence* (pp. 151–157).

Winston, P. H. (1978). Learning by creating and justifying transfer frames, *Artificial Intelligence, 10* (2), 147–172.

Winston, P. H. (1979) Learning and reasoning by analogy, *Comm. ACM, 23* (12), 689–703.

Wright, M., & Fox, M. (1983). The SRL users manual (Tech. Report), Pittsburgh, PA: Carnegie-Mellon University, Robotics Institute.

12 A Short Companion to the Naive Physics Manifesto*

David Israel

BBN Labs
Bolt Beranek and Newman
Cambridge, Massachusetts

1 Introduction

There is no reason to think that artificial intelligence, unlike other disciplines, has a unique goal. It is inspired, however, by a unique vision—of fully autonomous, flexibly intelligent, rational (though artificial) agents. Not all work in AI has that vision firmly in mind; to the contrary, many current efforts are directed toward the design and development of various "intelligence enhancers," prosthetic devices to aid human intellects. Some of the research in natural language understanding can be seen in this latter light; so, too, the work in expert systems. Still, what inspires much of the work, and even more of the interest and enthusiasm, is the vision of intelligent robots, creatures able to find out about, and respond adequately to, complex and changing environments which might well include other intelligent creatures, both natural and artificial. I think it proper to see the papers in this volume as contributions toward realizing that vision—whatever the motivations of the individual researchers.

2 What Is To Be Known?

What must an intelligent, though artificial, creature know, and what must it be able to do with what it knows? Of course, that depends on what the world it has to deal with is like and on what is expected of it. In particular, is it expected to know or to do serious science? Almost from the very beginnings of the field, those workers in AI who have had the robot vision before them have thought not (primarily) in terms of designing little Newtons and Einsteins, but rather of designing intelligent "lay-androids"—robots who know a good deal of what more or less every human being knows. This body of knowledge (belief) and know-how, indefinite in its scope and

---

* An earlier version of part of this essay was published as "The Role of Logic in Knowledge Representation" in *IEEE Computer*, October, 1983, *16* (10).

boundaries, often goes by the name of *common sense*. The beliefs in question are usually implicit, too obvious even to notice, let alone mention. Needless to say, the designers and builders of such robots may themselves have to be in possession of awe-inspiring bodies of scientific expertise. Still, the goal of the research could, without much distortion, be described as the development of artificial Everypersons, as knowledgeable and adaptable as, say, the average 10-year-old human.

2.1 The Problem of Perception

Of course, such a creature will need to have some sensory capacities, some analogues—at least—of vision, touch, and proprioception. Research on these faculties will draw on mathematically sophisticated work in physics and psycho-physics. Now, there *may* be a sense in which all of us, including our average 10-year-old, "implicitly knows" all this fancy mathematical physics, and again, our robot builders will certainly have to know this, and more, explicitly. But we need not suppose it to be any part of the plan that our robot either explicitly know such stuff or even be able to learn it—except, of course, to the extent that our average 10-year-old is able to learn it. This may, in part, explain the striking and lamentable lack of interaction between work in knowledge representation and work on "low-level," peripheral sensory processing. The more important explanation, of course, is the enormous difficulty of constructing systematic and well-motivated bridges across the chasms separating the proprietary vocabularies of peripheral processors and the vocabulary of our explicit commonsense beliefs about our environment, both natural and sociocultural. Whatever the causes, the almost complete silence of the essays in this volume on matters perceptual is an effect.

3 The Orthodox Strategy

It is assumed that the core of commonsense knowledge resides in general principles, as in the knowledge that objects fall unless they are supported; that if one goes outside in the rain, one is likely to get wet; that physical objects don't suddenly disappear; and that if a person wants something and believes there is a best way to go about getting it, then the person is likely to try that way of getting it.[1] "The AI problem" is: how to impart such knowledge to a robot? Or: how to design a robot with a capacity to reason and learn sufficiently powerful and fruitful that, when provided with some sub-body of this knowledge and exposed over time through the deployment of its sensors to a rich variety of experience, it will be able to generate enough of the rest to enable the robot to manifest intelligent adaptation to and exploitation of its environment.

   Nobody, anymore, thinks of designing "tabula rasa" self-organizing systems.[2]

---

[1] It is, then, further assumed that knowledge of the particular facts of its current situation are to be gained by deployment of the robot's sensory equipment, or simply by being told by some other intelligence. The particular examples, by the way, are due to Nils Nilsson (1982).

[2] See Minsky (1974).

But, crucially, the minds of robots will be clean slates at least in this regard: robots start out with no knowledge at all about the world they are going to inhabit. Let us assume that some, at least, of what *we* all know is innate—vouchsafed to us solely (or mostly) in virtue of our biological inheritance and that this inheritance is a necessary precondition for our learning the rest of what we know. Things are otherwise for artificial intelligences. Whatever implicit control know-how is taken as built into the computational architecture of the robot, it is taken for granted that the robot comes into the world knowing nothing about that world. Its designers and builders, then, have to get it started, by telling it at least some of what *they* know.

Beginning in the late 1950s, John McCarthy began to sketch a strategy in which the formulation of commonsense knowledge and belief in a formal logical language played a crucial role in the design of intelligent robots. One should conceive of the robot, at least with respect to its central, rational aspects, as a sentential automaton, whose abstract data structures are sentences of a formal language and whose interpreter is—or includes—a sound theorem prover for that language (relative to some semantic account). We impart commonsense knowledge to a robot by first formalizing and axiomatizing this knowledge, as completely as we can, and then telling it all to the robot.

Thus in "Programs with Common Sense," McCarthy (1968) assumed that "our ultimate objective is to make programs that learn from their experience as effectively as humans do." But how to begin? With the "Advice Taker," (McCarthy, 1968) a "proposed program for solving problems by manipulating sentences in formal languages":

> The main advantages we expect the advice taker to have is that its behavior will be improvable merely by making statements to it, telling it about its symbolic environment and what is wanted from it . . . [We] assume that the advice taker will have available to it a fairly wide class of immediate logical consequences of anything it is told and its previous knowledge. *This property is expected to have much in common with with what makes us describe certain humans as having common sense.* We shall therefore say that *a program has common sense if it automatically deduces for itself a sufficiently wide class of immediate consequences of anything it is told and what it already knows . . .*
>
> *We base ourselves on the idea that in order for a program to be capable of learning something it must first be capable of being told it.* In the early versions we shall concentrate entirely on this point and attempt to achieve a system which can be told to make a specific improvement in its behavior with no more knowledge of its internal structure or (its) previous knowledge than is required in order to instruct a human.

4 The Debate about Logic

Although the "Advice Taker" strategy has inspired much work in the field, it has not been without its challengers—and the debate continues. Witness Kolota (1982):

> Theoreticians . . . have reached no consensus on how to solve the AI problem—on how to make true thinking machines. Instead, there are two opposing philosophical

viewpoints and a flurry of research activity along these two directions. The different viewpoints were represented at a recent meeting of the American Association for Artificial Intelligence by Marvin Minsky and John McCarthy . . .

McCarthy believes that the way to solve the AI problem is to design computer programs to reason according to the well worked out languages of mathematical logic, whether or not that is actually the way people think. Minsky believes that a fruitful approach is to try to get computers to imitate the way the human mind works, which, he thinks, is almost certainly not with mathematical logic.

4.1 On the Role of Psychology

It is clear enough that humans, at least, are intelligent entities; moreover, we are them (or they are us). So even if one were not interested in the cognitive psychology of humans for its own sake, even if one were interested only in the design of artificial intelligences, one might very well think that a good strategy would be to discover as much as we could about how we humans do all the wonderful things we do—such as learn, form useful concepts and fruitful hypotheses—and then see to what extent we could design an entity with our cognitive architecture, an entity that processed information in very much the same way we do.

The two "camps" divide fairly sharply on the utility of psychologizing. Those who share Minsky's doubts about the relevance of logic typically accept the foregoing argument that the best way to proceed is to have the artificial imitate the natural. On the other hand, those who are most impressed with the power and precision to be gained by working in a formal language are typically both sceptical of our ability to discover anything much useful about how we really do what we do and least likely to be bothered by that inability—holding as they do to a vision of *artificial* intelligence as "a most abstract inquiry into the possibility of intelligence or knowledge" (Dennett, 1978). Thus also, McCarthy answers Minsky (in Kolata, 1982):

> Whether logical reasoning is really the way the brain works is beside the point, McCarthy says. "This is A(RTIFICIAL) I(ntelligence) and so we don't care if it's psychologically real."

Psychologically realistic or not, are logical formalisms appropriate media for representing our commonsense knowledge of the world?

4.2 On The Appropriateness of Logic

A question naturally arises as to the nature of these "well worked out languages of mathematical logic." Such languages were originally created and studied with an eye toward the goal of a precisely characterizable symbolic language within which all mathematical propositions could be expressed. More particularly, what was wanted was a language within which one could express a set of basic mathematical truths (axioms) from which all of the rest of mathematics could be generated by the application of a finite set of precisely characterized combinatorial rules of proof which could be shown to be truth (or validity) preserving.

As just characterized, the languages of mathematical logicians were not meant for "general" use. Their developers did not claim they were unrestrictedly universal symbolisms: that everything thinkable was adequately expressible in them. Indeed, it was not even required that everything sayable in any natural language be expressible in a formalized logical language. And surely much of commonsense knowledge is expressible in (e.g.) English. Of course the fact that these formalisms were not devised with an eye toward the expression of commonsense knowledge, that is, toward solving the AI problem, doesn't signify that they can't be so used.

To argue this last point, one must point to particular failures of representational adequacy, perhaps supplementing these pointers with an explanation of said failures in terms of the differences between mathematical knowledge and reasoning and commonsense knowledge and reasoning. But very little worthwhile in the way of such pointers has been forthcoming. (I argue for this judgment, at least a little, immediately below.) For the most part, those in the Minsky camp simply seem to assume that the enormity of the differences between mathematics and common sense, together with the fact that the formalisms of mathematical logic were meant for and are fine for the former, somehow *guarantee* the inadequacy of such languages for the latter. Moreover this guarantee is taken to absolve them of the responsibility to show this principled inadequacy in any detail. Let me simply note, and briefly comment on, some favorite themes.

Doubts *have* been raised about the adequacy or appropriateness, for example, of the "basic" language of logic—the language of the first-order predicate calculus. First, of course, it is not obvious that these translate into doubts about the adequacy of logical languages in general. Moreover, there is nothing in the spirit of the McCarthy camp to rule out the use of many different logical languages in addressing the representation problem.

Many of these critiques of "logic" or of "the predicate calculus" have been, at least in part, criticisms of some *particular* way of formally representing some body of knowledge. Such considerations are best understood as objections to the effect that the objects, properties and relations of the domain have been wrongly conceived (or wrongly represented). Instead, they seem to have been understood as objections to the language(s) of logic itself; as if adopting some logical language involved adopting some one particular way of "cutting the world (or any part of it) at its joints," a way that was arguably inappropriate to many domains and for many purposes.

As a representational formalism, a logical language is (just) a tool. Given a certain task, this tool can be used more or less well. For instance, Pat Hayes has argued persuasively that if the task at hand is to represent in a first-order language what an intelligent critter must know about liquids, then one should opt to include in one's ontology histories, four-dimensional space-time volumes. This move, which is conceptual, not primarily notational, represents a very different way of carving up the world than one that recognizes only three-dimensional objects and instants (or intervals) of time.[3] Both options, and others yet more weird, are realizable within a

---

[3] See Hayes' "Second Naive Physics Manifesto" and especially his "The Ontology of Liquids," Chapters 1 and 3, this volume.

standard first-order language. A commitment to standard logical formalisms does not carry along with it a commitment to a particular metaphysics or ontology, let alone to a particularly wrong-headed one.

Again, some critics of logic have stressed the indefinability of many common-sense concepts. There seems to be a presumption to the effect that to buy into logic is to buy into the ubiquity of formal, precise definitions for this, that, and the other; but this simply isn't so. There are, of course, cases where a mania for definitions might result from (or in) a wrong-headed way of conceptualizing one's domain— but such a mania need not arise from the language in which one expresses that representation. Indeed, one usually thinks of a logical language as giving one infinitely many "semantically atomic" descriptive constants; so there is scarcely any need to worry about running out of expressions whose logical type at least allows of indefinability (for more on this, see Brachman and Israel, 1983).

Another version of the aforementioned view is the impression that to formalize *means* to axiomatize concisely, to search for a minimal set of axioms, because that is what mathematical logicians do. It is of course true that mathematical logicians are ever on the lookout for elegant and simple characterizations and axiomatizations of various mathematical structures, but that is in no way forced on them by the nature of the representation systems they use. Moreover, as Hayes points out, there is not only no premium on elegance or "brevity" in formalizations of common-sense, there is essentially no chance of it (see "The Second Naive Physics Manifesto," this volume; I return to this point below).

5 Reasoning and Proof

> Does [the entity] reason? That is, do new beliefs arise that are *logical* consequences of previous beliefs? (McCarthy & Hayes, 1964; the emphasis is mine)

I believe that most of the historically important objections to the applicability of logic to the AI problem have been aimed not at the expressive capabilities of logical languages, but rather at the imputed claim that commonsense *reasoning* could be adequately captured by running a (provably) sound theorem prover over such a language.

The tendency to focus on reasoning, not representation, is evident, for example, in the Appendix to Minsky (1974) and in his recent *AI Magazine* article "Why People Think Computers Can't" (Minsky, 1982).

> Many AI workers have continued to pursue the use of logic to solve problems. This hasn't worked very well, in my opinion; *logical reasoning* is more appropriate for displaying or confirming the *results* of thinking than for thinking itself. That is, I suspect we use it less for solving problems than we use it for explaining the solutions to other people and—much more important—to ourselves.

A brief look at Minsky's criticisms of the "logistic approach" would, I think, support my claim about the tendency to mistake (perhaps quite appropriate) criticisms of views which equate thinking with proving for arguments for abandoning the use of formal logical languages in representation.[4] Minsky, thus, is best taken as objecting to the notion that thinking is proving, and to various of its alleged corollaries. For example, a good deal of his criticism focuses on exceptions and defaults and on the alleged inability of the logistic approach to handle them. On a more abstract level is his discussion of the inadequacy of logic in virtue of its monotonicity. I shall return to this latter point below. For now, let me briefly examine one of the alleged corollaries: the hang-up with consistency—that hobgoblin of little minds.

5.1 On Inconsistency

> I do not believe that consistency is necessary or even desirable in a developing intelligent system. No one is ever completely consistent. What is important is how one handles paradox or conflict, how one learns from mistakes, how one turns aside from suspected inconsistencies . . . The Consistency that Logic absolutely demands is not otherwise usually available—*and probably not even desirable!*. (Minsky, 1974)

Ignore the claim that the use of a logical language *demands* consistency—it does not. (By the way, if consistency is "probably not even desirable," why turn away from suspected instances of its failure?) Logic simply offers you a precise reconstruction of (various notions of) consistency and—if the sentences in question are all first-order sentences—it offers procedures for showing an inconsistent set to be inconsistent. There is no "logical" reason to require that common sense *is* consistent, especially if we have in mind "all of it"—that is, if we consider the one big commonsense theory that results from joining together the commonsense theory of ordinary three-dimensional objects, and the commonsense theory of human psychology, and the commonsense theory of action, and the commonsense theories of time, space, etc. Minsky urges us to take seriously the possibility of inconsistency—perhaps even within a relatively isolable chunk of common sense. There is no reason why those committed to the use of logic as a representation language for commonsense theories shouldn't take this advice to heart. Taking the possibility of inconsistency seriously is not to be confused with desiring it as an end in itself.

Moreover, and more to the point, I don't see what any of this has to do with the appropriateness of logical languages as representational formalisms. The use of a standard logical language does not debar one from handling inconsistency in more or less whatever way one thinks best.

It is true, in any standard system, that for any sentence S of the language of the system there is a derivation of S from a contradictory sentence—or inconsistent set

---

4 See Minsky (1974). I return to Minsky's criticisms toward the end of the paper.

of sentences. Speaking semantically: every sentence is a logical consequence of any unsatisfiable—inconsistent—set of sentences.[5] But the proof theory of such systems doesn't mandate what proofs should be "executed" by subjects—the theory merely describes what a proof is. The semantic account doesn't tell a subject what consequences he/she/it should draw; it just characterizes the relation of logical consequence among sentences.

Strictly speaking, "rules of inference" are relations among (sets of) sentences or proofs. As such, they have nothing *directly* to do with anyone's or anything's behavior. Just as in standard systems, one can derive any arbitrary sentence from a contradiction, so, too, in every system known to man—or at least to me—from any sentence S one can derive, for any n, the n-ary conjunction of S with itself, and also the n-ary disjunction. One can; that is, there is such a derivation. *But should one?* In all these cases, the answer depends on what one is up to, on one's goals and resources, etc. About all of this logic, with all its "rules," is respectfully silent. If there are any rules in this domain, it is best to think of them as rules for reasoning.

5.2 On Reasoning

Exemplary reasoning can often lead us from true beliefs to false ones. Indeed, reasoning typically involves going out on a limb a little, going beyond what we are sure of and what follows from what we are sure of. Thus reasoning can often lead us to give up some of the beliefs from which we began. This can happen even when we have not set out purposefully to put those beliefs to the test; contrast this with proofs by refutation or with reductio ad absurdum proofs in logic.

To take a simple case of modus ponens (almost everybody's favorite proof rule): suppose you accept—*among other things, of course; nobody has only two beliefs*— some sentence of the form if P then Q and suppose you also accept the antecedent. Should you, need you, accept the consequent? Surely not, for you may have tremendously good *overall* reasons for believing not-Q and these might lead you to give up, say, belief in either the conditional or its antecedent (see Israel, unpublished manuscript, for much more on this). Are you thereby flouting logic or being illogical? Neither. All logic can tell you is that *if* the premises you started from were true, then so would be the conclusion. Note: not another (relevant) word about what you should believe.

Another moral: Rules of proof are local; they apply to a given set of sentences in virtue of their individual syntactic forms. Reasoning, on the other hand, is typically more global—one must try to take into account all the relevant evidence in one's possession. Indeed, one must often try to get more evidence if that on hand is judged insufficient. That judgment, and judgments about the relevance and weights of evidence, are typically themselves the products of reasoning.

---

[5] In the above, the word "standard" can be understood as a technical term. A system is standard if it is a metatheorem that for any sentences S and T, there is a derivation of T from $\{S, \text{not-}S\}$ in that system. Needless to say, where there is a standard, there are deviations from that standard. There are logics, defined over perfectly vanilla first-order languages, with negation, within which, from a contradiction, only some things follow (see, e.g., Anderson & Belnap, 1975).

It is often assumed that the commitment to use a logical language as one's representation language carries with it ineluctably a commitment to some sound deductive apparatus as the *sole* nonperceptual generator of new knowledge or new beliefs. But the first commitment is independent of the second; the second, much more contentious than the first. The claim that deductively valid rules of proof are *all* that is required *is* an extraordinarily strong one. It imposes an extremely strong condition of adequacy on a formalization of commonsense knowledge; namely, that everything a robot needs to know, even in a constrained, but real environment, be a deductive consequence of the things we "tell" it (together with the particular facts delivered by its sensors). For on such an account, the only way a robot can learn new things (except those it learns by perceiving) is by deducing them from what it already knows. Quite independent of the question of how people do it, it's going to be awfully hard for us to arrange for artificially intelligent beings do it successfully that way. *Nota Bene:* This is not an argument, though, that we should give up trying to formulate as much as we can as systematically as we can; and the *other* papers in the volume consitute an argument that there is much to be gained in the attempt.

Having specified a formal, logical language and its semantics, one is free to specify any rules of transformation from sentences to sentences one likes or believes useful. They need not be sound; they need only be mechanically applicable. Notice: I speak of "transformation rules," not "deductive rules." That is, the conditions of their "legal" applicability must be decidable solely in virtue of the syntactic structures of sentences. For instance, we might be able to come up with such rules which embody useful principles of plausible or probabilistic reasoning, or of analogical reasoning. Again just as they need not be sound, they need not be nondomain-specific. For instance, their applicability *can* depend on the occurrences of particular nonlogical expressions in sentences as well as, or to the exclusion of, the occurrences of the logical constants. So, one could have a rule that sanctioned deriving the atomic sentence predicating "is a dog" of an individual constant from the atomic sentence predicating "is a mammal" of that constant; *similarly for* "*flies*" *and* "*is a bird*".

Holding that such rules need not be sound does not commit one to ignoring the semantics of the language in the specification of the rules. What some of us want is *a set of rules that, collectively, embody—in syntactically codifiable form—fruitful and generally reliable modes of reasoning.* These rules need not be our own; and they certainly need not be discovered by introspection. Still, the crucial point remains: it's hard to see how to go about devising mechanizable rules that embody rational principles of belief transformation and fixation unless one knows the meanings of the sentences on which those rules act. *This last consideration immediately suggests perhaps the strongest argument for using a formal, logical language: we can get our hands on precise accounts of what their sentences mean.*

It may appear that logical deduction is being opposed to reasoning. Really, though, the right way to put things is that deduction is a tool used in reasoning. Hence the inappropriateness of talk about "logical reasoning," especially if it carries the connotation that the reasoning that proof subserves is "illogical" or nonlogical. Indeed, and ironically, Minsky seems quite aware of the present point (Minsky, unpublished manuscript):

> But "Logic" simply isn't a theory of reasoning at all. It doesn't even try to describe how a reasoning process might work.

And if it doesn't even try, it can scarcely botch the job, can it?

5.3 What's Wrong with Monotonic Logic: Revisited

I should like to make this point in the particular context of the "problem with monotonic logic." In every logical system worthy of the name, the relation of semantic or logical consequence is monotonic: if a set of sentences S entails a sentence A, then every superset of S entails A. *Derivatively*, the notion of syntactic consequence is also monotonic, assuming, of course, that the rules of inference are sound. So if a sentence A is a syntactic consequence of a set S—if A is derivable from S, then A is derivable from every superset of S. Minsky puts the point as follows (1974):

> In any logistic system, all the axioms are necessarily "permissive"—they all help to permit new inferences to be drawn. Each added axiom means more theorems, none can disappear. There simply is no way to add information to tell such a system about the kinds of conclusions which should *not* be drawn!

McCarthy (in Kolata, 1982) makes the connection bewteen defaults and exceptions and non-monotonicity more explicit:

> A proper axiomatization is one in which a proof exists for all conclusions that are ordinarily drawn from these facts. But what we know now about common sense is that that's asking for too much. You need another kind of reasoning—nonmonotonic reasoning . . . If you know I have a car, you may conclude that you can ask me for a ride. If I tell you the car is in the shop, you may conclude you can't ask me for a ride. If I tell you it will be out of the shop in 2 hrs, you may conclude you can ask me. [As more premisses are added, the conclusion keeps changing.]

By my lights, the alleged defect of *logic* is no defect at all; indeed, it has nothing directly to do with logic. To repeat: Logic doesn't tell you what beliefs, other than the truths of logic, to hold on to; nor, other than the negations of the truths of logic, what to get rid of. That's the job of reasoning—which is surely in general a nonmonotonic process. Finding out or coming to believe new things often gives us good reason for repudiating old favorites; remember the case of modus ponens. Throwing away one's initial beliefs is in no way illogical—especially not if you throw them away because what they logically entail conflicts with what you have overwhelming reasons to believe. This, by the way, is one reason it's misleading to talk of "premises" in reasoning. Another reason has to do with the already mentioned global nature of reasoning—the fact that, in principle, it's nothing less than a whole theory that operates as one's starting point. Surely, it is odd to think of a theory as a premise in the technical sense of that term. (It's especially odd if one then thinks of a theory in the way logicians typically do, as a set of first-order sentences closed under logical consequence.)

The problem to which Minsky and McCarthy are addressing themselves is a deep one and McCarthy (1980), in particular,[6] has made a significant technical contribution in the area with his account of "circumscription". But the crucial point is that nothing in the debate about the nonmonotonicity of reasoning argues against the use of a standard logical language, with some standard semantic account, as a representation language for artificial intelligence. So long, that is, as "logic" is kept in its proper place.

5.4 On Axiomatization

If one looks at the history of science, one *can* see part of the force of Minsky's claim that "logical reasoning [sic] is more appropriate for displaying or confirming the *results* of thinking than for thinking itself." Axiomatic formalizations by logicians of a body of knowledge—when such formalizations are forthcoming at all—come after the scientists have done their work. But this does not mean that deductive inference has played no part, or only an insignificant part, in the scientific work. This last point is only contentious if one holds that the attempt to discern what follows from what, to discover the entailments of assumptions, is possible only in the context of a fully formalized theory; and *this* there is no good reason to believe. There can be no doubt that the major impetus behind the creation of formal languages has been precisely the goal of formal and systematic specifications of the relation of logical consequence or entailment. (After all, why should anybody be interested in the *syntax* of these artificial systems?) But there should also be little doubt that the "data" these theories of logical consequence are trying to systematize and extend are judgments of validity or consequence for arguments expressed in natural languages—including the languages of science and of informal mathematics.

As to the point about axiomatizations as afterthoughts: there is, I think, a common misidentification of formal axiomatization with (AAARRRGGHHH) "precisification" or systematic mathematicization. Formal axiomatization involves, as Hayes points out, systematically expressing some body of knowledge in a formal language for which notions of logical consequence and derivability can be defined. In the standard case, it means expressing the knowledge within the first-order predicate calculus (with identity). These are Tarski's "theories with standard formalization." If we have such beasts in mind, and *if we limit ourselves to uncontroversially empirical sciences,* formal axiomatizations are very few and far between, indeed. Those few have been produced by mathematical logicians interested in questions about minimal sets of axioms and independence of axioms, etc. It is very unclear what of real use a working physicist, say, can glean from axiomatiza-

---

[6] But not alone: see Special Issue (1980).

tions of Newtonian Mechanics or Special Relativity. Note, though, that nothing in the "Second Naive Physics Manifesto" rests on any claim about the universal importance of formal axiomatizations of bodies of empirical or nonmathematical scientific knowledge. One must keep in mind the goal: that of telling a robot enough of what it needs to know about its world to enable it to do what, say, we want it to do. Hayes isn't engaged in the Philosophy of Science; he's engaged in arguing for a particular strategy for designing artificial minds.

Moreover, with respect to the particular case at issue, that of representing commonsense knowledge, it can surely be argued that the "science" has long since done much of its job. Most of us already know a whole lot about the way the world works.[7] It's not that there are lots of new discoveries to be made; although it's also surely not that there are none. A significant part of the problem is precisely to make explicit and then to codify and systematize this knowledge. The philosopher P. F. Strawson (1959) makes much the same point about "descriptive metaphysics"— the attempt to "describe the actual structure of our thought about the world."

> It is consequently unlikely that there are any new truths to be discovered in descriptive metaphysics. But this does not mean that the task of descriptive metaphysics has been, or can be, done once for all . . . If there are no new truths to be discovered, there are old truths to be rediscovered.

To repeat my main point: There *may* be reasons for doubting the adequacy of logical formalisms for *this* task; but these need have nothing to do with the claims about the adequacy of deductively sound rules of proof.

6 Some Qualms and Quibbles

The main doubt that Hayes himself raises—only to dismiss—is whether the project can be done. But first we must ask ourselves: what are the criteria of adequacy here? The major ones are, of course: breadth, and depth or detail of coverage. Can these criteria be formalized; in particular, can we sensibly propose completeness as a criterion of adequacy?

What we have in mind here, of course, is the completeness of (first-order) theories, not the completeness of first-order logic.[8] Surely, the most we can hope for is a kind of "experimental" completeness—I take the term from Herbrand. It's hard to see how we could hope for a completeness proof; and harder to see what there is to fear from a proof of incompleteness.[9] Anyway, experimental completeness is just what Hayes seems to have in mind in "The Second Naive Physics

---

[7] Or at least: we have lots of beliefs about how it works. Here and throughout, I am simply ignoring the distinction between belief and knowledge, at least as regards common sense. My only excuse in this regard is that it seems positively *de rigeur* in AI discussions in this area.

[8] I return to each of these below—first, to completeness for logics; then, to completeness for theories.

[9] See the previous footnote.

Manifesto.'' Keep working until a lot of what you believe about some domain is captured; then think some more, see if what you come up with is already taken care of; if not, simply add some more sentences—the aim of all this activity being what Hayes calls ''conceptual closure'':

> This phenomenon is familiar to anyone who has tried to axiomatize or formalize some area. Having chosen one's concepts to start on, one quickly needs to introduce tokens for others one had not contemplated, and the axioms which pin down their meanings introduce others, and so on: until one finds suddenly there are enough tokens around that it is easy to say enough about them all, enough, that is, to enable the inferences one had had in mind all along to be made.

6.1 Minsky's Qualm

I would be remiss if I didn't address more directly what I take to be the heart of (e.g.) Minsky's qualms. Keep in mind that Hayes' strategy goes something like this: formulate in some logical formalism, say in a first-order theory, much of what we all know about the world and then figure out ways to ''install'' that knowledge into a robot in ways that allow it to make good use of that knowledge. Minsky's concern is, of course, that second stage. Roughly, his sense is that if we follow Hayes's strategy in its pure form, and do not allow considerations of ''heuristic adequacy'' to guide us in our efforts at representing what we know, then, when it comes time to impart the information to a machine, we'll discover insuperable obstacles in generating useful access to that information. I want first to look at the letter of his concern and then turn to its more interesting spirit.

Minsky (1974), in an appendix, offers some ''criticisms of the Logistic Approach.'' I should note that Minsky never says exactly what he means by the ''logistic (or: ''logical'') approach''—but he does characterize the approach as one that makes a complete separation between

1. ''Propositions'' that embody specific information
2. ''Syllogisms'' or general laws of proper inference

I think that Minsky has in mind both the distinction between the sentences of a logical language and rules of valid inference defined over them, *and*, what is a special instance of that distinction, the format of standard axiomatizations in such languages, consisting of axioms and, again, rules of inference. Thus (in Minsky, unpublished manuscript) he says: ''In one place lie all the 'facts' one knows about any special, particular domain, in the form of a collection of 'axioms'. In another, separate collection is everything one knows about 'valid reasoning' in general; these are called the 'rules of inference'.'' The claim seems to be that this separation somehow dooms efforts to apply the logistic approach to anything more than toy problems.

Now at this point vague yet terrifying memories of the dreaded *Declarative-Procedural Controversy* might begin to disturb the reader's peace of mind. Have no fear; I will not here attempt to add to what has already been said on this issue by my betters (see especially Hayes, 1977; Moore, 1982; Winograd, 1980). *Except, that is,* to remark again that very little of what was actually said in that debate bears in any way on the question of the appropriateness of logical languages as representation languages. Some of it would be relevant to that question if and only if one assumes or argues for the following: *standard logical formalisms—with one or another standard semantic theory—somehow, by their very nature, bring to ruin any attempt to devise "heuristically adequate" systems for their use.* But I, at any rate, have seen no such argument in the literature and I'll be darned if I can see why we should make the assumption. Not that I assume that the task is a trivial one; nor do I doubt the rationale behind the demand for good solutions if Hayes's design strategy is to be practicable. Of course, one might also demand that the proceduralists come up with at least one alternative—"non-logical"—formalism, arguably close in expressive power, which can be shown not to be liable to a difficult control problem in the face of very large bodies of information.

To repeat: I fail to see any reason, in principle, why the following claims from Minsky (1974) aren't just false:

1. But while the system can make deductions implied by its axioms, it cannot be told when it *should* or should not make such deductions.
2. The separation between axioms and deduction makes it impractical to include classificational knowledge about propositions.
3. Nor can we include knowledge about the management of deduction.

At bottom, I think, Minsky is motivated by a pronounced scepticism about the applicability to real cognitive systems—such as the human mind/brain—of the distinction between (a) the content of knowledge and (b) the structures in which that knowledge is realized—and the organization of such structures. Or: between (a) the symbolic expressions, e.g., sentences, in which knowledge is encoded and (b) the organization of and interconnections among such expressions. The "declarativists" took it for granted that one could and should distinguish what was known or believed—what one wanted to say and even the language in which one wanted to say it—from "organizational" principles devised with an eye toward the use of that knowledge, in particular principles of relevance and apropriateness which in turn underlay strategies of access, retrieval, and control. The declarativists could then say to the "proceduralists" that when dealing with large bodies of knowledge, such issues of procedural or control know-how were of course important and had somehow to be realized, either declaratively, through so-called "meta-knowledge" or embedded in the control strategies of one's theorem prover (see, especially Hayes, 1977; see also the discussion of "heuristic adequacy" in McCarthy & Hayes, 1969).

This response, though correct as far as it goes, does not really address Minsky's deeper sense that the distinctions in question can't be made; that one can't factor out—from the mind—what it knows and how what it knows is embedded in its adaptive global organization and principles of functioning. Finally, if I may speculate: it is this sense that lies behind Minsky's deepest doubts about "logical languages"; for these are really doubts about symbolic representational systems, at least as these have traditionally been conceived. It is this, also, that provides some of the impetus behind Minsky's current speculations about K-lines, C-lines, C-germs and the like (Minsky, unpublished manuscript). As I've said, I don't think that the likely responses will quiet Minsky's doubts; arguably, nothing beyond getting on with the proposed strategy will. Fair enough.

6.2 On Completeness with Respect to Validity

My main quibbles—and quibbles they are—have to do with Hayes's characterization of the import, for his program, of completeness results, or their absence. Hayes says:

> The main attraction of formal logics as representational languages is that they have very precise model theories, and the main attraction of first-order logic is that its model theory is so simple, so widely applicable, and yet so powerful.

AMEN TO THAT. Of course, one *very* nice thing about first-order logic is that we have complete proof procedures for its valid sentences; indeed, if some sentence is a logical consequence of some set of sentences, even an infinite set, we can prove that it is. As Hayes says, "We should treasure completeness theorems: they are rare and beautiful things." *AMEN,* again. But then he goes on to add:

> Without them, we have no good justification for our claims that we know how our theories say what we claim they say about the worlds we want them to describe. To emphasize this, consider enriching the formal language [of first-order logic] by introducing a new kind of symbol, say a quantifier M, which I claim means 'most', so that $MxP(x)$ means P is true of *most* things. I can easily give a model theory: $MxP(x)$ is true in a model just when P is true of more than half the universe . . . I can claim this, but the claim is premature until I can describe some mechanism of inference that captures that interpretation, generating all the inferences that it justifies and non that it refutes. [A sound and complete proof procedure—DI.] And this might be difficult. For some model theories we know it is impossible.

Despite Hayes's avowed intention to stick to the model-theoretic high road, I smell a whiff of Formalism here. It is fairly easy to prove that "most" is not definable in terms of "for all" and "for some" (together with "and," "or," and "not"). The same is true—and for essentially the same reason: the Compactness Property of first-order logic—for the notions of finite and infinite; that is, for the generalized quantifiers "there are finitely many," "there are infinitely many."[10] Such notions can be defined in logics stronger than first-order logic, such as second-order logic and/or various of its fragments or, indeed, in logics created precisely to

---

[10] The Compactness Theorem states that a set T of sentences is satisfiable or has a model if and only if every *finite* subset of T has a model.

handle such quantifiers (see Mostowski, 1957; Barwise & Cooper, 1980 for the notion of "generalized quantifiers".)

In general, these logics do not admit of sound and complete proof procedures; the logic which builds in the finite/infinite distinction doesn't, and full second-order logic doesn't even come close. But they do have quite well-developed model-theoretic accounts, and all of them admit of Tarski-style "semantic" definitions of truth. Indeed, the definition of truth for sentences of full second-order logic is a minor variant on that for first-order logic.[11]

To continue: imagine you are given a specification of a logic—and essential features of a model-theoretic account—for (e.g.) the quantifier "there are finitely many." Imagine as well that one can show that the model-theoretic account does the work you want it do; that is, you can apply your new logic (e.g.) to handle notions in algebra, where the notion of finitude or the distinction between, finite and infinite is often crucial. (For examples, see the introduction to Barwise, 1977.) Of course, you know full well that there can be no completeness result for that logic— and no compactness result, etc. But so what? What more does Hayes think one needs to enable one to say that the quantifier ("really"?) means "there are finitely many?" A completeness result would, no doubt, be nice; but I don't see why we should worry over much about its absence. Logicians don't worry *overmuch* about it.

Again, for those familiar with work on the semantics of programming languages: there can be no complete proof procedure for full first-order dynamic logic (Harel, 1979). Indeed, most significant fragments of the logic are in the same boat. Are, then, the claims about the interpretations of the modal operators in first-order DL "premature"—and never to be ripened?

This last case raises another. Thanks to Kripke et al., we now have completeness proofs for lots of quantified first-order modal logics. But have these proofs, or any one them, made good our previously premature claims to know what "necessarily" or "possibly" mean? *If anything* in this work has sharpened our understanding of these notions, it was the model theory. In particular, there was the astounding success of producing a semantic account of modal logics which gave backing to Leibniz's heuristic that necessity is truth in all possible worlds; possibility, truth in at least one. At the same time, we were given a tool to account systematically for the relations among the various standard modal logics—the tool consisting simply in wringing changes on a binary relation of relative accessibility between possible worlds. None of the above *required* completeness proofs. (This *is* a little glib.) Nor does any of it actually make clear what a possible world is, or whether one and the same individual can inhabit more than one of them, or which necessity, which

---

[11] The ease of this transition doesn't speak to the quite distinct point about the conceptual tractability of model-theory for second-order languages. This latter is the study of the relations between second-order theories and second-order structures, and of such structures themselves. And here, there can be little question that the beauty and order to be found in the model-theory of first-order languages are sadly wanting.

relation of relative accessibility between worlds is the right one, etc., etc. And, of course, it leaves untouched the evident circularity of defining *necessity* in terms of *possible worlds*.

Still, far be it from me to understate the importance and value of completeness results. In particular, such results sanction proofs of theoremhood and its lack via reasoning in the semantic metatheory. This, of course, is how such things usually get done—not by attempting to prove things *in* the formalism. And in this regard, note how different the situation would be if the only kinds of completeness proofs were based on thoroughly unintuitive, purely algebraic/topological *tours de force*; semantic accounts that yielded no insight into the "intended" interpretation of the logical constants.

A similar point can be made with respect to the best-known attempt to specify formally the semantics of natural language—Montague Grammer (Montague, 1974). (Until quite recently, it was the only serious attempt.) Montague gives a perfectly vanilla-flavored account of truth for arbitrary sentences of a very non-vanilla-flavored formal language. No complete proof procedures are in the offing. A bit of a shame, that; but what hangs on it? In particular, what if one chose to use, say, English as one's representation language? Surely we English speakers do so choose most of the time. Indeed, Hayes himself says:

> Initially, the formalizations [sic] need to be little more than carefully-worded English sentences. One can make considerable progress on ontological issues, for example, without actually formalizing anything, just by being *very* careful what you say.

Imagine—and this bit is hard—that the fragment of English actually used could be given a full treatment a la Montague, perhaps by way of translation into something like Montague's logical symbolism. We would thus have a clear specification—in the standard model-theoretic vein—of truth in a model for sentences of that fragment of English, hence of validity of sentences and of the consequence relation between sentences. But—ex hypothesis—no complete proof theory. Would we really be doomed not to know what the logical constants of English—or of the logic—mean?

The same kind of point *could* be made about nonlogical constants that appear in essentially incomplete formal theories, such as the constants for 0 and successor, addition and multiplication in formal number theory, or the membership relation in first-order set theories.[12] But (more than) enough. Let us return to the general question of completeness for formalizations of commonsense theories.

---

[12] Or, for that matter, a similar point can be raised about nonlogical constants in complete theories. Hayes raises this point, based on Herbrand's theorem—or more generally, on the Lowenheim-Skolem theorem—in section 4. I must admit that I don't really see why such worries should concern research workers in artificial intelligence—or anywhere else.

6.3 On Completeness of Commonsense Theories

So, what of the completeness of naive physics, or of other formal theories of the commonsense world? First, let me sketch an approach to questions of completeness. Imagine we have specified a model M for a first-order language, that is, some nonempty set A and appropriate correspondences between nonlogical constants and elements, functions and (other) set-theoretic constructs over A. The theory of M is the set of all sentences true in M. The theory of any model is, of course, a complete theory. Note that this conception has nothing to do with formal axiomatizability, finite or otherwise. What we have sketched is the model-theoretic approach to theories. Now in so far as the commonsense world, or aspects of it, can be presented as a structure of the right sort, we can be sure that there is a complete theory of the commonsense world—namely, the theory of that structure. But this way of looking at things *seems* to give us no handle on what the sentences in the theory of the structure might be.

Why then the detour through model theory? Simply this: we do know a lot about the commonsense world and we want to characterize that world as closely and fully as can. Just as we know a whole lot about the natural numbers, their properties and relations, and operations on them. That is to say, in both cases we have in mind an intended model or structure for our theory. We are not in the position of mere "symbol pushers."[13]

No doubt, we cannot specify the structure we're aiming to capture as we can, say, the structure of the natural numbers. Note that in this last instance we have a case of a complete theory, the theory of the relevant structure, which cannot be completely axiomatized—except, of course, by having the axiom-set simply be the set of all sentences true in the intended or standard structure. In the case of the commonsense world, we are in the position of specifying the intended structure precisely by expressing clearly and systematically as much as we can of our knowledge about it.

I have no qualm at all about our having no abstract "algebraic" characterization, by way of a specification of a structure, of the theory we're attempting to express. Logic cannot demand completeness of theories any more than it does consistency. In both cases, logical theory yields precise characterizations of the concepts involved, rendering them amenable to proof. In neither case, does logical theory tell us what to do in their absence.

6.4 On How to Stop Worrying about Completeness

Let me remind the reader of the point of all this. Hayes's strategy is that, for a while, some of us at least should "eschew control (= computational) issues" and concern ourselves solely with figuring out what we want to tell our robot and then putting that down, first off for ourselves, in some formalism with a precisely specified semantic account. His own work in the "Ontology of Liquids" and much

---

[13] Notice, for instance, Hayes's use of the model-theoretic technique of counter-examples in the brief example of the "axiomatic method" in section 3 of "The Second Naive Physics Manifesto."

of the other work in this volume is clear evidence of the fruitfulness of such an approach. My quibble, simply, is that I do not see the point in demanding that that formalism come with a complete proof procedure or that the resulting theory be complete.

When the time comes to install our commonsense knowledge in machines, a *possible* strategy is to design them essentially as theorem provers over first-order sentences. (But see secs. 5.2, 5.3 above.) If the representational formalism we used in the first phase of the design process, the one in which we put down what we all know, isn't the first-order predicate calculus, then we must translate or compile that representation into a first-order theory. Reasons for pursuing this as an implementation technique are that we already have a good deal of experience designing and building first-order theorem provers, *including both provably incomplete and not provably complete ones;* there is this nice uniform method—resolution—available, etc., etc. Many of these "practical" advantages of standard first-order logic are equally advantages over (e.g.) quantified first-order modal logics—which are also complete—and (e.g.) higher-order intentional logics a la Montague—which are not. So in a sense, I am urging that we may want to think of *the first-order predicate calculus as a universal machine-language for Knowledge Representation.*

In sum, then: with respect to the first phase of implementing a Hayesian strategy, what counts is a uniform, general symbolism with a clear semantic account and this requirement can be met without a completeness result in the offing. As to the second phase, where control (= computation) issues are of the essence: even if complete proof procedures are available for first-order logic, must—or *should*—our robot use one? Can't we, shouldn't we,—*mustn't we really*—allow some legitimate and potentially useful derivations to go forever unmade? Indeed, to be forever unmake-able.

7 Conclusion

There is one thing on which all can agree (Kolata, 1982):

> All efforts to solve the knowledge representation problem share [a] major obstacle, McCarthy explains. "The preliminary problem is to decide what knowledge to represent. The key thing that we have not got formulated [are] the facts of the commonsense world."

Thus, Minsky (1974):

> Just constructing a knowledge base is a major intellectual research problem. *Whether one's goal is logistic or not,* we still know far too little about the structure and contents of commonsense knowledge. A "minimal" commonsense system must "know" something about cause-and-effect, time, purpose, locality, process, and types of knowledge.

The essays in this volume constitute a sample of the best attempts to date to chip away at that "major obstacle" and to solve "that major intellectual research problem."

Acknowledgments

This research was supported in part by the Defense Advanced Research Projects Agency, monitored by the Office of Naval Research under Contract No. N00014-77-C-0378, and in part by the Office of Naval Research under Contract No. N00014-77-C-0371. Thanks as well to Candy Sidner, Andy Haas, and Lyn Bates—all of BBN—and Ken Forbus, of MIT and BBN, for helpful and, at times, painfully incisive, comments on this and earlier versions. Special thanks to Pat Hayes.

References

Special issue on non-monotonic logic. (1980, April). *Artificial Intelligence, 13* (1, 2).

Anderson, A., & Belnap, N. (1975). *Entailment*. Princeton, NJ: Princeton University Press.

Barwise, K. J. (1977). An introduction to first-order logic. In K. J. Barwise (ed.), *Handbook of mathematical logic* (pp. 5–46). New York: North Holland Publishing.

Barwise, J., & Cooper, R. (1981). Generalized quantifies and natural languages. *Linguistics and Philosophy, 4*, 159–219.

Brachman, R. J., & Israel, D. J. (1983). Some remarks on the semantics of representation languages. In M. Brodie, J. Mylopoulus, & J. Schmidt (Eds.), *Conceptual modelling: Perspectives from artificial intelligence, databases and programming languages*. New York: Springer Verlag.

Dennett, D. (1978). Artificial intelligence as philosophy and as psychology. In *Brainstorms* (pp. 109–126). Cambridge, MA: Bradford Books.

Harel, D. (1979). *First-order dynamic logic* (Lecture Notes in Computer Science, Vol. 68). New York: Springer Verlag.

Hayes, P. J. (1977). In defence of logic. *Proc. IJCAI-77* (pp. 559–565). Cambridge, MA: International Joint Conferences on Artificial Intelligence.

Israel, D. J. (1973). Achilles and the tortoise—A rematch. Unpublished manuscript.

Kolata, G. (1982, September 24). How can computers get common sense. *Science, 217*, 1237–1238.

McCarthy, J. (1968). Programs with common sense. In M. Minsky (ed.), *Semantic information processing* (pp. 403–418). Cambridge MA: MIT press.

McCarthy, J. (1980). Circumscription—A form of non-monotonic reasoning. *Artificial Intelligence, 13*(1,2), 27–39.

McCarthy, J., & Hayes, P. J. (1969). Some philosophical problems from the standpoint of artificial intelligence. In B. Meltzer & D. Michie (Eds.), *Machine Intelligence 4*. Edinburgh, Scotland: Edinburgh University Press.

Minsky, M. (1974). *A framework for representing knowledge* (AI Memo 306). Cambridge, MA: Massachusetts Institute Technology AI Lab.

Minsky, M. (1982). Learning meaning, Unpublished manuscript.

Minsky, M. (1982). Why people think computers can't. *AI Magazine, 3* (4), 3–15.

Montague, R. (1974). The proper treatment of quantification in ordinary English. In R. Thomason (Ed.), *Formal philosophy* (pp. 247–270). New Haven, CT: Yale University Press.

Moore, R. C. (1982). The role of logic in knowledge representation and commonsense reasoning.

Proceedings of the National Conference on Artificial Intelligence (pps. 428–433). American Association for Artificial Intelligence.

Mostowski, A. (1957). On a generalization of quantifiers. *Fundamenta Mathematica, 44,* 12–36.

Nilsson, N. (1982). Artificial intelligence: Engineering, science, or slogan? *AI Magazine, 3*(1), 2–8.

Strawson, P. F. (1959). *Individuals.* London: Methuen.

Winograd, T. (1980). Extended inference modes in reasoning by computer systems. *Artificial Intelligence, 13*(1,2), 5–26.

Author Index

Subject Index